LABOR RELATIONS
Development, structure, process

LABOR RELATIONS

Development, structure, process

JOHN A. FOSSUM

Graduate School of Business Administration
The University of Michigan

1979

Business Publications, Inc. Dallas, Texas 75243
Irwin-Dorsey Limited Georgetown, Ontario L7G 4B3

ISBN 0-256-02088-4
Library of Congress Catalog Card No. 78–61198

Printed in the United States of America

1 2 3 4 5 6 7 8 9 0 MP 6 5 4 3 2 1 0 9

To
all my parents
Peter, Almeda, Herb, and Jane

PREFACE

Each author has a specific purpose in mind in writing a text. Since I have a background in industrial relations in its broadest sense and teach primarily business students, I am most concerned with labor relations as one of a number of functional areas which involves business. In dealing with business administration students, I have found a good deal of both ignorance and prejudice when it comes to understanding the goals, purposes, and history of the organized labor movement within America. Thus, my primary audience is students who have a moderately sound grounding in business courses, but who for whatever reason (be it lack of preparation or unbalanced previous presentations) have not been exposed to the "other side" of labor relations.

The study of labor relations has suffered for some time from an overly descriptive orientation. Too many conclusions have been drawn from the study of single situations. There also has been too little done in attempting to include some major behavioral generalizations that would be drawn from research in the areas of individual and organizational behavior. I hope to remedy these deficiencies in this text. You will notice that I have been heavily influenced by what I consider to be a classic in the field: Richard E. Walton and R. B. McKersie's *Behavioral Theory of Labor Negotiations*. These authors were ahead of their time since behavioral courses were not then (1965) interested in such "worldly" subjects of study as unions, nor were labor relations courses likely to pay obeisance to some "fuzzy-thinking" hypothetical approaches. Some of the more recent references in this text mirror the acknowledgment we owe to Walton and McKersie's pioneering behavioral approach. The application of multiple methods and disciplines to the study of an area as complex as organized labor can only enhance our understanding of its many facets.

On the other hand, while an inclusion of general behavioral principles is important, an abdication of the richness of detail inherent in the heritage and major incidents of labor relations is to introduce a sterility that masks the process. Thus, I will introduce specific incidental material to exemplify the generalizations to be drawn. Labor relations rest on a foundation of two centuries in the United States. The understanding of the foundation is necessary to see why the edifice exists in its present form. We also must note that law has played an important part in labor relations in the United States. Interpretations by the various courts and the National Labor Relations Board have lent the specifics, but public policy reflects the mood of the electorate, and the electorate has generally favored collective bargaining.

I hope, then, you will see in this book a balanced approach: balanced from a labor or management viewpoint, and balanced from a behavioral or institutional orientation. In the development of my approach, I am indebted to many institutions and individuals, primarily to the many professors in the Industrial Relations Center of the University of Minnesota and the School of Labor and Industrial Relations of Michigan State University, who provided information and viewpoints which have influenced my thinking on the subject.

Specific acknowledgments also are necessary to credit those who have assisted in this immediate work. The thorough review and helpful comments of Hoyt Wheeler of the University of Minnesota and I. B. Helburn of the University of Texas steered me into fertile areas and out of shoal waters that I may not have recognized. They should not be held responsible for my shortcomings, however. My research assistant, Ray Brillinger, provided valuable bibliographic help. The Industrial Relations Reference Room in the Business School here at The University of Michigan greatly aided my preparation of this book. The librarian, JoAnn Sokkar, and her assistants, Mabel Webb and Phyllis Hutchings, located material and provided rapid assistance which speeded my work. A battery of secretaries waded through incredibly bad handwriting to turn out a readable manuscript. The longest suffering were Linda Graf, Shirley Dunham, and Judy Armstrong. Others who may have learned more than they ever wanted to know about various facets of labor relations are Therese Sester, Vicki Oppenheim, and Sue Gamble. Finally, my family has provided both support and perspective. Andy and Jean had to forgo weekends they deserved and my wife Alta gave in more ways than I might be willing to admit. First, she took up the slack where my work on this book detracted from family life. Second, she was a supportive but highly perceptive critic. What clarity you find here is owed to her to a large extent. Finally, she has always had a misplaced belief that ventures like these which I have essayed would be successful.

December 1978   JOHN A. FOSSUM

CONTENTS

1. INTRODUCTION 1

Statutes and contracts. Plan of the book: *Development. Structure. Process. Overview and the future. Questions, readings, and cases.* Overview.

2. THE EVOLUTION OF AMERICAN LABOR: I 10

Labor history: *Early unions and the conspiracy doctrine. Philadelphia cordwainers. Commonwealth v. Hunt. Pre-Civil War unions. The birth of national unions. National Labor Union. The Knights of Labor. The American Federation of Labor. Labor unrest. The IWW and the Western Federation of Miners. The boycott cases. Early legislation. World War I. The American plan. The end of an era. Union typologies.* Summary and prologue.

3. THE EVOLUTION OF AMERICAN LABOR: II 29

Industrial unions: *The industrial union leadership. Organizing the industrial work force.* Legislation: *Norris-LaGuardia Act (1932). National Industrial Recovery Act (1933). The Wagner Act (National Labor Relations Act, 1935).* Employer intransigence. Labor power: *Pre-World War II. World War II. Reconversion.* Restoring the balance: *Taft-Hartley Act.* Retrenchment and merger: *Merger. Corruption. Landrum-Griffin Act.* Legislative activity in the 1970s. Public sector union growth: *Executive Order 11491. Executive Order 11616. Executive Order 11838. State and local government.* Summary.

4. FEDERAL STATUTORY LABOR LAW 60

Overview. Railway Labor Act: *Overview.* Norris-LaGuardia Act (1932). Wagner and Taft-Hartley Acts (as amended): *Section 1. Section 2. Section 3. Section 7. Section 8. Section 9. Sections 10, 11, and 12. Sections 13 through 19. Sections 102–104. Title II. Title III. Summary.* Landrum-Griffin Act (1959): *Title I—Bill of rights for union members.*

Title II—Reports required of unions and employers. Title III—Trusteeships. Title IV—Elections. Title V—Safeguards for labor organizations. Title VI—Miscellaneous provisions. Summary. Summary.

5. **UNION STRUCTURE AND GOVERNMENT**   77

Union components: *The local union. Local governments and politics. International unions. National structure. The UAW. The Carpenters' Union. The USW. The IBT. The federation. State and local central bodies. Overview of the union hierarchy.* Union democracy. Union finances: *Operational receipts and disbursements. Pension administration.* Political action. Summary.

6. **FEDERAL AGENCIES INVOLVED WITH LABOR RELATIONS**   109

Branches of government. Department of Labor: *Labor-Management Services Administration. Occupational Safety and Health Administration. Employment and Training Administration. Bureau of Labor Statistics. Employment Standards Administration.* Executive agencies: *Equal Employment Opportunity Commission. Federal Mediation and Conciliation Service. National Labor Relations Board. National Mediation Board. Occupational Safety and Health Review Commission. Pension Benefit Guarantee Corporation.* Summary.

7. **THE BEHAVIORAL BASIS FOR UNIONS**   117

Motivation: *Expectancy theory. Schematic model.* Group behavior: *Group cohesiveness.* The union as an agent: *Dual allegiance. Management-union relationships.* Summary.

8. **UNION ORGANIZING CAMPAIGNS**   128

The catalyst for organization. The organizing campaign. Authorization cards: *No distribution or solicitation rules. Employer and union conduct. Representation elections.* Bargaining unit determination: *Legal constraints. Jurisdiction of the organizing union. The union's desired unit. The employer's desired unit. NLRB policy. Other issues in unit determination.* Employer and union campaigns: *Union strategy. Management strategy. Union tactics. Management tactics. The role of the NLRB. Employer communications. Union communications. 24-hour rule. Totality of conduct.* Election certifications: *Setting aside elections. Bargaining orders.* Employee responses to campaigns. The *Shopping Kart* decision. Who wins representation elections? Preview. Summary. Point and counterpoint.

9. **BARGAINING ISSUES**   164

Introduction to contract negotiations. Union and management goals: *Union goals. Management goals. Joint goals.* Legal requirements. Economic issues: *Form of pay. Magnitude of pay. Determinants of pay.*

Other considerations. Hours: *Overtime, Shift differentials and preference. Other considerations.* Terms and conditions of employment: *Job security. Safety and health. Work rules. Union security. Management rights. Grievance procedures. Strikes and lockouts. Training and apprenticeships. Duration of the agreement. "Zipper" clauses.* Prevalence of contract provisions in recent negotiations. Summary.

10. CONTRACT NEGOTIATIONS   199

Bargaining activities: *Prenegotiation activities. Negotiation requests. Bargaining meetings. Union presentation. Management response. Bargaining on specific issues. Strike authorization vote. Tentative settlement. Ability to continue operations (or take a strike).* Behavior in collective bargaining: *Distributive bargaining tactics. Integrative bargaining. Intraorganizational bargaining. A test of the model.* Summary.

11. IMPASSES AND THEIR RESOLUTION   261

Impasse definition. Third-party involvement: *Mediation. Mediator backgrounds. Mediator attitudes and personalities. Mediator training. Mediator activity. Fact-finding. Taft-Hartley fact-finding. Railway labor boards. Fact-finding and the issues. Interest arbitration. Review of "third-party" involvements.* Strikes: *Economic strike activity. Strike votes and going out. Picketing. Situs picketing. Construction industry. Ambulatory site. Multiple-use sites. Off-site picketing. Employer responses. Shut-downs. Continued operations. Rights of employers. Rights of strikers. Contracting-out. Overview.* Boycotts. Lockouts: *Perishable goods. Multiemployer lockouts. Single employer lockouts. Requirements for the use of a lockout.* The 1976 rubber strike: *Toward the strike. The approach of April 20. April 21–27—week 1. Week 2. Week 3. Week 4. Weeks 5 and 6. Week 7. Weeks 8, 9, and 10. Week 11. Week 12. Weeks 13, 14, and 15. Week 16. Week 17. Aftermath. Analysis. Initial positions and settlements.* Review. Summary.

12. SPECIAL BARGAINING PROCESSES AND TOPICS   306

Alternative negotiating sequences: *Boulwareism. Boulwareism and the duty to bargain.* Bargaining structures: *Coalition bargaining. Decisions on coalition bargaining. Conglomerates and multinationals. Multiemployer bargaining. Industrywide bargaining.* Bargaining units: *For representation and negotiation.* Special topics and methods: *Dispute resolution. Experimental Negotiating Agreement. Productivity bargaining. What is productivity bargaining? The Scanlon Plan. How does the Scanlon Plan work? Quality of working life. A case study.* Summary.

13. CONTRACT ADMINISTRATION   329

Issues in administration: *Discipline. Incentives. Work assignments. Individual personnel assignments. Hours of work. Supervisor doing production work. Production standards. Working conditions. Subcontract-*

ing. Past practice. Grievance procedures: *Steps in the grievance proce-dure. Time involved. Methods of dispute resolution. Striking over grievances. Discipline for wildcat strikes. Due process in grievance initiation. What is the employee entitled to?* Fair representation: *Indi-vidual rights under the contract.* Grievances and bargaining: *Union responses to management action. "Fractional bargaining." Union in-itiatives in grievances. Grievance types.* Innovations in grievance processing. Who files grievances? Summary.

14. GRIEVANCE ARBITRATION   351

What is arbitration? Development of arbitration: *Lincoln Mills. Steel-workers' trilogy. The 1962 trilogy. NLRB deferral to arbitration. Arbitration and grievance settlement. A judicial exception to defer-ral.* Arbitration procedures: *Prearbitration matters. Selection of an arbitrator. Sources and qualifications of arbitrators. National Academy of Arbitrators. American Arbitration Association. Federal Mediation and Conciliation Service. Prehearing. Hearing processes. Representa-tives for the parties. Presentation of the case. Posthearing. Evidentiary rules. Preparation of the award.* Procedural difficulties and their resolu-tion: *Expedited arbitration. Inadequate representation.* Arbitration of discipline cases: *Role of discipline. Evidence. Uses of punishment.* As-sessment of arbitration. Summary.

15. PUBLIC SECTOR LABOR COSTS   379

Jurisdictions and employees: *Occupational groups. Source of employ-ment. Levels of government.* State labor laws: *Impasse procedures.* Fed-eral policy: *Executive Order 10988. Executive Order 11491 as amended. Administration. Recognition. Agreements. Disputes and impasses. Un-fair labor practices. U.S. Postal Service. Overview.* Public employee unions. Public sector bargaining processes. Impasse procedures: *Fact-finding. Statutory role of the fact finder. Fact-finding results. Criteria for recommendations. Fact-finding overview. Arbitration. Interest arbi-tration variants. Arbitration criteria.* Trends in public sector bargain-ing. Summary.

16. HEALTH CARE ORGANIZATIONS   414

Jurisdictions: *What is a private nonprofit hospital? What is an em-ployee?* Bargaining unit determination: *Bargaining structures.* Health care unions. Special bargaining rules for hospitals: *Organizing. Timing of bargaining activities. Ally doctrine.* Health care bargaining issues. Impasse settlement. Patterns and effects of unions. Summary.

17. LABOR AND EQUAL EMPLOYMENT OPPORTUNITY   427

Equal employment opportunity: *Title VII—1964 Civil Rights Act. Seniority issues. Departmental versus plantwide seniority. Seniority systems and utilization. The Supreme Court and seniority.* Franks *v.* Bowman Transportation. Teamsters *v.* United States. *Summary.* Unions and discrimination: *Construction industry. Affirmative Action. Mandatory compliance. Industrial unions. Remedies for discrimination. Consent decrees and judicial determinations.* Albemarle Paper Co. *v.* Moody. EEOC et al. *v.* Detroit Edison Co. et al. American Telephone and Telegraph. *Steel industry consent decree. Summary.* Certification and discrimination: *Mansion House. Bekins Moving and Storage Co. of Florida. Handy-Andy, Inc.* Fair representation: Steele *v.* Louisville & Nashville Railroad. Hughes Tool Company. Local 12, United Rubber Workers *v.* NLRB. Emporium-Capwell *v.* Western Addition Community Organization. Summary.

18. COLLECTIVE BARGAINING IN THE FUTURE   451

Industrial change: *Employment distribution by industry. Production and nonproduction workers. Union penetration.* Occupational distribution. Demographic changes. Geographical shifts. Legislation: *Labor Reform Act of 1977. Public employee bargaining laws.* Inflation. The labor movement: *The leadership.* Conclusion.

AUTHOR INDEX   467

SUBJECT INDEX   470

1

INTRODUCTION

Probably the vast majority of the readers of this text have been employed at some time during their lives, either part-time or full-time. It is probably also safe to conclude that the majority of the readers have not been union members. We might also conclude with some safety that the readers also generally do not expect to hold jobs in the future in which they will be union members. But many may be in contact with a union in an observer or adversary role.

With these conclusions and projections in mind, the book will devote more space to an understanding of the role of unions in development of collective bargaining than that of management. We are going to presume that you have relatively little familiarity with unions, their development, the activities they are engaged in, and the methods and techniques used by both parties in the collective bargaining relationship. But we also assume that you have certain attitudes toward labor relations.

Unfortunately, most of our acquaintance with labor organizations is biased by the fact that most news reports of labor-management relations are focused on either national issues or spectacular events that occur. We can't fault newscasters and reporters for this—excitement is what draws viewers or sells newspapers—but it does not reflect the essence of day-to-day labor relations in the United States. Rather than the relationship being a continually contentious one, we will find that both parties have learned to accommodate to each other quite well, with overt disagreement reflected by strikes, lockouts, and injunctions occurring in few situations. The parties in collective bargaining recognize that any of these can occur, but both generally strive to minimize the possibility that such shows of strength will be necessary to resolve differences.

STATUTES AND CONTRACTS

As you proceed through the early chapters of this book on the history of the labor movement, you will note that the public has been concerned about labor relations for some time. It would be fair to say that, on balance, public opinion in the United States has not generally been favorable toward labor organizations. For example, a recent national poll found that only about 20 percent of the American people felt that national union leaders were individuals in whom the public could place their trust and confidence. At the same time, the public does not hold business executives in excess esteem either. If either business or organized labor were viewed as undeserving of trust and also able to cause difficulties for the public at large, we would expect some push for legislation to curb or regulate the conduct of the parties. You will see major legislation, spelling out the ground rules for collective bargaining, dates back to the early 1930s in the United States.

These statutes regulate what conduct is permissible for management and labor in their relationship with each other. As you study the development of the law, you will find that it has generally sought to balance the power of the contending parties and reduce the possibilities of major disruptions occurring. The parties themselves have done the same. As you study the negotiation and administration of contracts, you will see that both labor and management build in mechanisms to increase the certainty of their relationship for a specific period and include ways to resolve differences that occur during the life of the agreement without resorting to strikes.

PLAN OF THE BOOK

Our title, *Labor Relations: Development, Structure, Process,* was not haphazardly chosen. It is obvious from the first part that we are dealing with the employment relationship in unionized settings. But it may not be as obvious why we have included the other three nouns after the main title.

Development

Development is necessarily related to the present state of the labor movement. We need to understand how it has grown and evolved to its present state. What conditions are necessary for workers to form unions? Under what conditions has formation been successful? What involvement by the public contributes to or interferes with union progress? What issues seem to be of the greatest importance to union members? Why have some unions failed and others succeeded?

But development does not only focus on the growth and stabilization of organized labor in the United States, it also examines the response of employers to the advent of labor unions. How did they respond to unionizing attempts? What has been the character of their long-run accommodation to labor unions and the process of collective bargaining? In what sectors of the economy has unionization had a major impact? What are the present stances of business and public sector employers toward the labor movement, and where is the greatest present involvement in organization and change taking place?

Chapters 2, 3, and 4 address development issues. In Chapter 2, we will trace the growth of the labor movement through the end of the 1920s. Up until the 1930s, there was no significant broad national labor legislation regulating the conduct of labor relations. This lack of legislation was a major factor in the early pattern and growth of organized labor. Chapter 2 deals with some of the major early personalities of the labor movement, their political philosophies, and the tactics they advocated. We will also examine employers' responses and the impact of public pressure on unions, the pressure most often supporting management initiatives. Chapter 3 focuses on labor relations since 1930. Included in this chapter is the impact of the significant prolabor legislation of the 1930s and the birth of the Congress of Industrial Organizations (the first unions with any major success in organizing semi-skilled and unskilled workers).

Legislation was a major issue during most of the post-1920 period. The growth in power of the labor movement and the seeming inequality of its position vis-à-vis management stimulated balancing legislation after World War II. Evidence of corruption among some unions and in some collective bargaining relationships involving both unions and employers lead to regulating legislation in the late 1950s.

We will see that during the 1950 decade, labor reached a peak in its penetration of the work force as measured by the percentage of employees who were organized. From this peak we can trace the trends and conditions that have contributed to its present position as an employee representative.

Chapter 4 details the major provisions of present day federal labor law. In this chapter, we will examine what is and is not permissible employer and union conduct in the collective bargaining relationship. We will see what the rights of individuals are in joining or abstaining from membership in a labor organization and in working on its behalf. The chapter will tell us what the present scope of federal involvement is in the practice of labor relations. I think you will be surprised to see the degree to which the government's relationship is generally on an "arm's-length" basis. Part of our belief that the government is intimately involved stems from the fact that we usually receive our information from crises situations where it, in fact, does have some real public policy concerns.

This background in the development of the labor movement should help to explain for you why labor acts as it does in many situations. You will see that labor has continually been a minority organization on the American scene, and as such it is not unrealistic to see it act to defend itself and seemingly to act often in its own self-interest. There are not a great number of others who immediately come to its aid, so it naturally tends to fend for itself.

Structure

Chapters 5 and 6 deal with structural issues. In the structural area we are primarily concerned with the offices and institutions that either make up the labor movement or have major influences on it. Obviously one of the major institutions influencing the labor movement is the federal government. Many boards have been created to observe and regulate certain aspects of the employment relationship, particularly where it is also involved in collective bargaining.

Chapter 5 examines the labor movement in some detail. There we focus on the institutions of the labor movement at the local, national, and federation level. We will note that the worker has the greatest involvement with the local but that the real power of the movement does not reside in either the local or the federation itself, but in the many national or international unions which charter and monitor the locals and are the constituents of the federations. Within each level, we also want to examine the offices that have been created to administer the organization and explain the various services that are provided to individuals and subordinate levels of the labor movement.

Chapter 6 details the workings of the federal government as they relate to the labor movement. Here we concentrate primarily on the executive branch of government through the Department of Labor and the several autonomous boards and agencies which regulate employment relationships. Among these are the Equal Employment Opportunity Commission, the National Labor Relations Board, the National Mediation Board, the Federal Mediation and Conciliation Service, the Occupational Safety and Health Review Commission, and the Pension Benefit Guaranty Corporation. We will explore the jurisdictions of each, the types of issues or problems that each handles, and the internal organization which governs their operation.

Process

The *process* aspect of the text consumes the major portion of the chapters. While we have major concerns for how the labor movement got to be where it is and how its background influences its present behavior, we are primarily concerned with the patterns of practice that underlie labor relations in the United States. What are the processes involved in the organization of workers, the identification of bargaining issues, the negotiation of a contract, and the day-to-day administration of the agreement?

Chapter 7 is designed to give you a working knowledge of behavioral theories which will be useful to you in explaining behavior in both organizing and negotiating activities. In this chapter we will examine briefly the expectancy theory of motivation, the concept of group cohesiveness, and the role of the union as an agent of the employee. The agency role is critically important to the study of American labor since the labor organization is the representative of the employees in dealings with management in much the same manner as if you were selling a house and retained a real estate agent to handle the transaction for you.

Chapter 8 deals with union organizing campaigns. In this and other subsequent process chapters, you will see that we focus our attention on the practices of the parties, the application and interpretation of federal labor law as it relates to the practices, and variations we find related to the environment in which the activity takes place. In Chapter 8 we want to examine how a typical union organizing campaign is practiced, the role of the National Labor Relations Board in the process, and the effect that the conduct of both labor and management has on the perceptions of the employees and the outcome of the campaign.

In Chapter 9, we will assume that an organizational drive has been successful and move to an examination of the issues which labor considers to be important for bargaining purposes. Statutory law requires that employers and unions be willing to bargain over wages, hours, and terms and conditions of employment. What areas are covered within this rather broad definition? What criteria are used by labor organizations to determine what they will demand on the issues to be covered? The identification and specification of the number and level of bargaining demands is a necessary step before bargaining begins.

Chapter 10 will focus on negotiating activity. In this chapter, we will trace the usual bargaining relationship between the parties when a contract is being negotiated. We will cover in detail how the parties prepare for bargaining. We will place a great deal of stress on the psychological properties involved in bargaining and on the various modes of bargaining behavior that may be necessary to obtain a settlement. The focus of the chapter also recognizes the economic variables which influence the bargaining power of the contending parties.

Chapter 11 deals with bargaining impasses. While most negotiations are uneventfully concluded, a small percentage does not result in agreement. First, we will examine mediation processes. These are aimed at getting the parties together where communications have broken down so that offers and counteroffers can again be exchanged between the parties and a settlement reached. We will also examine strike and lockout activities. In the strike area, we want to define the multitude of different strikes that can take place and the role and rights of the strike participants within these. Finally, we will trace the chronology of a major national strike to see how resolution was ultimately achieved.

Chapter 12 is entitled "Special Bargaining Topics." This chapter will cover a range of innovative issues not covered in Chapters 9 and 10. In this chapter we will focus on strategies and issues that are not normally covered in most negotiations or labor agreements. For example, we will examine the major points of the Experimental Negotiating Agreement between the major steel producers and the United Steelworkers of America which has as a primary objective the avoidance of strikes over contract negotiations. We will also investigate bargaining outcomes which will simultaneously leave both the organization and its employees in a better position, such as the Scanlon Plan and Quality of Working Life programs.

Chapter 13 deals with contract administration. Once an agreement is concluded, how are the terms put into effect? What is the effect of a disagreement between the union and the employer over how a contract is interpreted? What are the rights of the union and the employer under the contract? How much certainty in its operations can management expect as a result of signing a contract?

Chapter 14 deals with grievance arbitration. Just as most contract negotiations are settled without a strike, the parties involved settle most contract interpretation disagreements. However, in some cases, agreement cannot be reached. Then what processes can be used to decide which of the two parties will prevail in a disagreement? Most contracts call for the arbitration of unresolved grievances. Arbitration is a process where a neutral third party hears evidence surrounding the dispute, gathers information about what portions of the contract were allegedly violated, and then renders a decision on the merits of the case. As you will note, many arbitration decisions are rendered on discharge and discipline cases and cases involved with the interpretation of work rules and assignments.

Thus, Chapters 7 through 14 deal with the core of the processes within labor relations. There are special cases, however. We touch on some special issues in Chapter 12 when we discuss special bargaining topics, but we are also concerned with some important variations given the type of employer we are examining. Chapters 15 and 16 deal with two special types of employers: government and private health care institutions. Both of these have some special rules and situations.

In the public sector there is no federal labor law. Each state makes its own rules about how labor relations are to be handled. For federal employees, the executive branch of government has established labor relations procedures. Since unionization varies substantially across states and the opinions of the populace among the states varies to a high degree, the legislation between states is not consistent in the application of rights and responsibilities by jurisdictions or occupations. One area where the differences are most prevalent is in the area of strikes. Some states permit strikes under certain conditions while others attach criminal penalties to striking. Some states permit bargaining; others do not. Some states permit public safety employees to bargain, but not other employees. Thus, the pattern is highly varied. In health care organizations, we are dealing generally with a widely varied work force in terms of skill levels. We are also dealing with a sector where work stoppages have a critical effect on the services provided. We can't tell a heart attack victim to resuscitate himself because hospital employees just went on strike. So some special rules have been devised to protect both the rights of patients to health care and the rights of employees to engage in protected labor activities in support of their demands.

Chapter 17 is also basically a process chapter, but it has some structural aspects to it. This chapter examines the impact of Title VII of the 1964 Civil Rights Act and Executive Order 11246 on the practice of collective bargaining. We will see in that chapter that the focus of the process aspects relates to issues surrounding seniority and the allocation of employment opportunities like the right to job retention during layoffs, promotions, and so forth. We will also see the influence that these civil rights changes have had on structure, primarily through the role of the government as a third-party monitor or enforcer of compliance with federal employment rules, especially in contract construction.

Overview and the future

The final chapter focuses on some of the probable future developments in the conduct of collective bargaining. We will examine the effects which will probably follow demographic changes in the U.S. labor force. Changing patterns of demands may influence settlements. Statutory law changes will also likely influence bargaining relationships.

This book will take the position that an understanding of labor relations requires an understanding not only of the issues that are involved in its practice, but also how these issues are raised and resolved, how patterns of individual behavior contribute to an overall whole, and how public policy impacts on the overall bargaining relationship.

Questions, readings, and cases

As you cover this text, you will notice that each chapter begins by introducing the subject and asking you to focus on some underlying issues or questions with which the chapter deals. These questions are primarily designed to suggest major areas of concern to the parties, to point out issues that should be explored to gain an understanding of the development, structure, or process, and to ask you to inquire about your personal conclusions over the issues raised.

At the end of most chapters there will be a set of discussion questions. These relate to relatively broad issues raised in the chapter or ask that you formulate a position for labor or management on one of these issues. We recognize that each of us may have some preconception or bias as to how an issue should be approached and whether or not management or labor is more likely to be "right" on a given issue. But these questions may help you to examine why you have taken the position you have in the past and to appreciate the manner in which the other side views the issue at hand.

A set of suggested readings is also included with each chapter. In these readings I have generally attempted to include readily available sources which are clearly written. For those with interests in a particular area we are covering (and where you have very complete library facilities in industrial relations) I would suggest that you use the footnotes for that issue as a start in tracking down the more technically oriented material.

Finally, many chapters have incident or case materials. There is a recurring set of incidents or cases related to a simulated organization, General Materials & Fabrication Corporation, a heavy equipment manufacturer. You will first become acquainted with GMFC after Chapter 10 through the mock negotiation exercise where you are asked to join a bargaining team to negotiate a new contract between GMFC and Local 384. Later you will see that there are contract administration and arbitration issues which follow from the GMFC-Local 384 contract. These exercises should help you to gain a greater appreciation of the processes involved in the collective bargaining relationship.

You may wonder why this is a simulated organization rather than a real one. I think, first, that there is enough detail injected into GMFC that realism is preserved. But second, and more important, since GMFC is a simulated organization, there is no "textbook" or historical solution that is applicable. The environment in which labor relations takes place is fluid and the solution which was reached or the agreement which was negotiated in 1976 may not be applicable to the situation you will study in 1979, 1980, or 1981. National health insurance may be a reality in 1980, so a contract negotiation that places a good deal of stress on a health insurance issue would be obsolete. Cost-of-living clauses may increase or decrese in importance depending on our experience with inflation. Thus, the simulation allows you to place the organization in a more realistic perspective as you actually deal with it. The simulation is also realistic enough so that you can apply the results of other similar negotiations and settlements to your examination of the processes and issues.

OVERVIEW

In this text, I have tried to include information which will increase your ability to understand labor relations as it is practiced in the United States. This understanding must be based on the evolution and development of the labor movement to its present form, the subject matter and jurisdiction of labor law, and the practices of the two major parties to the process, management and labor.

I think you will find the subject interesting. In teaching courses in organizational behavior, personnel management, and labor relations, I have always found that there is a greater degree of intrinsic interest in labor relations on the part of most students than for the other two. Perhaps this is because we are likely to have strong attitudes about what we think are the proper roles each party should take in the process and notions about which side should be blamed for the problems that we feel surround labor relations. I would not expect that your basic posture toward labor relations would change as a result of either this book or the course you are in, but I would expect that you will have a far greater understanding of why the parties act as they do and a far greater willingness to agree that in most instances both do a good job of representing their constituents and arriving at means for settling conflicts which minimize disruptions in their organizations and, as a result, minimize disruptions to the public at large.

2

THE EVOLUTION OF
AMERICAN LABOR: I

To understand the present position of the American labor movement, we need to know something about the events, personalities, and philosophies that shaped it. What are the concerns of the labor movement and how do they differ in the United States from those in other countries? How has the movement grown and in what areas does its major strength lie? In the next three chapters we will examine the major historical stream of American labor; trace the evolution, growth, and demise of major labor organizations; and present an overall philosophy of the American labor movement. As a hint of what will follow in the area of union philosophy, let me suggest that American labor has predominantly been "results" rather than "ideologically" oriented and that the surviving labor organizations have adapted to change and have been responsive to member needs.

In this chapter we will concentrate on the path the labor movement has traveled since the nation's founding to the end of the 1920s. Particular points that you should look for include:

1. The legal and public policy climate surrounding early American labor relations. Legislators, judges, and the news media all had major influences on early labor relations.
2. The development of a surviving form for the American labor movement. Be aware of the properties which appear to be necessary for success in the United States. Ask whether the ingredients change over time.
3. Identify the events which contributed to and detracted from union growth. Do these still operate in the same manner?
4. Watch the personalities of the major actors within the labor movement. How have they contributed to union growth?

LABOR HISTORY

Early unions and the conspiracy doctrine

Just as the United States has recently celebrated its bicentennial year as a nation, the American labor movement is beginning the celebration of the bicentennial of its birth. In 1778, the first concerted collective action to win a wage increase was successfully implemented by the New York journeyman printers.[1] As we will note, however, the growth of unions in the United States did not keep pace with the growth of the country during most of the following 200 years. Substantial impediments were raised by legal decisions, the predominantly rural nature of 19th century America, and substantial numbers of relatively unskilled immigrants competing for jobs at relatively low wages. In fact, in the area of wages most collective actions taken through its first hundred years were aimed at resisting wage cuts rather than attempting to gain increases.

Philadelphia cordwainers[2]

The Federal Society of Journeymen Cordwainers (shoemakers) was organized in Philadelphia in 1794. Their banding together resulted from some substantial changes in the manner in which shoes were marketed. Up until about 1790, journeymen had been almost exclusively involved in the manufacture of "bespoke" (custom) work. Masters took orders and supplied materials for the journeymen who produced a pair of shoes or boots for an agreed upon rate. Obviously this arrangement required that the customer be willing to wait for the completion of the boots or shoes. Since this arrangement was inconvenient to many customers and expensive as well, three other market classes (besides "bespoke" work) were developed by the masters. These were "shop," "order," and "market" work. In turn, each commanded a lower price than its predecessor, and the master attempted to discriminate in wage rates depending on the type of market being supplied. "Shop" work was for the master's stock, "order" work for wholesalers, and "market" work to sell in the public market. The journeymen cordwainers responded by attempting to fix wages at the rate paid for "bespoke" work. This attempt was a forerunner of the union demand for equal pay for equal work.

---

[1] U.S. Department of Labor, Bureau of Labor Statistics, *A Brief History of the American Labor Movement*, Bulletin 1000, revised (Washington: Government Printing Office, 1970), p. 99.

[2] For a thorough analysis of this group, see John R. Commons, *Labor and Administration* (New York: Macmillan, 1973), pp. 210–64.

The refusal of the cordwainers to work at different rates dependent on the ultimate market for their output was seen by the employers as a criminal act. The courts found that the collective action of a few persons in pursuit of their selfish interests contravened the interests of citizens in general and was, hence, a criminal conspiracy. Each member of the union was fined $8 upon conviction.[3] Under the criminal conspiracy doctrine, a union could be punished if either its *means* or *ends* were deemed illegal by the courts.

BOX 2–1
Charge to the jury in the *Philadelphia Cordwainers* case

"What is the case before us? . . . A combination of workmen to raise their wages may be considered in a twofold point of view: one is to benefit themselves . . . the other is to injure those who do not join their society. The rule of law condemns both. . . . [T]he rule in this case is pregnant with sound sense and all the authorities are clear on the subject. Hawkins, the greatest authority on criminal law, has laid it down, that a combination to maintaining one another, carrying a particular object, whether true or false, is criminal. . . ."

Source: Condensed from 3 Commons and Gilmore 228–233, which was partially reprinted in Jerre S. Williams, *Labor Relations and the Law*, 3d ed. (Boston: Little, Brown, 1965), p. 20.

Commonwealth v. *Hunt*

In 1842, this approach was softened substantially by the Massachusetts Supreme Court decision in *Commonwealth* v. *Hunt*.[4] This decision set aside the conviction of members of the Boston Journeymen Bootmakers' Society for refusing to work in shops where nonmembers worked for less than the negotiated rate. The court held that the Society's action was primarily to convince nonmembers to join the organization rather than to secure criminal ends. Thus, the court refused to enjoin organizing activities but still might enjoin the activities and purposes of the organized group.[5]

---

[3] Jerre S. Williams, *Labor Relations and the Law*, 3d ed. (Boston: Little, Brown, 1965), p. 18.

[4] 4 Metcalf 111 (1842).

[5] Williams, *Labor Relations and the Law*, p. 22.

BOX 2–2

Interpretation of conspiracy doctrine under *Commonwealth* v. *Hunt*

"The manifest intention of the association is to induce all those engaged in the same occupation to become members of it. Such a purpose is not unlawful. It would give them a power which might be exerted for useful and honorable purposes, or for dangerous and pernicious ones. If the latter were the real and actual object and susceptible of proof, it should have been specially charged. . . . In this state of things, we cannot perceive that it is criminal for man to agree to exercise their acknowledged rights in such a manner as best to subserve their own interests."

Source: 4 Metcalf 129, as contained in Jerre S. Williams, *Labor Relations and the Law*, 3d ed. (Boston: Little, Brown, 1965), p. 22.

Pre–Civil War unions

During the first half of the 19th century, unions were faced with a number of problems. These included employers who did not see them as legitimate organizations, courts which enjoined and punished collective activity, and competition from a growing supply of immigrant labor. Even in the face of all these impediments, collective activity still occurred. Most of this was among skilled artisans, such as the cordwainers, but even unskilled textile workers in Massachusetts became involved.

Workingmen's parties were organized and contributed to the election of President Andrew Jackson.[6] Following Jackson, Martin Van Buren promulgated an executive order decreasing the length of the workday for federal employees to ten hours. Unions in major U.S. cities successfully used the strike as a mechanism for securing wage increases. Memberships in union ranks swelled in the early 1830s. But economic conditions soon tipped the scales in favor of employers, and union activity waned where membership might threaten continued employment.

The birth of national unions

Beginning in the 1850s, a number of national trade unions were formed. Among the unions formed at this early stage, the National

---

[6] See Foster Rhea Dulles, *Labor in America*, 3d ed. (New York: Crowell, 1966), pp. 35–52.

Typographical Union has survived to the present day. Until the end of the Civil War, the unions that had been organized were representative only of certain trades or industries. This pattern ultimately prevailed in American union organization, with workers belonging to unions representing their skills or industries. After the Civil War, however, the first major movements were national in scope, without craft or industry distinction.

National Labor Union

The National Labor Union was founded in a convention at Baltimore in 1866. Its goals were largely political and reformist in nature rather than economic or immediate. Its leader, William Sylvis, had been instrumental in organizing the National Molders' Union in 1859. Among the goals of the National Labor Union were the establishment of the eight-hour day, the establishment of consumer and producer cooperatives, the reform of currency and banking laws, a limitation on immigration, and the establishment of a federal Department of Labor.

The NLU was open not only to trade union members, but also to other interested and sympathetic individuals. For example, the women's suffrage movement attempted to get the NLU to endorse its position. Suffragettes were prominent at its national meetings.

Sylvis was the backbone of the NLU, but with his death in 1869 and the NLU's subsequent alliance with the Greenback party in 1872, the movement failed. The lack of leadership and inattention to immediate problems contributed most to the NLU's demise.[7] But the first attempts at nationally coordinating labor organizations had begun and would ultimately be successful.

The Knights of Labor

The Knights of Labor was organized in Philadelphia in 1869. Its goals and membership were different from those ultimately embodied in the U.S. labor movement, but it was closer to the final pattern than was the National Labor Union. It was part labor organization and part fraternal lodge. Workers were organized on a city-by-city basis across crafts rather than primarily along craft lines. The Knights of Labor held that all workers had common interests which blurred craft distinctions.

From a philosophical standpoint, the Knights of Labor were more willing to recognize the short-term legitimacy of capitalism than was

---

[7] See Dulles, *Labor in America*, pp. 100–113.

the NLU. The leaders of the Knights, Uriah Stephens first, followed by Terence Powderly, were essentially idealists and took positions such as favoring arbitration over strikes. Employers used these prestated strategic positions to their advantage. As we'll note, in confrontation situations, the rank and file were generally ahead of the leadership in their advocacy of collective action to counter employer initiatives.

As often occurred during the 19th century, the country entered a depression in the beginning of the 1880s. In the past these periods had usually taken their toll on labor organizations, but this time the strength of the Knights of Labor grew. In a number of railroad strikes in 1882 and 1883, the Knights of Labor successfully organized workers and won their demands, a sharp contrast to the crushing defeat railroad strikers suffered in 1877. Later, in 1885, when Jay Gould, the railroad financier, attempted to break the union by laying off its members, the union's strike on the Wabash Railroad and its refusal to handle Wabash rolling stock on other lines forced Gould to cease discriminating against Knights of Labor members. The nationally publicized negotiations surrounding this dispute gave added impetus to organization so that by the middle of 1886 the membership in the Knights of Labor had reached 700,000.[8]

Chamberlain and Cullen[9] point out the irony involved in the Knights's success against Jay Gould. A large influx of new members entered the ranks, to gain the same types of concessions from their employers that Gould had given. But the position of Powderly and the other executives was much more long-run in its orientation than the satisfaction of day-to-day grievances. They did not espouse a collective bargaining approach which would lead to an ultimate goal on a piecemeal basis. They were also firmly opposed to the strike as a weapon for pressuring employers. The long-run perspective of the leadership and its belief in "rational" processes for achieving ultimate objectives is typified by these quotes from Powderly and Knights of Labor publications: "You must submit to injustice at the hands of the employer in patience for a while longer." In another instance, "Do not strike, but study not only your own condition but that of your employer. Find out how much you are justly entitled to, and the tribunal of arbitration will settle the rest."[10]

The reformist and long-run objectives were inconsistent with the immediate results sought by the new membership. To some extent, the differences between the ascetic Powderly as leader and the inter-

---

[8] Ibid., pp. 139–41.

[9] Neil W. Chamberlain and Donald E. Cullen, *The Labor Sector*, 2d ed. (New York: McGraw-Hill, 1971), pp. 97–98.

[10] Ibid., p. 98.

ests of the burgeoning rank and file hastened the decline of the Knights. Besides the leadership-membership cleavages, an antagonistic press increasingly linked anarchy and radical action to the Knights of Labor. Public pressure, internal power vested in individuals with reformist sentiments, and an inability to get employers to arbitrate all contributed to the decline of the Knights' membership to 75,000 by 1893. But the withering of the Knights of Labor did not bring an end to national organizations. In fact at the height of the Knights of Labor's success, the first enduring national federation was formed.

BOX 2–3
The ascetic Terence Powderly on labor picnics

"I will talk at no picnics. When I speak on the labor question, I want the individual attention of my hearers, and I want that attention for at least two hours, and in that two hours I can only epitomize. At a picnic where the girls as well as the boys swill beer I cannot talk at all. . . . If it comes to my ears that I am advertised to speak at picnics . . . I will prefer charges against the offenders for holding the executive head of the Order up to ridicule. . . ."

Source: Foster Rhea Dulles, *Labor in America: A History*, 3d ed. (New York: Crowell, 1966), p. 135.

The American Federation of Labor

The American Federation of Labor (AFL) was created in a meeting of national unions in Columbus, Ohio, in 1886.[11] The AFL was born out of the frustration of craft unionists with the mixing of skilled and unskilled workers in Knights of Labor locals and the increasingly reformist orientation of that movement.[12] The Knights of Labor also tended towards centralization of authority, which diminished the autonomous power of individual craft unions.

Twenty-five national labor groups representing about 150,000 members initially formed the federation. It is worth noting that the individual craft unions maintained autonomy and control over aspects related to their trades, while ceding authority to the AFL to settle disputes among them.[13] The AFL was formed by unions of skilled employees. During most of the rest of its history, it maintained a skilled worker, or craft, orientation and an antipathy toward involving unskilled workers in its unions.

---

[11] Dulles, *Labor in America*, 161.

[12] Craft is used to mean a particular skilled trade, normally requiring an apprenticeship period to learn the skill, for example, carpentry, typography, tailoring.

[13] Dulles, *Labor in America*, 161.

In terms of philosophical divergences, the AFL concentrated on winning tangible gains for its members. In this regard, it concentrated on wages and hours as bargaining issues and entered into collective agreements with employers. Its conduct of bargaining aimed at rationalizing and making more certain employment relationships by contracting with regard to conditions of employment.

Much of the early direction of the AFL was a result of the philosophies of its first president, Samuel Gompers. By trade Gompers was a cigarmaker. As a member of the New York local of the Cigarmakers, he had seen radical action punished by civil authorities and had experienced the Knights of Labor advocacy of unskilled demands within the cigarmakers. As a labor leader, these experiences led Gompers to pay close attention to the workers he *presently* represented, not necessarily the interests of all laborers. Experience also led him to take a pragmatic approach, seeking gains at the bargaining table rather than through legislation. His direction was pragmatic, not ideological, and his long incumbency (1886–1924 except for one year) is in large part responsible for the "business" orientation of U.S. unions.

Gompers and other early leaders such as Adolph Strasser cemented the base on which the American trade movement has stood. Their approach was to accept the system as it existed and work within it. Given the system, they were primarily concerned in improving the lot of the workers they represented. This approach is basically undisturbed in the present agency approach taken by unions in representation.

BOX 2–4
Testimony of Adolph Strasser, President of the International Cigarmakers'
Union before the Senate Committee on Education and Labor, 1885

Q: You are seeking to improve home matters first?

Strasser: Yes, sir, I look first to the trade I represent . . . the interests of the men who employ me to represent their interests.

Q: I was only asking you in regard to your ultimate ends.

Strasser: We have no ultimate ends. We are going on from day to day. We fight only for immediate objects—objects that can be realized in a few years.

This pragmatic, business oriented viewpoint necessarily limited the AFL from major societal reform initiatives. The AFL approach has been to advocate legislation only in situations where it cannot bargain successfully for its objectives. As such, its legislative initiative also is fairly narrow and membership oriented. Perhaps the immediacy and absence of an underlying value is best typified in the answer, attributed to Gompers, to a question asking what labor's goals were: "More, more, more."

Another aspect of the pragmatic genius found in the founders of the AFL was their structural designing of the federation. Its early structure has generally been broadly maintained to the present (presented in detail in Chapter 4). This structure preserves the general autonomy of the international unions and makes the locals subsidiary to them. This approach serves two purposes: First, the leaderships' focus is toward the job problems unique to the trade it represents; second, discipline is maintained over the activities of the locals to present a more united and rational front when initiating actions or responding to management.

Labor unrest

The last three decades of the 19th century and the first decade of the 20th century saw some of the bitterest labor struggles the United States has ever experienced. This era was characterized by frequent financial panics resulting in depressions, continuing adamance of owners in refusing to recognize or negotiate with labor unions, and the willingness of the government to intervene on the side of the employers. Some of the unrest was localized and grew out of either radical political action or the nationalistic solidarity of immigrant groups, but much was of a general nature within an area or industry.

In one of the first outbursts, coal miners in Pennsylvania struck when mine operators unilaterally cut wages below an agreed minimum. As the strike lengthened, some miners returned to work, but a few diehards formed a secret organization which became known as the "Molly Maguires" to continue to resist the mine owners. This group sabotaged the mines, threatened owners and foremen, and conducted other terrorist activities until it was infiltrated by James McParlan, a Pinkerton detective hired by the owners. As a result of his testimony in 1875, 10 of the Molly Maguires were hanged, and another 14 were jailed, ending the mine warfare.[14]

In the summer of 1877, after the railroads had cut wages while maintaining high dividends, rail employees in the East struck and in some instances seized railway property. In Pittsburgh, federal troops were called in to retake railway property. Before this was accomplished, 25 people had been killed. Widespread rioting broke out. Railroad property was burned and local business establishments were looted.[15]

---

[14] Ibid., pp. 117–18.
[15] Ibid., pp. 119–20.

In 1886, violence broke out at the McCormick Harvester plant in Chicago when strikers and strikebreakers fought. The police intervened and four persons were killed. To protest the use of police, a meeting was called for Haymarket Square in Chicago on May 4. As the peaceful meeting was dispersing, the police arrived and ordered everyone to leave. Just then, a bomb exploded among the police, killing one. Before the battle was over, 7 more police and 4 workers were killed, and over 100 injured. The riot was blamed on anarchists. Eight were rounded up and charged with murder. Seven of the eight were ordered hanged and the eighth imprisoned. All (who were still alive) were subsequently pardoned six years later.[16]

Two major strikes in the 1890s helped to shape the constituency of the labor movement and to cast doubt upon the power of industrial employees to win their demands. These were the Homestead strike of the Carnegie Steel Company in 1892 and the Pullman Company strike in 1894.

Homestead workers refused to accept a company ordered wage cut and were then locked out by Henry Frick, Carnegie's general manager. The workers assumed that Frick would attempt to secure the plant and reopen it using strikebreakers. To reopen the plant, Frick had barged 300 armed Pinkerton detectives up the Monongahela River behind the plant. As they neared the works, the entrenched workers opened fire on them. The battle raged all day. The workers attempted to sink the barges with a small cannon and poured oil into the river, setting it on fire. The Pinkertons surrendered.

The workers' victory was short-lived, as the governor called out the militia and took over the plant. When it was reopened, Frick staffed it largely with strikebreakers. The union was crushed, and in fact, serious attempts to organize the steel industry were not made again until the 1930s.[17]

The Pullman strike of 1894 began as a local issue but took on nationwide proportions before being crushed by the combined use of federal troops and court injunctions. The Pullman Company produced railroad cars. Pullman workers lived in company-owned houses and paid rent for their occupancy. They had no other choice as to living accommodations as the company required them to use company-owned housing. In 1893, the company laid off half of its employees and cut the wages of those remaining up to 40 percent. There was no corresponding reduction in rents, and the company continued to pay dividends to stockholders.

Pullman employees attempted to get the owners to adjust their

---

[16] Ibid., pp. 123–25.
[17] Ibid., pp. 166–69.

economic grievances. The company refused and discharged several of the leaders. Reacting to this, the Pullman locals of the American Railway Union struck. The company refused the union's offer to have the differences arbitrated, and as a result, Eugene Debs, the ARU leader, ordered ARU members not to handle Pullman rolling stock.

This action meant that railroad employees throughout the country would stop trains and uncouple cars manufactured by Pullman. The railroads retaliated by discharging employees found to be cutting out Pullman cars. But whole train crews quit and abandoned their trains if one of their members was discharged.

One strategy used by the rail owners led to the ending of the strike. In assembling trains, Pullman cars were connected to U.S. mail cars. Then if the Pullman cars were later uncoupled, the mail car might also be cut out, leading to charges of interference with the mail—a federal offense. When this occurred, the rail managers gained the intervention of the government in supplying federal troops and permanently enjoining conduct interfering with mail delivery and the movement of goods in interstate commerce. Debs was sent to jail for conspiracy to obstruct the mails, and the strike was broken.[18]

With the failure of these early industrial actions, members of one faction of the labor movement became convinced that the capitalistic system must be replaced by socialism if worker goals were to be achieved. These revolutionary unions were spawned in the West in the mining and timbering industries and in the East as a result of the Pullman strike.

The IWW and the Western Federation of Miners

The inability of the Knights of Labor to win important settlements and the antipathy of the AFL to industrial organization led to some more radical approaches. Just as Eugene Debs's jail term convinced him that revolutionary unionism and the abolition of capitalism was necessary, so too did the results of numerous mine strikes and wars convince "Big Bill" Haywood that miner solidarity and resistance was the answer to employer resistance.

Haywood was active in organizing the Western Federation of Miners which was once affiliated with the AFL. It withdrew from the federation in 1897. After the long-smoldering Cripple Creek, Colorado, strike was crushed in 1904, the Western Federation of Miners realized it needed national support. Thus, in 1905, Haywood, Debs, and other leading socialists banded their unions together to form the Industrial Workers of the World.[19]

---

[18] Ibid., pp. 171–79.
[19] Ibid., pp. 208–11.

BOX 2–5
Preamble to the IWW constitution

The working class and the employing class have nothing in common. There can be no peace so long as hunger and want are found among millions of working people and the few who make up the employing class have all the good things of life.

Between these two classes a struggle must go on until the workers of the world organize as a class, take possession of the earth and the machinery of production, and abolish the wage system.

We find that the centering of management of the industries into fewer and fewer hands makes the trade unions unable to cope with the ever growing power of the employing class. The trade unions foster a state of affairs which allows one set of workers to be pitted against another set of workers in the same industry, thereby helping defeat one another in wage wars. Moreover, the trade unions aid the employing class to mislead the workers into the belief that the working class have interests in common with their employers.

These conditions can be changed and the interest of the working class upheld only by an organization formed in such a way that all its members in any one industry, or in all industries if necessary, cease work whenever a strike or lockout is on in any department thereof, thus making an injury to one an injury to all.

Instead of the conservative motto, "A fair day's wage for a fair day's work," we must inscribe on our banner the revolutionary watchword, "Abolition of the wage system."

It is the historic mission of the working class to do away with capitalism. The army of production must be organized, not only for the everyday struggle with capitalists, but also to carry on production when capitalism shall have been overthrown. By organizing industrially we are forming the structure of the new society within the shell of the old.

Immediately embroiled in internal political struggle, the IWW was decimated by the withdrawal of the Western Federation of Miners in 1906, but "Big Bill" Haywood stayed with the IWW. There is no doubt that its rhetoric was radical. Whether or not its demands were radical is another question. When involved in collective action, the IWW's usual demands related to wages and hours rather than usurpation of the management function.[20] And although it was involved on occasion in violence related to strikes, these incidents were often begun by management action similar to that which faced the 19th century industrial labor movement. It's important to note, however, that the *purpose* of

---

[20] Joseph G. Rayback, *A History of American Labor* (New York: Free Press, 1966), p. 248.

the IWW was not to achieve better wages and working conditions—rather it was to abolish the wage system. This may be one of the reasons that it had little success in building permanent organizations.

Perhaps the most successful IWW strike occurred in Lawrence, Massachusetts, in 1912 after the textile workers had suffered a wage cut. Although most of the workers were unorganized, 20,000 walked out and IWW organizers took over the direction of the strike. After two months in which several violent incidences occurred, some perpetrated by the owners and local authorities, others resulting from clashes with strikebreakers, worker demands were met and the mills reopened.[21]

But the IWW lost a subsequent textile strike in 1913 in Paterson, New Jersey. This outcome, coupled with the advent of World War I, in which the IWW took the position that its members would fight for neither side since only the capitalists would benefit, led to its demise. "Big Bill" Haywood and other leaders were tried and convicted of sedition for allegedly obstructing the war effort. The IWW was effectively finished.[22]

The boycott cases

The strike was not the only weapon used against employers by labor organizations during the pre–World War I period. While local employees struck, national unions urged boycotts of struck or "unfair" products on other union members and the general public. Two major national boycotts led to sharp legal reverses for labor organization. These were the *Danbury Hatters* and *Bucks Stove* cases.

Both of these involved nationwide boycotts to support strikes. In the *Danbury Hatters* case, the employer, D. E. Loewe and Company, retaliated by filing charges against the union for conspiring to restrain trade, a violation of the Sherman Antitrust Act. If a restraint were found, actual damages could be punitively trebled. The union lost and for a time it appeared individual members would have to pay damages, but the AFL and the United Hatters' national organization passed the hat and paid the fines.[23] In the *Bucks Stove* case, a federal district court enjoined the boycott and held, among others, Samuel Gompers in contempt of court. The old spectre of the conspiracy doctrine was reappearing in the application of court injunctions to union actions. And, in fact, strike activity, union organizing, and other union activities were being increasingly interpreted by lower federal courts as

---

[21] Dulles, *Labor in America*, pp. 215–19.

[22] Ibid., pp. 219–22.

[23] Ibid., p. 197.

actions leading to a restraint on interstate commerce and hence, enjoinable and punishable.[24]

Early legislation

The early attempts by unions to engage in collective action on an industrial scale had been generally met with a two-pronged attack: adamant resistance by employers and injunctive relief to employers by the courts. In an effort to balance the power between the conflicting parties and to substitute statutory law for court-made common law, Congress began to consider labor legislation toward the end of the 1890s. The Erdman Act was the first federal labor statute, passed in 1898, guaranteeing that railroad employees could not be discriminated against for union membership. However, this, and subsequent, acts were subject to judicial review, and the Erdman Act was held unconstitutional in 1908 as an abridgement of personal liberty and the rights of property.[25]

The rulings of the federal courts in the *Danbury Hatters* and *Bucks Stove* cases applied the Sherman Antitrust Act to union activity. Union leaders felt this application essentially hamstrung collective activity. With the election of President Woodrow Wilson and a Democratic Congress, labor felt that legislative relief would be forthcoming. In 1914, their hopes were realized with the passage of the Clayton Act which was hailed by Samuel Gompers as "the industrial Magna Carta upon which the working people will rear their structure of individual freedom."[26]

Two sections of the Clayton Act, 6 and 20, removing labor from the jurisdiction of the Sherman Act and limiting the use of federal injunctions, contributed to Gompers's euphoria. The enthusiasm was short-lived, however, since the ambiguity of the act's wording, ultimately led to judicial interpretations of its meaning which disappointed labor.[27] In fact, the Supreme Court held in *Duplex Printing Co. v. Deering*[28] that, although the antitrust laws could not be construed as rendering trade unions illegal per se, their actions might be still considered to restrain trade. Second, the court held that a strike terminated the normal employer-employee relationship, thereby removing

---

[24] Rayback, *A History of American Labor*, pp. 224–26.

[25] Arthur A. Sloane and Fred Witney, *Labor Relations*, 2d ed. (Englewood Cliffs, N.J.: Prentice-Hall, 1972), p. 64.

[26] Samuel Gompers, "The Charter of Industrial Freedom," *American Federationist*, vol. 21 (November 1914), pp. 971–72.

[27] S. I. Kutler, "Labor, the Clayton Act, and the Supreme Court," *Labor History*, vol. 3 (1962), pp. 19–38.

[28] 254 U.S. 445 (1921).

the protection against injunctions for lawful employee activities.[29] Thus, the Clayton Act lost whatever teeth labor believed it had.

World War I

While World War I spelled the end of the IWW, AFL unions made solid gains. During 1917, a large number of strikes, many fomented by the IWW, protested static wages during a period of steadily advancing prices. To reduce the incidence of strikes, the National War Labor Board was established in 1918 and included five representatives each from labor and management, with two members as cochairmen to represent the public interest. Labor's right to organize and bargain collectively was recognized by President Wilson's administration as the *quid pro quo* for ending strikes. By the end of the war, average earnings of even semiskilled union members exceeded $1,000 annually, and the AFL had grown by over a million members to over 4 million in 1919.[30]

The American plan

A variety of factors combined to make inroads on labor's growth after World War I. First, the 1920s were a decade of relative prosperity and freedom from economic panics. The flow of immigrants was declining, reducing the pressure on competition for jobs among unskilled workers. Second, just as the extremist bell had been tied on the neck of labor in the 1880s through the allegation that it was in league with radicals and anarchists, the same was the case in the late 1910 decade. Several prominent members of the IWW had been prosecuted for sedition. While they did not represent large portions of the labor movement, they became symbols of its danger in the public's eyes. At the same time the Bolsheviks had gained power in Russia, and warnings were made that this pattern could occur in the United States as well if trade unions became too strong.

Against this backdrop, employers began subtly to associate the union movement with foreign subversives. They also questioned whether it was appropriate for workers to be represented by union officials who may have no close employment ties with their plant. They also championed the open shop which was ostensibly aimed at preserving the freedom of employees to refrain from joining unions. But the freedom to join was not as zealously protected and, in fact, was

---

[29] Dallas L. Jones, "The Enigma of the Clayton Act," *Industrial and Labor Relations Review*, vol. 10 (1957), pp. 201–21.

[30] Dulles, *Labor in America*, pp. 226–28.

discouraged through the use of "yellow-dog" contracts which applicants and employees were required to sign indicating they were not then nor would they become union members.

Local communities organized open shop committees to protect local citizens from outside labor organizers. Reinforcing the local control-local concern idea, many employers did improve wages and working conditions in unorganized plants. Where organizing took place, employers encouraged the workers to establish an organization at the local level, autonomous from a national union, but not necessarily autonomous of the employer.[31]

BOX 2–6
Speech by Charles M. Schwab, Chairman of the Board of Bethlehem Steel to a Chamber of Commerce audience, 1918

"I believe that labor should organize in individual plants or amongst themselves for the better negotiation of labor and the protection of their own rights; but the organization and control of labor in individual plants and manufactories, to my mind, ought to be made representative of the people in those plants who know the conditions; that they ought not to be controlled by somebody from Kamchatka who knows nothing about what their conditions are."

Source: Charles M. Schwab, "Capital and Labor," *A Reconstruction Labor Policy,* Annals of the American Academy of Political and Social Science (January 1919), p. 158.

The end of an era

The 1920s was a decade of transition for the United States in many ways. Organized labor was not untouched by the changes which occurred. The country was shifting from an agriculturally oriented society to one which had an industrial base. Henry Ford had introduced the assembly line, and job skill demands declined in many areas, creating an industrial rather than a craft orientation. Immigration to the United States was limited by quotas so that the influx of unskilled or impoverished potential employees dwindled to a trickle. And while the AFL was taking a stand-pat approach to industrial organization, some of its newer, although nonrevolutionary, leaders began to see the importance of organizing unskilled workers.

Prior to the 1920s, public policy had generally left the development and interpretation of labor law to the courts. As we have seen, the

---

[31] See Chamberlain and Cullen, *The Labor Sector,* pp. 109–10; and Philip Taft, *Organized Labor in American History* (New York: Harper & Row, 1964), chap. 17.

rulings of the courts were predominantly in favor of business, severely restricting the lawful boundaries of union action. The World War I experience and a more sympathetic Congress showed that the conduct of labor-management relations needed some explicit ground rules. This decade spawned the first permanent labor legislation and pointed toward the advent of later legislation.

By the end of the 1920s, American labor could not be adequately described in terms of a stage of development. Looking at the surface of the AFL, one might describe it as a withering, elderly, senile recluse, attending only to its own interests, conserving a shrinking base. Examining the changing role of industry, it might be described as a sleeping giant awaiting the dawn. In terms of internal politics, it might be seen as a festering mass of irreconcilable factions. But regardless of the factionalism, it did have a mainstream and a distinctive flavor subscribed to by most which was vital and unique to the American labor movement. We need now to turn to an explanatory examination of this philosophy and the causes of union evolution.

Union typologies

In 1921, Robert Hoxie established a classification of unions in terms of their goals.[32] His classification is still useful. Hoxie recognized four categories of unions: uplift, revolutionary, business, and predatory. Uplift unionism was concerned with social issues and aimed at the general betterment of educational, monetary, and labor-management systems. The National Labor Union is an example of this type. Revolutionary unions were primarily oriented toward changing the fabric of society, overthrowing the capitalistic system, and replacing it with worker ownership. The IWW serves as the prime American example of this type. Business unionism relates to the representation of employees' employment interests. It is primarily concerned with regulating wages, hours, and terms and conditions of employment. It is represented by the AFL unions. This philosophy was typified by Adolph Strasser, one of the AFL's founders in 1883, when he testified in Congress, "We have no ultimate ends. We are going on from day to day. We are fighting only for immediate objects—objects that can be realized in a few years." Predatory unionism occurs when the union's prime goal is to enhance itself at the expense of the workers it represents.

No U.S. union exists in one of these absolute pure forms, but most appear to duplicate the characteristics of business unionism, being concerned with immediate goals and accepting the system as it is and

---

[32] Robert F. Hoxie, *Trade Unionism in the United States* (New York: Appleton-Century, 1921).

working for its goals within that system. As we move along, we will see where this predominant approach has contributed to its durability and also where it has missed chances to contribute to meaningful changes involving the mainstream of American society.

SUMMARY AND PROLOGUE

The following major points should be apparent to students examining the early U.S. labor movement.

1. Labor organizations have been an integral part of the nation's growth at all stages.
2. At least until the end of the 1920s labor was faced with a hostile national environment.
3. Most of labor's activities could be and were enjoined by the courts when and if they were effective.
4. Most successful labor leaders were concerned about labor's role in representing their members' immediate concerns and in refraining from advocating idealist positions.

In summary, labor has passed over several hurdles in its early organization: the conspiracy doctrine, initial uplift union movements, the link with radicals, and injunctions aimed at union activities. Personalities shaping the American labor movement include Terence Powderly and Uriah Stephens, Samuel Gompers and Adolph Strasser, Eugene Debs and "Big Bill" Haywood.

As we noted, the 1920s was a decade of retrenchment. Underneath the surface there was a growing interest in industrial union organization, particularly by John L. Lewis, president of the United Mine Workers.

Interest in labor legislation was growing. Then in late 1929, the depression began. The following decade—the 1930s—saw most of our present labor legislation being shaped and many of our present-day industrial unions being formed. It was a decade of turbulence, formation, and definition and a necessary adolescence for America's labor-management relations to endure to reach adulthood and relative maturity.

SUGGESTED READINGS

AFL–CIO. *Unions in America: Labor and the Bicentennial* (Washington: AFL–CIO, 1976).

Brecher, Jeremy. *Strike*. (San Francisco: Straight Arrow, 1972).

Cohen, Sanford. *Labor in the United States*, 4th ed. (Columbus, O.: Merrill, 1975).

Dulles, Foster Rhea. *Labor in America: A History*, 3d ed. (New York: Crowell, 1966).

Jones, Mary. *The Autobiography of Mother Jones* (Chicago: Illinois Labor History Society, 1972).

Lens, Sidney. *The Labor Wars: From the Molly Maguires to the Sitdowns* (Garden City, N.Y.: Doubleday, 1974).

Marshall, F. Ray. *Labor in the South* (Cambridge, Mass.: Harvard University Press, 1967).

Morris, Richard B., ed. *The American Worker* (Washington: Government Printing Office, 1976).

Soltow, Martha Jane, and Wery, Mary K. *American Women and the Labor Movement, 1825–1974: An Annotated Bibliography* (Metuchen, N.J.: Scarecrow Press, 1976).

Taft, Philip. *Organized Labor in American History* (New York: Harper and Row, 1964).

U.S. Bureau of Labor Statistics. *A Brief History of the American Labor Movement*, Bulletin 1000 revised (Washington: Government Printing Office, 1970).

DISCUSSION QUESTIONS

1. Trace the evolution of the legal status of American unions. What activities were restricted by laws and courts? Did constraints increase or decline with time?
2. What were the major contributing causes to the failure of uplift unionism?
3. What were the advantages and disadvantages of taking a "business union" approach as opposed to advocating a labor political party?
4. Who were the leading personalities in 19th century labor relations? Which ones contributed to the definition of labor relations in the United States?

3

THE EVOLUTION OF
AMERICAN LABOR: II

To say that the Great Depression of the 1930s caused a reorientation of many American social institutions would be an understatement. Increased regulation of private business activities resulted. The economic security of wage earners was protected. Government assumed the role of employing persons out of work. Government fiscal policy was expressly tailored to affect the economy. And American labor emerged with legislation guaranteeing its legitimacy and protecting many of its activities.

Immediately following the Depression and its labor surpluses were World War II and its labor shortages. The growth of union power resulting from legislation and employer demands for labor made itself felt on the consuming economy after the war was over. This situation led to balancing legislation which has since served as a model for the government's approach to labor-management relations. That approach is roughly to balance the power held by labor and management and to encourage them to settle their differences in a prescribed collective manner without outside interference so long as the public's well-being is not seriously threatened.

In this chapter, we will examine the development of industrial unions, their split with the AFL and subsequent reunification, the effect of federal labor law, the incorporation of administrative procedures occasioned by the laws and World War II, and the thrust of unionization into the public sector of employment. As you move through this chapter you should be on the lookout for several major themes or issues which have had an effect on the evolution of our labor relations system. Among these are:

1. The continuing opposition of the AFL to industrial organization.
2. The shift in public sentiment towards unions in the 1930s and away in the later 1940s, and the influence of this shift on union success.

3. The conflict between revolutionary and business union factions in the newly founded industrials.
4. The role of legislation in creating an atmosphere for collective bargaining, seeking to balance the power of the contending parties, and introducing rules constraining the behavior of both (toward each other and toward individual employees or members).

INDUSTRIAL UNIONS

Up to the 1930s, organization of industrial unions had been generally unsuccessful. We have previously noted that this lack of organizing success was due to a number of factors. Among these were the facts that the supply of unskilled workers was continuously increased by a stream of immigrants, the relative disinterest in industrial organization shown by the AFL, and the tendency of industrially oriented unions to adopt revolutionary goals. By the middle 1930s a new set of circumstances had evolved which created an atmosphere more favorable for industrial organizing. The Depression and legislative initiatives in labor-management relations helped. Established union leaders with a business union orientation took up the industrial organizing crusade. Elected officials became more tolerant of, or actively in favor of, union activity.

The industrial union leadership

The early leadership of Eugene Debs and "Big Bill" Haywood had lapsed for more than a decade when industrial organizing efforts resumed. This time the leadership came from within the AFL. John L. Lewis and other officials of the United Mine Workers (UMW), an AFL union, spearheaded the drive over the objections of the craft unions.

Lewis was an established leader within the AFL, but his UMW was faced with membership problems in a declining industry. A realist, Lewis decided it was time, in the 1930s, to make a push for industrial organizing. He was not prepared for the adamant opposition to industrial unionism which he met within the AFL. In an acrimonious debate at the 1935 AFL convention, Lewis and "Big Bill" Hutcheson, president of the Carpenters' Union, actually came to blows. The convention voted 18,000 to 11,000 to uphold craft unionism and not embark on industrial organization. After the convention, leaders of the UMW (Lewis and Philip Murray), the Amalgamated Clothing Workers (Sidney Hillman), the International Ladies' Garment Workers (David Dubinsky), the Typographical Union (Charles Howard), the Textile Workers (Thomas McMahon), the cap and millinery department of the United Hatters (Max Zaritsky), the Oil Field, Gas Well, and Refining

Workers (Harvey Flemming), and the Mine, Mill, and Smelter Workers (Thomas Brown) met to form the Committee for Industrial Organization (CIO).[1]

BOX 3–1
Lewis and Hutcheson at the 1935 AFL convention

The industrial union report was defeated, but the question kept recurring. Delegates from rubber, radio, mine, and mill kept urging a new policy. Their way was blocked, though, not least by the towering figure of Big Bill Hutcheson, powerful head of the Carpenters' Union. Hutcheson and Lewis had always held similar views and frequently worked together. Like Lewis, Hutcheson was a big man, 6 feet tall and 220 pounds. When a delegate raised the question of industrial unionism in the rubber plants, Hutcheson raised a point of order. The question had already been settled, he contended. Lewis objected; the delegate should be heard on a problem facing his own union. "This thing of raising points of order," he added, "is rather small potatoes."

"I was raised on small potatoes," Hutcheson replied.

As Lewis returned to his seat, he paused to tell Hutcheson that his opposition was pretty small stuff. "We could have made you small," was the reply. "We could have kept you off the executive council, you crazy bastard."

Lewis swung a wild haymaker. It caught Hutcheson on the jaw; the two men grappled, crashed against a table, and fell awkwardly to the floor. President Green wildly hammered his gavel as delegates tried to separate the two heavyweights.

Source: David F. Selvin, *The Thundering Voice of John L. Lewis* (New York: Lathrop, Lee, & Shepard, 1969), pp. 103–104.

Organizing the industrial work force

Major efforts were begun to organize workers in basic industries: steel, textiles, rubber, autos. Philip Murray headed the Steel Workers Organizing Committee (SWOC) which succeeded in establishing 150 locals totaling over 100,000 members by the end of 1936. In early 1937, through the secret efforts of John L. Lewis and Myron Taylor, head of U.S. Steel, SWOC was recognized as the workers' bargaining agent, the 8-hour day and 40-hour week were granted, and a wage increase was won. The other steel firms were not so readily organized, and violence broke out as ten strikers were killed by Chicago police on Memorial Day 1937.[2]

---

[1] Joseph G. Rayback, *A History of American Labor* (New York: Free Press, 1966), pp. 348–50.

[2] Foster Rhea Dulles, *Labor in America*, 3d ed. (New York: Crowell, 1966), pp. 299–302.

The auto workers were next. Despite the relatively high wages pioneered by Henry Ford, the jobs were tedious and fatiguing, and the owners had established private police forces to keep the workers in line.[3] Initial organizing began in 1936. By the end of the year the United Automobile Workers (UAW) under its president, Homer Martin, sought recognition from and bargaining with General Motors. GM refused, but worker sentiments were strong enough so that "quickie" strikes against the company resulted.[4]

Then in late 1936 the UAW embarked on a strategy which was successful in forcing GM recognition and negotiations. This was the "sit-down" strike. Auto workers in the Fisher body plants of GM in Flint, Michigan, refused to leave their work places and took over the plants. GM viewed this as criminal trespass, but the workers asserted that job rights were superior to property rights. Injunctions were obtained to oust the workers, but these were ignored. Attempts to persuade Governor Frank Murphy to mobilize the militia to enforce the injunction failed. Realizing that the workers could hold out, GM capitulated in February 1937, agreeing to recognize the UAW and promising not to discriminate against union members.[5]

BOX 3–2
Telegram from sit-down strikers to Governor Murphy

"Governor, we have decided to stay in the plant. We have no illusions about the sacrifices which the decision will entail. We fully expect that if a violent effort is made to oust us many of us will be killed and we take this means of making it known to our wives, to our children, to the people of the state of Michigan and of the country that if this result follows from the attempt to eject us you are the one who must be held responsible for our deaths."

Source: Sidney Fine, *Sit-Down: The General Motors Strike of 1936–1937* (Ann Arbor: University of Michigan Press, 1969), p. 278.

A short time later, this tactic was used successfully to organize Chrysler Corporation workers as well as glass, rubber, and textile workers. Industrial unionization had been achieved. In fact, by the

---

[3] Martin J. Gannon, "Entrepreneurship and Labor Relations at the Ford Motor Company," *Marquette Business Review*, vol. 16 (Summer 1972), pp. 63–75.

[4] Rayback, *A History of American Labor*, p. 353.

[5] Sidney Fine, *Sit-Down: The General Motors Strike of 1936–1937* (Ann Arbor: University of Michigan Press, 1969).

end of 1937, the CIO union membership of 3,700,000 exceeded membership in the older AFL by 300,000.[6]

LEGISLATION

Organized labor did not achieve overnight success in its efforts to unionize workers. But by the 1930s, public policy towards unions had shifted radically from the previous two decades. In the past, until the Railway Labor Act in 1926, no legislation had been implemented which facilitated organization or bargaining. Courts had consistently enjoined unions from striking, organizing, picketing, and other activities, even if peacefully conducted. State laws regulating injunctive powers of state courts were likewise struck down by the Supreme Court in *Truax* v. *Corrigan*, a case testing an Arizona statute.[7]

Norris-LaGuardia Act (1932)

By the time the Norris-LaGuardia Act was passed in 1932 Congress favored collective bargaining. In view of earlier judicial decisions, it pointed out the fact that capital had been collectivizable through incorporation while labor was not. At that time, acceptance of a collective bargaining relationship had to devolve from a voluntary employer action.[8]

To grant organized labor relief from federal court injunctions for collective activity, the act guarantees the right to strike for any purpose, the right to pay strike benefits, the right to picket, the right to ask other employees to strike, the right financially to aid persons involved in court actions over labor disputes, the right to meet on strike strategy, and the right to organize using nonemployees by severely restricting the power of federal courts to issue injunctions in labor disputes. The act also forbade federal courts from enforcing the "yellow-dog" contract, which required employees or job applicants to agree, as a condition of employment, not to join a labor union. Previously, if one joined after signing such an agreement and were discharged as a result, federal courts could and did uphold the discharge.[9]

While the Norris-LaGuardia Act protected numerous previously enjoinable activities, it was neutral policy—not opening up any right to

---

[6] Rayback, *A History of American Labor*, pp. 354–55.

[7] 257 U.S. 312 (1921).

[8] Benjamin J. Taylor and Fred Witney, *Labor Relations Law*, 2d ed. (Englewood Cliffs, N.J.: Prentice-Hall, 1975), pp. 144–46.

[9] *Hitchman Coal Co.* v. *Mitchell*, 245 U.S. 229 (1917).

demand employer recognition. Other than the removal of the yellow-dog contract, there were still no explicit federal ground rules for employer conduct in labor-management relations. This would be changed following the inauguration of President Franklin D. Roosevelt.

National Industrial Recovery Act (1933)

The National Industrial Recovery Act (NIRA), adopted in 1933, was not principally labor legislation. In fact, as a major part of the bill, employers were encouraged to band together and set prices and production quotas through industrial codes. To complete an industrial code, however, employers were required to include a provision enabling employees to bargain through representatives of their own choosing, free from employer interference.

NIRA survived for only two years before it was found to be unconstitutional. For labor, it is perhaps fortunate that it did not survive, since the law included no enforcement mechanism to guarantee rights to organize. It did, however, sow the seeds for the first piece of comprehensive labor legislation enacted in the United States.[10]

The Wagner Act (National Labor Relations Act, 1935)

The NIRA was beginning to bog down even before it was ruled unconstitutional.[11] Big business objected to the requirement to include the legitimization of union activities in their codes while smaller businesses objected to the monopoly powers inherent in the codes. Unions lost their safeguards when the NIRA was wiped out, although the 1934 amendments to the Railway Labor Act secured them for some transportation employees. The Wagner Act was rolled into place to resecure organizational rights included in the NIRA as well as to specify activities which, if practiced by employers, would be illegal.[12]

Section 7 is the heart of the act, specifying the rights of employees to engage in union activities: "Employees shall have the right to self-organization, to form, join, or assist labor organizations, to bargain collectively through representatives of their own choosing, and to engage in concerted activities, for the purpose of collective bargaining or other mutual aid or protection." To specify the types of actions which would be presumed to interfere with Section 7 rights, Congress created Section 8. Section 8 broadly forbade interference with em-

---

[10] Taylor and Witney, *Labor Relations Law*, pp. 147–48.

[11] *Schecter Poultry Corp.* v. *United States*, 295 U.S. 495 (1935).

[12] Dulles, *Labor in America*, pp. 273–75.

ployees' rights to be represented and to bargain, to have their labor organizations free from employer dominance, to be protected from employment discrimination for union activity, and to be free from retaliation for accusing the employer of an unlawful (unfair) labor practice.

To investigate violations of Section 8 and to determine whether or not employees desired representation, the Wagner Act established the National Labor Relations Board (NLRB), whose major duties were to determine which, if any, unions were the employees' choice to represent them collectively and to hear and rule on alleged unfair labor practices.

The Wagner Act also statutorily established the agency relationship between the union as bargaining agent and the employee. Where a union was certified as the choice of the majority of employees all employees in that unit, regardless of union membership, would be represented by the union on issues of wages, hours, and terms and conditions of employment.

The Wagner Act did not apply to all employers and employees, although a major portion of the private sector was covered. Specifically exempted were the following employers: federal, state, and local governments, those subject to the Railway Labor Act, and labor organizations (except when acting as employees). Employee groups specifically exempted were agricultural laborers, domestic employees, and family workers.

The passage of the Wagner Act did not immediately presage a shift in U.S. labor relations, however. With the NIRA recently having been declared void by the Supreme Court and with Section 7 of the Wagner Act closely duplicating the NIRA section, some employers expected the courts to rule against Congress on a constitutional challenge.

EMPLOYER INTRANSIGENCE

Congressional investigators disclosed that between 1933 and 1937 companies had systematically spied on union activities, infiltrated union government, and spent almost $10 million for spying, strike-breaking, and munitions. In strike preparations, Youngstown Sheet and Tube had amassed 8 machine guns, 369 rifles, 190 shotguns, 450 revolvers, 109 gas guns, 3,000 rounds of gas, and almost 10,000 rounds of shotgun shells and bullets. Republic Steel had purchased almost $80,000 worth of repellent gases and was allegedly the largest nonlaw enforcement arsenal in the United States.[13]

---

[13] Ibid., pp. 277–78.

Another device employers used was a strategy called the "Mohawk Valley" formula, which was aimed at linking unions with agitators and Communists, organizing back-to-work drives, getting local police to break up strikes, and aligning local interests against the focus of union activities.[14]

While employers doubted the constitutionality of the Wagner Act and remained adamant in opposing union activity, workers viewed the congressional action as a legitimation of their position. The Act had created a mechanism for determining whether or not unions represented units of employees. The fact that almost half of strikes between 1935 and 1937 were not over bargaining issues, but to obtain recognition, reflects the adamancy of employers as well as the new militancy of unions. Both sides had reasons to believe their positions to be valid. Management had seen a long line of Supreme Court decisions adverse to labor, not the least of these being the striking down of the NIRA which was partially similar to the Wagner Act. Labor had seen sympathy for its position grow throughout the country and, with President Roosevelt consolidating his position through the overwhelming electoral endorsement of the New Deal in 1936, felt the court would find it difficult to invalidate the law.[15]

The answer came on April 12, 1937, with the Supreme Court's decision in the *Jones & Laughlin* case.[16] The NLRB had previously determined that Jones & Laughlin had violated the Wagner Act by coercing employees and discriminating against union members. It had ordered ten employees reinstated with back pay and told the firm to cease its unfair labor practices. The appeals court had held that the board's action was beyond the range of federal power, but the Supreme Court agreed to review the case.

By a 5–4 majority, the Supreme Court sided with the board and upheld the validity of the Act. The court held first that Congress may regulate employer activities under the Constitution's commerce clause. Second, it reaffirmed the right of employees to organize and recognized Congress's authority to restrict employer activities likely to disrupt organization. Third, the court ruled that manufacturing, even if conducted locally, was a process involving interstate commerce. Fourth, the effects of Jones & Laughlin's antiunion activities would have a significant possible effect on interstate commerce. Fifth, it is reasonable for Congress to set rules and procedures governing employees' rights to organize. Finally, the Court found that the board's conduct at the hearing and its orders were regular, within the meaning of the Act, and protected.

[14] Ibid., p. 278.

[15] Taylor and Witney, *Labor Relations Law*, pp. 161–64.

[16] *NLRB* v. *Jones & Laughlin Steel Corp.*, 301 U.S. 1 (1937).

Thus, the Wagner Act passed the Supreme Court's test and opened an era of rapid industrial organization.

LABOR POWER

Pre–World War II

The momentum gained by the CIO in its split with the AFL continued for the remainder of the 1930s. Both federations also engaged in raids of each other's members with employers helplessly caught in the midst of these disputes. These jurisdictional disputes[17] created public hostility and led to some state legislation outlawing certain union activities.

While labor had been instrumental in getting its friends elected since the Depression began, its ranks began to split in 1940 when John L. Lewis announced his support for Wendell Wilkie, abandoning President Roosevelt. The split began in 1937 when Lewis felt the federal government had not done enough to aid labor. He obviously expected help from the Democratic administration in exchange for labor's campaign assistance during the GM sit-down strike when he said: "For six months the economic royalists represented by General Motors contributed their money and used their energy to drive this administration [Roosevelt's] out of power. The administration asked labor for help and labor gave it. The same economic royalists now have their fangs in labor. The workers of this country expect the administration to help the workers in every legal way and to support the workers in General Motors plants."[18]

Roosevelt did nothing except urge meetings between the UAW and the company. Later, during the "Little Steel" campaign, Roosevelt incurred Lewis's wrath by criticizing labor and management jointly: "a plague o' both your houses." Lewis responded by chastising Roosevelt. "It ill behooves one who has supped at labor's table and who has been sheltered in labor's house to curse with equal fervor and fine impartiality both labor and its adversaries when they become locked in deadly embrace."[19]

During the prewar period, it became apparent that an increasingly large number of industrial union staff positions were held by Communists. This group broke the line in President Roosevelt's support for the Allies after Germany and Russia signed their nonaggression pact in 1939.

---

[17] A jurisdictional dispute occurs when two or more unions claim to (1) simultaneously represent or attempt to bargain for the same employee group; or (2) simultaneously assert that its members are entitled by contract to a certain class of work.

[18] Rayback, *A History of American Labor*, p. 368.

[19] Ibid., p. 368.

Nineteen forty-one was a crisis year for labor-management relations. Labor's ambivalent stand toward the war (among the industrials) had allowed employers to brand them as nonpatriotic. While this stand shifted when Philip Murray became the president of the CIO in 1940, the label was not entirely removed. Employers refused to recognize unions, although union organizing of Ford and "Little Steel" was finally successful. Perhaps for the first time labor's goal of "more, more, more now" was becoming intolerable to the general public. Over 4,300 strikes broke out in 1941, involving in excess of 8 percent of the work force. This widespread industrial disruption would probably have been moderated by congressional action had it not been for the attack on Pearl Harbor involving the United States in World War II.[20]

World War II

At the outbreak of World War II, both the AFL and CIO and management pledged to produce together to meet the war effort. Labor pledged not to strike if a board was established to handle unresolved grievances. Management did not entirely concede and, as a result, President Roosevelt established the National War Labor Board (NWLB). As the war got underway, prices rose more rapidly than in the previous several years. Labor's demands for wage increases grew, but the NWLB attempted to maintain a policy whereby wage increases (unless not recently attained) would be equal to changes in the cost of living. Labor objected to the dual check of collective bargaining and the NWLB on wages, but the policy was not changed.[21]

While no-strike pledges had been given, in 1945, 4,750 strikes involving 3,470,000 workers with 38,000,000 man-days lost were recorded. This exceeded the prewar high of 28,400,000 in 1937. Major sporadic strikes in the coal industry, led by John L. Lewis, were particularly evident to the public. At one point the coal mines had to be seized and run by Secretary of the Interior Harold Ickes.[22]

The strike activity presages some postwar legislative developments with the passage over President Roosevelt's veto of the War Labor Disputes Act. This act authorized the seizure of plants involved in labor disputes, made strikes and lockouts in defense industries a criminal offense, required 30 days' notice of a pending dispute to the NWLB, and required the NLRB to monitor strike votes.[23]

---

[20] Ibid., pp. 370–73.

[21] Philip Taft, *Organized Labor in American History* (New York: Harper & Row, 1964), pp. 546–52.

[22] Ibid., pp. 553–56.

[23] Ibid., p. 557.

BOX 3–3
Comments by President Roosevelt on coal strikes during 1943

On June 23d, the President issued a statement in which he said that "the action of the leaders of the United Mine Workers coal miners has been intolerable—and has rightly stirred up the anger and disapproval of the over-whelming mass of the American people."

He declared that the mines would be operated by the government under the terms of the board's directive order of June 18th.

He stated that "the government had taken steps to set up the machinery for inducting into the armed services all miners subject to the Selective Service Act who absented themselves, without just cause, from work in the mines under government operation." Since the "Selective Service Act does not authorize the induction of men above 45 years into the armed services, I intend to request the Congress to raise the age limit for noncombat service to 65 years. I shall make that request of the Congress so that if at any time in the future there should be a threat of interruption of work in plants, mines or establishments owned by the government, or taken possession of by the government, the machinery will be available for prompt action."

Source: Arthur Suffern, "The National War Labor Board and Coal," in *The Termination Report of the National War Labor Board,* vol. 1: Industrial Disputes ánd Wage Stabilization in Wartime (Washington: Government Printing Office, 1948), p. 1099.

While this overview of World War II has not reflected accommodation and innovation, the evidence reveals they were there. In only 46 of 17,650 dispute cases going before the NWLB did the parties fail to reach or accept agreements. And the war experience led to a widespread acceptance of fringe benefits in lieu of wage increases. Holidays, vacations, sick leaves, and shift differentials began to be approved as parts of labor contracts by the NWLB. Labor shortages led for the first time to policies advocating equal employment opportunities for minorities and equal pay for men and women in the same jobs.[24]

Reconversion

As the war ended, consumers anticipated the return of goods unavailable during the war. Labor looked forward to wage increases after the cost-of-living changes during the war. The inevitable clash of labor and management led to the greatest single yearly period of labor conflict in U.S. history. During this period, 4,630 strikes involving

---

[24] Ibid., pp. 559–62.

4,900,000 workers losing 119,800,000 man-days (or 1.62 percent of total days available) occurred between August 1945 and August 1946. Most major industries were affected, with major strikes being called in coal, rails, autos, and steel. These were settled with wage increases averaging about 18.5 cents per hour and some, especially in steel, resulted in price increases as well.[25]

The end of the war, the strikes, and the election of a more conservative Congress led to legislation to balance the power of the unions and management.

RESTORING THE BALANCE

The Wagner Act had been passed during a period where industrial organizing was just beginning and where the array of weapons employers had with which to battle labor was overwhelming. The Wagner Act had aimed to strike a balance between the contenders. Over the ten years since its passage, however, the challenger had now become the champion. The strikes of 1941, the coal problems during World War II, and the labor difficulties encountered in 1946, all had their effect on stimulating legislation to expand and clarify rules to be applied to the practice of U.S. labor relations.

While the Wagner Act had addressed only employer unfair labor practices, critics of the labor movement argued that unions could also engage in tactics which might coerce individual employees and constitute a refusal to bargain collectively. The balancing legislation was contained in amendments and additions to the Wagner Act entitled the Labor Management Relations Act of 1947, better known as Taft-Hartley.

Taft-Hartley Act

Employee rights were expanded in Section 7 to include not only the right to join, but the right to refrain from, union activities unless a contract between an employer and a union required union activity. In most cases this right to refrain allowed collective bargaining agreements to require, at most, joining a union or paying dues. But Congress went even farther than that in adding Section 14(b) which enabled states to pass even more restrictive legislation regarding employees' rights to refrain from union activities. In these states so-called right-to-work laws make illegal any contract provision requiring union membership as a condition of employment. Most of the states passing right-to-work laws have been either southern or predominantly ag-

---

[25] Ibid., pp. 563–78.

ricultural states where union strength has never been high.[26] Efforts at passage in Ohio and California failed in 1958, and Indiana voters repealed a state statute in 1965. Right-to-work laws are highly emotional issues both to their proponents and their opponents. Organized labor refers to them as "right-to-wreck" laws, enabling nonmembers to act as free riders utilizing union gains applicable to an entire bargaining unit without contributing money or effort to the cause. Proponents see the laws as essential to one's freedom of association and protective of one's right to join or not join organizations. The heat of the rhetoric on both sides is probably greater than the impact of the statutes.

Section 8 was amended to restrict a union's treatment of its members, recognizing the agency role the union plays for all bargaining unit members. Unions were required to bargain in good faith with employers and were forbidden from striking to gain recognition or to put pressure on outside, uninvolved second parties to get at a primary employer.

Title II was an entirely new addition to U.S. labor legislation. First, it established the Federal Mediation and Conciliation Service (FMCS) to help in the settlement of unresolved contractual disputes. These acts of assistance could be requested by the parties or offered directly by the FMCS. Second, provision was made for intervention in strikes likely to create a national emergency. If the president determined that a current or pending labor dispute imperiled the nation, he could convene a board of inquiry to find the issues and the positions of the parties. If he then believed that it was a national emergency, the attorney general could seek to have the strike or lockout enjoined for 80 days. During the first 60 days the parties would continue negotiations. At the end of this period, if agreement had not been reached, the board of inquiry would report the last positions of both parties. The NLRB would then hold an election in which union members would vote to accept or reject management's last offer. The results of the election would then be certified by the end of the 80 days. If the membership voted to accept, the contract was made; if to reject, they were free to strike, although the president is directed to submit a report to Congress so that Congress may consider taking action.

Title III dealt with suits by and against labor organizations. Suits seeking damages from either employers or unions for violating labor contracts were permitted. Recovery of damages was restricted to the assets of the organization, not the individual members. Union officials were forbidden to accept money from employers, and it was unlawful

---

[26] Alabama, Arizona, Arkansas, Florida, Georgia, Iowa, Kansas, Louisiana, Mississippi, Nebraska, Nevada, North Carolina, North Dakota, South Carolina, South Dakota, Tennessee, Texas, Utah, Virginia, and Wyoming.

BOX 3–4
Union position on Taft-Hartley

At this moment Congress is rushing headlong into one of the worst legislative blunders in history—the enactment of repressive and restrictive labor bills which would disrupt and demoralize labor-management relations if they become law.

The whole purpose of this legislation—regardless of the hypocritical claims of its sponsors—is to destroy the power of trade unions to serve the workers of America effectively.

The American Federation of Labor hereby declares war against this legislation—an all-out war for the preservation of the life of free trade unionism in America.

Whether the proponents of the pending legislation realize it or not, they are opening the door to fascism in America by impairing freedoms basic to the American way of life, and they are likewise encouraging the subversive enemies of democracy to foment a class struggle in our land which would weaken our nation's leadership on the international front.

To carry on the fight against this impending evil, the executive council is preparing to rally the entire membership of the American Federation of Labor and to mobilize a substantial portion of trade union resources for a program of concerted action. Details of this program, aimed at awakening the American people to the dangers contained in this legislation, will be announced later.

The sponsors of the House and Senate bills are trying to make labor the goat for all the ills which the nation has suffered since the war ended. They claim they have a mandate from the American people to enact laws which would place trade unions in a straight-jacket. That is a false and specious assertion.

Clever politicians in Congress, aided and abetted by the powerful National Association of Manufacturers and other special interests, have taken advantage of public impatience over high prices, scarcities of peacetime necessities, and other postwar maladjustments. They have tried to make the public believe that once the trade unions are stripped of the power to protect the interests of the nation's workers, all these economic problems will be solved.

To justify the drive against organized labor, our opponents in Congress have sought to give the public a distorted picture of the state of labor-management relations in this country by bringing in a few recalcitrant and spiteful employers to air their grievances at open hearings, while they have studiously ignored the many thousands of American employers who enjoy satisfactory relations with unions.

On this flimsy basis, relying on ballyhoo instead of a fact-finding investigation, Congress is now about to cripple and rip apart the fabric and techniques of successful and effective collective bargaining, which is the only democratic and fair machinery for the establishment and maintenance of industrial peace and high production.

BOX 3–4 (*continued*)

There is no question that the people of this country want peace on the industrial front. But they have too much good sense to hold the workers and their trade unions responsible for every dispute and strike that occurs. They know that it takes two to make a quarrel and that management is at least equally responsible for such strife as develops. And they know that the basic cause of most of the strikes that have taken place since V-J Day was the refusal of management to pay wages which would enable the masses of our people to maintain the American standard of living in the face of the economic dislocation and the inflated cost of living which we inherited from the war.

Unfortunately, the American people have been kept ignorant of the fact that collective bargaining is working successfully under our present laws whereever and whenever management practices it sincerely with trade unions and that there are a thousand unpublicized cases of agreement between employers and unions for each disagreement which is played up in the headlines. In the name of drastic treatment of these exceptional cases, Congress is voting legislation which would make agreements impossible in the vast majority of cases.

If such legislation becomes law, it will wreck production in America and flood the nation with industrial strife. The workers of America will never submit to slavery, nor will they work against their will under conditions which are obnoxious to them. They have no intention of meekly acquiescing in legislative robbery of the gains they have won through their trade unions after long years of patient effort.

Freedom is the most precious asset of the American people. Abrogation of the freedom of American workers by legislative action must lead inevitably to the undermining of the freedoms of those in all other walks of life. Let businessmen, especially, keep in mind that the free enterprise system depends upon the freedom of labor and will be jeopardized if labor is enslaved.

The provisions in the pending legislation which would restore government by injunction constitute a direct invasion of fundamental American liberty. The black history of the abuses of the labor injunction by the courts in the past should serve as a bar against its future employment. To make kings of judges, as a recent decree—more royalistic than judicial—permitted, is repugnant to a free America.

The executive council calls upon President Truman to show real statesmanship and leadership in this crisis. It is up to him to stand by the principles he has repeatedly enunciated and to withstand powerful pressure from the moneyed interests and their Congressional lackeys. It is his duty to protect the interests of American workers and the American people as a whole by vetoing the final, illegitimate off-spring of the current House and Senate labor bills.

Source: *American Federationist*, vol. 58 (April 1947), pp. 2–3.

for employers to offer inducements to them. This title further provided that boycotts to force an employer to cease doing business with others were illegal. Corporations and labor unions were forbidden to make political contributions. Finally, federal employees were forbidden to strike.

The overall thrust of the legislation was to balance the relative power of the contenders and to provide mechanisms through the FMCS and national emergency dispute procedures to reduce the likelihood of a recurrence of the 1946 labor strife. Since the bill represented a retreat from the initiatives labor had previously enjoyed, it was (to say the least) not greeted with enthusiasm in that quarter. But the bill satisfied business, the Congress, and the public. The bill passed by wide margins in both houses, was vetoed by President Truman, and repassed over his veto.

RETRENCHMENT AND MERGER

The AFL and CIO both regarded the Taft-Hartley Act as a "slave labor" bill. They saw the possibility that labor disputes would be again subject to injunctions through the national emergency procedures. Actually, these procedures have been used sparsely.

In one major case where it could have been used, President Truman seized the nation's steel mills in 1952 rather than invoke the national emergency steps. When the Supreme Court declared his action unconstitutional, he was forced to return operations to management and a strike ensued. We will examine the mechanisms and uses of Taft-Hartley injunctions in greater detail in Chapter 11.

Organized labor realized two things following Taft-Hartley. First, it would have to exert more influence in legislative activity and adopt a more publicly advocative stance on issues concerning labor. Second, the strength of labor had been equalized in relation to that of management by the Taft-Hartley Act. The time had come to direct labor's energies toward unity rather than division. The old guard present at the sundering of the AFL was disappearing. Green and Murray both died in 1952. This resulted in George Meany becoming president of the AFL and Walter Reuther becoming president of the CIO. John L. Lewis's UMW was unaffiliated, thereby greatly reducing the historic friction.[27]

Merger

The first step toward rapprochement was the ratification of a no-raid agreement by both the AFL and CIO conventions in 1954. A Joint

---

[27] Dulles, *Labor in America*, pp. 360–72.

BOX 3–5
George Meany on labor's role

Plain realism dictates, therefore, that our thinking about the America of the quarter century ahead must be limited to goals rather than to predictions. Yet long-range goals, if they are meaningful, originate in the world of today and are shaped by one's tradition and one's philosophy. In a single man's lifetime, 25 years is a long time, perhaps half the span of his mature, vigorous life. Institutions, and the men who reflect them, have a longer perspective than individuals alone, and in the A.F. of L. our traditions and our philosophy have emerged from an experience of 75 years. Our goals can be understood only in terms of that experience. Moreover, the goals of a future but a quarter of a century away will not appear so unreal when measured against a philosophy hammered out by millions of Americans over the course of three quarters of a century.

Our goals as trade unionists are modest, for we do not seek to recast American society in any particular doctrinaire or ideological image. We seek an ever-rising standard of living. Sam Gompers once put the matter succinctly. When asked what the labor movement wanted, he answered "More." If by a better standard of living, we mean not only more money but more leisure and a richer cultural life, the answer remains, "More."

But how do we get "more"? Imperfect in many details as our system may be, this country has adopted a flexible method for increasing the standard of living while maintaining freedom. It is the method of voluntary collective bargaining, of free decision making outside the coercions of government, in the solution of economic disagreement. And it is through the give-and-take of collective bargaining that we seek to achieve our goals.

Source: George Meany, "What Labor Means by 'More,' " *Fortune,* Vol. 26 (March 1955), p. 92.

Unity Committee was also established to explore ways to devise a merger. On February 9, 1955, a merger was announced forming the combined AFL–CIO. George Meany became president of the merged federations.[28]

Meany expounded the merged federation's goals in 1955. He reendorsed Gompers's concept of "more" as it applied to one's standard and quality of living. He reiterated labor's commitment to collective bargaining. He was unwilling to involve labor in management but demanded that management's stewardship be high.[29] Essentially, his essay was a reiteration of the goals and past behavior of the union movement; careful member oriented activity, yet with a degree of social concern recognizing that advances for its members may lead to advances for society.

---

[28] Ibid., pp. 372–74.

[29] George Meany, "What Labor Means by 'More,' " *Fortune,* vol. 26 (March 1955), pp. 92–93.

The merged AFL–CIO did not become a more powerful movement. In fact, in terms of union penetration it reached its peak in 1956 with about one third of the nonagricultural work force unionized. By 1964, this proportion had fallen to 30 percent, and an absolute decline of 700,000 members was recorded. Part was due to less aggressive organizing, some to better nonunion employee relations, and a portion to the reduced relative proportion of blue-collar manufacturing workers. Whatever the reasons, the 1956–1965 decade was one of malaise and retreat for the labor movement.[30] Unions did not gain stature in the public eye either, but they did gain some unwanted notoriety as congressional investigators uncovered gross malfeasance by some major national union officers.

Corruption

In 1957 the Senate Select Committee on Improper Activities in the Labor Management Field convened its investigations under Chairman Senator John L. McClellan. For the next two and a half years, the American public was exposed to televised hearings with wholesale invocations of Fifth Amendment privileges by a parade of labor officials.

The Teamsters Union drew the lion's share of the spotlight as witnesses disclosed that its president, Dave Beck, had converted union funds to his own use, borrowed money from employers, and received kickbacks from labor "consultants." James R. Hoffa was accused of breaking Teamster strikes and covertly running his own trucking operation. "Sweatheart" contracts, offering substandard benefits and guaranteeing labor peace, were uncovered in the New York area in unions chartered by the Teamsters and operated by racketeers.

Other unions such as the Bakery and Confectionary Workers, Operating Engineers, Carpenters, and United Textile Workers were also involved. Management contributed to the corruption by providing payoffs for "sweetheart" contracts preventing others from organizing but paying substandard rates.[31]

The publicity associated with the hearings cast a pall over the entire labor movement. By inference, all labor was corrupt. The AFL–CIO investigated internally and considered charges against the Allied Industrial Workers, Bakers, Distillers, Laundry Workers, Textile Workers, and Teamsters. The Textile Workers, Distillers, and Allied Industrial Workers agreed to mandated changes. The Bakers, Laundry Workers, and Teamsters did not, and were expelled from the AFL–

---

[30] Dulles, *Labor in America,* pp. 377–81.

[31] Taft, *Organized Labor in American History,* pp. 698–704.

BOX 3–6

Congressional Testimony in the Teamsters Investigation

Mr. Kennedy. And were the funds of the Teamster fund taken from the international union here in Washington to pay your own personal bills?

Mr. Beck. I decline to answer on the Fifth Amendment.

Mr. Kennedy. And were Teamster funds taken from the Los Angeles local to buy an automobile for you and then the Los Angeles local reimbursed by the Teamster Union funds in Seattle?

Mr. Beck. I decline to answer on the Fifth Amendment.

Mr. Kennedy. Were any of the funds taken out of the Teamsters Union in Seattle and put in your own personal bank account since January 1, 1951?

Mr. Beck. I decline to answer on the Fifth Amendment.

Mr. Kennedy. And were cashiers checks used for your own personal benefits, since January 1, 1951?

Mr. Beck. I decline to answer on the Fifth Amendment.

Mr. Williams. Mr. Chairman, I will stipulate for the record that the witness will assert his rights under the Constitution to each of these questions which Mr. Kennedy is now reading. He is reading all 52 of them.

The Chairman. Since counsel stipulates that these questions are being asked, the Chair will order all of them inserted in the record at this point.

I understand that counsel is going to advise his client, and the client is going to act upon that advice and decline to answer all questions pertaining to these matters by invoking the Fifth Amendment?

Mr. Williams. That is right, sir. We will so stipulate.

(Questions referred to follow:)

Dave Beck—Some 52 ways in which Dave Beck misused his authority, position, and trust as president of the Western Conference of Teamsters and subsequently as president of the International Brotherhood of Teamsters

1. Misappropriation of Teamster funds by payments to John Lindsay and John Lindsay Construction Co. in connection with work done on his own real estate development and renovations on his home in Seattle.

2. Misappropriation of Teamster funds by direct payments to Nathan Shefferman from Teamster accounts for payment of Beck's personal bills.

3. Misappropriation of Teamster funds by indirect payments from Teamster funds in the Seattle Teamsters' accounts in Los Angeles; thence, payments to Nathan Shefferman in payments of personal bills of Dave Beck.

BOX 3–6 (*continued*)

4. Misappropriation of Teamster funds by payments from the international union to Nathan Shefferman for the personal bills of Dave Beck.

5. Misappropriation of Teamster funds by the purchase of a personal automobile paid by Los Angeles Teamsters local; this local was later reimbursed with funds from the Western Conference of Teamsters.

6. Misappropriation of Teamster funds by using these funds to pay Beck's own personal bank loan.

7. Misappropriation of Teamster funds in connection with the purchase of cashier checks, which purchasers were charged to Teamster bank accounts and the proceeds used for his personal use.

8. Misappropriation of Teamster funds by causing the Joint Council No. 28 Building Association to obtain loans, the proceeds of which went directly to Beck's bank account.

9. Ordering the payment of Teamster funds to two news reporters writing his biography.

10. The funneling of some $9 million of Teamster funds through the National Mortgage Co., in which a relative purchased a one-third interest with money received from Beck.

11. The obtaining of Teamster insurance from an insurance company in which his family had an interest.

12. Obtaining a share of the commission on the purchase of a mortgage from the Lanphar Co. by the Teamsters Union.

13. Obtaining a share of commission on purchase of Federal National Mortgage Insurance Agency mortgages with Teamster funds through National Mortgage Co.

14. Obtaining share of commission on purchase of 35 miscellaneous loans with Teamster funds through National Mortgage Co.

15. Obtaining Teamster funds to purchase contracts which were then sold to the Ray Leheney memorial fund at a considerable profit to himself.

16. The acquisition of land at Parkwood No. 1 in Snohomish County, Wash., and the immediate sale to the Linton Construction Co. at a considerably higher price, the ultimate financing being handled with Teamster funds.

17. The acquisition of land at Firwood Park in Snohomish County, Wash., and its immediate sale to the Linton Construction Co. at a substantial profit, the ultimate financing being handled with Teamster funds.

18. The obtaining for a friend and business partner, brokerage commissions paid by T. J. Bettes, Lambrecht Realty Co., A. D. Robbs, and the PBC Investment Co., which concerns received Teamster funds in connection with sale of mortgages.

BOX 3–6 (*continued*)

19. Borrowing $273,000 at 3½ percent interest from the Occidental Life Insurance Co., which company was the insurer for the Western Conference of Teamsters.

20. Subsequently borrowing another $40,000 at 3½ percent interest from the Occidental Life Insurance Co.

21. For his own personal benefit and without cost, requested the Occidental Life Insurance Co. to make an appraisal of the Vista Delmar property.

22. For his own personal benefit, requested the Occidental Life Insurance Co. to make an appraisal of the Griffith-Dulien property in Los Angeles.

23. Purchase of property adjoining Teamster building in Los Angeles through the facilities of the Occidental Life Insurance Co.

24. Sale of the adjacent property to the Los Angeles Teamsters' headquarters some 8 months later for $5,000 personal benefit.

25. Borrowing at various times substantial sums of money from the Seattle First National Bank at 3 and 3½ percent interest, which Beck's own financial counsel stated was an unusually favorable transaction for Beck and necessary for the bank because it was a depository for Teamster funds.

26. The purchase of insurance for personal use paid for by Teamster funds.

27. The payment of relatives' expenses with Teamster's funds at 1952 convention.

28. The purchase of furniture and other items for the Teamster Union through a company in which his family had a financial interest.

29. His personal activity in the sale of toy trucks to the Teamster Union for the financial benefit of his family.

30. The obtaining of funds from the Fruehauf Trailer Co. and the Associated Transport Co., a New York trucking company with whom the Teamsters have contracts, for his family's toy truck business.

31. The obtaining of a part of a $200,000 loan from the Associated Transport Co.

32. The obtaining of part of a $200,000 loan from the Fruehauf Trailer Co. after the Teamsters had loaned that company $1,500,000.

33. The free transportation of boat for his son from Detroit, Mich., to Seattle, Wash., by the Fruehauf Trailer Co.

34. The free use of an automobile and a chauffeur for his personal transportation in visiting in Europe provided by the Fruehauf Trailer Co.

35. The free use of a chauffeur and car provided by Fruehauf Trailer Co. for his niece and companion when they were touring Europe.

36. The free use of the Fruehauf Trailer Co.'s airplane on three or four occasions.

BOX 3–6 (*concluded*)

37. The free use of four refrigerated trailers obtained from the Fruehauf Trailer Co. for the benefit of the Sunset Distributing Co. in which his family has an interest.

38. The payment with Teamsters' funds of transportation for his niece and companions from Paris to London.

39. The purchase of land adjoining the Teamsters' building and subsequently leasing the same for parking purposes to the Teamsters.

40. The channeling of more than $165,000 of Teamster business to a service station owned by himself and Brewster.

41. The purchase of land adjoining the Seattle Teamsters' building and the subsequent sale of a portion thereof at an excessively high price to the Teamsters' Union.

42. The obtaining of the rights to distribute Anheuser-Busch beer by K. & L. Beverage Co. in the states of Washington and Alaska. During this period of time at least 50 percent of the employees of Anheuser-Busch were members of the Teamsters Union.

43. The use of the union's power to have Dave Beck, Jr., made president of the K. & L. Beverage Co.

44. Mr. Beck's intercession in a strike of other unions for the benefit of and at the request of the Anheuser-Busch Co.

45. The contacting of Occidental Life Insurance Co. and other concerns for the purpose of getting business for National Mortgage, Inc.

46. His insistence that a fee be paid to Donol Hedlund in connection with the St. Louis Teamster building.

47. The sharing in the $12,000 commission paid to Nathan Shefferman in connection with the purchase of land for the Teamsters in Washington, D.C.

48. Allowing the Teamsters to pay a fee to Nathan Shefferman for allegedly performing the services of effecting a savings in the Teamsters in the acquisition of the land for its Washington, D. C., building while knowing no such services were performed.

49. Use of Sam Basset, attorney for the Teamsters and paid for by them, for his own personal benefit.

50. Use of Simon Wampoid, attorney for the Teamsters and paid for by them, for his own personal benefit.

51. The payment of over $15,000 of union funds to cover the salary and expenses of Stewart Krieger during the time that he was representing Beck at the K. & L. Distributing Co.

52. The use of the International auditor, Fred Verschueren, Sr., in connection with the operation of personal business.

Source: U.S. Congress, 1st sess., 85th Congress, *Hearings before the Select Committee on Improper Activities in the Labor or Management Field*, part 7 (Washington: Government Printing Office, 1957), pp. 2383–85.

CIO in 1957.[32] Meantime the congressional investigation led to legislation to reduce the likelihood of corrupt practices and also to amend the Taft-Hartley Act.

Landrum-Griffin Act

As a result of its investigations considerable legislative interest in monitoring internal union affairs was expressed. In 1959, Congress passed legislation which gave the Department of Labor greater power to audit union financial and political affairs. The Landrum-Griffin Act, formally titled the Labor-Management Reporting and Disclosure Act of 1959, also amended portions of the Taft-Hartley Act.

The Landrum-Griffin Act contains seven major titles. Title I was aimed at establishing rights of individual union members to freedom of speech, equal voting rights, control of dues increases, retention of the right to sue, and rights to copies of labor agreements under which they worked. Title II required of labor organizations periodic reports of official and financial activities to the secretary of labor, reports of financial holdings of officers and employees of unions, and reports by employers of financial transactions with unions. Title III required reporting of trusteeships (in which the national union takes over a local union's operation) and specified conditions under which trusteeship is allowed. Title IV dealt with internal union elections, setting maximum terms of office and requiring secret ballot elections. Title V required bonding of officers, restricted loans, and prohibited recently convicted felons from holding office. Title VI contained miscellaneous provisions, including the prohibition of extortionate picketing.

Title VII amended the Taft-Hartley Act. Major changes here strengthened the prohibitions against secondary boycotts (through which employers cease doing business with a struck or nonunion firm), restricted the use of picketing unorganized employers to force recognition, made illegal "hot cargo" clauses in labor agreements wherein employers agree not to use nonunion goods, reestablished the legality of what amounts to a closed shop in building and construction, and established minimum levels of economic activity necessary before the NLRB would assert its jurisdiction in representation and unfair labor practice cases.[33]

LEGISLATIVE ACTIVITY IN THE 1970s

In the 1970s there have been several legislative initiatives to modify and expand Taft-Hartley. One of these has been successful. In

---

[32] Ibid., p. 704.

[33] A closed shop requires that one be a union member as a condition of initial employment.

1974, the coverage of the Taft-Hartley Act was extended to employees of private nonprofit hospitals. Additional rules governing collective bargaining in private health care facilities were also fashioned. We will explore the implications of these changes in greater detail in both Chapters 4 and 16.

There have also been efforts to override a significant Supreme Court decision establishing rules on picketing for the construction industry. A bill was passed by Congress in late 1975 allowing a construction union which had a dispute with one of a number of contractors on a site to picket the whole site rather than only its reserved gate. This so-called common situs picketing would establish more pressure for settlement since all workers would likely refuse to cross picket lines established to cover all entrance gates. As an inducement to gain the support of a sufficient number of congressmen, a comprehensive construction bargaining mechanism aimed at establishing regional and national control of settlements was included. This section was largely conceived and fashioned by Secretary of Labor John Dunlop. All parties predicted the bill would be signed into law since President Ford had indicated he would sign if the comprehensive bargaining title were included. But in January 1976, he vetoed it. Labor reintroduced the bill after President Carter's inauguration without the bargaining titles, and it failed to pass.

Stung by this defeat, labor recognized that it would have to lobby more vigorously for future legislation. It also has indicated that it will evaluate candidates on more narrowly defined, labor oriented issues when endorsements and political aid are to be given in the near future.

In 1977, a bill amending Taft-Hartley to make organizing and representation easier for unions was introduced. The Taft-Hartley Act would also impose punitive damages on employers who intentionally interfered with employees' Section 7 rights. A great deal of acrimony surrounds this bill with both labor and management apparently exaggerating its supposed equity or punitive aspects. The labor reform bill was passed by the House but failed, by one vote, to survive a Senate filibuster during the summer of 1978.

Finally, attempts were made in the mid-1970s to introduce and pass a Wagner Act type of law for employees of federal, state, and local governments. The prime movers behind this were the National Education Association, the American Federation of Teachers (AFL–CIO), and the American Federation of State, County, and Municipal Employees. While there was some initial optimism by labor about its chances of being debated and passed, this vanished in the dust clouds surrounding the virtual financial collapse of New York City. Critics argued that public employee unions were already too powerful, as evidenced by high pay rates and heavy future pension liabilities cities and states had incurred through bargaining. We will briefly overview some of the changes taking place in the public sector next but will reserve a detailed discussion for Chapter 15.

BOX 3–7
Statements by Robert Georgine, president of the Building and Construction Trades Department, AFL-CIO

Statement after House and Senate passage of common situs picketing bill

Justice finally has prevailed, as it almost always does under the democratic procedure of the United States—if infinite patience is practiced, frustration husked, disappointment checked, and dedication to a principle maintained by driving determination.

The Senate of the United States has joined the House of Representatives in passing legislation that will end the 26 years of special unfairness levied against the building and construction trades unions by permitting them to picket a construction site in the same proper manner that the laws of the nation allow other unions to picket in support of their grievances.

It will be some time before the bill, approved by the Senate and the House of Representatives, actually becomes the law of the land. The measure now must be considered by a conference committee and then resubmitted to both houses for final passage.

Then, when that procedure has been completed, the bill must be signed by President Ford who, like Presidents Truman, Eisenhower, Kennedy, Johnson, and Nixon, has stated his belief in the fairness of the provisions.

But the crucial legislative action of the last few days comes at a most appropriate time—on the eve of Thanksgiving. And that should be the reaction of building and construction tradesmen to the magnificent developments—thankfulness.

It is very tempting because of the lengthy struggle, because of the tactics of our opponents, because of our own efforts to raise our arms and voices in claim of great victory.

Certainly, the technicians of the AFL–CIO building and construction trades department have done a remarkable job.

Beyond doubt, the general presidents of our 17 affiliated national and international unions, their staffs and their members have given the department tremendous support, as have the state and local building trades councils.

But, in a sense, this has not been the attainment of any goal except that which we, as citizens of the United States, fully deserved—a first-class status with rights neither superior nor inferior to those of all other citizens.

We sought not power or glory. We pleaded for equal treatment.

Therefore, I do not think it necessary, desirable, or appropriate to boast of any personal kind of triumph or proclaim it by public demonstration.

BOX 3-7 (*continued*)

Rather, we should express thanks to other AFL–CIO unions and departments; thanks to the congressmen and senators who, in the face of some of the most extreme pressure ever applied on Capitol Hill, had the strength of character and the moral fiber to cast their votes for equality, instead of expedience; for justice and fairness, instead of political favor and partisanship.

I want to thank all of you for your tremendous assistance over a long period of time in helping justice prevail.

Statement after President Ford's veto

"The President of the United States has vetoed an administration bill, endorsed by every President since Harry Truman, Republican and Democrat alike.

"The veto of the situs picketing bill is a national tragedy.

"It denies four million of our citizens equal treatment under law. It eliminates the possibility of bringing stability to the construction industry under the terms of the Collective Bargaining Act.

"More important than any other consideration, it reveals that the President of the United States is not a man of his word. Publicly and privately, Mr. Ford assured us that if the building and construction trades would agree to certain stipulations—which in good faith we did, although some were hard to swallow—he would approve the equal treatment legislation.

"It is one thing to change your mind on account of reasonable argument and discussion. It is quite different when you surrender to pressure and such blackmail threats as the warning that a number of Republican state and finance chairmen would resign if Mr. Ford signed the bill.

"The President's explanation that the enactment of the bill under present economic conditions could lead to more idleness for workers, higher costs, and a slowdown in the construction industry is absolutely untrue.

"It demonstrates that he is listening to emotional opponents not restricted to the truth in their advice to him and is disregarding the counsel of the one man in his administration who knows the construction industry both academically and practically—the secretary of labor.

"I am saddened by his decision, not alone as president of the building and construction trades department but as an American citizen. I am deeply hurt because President Ford caved in to a powerful, selfish, antiunion minority.

"The person in the office of the Presidency of the United States now has lost the confidence of the working people of this country because he has knuckled under and broken his pledge."

Source: *Daily Labor Report,* November 21, 1975, pp. A8–A9 and December 23, 1975, p. A11.

BOX 3–8A
Positions of labor and Chamber of Commerce on proposed labor reform

And, with your pleasure, I would like to introduce, Mr. George Knee, president of the Rhode Island Workers Union.

Senator Chaffee. Mr. George Knee is with you. We welcome you, Mr. Knee. Do you have a statement, or are you going to supplement?

Mr. Knee. I just had a few brief remarks in summary. Our experience—we are a new union, an independent union, that began in the early part of 1976. We have been involved in approximately ten cases, either discharge cases or organized elections with the National Labor Relations Board.

And, in that limited amount of time, I think it would be very clear that anyone who has been involved in union organizing could start a very successful management consulting firm, with one basic principle, and that would be to urge employers to break the law—very clearly, just break the law, have no regard for it, because there is absolutely no penalty for it—and that in the long run, you are going to save money because it is going to discourage the union organizing campaign. The most you are going to have to do is hire somebody back.

I think that we have just seen utter contempt on the part of employers for the law. They know the law. To them, it is a toothless piece of paper that they just disregard.

I would just like to give a concrete example of the effect that the utter contempt for this law has on workers. We were involved in a case with the Grand Islander Nursing Home, where an employee with 2½ years' service called us up and set up a union meeting for 3 o'clock, after work. She was brought into the boss's office at 2:30 and was told that her attitude toward the patients had changed, she was not a very good worker anymore, and after 2½ years, she was to be terminated on the spot.

Thirty employees came to the meeting at 3 o'clock, and when she walked into the room, and the word got around that she had been fired, five employees got up and walked out of the room, out of fear.

We tried to schedule another meeting to see if people were going to be angry, or whether they were going to be fearful. Eight people came.

We have been involved in other cases where the same situation happens, where the lawyers and the consulting firms that are hired by the management just tell them to break the law.

It becomes very difficult as a union organizer, and very embarrassing, to sit with a group of workers when they ask questions about, "I have heard that there is a lw that protects workers. What are my rights?" And you have to sit there and tell them that quite simply they have no rights, and that, yes, there are laws that protect workers, but quite frankly, the boss is going to violate them, the boss is going to pay no attention to them, and the NLRB, through the delays in the tactics and the legal maneuvering, will make sure that it means nothing.

Source: Testimony of George Knee, president of Rhode Island Workers Union before Senate Committee on Human Resources, reported in *Daily Labor Report,* "Special Supplement," February 6, 1978, p. 3.

BOX 3–8B

The U.S. Chamber of Commerce predicts that if the administration's labor law reform bill (H.R. 8410, S. 1883) is enacted the resulting increases in unionization could contribute to inflation, layoffs, small business failures, and higher taxes.

The report was the latest of various conflicting surveys and polls issued by labor and management groups to reinforce their positions on the measure.

The chamber developed two sets of statistics, one on the basis of a projected 12 percent increase in unionization, and another based on a 6 percent increase. Using the 12 percent projection, the chamber predicted that by 1985:

1. Labor costs could rise by 7.4 percent;
2. Labor costs could rise even more sharply for small businesses by an estimated 9.3 percent and cause them to lose business to larger firms;
3. Consumer prices could rise by at least 3.6 percent more by 1985, or about an 0.5 percent higher inflation rate each year, causing a decline in the purchasing power of the average family of four or more than $1,000;
4. The increase in unionization could cause a loss of two million jobs. However, the chamber said 1.3 million of those workers might find work in the nonunion sector. The net job loss thus would be 700,000. "Those ultimately losing jobs would be less skilled young, minority, female, and older workers, those least able to protect themselves," the report states;
5. If federal public service jobs were provided for each of the net jobs lost, federal taxes and spending could increase by $7 billion and taxes could increase by $116 yearly for the average family, according to the report.

The report, prepared by Jack Carlson, vice president and chief economist for the chamber, said more unionization would increase labor costs for this reason:

"Unionization is associated with both higher direct labor costs and lower productivity because of stringent work rules and more frequent work stoppages. Therefore, the bill, if enacted, would add to cost-push inflation. If, as some people expect, the bill encourages an additional 12 percentage points of employed workers to be unionized by 1985, then labor costs for each product or service could increase by 7.4 percent."

Source: *Daily Labor Report,* January 16, 1978, p. A10.

PUBLIC SECTOR UNION GROWTH

As private sector unionization had sunk into the doldrums in the late 1950s and early 1960s, public employees became increasingly interested in unionization. In the federal service, the Taft-Hartley Act forbids strikes. Most states also forbid strikes by public employees. Such statutes also generally make the strikers ineligible for any gains won by striking, and many included summary discharge as a penalty. Concommitantly, most federal and state statutes had no mechanism for the recognition of bargaining representatives.

In 1962, President Kennedy signed a breakthrough for federal employee unions, Executive Order 10988. This order enables a majority union to bargain collectively with a government agency. Negotiations open to the union essentially related to terms and conditions of employment, not wage levels. Unions could not represent employees if they advocated strikes or the right to strike. While a grievance procedure was outlined, final determination was to be made by the federal government, not an impartial arbitrator.[34]

Executive Order 11491

President Nixon signed Executive Order 11491 to be effective on January 1, 1970. The changes and additions to 10988 were provisions requiring secret ballot elections for recognition, establishing procedures for determining appropriate bargaining units, requiring Landrum-Griffin type reporting by unions, and granting arbitration as a final settlement procedure for grievances. Unfair labor practices were specified, and procedures for redressing them were created. The Federal Labor Relations Council was established. Finally, a Federal Impasse Panel was created to render binding decisions in cases where collective negotiations had reached an impasse. This provision ameliorates the statutory no-strike provisions facing federal government employees.[35]

Executive Order 11616

This order was implemented in August 1971. Some changes introduced here allowed professionals in an agency to decide whether or not to join a bargaining unit, allowed individuals to pursue unfair labor practice charges through grievance channels or through the assistant secretary of labor for labor-management relations, required a grievance procedure in exclusive units, but weakened arbitrability, and allowed some negotiation on government time.[36]

Executive Order 11838

Executive Order 11491 required the Federal Labor Relations Council to review the status of labor relations at the federal level and

---

[34] Taylor and Witney, *Labor Relations Law*, pp. 545–49.

[35] Ibid., pp. 550–53.

[36] Ibid., pp. 553–55.

report to the president. As a result of its recommendations in 1974, President Ford issued Executive Order 11838. This order provided for the consolidation of some bargaining units, increased the area covered in negotiations, and dealt with structural aspects of the FLRC.[37]

State and local government

Since there is no federal law asserting jurisdiction over state and local employees, the laws and development of public employee unions differ substantially. For most areas, the development is a relatively recent phenomenon, with police and firefighters being more likely to have specific laws enabling organization and specifying bargaining. On occasion unionized employees have been acquired when previously private employers such as local transit companies have been assumed by public authorities. We will detail the development and growth of labor in public areas in Chapter 15.

SUMMARY

The period from 1930 to the present has seen labor-management relations move from an essentially "no holds barred" approach to one where the guidelines and rules surrounding the overall bargaining relationship are well established. As this change has occurred, there has been a continuation in the long line of "business union" leaders that began with Samuel Gompers. Some flamboyant and charismatic leaders, like John L. Lewis and Walter Reuther, have been part of the scene. Reuther, of the recent labor leaders, was probably the most overtly oriented toward broad public policy issues, but all have led their unions toward primarily economic ends of importance to the membership.

Within labor the most important issues were related to the unwillingness of the AFL to organize industrial workers which resulted in the formation of the CIO. The struggle for organization brought early involvement of individuals with socialistic or communistic ideological perspectives. However, the nonaggression pact between Germany and Russia, and the Communists' lack of enthusiasm for America's involvement in World War II all led to their exit from the labor movement. The ideological movement of the maturing CIO toward complete business unionism hastened the day merger could be contemplated.

The passage of the Taft-Hartley Act rebalanced labor and management power in the United States. With the retrenchment that fol-

---

[37] Murray A. Nesbitt, *Labor Relations in the Federal Government Service* (Washington: Bureau of National Affairs, 1976), p. 133.

lowed, it became increasingly apparent to labor leaders that merger was in their best interests. Contrary to employer fears, the merged federations were not significantly more powerful than they had been.

With significant portions of private industry organized, particularly in heavy manufacturing and skilled trades, labor had to shift its emphasis in organizing toward the public sector in the 1960s. This is the major area where growth and change now takes place.

SUGGESTED READINGS

Bernstein, Irving. *The Turbulent Years: A History of the American Worker, 1933–1941* (Boston: Houghton Mifflin, 1970).

Fine, Sidney. *Sit-Down: The General Motors Strike of 1936–1937* (Ann Arbor, Mich.: University of Michigan Press, 1969).

Howe, Irving, and Widick, B. J. *The UAW and Walter Reuther* (New York: Random House, 1949).

Reuther, Victor G. *The Brothers Reuther and the Story of the UAW* (Boston: Houghton Mifflin, 1976).

See also the general labor history sources listed at the end of Chapter 2.

DISCUSSION QUESTIONS

1. Why do you think the AFL was reluctant to organize industrial workers during the early 1930s?
2. What were the major reasons for the rapid increase in labor's power during the 1930s and 1940s?
3. Why didn't the industrial unions embrace uplift or revolutionary unionism instead of business unionism?
4. Who were the most effective union leaders during the 1930s and 1940s? What are your criteria for effectiveness? Would these same leaders be likely to be effective now?

4

FEDERAL STATUTORY
LABOR LAW

In this chapter we will explore in some detail the substance and coverage of federal law as it relates to collective bargaining. The relevant laws include the Railway Labor Act, the Norris-LaGuardia Act, the Wagner Act (as amended by Taft-Hartley and later changes), and the Landrum-Griffin Act. Our plan in this chapter is to detail the areas and conduct regulated by the acts and the employee groups they apply to.

As you go through this chapter, keep the following points in mind:

1. What specific types of activities are regulated?
2. In what areas has regulation been extended or retracted?
3. What employee groups are included or exempted from various aspects of the regulations?

OVERVIEW

As we noted in Chapters 2 and 3, statutory labor law is relatively recent in U.S. history. The laws which currently outline the conduct of organizing and collective bargaining date back only to 1926 when the Railway Labor Act was enacted. Since then, four other significant pieces of legislation have followed. Norris-LaGuardia (1932), Wagner (1936), Taft-Hartley (1947), and Landrum-Griffin (1959). The Wagner and Taft-Hartley Acts were combined to form the Labor Management Relations Act of 1947. This was subsequently amended in several areas by the Landrum-Griffin Act. Each of these has served to clarify the roles of management and labor from a public policy perspective. While these five acts may not seem as if they are a significant number, it is important to remember that the conduct of labor relations may be much more rule oriented in the United States than in some European countries.

In this chapter on labor law we will present a broad overview in tabular form and then discuss the legislation in its detailed application. Table 4–1 lists each piece of major legislation and areas of labor relations to which it applies.

RAILWAY LABOR ACT

The Railway Labor Act applies to rail and air carriers. Employees in these industries fall within this act's jurisdiction instead of the Taft-Hartley Act. As the act is written, an employee under its jurisdiction is considered to be a nonsupervisor or subordinate official. The act claims to have five general purposes:

1. The avoidance of service interruptions.
2. The elimination of any restrictions on joining a union.
3. The guaranteeing of the freedom of employeees in any matter of self-organization.
4. The provision for prompt dispute settlements.
5. The enabling of prompt grievance settlements.

Within Section 2, a number of general duties are prescribed. First, the carriers and employees are called upon to maintain agreements relating to pay, rules, and working conditions, and to settle disputes about these to avoid the interruption of services. Second, the disputes are to be settled by representatives of the carriers and the employees. Third, the parties cannot influence the choice of the other's representative, and the chosen representative need not be an employee of the carrier. Fourth, employees are free to choose a representative by majority vote, and this representative shall be free from any dominance or financial relationship to the carrier. Fifth, no one can be forced to refrain from union membership or activities as a condition of employment. Sixth, a procedure for settling grievances must be established consistent with the provisions of the act. Seventh, no aspect of pay, rules, or working conditions can be unilaterally changed by the employer if covered in a contract. Eighth, carriers must notify employees of their intent to comply with the act. Ninth, the National Mediation Board (established by the Railway Labor Act) will determine majority status of a union where questioned. Tenth, criminal penalties for violations of this act are established. Eleventh, if unions are shown to be nondiscriminatory in fees and dues, union shop clauses may be negotiated with the carriers.

Section 3 established the National Railroad Board of Adjustment. The Board consists of equal numbers of union and management members and is empowered to settle grievances between carriers and unions which are not settled at the chief executive level of both parties. If the Adjustment Board is deadlocked on a grievance, it must

TABLE 4–1
Major federal labor laws and provisions

	Railway Labor	Norris-LaGuardia	LMRA	Landrum-Griffin
Jurisdiction	Rail and airline employees below managerial levels.	All employers and labor organizations.	Nonmanagerial employees in private industry (nondomestic and non-agricultural) not covered by Railway Labor Act.	Employers and labor organizations within Railway Labor or LMRA jurisdiction.
Individual rights guaranteed	Organization for bargaining, majority choice of representative, no yellow-dog contracts, dispute settlement and procedures.	No yellow-dog contracts, no injunctions for nonviolent union activities.	Organization and concerted activity; if represented, employer must bargain; union may not unequally represent.	Procedures for redressing internal union problems, specification of illegal internal activities, trusteeships regulated.
Employer rights guaranteed			Secondary boycotts unlawful, union must bargain, hot cargo clauses illegal, suits for breach of contract.	
Agencies created	National Mediation Board, National Board of Adjustments.		National Labor Relations Board, Federal Mediation and Conciliation Service.	
Impasse procedures	Mediation, voluntary arbitration, emergency boards.		FMCS volunteers assistance, national emergency procedures for major disputes.	

obtain a referee to hear the case and make an award. Awards are binding on the parties, and prevailing parties may sue in federal district courts for orders enforcing the awards.

Section 4 established the National Mediation Board, composed of three members appointed by the president. Section 5 details the functions of the board. First, the board's services may be offered or requested to mediate a bargaining dispute. If agreement is not reached through mediation, the board is to urge the parties to arbitrate. Second, the board may be called upon to interpret mediated contract agreements. Third, where the parties to a dispute cannot agree on a mutual arbitrator, the board is empowered to appoint one.

Section 6 requires a 30-day notice be given of an intent to renegotiate a contract.

Sections 7, 8, and 9 deal with arbitration, the selection of arbitrators, procedures, and the enforcement of awards.

Section 10 states that in case the National Mediation Board determines that a dispute will deprive a section of the country of transportation, the president is empowered to establish an emergency board of neutrals. The emergency board has a fact-finding duty in the dispute, and no party involved in the dispute may change employment conditions within 30 days of the board's filing of conclusions.

Sections 11 through 13 extend coverage of the act to common carriers by air.

Overview

By comparison with the later acts, the Railway Labor Act is a cumbersome piece of legislation with a good deal of government rule making on how disputes are to be handled. You will notice in subsequent bills that these are generally left up to the parties. One should temper criticism of the act, however, by observing that the technological changes which railroads faced followed the passage of the act meant that a great deal of controversy would be likely to ensue. With the advent of diesel locomotives, firemen were seen by the carriers as redundant. Rather than facing slow attrition as would occur in most industrial unions, here a single craft was faced with the possibility of sudden extinction. A further assessment of the Railway Labor Act's relative effectiveness will be covered in Chapter 12 on impasse procedures.

NORRIS-LaGUARDIA ACT (1932)

The Norris-LaGuardia Act was the first piece of legislation drafted to protect the rights of unions and workers engaged in union activity.

It is comprehensive in its application to workers and firms and absolute in its prescriptions. As we will see in our discussion on contract administration and arbitration, the federal court system has been extremely reluctant to allow any loopholes to develop in its enforcement.

The Norris-LaGuardia Act has two major purposes. First, it forbids federal courts to issue injunctions against a variety of union activities which are specifically cited in the act. Second, it forbids employers from requiring employees to sign so-called yellow-dog contracts in which they agree that continued employment is dependent on abstention from union membership or activities. These contracts had been upheld as legal by the Supreme Court in the *Hitchman Coal* case.[1]

This act recognizes that freedom to associate for collective bargaining purposes may be seen as the corollary of the collectivization of capital through incorporation. Injunctions and yellow-dog contracts act to interfere with this freedom of association. Therefore, the Norris-LaGuardia Act forbids agreements not to join a union or to quit if one joins.

Besides the absolute prohibition of yellow-dog contracts, a number of activities are specified as outside the scope of injunctive relief. This applies regardless of whether the act is done by a single individual or a group or union. The following cannot be enjoined:

1. Stopping or refusing to perform work.
2. Union membership.
3. Payment or withholding of strike benefits, unemployment benefits, and the like to people participating in labor disputes.
4. Aid or assistance for persons suing or being sued.
5. Publicizing a labor dispute in a nonviolent, nonfraudulent manner.
6. Assembly to organize.
7. Notifying anyone that any of these acts are to be performed.
8. Agreement to engage or not engage in any of these acts.
9. Advising others to do any of these acts.

The Norris-LaGuardia Act also finally and completely lays to rest the 18th century "conspiracy doctrine." Section 5 prohibits courts from enjoining any of the activities mentioned above on the basis that persons interested in pursuing normal activities of a labor organization are conspiring. The effects of the *Danbury Hatters*[2] decision (which required union members to pay boycott damages) was also substantially diminished by Section 6. That section holds that an individual or

---

[1] *Hitchman Coal & Coke Co.* v. *Mitchell*, 245 U.S. 229 (1917).

[2] *Loewe* v. *Lawlor*, 208 U.S. 274 (1908).

labor organization may not be held accountable for the unlawful acts of its leadership unless they were clearly directed or ratified by the membership.

To insure that the act did not become an endorsement of violent and destructive actions, Section 7 was created. This section states that an injunction may be issued where:

1. Substantial or irreparable injury to property will occur.
2. Greater injury will be inflicted on the party requesting the injunction than the injunction would cause on the adversary.
3. There is no adequate legal remedy.
4. Authorities are either unable or unwilling to give protection.

For the injunction to be granted, the union must be given the opportunity for rebuttal. If an immediate restraining order is sought and there is not sufficient time for an adversary proceeding, the employer must deposit a bond to compensate the union for possible injuries done to it by the injunction. The section also requires that injunctions be surgical rather than broad-brush since the injunction is to be issued against only those persons or associations actually causing the problems.

Section 8 further restricts the injunction granting powers by requiring that the requester must have tried to settle the dispute before asking for the injunction. Section 9 states that the injunction cannot be issued against all union activities in the case, only those leading to the injury. For example, mass picketing might be enjoined, if violent; but the strike, payments of strike benefits, and so on, cannot.

While the Norris-LaGuardia Act does not require that an employer recognize a union or bargain with it, it does go the first step in giving labor some leverage in organizing and bargaining activity. Labor could, henceforth, bring pressure on the employer in bargaining through strikes, boycotts, and the like, without worrying about federal court injunctions.

WAGNER AND TAFT-HARTLEY ACTS (AS AMENDED)

The Wagner and Taft-Hartley Acts were enacted 11 years apart, but the Taft-Hartley was to a large extent an amendment of and extension to the Wagner Act. In 1959, the Landrum-Griffin Act extended the amending process. All of these legislative initiatives were basically aimed at making clear the public policy preference for collective bargaining as the desired mode for resolving differences in the employment relationship and for roughly balancing the power of labor and management. As such, the Wagner Act, passed during a period of relative weakness for organized labor, only spoke to employer practices. As the pendulum swung in the other direction, the Taft-Hartley amendments added labor practices to the prsocribed list. Finally, the Landrum-Griffin Act attempted to "fine-tune" the statutes consistent with day-to-day realities. We will now examine the major provisions of the labor relations acts.

Section 1

This is the findings and policies section of the act. Congress concluded that actions by employers denying the right to organize and refusing to bargain impaired the free flow of commerce and led to industrial strife. Equality of bargaining power between employers and employees could only be assured where employees had the right to bargain collectively. This process could be interfered with through both employer and union practices coercing individuals attempting to exercise their rights or denying the opportunity for negotiated settlements through refusals to bargain.

Section 2

Section 2 defines the terms used in the act. From our standpoint, the most important definitions are related to the terms *employer, employee, supervisor,* and *professional employee.*

Employer. An employer is an organization or a manager acting on behalf of the organization. However, certain types of organizations are specifically excluded from the act's jurisdiction. These are federal, state, and local governments or any organizations which are wholly owned by these agencies; persons subject to the Railway Labor Act; and union representatives when acting as bargaining agents.

Employee. An employee does not necessarily have to be a member of an organization against which a labor dispute is directed. For example, if firm A is being struck and employees of firm B refuse to cross the picket lines, even though no dispute exists with B, B's workers are considered "employees" for labor-management relations purpose under the act. An individual also is considered to remain an employee if on strike for a contract, or on strike or being discharged as the result of an employer unfair labor practice. Employees are considered to remain within this definition, even if employers do not consider them as employees, until they take new employment at or above a level equivalent to their previous jobs. Domestic workers, agricultural workers, independent contractors,[3] supervisors, individuals employed by a spouse or parent,[4] or persons whose rights are specified by the Railway Labor Act are excluded.

---

[3] *P. Q. Beef Processors, Inc.,* 231 NLRB 179 (1977).
[4] *Viele & Sons, Inc.,* 227 NLRB 284 (1977).

Supervisor. A supervisor is someone who has the authority to make personnel decisions and administer a labor agreement through the use of independent judgment. Examples of personnel decisions include hiring, firing, adjusting grievances, work assignment, salary decision, and so forth.

Professional employee. A professional is considered to be an employee whose work is intellectual in character, requiring independent judgment or discretion, where performance cannot readily be measured on a standardized basis and where the skills are learned through a prolonged, specialized program of instruction.

Section 3

This section establishes the National Labor Relations Board. The board consists of five members appointed by the president and confirmed by the Senate. Members serve five-year terms and may be reappointed. One member, designated by the president, is the chairman of the board.

The board may delegate its duties to any group of three or more members. It also can delegate authority to determine representation and election questions to its regional directors. The board also has a general counsel who has the responsibility of investigating charges and issuing complaints.

Sections 4 through 6 relate to salaries, locations, and administrative procedures used by the board.

Section 7

This section was the heart of the original Wagner Act and still represents the embodiment of public policy toward the individual worker and collective bargaining. As amended, Section 7 reads:

> Employees shall have the right to self-organization, to form, join, or assist labor organizations, to bargain collectively through representatives of their own choosing, and to engage in other concerted activities for the purpose of collective bargaining or other mutual aid or protection, and shall also have the right to refrain from any or all of such activities except to the extent that such right may be affected by an agreement requiring membership in a labor organization as a condition of employment as authorized in Section 8(a)(3).

Section 8

Section 8 specifies the actions of employers which would constitute a violation of an employee's Section 7 rights and includes union violations of Section 7 and refusals to bargain with an employer. Part (a) deals with employer practices, part (b) with those of unions.

Employer unfair labor practices. An employer may not interfere with an employee engaging in any activity protected by Section 7. The employer may not assist or dominate any labor organization. For example, if two unions are vying to organize a group of workers, an employer may not recognize one to avoid dealing with the other or express a preference for one over another.

An employer may not discriminate in hiring, assignment, or other terms of employment on the basis of union membership. However, employers and unions may negotiate contract clauses requiring union membership as a condition of continued employment (a union shop agreement). But if such a clause is negotiated, the employer cannot discriminate against nonmembership if the union discriminatorily refuses to admit an employee to membership.

Employees may not be penalized or discriminated against for charging an employer with a violation of the act.

Finally, employers may not refuse to bargain with a union over issues of pay, hours, or other terms and conditions of employment.

Union unfair labor practices. Unions may not coerce employees in the exercise of Section 7 rights. But this does not limit union internal rule making, discipline, fines, and so forth. Unions cannot demand or require that an employer violate Section 8(a)(3) by discriminating against a given employee or to discriminate against an employee who has been denied union membership except for failure to pay union dues.

Unions are also forbidden from engaging in or encouraging individuals to strike or to refuse to handle some type of product or work where the object is to accomplish any of the following ends:

1. Forcing an employer or self-employed person to join an employer or labor organization, or to cease handling nonunion products (except in certain cases detailed later).
2. Forcing an employer to bargain with an uncertified labor organization, that is, one whose majority status has not been established.
3. Forcing an employer to cease bargaining with a certified representative.
4. Forcing an employer to assign work to employees in a particular labor organization, unless he has been ordered to do so or has previously bargained to do so.
5. Requiring excessive initiation fees for union membership.
6. Forcing an employer to pay for services not rendered.
7. Picketing an employer to force recognition of the picketing union where: (*a*) the picketing group has not been certified as the employees' representative, (*b*) and either there has not been a union election within the past 12 months or the picketing union requests

a representation election within 30 days after picketing begins, (*c*) but nothing can prohibit a union's picketing to advise the public that an employer's employees are not unionized, and the picketing does not interfere with pickups and deliveries.

Protected activity.   Where there is no evidence of threat, reprisal, or promise of benefit, the parties involved in collective bargaining activities are free to express views in any form.

Duty to bargain.   It is the mutual duty of unions and employers to bargain in good faith about wages, hours, terms and conditions of employment. Each must also be willing to meet at the request of the other to negotiate an agreement, to reduce it to writing, and to interpret its meaning when a disagreement arises. Neither party is required to concede any issue as a necessary condition for the demonstration of good faith bargaining. Rules are also set forth requiring the notification of the Federal Mediation and Conciliation Service (FMCS) as a condition for contract modification. Specific, and more stringent, requirements are laid out for health care organizations.

Prohibited contract clauses.   Except in the construction and apparel industries, employees and unions cannot negotiate contracts providing that particular products of certain employers will not be used. This is the so-called hot cargo issue. For example, a trucking union could not negotiate a contract which would not require them to haul goods manufactured by a nonunion employer. But a construction union could refuse to install nonunion goods if a contract clause had been negotiated.

Construction employment.   Contractors can make agreements with construction unions even where there has been no demonstration of majority status. The agreements may also require union membership within seven days of employment and also require that the union be given an opportunity to refer people for existing job openings. The agreements may also provide for apprenticeship training requirements and may give preference in job openings to workers with greater past experience.

Health care picketing.   A union anticipating a strike or picketing at a health care facility must notify the FMCS ten days prior to commencing the activity.

Section 9

Section 9 deals with representatives and elections. The act provides that if a majority of employees in a particular unit desire representation by a labor organization, all employees (regardless of union membership) will be represented by the union regarding wages, hours, and terms and conditions of employment. Individuals can present and have their own grievances adjusted if the adjustment is not inconsistent with the contract.

It is up to the NLRB to determine what group of employees constitutes an appropriate unit for a representation election and subsequent bargaining. There are some limitations to its discretion, however. First, it cannot include professional and nonprofessional employees in the same unit unless a majority of the professionals desire inclusion. Second, it cannot deny separate representation to a craft solely on the basis that it has been a part of a larger unit determined to be appropriate by the board. Third, it cannot include plant guards in the same unit as other workers or certify a union which represents both guards and other types of employees in diverse units. It should also be remembered that supervisors are not employees as defined by the act; so, for example, a unit of production supervisors would be inappropriate.

Where there is a question about a union's majority status, the board is authorized to hold elections (subject to certain constraints detailed in Chapter 8). The board may also conduct elections to determine whether an existing union maintains a continuing majority status.

Sections 10, 11, and 12

This section deals with the prevention of unfair labor practices and procedures used by the NLRB in investigating and remedying them. If the board finds that an unfair labor practice occurred, it can issue cease and desist orders, require back pay to make injured persons whole, and petition a court of appeals for enforcement of its orders.

Section 11 deals with the procedures the NLRB has available to obtain evidence, such as subpeonas. Section 12 provides for criminal penalties for persons interfering with board activities.

Sections 13 through 19

These sections limit the applicability of other sections. Section 13 indicates that nothing in the act limits the right to strike. Section 14(a) holds that supervisors cannot be prohibited from belonging to a union, but an employer need not recognize membership for bargaining purposes. Section 14(b) is one of the most controversial in the act. This section permits the passage by states of so-called right-to-work laws. In states with these laws, employees who are represented by unions cannot be compelled to join a union or pay dues as a condition of employment. Section 14(c) allows the NLRB to decline jurisdiction in cases where the impact on commerce is judged to be insignificant, but state agencies can assert jurisdiction if the Board declines. Section 15 deals with bankruptcies. Section 16 is a "savings clause" indicating that if some section is held to be invalid, the remainder of the act will not be affected. Section 17 provides for citations to the act. Section 18 provides that the CIO and AFL have a grace period until December 22, 1949, and November 7, 1947, to file their constitutions and by-laws with the Secretary of Labor if they desire to be considered labor organizations under Section 9. Section 18 has no current application because the time deadlines have been exceeded and the portions of Section 9 it refers to were repealed by the Landrum-Griffin Act in 1959. Finally, Section 19 provides that employees of health care organizations whose religious beliefs preclude union membership may donate a sum equal to union dues to a nonreligious charity in lieu of membership in union or agency shops.

Sections 102–104

These relate to the effective date of changes in the act. None of these sections is presently of any importance.

Title II

This title begins the major additions that were made to the act. Obviously, some of those previously mentioned, such as union unfair labor practices were important, but the additions break new ground in public policy toward unions.

Title II, Section 201, indicates that it is in the public interest to maintain stable labor relations. If there are problems between the parties which interfere with this stability, the government should be able and willing to offer assistance. Thus, Section 202 created the FMCS, whose duties (defined in Section 203) are to offer its mediation services whenever a dispute threatens to interrupt commerce or where it involves a health care organization. The FMCS is directed to emphasize services in contract negotiations and not grievance settlements.

A second major feature of Title II is the national emergencies sections. If there is a labor dispute which, in the opinion of the president, will imperil the nation, a board of inquiry may be appointed to look into the issues surrounding the dispute. After the board of inquiry submits its report, the attorney general may be directed to ask a district court to enjoin a strike or lockout. If the court agrees that the dispute is involving a substantial area and if national security is threatened, an injunction against the strike or lockout may be issued. If an injunction is ordered, the board of inquiry is reconvened and is charged with the duty of monitoring the settlement process. If an agreement is not reached after 60 days, the board reports the position of labor and management and includes management's last offer. Over the next 15 days the NLRB takes a ballot among the employees to determine whether a majority favors accepting management's last offer. Five more days are taken to certify the results. At this time (or earlier if a settlement was reached), the injunction will be discharged. If a settlement was not reached, the president forwards the report of the board, the election results, and his recommendations to Congress for action.

Title III

This title speaks to suits by and against labor organizations. The title enables unions to sue on behalf of its members and to be sued and found liable for damages against its organizational (but not member's individual) assets.

The title also forbids financial dealings between an organization and the representatives of its employees. Union agents were forbidden from demanding payment for performing contractual duties. Certain regulations related to the establishment of trust funds are also included.

Unions and corporations were forbidden to make political contributions in any elections involving the choice of federal office holders.

Titles IV and V have other miscellaneous provisions of no particular importance to the overall application of federal labor law.

Summary

The important aspects of the LMRA relate to the establishment, function, and powers of the NLRB, the delineation of employer and union unfair labor practices; the promulgation of rules governing representation and certification; the creation and functions of the FMCS; and the national emergency injunction procedures. These aim at balancing the power of labor and management and interjecting the public's interest in stabilizing industrial relations.

LANDRUM-GRIFFIN ACT (1959)

The Landrum-Griffin Act was essentially the result of the concern of Congress that there was too great an opportunity for unions and managements to engage in corrupt practices. This act, formally named the Labor-Management Reporting and Disclosure Act of 1959 (LMRDA), regulates internal activities of both labor and management. The

Landrum-Griffin Act applies not only to areas under Taft-Hartley jurisdiction, but also to those within the purview of the Railway Labor Act.

Title I—Bill of rights for union members

Section 101 provides that union members are to have equal rights and privileges in nominating, voting, participation in referenda, meetings, and so forth. Each member is to be afforded an opportunity to be heard and to oppose the directions of the leadership insofar as this opposition does not interfere with the union's legal obligations. Dues, initiation fees, and assessments cannot be increased without the majority of members voting approving the increase. Members' rights to sue their labor organizations are guaranteed as long as they have exhausted internal union procedures and are not aided by an employer or employer association. Finally, members of labor organizations cannot be expelled unless due process consistent with this section is followed.

Section 104 provides that copies of the labor agreement between the employer and the union be available to any member desiring a copy.

Title II—Reports required of unions and employers

Section 201 provides that all labor organizations have constitutions and by-laws deposited with the Secretary of Labor. Reports must be filed by unions annually, detailing assets and liabilities, receipts, salaries and allowances of officers, loans made to officers, loans made to businesses, and other expenditures as prescribed by the Secretary of Labor. The report must also be made available to the membership.

Section 202 requires that *every* officer and employee of a labor organization (except clerical and custodial employees) submit a report to the Secretary of Labor annually detailing any family income or transaction in stocks, securities, or other payments (except wages) made by a firm with which it represents employees; or operated a business which had substantial dealings with these firms; or any payments made by a labor consultant to such a firm.

Section 203 requires employer reports on payments made to union officials (even if only to reimburse expenses); payments made to employees to convince other employees to exercise or not exercise their rights to organize and bargain collectively; payments made to obtain information about labor organizations or individuals involved in disputes with the employer; and agreements with or payments to a labor relations consultant whose purpose it is to influence workers in their choice of utilizing Section 7 (LMRA) rights.

Title III—Trusteeships

On occasion a union will take over one of its subsidiaries for breaching the constitution or by-laws. To reduce the possibility that trusteeship is imposed simply to stifle dissent, Title III requires that the trusteeship be imposed only to restore democratic procedures, correct corruption or financial malpractice, assure performance of collective bargaining agreements, or other legitimate union functions. If a union imposes trusteeship on one of its subsidiaries, it must file a report with the Secretary of Labor detailing the reasons for the takeover. It must also disclose the subsidiary's financial situation. A labor organization exercising a trustee relationship cannot move assets from the organization it took over or appoint delegates to conventions from it (unless they were elected by secret ballot of the membership).

Title IV—Elections

This title requires that international unions elect their officers either through referenda or by convention delegates who were elected by secret ballot. These elections must take place at least every five years. Local union officers must be elected by secret ballot of the membership at least once every three years.

No member in good standing can be denied voting or candidacy privileges. Unions may not use dues or other funds collected from their constituents to pay for campaigning for particular candidates. Membership roles must be made equally available to all candidates for campaign purposes.

If a complaint is filed about violations of provisions of Title IV and a Labor Department investigation discloses that they occurred, a civil suit may be filed to invalidate the election. If this occurs, the Secretary of Labor conducts a new election and certifies the results.

Title V—Safeguards for labor organizations

First, Title V holds that union officials are responsible to see that union property is used only for purposes consistent with its constitution. Union members can sue officials in court for the recovery of misappropriated assets if the union will not adequately handle the problem internally. Union officials must also be bonded to meet the requirements of Title V. Employees or officials of unions are prohibited in borrowing more than $2,000 from their unions. Finally, persons convicted of a variety of felonies may not serve as union officials or labor consultants within five years of their conviction.

Title VI—Miscellaneous provisions

A number of nonprocedural clauses are of interest here. First, Section 602 forbids picketing of a nature to force an employer to make payments (other than wage increases or employee benefits) as a condition for its removal. This is called extortionate picketing. Second, Section 609 forbids unions from disciplining members for exercising any right given by the act.

Summary

The Landrum-Griffin Act generally is aimed at checking the power of unions over individual members and for safeguarding union assets from possible corrupt practices. All unions and some employers are faced with increased paperwork as a result of the legislation.

SUMMARY

Federal labor law presently applies to most private sector employers. Rail and air transport falls within the Railway Labor Act while the Labor Management Relations Act governs the remainder. Basic provisions of the laws include the rights of individuals to engage in concerted activity free from employer interference, the right to organize and bargain, and the right to contract.

The acts lay out ground rules for the bargaining relationship and rules for the conduct of internal activities of employers and unions relative to their bargaining relationships and memberships.

Federal agencies such as the NMB, NLRB, and FMCS were created by these statutes to monitor and assist ongoing bargaining relationships.

Since the 1930s public policy has seemed to favor collective bargaining as a method for dispute settlement and wage determination where workers desire it. To foster a climate for these activities, Congress has generally made rules to broadly balance the powers of the parties in the bargaining relationship. Congress has also been careful to protect the rights of individuals in engaging in union activity and in being protected from arbitrary treatment by either employers or unions.

DISCUSSION QUESTIONS

1. In the absence of federal labor laws, what do you think the scope and nature of labor relations would presently be in the United States?
2. Should workers now under the Railway Labor Act be brought within jurisdiction of the LMRA?
3. Are the laws strong enough in the preservation of individual rights?
4. To what extent should the federal government have power to intervene in collective bargaining activities?

SUGGESTED READINGS

Rothman, Stuart. *A Layman's Guide to Basic Law under the National Labor Relations Act* (Washington: NLRB, 1962).

Sherman, Herbert L., Jr. *Unionization and Collective Bargaining*, 2d ed. unit 1 in Labor Law Group Trust, eds., *Labor Relations and Social Problems* (Washington: Bureau of National Affairs, 1972).

Taylor, Benjamin J., and Witney, Fred. *Labor Relations Law*, 2d ed. (Englewood Cliffs, N.J.: Prentice-Hall, 1975).

5

UNION STRUCTURE AND GOVERNMENT

One of the first things a student of labor relations should recognize is that the two parties contending with each other in collective bargaining are organized differently. Employers usually have some specific objectives to be pursued and purchase the labor of individuals for the accomplishment, directly or indirectly, of these objectives. Employees have little voice in what the objectives will be; employing organizations are generally operated in an autocratic manner. On the other hand, labor unions are political organizations. The leadership is elected by the membership and must remain generally responsive to membership desires to maintain incumbency. Thus, the behavior of the parties differs because of the different constituencies they serve and the manner in which organizational leaders are chosen.

In this chapter we will examine the components and interrelationships of union organization. As such, we also must detail the points at which these components relate to nonunion organizations. We will also describe the functions of unions and how these relate to the membership. As you are reading this chapter, you should be concerned with the following general areas or questions.

1. What are the major organizational levels within the labor movement?
2. Where is the real locus of power in the direction of labor as an organized entity?
3. What are the lines of authority between the local, the international, and the AFL–CIO?
4. How do international unions differ in their organizational structure and politics?
5. To what extent are unions autocratically or democratically governed?
6. How does a union's structure relate to the manner in which an industry is organized?

UNION COMPONENTS

There are several formalized components at different hierarchical levels of the U.S. labor movement. Initially, we will deal with the three predominant components and later relate these to others. These are the local union, the national union, and the labor federation.

The local union

The local union is the institution through which the individual deals with the employer on a day-to-day basis. There is no strict definition of a local union in terms of size, geographical jurisdiction, or numbers of employers with which it deals. Barbash notes that local unions exercise jurisdiction along four major dimensions: (1) the specific duties workers perform or the industrial classification in which they are employed (craft and industrial jurisdictions), (2) a specified geographical area, (3) the specific purpose of the jurisdiction (organizing, bargaining, and so on), and (4) the level of union government applying the jurisdiction.[1] The exact definition of a local's constituency can then vary within these parameters. As examples, Barbash points out that Local 12 of the United Auto Workers in Toledo, Ohio (an amalgamated local), represents employees among several employers in different industries; Local 65 of the Retail, Wholesale, and Department Store Union in New York City represents over 32,000 workers employed by 2,000 establishments; Local 3 of the Operating Engineers covers portions of four western states; and Local 459 of the IUE, based in New York, bargains with employers in Milwaukee, New Orleans, and Chicago.[2] These are exceptions, however. In most instances local unions tend to be confined to a specific municipality, representing workers in a single industry or job classification, and frequently bargaining with a single employer.

The jurisdiction of a union will tend to affect some of its structural properties. Sayles and Strauss suggest that jurisdiction will affect a local's size, constitution, officers, committees, steward appointments, social activities, and field representatives.[3] If a local is restricted to a single plant or employer in a relatively small geographical area, it will tend to administer itself largely through elected officials who serve on a part-time basis. On the other hand, locals interested in expanding to other employers or currently dealing with multiple employers will

---

[1] Jack Barbash, *American Unions: Structure, Government, and Politics* (New York: Random House, 1967).

[2] Ibid., pp. 12–14, 43.

[3] Leonard R. Sayles and George Strauss, *The Local Union*, rev. (New York: Harcourt, Brace, & World, 1967), pp. 2–5.

often create a position designated as "business agent." The business agent's job is to make sure the contractual rights of members are not being violated. Frequently, business agents are also responsible for referring union members to available employment. The use of business agents is perhaps most pervasive in the construction industry where union members frequently have only transient relationships with a single employer and move from project to project as work is finished and becomes available elsewhere.

Typical local unions elect and appoint a variety of officeholders and committee members. Generally officers would include a president, vice president, recording secretary, financial secretary, treasurer, sergeant at arms, and trustees.[4] Unless the local is quite large, these posts are generally unpaid.

Two major committees operate within most local structures. These are the executive committee (made up of the local's officers) and the grievance or negotiating committee. The executive committee establishes local policy while the negotiating committee reviews and acts upon the merits of members' grievances and negotiates over grievances and contractual changes with management. Other committees deal with organizing and membership, welfare, recreation, and political action.

At the grass roots level, the union elects or appoints stewards. Stewards are responsible for insuring that management, particularly first-line supervision, complies with the contract. When grievances are presented, the steward frequently acts as a spokesperson for the aggrieved union member. Stewards also perform routine functions such as collecting dues and soliciting participation in union social activities. Many collective bargaining contracts recognize the vulnerability of the steward's advocative position by according incumbents superseniority. As long as one remains a steward, the incumbent is, by definition, the most senior member of that seniority unit.

Local government and politics

Local union political activity bears many resemblances to municipal politics. There is generally only moderate interest in union elections, and incumbents generally are reelected unless some critical issue has been mishandled, at least in the eyes of the rank and file members. The local typically holds regular meetings to handle its business. These meetings may be characterized best by drawing an analogy between them and the traditional New England town meet-

---

[4] Ibid., p. 3.

ing. However, in most cases attendance is low, limited to officers and a few activists.

Two aspects of local government and politics bear examination: (1) the type of business conducted by unions in their meetings, and (2) the degree to which the local union is democratically operated. Union business meetings are generally fairly mundane unless contract negotiations are approaching. Most routine meetings deal with detailed reporting of disbursements, reading of communications, and detailing of pending grievance procedures. Attendance at meetings is generally quite low; Sayles and Strauss reported figures of between 1 percent and 33 percent, with smaller locals having higher figures and locals with more highly skilled workers having higher attendance levels.[5] They also note that the major content of the meeting also affects attendance. In examining a newly organized local of utility workers, they found that the highest attendance level was 42 percent for the contract ratification; and only exceeded 15 percent in 3 of the other 16 meetings (18 percent for a discussion of contract demands, 20 percent for an election of temporary officers, and 18 percent for a report on the completed contract).[6]

The fact that so few members attend raises questions about how broadly supported local unions are and how democratically they can be run. Ironically, member interest seems to be low at the local level although this is the level at which most of the members' relations with management are determined. One could draw a parallel here between participation in local union affairs and municipal government. Typically, electoral turnouts are far lower for local government elections than for national presidential elections.

With this in mind, are local unions run democratically? If we require that democracy include two or more relatively permanent recognized factions, the answer must generally be "no." But if democracy only demands that the leadership be open to dissent and responsive to individuals and groups, the answer is generally "yes." A degree of democracy in union organization is generally a constitutional requirement within the local through the specification of electoral proceedings and terms of office. From a statutory standpoint, the Landrum-Griffin Act requires locals to conduct elections no less often than once every three years. And also, by statute, unions which have been certified as the representatives of specific bargaining units are exclusive representatives for all employees in the unit and must apply the terms of the contract equally to all bargaining unit employees.

In their study, Sayles and Strauss concluded that on the whole

---

[5] Ibid., p. 97.

[6] Ibid., p. 98.

unions are relatively democratic. Pressure by the membership to handle grievances and improve conditions requires a degree of response by union officers. On the other hand, if management is difficult to deal with, the pressure to maintain a united front may lead to the suppression of dissent.[7] One aspect that must be recognized in examining union democracy is the individual member's degree of commitment to union activity. While most would not move to get rid of the union, many were not involved in its original organization and may view the union simply as their agent in employment matters. In return for dues rendered to the union, the union is expected to represent the employee(s) and to relieve them of the effort and detailed work involved in regulating the employment relationship. What the members may want is a fair return for their dues, not a chance to participate in and devote effort to an organization.

Up to this point, one might have viewed the local union as an essentially autonomous, free-standing organization. In most cases it is not. It may owe its existence to, and almost certainly must comply with the directives of, its parent international.

International unions

International unions establish jurisdiction over the organization of workers in specific crafts, industries, or other job territories. They are called "internationals" because most have members in Canada or Mexico (less often) as well as in the United States. As we noted earlier in our examination of the evolution of labor in the United States, the national or international union holds predominant power in the union movement. Most local unions are chartered by a parent national, and many local activities are constrained or must be approved by the national body. These will be explored later when we examine the relationships between the various union bodies.

In its 1973 directory, the U.S. Department of Labor's Bureau of Labor Statistics listed 175 national unions and 37 professional or state employee associations. One hundred eleven were affiliated with the AFL–CIO, accounting for about 79 percent of total union membership in the United States.[8] In 1972, 53 unions and associations had over 100,000 members. Over half of union membership is concentrated in the ten largest national unions and associations. Table 5–1 lists unions and associations with 100,000 or more members in 1972.

---

[7] Ibid., pp. 143–57.

[8] U.S. Department of Labor, Bureau of Labor Statistics, *Directory of National Unions and Employee Associations 1973* (Washington: Government Printing Office, 1974), p. 1.

In 1972, over 71,000 locals were affiliated with national unions. Associations had almost 14,000 additional chapters affiliated. In terms of size, more national unions had fewer than ten locals than any other category, but the median was between 100 and 200 affiliates. Seventeen internationals claimed 1,000 or more locals each.

The international union operates in some ways as a local union does, but it is a full-time operation. Officers are full-time unionists, and departments, with specialists to handle specific functions, are established in place of the standing committees which are formed within the local. In most unions, the elected officials are chosen by the union convention which, by law, must meet at least every fifth year. The convention consists of delegates designated by each local and sent on a per capita basis. The union convention assumes much the same flavor as a political convention. If the national leadeship is strong, it has some power in seeing to it that convention delegates favor the incumbents. The internal structure of the national union helps to insure this outcome.

TABLE 5–1
**National unions and employee associations reporting
100,000 members or more, 1972***

Organization	Members
Union	
Teamsters (Ind.)	1,855,000
Steelworkers	1,400,000
Automobile workers (Ind.)	1,394,000
Electrical (IBEW)	957,000
Carpenters	820,000
Machinists	758,000
Retail clerks	633,000
Laborers	600,000
Meat cutters	529,000
State, county	529,000
Service employees	484,000
Hotel	458,000
Communications workers	443,000
Ladies' garment	428,000
Operating engineers	402,000
Paperworkers	389,000
Clothing workers	365,000
Musicians	315,000
Government (AFGE)	293,000
Electrical (IUE)	290,000
Teachers	249,000
Transportation union	248,000
Postal workers	239,000
Railway clerks	238,000
Plumbers	228,000
Letter carriers	220,000
Mine workers (Ind.)	213,000

Table 5-1 (*continued*)

Organization	Members
Painters	208,000
Retail, wholesale	198,000
Rubber	183,000
Iron workers	176,000
Textile workers	174,000
Oil, chemical	172,000
Electrical (UE) (Ind.)	165,000
Fire fighters	160,000
Sheet metal	153,000
Transport workers	150,000
Bricklayers	149,000
Bakery	146,000
Maintenance of way	142,000
Boilermakers	132,000
Transit union	130,000
Printing pressmen	115,000
Typographical	115,000
Graphic arts	106,000
Woodworkers	106,000
Railway carmen	104,000
Government (NAGE) (Ind.)	100,000
Associations	
Education association	1,166,000
Civil service (NYS)	202,000
Nurse association	157,000
Police	125,000
California	103,000

* Based on union and association reports to the Bureau of Labor Statistics with membership rounded to the nearest thousand. All unions not identified as (Ind.) are affiliated with the AFL–CIO.

Source: U.S. Department of Labor, Bureau of Labor Statistics, *Directory of National Unions and Employee Associations 1973* (Washington: Government Printing Office, 1974), p. 74.

National structure

In 1962, a series of works on trade union government was published. From this series, we will abstract a structure of four unions: the United Automobile, Aerospace, and Agricultural Equipment Workers of America (UAW), the United Steelworkers of America (USW), the United Brotherhood of Carpenters and Joiners (Carpenters), and the International Brotherhood of Teamsters, Chauffeurs, Handlers, and Warehousemen (IBT). The first two are industrial unions, the third a craft union, and the fourth a mixture of craft and industrial approaches. Obviously, these unions have changed their structures to some extent over time, but their overall jurisdictions and development have not changed as rapidly.

The UAW[9]

The UAW asserts jurisdiction over workers in automotive, aerospace, and agricultural equipment industries. It has also recently begun to organize clerical employees in firms and units outside these industries. The UAW is an explicitly industrial union, organizing persons in a variety of skills and occupations for a given plant or employer. Thus, electricians in an auto plant are more likely to belong to the UAW, for example, than to the International Brotherhood of Electrical Workers.

As an industrial union, the UAW was a member of the CIO during the years when separate federations existed. The CIO had originally been piloted by John L. Lewis and Philip Murray, both from the United Mine Workers. Murray later became president of the United Steelworkers and simultaneously held the presidency of the CIO. In 1952 Murray died and Walter Reuther, the president of the UAW, assumed the reins of the CIO. This change, coupled with the ascension of George Meany of the AFL presidency upon William Green's death in 1952, left both federations with chief executives who were not a part of the original schism of the 1930s. In 1955, when the two federations merged, Meany became president and Reuther vice president. It demonstrates the relative autonomy of the national unions vis-à-vis the federation that Reuther pulled the UAW out of the AFL–CIO in 1968 and with the Teamsters formed the Alliance for Labor Action (which we will examine later).

Since the automobile industry is concentrated among a relatively small number of primary manufacturers and since their plants are usually quite large, the UAW is organized along lines which match the departments of the firms with which they bargain, and its locals tend to be quite large. The departmental matching between the union and specific manufacturers (for example, General Motors department) leads to or follows from companywide bargaining on economic issues and the desire of the union to establish uniformity of treatment among members doing equivalent work. As we will examine in detail when we look at collective bargaining, the departments still leave enough latitude for locals to bargain over local plant work rules.

Departmentalization takes place in unions much as in business or other organizations. Some departments handle specific groups of workers according to employer, some serve members according to geographical location, and some provide specialized services to the organization in the form of staff functions.

The headquarters of the UAW is located in Detroit at Solidarity House. About one third of the national's officers and employees are based there, while another two thirds work out of the Washington and

[9] See Jack Stieber, *Governing the UAW* (New York: Wiley, 1962), pp. 92–130.

regional offices. Except for clerical and maintenance employees, most national union employees rose from rank and file membership and have experience in various laboring jobs in the industries represented by the UAW. Employees classified as "international representatives," which constitute a large group, must have been members of the UAW in good standing for at least a year before appointment.

The international office staff consists of the president, administrative assistants to the president, the secretary-treasurer, and the departmental vice presidents. Each national department (for example, Ford) has a National Department Council consisting of delegates from that department's locals. In turn, these form subcommittees based on common interests of the members such as seniority, work rules, and so on. These subcommittees designate members to be a part of the National Negotiating Council from that department to bargain with management on future contracts.

There are also a number of regional staffs. Thus, primary responsibilities relate to organizing activities and assisting remote locals or locals not affiliated closely with a national department in administration, negotiation, and grievance handling. Frequently international representatives are given the responsibility of assisting designated locals and also to serve as regional experts on certain topics (for example, time study). Figure 5–1 details the present organizational structure of the UAW.

The Carpenters' Union[10]

In contrast to the UAW, the Carpenters' Union is organized along craft or occupational skill lines. To be a member one must be:

> An apprentice or Journeyman Carpenter or Joiner; Millwright; Pile Driver, Bridge, Dock and Wharf Carpenter, Underprimer and Timberman; Shipwright, Boat Builder, Ship Carpenter, Joiner and Caulker; Cabinet Maker, Bench Hand, Stain Builder, Millman; Floor Layer and Finisher; Shingler; Sider; Insulator; Accoustie or Dry Wall Applicator; Shorer and House Mover; Logger, Lumber and Sawmill Worker; Furniture Worker, Reed and Rattan Worker; Casket and Coffin Maker; Box Maker; Railroad Carpenter and Car Builder; and all those engaged in the operation of woodworking or other machinery required in the fashioning or milling of products used in the trade, or engaged as helpers to any of the above divisions or subdivisions, or the handling of material on any of the above divisions or subdivisions.[11]

---

[10] See Morris A. Horowitz, *The Structure and Government of the Carpenters' Union* (New York: Wiley, 1962), pp. 9–62.

[11] Constitution of Carpenters' Union, as amended April 1959, Section 42F, p. 30, as quoted from Horowitz, ibid., p. 4.

FIGURE 5–1

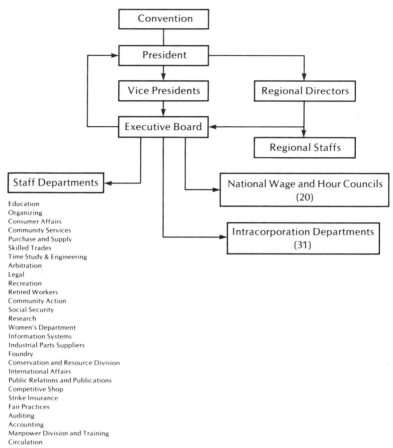

Education
Organizing
Consumer Affairs
Community Services
Purchase and Supply
Skilled Trades
Time Study & Engineering
Arbitration
Legal
Recreation
Retired Workers
Community Action
Social Security
Research
Women's Department
Information Systems
Industrial Parts Suppliers
Foundry
Conservation and Resource Division
International Affairs
Public Relations and Publications
Competitive Shop
Strike Insurance
Fair Practices
Auditing
Accounting
Manpower Division and Training
Circulation

Source: Abstracted from *You and Your Membership in the UAW,* publication 383, December 1974; *The UAW . . . A Union that Gives Service,* publication 342, July 1974; Leonard Woodcock, *Report to the 24th Constitutional Convention* (Detroit: United Auto Workers, 1974).

The structure of the Carpenters' Union differs from that of the typical industrial union since it represents a narrower occupational group and deals generally with smaller employers. It is also less concerned with nationwide bargaining since employees of contractors generally come from a rather limited geographical area. On the other hand, it spends a greater amount of effort in protecting its jurisdiction against encroachments of other recognized trades and nonunion contractors.

Similar to most unions, the Carpenters' Union has as its ultimate governing body its national convention, consisting of delegates sent by its affiliated locals. The convention is responsible for electing national officers and for amending the organization's constitution. Each local has at least one representative with additional delegates apportioned according to size. Since the apportionment is not directly dependent on size, there is some bias toward smaller locals inherent in the convention composition.

A full-time executive branch operates the union between conventions. This consists of the general president, first and second vice presidents, general secretary, general treasurer, and an executive board. The members of the board are elected executives and representatives from ten geographical districts within the international. The board's primary functions are to handle grievances and appeals from locally imposed sanctions, authorize strikes, and adjudicate jurisdictional disputes.[12]

Besides the executive board, there are staff departments to advise the international and the locals. The major staff departments are legal, research, publications, pensions, and general representation. The administration of pensions by the international is typical of those in the building trades since the transience of jobs and the relatively small size of most contractors would make employer administration cumbersome and uncertain. The union is the only institution with a degree of permanence in the tradesman's employment, and hence, it is the logical organization to administer long-term personnel programs.

Generally speaking, a great deal of autonomy is exercised by union locals. They negotiate and administer their own contracts. They refer members to jobs (subject to the requirement that a member of one local in good standing can transfer to another local to enhance employment opportunities). And they handle local grievances, primarily by striking, since arbitration generally takes longer than one is likely to remain on a given job. The locals do sacrifice autonomy to the district councils in the establishment of work rules and to the national on bargaining with national contractors and the settlement of jurisdictional disputes.

The structure of the union is thus seen as being dependent on the structure of the employing industry. In the UAW, the international retains substantial control over bargaining and organization in a relatively concentrated industry while local Carpenters' unions exercise substantial autonomy in an industry with many relatively small employees.

---

[12] A jurisdictional dispute can arise where two or more unions claim representation rights for the same employees or members of two or more unions claim entitlement to certain work. For example, should rain gutters be nailed in place by carpenters or sheet metal workers?

The USW[13]

The USW is the largest industrial international affiliated with the AFL–CIO. As we noted in Chapter 3, the Steelworkers were nurtured by John L. Lewis, Philip Murray, and the United Mine Workers. The forerunner of the USW, the Steel Workers Organizing Committee (SWOC) was an early outgrowth of the CIO in the 1930s. Unlike the UAW, the major resistance to the rise of the USW did not come from the leading producer, U.S. Steel, but from smaller producers, referred to as the "Little Steel" group. While U.S. Steel is still the leader in negotiations, most bargaining innovations and pattern breaking have occurred among some of the smaller factors in the basic steel industry. For example, in 1959 Kaiser Steel broke the united industry front by negotiating gain sharing on productivity and job security against technological change with the USW.

Like the UAW, the USW has many members employed in its basic industry, but it also exercises jurisdiction in many other industries, that is, those which fabricate, mine, or use metal in raw and finished forms. This multiindustry jurisdiction has led to part of the organizational structuring of the USW, the industry conferences. Figure 5–2 shows the current USW industry conferences, their memberships, and their jurisdictions. We will return to a discussion of the industry conference function as we portray the USW organization. You will probably notice on the industry conference figure the title "United Steelworkers of America, AFL–CIO/CLC." The term "CLC" has not been introduced to you before this. CLC means Canadian Labor Congress, a group of federated unions representing workers in Canada. The Steelworkers are one of the major elements in Canadian labor.

The union is ultimately governed by its biennial convention, which has the responsibility for amending its constitution. Steelworkers elect their international officers by referendum among the total membership. This provision has led to some lively past campaigns and a significant leadership change in 1965. At that point, I. W. Abel was elected president to succeed David McDonald. The campaign centered to some extent on the issue that McDonald was too close to management in terms of his personal tastes, style of living, and willingness to seek cooperative solutions to industry problems. Abel won a close election. Another group, called "Dues Protest" and centered in western Pennsylvania, has also frequently opposed the USW leadership.[14] One other major factor involved in USW factionalism is the fact that both the Pittsburgh-Youngstown and the Chicago-Gary areas are major steel producers and strong regional leaders emanate

---

[13] For an expanded treatment see Lloyd Ulman, *The Government of the Steel Workers' Union* (New York: Wiley, 1962).

[14] Ibid., pp. 141–48.

FIGURE 5–2
Industry conferences United Steelworkers of America, AFL–CIO/CLC

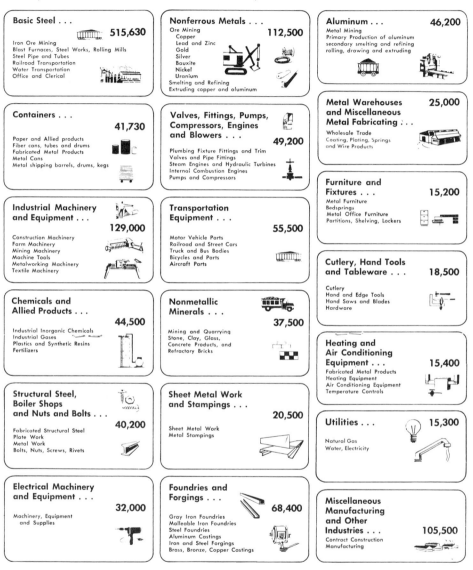

Source: *The Union,* pamphlet no. RP 302–A (Pittsburgh, Pa.: United Steelworkers of America, 1975).

from each. The most recent election took place in 1977 to replace the
retiring Abel. The choice of the incumbent officers was Lloyd
McBride, while Ed Sadlowski represented the dissident Chicago-Gary
group. It is ironic that the Abel organization was accused of the same
type of initiatives toward cooperation by Sadlowski that Abel had

accused McDonald of a dozen years before. McBride won a close election, but there will probably be some difficulty for the leadership in consolidating its position since it has been argued that Sadlowski carried a majority of basic steelworkers but lost in other industry conferences. USW politics are not dull. The current structure of the union is shown in Figure 5–3.

In terms of departmentalization, we will examine the industry conference first and then move to the general departments. As a major international industrial union, the USW is far flung geographically and is diversified across several industries involved in the extraction, pro-

FIGURE 5–3
Organization of the Steelworkers' Union

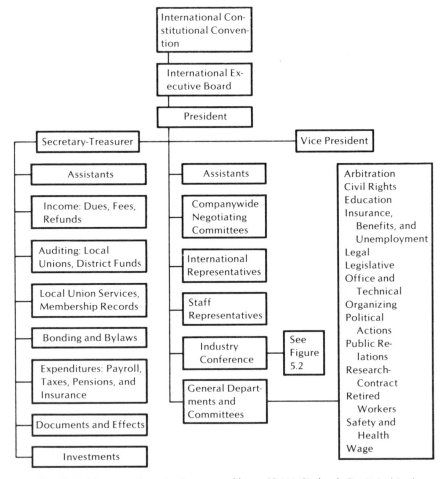

Source: Adapted from *How the Union Serves*, pamphlet no. PR 225 (Pittsburgh, Pa.: United Steelworkers of America, 1975).

BOX 5–1
Campaign positions taken by Lloyd McBride and Ed Sadlowski during 1977 USW election

Lloyd McBride.   Basically, the philosophy that I have about the union is that when I became an employee of the union, I then was taking the membership's money, I was in the pay of the union, and I understood my job as a representative of the union was to build and preserve the union.

Well, the difference, as I see it: I feel that my acceptance of a position of pay for the union committed me to build the union. This entails all of the acts and conduct which makes the union attractive to our membership.

Newman.   You mean and also not to criticize it.

McBride.   Not—to speak freely in the decisions that are made policywise. But whatever the decision was on the board, I then accepted it, and that was the policy of the union. I bowed then to the superior knowledge and common consent and at least the thinking by vote of responsible people on the board. I don't know it all.

Sadlowski, on the other hand, sits on the board, debates the issues, votes, and then goes out and criticizes whatever is done after he loses his particular point. This is where he has failed the union and did it a disservice, in my opinion.

Newman.   Union service, in McBride's vocabulary, is disservice in Sadlowski's, whose first priority is to open up the union.

Sadlowski.   The type of crap that goes on from that podium, with the fast gavel, when the question at hand is one that the chairman doesn't want to hear, or the booing and the shouting and the cheering and the clapping and the stomping and the pushing and the shoving, that doesn't belong. And that change is long overdue.

If you talk about Munich beer halls, it's reminiscent, you know, of Las Vegas convention centers.

McBride's whole platform and the whole theme is "Let us continue," or "Follow along the same roads and policies of I. W. Abel." Well, that's not good enough in 1976. It wasn't good enough ten years ago, and it's sure as hell not good enough today.

Newman.   But what specific things do you offer?

Sadlowski.   Now the membership will give you the direction, and then look for the leader to lead and find ways in order to develop that.

Newman.   That's very unspecific.

Sadlowski.   Well, that was a very unspecific question.

Newman.   No. Now, what. . . .

Sadlowski.   Are you saying what the programs are or the policies?

Newman.   No, no, not—it doesn't have to be programs or policies. But really, what—are—do you really see yourself as offering?

Sadlowski.   Change.

BOX 5–1 '*continued*)

Newman.   In what direction?

Sadlowski.   Change in the direction of leading the union in a more responsive institution to the membership. The historic role of labor up until a few years ago, Steelworkers specifically with the steel industry, was one of an adversary role, with United States Steel and Bethlehem Steel, et cetera.

I don't find anything compatible with the Steelworkers' Union and United States Steel, nothing whatsoever, nothing whatsoever.

Newman.   In Ed Sadlowski, McBride is fighting an ideology. Its cement is the desire of workers for control of union decision making, and a potent ingredient is a deep-seated hostility to industry.

While the current union leadership typically works out difficulties with industry behind the scenes quietly with mutual accommodation, Sadlowski's style is to view himself as the implacable enemy of industry.

I asked Lloyd McBride if he followed this line.

McBride.   No, I would not say I'm an implacable enemy of industry. There is a place for industry in our free economy system. I think that I would be an implacable enemy of tyranny in industry, of unfair conditions in industry, of unfair wages. I would certainly be an implacable enemy of anything that would run counter to the best interests of our membership.

I don't think that anyone who is an implacable enemy of industry can competently represent the best interests of our membership. This is a totally biased, unreasonable attitude.

Sadlowski.   I think that the ultimate (aim) of the labor leader in this country has to be one of taking a guy out of a coal mine and off of an open-hearth floor. And I strongly advocate that we find ways of making steel on an open-hearth floor with machines, and the people that were there be benefited monetarily by virtue of being displaced by the machines, so they can go out and find out what the hell the good life that a lot of public people talk about is all about. Eh?

There's nothing romantic, contrary to what some people write with pencils and pens, about working in a goddam—excuse the expression—no, don't excuse it—open hearth or a blast furnace.

Source: Interview by Barbara Newman of National Public Radio with Lloyd McBride and Edward Sadlowski as reported in *John Herling's Labor Letter*, October 23, 1976.

---

cessing, fabrication, and consumption of metals. Presently there are 24 geographical districts in the United States and Canada, each of which elects its own district director. The international services the district through staff representatives appointed by the USW president but who report to the district director. The major function of the district organization is to service the locals in its area. Some districts are relatively large geographically, such as district 38 which includes North and South Dakota, Montana, Wyoming, Colorado, New Mexico, Idaho, Utah, Arizona, Washington, Oregon, Nevada, California, and Hawaii. On the other hand, the steel producing belt from Milwaukee through Buffalo, encompassing Wisconsin, Illinois, Michigan, Ohio, Indiana, Pennsylvania, and New York contains all or parts of 14 of the 24 districts.

The industry conferences were organized in 1966 to coordinate bargaining and recognize the particular unique concerns of each industrial group. Overall, the aims of the industry conferences were to establish concurrent contract expiration dates, wages, and benefits across employers within an industry. This new setup has allowed each industry to have a greater voice in its own negotiations and, in turn, less impact on the negotiations outside their group which had taken place through a diversity of representatives on the international wage committee.[15]

The general departments of the union are primarily responsible for assisting the districts (and their locals) in organizing new locals, arbitrating grievances with employers, providing data for negotiations, upgrading work and safety standards, providing education and information to members and others, influencing legislation and political campaigns, and servicing retired workers. These departments are typical of those encountered in other industrial unions.

The financial backing for the international comes from individual member dues. Currently, the first $6 in dues is split equally between the local and the international. Any excess over $6 monthly is divided 40/40 between the local and the international with the remaining 20 percent allocated to the strike and defense fund.[16] Frequently, unions will step up dues levels in situations where strikes are anticipated so that strike benefits from strike funds will last through the duration.

The USW is somewhat similar to the UAW in organization. The membership has a major influence on its direction since the president is elected by referendum, not by the convention. In turn, the president has great power to influence local behavior through his appointive power in designating staff representatives who, in turn, service the locals. On occasion dissident USW locals have been asked to discipline their leaders, but the internal judicial process, which must begin at the local, usually results in acquittal.

---

[15] *USWA Industry Conference*, pamphlet no. PR 198 (Pittsburgh, Pa.: 1970), pp. 3–4.

[16] *How the Union Serves*, pamphlet no. PR 225 (Pittsburgh, Pa.: United Steelworkers of America, 1975).

The IBT[17]

The Teamsters' Union is perhaps the closest thing there is in the United States to a general union. In the past, its jurisdiction was primarily limited to trucking and warehousing, but with its expulsion from the AFL–CIO, it has broadened its jurisdiction to cover all workers, without limitation.[18] Teamster members now not only drive but are retail workers, manufacturers and assemblers, police, brewery workers, food processors, agricultural workers, and so on.

Similar to other unions, the international convention amends the constitution and elects officers. Delegates to the convention include international officers, members of various joint councils and conferences, and local union delegates. The local delegates are elected by the local's executive board and not the rank and file membership. This fact, coupled with the long duration (five years—the maximum permissible lapse under current federal law) between conventions, serves to isolate the leadership from membership demands of nonofficer factions.

The top executive ranks of the Teamsters consist of the general president, the general secretary-treasurer and 15 vice presidents. These officers make up the executive board. They may also have duties as international directors of Teamster conferences. Currently, five area conferences exist. These are the Eastern, Southern, Central, Western, and Ohio conferences of Teamsters. There are also eleven trade conferences somewhat similar in composition, but not necessarily in activity, to the USW industrial conferences. These are: airline; automotive, petroleum, and allied trades; baking; brewery and soft drinks; building materials and construction; communications; freight; food processing; laundry; warehouse; and household goods, moving and storage.

The joint councils are semiautonomous bodies which administer activities among affiliated locals. Each local is required to belong to a joint council and must get its permission to contract or to strike. The joint council is indirectly controlled by the IBT executive branch which must approve or disapprove certain recommendations made about a local.[19]

The Teamsters are perhaps the least democratic and most centralized of the national unions examined here. It is also atypical in terms of its inclusive jurisdiction and the structure of its bargaining relationship. Similar to the craft unions, it represents a large number of

---

[17] For more details on the Teamsters see Sam Romer, *The International Brotherhood of Teamsters: Its Government and Structure* (New York: Wiley, 1962) and Arthur L. Fox, II, and John C. Sikorski, *Teamster Democracy and Financial Responsibility* (Washington: Professional Drivers Council for Safety and Health, 1976).

[18] Romer, *The International Brotherhood of Teamsters*, pp. 8–11.

[19] Fox and Sikorski, *Teamster Democracy and Financial Responsibility*, pp. 1–7.

similarly skilled employees (truck drivers) in a single industry (interstate trucking). But unlike the craft unions where collective bargaining agreements seldom exceed statewide scope, the Teamsters have a national master agreement with trucking operators. Paradoxically, this master agreement consolidates the power of top leaders in negotiations but could be the one instrument that might lead to the rise of local discontent over terms a given area might feel are inadequately addressed, given their past bargaining success.

The Teamsters is the nation's largest international and is continuing to grow rapidly. They also continue to be cloaked in relative operational secrecy with nagging doubts about the interests of some of their officers and the legality of some of their actions.

The federation[20]

The AFL–CIO is a federation of 109 national unions banded together to provide some overall direction to the labor movement and technical assistance to individual nationals. It also has a number of independent local unions as direct affiliates. To maintain membership in the AFL–CIO, a national union must comply with the federation's Ethical Practices Code, demonstrate a lack of dominance by non-democratic ideologists, and agree to submit interunion disputes to mediation and adjudication within the AFL–CIO.

The organization of the AFL–CIO is complex due to its federal nature and its simultaneous relationship as coordinator of national union interests and director of state and city central body activities. Figure 5–4 gives the general organization of the AFL–CIO. At the top is the biennial national convention. Delegates are apportioned to the nationals on the basis of size and are elected or appointed consistent with individual national union policy. Other delegates are sent by directly affiliated locals, state and city central bodies, and national industrial and trade departments. The national convention amends the constitution, elects officers, and expresses official positions of the federation. The national convention elects the president and 33 vice presidents who together make up the executive council. As an adjunct, the general board consists of the executive council and presidents of each affiliated national as well as representatives from each of the constitutionally described departments within the federation.

The ongoing business of the AFL–CIO, like the nationals, is handled by the top executives, their staffs, and the constitutional departments. One could say that, similar to business organizations, the AFL–CIO has elements of both *functional* and *product-line* organiza-

---

[20] For an overview see *This Is the AFL–CIO*, pamphlet no. 20 (Washington: AFL–CIO, 1976).

FIGURE 5–4
Organization chart of the AFL–CIO

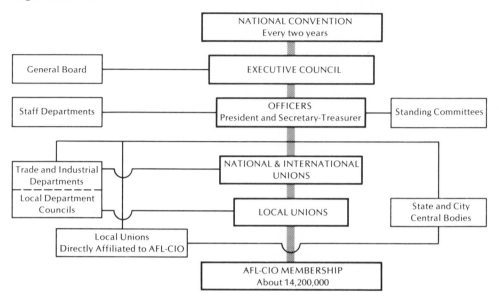

Source: *This Is the AFL–CIO,* pamphlet no. 20 (Washington: AFL–CIO, 1976), p. 15.

tions within it. By functional, we mean the organization structure is established in terms of what departments do that is of a specific, nonoverlapping nature. By product-line, we mean an organization structures itself around the specific separate goods and services it produces.

The product-line aspect relates to the trade and industrial departments. These are groupings of unions with relatively similar interests and industrial orientation. Currently there are seven such departments: building and construction trades, maritime trades, metal trades, railway employees, industrial union, union label and service trades, and the public employee department.

The functional portion of the organization consists of the various standing committees and their equivalent staff departments. These departments are involved in the normal ongoing federal activities. The following staff departments and their allied responsibilities are presently included in the AFL–CIO.

1. Organizing. Field representatives of the department of organizing and field services encourage and assist unorganized workers or local unions in unionization campaigns.

2. Legislation. The department of legislation prepares official positions; provides testimony on relevant legislation dealing with labor, social issues, and foreign policy; and lobbies with congressmen and representations.

3. Politics. The committee on political education evaluates legislative records of federal, state, and local candidates, and provides political information to the membership.

4. Community services. The department of community services coordinates activities with and assists local charitable and community service agencies during fund drives, local crises, and regional disasters.

5. International affairs. The department of international affairs maintains a liaison with trade unions in the free world.

6. Civil rights. The department of civil rights polices union violations of civil rights and pursues liaison activities with state and federal civil rights agencies.

7. Urban affairs. In this area the department of urban affairs encourages the investment of pension funds in mortgages for union members, coordinates apprenticeship programs for minorities, and works toward the increased utilization of urban human resources.

8. Education. The department of education prepares curricula for the training of union members in the principles of trade unionism.

9. Social security. The department of social security advises affiliates on matters relating to social security, unemployment insurance, and workmen's compensation.

10. Research. The department of research analyzes economic trends and the effects of legislative and economic policy on collective bargaining. It also maintains specialists in industrial engineering, consumer affairs, and natural resources problems.

11. Public relations. The department of public relations maintains liaison with the media and communicates the official position of the federation on current issues.

12. Publication. The department of publications serves as the major link between the federation and the individual member. It publishes the weekly *AFL–CIO News* and the monthly *AFL–CIO American Federationist*.

Besides these product-line and functional departments, the AFL–CIO has a direct relationship with over 900 state and local central bodies. In terms of their makeup, these bodies reflect the composition of the parent AFL–CIO and the particular industrial mix of that geographical area. The state and local centrals are directly responsible to the AFL–CIO and not to the internationals. A good example of this subordinate relationship occurred in 1972 when the AFL–CIO refused to endorse a presidential candidate. However, the Colorado Labor Council did endorse Senator McGovern. As a result of this action the AFL–CIO revoked the Colorado group's charter, successfully defended their actions in the federal courts, and forced the resignation of the president, Herrick Roth. By its rules, state central bodies were not permitted to endorse presidential candidates independent of AFL–CIO action, hence the revocation.[21]

Another labor federation, the Alliance for Labor Action (ALA) was founded in 1968 after the UAW had withdrawn from the AFL–CIO. Like politics, labor federations may also occasionally produce some strange bedfellows. In this case it was the Teamsters. It appears that the primary overt motive of both was to enhance their abilities to organize. With its withdrawal from the AFL–CIO, the UAW could expand its jurisdiction to nonauto workers quite readily. The Teamsters already viewed themselves as having a broad jurisdiction. Both joined forces in a concentrated drive to organize workers in Atlanta.

The less apparent reason for the ALA was Walter Reuther's disenchantment with the AFL–CIO in introducing and supporting progressive public policies. He viewed the ALA as a new federated effort toward directing labor on a more broadly advocative approach.

The long GM-UAW strike of 1970 was the first major event which led to the death of the ALA. From a $120 million surplus in its strike fund, the UAW was strapped with loans to the Rubber Workers, Steelworkers, and Teamsters by the time a new contract was signed. It had to pull back from an activist approach in organizing and run a low-profile operation until it returned to financial health. These strains, combined with Walter Reuther's untimely death in a plane crash, signaled the end of the ALA.[22]

State and local central bodies

State and local central bodies are primarily involved in political and lobbying activities. Major stress is given to endorsements of state and local candidates and testimony and lobbying on local and state legislative matters. The major difference between the parent AFL–CIO and state and local central bodies revolves around the fact that the AFL–CIO is predominantly made up of affiliated internationals while state and local centrals draw on affiliation with local unions. Figure 5–5 shows the relationship of state and local central bodies to other labor union organizations.

---

[21] *Rules Governing AFL–CIO State Central Bodies*, publication no. 12 (Washington: AFL–CIO, 1973), p. 21.

[22] See Karl F. Treckel, *The Rise and Fall of the Alliance for Labor Action (1968–1972)* (Kent, Ohio: Center for Business and Economic Research, Graduate School of Business Administration, Kent State University, 1975).

FIGURE 5–5
Structure of the labor movement

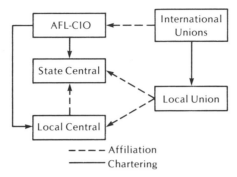

Source: Adapted from Joan G. Kilpatrick and Miles
C. Stanley, *Handbook on Central Labor Bodies: Functions and Activities,* West Virginia University Bulletin,
series 64, no. 4–6, October 1963, p. 5.

Overview of the union hierarchy

It is apparent in the constitutions, organization, and operation of the labor movement, presently and in the past, that the major locus of power resides in the various internationals and that locals and the federation derive their power from that delegated to them by the internationals. That this is true in fact as well as in statement is shown through the inability of the AFL–CIO to produce any substantial effects on the IBT as a result of its suspension and is continually shown through the power of the national to place recalcitrant locals under trusteeship (although this is seldom done).

The local union is structured to handle the day-to-day activities of the membership. Much of its effort is spent on policing the contract and pursuing grievances. It may have a major voice in negotiating work rules and the economic package in smaller industries and isolated markets. As we will note in greater detail, the local must defer to or gain permission from the international in many functions, particularly negotiating and strike activities.

The international unions maintain the expertise to deal with collective bargaining, political, legislative, and educational issues. One could compare the international to the corporate staff division of a large company where policies are developed, actions are audited to ensure conformity to policy, and advice is given to generalists in the plants (or locals) on specific issues. While the international convention is the ultimate governing body of the international, many international presidents have broad powers under their constitutions to take interim actions and also to influence the delegate composition of future conventions markedly.

The AFL–CIO serves the same function as a trade association, a chamber of commerce, or a national association of manufacturers. It coordinates activities among the internationals and makes their voices heard in a more amplified tone than they would singly. The federation's prime functions are informational, integrative, and advocative in nature. Its greatest areas of autonomy relate to legislative and political processes.

UNION DEMOCRACY

Whether or not unions are democratic has been a subject of considerable debate. The debate centers around two major areas: (1) whether they do behave democratically through the expression of majority and minority viewpoints and rely on the will of the rank and file, and (2) whether they should be democratic. We might also draw another definition of democracy that is often a mislabeling of the term; that is, due process. Do the various labor organizations incorporate a structure which allows individual members to obtain rights and benefits guaranteed by their union and to be free from arbitrary and capricious conduct which would be nonreviewable? In our discussion here, we will focus on the organization, not the individual. But we will take up the individual again when we discuss the duty of fair representation.

Union democracy is an important issue since the role of the union in one's employment is often critical. Under U.S. labor law we know that two elements make democracy exceedingly important. First, U.S. law provides for the concept of exclusive agency. If the union in question is the certified agent, it must represent all employees in the unit, and as a corollary, no employees can unilaterally bargain mandatory issues for themselves. Second, unions may negotiate labor contracts requiring employees to be union members as a condition of continued employment. But if they do so, members can only be expelled for nonpayment of dues. Democracy would demand that members conscripted in this way must have a voice.

One critical fact in collective bargaining legislation, which is often ignored, seems to guarantee at least some level of democracy on important issues to union members at the bargaining unit level. That provision entitles bargaining unit members to request certification or decertification of a designated union as their representative on the basis of majority rule. This rule does not, however, guarantee democratic behavior in union institutions. In fact, in an amalgamated local union representing a variety of employees across employers, one faction that is dissatisfied may have relatively little effect on the thrust and direction of the local. But this is not much different than what we find in municipal, state, and federal politics. Often a faction finds its taxes increasing or zoning decisions going against its wishes, but it has an opportunity to express its dissatisfaction and may attempt to persuade other factions to join with it later to oust the present leadership.

Even with the legal safeguards, the existence of democracy is still an issue. In the United States, our cultural values place a high priority on democratic institutions. Legislation requiring public bodies to deliberate openly reflects our concern for democratic behavior as an inherent right of organizational members. One might argue that we do not require the same of business organizations, but a distinction exists. The owners (stockholders) of business organizations have democratic rights specified in their organization's charter and guaranteed by laws of incorporation. Employees of these firms are not viewed as members of the corporation under the law, but as individual or collectivized vendors of labor to the purchasing firm.

The degree to which unions, at their various levels, are open and democratic depends on both the constitutional structure of the union and the behavior of the membership on issues which allow democratic choice. At the national level, there are two constitutional provisions which will affect the degree to which democracy is present. The first relates to the mode by which the general president is elected. A referendum of the entire membership will tend to encourage nonincumbents and factions. Election by a convention delegate vote suppresses factionalism, particularly if it is issue, rather than geographically, based. Second, the degree to which union posts are appointive rather than elective would tend to reduce democracy, since the maintenance of appointed positions depends upon the continued incumbency of the chief executive. Further, if the composition of delegates to the international convention includes not only those selected at a local level, but also those appointed officials selected by the incumbent, the chances of mounting a successful drive to oust the incumbent is virtually impossible.[23]

There is some evidence to show that turnover of union officials is inversely related to their pay.[24] This suggests that a career orientation would tend to create a vested interest in maintaining the incumbent or providing means to save one's job. Besides being related to lower salaries, turnover seems to be higher at local rather than national levels, reflective of the greater likelihood that a dispute over leadership practices is to be more pervasive on a locally focused issue and that elections tend to offer more direct impact from the membership

---

[23] The PROD report alleges that this type of arrangement perpetuates Teamster leadership. See Fox and Sikorski, *Teamster Democracy and Financial Responsibility.*

[24] Leon Applebaum and Harry R. Blaine, "Compensation and Turnover of Union Officers," *Industrial Relations*, vol. 14 (May 1975), pp. 156–57.

(referendum).[25] Even so, turnouts for local elections seldom exceed 10–20 percent, allowing local leaders and "in-groups" to control the organizations effectively.

Most labor organizations do not contain the elements necessary to ensure democracy as it is usually defined. There is not, for example, an ongoing opposition, recognized and tolerated by the incumbents. Instead, there is a tendency at both the local and national level to view internal dissent as divisive and counterproductive. Dissenters are seen as being in league with the common enemy: management. Any internal conflict which requires energy to resolve is seen as taking away from the strength to resist the employer collectively.

In their classic study of the International Typographical Union, Lipset, Trow, and Coleman[26] explore the conditions which appear to be necessary for traditional democracy to flourish. They see a pluralistic constituency as being necessary for democracy. More than two factions are necessary and coalitions of these factions must change over time if domination by one group is to be avoided. Since members will have belonged to winning and losing coalitions over time, it is to nearly everyone's interest to establish and protect rights of members of the current minority. They also note that a union must feel relatively secure from external threat (decertification, intransigent bargaining, and so forth) before it can afford democracy. This phenomenon has been observed in other contexts and in small groups where cohesiveness (that is, intolerance of deviant behavior and individual subscription to group goals) increases as a result of external threat.[27]

One thing we must remember in our examination of union democracy is that the union member is simultaneously an employee. The union may be seen as necessary to the introduction of some semblance of democracy in the employment relationship. Just as a political pressure group may demand internal discipline to influence a demo-

---

[25] Leon Applebaum, "Officer Turnover and Salary Structures in Local Unions," *Industrial and Labor Relations Review*, vol. 19 (1966), pp. 224–30.

[26] Seymour M. Lipset, Martin A. Trow, and James S. Coleman, *Union Democracy: The Internal Politics of the International Typographical Union* (Glencoe, Ill.: Free Press, 1956).

[27] On group cohesiveness, see Dorwin Cartwright, "The Nature of Group Cohesiveness," in Dorwin Cartwright and Alvin Zander, eds., *Group Dynamics: Research and Theory*, 3d ed. (New York: Harper & Row, 1967), pp. 91–109. From an historical standpoint, the United States, with long democratic traditions, has on occasion been guilty of grossly undemocratic suppression of real or perceived dissent resulting from an external threat. For example, thousands of Japanese-Americans—U.S. citizens—were interned during World War II to remove them supposedly from the opportunity for committing treasonous and seditious acts even though none had any previous history of such activity.

cratic process collectively, a union might also suppress internal dissent to enable it to play an advocate role of some power in the collective bargaining process. Chamberlain and Cullen call this "functional democracy" and argue that the (at least) two-party system, necessary for democracy to occur, consists of the employer and the union, not some requirement that at least two factions exist and are tolerated in the union.[28]

Another point that has been raised in relation to union democracy is the fact that union members are entitled to due process under at least two sets of rules. Cook[29] points out that a dual system of governance exists within the union structure. One set of rules is contained in the local union's constitution, the other in the collective bargaining agreement between the employer and the union as bargaining agent. Each set of rules is administered by separate sets of officials (although some individuals may hold dual offices). For the local's operation there are elected a president, secretary-treasurer, executive board, and other officials, as needed. To administer the agreement, a negotiating committee and stewards are elected. Thus, there is an internal check and balance system to help insure that the contract is administered fairly for all bargaining unit members and that the contract in an individual unit is not contrary to union philosophies. Figure 5–6 should help you to conceptualize the idea of dual governance. Assume here a local which includes three bargaining units in an open shop industry. There are three separate contracts administered by the local through three separate negotiating committees. Each bargaining unit's union members are eligible to vote for the officers of the local. The shaded area represented workers who have union and bargaining unit membership, while those outside the local circle are only bargaining unit members.

The question then of whether or not unions are democratic boils down to: how democratic? They are probably less democratic than governmental units. But they probably can be less democratic with fewer problems. Union members generally are interested in similar types of outcomes, view the union as their agent, and evaluate that agency on the outcomes it produces rather than on an ideological stand of a faction.[30] The union member does not generally feel a need to be "protected" from his union. On the contrary, it is management that he is worried about. Besides, if the union member is concerned about the

---

[28] Neil W. Chamberlain and Donald E. Cullen, *The Labor Sector*, rev. ed. (New York: McGraw-Hill, 1971), pp. 194–96.

[29] Alice H. Cook, "Dual Governance in Unions: A Tool for Analysis," *Industrial and Labor Relations Review*, vol. 15 (April 1962), pp. 323–49.

[30] Sayles and Strauss, *The Local Union*, p. 141.

FIGURE 5–6
Dual governance in unions

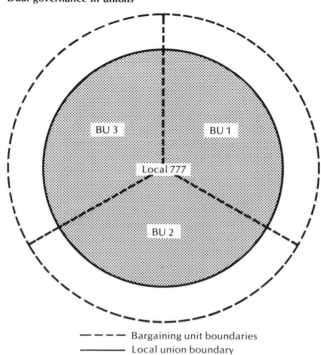

- - - - Bargaining unit boundaries
———— Local union boundary

direction of his union, he can, at the very least, attempt to have it decertified or replaced with another. There are enough legal safeguards to require responsiveness, if not democracy, and that appears to be enough for most members.

UNION FINANCES

Union finances are generally related to two different functions. The first relates to the day-to-day operations and functions of the union organization while the second relates to the fiduciary obligation of officers in some unions in the collection, trusteeship, and disbursement of pension and welfare benefits to members. This latter function is usually found in craft unions or unions where the employers in represented industries are too small or marginal to administer their own pension programs.

Operational receipts and disbursements

Three major sources of revenue are available to the various union entities. These generally are dues from members; fees, fines, and assessments from members; and investment income. Dues and fees are generally collected at the local level. The only entity that depends on the dues themselves are the locals. The internationals and the AFL–CIO level depend upon a per capita tax on the local's membership to maintain affiliation. The current AFL–CIO per capita tax is 13 cents monthly while many internationals collect about 50 percent of dues payments for international operations.[31] Dues vary widely among unions, with some requiring a flat fee, others scaled to earning levels. The dues usually have minimum and maximum levels set by the parent international with the local given flexibility to adjust within those limits. Occasionally an assessment is added to replenish or maintain strike funds.

Unions also require new members to pay initiation fees. These can vary widely with about two thirds of international unions allowing the local to determine the rate with some latitude. As of 1968, internationally set fees ranged from nothing to $1,000, with a modal level of $5.[32]

A U.S. Department of Labor report found local unions receiving a total of $1.857 billion during 1970. Of this amount, 71 percent came from dues; while 12 percent came from fees, fines, and assessments; and 17 percent from other sources. Just over $1.8 billion was disbursed, with 38 percent going for per capita taxes to affiliated bodies, 28 percent to officer and employee salaries, almost 10 percent for office and administrative expenses, about 7 percent to member benefits, and about 17 percent to other items. National union receipts totaled $1.380 billion of which 44 percent came from per capita taxes; 4 percent from fees, fines, assessments, and work permits; and 52 percent from investments and other sources. The nationals' income from nondues sources provides over half of their revenues. Investments in securities, real estate, and other ventures reflect the business orientation of U.S. unions. National unions spent $1.344 billion with 9 percent going toward affiliation payments, 18 percent for salaries, 7 percent for office and administrative expenses, 1 percent for loans, 25 percent for benefits, and the other 40 percent for other payments.[33]

---

[31] *This Is the AFL–CIO*, p. 5.

[32] Edward Curtin, *Union Initiation Fees, Dues, and Per Capita Tax—National Union Strike Benefits* (New York: National Industrial Conference Board, 1968), p. 3.

[33] U.S. Department of Labor, *Union Financial Statistics, 1960–1970* (Washington: Government Printing Office, 1972).

Pension administration

Pension plans are frequently administered by craft unions and other unions where employers are small. In the craft unions, dues are generally greater than those in industrial unions, and a portion is set aside for future benefits. Other unions require the employer to make a per capita payment, as in the Teamsters national agreement (1976) calling for $25 per employee per week in pension payments. In the coal industry a royalty on coal tonnage is negotiated, and this income is used to pay retirement benefits.

The administration of pension programs has become an increasingly important issue for both union administrators and members. With the passage of the Employee Retirement Income Security Act of 1974, both employer and union pension administrators are required to follow practices to safeguard the contributions made toward retirement. Certain investment practices, such as risky loans or low interest loans, are illegal. Investments in one's own organization are also largely precluded. Recently officials of the Teamsters Union have been under fire for alleged mismanagement of pensions. An agreement was recently reached to enable Department of Labor oversight of pension activities.

POLITICAL ACTION

While labor in the United States does not field its own political party or monolithically deliver votes or endorsements, it is active politically. Over time its activism, in terms of scope, has waxed and waned. In recent years, perhaps Walter Reuther is the best example of a union leader advocating a broadly based legislative program including aspects of no direct concern to labor. Recently, however, the AFL–CIO's approach has been to concentrate its activities on issues having a direct consequence on its membership such as reforming existing labor laws, tariffs and trade, and economic stimulation.

Labor organizations provide endorsements and information about union positions through Committees on Political Education (COPE). Efforts to register people to vote and get them to the polls are undertaken. Records are kept of votes on labor-related issues rendered by senators, representatives, and legislators. Lobbying in support or in opposition of legislation is done at the state and federal level.

While organized labor tends to support Democratic party candidates, it does not always do so. For example, the Teamsters (and some others) endorsed President Nixon over Senator McGovern in 1972. On other occasions it "sits on its hands," as it did generally in 1972 for the presidential race. Probably the best description of labor's approach to political action is the motto: "Reward your friends and punish your enemies."

SUMMARY

Organized labor is essentially a three-tiered structure with the power concentrated at the second level. The levels are local, national, and AFL–CIO. At the local level, the most typical structure is the single bargaining unit local. Multiemployer units are perhaps most common in the construction industry. National unions are of two major types: craft, representing workers in a specific occupation; and industrial, representing occupations in a specific industry. The AFL–CIO is the only major U.S. labor federation with about 75 percent of union members affiliated.

While the local is the workers' direct representative, members' interest in internal affairs is generally low. They appear to view the union as their employment agent allowing a cadre of activists to control its internal politics.

International union structures, particularly the industrials, adapt both to the breadth of the constituencies and the concentration within their industries. For example, the UAW has a "General Motors department" and the USW has a "basic steel" component in its industry conference.

Whether or not unions operate democratically depends on your definition of the term. Most do not have two-party systems, and many equate dissent with attempts to undermine union goals. On the other hand, local officers are directly elected, and international officials are chosen in a manner similar to a presidential nominating convention. Unions do introduce democracy into the work setting by requiring a bargained contract. Within unions the checks and balances initiated through the union's constitution and its contracts serve to increase democracy or safeguards for members.

SUGGESTED READINGS

Barbash, Jack. *American Unions, Structure, Government, and Politics* (New York: Random House, 1967).

Bok, Derek C., and Dunlop, John T. *Labor and the American Community* (New York: Simon & Schuster, 1970).

Chamberlain, Neil W., and Cullen, Donald E. *The Labor Sector*, rev. ed. (New York: McGraw-Hill, 1971).

Cook, Alice H. *Union Democracy: Practice and Ideal* (Ithaca, N.Y.: New York State School of Industrial and Labor Relations, Cornell University, 1963).

Estey, Martin. *The Unions: Structure Development and Management,* 2d ed. (New York: Harcourt Brace Jovanovich, 1976).

Richardson, Reed. *American Labor Unions: An Outline of Growth and Structure,* 2d ed. (Ithaca, N.Y.: New York State School of Industrial and Labor Relations, Cornell University, 1970).

Roth, Herrick. *Labor: America's Two-Faced Movement* (New York: Petrocelli/Charter, 1975).

Sayles, Leonard R., and Strauss, George. *The Local Union,* rev. ed. (New York: Harcourt, Brace, & World, 1967).

Seidman, Joel, ed. *Trade Union Government and Collective Bargaining* (New York: Praeger, 1970).

Tannenbaum, Arnold S. "Unions." In James G. March, ed., *Handbook of Organizations* (Chicago: Rand-McNally, 1965), pp. 710–63.

DISCUSSION QUESTIONS

1. Herrick Roth was forced to resign as the leader of the Colorado labor council as a condition for its reinstatement in the AFL–CIO. He had led the drive to endorse McGovern in 1972. If Roth had been a regional manager in a business organization, would the outcome have been the same?

2. If you were recommending an organizational structure for a national union, what factors would you advise that it take into account (for example, industrial concentration, occupations it represents, and so on)?

3. Should unions at all levels be involved in the endorsement of political candidates?

4. What could a union local do to increase the involvement of its membership?

5. Defend or attack the usual method of electing an international president through local delegates and international staff members at the convention.

6

FEDERAL AGENCIES INVOLVED
WITH
LABOR RELATIONS

The legislation we described in Chapter 4 established several governmental agencies. Other agencies also influence labor relations directly but have not been mentioned to this point. This chapter gives you an overview of the major government agencies and their organizational relationships as they were in 1977. Reorganizations take place from time to time so that the present structure may differ somewhat from what exists as you read this chapter.

BRANCHES OF GOVERNMENT

All three branches of government: legislative, executive, and judicial are involved in private sector labor relations. The legislative branch writes and amends the law; the executive agencies implement and regulate within the law; and the judicial branch examines the actions of the other two in the light of the Constitution and the statutes and common law. Figure 6–1 presents the organization of the federal government.

DEPARTMENT OF LABOR

The Department of Labor, created as a cabinet department in 1913, has a broad charter:[1]

> The purpose of the Department of Labor is to foster, promote, and develop the welfare of the wage earners of the United States, to improve their working conditions, and to advance their opportunities for profitable employment. In carrying out this mission, the department adminis-

---

[1] Office of the Federal Register, National Archives and Record Service, General Services Administration, *U.S. Government Manual* (Washington: Government Printing Office, 1977), p. 360.

FIGURE 6–1
The government of the United States

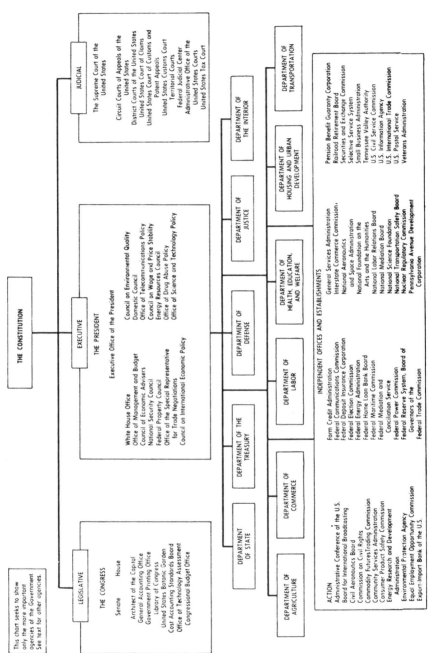

This chart seeks to show only the more important agencies of the Government. See text for other agencies.

THE CONSTITUTION

LEGISLATIVE

THE CONGRESS

Senate House

Architect of the Capitol
General Accounting Office
Government Printing Office
Library of Congress
United States Botanic Garden
Cost Accounting Standards Board
Office of Technology Assessment
Congressional Budget Office

EXECUTIVE

THE PRESIDENT

Executive Office of the President

White House Office
Office of Management and Budget
Council of Economic Advisers
National Security Council
Federal Property Council
Office of the Special Representative for Trade Negotiations
Council on International Economic Policy

Council on Environmental Quality
Domestic Council
Office of Telecommunications Policy
Council on Wage and Price Stability
Energy Resources Council
Office of Drug Abuse Policy
Office of Science and Technology Policy

JUDICIAL

The Supreme Court of the United States

Circuit Courts of Appeals of the United States
District Courts of the United States
United States Court of Claims
United States Court of Customs and Patent Appeals
United States Customs Court
Territorial Courts
Federal Judicial Center
Administrative Office of the United States Courts
United States Tax Court

DEPARTMENT OF STATE
DEPARTMENT OF THE TREASURY
DEPARTMENT OF DEFENSE
DEPARTMENT OF JUSTICE
DEPARTMENT OF THE INTERIOR
DEPARTMENT OF AGRICULTURE
DEPARTMENT OF COMMERCE
DEPARTMENT OF LABOR
DEPARTMENT OF HEALTH, EDUCATION, AND WELFARE
DEPARTMENT OF HOUSING AND URBAN DEVELOPMENT
DEPARTMENT OF TRANSPORTATION

INDEPENDENT OFFICES AND ESTABLISHMENTS

ACTION
Administrative Conference of the U.S.
Board for International Broadcasting
Civil Aeronautics Board
Commission on Civil Rights
Commodity Futures Trading Commission
Community Services Administration
Consumer Product Safety Commission
Energy Research and Development Administration
Environmental Protection Agency
Equal Employment Opportunity Commission
Export-Import Bank of the U.S.

Farm Credit Administration
Federal Communications Commission
Federal Deposit Insurance Corporation
Federal Election Commission
Federal Energy Administration
Federal Home Loan Bank Board
Federal Maritime Commission
Federal Mediation and Conciliation Service
Federal Power Commission
Federal Reserve System, Board of Governors of the
Federal Trade Commission

General Services Administration
Interstate Commerce Commission
National Aeronautics and Space Administration
National Foundation on the Arts and the Humanities
National Labor Relations Board
National Mediation Board
National Science Foundation
National Transportation Safety Board
Nuclear Regulatory Commission
Pennsylvania Avenue Development Corporation

Pension Benefit Guaranty Corporation
Railroad Retirement Board
Securities and Exchange Commission
Selective Service System
Small Business Administration
Tennessee Valley Authority
U.S. Civil Service Commission
U.S. Information Agency
U.S. International Trade Commission
U.S. Postal Service
Veterans Administration

Source: Office of the Federal Register, National Archives and Record Service, General Services Administration, *U.S. Government Manual* (Washington: Government Printing Office, 1977), p. 28.

ters more than 130 federal labor laws guaranteeing workers' rights to safe and healthful working conditions, a minimum hourly wage and overtime pay, freedom from employment discrimination, unemployment insurance, and workers' compensation. The department also protects workers' pension rights; sponsors job training programs; helps workers find jobs; works to strengthen free collective bargaining; and keeps track of changes in employment, prices, and other national economic measurements. As the department seeks to assist all Americans who need and want to work, special efforts are made to meet the unique job market problems of older workers, youths, minority group members, women, the handicapped, and other groups.

The primary areas of interest for students of labor relations are associated with the assistant secretary for labor-management relations, the assistant secretary for occupational safety and health, the assistant secretary for employment and training, and the commissioner of labor statistics. The entire major organization of the Department of Labor is shown in Figure 6–2.

Labor-Management Services Administration

LMSA is responsible for collecting reports from employers and unions as required by the Employee Retirement Income Security Act of 1974 (ERISA) and the Labor Management Reporting and Disclosure Act (LMRDA). The LMSA also provides research assistance in collective bargaining for long-range changes (for example, automation) and immediate negotiations. The LMSA administers the executive orders pertaining to federal employees by determining appropriate bargaining units, supervising representation elections, ruling on unfair labor practices, and deciding the arbitrability of grievances.

Occupational Safety and Health Administration

OSHA is responsible for the interpretation and enforcement of the Occupational Safety and Health Act of 1970. It investigates violations and through hearings held by Department of Labor administrative law judges assesses penalties.

Employment and Training Administration

Of the various agencies with the ETA, the Bureau of Apprenticeship and Training is the one probably closest to labor relations. The BAT assists employers and unions in establishing high-quality worker training programs to ensure consistent standards across jurisdictions.

FIGURE 6-2
Department of Labor

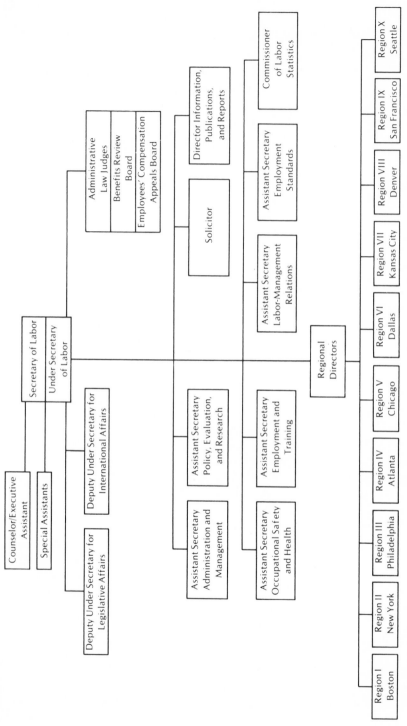

Source: Office of the Federal Register, National Archives and Record Service, General Services Administration, *U.S. Government Manual* (Washington: Government Printing Office, 1977), p. 361.

Bureau of Labor Statistics

The BLS collects, maintains, and publishes data which interested persons use to assess the current state of the economy, nationally, regionally, or locally. It publishes the Consumer Price Index, conducts area wage surveys, and provides unemployment data as part of its activities.

Employment Standards Administration

Several offices within the ESA are important to unions and employers. The wage and hour division enforces provisions of the Fair Labor Standards Act governing overtime, minimum wage, and child labor. The Office of Federal Contract Compliance Programs monitors federal contractor actions in affirmatively hiring and employing women, minorities, and the handicapped. The Women's Bureau is charged with promoting the welfare of working women. Finally, the Office of Workers' Compensation Programs administers federal programs for longshore workers and miners suffering from "black lung" diseases.

EXECUTIVE AGENCIES

Equal Employment Opportunity Commission

The EEOC was established through Title VII of the 1964 Civil Rights Act. It receives and investigates charges that employers or unions have violated Title VII. If it finds violations, it first attempts to conciliate to reach a settlement with the charged party. It may enter into consent decrees administered by the federal district courts. Where voluntary agreements are not reached, the EEOC grants the right to sue to the charging party or intervenes on behalf of the party by suing in a federal district court.

The EEOC is also empowered to publish employment regulations consistent with Title VII. To determine patterns of compliance with the Civil Rights Act, it gathers employment statistics from all covered employers on a periodic basis.

Federal Mediation and Conciliation Service

The FMCS was established by the Taft-Hartley Act in 1947. There are a variety of functions performed by the FMCS. Probably the most prominent is its mediation efforts in labor-management negotiations. It mediates either through invitation or on its own motion. But the mediators have no power to impose settlements or regulate bargaining activity.

The FMCS also maintains listings of arbitrators from which it selects panels to settle contractual disputes if private parties request them. In its decision to list or delist an arbitrator, it applies rules that have been established by the FMCS to assess qualifications.

National Labor Relations Board

The NLRB was established in 1935 by the Wagner Act. Its two primary functions are to determine whether or not groups of employees desire union representation or not and whether unions or companies have committed unfair labor practices as defined by federal law. The NLRB has jurisdiction over most profit-making employers (subject to certain minimum revenues generated), employees of private nonprofit hospitals, and the U.S. Postal Service.

Figure 6–3 shows the board's organization. The general counsel coordinates much of the board's activity, since determinations are made by that office on whether to proceed against an employer or union once a complaint has been filed. The board does not initiate action but only responds to complaints from the parties. If a complaint is received, the regional office will attempt to gain a mutually agreed to settlement. If this is not achieved, then the case is handled at a national level. For representation cases, if a regional director declines to handle the case, a petition may be filed with the board. In unfair labor practice cases, the general counsel to the NLRB determines whether or not to proceed. Cases involving unfair labor practices are heard by administrative law judges assigned to the board. If a party to the case disagrees with the law judge's conclusions, the board will review the case.

If a decision of the NLRB is not complied with, the board may petition a United States Court of Appeals for enforcement. Board orders must be publicized to employees and/or union members. The board may issue "cease and desist" orders, "bargaining orders," and decisions which make employees whole for illegal personnel actions such as terminations for union activity.

National Mediation Board

The NMB was established in 1934 by an amendment to the Railway Labor Act. Its responsibilities are to mediate contract disputes between covered carriers and their unions and to certify representatives of employees for bargaining purposes. It refers grievances to the National Railroad Adjustment Board. The NMB may appoint a referee to assist in making NRAB awards where the panel is deadlocked.

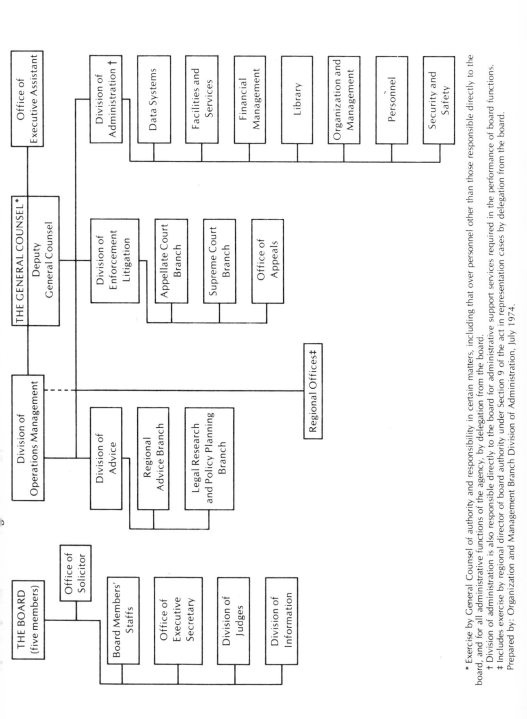

THE BOARD (five members)

Office of Solicitor

Board Members' Staffs

Office of Executive Secretary

Division of Judges

Division of Information

Division of Operations Management

Division of Advice

Regional Advice Branch

Legal Research and Policy Planning Branch

Regional Offices‡

THE GENERAL COUNSEL*
Deputy General Counsel

Division of Enforcement Litigation

Appellate Court Branch

Supreme Court Branch

Office of Appeals

Office of Executive Assistant

Division of Administration †

Data Systems

Facilities and Services

Financial Management

Library

Organization and Management

Personnel

Security and Safety

* Exercise by General Counsel of authority and responsibility in certain matters, including that over personnel other than those responsible directly to the board, and for all administrative functions of the agency, by delegation from the board.
† Division of administration is also responsible directly to the board for administrative support services required in the performance of board functions.
‡ Includes exercise by regional director of board authority under Section 9 of the act in representation cases by delegation from the board.
Prepared by: Organization and Management Branch Division of Administration, July 1974.

The NMB is also responsible for notifying the president if a mediated dispute is unsettled and threatens to cripple transport in some section of the country. The president may then appoint an emergency board to study the situation and make recommendations.

Occupational Safety and Health Review Commission

OSHRC was established in 1970 by the Occupational Safety and Health Act. While most OSHA cases are handled in the Department of Labor, where disputes between the government and employers cannot be resolved, OSHRC reviews the case and renders a judgment. Most of the judgments are made by OSHRC's administrative law judges although their conclusions can be appealed to the commissioners. Enforcement of commission orders is handled through the appeals court system.

Pension Benefit Guarantee Corporation

PBGC was established by the Employee Retirement Income Security Act of 1974. Its primary mission is to insure the vested pension benefit rights of employees covered by private noncontributory pension programs. Employers pay insurance premiums to fund the plan, and these premiums are used to pay pensions where plans become insolvent.

SUMMARY

In our system of government the legislative department enacts the laws, the executive department carries them out, and the court system tests their validity and rules on conduct within their purview.

As a cabinet department, the Department of Labor is primarily responsible for the implementation of human resource programs and monitoring activities. It has little direct influence on collective bargaining.

Rule making, interpretive, and assistance agencies have major influences on employers, either through direct intervention or regulation. The EEOC and NLRB are probably the two having the greatest impact.

DISCUSSION QUESTIONS

1. Looking at Figure 6–1, should the human resource and labor relations functions of the federal government be reorganized? If so, how?
2. Should administrative agencies such as the NLRB be allowed to render administrative law decisions which can be enforced by the courts? Or should an agency be required to go directly to court?

7

THE BEHAVIORAL BASIS FOR UNIONS

To this point we have focused on the historical development of, public policy stance toward, and internal structure of, labor unions. Many of the instances we examined in the historical context give us some insight about the genesis and survival power of unions, but they do not describe it in any systematic way. In this chapter we will apply some of what is known about the reasons behind individual, group, and organizational behavior to an explanation of union activity.

As we go through this chapter, keep these questions in mind:

1. What appear to be the necessary conditions for organizing activity to begin?
2. Does the character of union participation remain the same among individuals over the course of their membership in the organization?
3. What is the effect of employer pressure on the behavior of present and potential union members?
4. What roles does the local union assume over time in relation to the employer?

MOTIVATION

When broken down to their elemental components, groups and organizations are made up of individuals. To establish the groups or organizations, individuals must make choices to join and engage in behavior necessary to create and sustain the group. Groups and organizations differ somewhat. We can usually think of an organization as a group of individuals with some set of established rules specifying their roles and the purposes of acting together. Groups are more informal collectives that have either social ends in mind or have no long-run perspective.

In this section we want to examine some basic concepts of motivation that will help to explain why organizing occurs and why some employees or industries or occupations are largely organized while others are not.

Expectancy theory

Probably the most widely recognized model of individual motivation during the past 15 years has been an approach called expectancy theory. This approach is unique when compared to other motivation theories in that it recognizes that individuals differ widely in terms of the things they desire to achieve. Some people find major satisfactions in money, others in interesting work, others in rapid and significant achievement, and still others in friendly social relations. Not only do we find this diversity across individuals, but also within them. For example, a person may find satisfaction in all four of the outcomes we just mentioned, although there may be at least a rank order in preference among them. The second unique aspect of expectancy theory is that individuals are presumed to make conscious choices about the courses of action they will take to achieve the outcomes that are important to them. Within our context here, what this basically means is that an individual should evaluate whether or not belonging to a union which will bargain with the employer will result in greater outcomes than being unorganized.

Schematic model

There have been a number of versions of expectancy theory proposed. Some are mathematical in nature,[1] others diagrammatic.[2] The diagrammatic models are probably more instructive to the beginning student of motivation but are too general when it comes to evaluating the complexity of the decision-making process. We will present a diagrammatic model in Figure 7–1 and then concoct a relatively realistic example to show how expectancy theories of motivation can be

---

[1] Cf. Victor H. Vroom, *Work and Motivation* (New York: Wiley, 1964); and Robert J. House and Mahmoud A. Wahba, "Expectancy Theory in Managerial Motivation: An Integrative Model," in Henry L. Tosi, Robert J. House, and Marvin D. Dunnette, eds., *Managerial Motivation and Compensation* (East Lansing, Mich.: Division of Research, Graduate School of Business Administration, Michigan State University, 1972), pp. 127–33.

[2] Cf. Lyman W. Porter and Edward E. Lawler, III, *Managerial Attitudes and Performance* (Homewood, Ill.: Irwin-Dorsey, 1968); John P. Campbell, Marvin D. Dunnette, Edward E. Lawler, III, and Karl E. Weick, *Managerial Behavior, Performance, and Effectiveness* (New York: McGraw-Hill, 1970); and Edward E. Lawler, III, *Pay and Organizational Effectiveness* (New York: McGraw-Hill, 1971).

FIGURE 7–1
A motivation model

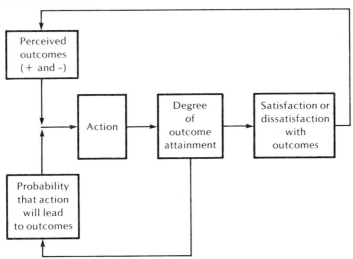

applied to explain individual behavior in union organizations and campaigns.

Figure 7–1 suggests that individuals have certain outcomes that are important to them and certain beliefs about whether or not they can achieve these outcomes. The outcomes and beliefs lead to taking some type of action to attain or avoid them. The effort or action may or may not lead to their achievement, but the degree to which the effort does lead to achievement of positive outcomes should increase the likelihood of this action or behavior in the future.

Figure 7–2 depicts a hypothetical belief system for two employees in a situation where organizing is being considered. The figure suggests that each employee considers the outcomes likely from organization. Here we have specified the same set for both as an example, but there is no reason why they should overlap to any extent, especially if there are major individual differences separating the two. If you look at the outcomes and their valuations, you see differences between the two individuals. A positively values a union leadership position while B apparently attaches no positive or negative value to it. Other differences also exist, such as for individual treatment.

The next explanatory component links the outcomes with the result of an action; in this case, success or failure in organizing. For individual A, organizing is associated with six positive and two negative outcomes. Failure to organize leads to one positive, one negative, and two neutral items. If individual A believes that taking action will increase

FIGURE 7–2
Beliefs about organizing

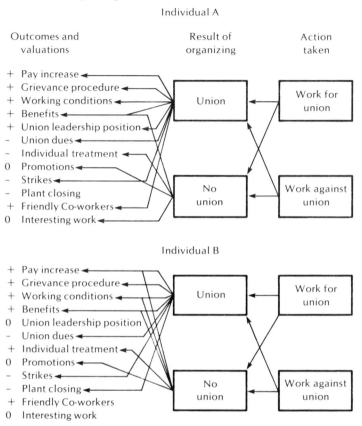

the likelihood of unionization, we would expect efforts to do so since the greater net balance of positive outcomes is seen as following from a union. Individual B, on the other hand, expects four positives and three negatives from a union, and four positives and a neutral from no union. We would predict B would oppose the union.

You can also see from this diagram that some consequences or outcomes could follow directly from the action taken rather than the result of the action. For example, if a large proportion of fellow workers favors the union, work against the union, whether successful or not in preventing unionization, will probably have a direct effect on having "friendly co-workers."

Another thing to consider here is the degree to which an individual expects that an action taken will lead to a result. For example, if individual A feels that neither working for nor against the union will affect the organizing campaign outcomes, then we would expect no effort. Why? It's easier. On the other hand if individual A feels that an effort is necessary for organization, we would predict it.

You might say that this model makes it very difficult to predict what people in a group will do. That's the case if they are extremely diverse in their backgrounds or they have widely differing beliefs as to what actions will lead to results or what outcomes will follow from results. But we might expect a number of things to reduce this diversity.

People see other avenues beside union membership to attain valued outcomes. For example, if promotions and interesting work were highly valued and these were unattainable on the jobs considered for unionization, many of the employees desiring these would probably have left. Also, those things that have been positive job outcomes in the past and have been achievable are now increasingly important to the employees. Thus, union attempts may begin because management withholds rewards or changes the system so that rewards are different from what people in the jobs value.

The degree to which unionization is seen as leading to the attainment of positive outcomes and the avoidance of negative outcomes may also be changed through campaign attempts. Both labor and management attempt to direct employees towards a stronger belief that the results of unionization will have positive and negative consequences, respectively.

GROUP BEHAVIOR

There are a variety of reasons for why groups come into being. Some evolve naturally because of mutual interests and similarities. Others are created to counter a perceived danger or threat. This type of "wagon-circling" is a pervasive phenomenon. For example, studies of inexperienced combat troops in World War II found that they tended to group when under fire even though spreading out reduced their vulnerability in an attack. Some studies have also indicated that assisting or affiliating behavior requires that the threat be applicable to a majority of a collection of individuals for group activities to occur.[3]

Group cohesiveness

Group cohesiveness is reflected through a generally lower variance in the behavior of group members. Many studies show, for example, that the productivity of certain work groups remains relatively constant over time and varies little among members.

---

[3] Cf. Stanley Schacter, *The Psychology of Affiliation: Experimental Studies of the Sources of Gregariousness* (Stanford, Cal.: Stanford University Press, 1959).

What are the underlying reasons for cohesiveness? First, the members of the group are likely to hold to the same basic norms or values. They believe in the same goals and methods for their attainment. Second, there is probably a good deal of similarity in age, seniority, and other background characteristics. Third, there is probably a group leader who has been chosen by the group on an informal basis. This member often has values which are the closest to the overall values of the group. Finally, cohesiveness may be a function of external threat.

If external threat increases cohesiveness, how does it do so, and is the relationship linear or at least monotonic? To answer the first part of this question, we might go back to expectancy theory. If someone perceives that negative outcomes will occur if one must act alone, but not if one acts within a group, then there are positive consequences in group behavior. If a united front is perceived as strength, then cohesiveness should be high. Thus, if an employer is unwilling to grant a wage increase to a single employee and dares the employee to quit over the refusal, the same employer may not be willing to risk the effects of the denial of a concerted demand for a wage increase. However, how far would we expect group members to go in individually sacrificing for the good of the group? Where the benefits perceived from remaining a group member are outweighed by losses from membership, then cohesiveness will break down. As Figure 7–3 shows, the hypothetical relationship between threat and cohesiveness is an inverted U. We would expect in most situations that the down side of the curve would not be encountered where management adheres to presently enacted labor legislation. However, we would also say that a labor group engaging in illegal activity such as sabotage and violence may also risk decreasing cohesiveness as the possible threat of legal

FIGURE 7–3
Hypothesized relationship between threat and cohesiveness

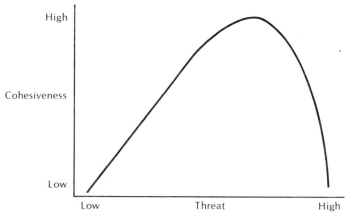

action increased or the actions were inconsistent with the general values of group members.

Since similarity in values and backgrounds making up the union are not directly within its control, there is only one major avenue open to it to maintain cohesiveness: perceived threat from management. Employers select the individuals who will become members of the group when old members leave. (Although union contracts may introduce criteria like seniority.) The law requires that unions permit membership to all employees where union or agency shops are negotiated. Thus, similarity is outside its control. To maintain cohesiveness through threat some degree of adversarial relationship must be necessary. Thus, it may be to the union's *benefit* for management to take action against individuals or the group which are rebuffed, modified, or rescinded through what members perceive as group action.

THE UNION AS AN AGENT

Perhaps a more plausible explanation than maintaining threat levels is the concept of agency in the labor relations process. Again, if we go back to expectancy theory predictions of behavior, we would expect an individual to engage in organizing activity to form a union if that would lead to a better or best set of outcomes. But unless union leadership or activity were a very important outcome, interest might well wane among individuals in a rather large unit. Why then do unions survive in this climate? Perhaps the answer is that members see the union as a better instrument for achieving outcomes important to them than by doing it individually. The union's expertise in the employment relationship provides a match for the employer experts. Our study of local unions in Chapter 5 would seem to confirm the idea that most members are interested in the job and monetary gains potentially available through union activity and relatively disinterested in administration or active participation.

Dual allegiance

A union member who is employed is obviously a member of two different organizations at the same time: the employer's operations and the union. On its face, it would seem that this dual membership would create severe problems for the employer if union members were militant and for the union if the membership viewed it as having a primarily agent role. This generally is not the case, however. Reviewing research in this area, Stagner and Rosen conclude that the evidence would indicate that favorable attitudes toward the union or company are usually related to favorable attitudes toward the other.[4] The employees surveyed, largely blue-collar industrial workers in mature bargaining relationships, don't find this a problem.

What might we predict in other situations? Much of what we speculate on in this section is purely hypothetical, but some secondary support exists to lend credence to the speculation. We might expect dual allegiance to be higher where the union is viewed as an agent and where its agency is positively evaluated. Here the union is a necessary facet in the employee's life but is not the central overriding influence. We might also expect dual allegiance to be high where one's work is not the most important segment of one's life. In this instance, the values employees hold may consign work to an instrumental role: It is valued because it provides the means (money) to gain other important ends.

A large number of studies have been done over the past 15 years, attempting to identify individual characteristics which are related to reactions to job or task design. Some of the conclusions from these studies would indicate that (other things held constant) rural workers prefer jobs with greater responsibility, autonomy, and identity with the final product than do urban workers.[5] Individuals endorsing the so-called Protestant work ethic prefer jobs with these same attributes.[6] Workers who express preferences for growth and development through the job react positively to these broadened and enriched jobs.[7] The findings coincide well with a hypothesis raised by Hulin and Blood that workers who did not prefer jobs with these types of characteristics did not see work as a central part of their lives but rather as an instrument for other ends.[8] Thus, work was primarily a tool to obtain economic ends.

We might predict then that for workers who were interested in instrumental job outcomes allegiance to the union would be high since its agency role is focused toward these types of ends. Where the union had low agency, for example, in areas where some of the primary job outcomes were inherent in the individual's reaction to the components of the job, allegiance to the union would be low. Where

[4] Ross Stagner and Hjalmer Rosen, *Psychology of Union-Management Relations* (Belmont, Cal.: Wadsworth, 1965), pp. 70–72.

[5] Arthur N. Turner and Paul R. Lawrence, *Industrial Jobs and the Worker* (Boston: Graduate School of Business Administration, Harvard University, 1965).

[6] John P. Wanous, "Individual Differences and Reactions to Job Characteristics," *Journal of Applied Psychology*, vol. 59 (1974), pp. 616–22.

[7] J. Richard Hackman, "Work Design," in J. Richard Hackman and J. Lloyd Suttle, eds., *Improving Life at Work: Behavioral Science Approaches to Organizational Change* (Santa Monica, Cal.: Goodyear, 1977), pp. 96–162.

[8] Charles L. Hulin and Milton R. Blood, "Job Enlargement, Individual Differences, and Worker Responses," *Psychological Bulletin*, vol. 69 (1968), pp. 41–55.

the job had high instrumentality for meeting the needs of the individual as he or she saw them, either economic or stemming from job components, allegiance to the company would be high. Figure 7–4 graphs an hypothesized interaction between agency and instrumentality as it affects company and union allegiance. Given this situation we would expect dual allegiance to be highest in situations where the goals of the workers are congruent with the types of ends for which collective bargaining is generally successful in gaining. For unions representing workers with high job content needs, we would expect less allegiance unless they were able to negotiate contracts which provided for greater individual control over the work.

FIGURE 7–4
Allegiance, agency, and instrumentality

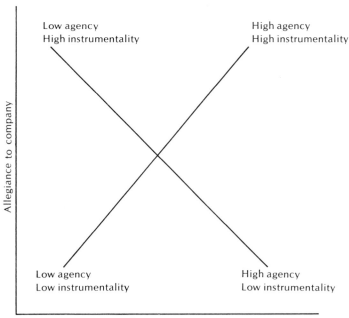

Management-union relationships

We don't have to argue about which came first, the chicken (management) or the egg (the union) in management-union relations. It's obvious that if there were no employer there would be no employees and, therefore, no union. But it is also obvious that we do not have a host-parasite relationship with the union feeding off the gains of management. The relationship is much more symbiotic than either side, in its usual adversary stance, is willing to admit. It is obvious that the union cannot survive in the absence of the firm or organization. Thus, it is to its benefit to frame its demands in such a way as to insure mutual survival. It may, on occasion, be a primary vehicle for convincing its membership (the firm's employees) of a necessary austerity position taken by management for survival. Because it is the agent of the employees, the belief in its interpretation may be higher than it would be if the same communication were made by management.

This raises another important point within the management-union relationship. Most contracts require some duty on the union's part to enforce the contract among the membership. When problems occur, management may reduce the effort needed to solve the problem by contacting the union representatives and reminding them of their members' contractual obligations.

SUMMARY

Organizations and groups are found because individuals perceive membership to be of benefit to them when compared to its costs. One method of predicting individual behavior and organizing activity is through the use of expectancy theory. This theory would predict that unionization would be likely where the perceived results of union activity are high and the probability that collective action would lead to successful unionization was believed to be high.

Groups in organizations vary in their cohesiveness. Cohesiveness appears to be higher among groups where members are highly similar in background characteristics and beliefs. External threat at moderate levels also serves to increase cohesiveness. Cohesiveness is reflected in the lower variance of individual behavior within the group setting.

Expectancy theory also helps to explain the survival power of unions through their roles as agents of workers. If agency is more instrumental for obtaining positive and avoiding negative outcomes, then it is more effortful for individuals to do it themselves. Thus, agency would survive.

SUGGESTED READINGS

Cartwright, Dorwin, and Zander, Alvin, eds. *Group Dynamics: Research and Theory,* 2d ed. (Evanston, Ill.: Row, Peterson, 1960).

Lawler, Edward E., III. *Motivation in Work Organizations* (Monterey, Cal.: Brooks/Cole, 1973).

Stagner, Ross, and Rosen, Hjalmer. *Psychology of Union-Management Relations* (Belmont, Cal.: Wadsworth, 1965).

Vroom, Victor H. *Work and Motivation* (New York: Wiley, 1964).

Weick, Karl E. *The Social Psychology of Organizing* (Reading, Mass.: Addison-Wesley, 1969).

DISCUSSION QUESTIONS

1. At what point would threat begin to break down cohesion? (Think of situations described in Chapters 2 and 3.)
2. What types of employment do you feel are essentially not organizable by unions? Defend your position.
3. To what extent do you believe that similarity in worker backgrounds is necessary for unionization?

8

UNION ORGANIZING CAMPAIGNS

Now that we have examined the theory of organizing from the standpoint of the worker, we need to examine the actual process of union organizing. In this regard we will look at the flow of the organizing process, the strategies of unions and managements, and the behavior of those involved. We will also look at the role of public policy in labor relations through the constraints of legislation, defining court decisions, and the administrative apparatus of the National Labor Relations Board.

As you study this chapter, you should consider the following questions:

1. What strategies and tactics are used by employers and unions in organizing campaigns?
2. What apparent effects do these strategies have on the outcome of a campaign?
3. What procedures are followed by the NLRB in representation elections?
4. Who decides what groups of employees will be represented by a given union as their bargaining agent?

THE CATALYST FOR ORGANIZATION

Attempts at organizing unrepresented workers are spurred at either the local or national level. National organizing campaigns usually involve sending full-time organizers to a specific set of locations to encourage or assist local employees in establishing a union. A typical example of a national organizing attempt might be found when a unionized firm establishes a new plant which is not covered by an existing contract. The union representing the established employees may then attempt to organize the new group to bring the firm's practices at the new plant into line with those in the rest of the organization. Other national organizing attempts may occur when the firm which is the target is in a predominantly unionized industry.

Other organizing attempts take place as the result of efforts at the local level. Here the employees (at least some portion) determine that they would be better off if they could collectively bargain with the employer. Issues may be either economic or job-related. The motivational aspects involved in local campaigns are those we just discussed in the last chapter. Employers have frequently used attitude surveys to assess their vulnerability to organization, suspecting that unfavorable attitudes held by employees are predictive of future organizing efforts. There is probably some validity to this belief, since a cross-sectional study of voters in union representation elections found that dissatisfied employees were significantly more likely to favor bargaining and vote for a union to represent them.[1]

THE ORGANIZING CAMPAIGN

The organizing campaign often is the most turbulent period of labor relations the union and employer ever experience. There are a number of reasons for this which we must remember as we examine the conduct of the parties during the campaign. First, some issue has probably served as a stimulus for organizing activity. Employees may believe collective action is necessary either to insulate them from capricious employer conduct or to gain economic or other benefits equivalent to similar workers in other firms. Second, management correctly views unionization as leading to a limitation in unilateral decision-making power in personnel matters and may cost the firm money. Third, it is generally true that neither party is experienced in labor-management relations. This inexperience may lead to questionable conduct by both parties in the organizing process.

In our examination of organizing we will trace the activities that take place in campaigns, point out typical patterns and exceptions, and describe the legal basis for present NLRB policy toward organizing. Figure 8–1 presents a generalized sequence of organizing events.

As you can see, organizing activity leads to an authorization card campaign. This activity seeks to obtain the employees' commitment to the union by authorizing it to act as their bargaining representative. In signing an authorization card, the employee may empower the union to act as his or her agent in negotiating wages, hours, and terms and conditions of employment. Figure 8–2 is an example of an authorization card.

---

[1] Julius Getman, Stephen Goldberg, and Jeanne B. Herman, *Union Representation Elections: Law and Reality* (New York: Russell Sage Foundation, 1976), p. 55.

FIGURE 8–1
Sequence of organizing events

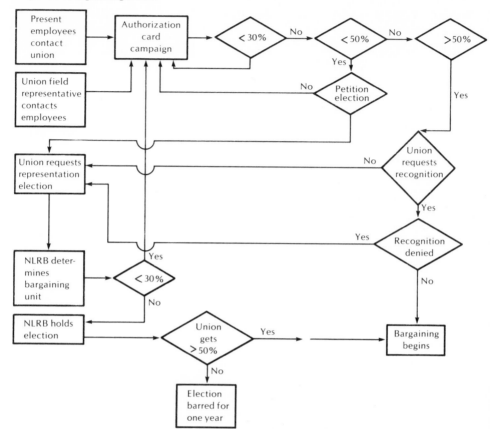

The first formal level of organization is to have 30 percent of employees enrolled through authorization card signatures. This level is necessary for the NLRB to determine whether or not employees will be represented. If over 30 percent are signed up, the union can (but usually doesn't) petition for a representation election. Normally it will try to establish a majority of signers within its intended bargaining unit. If over 50 percent are signatories, the union may directly demand recognition from the employer. Usually, employers refuse these demands, but they may legally recognize the union if the union can clearly establish its majority status.

When a union believes that it represents a majority of the workers but is refused recognition, it normally petitions the National Labor Relations Board (NLRB) to hold a representation election. The board

FIGURE 8–2
Authorization card

YES, I WANT THE IAM

I, the undersigned employee of

(Company)

authorize the International Association of Machinists and Aerospace Workers (IAM) to act as my collective bargaining agent for wages, hours and working conditions. I agree that this card may be used either to support a demand for recognition or an NLRB election, at the discretion of the union.

NAME (print)_____ DATE_____

HOME ADDRESS_____ PHONE_____

CITY_____ STATE_____ ZIP_____

JOB TITLE_____ DEPT._____ SHIFT_____

SIGN HERE **X**

NOTE: This authorization to be SIGNED and DATED in Employee's own handwriting. YOUR RIGHT TO SIGN THIS CARD IS PROTECTED BY FEDERAL LAW.

RECEIVED BY (Initial)_____

establishes its jurisdiction and determines which employees should be included in a bargaining unit if the union wins the election. We will discuss bargaining unit determination in some detail in this chapter. For our immediate purposes, it suffices to say that bargaining units usually are made up of employees with common interests, as determined by the board, within limits set by legislation.

If the NLRB finds that the union has authorization cards from more than 30 percent of the employees in the defined bargaining unit, an election is ordered, and employees eligible to vote are identified. If the union achieves a majority of the votes cast, the board certifies it as the employees' bargaining agent and negotiations on a contract can begin. If the union loses, the board certifies the results, and no representation election may be conducted in that unit for a one-year period. So far we have limited our discussion to the case where only one union is seeking recognition. Multiunion organizing problems are discussed later in our section on representation elections.

The activities specified above seem rather cut and dried, but they aren't. A number of formidable road blocks may be naturally encountered or imposed in organizing attempts. Some of these are legal, others are not. We need to trace the activities of the parties through the process to see what leads to successful organizing attempts and successful employer strategies for stopping unionization. As we continue into union and employer strategies and tactics, we will detail reasons why both take particular "value" positions on recognition.

AUTHORIZATION CARDS

Obtaining authorization cards is a crucial part of the union's organizing campaign, since evidence of employee support may be used to gain either outright recognition or an NLRB election. A critical problem facing organization attempts is access to the employer's work force. Most employers are not in favor of unionization of their unorganized employees, and many have rules forbidding or limiting access to employees on company property or during work time.

No distribution or solicitation rules

As a company policy, most employers prohibit solicitations by any organizations on company property or on company time. The effect of these policies is to prohibit labor organizers from gaining easy access to their employees. An organizing campaign becomes much more difficult if workers must be contacted off-the-job, especially when the organizer may not even know where workers live.

These rules require a general modification in organizing strategy if the initial impetus comes from outside the organization. There has been a line of Supreme Court decisions which differentiates between the rights of "employee" and "nonemployee" organizers in their attempts to solicit membership. Generally, these rulings allow employees to solicit fellow workers on company premises (during nonworking time) unless a clear showing can be made that the solicitation interferes with production.[2] On the other hand, nonemployee organizers (for example, international field representatives) can, in most instances, be prohibited from soliciting on company property.[3] The effect of these decisions is to require very early internal interest in the plant if the drive is likely to be successful.

There are special cases where a union organizer may solicit on the company's property. These occur where there is no other reasonable access to the employees, as in remote operations (for example, logging), or where workers live in a company town.[4] On the other hand,

---

[2] *Republic Aviation Corp.* v. *NLRB;* and *NLRB* v. *LeTourneau Co.,* 324 U.S. 793 (1945).

[3] *NLRB* v. *Babcock & Wilcox Co.; NLRB* v. *Seamprufe, Inc.;* and *Ranco, Inc.* v. *NLRB,* 351 U.S. 105 (1956).

[4] *Marsh* v. *Alabama,* 326 U.S. 501 (1946).

organizers may not take advantage of the quasi-public nature of some of the company's property, like retail store parking lots or shopping malls, to solicit workers.[5]

Employers may counter some of these allowances by requiring employees to leave working areas and the plant immediately after their shifts end to lessen the chance of solicitation occurring.

Employer and union conduct

Once the authorization campaign begins, both employers and unions enter a period where their actions are under considerable scrutiny. The labor laws provide that individuals cannot be coerced or restrained in their rights to engage or not to engage in concerted activity or to be represented by agents of their own choosing. This means that neither party may legally interfere with an employee's right to free choice to join or not to join a union.

Unions obviously believe it is to the benefit of employees to be represented. In any organizing campaign its members are initially in the minority. And we have seen earlier that the NLRB requires at least a 30-percent authorization card showing to signify substantial interest in organization. Thus the union is faced with a delicate early strategy problem: It must publicize its activities enough to induce others to join, but it does not want the employer to know of the activities until they would seem to be irreversible. Where a union suspects that an employer will retaliate against employee union organizers, it may deliberately inform the company of the activists' names so the company cannot later plead that its disciplinary actions were not based on antiunion feelings.[6]

Employers must take care that they do not treat employees differently as a result of their union activity. Once an organizing campaign begins, it is important that the employer take particular pains to carry out personnel practices consistent with past practices and equally across workers. Box 8–1 illustrates an appeals' court's decision in an extreme case of a personnel practice reversal toward an individual.

For its part, the union may also encounter difficulties in its campaign. For example, employees may not want to sign authorization cards which appear to commit them to union membership even though they might favor organization. Employees may also worry that the employer will find out they are interested in unionization. If cards

---

[5] *Central Hardware Co.* v. *NLRB*, 407 U.S. 539 (1972); and *Hudgens* v. *NLRB*, 91 LRRM 2489 (U.S. Supreme Court, 1976).

[6] Stephen I. Schlossberg and Fredrick E. Sherman, *Organizing and the Law*, rev. ed. (Washington: Bureau of National Affairs, 1971).

BOX 8–1

Edward G. Budd Manufacturing Co. v. *NLRB,* United States Court of Appeals, Third Circuit, 1943, 138 F.2d 86

Biggs, Circuit Judge. . . .

The complaint, as subsequently amended, alleges that the petitioner, in September 1933, created and foisted a labor organization known as the Budd Employee Representation Association upon its employees and thereafter contributed financial support to the association and dominated its activities. The amended complaint also alleges that in July 1941 the petitioner discharged an employee, Walter Weigand, because of his activities on behalf of the union . . .

The case of Walter Weigand is extraordinary. If ever a workman deserved summary discharge it was he. He was under the influence of liquor while on duty. He came to work when he chose, and he left the plant and his shift as he pleased. In fact, a foreman on one occasion was agreeably surprised to find Weigand at work and commented upon it. Weigand amiably stated that he was enjoying it. He brought a woman (apparently generally known as the "Duchess") to the rear of the plant yard and introduced some of the employees to her. He took another employee to visit her, and when this man got too drunk to be able to go home, punched his time card for him, and put him on the table in the representatives' meeting room in the plant in order to sleep off his intoxication. Weigand's immediate superiors demanded again and again that he be discharged, but each time higher officials intervened on Weigand's behalf because as was naïvely stated he was "a representative" (of the association, found to be a dominated union). In return for not working at the job for which he was hired, the petitioner gave him full pay and on five separate occasions raised his wages. One of these raises was general; that is to say, Weigand profited by a general wage increase throughout the plant, but the other four raises were given Weigand at times when other employees in the plant did not receive wage increases.

The petitioner contends that Weigand was discharged because of cumulative grievances against him. But about the time of the discharge it was suspected by some of the representatives that Weigand had joined the complaining CIO union. One of the representatives taxed him with this fact, and Weigand offered to bet a hundred dollars that it could not be proved. On July 22, 1941, Weigand did disclose his union membership to the vice chairman (Rattigan) of the association and to another representative (Mullen) and apparently tried to persuade them to support the union. Weigand asserts that the next day he, with Rattigan and Mullen, were seen talking to CIO organizer Reichwein on a street corner. The following day, according to Weigand's testimony, Mullen came to Weigand at the plant and stated that he, Mullen, had just had an interview with Personnel Director McIlvain and Plant Manager Mahan. According to Weigand, Mullen said to him, "Maybe you didn't get me in a jam." And, "We were seen down there." The following day Weigand was discharged.

BOX 8-1 (*continued*)

As this court stated in *National Labor Relations Board* v. *Condenser Corp.,* . . . 3 Cir., 128 F.2d at page 75, an employer may discharge an employee for a good reason, a poor reason, or no reason at all so long as the provisions of the National Labor Relations Act are not violated. It is, of course, a violation to discharge an employee because he has engaged in activities on behalf of a union. Conversely an employer may retain an employee for a good reason, a bad reason, or no reason at all, and the reason is not a concern of the board. But it is certainly too great a strain on our credulity to assert, as does the petitioner, that Weigand was discharged for an accumulation of offenses. We think that he was discharged because his work on behalf of the CIO had become known to the plant manager. That ended his sinecure at the Budd plant. The board found that he was discharged because of his activities on behalf of the union. The record shows that the board's finding was based on sufficient evidence. . . .

---

are not explicit in establishing an agency relationship, they may be useless in later attempting to establish a majority status.[7]

Representation elections

As we noted in Figure 8–1, if substantial interest in representation (or decertification) is shown, the union (or the employer in the absence of an interest showing) can petition the NLRB to hold a representation election to determine the desires of the employees. A number of issues are relevant in our discussion of elections. Among these are the conduct of the parties, the employees to be included in the proposed bargaining unit, and the role of the NLRB. We will trace the steps in the election effort and lay out a timetable, detailing the activities of the parties; the union, employer, and NLRB.

Recognition requests. A variety of paths lead to representation elections. An election can take place initially to determine whether or not employees desire representation or to ascertain whether the union continues to retain majority status. This latter type is called a decertification election. Figure 8–3 details the specific avenues toward election.

There are a number of ways in which a recognition request is made. The most common occurs when the union has obtained authorization cards from a majority of the employees it desires to represent. Usually the union will not make its request until at least 55 percent or more are enrolled. The union prefers to have a margin of safety so that, among

---

[7] Ibid., p. 51.

FIGURE 8-3
Avenues to election petitions

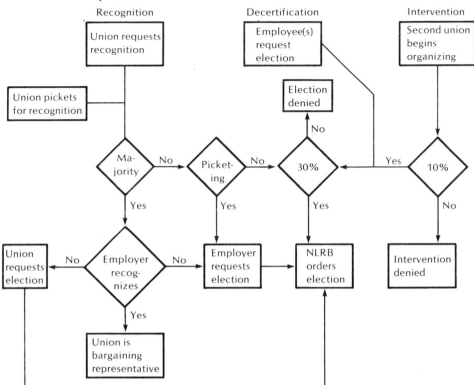

other things, its status can sustain a challenge by the employer who may assert that certain employees are not eligible to belong to or be represented or vote in the unit. When the employer is faced with a recognition request, it will most often refuse to accede to it, claiming that a doubt exists as to the union's majority status. The union may offer to have a neutral third party match the authorization card signatures with a list of employees to establish that a majority actually exists. If the employer has evidence that a majority exists and is satisfied with the appropriateness of the proposed bargaining unit, recognition can be voluntarily granted.

A union may also seek recognition by picketing an unorganized employer for a period up to 30 days, demanding that it be recognized as the employees' bargaining representative. If this occurs, the employer can directly petition the NLRB to hold an election among the employees the union seeks to represent. If the union fails to obtain a majority, further recognitional picketing constitutes an unfair labor practice.

Election petitions. An election petition may be filed with the board by a labor organization, an employer, or an individual. However, in certain types of elections, employers are precluded from filing petitions since early petitions could lead to a showing of inadequate union interest to pursue the election. A union may file a petition if it can prove that sufficient interest (30 percent) exists to hold an election. In its petition or within 48 hours, proof (for example authorization cards) must be affirmatively shown that a sufficient level of interest exists. With its petition, the union must also define the group of employees it intends to represent if certified. This is its preferred bargaining unit. If an employer has had a recognition demand from a union (for example recognitional picketing) the employer can directly petition the board to hold an election but must also provide proof of the recognition demand. A union or an employee (but not an employer) can file a decertification petition. This petition must allege that the present union is no longer the choice of a majority of employees and they desire its removal as bargaining agent. The 30 percent interest requirement exists here as well.

When a petition has been received, the NLRB will request the employer to supply a current list of employees in the proposed or present unit so the board may confirm the presence or absence of sufficient (30 percent) interest.

Preelection board involvement. The NLRB begins by investigating the employer involved in the election petition. Certain requirements must be met before jurisdiction will be exercised by the board. These requirements vary according to the type of business involved. For example, nonretail businesses must do at least $50,000 of business in interstate commerce to be included. If the board takes jurisdiction there are a number of avenues open. Figure 8–4 details preelection board procedures.

There are two major avenues that are available to the parties in the election. The first is a consent election where the parties agree, without formal hearing, as to the scope of the proposed bargaining unit and which employees will be eligible to vote in an election. The second avenue is a board-directed election where, after hearings, the NLRB regional director determines the appropriate bargaining unit and the eligible voters.

If the board directs an election, the employer is required to provide the board and union a so-called Excelsior list containing the names and addresses of employees in the proposed bargaining unit.[8] This list

---

[8] *Excelsior Underwear, Inc.,* 156 NLRB 1236 (1966).

FIGURE 8–4
NLRB involvement: Petition to election

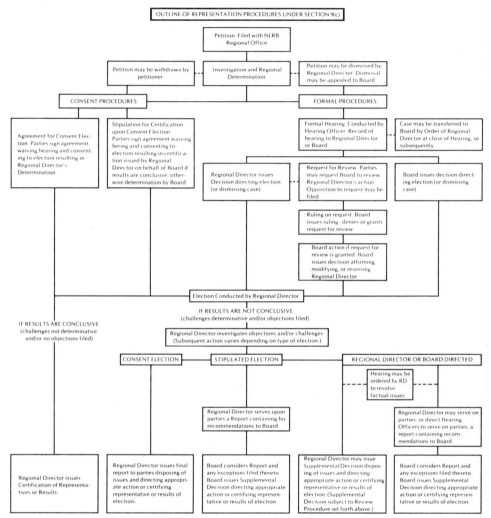

OUTLINE OF REPRESENTATION PROCEDURES UNDER SECTION 9(c)

Petition. Filed with NLRB Regional Office

Petition may be withdrawn by petitioner.

Investigation and Regional Determination.

Petition may be dismissed by Regional Director. Dismissal may be appealed to Board.

CONSENT PROCEDURES

FORMAL PROCEDURES

Agreement for Consent Election. Parties sign agreement waiving hearing and consenting to election resulting in Regional Director's Determination.

Stipulation for Certification upon Consent Election. Parties sign agreement waiving hering and consenting to election resulting in certification issued by Regional Director on behalf of Board if results are conclusive; otherwise determination by Board.

Formal Hearing. Conducted by Hearing Officer. Record of hearing to Regional Director or Board.

Case may be transferred to Board by Order of Regional Director at close of Hearing, or subsequently.

Regional Director issues Decision directing election (or dismissing case).

Request for Review. Parties may request Board to review Regional Director's action. Opposition to request may be filed.

Board issues decision directing election (or dismissing case).

Ruling on request. Board issues ruling - denies or grants request for review.

Board action if request for review is granted. Board issues decision affirming, modifying, or reversing Regional Director.

Election Conducted by Regional Director

IF RESULTS ARE NOT CONCLUSIVE
(challenges determinative and/or objections filed)

IF RESULTS ARE CONCLUSIVE
(challenges not determinative and/or no objections filed)

Regional Director investigates objections and/or challenges
(Subsequent action varies depending on type of election.)

CONSENT ELECTION

STIPULATED ELECTION

REGIONAL DIRECTOR OR BOARD DIRECTED

Hearing may be ordered by RD to resolve factual issues.

Regional Director serves upon parties a Report containing his recommendations to Board.

Regional Director may serve on parties, or direct Hearing Officers to serve on parties, a report containing recommendations to Board.

Regional Director issues Certification of Representatives or Results.

Regional Director issues final report to parties disposing of issues and directing appropriate action or certifying representative or results of election.

Board considers Report and any exceptions filed thereto. Board issues Supplemental Decision directing appropriate action or certifying representative or results of election.

Regional Director may issue Supplemental Decision disposing of issues and directing appropriate action or certifying representative or results of election. (Supplemental Decision subject to Review Procedure set forth above.)

Board considers Report and any exceptions filed thereto. Board issues Supplemental Decision directing appropriate action or certifying representative or results of election.

must be provided within seven days after the direction of an election. Then after another 10 days, but not more than 30 days after the direction, the election will normally be held.

The election. The NLRB supervises the election which is done by secret ballot. Both company and union observers may challenge the eligibility of voters but may not prohibit voting of any individual. Challenges are ruled on subsequent to the election. After the election the ballots are counted, and the choice receiving a majority of *votes cast* will be declared the winner. If more than two alternatives (two different unions, and no union, for example) are on the ballot and none obtains an absolute majority, a runoff will be held among the two highest recipients of votes. Figure 8–5 is an example of an NLRB election ballot.

FIGURE 8–5
Specimen NLRB ballot

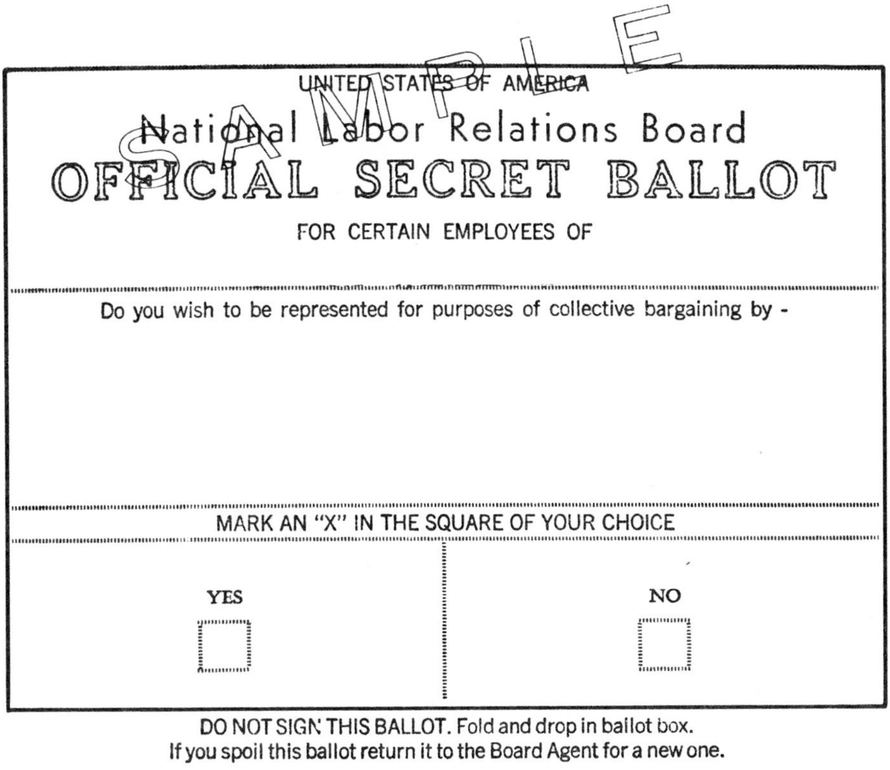

UNITED STATES OF AMERICA
National Labor Relations Board
OFFICIAL SECRET BALLOT
FOR CERTAIN EMPLOYEES OF

Do you wish to be represented for purposes of collective bargaining by -

MARK AN "X" IN THE SQUARE OF YOUR CHOICE

YES	NO
☐	☐

DO NOT SIGN THIS BALLOT. Fold and drop in ballot box.
If you spoil this ballot return it to the Board Agent for a new one.

After the election when any challenges have been resolved, the regional director will certify the results. If the union wins, it becomes the exclusive bargaining representative of the employees in the bargaining unit and is entitled to begin negotiations on a contract. If the employer wins, no election petition will be honored by the NLRB for a one-year period. In effect, certification guarantees the union or nonunion status of a bargaining unit for a period of at least one year.

BARGAINING UNIT DETERMINATION

An inextricable part of the organizing process is determining what group of employees would be represented by the union, if successful in its organizing attempts. Bargaining units are shaped by a variety of factors. Among the primary issues to be considered are (1) legal constraints, (2) the constitutional jurisdiction of the organizing union, (3) the perceptions of the union as to organizing and bargaining success, (4) the desires of the employer in resisting organization or promoting stability in the bargaining relationship, and (5) the philosophy of the NLRB in unit determination.

Bargaining units may differ depending on whether we are referring to organization and representation or to contract negotiation. For example, several retail stores in a given chain may constitute an appropriate bargaining unit for representation election purposes; while for bargaining purposes, several retail stores, owned by different companies, may associate in multiemployer bargaining. Our discussion of bargaining unit determination will be concerned only with representation activities. Bargaining modes will be discussed later.

We will note that certain legal constraints limit the potential scope of a bargaining unit, but within these constraints the contending parties, labor and management, are free to determine an appropriate unit jointly. This is the procedure we encountered as part of the consent election process. If no agreement is reached, the NLRB has the responsibility for determining unit appropriateness.

Legal constraints

Section 9(b) of the Labor-Management Relations Act of 1947 details the constraints that are placed on consent between the parties or the NLRB's decision-making powers in unit determination. First, no unit can be comprised of both professional and nonprofessional employees without the express approval of a majority of the professionals. Professional employees are those whose occupations primarily involve work of a nonrepetitive, varied, and intellectual nature. Second, a separate craft unit within an employer's operation may not be precluded simply because the board has earlier included it in a broader group. We will find that this subsection has been rather liberally interpreted by the board in continuing inclusion of craft groups in larger units. Third, no bargaining unit may consist of both guards hired by employers to enforce the company's rules and other employees. Fourth, supervisors and managers are precluded from inclusion and/or collective bargaining since their roles as agents of the employer place them outside the category of an employee as defined in Section 2 of the Wagner Act.

Other than those proscriptions, the board is free to develop its own rules for bargaining unit determination.

Jurisdiction of the organizing union

You will recall in our discussion of the Carpenters' Union that its constitution specified the scope of its jurisdiction in terms of the occupations it would enroll. As we noted in the union organization area, most unions specifically concentrate on organizing in certain occupations or industries. There are exceptions, such as the Teamsters, but generally unions do not stray far from their traditional jurisdictions.

If an AFL–CIO union is attempting to organize where another AFL–CIO union already exists, the NLRB will notify the AFL–CIO when an election petition is filed to allow the federation to adjudicate the problem internally according to its constitution. These proceedings almost always solve the jurisdictional problem, since one of the conditions of AFL–CIO affiliation is the agreement to let the federation resolve internal disputes.

The union's desired unit

The union is faced with several problems in deciding what bargaining unit configuration it will pursue. The type of union involved in organization will also probably predict preferred bargaining unit makeup. A union also must balance the optimal configuration of a unit from a recognitional standpoint against what might be conflicting objectives in later contract negotiations.

We would expect that a craft union would seek a bargaining unit which includes only workers of relatively similar skills. Industrial unions would tend to be inclusive, seeking recognition for all employees (coverable under the law) within a given plant or company.

To be able to bargain, the union must be able to demonstrate majority status to gain recognition. Therefore, a union might suggest an appropriate unit as one where a majority exists or one which it believes will be easiest to organize. On the other hand, it would be futile from a bargaining standpoint to organize a unit which had little impact on the company's business if it were to strike. For example, it might be relatively easy to gain a majority in a unit of janitorial or custodial employees in a manufacturing plant but relatively hard to negotiate a favorable contract, since the employer could readily subcontract the work for little incremental cost during a strike.

The goals of the union, then, are twofold: (1) the establishment of a "winnable" unit, and (2) the definition of a unit which will have some bargaining power with the employer.

The employer's desired unit

The employer's desired unit is often different from (but not necessarily diametrically opposite) what the union wants. The employer may prefer the unit to be specified so that the greatest likelihood of a union defeat exists. If a craft union is organizing, this means that the employer will generally favor a plantwide unit. In some circumstances, the employer will seek to narrow the unit so that groups strongly in favor of the union will not lead to a majority among a variety of groups that marginally support management. Figure 8–6 details a situation where management might argue for a smaller unit than the organizing union desires.

FIGURE 8–6
Conflicting unit desires

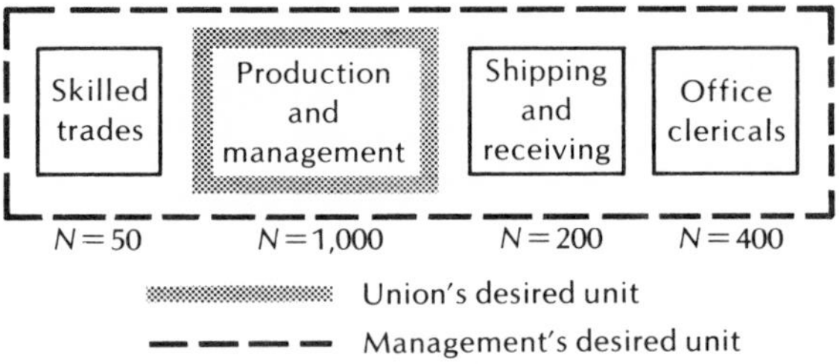

	ST	P and M	S and R	OC	Total
Percent pro-u	40	76	45	30	60
Percent pro-m	60	24	55	70	40
Number pro-u	20	760	90	120	990
Number pro-m	30	240	110	280	660

The firm also would like the unit configured so that the union's bargaining power would be minimized if it obtained recognition. Thus, it might desire functionally independent units that would allow continued operation if a strike occurred. On the other hand, it would avoid fragmented units that might require continuous bargaining due to different contract expiration dates and the likelihood of excessive demands by single units to avoid a siege of rotating strikes among the unions.

Both parties also have a long-run vested interest in a stable bargaining relationship. The union needs to be perceived by its members as meeting their particular needs while the organization needs to introduce and maintain a high degree of predictability in its labor relations.

NLRB policy

One of the most crucial determinants of bargaining unit appropriateness is the policy of the NLRB. There is substantial evidence that the board has not consistently exercised a uniform decision-making process in unit determination. Abodeely has thoroughly traced the evolution of present board policy in bargaining unit determination.[9] He concludes that the present posture is more straightforward than in the past, but both employers and unions face a great deal of uncertainty as to the outcome of a contested bargaining unit determination.

Some of the tests that Abodeely finds the NLRB has used include the following:

1. *Community of interests.* In a 1952 decision the NLRB felt that mutuality of interests in bargaining for wages, hours, and working conditions was paramount.[10] A bargaining unit where the goals of one group of employees were contrary to others would not be appropriate. This factor is difficult to interpret, however, because there is no benchmark used to define necessary similarity between employee groups or the scope of attributes included to establish a community of interests.

2. *Geographical and physical proximity.* The more separated in distance two or more locations might be, the more difficult it might be for a single union to represent employees. This factor may be considered and given considerable weight when the employer's policies differ substantially across locations.

3. *Employer's administrative or territorial divisions.* If labor relations or personnel management within a firm were uniform over a given territory (for example, 46 grocery stores in chain X located in a five-county area in southeastern Michigan managed as a territorial subdivision of a multistate chain), then this unit rather than a single store or subset may be most appropriate.

4. *Functional integration.* This factor relates to the degree to which all potentially includable employees are required to maintain the company's major production processes. For example, in its decision in the *Borden Co.* case the board recognized that while 20 different facilities were involved in the seemingly independent processes of manufacturing (3) and distribution (17), and had varying personnel

---

[9] John E. Abodeely, *The NLRB and the Appropriate Bargaining Unit*, Labor Relations and Public Policy Series, report no. 3 (Industrial Research Unit, Department of Industry, Wharton School of Finance and Commerce, University of Pennsylvania, Philadelphia, 1971).

[10] *Continental Baking Co.*, 99 NLRB 777 (1952).

policies, an appropriate unit would contain all 20 plants because of the interrelationships between facilities which were necessary to market the product.[11]

5. *Interchange of employees.* If employees are frequently transferred across plants or offices, their community of interest may be more similar, leading the board to designate a multiplant unit.

6. *Bargaining history.* In applying this factor, the board may take into account the past practices of the union and employer (if it were a decertification or unit clarification election) or typical industry practices in bargaining. For example, if an employer had a companywide unit which had served the mutual bargaining interests of both the employer and union, the board would probably leave it undisturbed.

7. *Employee desires.* Early in the board's history, the Globe Doctrine was developed.[12] Where a bargaining history involving several units exists, the board may allow employees to vote for or against their inclusion in a more comprehensive unit.

8. *Extent of organization.* The board may consider, after the foregoing factors are analyzed, the degree to which organization has taken place in a given proposed unit. While this is not to be considered the prime factor,[13] The Supreme Court has concluded that the board could consider it since Section 9 of the labor act also requires the board to consider the necessity for allowing employees the fullest freedom in exercising their rights.[14]

We can see that many of these factors are interrelated. For example, employee interchange is more likely to occur within a defined administrative unit, and, in turn, an interchange should establish a broader community of interests. Thus, the board's determinations frequently rest on several factors. While these factors are generally utilized, Abodeely points out that there have been exceptions to each of these rules in the board's determinations.[15]

Craft severance. The term *craft severance* means that a group of employees with a substantially different community of interests than the overall unit is allowed to establish itself as a separate unit. Craft severance can occur during initial unit determination or from a desire of presently represented employees to leave their bargaining unit.

The current board thinking on craft severance is enunciated in what is known as the Mallinckrodt Doctrine.[16] Here, a group of instrument

---

[11] *Borden Co., Hutchinson Ice Cream Div.,* 89 NLRB 227 (1950).

[12] Abodeely, *The NLRB and the Appropriate Bargaining Unit,* pp. 65–67.

[13] Section 9(c)(5).

[14] *NLRB v. Metropolitan Life Insurance Co.,* 380 U.S. 438 (1965).

[15] Abodeely, *The NLRB and the Appropriate Bargaining Unit,* pp. 7–86.

[16] *Mallinckrodt Chemical Works,* 162 NLRB 387 (1966).

mechanics sought severance from a larger unit of production and maintenance employees. The petition was denied by the NLRB, which reasoned that the instrument mechanics were integrally involved in the production process and that the interests of the employer and the industrial union representing the unit had to be considered in deciding upon the severance request. The board enumerated a set of tests or rules concerning severance: (1) whether the group desiring severance is either a skilled trades group or a functionally separate group with a tradition of separate representation; (2) the historical bargaining patterns of the present unit and the degree of disruption likely if severance were granted; (3) the degree to which the proposed new unit has maintained its distinct separateness in the established unit; (4) the collective bargaining history in the industry; (5) the degree of integration in production; and (6) the degree of experience of the union desiring severance as a representative for that craft.[17] Thus severance from an existing unit was made very difficult.

Severance or establishment of separate units is somewhat easier during initial organization. In several initial organization cases, craft severance has been allowed where there is a recognizable difference in the communities of interest and where there is no prior contrary bargaining history.[18] The degree of functional integration in the production processes for the firms involved in these cases was not substantially different than Mallinckrodt's.

What factors are used? The answer to the question of what factors are used depends upon whether the determination relates to initial representation or severance. For severance, it appears that the overriding factor is bargaining history, buttressed by the degree of functional integration in an employer's operation. For representation, community of interest and functional integration are important. The workers' community of interest is affected to a great extent by the production process, employee interchange policies, geographical proximity, and administrative division. There are no hard and fast rules, however, and the board determines bargaining unit appropriateness on a case-by-case basis.

There are few precedents for employers or unions to rely on in unit determinations since NLRB bargaining unit determinations are not "final orders" and, therefore, not appealable. If an employer is dissatisfied with the bargaining unit's appropriateness, the only recourse to gain judicial review is to refuse to bargain and then have the courts

---

[17] Ibid., p. 397.

[18] *E. I. DuPont de Nemours & Co.*, 1962 NLRB 413 (1966) and *Anheuser-Busch, Inc.*, 170 NLRB No. 5 (1968).

determine whether or not the board established an appropriate unit.[19] In most cases, the courts will leave the determinations undisturbed.

Other issues in unit determination

The structure of organizations changes over time. What might initially have been an appropriate unit may not be at the present time. Major factors involved in the continuing definition of a unit relate to company growth and acquisitions, reorganization and reclarification of jobs, or the assumption of ownership by another firm.

Accretion. Accretion occurs when a new facility is included in the bargaining unit or when an existing union in an organization gains representation rights for persons previously represented by another union. The NLRB generally applies the same standards to accretion as it does to initial unit determination. There is some evidence, however, that the board tends to give extra weight to the desires of employees in the unit subject to accretion.

Reorganization and reclassification. Occasionally an employer will reclassify the jobs performed by employees or will reorganize administrative units. These changes might now make a previously defined bargaining unit inappropriate. The parties may redefine the unit by consent. Failing this, the employer would have to refuse to bargain and the union file an unfair labor practice charge in order for the board to reexamine appropriateness.

Successor organizations. Generally speaking, a firm that takes over another company or merges with another assumes the contractual bargaining obligations accrued up to the time of the merger.[20] An employer who assumes the operations of another where the employees simply change employers is obligated to recognize the union but need not honor the predecessor's contract with the union.[21] But a substantial apparent continuity in operations does not so obligate where the union lacks majority status, even if the absence of a majority is due to layoffs and new hires by the successor.[22]

EMPLOYER AND UNION CAMPAIGNS

After an election has been agreed to or ordered by the NLRB, both sides campaign to win the election. In this section of the chapter, we

---

[19] Abodeely, *The NLRB and the Appropriate Bargaining Unit*, pp. 28–29.

[20] *John Wiley & Sons, Inc.* v. *Livingston*, 376 U.S. 543 (1964).

[21] *NLRB* v. *Burns International Security Services*, 406 U.S. 272 (1972).

[22] *Howard Johnson Co., Inc.* v. *Detroit Local Joint Executive Board, Hotel and Restaurant Employees & Bartenders International Union, AFL–CIO,* 417 U.S. 249 (1974).

will discuss (1) union strategy, (2) employer strategy, (3) the role of the NLRB and its criteria for fair elections, and (4) the reaction of employees to organizing campaigns and the possible illegal conduct of one or both parties.

Union strategy

Earlier in our chapter on organizing theory, we stressed that an individual might see benefits in belonging to a union if that membership was seen as leading to more certain attainment of important outcomes. This means that a successful union campaign should stress issues that are important to employees and show them how the union will enable these ends to be achieved through unionization.

What issues do unions stress? A study of 33 representation elections showed that 15 issues were raised by the union in at least half of these elections.[23] Table 8–1 gives these issues and the number of elections in which each was raised by the union. These issues aim at calling attention to inequitable or threatening treatment by the employer, creating

TABLE 8–1
Prevalent union campaign issues

Issue	Number of campaigns
Union will prevent unfairness, set up grievance procedure/seniority system	27
Union will improve unsatisfactory wages	26
Union strength will provide employees with voice in wages, working conditions	26
Union, not outsider, bargains for what employees want	24
Union has obtained gains elsewhere	23
Union will improve unsatisfactory sick leave/insurance	21
Dues/initiation fees are reasonable	21
Union will improve unsatisfactory vacations/holidays	20
Union will improve unsatisfactory pensions	20
Employer promises/good treatment may not continued without union	20
Employees choose union leaders	18
Employer will seek to persuade/frighten employees to vote against union	18
No strike without vote	18
Union will improve unsatisfactory working conditions	17
Employees have legal right to engage in union activity	17

Source: Adapted from Table 4–3 in *Union Representation Elections: Law and Reality*, by Julius G. Getman, Stephen B. Goldberg, and Jeanne B. Herman, © 1976 by Russell Sage Foundation, New York.

---

[23] Getman, Goldberg, and Herman, *Union Representation Elections*, pp. 80–81.

a strong impression that the union's agency role will yield important gains to the employee, countering expected employer positions, and establishing the legitimacy of the union and union activity. Figure 8–7 is a specimen of union campaign information.

FIGURE 8–7
Union campaign information

Wherever the boss holds a meeting whether it's in the laundry, or house keeping, or in dietary, or in Nursing, the boss acts like they know how bad conditions were. If they worked one day sweat-
ing the laundry or one day cleaning a bedpan or one day as a dishwasher, they would know how bad conditions are in less than one day!!

Money is fine and benefits great and we know
if we had 1199 Union fighting for us
all the time we really would make
a decent living. We are going to continue to fight for
more and more dollars and in addition add the one thing
that assures a permanent set of future raises with a permanent job!!
1199 UNION JOB SECURITY

Management strategy

Management generally tends to emphasize that unions may be run by outsiders who are less concerned than the employer with employee welfare, that conditions may not improve after unionization, and that employees will be deprived of a direct link with management as to their individual wages, hours, and working conditions. Table 8–2 displays the issues emphasized most often by management in the campaigns studied by Getman, Goldberg, and Herman.

TABLE 8–2
Prevalent management campaign issues

Issues	Number of campaigns
Improvements not dependent on unionization	28
Wages good, equal to/better than under union contract	27
Financial costs of union dues outweigh gains	26
Union is outsider	26
Get facts before deciding, employer will provide facts and accept employee decision	25
If union wins, strike may follow	23
Loss of benefits may follow union win	22
Strikers will lose wages, lose more than gain	22
Unions not concerned with employee welfare	22
Strike may lead to loss of jobs	21
Employer has treated employees fairly/well	20
Employees should be certain to vote	18

Source: Adapted from Table 4–2 in *Union Representation Elections: Law and Reality*, by Julius G. Getman, Stephen B. Goldberg, and Jeanne B. Herman, © 1976 by Russell Sage Foundation, New York.

Management typically communicates with employees to urge them to oppose the union. Figure 8–8 is an example of management material which urges employees to vote against the union.

Union tactics

After a significant showing is demonstrated by an election petition, the union's tactics become more open and public. There are three reasons for this. First, the union's major adherents have already signed up so that each additional prounion vote will become increasingly harder to obtain. Second, since the employer is now definitely aware of the campaign, there is no need for secrecy. And, third, some employer tactics against the union which would have been fair before organizing activity became known may now have become illegal.

During the preelection period, the union may attempt to show its

FIGURE 8–8
Specimen employer communication

Home mailing

Dear Fellow Employee: Wednesday

At our plant gate yesterday, the union distributed a leaflet in which it discussed how it will back up its demands at our company.

In other words, the union is stating that it can fulfill its promises by the use of force. This is absolutely untrue. While the union can make promises and threaten to force us to do things, it is the company which pays your wages and provides you with benefits.

I think you should know some facts about what the union <u>cannot do</u> to your company, and some of the things they <u>can do</u> to you.

First, let's look at what it <u>cannot</u> force your company to do:

1. It cannot force the company to agree to any proposal that the company is unwilling or unable to meet.
2. It cannot increase any wages or benefits unless the company feels it is in its best interest to do so.
3. It cannot guarantee job security or furnish you a day's work or a day's pay.

Now let's look at what it <u>can</u> "force" employees to do:

1. It can force the employees to pay dues each and every month where there is a union shop clause in the contract.
2. It can force members to stand trial and pay fines for violation of any of the provisions of the "book of rules" (constitution).
3. It can force members to pay assessments whenever the union treasury requires more money.

Consider the many advantages and benefits you now enjoy. These have been provided without a union. Consider the many disadvantages of union membership. When you do, I am sure you will vote "no."

Sincerely,

General Manager

Source: Louis Jackson and Robert Lewis, *Winning NLRB Elections*, (Practising Law Institute, New York © 1972), p. 134.

strength by the wearing of campaign buttons or tee shirts. The union holds meetings during nonwork time and utilizes the "Excelsior" list the company must provide to it to make personal contacts at the homes of workers.

Frequently, the union will stress differences between wages, hours, and working conditions in the target organization as compared with others. Unions are at an advantage here compared to management since they can speculate on expected changes likely to occur after organization while the employer must not communicate future benefits which might result if organization fails.

Management tactics

As we will soon see, management tactics have been constrained much more than those of the union by the NLRB, but one major advantage still remains: its access to employees.

Jackson and Lewis suggest that employers should engage in several tactics to counteract a union campaign.[24] These authors advise employers to begin large-scale communications efforts toward employees, including mass meetings, small group discussions with management representatives, and individual interviews to give information on *present* (not anticipated) company personnel programs. Supervisors may be a key management group in communicating with rank and file employees and would thus need extensive briefings on the company's position and the type of conduct which may lead to unfair labor practice charges.

The role of the NLRB

It is the NLRB's responsibility to conduct the election and certify the results. Along with the responsibility for conducting the election, it may have to determine whether the preelection conduct of the parties has tainted the results.

It is obvious that a variety of strategies and tactics are available to both parties during the campaign. The NLRB may have to decide when a specific tactic is unfair. From an overall standpoint, the board has stated that an election should "provide a laboratory in which an experiment may be conducted, under conditions as nearly ideal as possible, to determine the uninhibited desires of employees."[25]

There are a number of areas in which the board examines employer conduct. These revolve around the use of interrogation, the scheduling of meetings, the content of communications, and campaigning during the last day prior to an election. Besides these specifics, the board may also assess the "totality of conduct" of a party to an election.

Interrogation. The NLRB's *Blue Flash Express* decision established for the first time that an employer's questioning of employees about union membership is not, in itself, illegal.[26] Interrogation would probably be legal if the reason for its use is to establish whether or not a union's majority status claim is supportable. Elaborating on the issue, the Second Circuit Court of Appeals established some tests to deter-

---

[24] Louis Jackson and Robert Lewis, *Winning NLRB Elections* (New York: Practising Law Institute, 1972).

[25] *General Shoe Corp.*, 77 NLRB 127 (1948).

[26] *Blue Flash Express Co.*, 109 NLRB 591 (1954).

mine whether or not interrogation would be unfair. These tests are as follows:

1. Is there a history of employer hostility toward unions?
2. Is the information likely to be used to take action against a particular individual?
3. Is the questioner a high-level manager?
4. Does the interrogation take place in an intimidating atmosphere?
5. Are the responses to the questions truthful (indicating a lack of fear on the part of the respondent)?[27]

These very precise definitions of what is lawful make it highly likely that an employer will be charged with an unfair labor practice if interrogation takes place.

Employer communications

Generally speaking, the employer may conduct meetings where employees are required to attend, on company premises and during working hours, to hear representatives of management speak in opposition to the union.[28] However, if the employer has a broad no-solicitation rule barring communication during nonworking time (as in a retail establishment), the employer may be required to give equal access to the union.[29]

Under its Excelsior rule requiring the company to supply names and addresses of employees in the election unit, the union gains an ability to have access to individual employees.

In the past, the NLRB has been essentially concerned with two issues in examining the substance of employer communications: (1) the degree to which the information would threaten or coerce employees in exercising representation rights, and (2) the truthfulness of the communication. These tests have recently been relaxed with the board's ruling in the *Shopping Kart* case which we will discuss later.[30] However, actions are viewed differently than communications. For example, an employer may not provide improved benefits during an election campaign unless they were scheduled to go into effect prior to the commencement of the organizing activity.[31]

---

[27] *Bourne* v. *NLRB*, 322 F.2d 47 (1964).

[28] *Livingston Shirt Corp.*, 33 LRRM 1156 (1953).

[29] *May Department Stores Co.*, 136 NLRB 797 (1962).

[30] *Shopping Kart Food Market, Inc.*, 228 NLRB 190 (1977).

[31] *NLRB* v. *Exchange Parts Co.*, 375 U.S. 405 (1964).

Union communications

From an access standpoint, unions generally have no standing to require equal time for addressing employees. The union instead must make its pitch through outside meetings, telephone calls, or visits to employees' homes.

24-hour rule

Because it would be almost impossible for a union or an employer to rebut a last minute campaign statement, the NLRB ruled in the *Peerless Plywood* case that no employer or union can hold captive audience presentations within 24 hours directly preceding the election.[32]

Totality of conduct

In the *Virginia Electric and Power* case, the Supreme Court agreed that the NLRB could find that the totality of an employer's conduct was such that an atmosphere of threats or reprisals existed which could taint the election process.[33] While no single specific act, in itself, might demand remedial action, all of them collected together could lead one to conclude that the employer was attempting to coerce or intimidate employees and, therefore, justify setting aside the election.

What effect would violations of these doctrines have on an election? What would happen normally if no violations occurred? These areas we will explore when we look at postelection procedures.

ELECTION CERTIFICATIONS

After the election has been conducted, the board counts the ballots to determine which alternative, if any, received a majority of the votes cast. If there are no objections by the parties to the election over challenged ballots which could call the majority into question and if no charges alleging unfair campaign tactics are filed, the NLRB certifies the results. If a union has received a majority vote, it becomes the exclusive representative of the employees in the election unit and can begin bargaining with the employer. If the union has lost, the holding of an unchallenged election creates a bar to another election for a one-year period.

Even if a union which has won an election were to lose its majority

---

[32] 107 NLRB 427 (1953).

[33] *NLRB* v. *Virginia Electric & Power Co.*, 314 U.S. 469 (1941).

status within the year, the board will not order a new election. The Supreme Court and the board reason that certification is the equivalent of a term in office for an elected official, even if the official's constituency no longer supports him.[34] If the union loses, it cannot call for another election, even if it subsequently attains majority status, until one year elapses. This election also precludes another union from requesting an election during the year.

If the union fails in the election, the employer still cannot legally take action against its supporters. Even though they are not represented by the union, they are protected by the laws which forbid discrimination on the basis of union activity.

Setting aside elections

If challenges to elections are filed, and the board finds that the alleged activity occurred and interfered with the employees' ability to make a reasoned choice, the election will be set aside and rerun. If the violations are trivial, the board proceeds to issue a certification of the results.

Bargaining orders

In some cases, improper actions of a party are considered by the board to be so powerful that the inherent strength of the opposition is eroded. For example, assume that a majority of employees had signed authorization cards and attended union organizing meetings. Assume also that the employer threatened cutbacks in the operation if the union won, possible plant closings, or likely strikes over bargaining issues, and that it interrogated employees. Then, when the election is held, the union loses and files a charge alleging that the employer's inflammatory and threatening statements have undermined an actual union majority. The board may remedy the situation through a bargaining order, requiring the employer to recognize and negotiate with the union. The reasoning behind this remedial approach is that, had it not been for the employer's illegal conduct, the union would have won.[35] The employer will not be allowed to benefit from its illegal activity. Although we will see later that the board is now allowing both employers and unions more latitude in campaign communications than it has in the past.

---

[34] *Brooks* v. *NLRB*, 348 U.S. 96 (1954).
[35] *NLRB* v. *Gissel Packing Co.*, 395 U.S. 575 (1969).

EMPLOYEE RESPONSES TO CAMPAIGNS

This section is a brief summary of some of the more important findings of a study previously referred to, conducted by Getman, Goldberg and Herman, which examines how employees involved in organizing campaigns react to employer and union campaign tactics, both fair and unfair in elections. They begin by enumerating the assumptions the NLRB has previously made about elections. These include:

1. Employees are attentive to the campaign.
2. Employees will interpret ambiguous employer statements as threats.
3. Employees are unsophisticated about labor relations.
4. Free choice is fragile.
5. Both the union and the employer should have approximately equal access to the voters.
6. Authorization card-signing is not as clearly indicative of employee choice as an election.[36]

To test the validity of these assumptions, 31 representation elections were intensely studied. Interviews were conducted with employees, and questionnaire data were gathered. In examining factors related to a vote for the union, they found that positive attitudes toward unions in general and job dissatisfaction were highly predictive.[37] Personal characteristics of prounion voters included: (1) under 24 years of age, (2) belonging to a minority, (3) less than one year's seniority, (4) wages less than $2 per hour, and (5) having voted for a union in previous NLRB election (not necessarily involving the same company).[38] Most of the people involved in the elections had close relatives who were union members and a sizable portion had been voters in previous NLRB elections. These findings cast doubt on the assumption (number 3, above) that employees are unsophisticated about labor relations.

Employees did not appear to respond to the multitude of issues raised in the campaign (number 1, above). During the campaigns, management raised almost 30 issues, on the average, with employees remembering about 3. Unions campaigned on an average of 25 issues with employees remembering about 2.[39] Of the issues which management stressed, only four were remembered by even one third of the

---

[36] Getman, Goldberg, and Herman, *Union Representation Elections*, pp. 7–21.

[37] Ibid., p. 61.

[38] Ibid., p. 67.

[39] Ibid., p. 75.

employees. These were: improvements not necessarily dependent on unionization; new management has recently taken over; plant closing or moving may follow unionization due to business conditions; and the financial costs of union dues will outweigh union gains. For the union, three issues were remembered by one third or more: Union will improve unsatisfactory wages; union will prevent unfairness by establishing grievance and seniority systems; and union will improve generally unsatisfactory working conditions.[40]

Another interesting finding is that persons who saw job loss themes in the employer campaign flowing from unionization were less likely to vote for the company. A simple threat of job insecurity did not seem to deter those who remembered it most clearly from voting for the union.[41]

Meeting attendance, either at union or management sponsored gatherings, was significantly related to a familiarity with issues but had little effect on voting if the meeting was company sponsored. Persons who expressed familiarity with the issues were more likely to vote for the side expressing issues they remembered. For example, three of the four most familiar management issues were given as reasons for voting against the union while the three most familiar union issues had the most influence on prounion votes.[42]

Generally speaking, unions won elections only in units where authorization card majorities existed prior to filing the petition for an election. Between the petition and the election, average erosion of union support was about 4 percent. Attendance at union meetings (which is not compulsory since unions have no equal-time rights) appears to motivate undecided employees toward the union. No clear-cut answers as to why some undecided employees vote for the company was given, but exposure to company information may play a role.[43]

Given the relative inexperience of many employers in election campaigns or, in some cases, a "win at any cost" strategy, illegal activity may well occur during the campaign. These incidents upset the "laboratory conditions" the NLRB has seen as necessary for free choice in the election. Few data have actually been gathered previously to test the effects of illegal practices on voting patterns. In examining preelection conduct, the board may certify the election, either because no violations occurred or those that did were trivial; it may set aside the election and order a rerun; or it may find that the employer's

---

[40] Ibid., pp. 78–81.
[41] Ibid., pp. 87–88.
[42] Ibid., pp. 95, 98–99.
[43] Ibid., pp. 100–108.

conduct was so grossly unlawful that it destroyed the union's majority status. In that event it may order the employer to recognize the union regardless of the fact that the union lost. In the Getman, Goldberg, and Herman study, an NLRB administrative law judge examined the campaigns of each election and found violations in 22 of the 31. Nine had violations so serious that a bargaining order would have been imposed under rules existing at that time. If unlawful campaign activities do not affect elections, then NLRB postelection hearings may result in employees not being able to exercise their choice freely. The study found that union supporters were not more likely to switch their vote in a tainted campaign than a clean campaign.[44] Campaign tactics, in terms of information transmission, may be effective since postpetition activity results in a general slight erosion of union support, but the type of tactics, legal or illegal, used in the campaign do not.

THE *SHOPPING KART* DECISION

In 1977 the NLRB reversed the *Hollywood Ceramics* doctrine. Its earlier position held that if substantial false communications were made in a campaign and the opponent did not have time to respond, the election results could be set aside and a new election ordered.[45] Relying heavily on the results of the Getman, Goldberg, and Herman study, a board majority in the *Shopping Kart* case held that distortions of fact by a union during an organizing campaign were not sufficient to set aside an election which the union had won. In this case, on the night before the election the contending union's business agent told Shopping Kart employees that the firm's profits were $500,000 when they had actually been $50,000. Under the *Hollywood Ceramics* rule the board could have ordered a new election. It chose not to do so and repudiated its previous doctrine. The majority opinion of the board stated that it "will no longer probe into the truth or falsity of parties' campaign statements."[46]

WHO WINS REPRESENTATION ELECTIONS?

In 1975 over 575,000 persons were eligible to vote in NLRB-conducted representation elections. In all, 8,687 elections resulting in certifications were held. Of these, 7,729 were requested by unions or employees to obtain initial representation (RC cases), 332 were filed

---

[44] Ibid., pp. 110–16

[45] *Hollywood Ceramics Co.*, 140 NLRB 221 (1962).

[46] *Shopping Kart Food Market, Inc.*, 228 NLRB 190 (1977).

by employers (RM cases), 516 were filed by employees seeking decertification (RD cases), and 110 were filed by employees requesting deauthorization of union shop clauses (UD cases). Table 8–3 gives data on election frequency and numbers of employers involved.

TABLE 8–3
Types of elections resulting in certification in cases closed, fiscal year 1975

		Type of election				
Type of case	Total	Consent	Stipulated	Board-directed	Regional director-directed	Expedited elections under 8(b)(7)(C)
All types, total:						
Elections	8,687	1,011	5,872	82	1,707	15
Eligible voters	576,536	30,588	398,888	10,221	136,622	217
Valid votes	508,031	26,412	352,033	8,815	120,595	176
RC cases:						
Elections	7,729	865	5,294	75	1,491	4
Eligible voters	533,576	27,416	369,536	9,950	126,584	90
Valid votes	471,933	23,688	326,851	8,586	112,731	77
RM cases:						
Elections	332	55	205	7	54	11
Eligible voters	11,527	988	9,221	271	920	127
Valid votes	9,953	835	8,028	229	762	99
RD cases:						
Elections	516	72	355	0	89	0
Eligible voters	23,817	1,637	18,331	0	3,849	0
Valid votes	20,110	1,412	15,632	0	3,066	0
UD cases:						
Elections	110	19	18	0	73	—
Eligible voters	7,616	547	1,800	0	5,269	—
Valid votes	6,035	477	1,522	0	4,036	—

Source: *Fortieth Annual Report of the National Labor Relations Board* (Washington: Government Printing Office, 1975), p. 225.

Table 8–4 shows the size of bargaining units, number of employees eligible to vote, total elections, and percent won by a union. As you can see, over half of all elections were conducted in units of less than 40 employees. As you also can see, representation rights were won in less than 50 percent of all elections and generally in only one third or less in bargaining units of over 200 employees. Organization appears to be most successful where the net gain to the international union is the smallest. One might conjecture that externally motivated campaigns would be more likely at larger plants, but less successful than internally motivated organizing attempts. It may also be that the easily organized large plants have already been "creamed off" through earlier organizing campaigns.

TABLE 8–4
Election results and employees involved by unit size (RC and RM)

Size of unit	Number eligible	Total elections	Percent won by union
10 to 19	51,415	3,743	57.0
20 to 29	23,905	993	49.9
30 to 39	22,974	674	44.4
40 to 49	20,934	474	48.1
50 to 69	32,114	552	42.2
70 to 99	37,198	449	42.8
100 to 149	53,873	443	41.3
150 to 199	33,605	196	36.2
200 to 299	53,163	221	29.9
300 to 399	41,175	121	30.6
400 to 499	24,832	57	33.3
500 to 999	65,409	93	33.3
1,000 to 1,999	40,130	33	18.2
2,000 to 2,999	14,628	6	33.3
3,000 to 9,999	16,640	4	50.0

Source: Adapted from *Fortieth Annual Report of the National Labor Relations Board* (Washington: Government Printing Office, 1975), pp. 246–47.

Why might this occur? Larger plants probably have more diversity in terms of occupations, cover a wider geographic area (making communications difficult), and have a variety of different supervisors. In a larger plant, the dissatisfaction that might be necessary to start and maintain an organizing drive is not sufficiently general, in many cases, to lead to union success.

PREVIEW

Now that we have examined the process of organizing, we will assume that a union has won representation rights. What takes place now? How do the parties adjust to their new roles which call for ultimate agreement, given their past extreme adversary positions? What issues do they have to settle? What tactics are used? What methods are available to break stalemates? These and other issues immediately await us in our examination of the collective bargaining process.

SUMMARY

Organizing is an extremely complex issue involving unions, employers, and the NLRB. The union goal is to organize a majority of employees while the employer seeks to avoid organization. The NLRB's role is to preserve the free choice of employees to be represented or remain unorganized.

Crucial aspects of organization include the authorization card campaign, bargaining unit determination, the postelection campaign, and certification. The NLRB's decisions on bargaining units and unfair campaigning charges have important bearings on many election outcomes.

Recent results show that most union victories occur in smaller election units where employees may be more homogeneous or closer together geographically. Recent behavioral research suggests that the NLRB's past preoccupation with unfair campaign practices may not be necessary to preserve free choice in representation elections.

SUGGESTED READINGS

Abodeely, John E. *The NLRB and the Appropriate Bargaining Unit* (Philadelphia: Industrial Research Unit, Wharton School of Finance and Commerce, University of Pennsylvania, 1971).

Getman, Julius; Goldberg, Steven; and Herman, Jeanne B. *Union Representation Elections: Law and Reality* (New York: Russell Sage Foundation, 1976).

Jackson, Louis, and Lewis, Robert. *Winning NLRB Elections: Management's Strategy and Preventive Programs* (New York: Practising Law Institute, 1972).

National Labor Relations Board. *Your Government Conducts an Election for You on the Job* (Washington: Government Printing Office, 1966).

Schlossberg, Steven I., and Sherman, Frederick E. *Organizing and the Law*, rev. ed. (Washington: Bureau of National Affairs, 1971).

Silverberg, Louis G. *How to Take a Case before the National Labor Relations Board*, 3d ed. (Washington: Bureau of National Affairs, 1967).

DISCUSSION QUESTIONS

1. Did the NLRB go too far in its *Shopping Kart* decision, or should employees be expected to be able to evaluate campaign communications by themselves?
2. What are the advantages and disadvantages of craft severance for employees, employers, and unions? What positions would you expect each to take if the issues were raised?
3. Should union organizers have greater or less access to employees in organizing campaigns than they do now?
4. What do you think explains the relatively poor record for unions in attempting to organize in large bargaining units?

Case

Doug Kellogg had just graduated from Midwestern University with a business administration bachelor's degree. In the fall he expected to return to begin work on his master's in industrial relations. He felt he would have a good head start on his program since he had landed a summer internship in the personnel and industrial relations department of General Computer Corporation. He was assigned as an administrative assistant to Ed Wheeler, the director of industrial relations. Wheeler reported, in turn, to Dick Snyder, the vice president of personnel and industrial relations.

With the exception of one small subsidiary that it had recently acquired, none of GCC's 10,000 production and maintenance employees were unionized. The company felt it had taken pains to provide wages, benefits, and working conditions at levels equal to or above its unionized competitors for labor. All of its local plants had been built within the past ten years, were air conditioned, and had ample parking and cafeteria facilities. Its wages and benefit packages were purposely structured to match prevailing local union contracts for comparable employees. These efforts were not altogether altruistic since the company felt it would have substantially more freedom to make decisions about its operations if it remained nonunion.

The first assignment Ed had given Doug was to update the salary survey information they had gathered the previous December. Doug decided he would call other employers in the area to find out what they were paying workers in comparable jobs and grade levels. (Companies frequently cooperate in these types of surveys.) Since pay at GCC had not been changed since December (usually done just after survey data were taken), he was not surprised to find the pay at GCC slightly lower than competitors. Exhibit 1 shows GCC's pay as a percentage of local area pay for comparable grade levels the previous December.

EXHIBIT 1
GCC pay comparison (Central City plants)*

Grade level	Production workers			Maintenance and other nontechnical workers		
	Number of employees	December	June	Number of employees	December	June
1	602	102	98	151	99	94
2	219	100	97	147	101	97
3	84	103	99	136	98	96
4	36	100	96	79	100	100
5	13	99	94	34	102	98
6	6	101	98	27	100	96
7	4	103	98	25	99	93
8	2	100	96	10	102	99

Note: Pay in each grade is about 10 percent greater than immediately lower grade; for example, pay in Grade 2 is 110 percent of Grade 1.
* All figures are calculated as follows:

$$\frac{\text{GCC pay in grade}}{\text{All surveyed firms' pay in grade}}$$

Revised: December and June annually.

Shortly after he completed the survey, an urgent call came in for Mr. Wheeler from Frank Page, the personnel manager at their largest manufacturing facility, Mainframe Operations. Since Mr. Wheeler was out of town for the day, Doug took the call. Page told him that he had heard a reliable rumor that 20 of the 25 truck drivers at the plant had signed authorization cards with the Teamsters' Union, that they were dissatisfied with their pay, and were going to demand recognition for the Teamsters as their bargaining agent at the beginning of the following week. After Doug hung up, he decided he should get as much data together as possible for Mr. Wheeler to brief him when he came in tomorrow.

First, he obtained the job description for the truck driver's position. Then he recalled the firms he had just contacted in his salary survey to find out what they were paying their intracity truck drivers. GCC apparently had dropped the ball, because wages at competitive firms averaged 50 percent higher. The problem began to look more and more serious since almost half of the Central City employees were located at Mainframe Operations, and any labor trouble there would have an extremely disruptive influence on the total organization.

Once he had gathered the pay and job description data (Exhibit 2) he decided to formulate a strategy to recommend to Mr. Wheeler when he returned tomorrow. If you were Doug Kellogg, what would you recommend? What actions should Mr. Wheeler take in this situation? What do you see the consequences as being? What risks are involved? Would your recommendations be the same if a strike was to be avoided at all costs?

EXHIBIT 2

GENERAL COMPUTER CORPORATION
JOB DESCRIPTION

Intraplant Truck Driver

Grade: 3
Position code: 047
Job family: Maintenance

Duties

Under the supervision of the plant transportation department foreman, job holder loads and unloads manufactured goods and components into and from assigned vehicle. Drives vehicles between plants in same city. Operates vans, straight trucks, and short trailer semis. Checks trucks for safety equipment, reports and records equipment malfunctions. When not driving or loading performs duties in loading or production area as assigned.

Specifications

Chauffeur's license
No disabling health problems
Vision correctable to 20/20
Ability to lift and move up to 100 lbs.
Insurance on company motor vehicle policy

Point and
Counterpoint

Over the last few years several organizing drives have received a great deal of publicity and have often involved public figures in taking advocative stands. For one of these organizing campaigns, trace the progress from the spark that catalyzed the process to its conclusion or present state. Attempt to identify the tactical errors made by either party. Determine how the public at large responded, either through consumer behavior or through legislation. Then, develop a strategy for one of the two parties that would appear to you to gain it the maximum benefit at the least cost. To do this, you must identify the goals of the organization and the mechanisms available to achieve these goals. The campaigns are:

1. Farah Manufacturing and the Clothing Workers (ACWA),
2. J. P. Stevens and the Clothing and Textile Workers (ACTWA),
3. California grape and lettuce growers and the United Farm Workers and Teamsters (UFW & IBT), and
4. General Motors new southern plants and the Auto Workers (UAW).

Some periodicals that should give you a flavor (sometimes biased) for these include:

Advance (ACWA)
American Federationist (AFL–CIO)
Business Week
Daily Labor Report
Forbes
Fortune
Labor Unity (ACTWA)
Nation
Nation's Business (Chamber of Commerce)
New Republic
New York Times Magazine
Ramparts
Rolling Stone
Solidarity (UAW)
Textile Labor (TWUA)
Textile World
U.S. News & World Report
The Wall Street Journal

9

BARGAINING ISSUES

The practice of collective bargaining may have some parallels to the installation of a new production process in a plant. During the installation phase (organizing), new machinery may require some alterations to the plant. Once it is installed, operators have to learn its capabilities and how to run it (recognition). Then the process is started for the first time (initial bargaining). Unanticipated problems surface and the capabilities of the new system are explored. As more experience is gained, the process smoothes out (continued bargaining experience). Periodically, the new equipment experiences minor breakdowns and must be repaired (grievance procedures). The initial installation is a one-time procedure. What follows recurs on a predictable cycle (contract negotiation) unless maintenance is neglected. Figure 9–1 is a representation of the simplified process.

INTRODUCTION TO CONTRACT NEGOTIATIONS

A number of subjects are central to an understanding of bargaining. While all are inextricably intertwined, we will treat them as discrete subject areas. The aspects we will deal with include (1) bargaining issues, (2) negotiating strategy, (3) impasses and their resolution, and (4) special bargaining patterns. This chapter will deal with bargaining issues. In it, we will examine the goals of labor and management in bargaining, the effects of the environment in which the union and management perceive themselves as operating, and the role of public policy as contained in statutes and interpreted by the NLRB and the courts.

The first aspect of the establishment of a contract that we want to examine is the portions of the employment relationship that will be agreed to and specified. As you go through the chapter, you will recognize that some are explicitly economic, like wages. Others have

FIGURE 9–1
Simple collective bargaining cycle

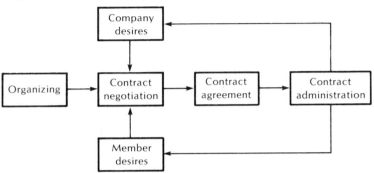

economic undertones like seniority, promotional issues, and job standards. Keep your focus on a number of key points and questions:

1. What subjects may the parties be legally required to consider if one requests their consideration?
2. How do unions and employers compare themselves to similar companies or unions?
3. What is the prevalence of certain issues in negotiated contracts?
4. What types of issues do unions and employers see as tradeoffs for each other?

UNION AND MANAGEMENT GOALS

While a negotiated contract will ultimately be specific to a particular plant, company, or industry within which bargaining takes place, there are some general considerations that labor and management are each presumed to find important. We will briefly examine these.

Union goals

Economists have suggested that there are two major goals of labor organizations: higher wages and increased membership.[1] At any given time, labor is presumed to prefer increases of both. But in its dealings with management, the union must usually choose between one or the other of the goals. If wages increase relative to other firms, an employer might necessarily reduce employment (membership) to remain competitive. If an employer is to be motivated to expand employment,

[1] Allen M. Cartter, *Theory of Wages and Employment* (Homewood, Ill.: Richard D. Irwin, Inc., 1959), pp. 88–94.

then wages must rise only slowly. On occasion unions may believe that they can simultaneously increase wages and membership through bargaining. For example, the UAW successfully demanded a wage increase and more paid time off for its members during the 1976 auto negotiations. It may have believed that an increase in time off would require the auto companies to hire new workers (members) to work the time off given by the new contract if the automakers were to be able to operate at equivalent production levels. Only time will tell whether their strategy was successful. Generally speaking, we would predict that a union would first seek wage gains for present members before pursuing expanded employment. Figure 9–2 gives a theoretical

FIGURE 9–2

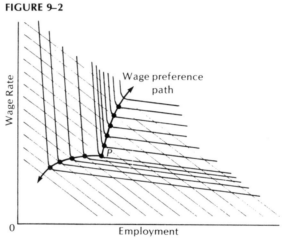

Source: Allan M. Cartter, *Theory of Wages and Employment* (Homewood, Ill.: Richard D. Irwin, Inc., 1959), p. 91.

progression of its demands. The reason that the theoretical preference path is not straight stems from the premise that current union members may not equally value employment changes and wages. For example, members may prefer wage increases more than having new workers added to the plant. When facing a cutback, they may prefer receding employment to wage cuts. This latter premise is reflected in practice by seniority rules for layoffs.

The union does not live in a vacuum while formulating its demands. It receives information about the firm with which it's negotiating and its external environment. The very issues that lead to initial organization that we discussed in Chapter 7 continue to influence the formulation of union demands. Perceptions of inequity and threat, goals that are important to members, all influence the path of bargaining and the choice and magnitude of issues.

From an equity and goal orientation standpoint, negotiations may proceed on a number of issues. These may relate to wages, hours, work rules, union security, and so on. Generally, discussions of great magnitude center around the wage theme, and it is this one we will examine briefly.

General wage issues.   Three criteria are suggested as the major factors in the structure of wage demands: equity within and across firms, ability to pay, and standard of living. These suggest that unions will be motivated to make a number of comparisons in formulating wage demands.

Equity.   From an equity standpoint, unions would expect wages to be consistent with levels of equivalent nonunion jobs in the firm. They would also expect some fringe benefit package equivalence across jobs. This would particularly apply to benefits of an insurance nature where the risks would generally be equivalent regardless of job or salary level. Unions also pay attention to bargains forged in other industries. Very often the steel or auto settlements are viewed as pattern setters for demands. The long Rubber Workers strike during 1976 was at least partially due to the fact that wage levels for production workers, which had compared closely to auto workers in the past, were now substantially lower than auto workers. Unions also attempt to introduce uniformity of wage rates for the same jobs in different locations of the same company. For example, an auto assembly worker at Ford's Twin Cities (Minnesota) assembly plant earns the same rate as another in a similar job in Wixom, Michigan.

Ability to pay.   A second component is "ability to pay." While this component takes two major forms, the prevalent rationale is usually related to the profitability of the firm. If a company has done well recently, unions are not reluctant to demand larger than normal increases. While some believe that similar attention to profits is not paid on the downside, evidence exists to show that unions do give some consideration to an employer's difficulties. For example, the UAW extended its expiring contract with American Motors for seven months in 1977 rather than attempting to demand a settlement consistent with the Big Three auto pattern set in late 1976. Unions do not generally agree to a wage retreat, however, assigning some of the blame for losses or low profits to management errors over which the union has no say or control. Another form of the ability to pay issue is associated with the proportion of a company's total costs that are associated with labor. Generally speaking, the less labor intensive (lower the share of costs going to labor) a firm is, the greater is its ability to pay. Table 9–1 shows why this is the case. Simply put, the same percentage pay in-

TABLE 9–1
Cost comparisons for labor and capital intensive firms

	Labor intensive firm	Capital intensive firm
Material cost	$ 500,000	$ 500,000
Capital cost	100,000	400,000
Labor cost.........................	400,000	100,000
Total cost	$1,000,000	$1,000,000
Cost of 10 percent wage increase	40,000	10,000
New total cost	$1,040,000	$1,010,000

crease for labor and capital intensive firms results in widely disparate cost impacts.

Standard of living. The third criterion is "standard of living." This component can also take on two meanings. The first relates to the stability of one's real wages. By real wages we mean the purchasing power of one's wages. If prices rise by 10 percent for the things the average worker buys, but wages rise only 6 percent over the same period, real wages have been eroded by 4 percent. Cost-of-living adjustments (COLA) are aimed at maintaining parity between wages and prices over time. Standard of living issues also can arise when unions believe that their members' purchasing power needs improvement to enable them to enjoy higher qualities of goods and services; for example, home ownership rather than rental. Obviously, there are some comparison or equity aspects included here, but the comparison is with society in general, not with other specific worker groups.

Components of wage demands. Figure 9–3 represents the components of wage demands we have just discussed. The equity issues relate to both internal and external comparisons, ability to pay to profits, and standard of living to real wages and absolute improvement. While equity issues were discussed first, you should not draw the conclusion that any of these pay issues is, *a priori*, more important than another.

Union security. Another major issue of concern is the union's security as the representative of the employees. It established itself at some point as the majority representative of the employees, and it wants to continue in this role. It would prefer to negotiate a contract which eases its job in recruiting new members, retaining old ones, and collecting dues.

Job security. A final pervasive demand centers around job property rights. Unions believe that workers have established an inherent value in their jobs and that this value grows with their tenure in the

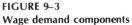

FIGURE 9–3
Wage demand components

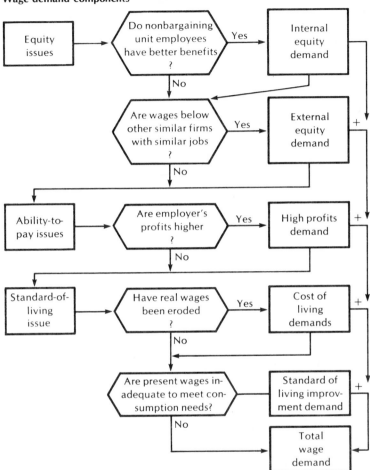

firm. To rationalize promotional opportunities and layoff procedures, unions generally demand that seniority serves as the sole or major criterion in personnel decision making. Seniority serves not only as an underlying norm among workers but also as a readily and simply measurable yardstick which is clearly recognized and applied by union members.

Management goals

There are probably three major management considerations. One is to obtain a degree of certainty in its employee relations. The second is to remain competitive with other firms. The third is to resist the erosion of management prerogatives. While the union is generally pressuring for "more," the company is usually not in a position of offering "less" but is attempting to hold the line. Therefore, management considerations are essentially defensive by nature.

Certainty. Certainty is highly related to the length of the contract, the scope of the bargaining unit, and contract expiration dates. Companies prefer long-term contracts because each succeeding negotiation obviously introduces the possibility that the union will modify or escalate its demands. Employers also prefer to deal with a single unions generally demand that seniority serves as the sole or major crite- plant. If this is not possible, due to multiple bargaining units, employers prefer common expiration dates so each union cannot whipsaw the employer by bargaining consecutively.

Competition. Employers also resist demands which place them at a disadvantage when compared with other firms in the same industry. Since employers have relatively little control over what other employers and unions do, the general trend is to reduce the range of possibilities for settlements which might be disadvantageous. Primary modes for this are multiemployer bargaining among a collection of small firms and industrywide bargaining where several large producers prevail, as in the steel industry. In some industries (for example, autos), unions pick a target company to set a settlement pattern. That company is placed at a competitive disadvantage because if a strike ensues its competitors continue to produce and sell while the target negotiates.

Management rights. Finally, management treasures the privilege of decision making and resists erosion of its prerogatives. Employers make a point of reserving the right to take certain actions on a unilateral basis through management rights clauses.

Joint goals

While the demands of both parties tend to be distributive in nature, that is, one's gain is the other's loss, the anticipated long-term relationship between a union and employer produces a need for a system to resolve disputes in contract interpretation and implementation. This joint need leads to the inclusion of grievance procedures. These formalize the process for handling problems of contract interpretation and application. Generally speaking, these provide for conferences between union and management representatives to resolve contractual disputes. If the parties cannot dispose of the issue, most procedures call for arbitration by an independent third party. In exchange for this agreement by management to let an outsider judge its decisions, the union agrees to forego strikes during the term of a contract through a no-strike clause.

Given these individual and joint goals, what broad constraints are imposed on bargaining conduct in relation to issues in the federal statutes and their interpretation?

LEGAL REQUIREMENTS

Section 8(d) of the Labor-Management Relations Act of 1947 sets forth in one sentence the essence of collective bargaining in the United States.

> For the purposes of this section, to bargain collectively is the performance of the mutual obligation of the employer and representative of the employees to meet at reasonable times and confer in good faith with respect to wages, hours, and other terms and conditions of employment, or the negotiation of an agreement, or any question arising thereunder, and the execution of a written contract incorporating any agreement reached if requested by either party, but such obligation does not compel either party to agree to a proposal or require the making of a concession.

The fact that such an important process as bargaining is dealt with in such broad terms has had impact on both the practice of bargaining and the issues involved. For example, in terms of process, what does "good faith" mean? On issues, what do "wages, hours, and other terms and conditions of employment" signify? Unions, employers, the NLRB, and the courts have all grappled with these issues. Novel demands and bargaining strategies are challenged to determine whether or not they conform to the current interpretation of the statute. Later we will examine the definition of "good faith" and its impact on process. Here we will study the meaning of "wages, hours, and other terms and conditions of employment" to identify bargaining issues.

Bargaining issues can be divided into three legal categories: mandatory, permissive, and prohibited. Mandatory issues are those which fall within the definition of wages, hours, and other terms and conditions of employment. The first two classifications are fairly apparent, dealing with economics and work schedules. "Terms and conditions of employment" is a more complex concept. A reasonable test of whether or not an issue is within this area is to ask if the practice would have a direct and immediate effect on union members' jobs. An example might be a plant closing or reassignment of work from one group to another. Permissive issues are those which may be raised but need not be responded to by the party asked since they have no provable direct impact on jobs. An example here might be a demand by a union to participate in the establishment of company pricing policies. Prohib-

TABLE 9–2
Items mandatory for bargaining

Wages
Hours
Discharge
Arbitration
Holidays—paid
Vacations—paid
Duration of agreement
Grievance procedure
Layoff plan
Reinstatement of economic
  strikers
Change of payment from hourly
  base to salary base
Union security and checkoff
Work rules
Merit wage increase
Work schedule
Lunch periods
Rest periods
Pension plan
Retirement age
Bonus payments
Price of meals provided by
  company
Group insurance—health,
  accident, life
Promotions
Seniority
Layoffs
Transfers
Work assignments and transfers
No-strike clause
Piece rates
Stock purchase plan
Workloads
Change of employee status to
  independent contractors
Motor carrier—union
  agreement providing that
  carriers use own equipment
  before leasing outside
  equipment
Overtime pay
Agency shop
Sick leave
Employers insistence on clause
  giving arbitrator right to
  enforce award
Management rights clause

Cancellation of seniority upon
  relocation of plant
Discounts on company products
Shift differentials
Contract clause providing for
  supervisors keeping seniority
  in unit
Procedures for income tax
  withholding
Severance pay
Nondiscriminatory hiring hall
Plant rules
Safety
Prohibition against supervisor
  doing unit work
Superseniority for union
  stewards
Checkoff
Partial plant closing
Hunting on employer forest
  reserve where previously
  granted
Plant closedown and relocation
Change in operations resulting
  in reclassifying workers from
  incentive to straight time, or
  cut work force, or installation
  of cost-saving machine
Plant closing
Job posting procedures
Plant reopening
Employee physical examination
Union security
Bargaining over "bar list"
Truck rentals—minimum rental
  to be paid by carriers to
  employee-owned vehicles
Musician price lists
Arrangement for negotiation
Change in insurance carrier and
  benefits
Profit-sharing plan
Company houses
Subcontracting
Discriminatory racial policies
Production ceiling imposed by
  union
Most favored nation clause

Source: Reed Richardson, "Positive Collective Bargaining," in Dale Yoder and H. G. Heneman, Jr., eds., *Employee and Labor Relations,* vol. 3 of the *ASPA Handbook of Personnel and Industrial Relations* (Washington: Bureau of National Affairs, 1976), p. 7–128.

ited issues are those that are statutorily outlawed, such as demands that an employer use only union-produced goods. Another distinction between mandatory and permissive issues is that neither party can go to impasse (refuse to agree on a contract) over a permissive issue. Table 9–2 gives a list of issues which are considered mandatory, if raised, under present interpretations. The inclusion of an issue in this table does not mean that a union will demand it or that it ultimately be included in a contract.

Now that we have a general overview for the study of bargaining issues, we will examine some of the major specific features included in the contract.

ECONOMIC ISSUES

There are three major features related to any economic issue in a package: the form of the pay, its magnitude, and how it is determined. The form of pay is generally divided into two major areas: (1) direct pay to the employee, and (2) fringe benefits which are, generally, insurance, deferred payments, or quasi-payments in kind. Magnitude is self-explanatory. Determination of pay is one of the most complex issues since it inextricably involves equity issues important to the union and performance issues important to the company.

Form of pay

It is obvious that pay for work performed is a mandatory issue in bargaining. But there has been some past controversy about whether other economic benefits like accident or health insurance, tuition refunds, and so on, are mandatory bargaining issues. This was settled in 1948 when the 7th Circuit Court ruled in the *Inland Steel* case that fringe benefits were within the mandatory area.[2] So, at this point, we have a relatively simple type (money wages), and some relatively complex types (fringe benefits). This latter type is what we will dwell on in our examination.

Economic components which are not received in the form of immediate money wages usually are either received as insurance or deferred compensation. Insurance typically applies to hospital and medical needs, life, disability, and dental benefits. Deferred compensation usually takes the form of retirement and pension plans. There are advantages and disadvantages to nonmonetary wage forms. For the employee, the benefit of the form depends partly on usage. Unmarried persons need life and family health care less than those who are mar-

---

[2] *Inland Steel Co.* v. *NLRB*, 170 F.2d 247 (1948).

ried. On the other hand, the aggregate value of the benefits is untaxed. When the company directly purchases insurance, the value is not reported as income to the recipient. A wage earner purchasing an equivalent amount would have already been taxed on the money which he pays for the individually purchased benefit.

As we will note later when we examine the determinants of pay, money may be the form of any one of a variety of negotiated benefits, such as holiday pay.

Employers, in particular, have become much more concerned recently about the form of pay. In the past, the form of the economic package had generally been considered the union's province. If an employer was willing to give an equivalent of 50 cents per hour in wages, it did not concern the employer how this was apportioned. Figure 9–4 represents an example of this approach. As benefits be-

FIGURE 9–4
Wage forms

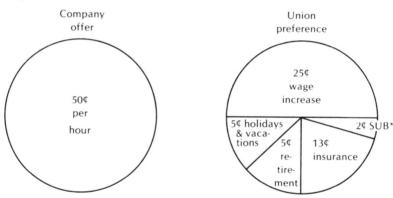

* Supplementary unemployment benefits (SUB).

came more complex, and as medical, dental, and other health care costs began to escalate, employer interests in the division of the package became critical. Table 9–3 details what might happen to costs over the course of a contract. Given that employers desire certainty or predictability in the effects of the contract, resistance to fringes where future costs are unknown would be expected since fringe packages generally specify coverages, not costs. The example in Table 9–3 shows that an original health insurance program costing 30 cents per hour at contract time becomes 45 cents per hour if the carrier increases rates by 50 percent (unfortunately not unusual). The second example reflects the fact that fringes are not as easy to control as wages. In this example, the employer effects a one-third cutback in hours worked.

TABLE 9-3
Cost per employee for wage and fringe increases*

	Present rate	Total cost/year	Increase offered	Anticipated cost	Possible cost†
Health insurance rate increase					
Wage cost	$5/hr.	$10,400	40¢/hr.	$11,232	$11,232
Health insurance	$100/mo.	1,200	30¢/hr.	1,824	2,736
Total cost		$11,600‡	($52 more/mo. in insurance)	$13,056§	$13,968#
Reduction in hours worked					
Wage cost	$5/hr.	$10,400	40¢/hr.	$ 7,488	$ 7,488
Health insurance	$100/mo.	1,200	($52 more/mo. in	1,824	2,736
Total cost		$11,600	insurance)	$ 9,312‖	$10,224**

* Assumes standard work year of 2,080 hours.
† Assumes 50 percent increase in premiums for similar coverage by carrier.
‡ Cost per hour is $5.58.
§ Cost per hour is $6.28.
‖ Cost per hour is $6.71.
Cost per hour is $6.72.
** Cost per hour is $7.37.

Since wages are not paid for unworked hours, costs are reduced when hours are reduced. But since health insurance is paid by the person, costs of this fringe benefit still increase by 50 percent even though only two-thirds as many hours are worked. Thus, you can see that the form of pay is an important item to the employer.

Retirement benefits is an area that has plagued both unions and management. For management, before sound financial funding was required by the Employee Retirement Income Security Act of 1974 (ERISA), an aging labor force could easily result in staggering yearly costs for pensions where employers paid them from current receipts. Unions had the same problem. For example, increases in the number of retired coal miners in the 1950s and 1960s, coupled with a reduction in coal production, caused the United Mine Workers continually to demand higher tonnage royalties on coal to support the pension plan. Even though some increases were negotiated, they were not enough to stop the erosion in the dollar level of benefits.

Since our federal wage and hour laws (for example, Fair Labor Standards Act) require employers to pay a 50-percent penalty for working an employee more than 40 hours in a given week, we might expect that an employer would always prefer to hire new employees when more work is needed. But overtime penalties do not apply to fringe benefits. If fringes exceed 50 percent of the basic pay rate, in the absence of a higher premium written into the contract an employer would prefer overtime. There have been arguments raised that fringe benefits are a barrier to employment expansion.[3] There is also evidence that fringes are now equal to about 35 percent of salaries, on the average.[4] If the trend continues, labor's position may not only restrict new entries, but reduce opportunities for its present membership. And where fringes are below 50 percent, if costs incidental to hiring plus fringes exceed that of the overtime premium, new hiring will be resisted.[5]

Magnitude of pay

The amount and mix of pay and fringes varies from industry to industry. Tables 9–4 and 9–5 shed some light on the magnitude of representative wage and fringe levels, respectively. What these tables show is that industry patterns differ. Skilled trades, particularly construction trades, have substantially higher wage rates, but fewer company paid benefits.

Determinants of pay

There are a large variety of pay determinants. Perhaps the simplest occurs in the area of fringe benefits. For health and other insurance benefits the usual determinant is simply whether or not one was employed as of a certain date, usually the first of the month.

A second major area that applies across all jobs in a bargaining unit is a cost-of-living adjustment (COLA). Cost-of-living adjustments, once negotiated, are generally outside of the control of the parties, since wage changes are dependent on changes in the Consumer Price Index published by the Bureau of Labor Statistics in the U.S. Department of Labor. Usually these clauses automatically increase pay by a predefined magnitude (for example, 1 cent per hour) for every increase of a certain amount (for example, 0.3 index points) in the CPI. Some COLA clauses have a cap, that is, a maximum increase that may be given over a certain period. Caps increase company certainty but allow for the possibility of an erosion in real wages.

Wages, while straightforward in magnitude, may be very complex in their determination. Generally speaking, companies would prefer to tie them to productivity since labor costs would be readily predictable and higher productivity might result from magnitude of pay being tied to the amount of output. On the other hand, unions usually object

---

[3] Joseph Garbarino, "Fringe Benefits as Barriers to Expanding Employment," *Industrial and Labor Relations Review*, vol. 17 (April 1964), pp. 426–42.

[4] U.S. Chamber of Commerce, *Employee Benefits*, 1975 (Washington, 1976).

[5] John A. Fossum, "Hire or Schedule Overtime? A Formula for Minimizing Labor Costs," *Compensation Review*, vol. 1, no. 2 (1969), pp. 14–22.

TABLE 9–4
Pay levels by industry

Average hourly earnings (dollars)

Year	Total private	Mining	Contract construction	Manufacturing			Transportation and public utilities	Wholesale and retail trade			Finance, insurance, real estate [2]	Services
				Total	Durable goods	Nondurable goods		Total	Wholesale	Retail		
1947	$1.13	$1.47	$1.54	$1.22	$1.28	$1.15	(3)	$0.94	$1.22	$0.84	$1.14	(3)
1948	1.23	1.66	1.71	1.33	1.40	1.25	(3)	1.01	1.31	.90	1.20	(3)
1949	1.28	1.72	1.79	1.38	1.45	1.30	(3)	1.06	1.36	.95	1.26	(3)
1950	1.34	1.77	1.86	1.44	1.52	1.35	(3)	1.10	1.43	.98	1.34	(3)
1951	1.45	1.93	2.02	1.56	1.65	1.44	(3)	1.18	1.52	1.06	1.45	(3)
1952	1.52	2.01	2.13	1.65	1.75	1.51	(3)	1.23	1.61	1.09	1.51	(3)
1953	1.61	2.14	2.28	1.74	1.86	1.58	(3)	1.30	1.70	1.16	1.58	(3)
1954	1.65	2.14	2.39	1.78	1.90	1.62	(3)	1.35	1.76	1.20	1.65	(3)
1955	1.71	2.20	2.45	1.86	1.99	1.67	(3)	1.40	1.83	1.25	1.70	(3)
1956	1.80	2.33	2.57	1.95	2.08	1.77	(3)	1.47	1.94	1.30	1.78	(3)
1957	1.89	2.46	2.71	2.05	2.19	1.85	(3)	1.54	2.02	1.37	1.84	(3)
1958	1.95	2.47	2.82	2.11	2.26	1.91	(3)	1.60	2.09	1.42	1.89	(3)
1959	2.02	2.56	2.93	2.19	2.36	1.98	(3)	1.66	2.18	1.47	1.95	(3)
1960	2.09	2.61	3.08	2.26	2.43	2.05	(3)	1.71	2.24	1.52	2.02	(3)
1961	2.14	2.64	3.20	2.32	2.49	2.11	(3)	1.76	2.31	1.56	2.09	(3)
1962	2.22	2.70	3.31	2.39	2.56	2.17	(3)	1.83	2.37	1.63	2.17	(3)
1963	2.28	2.81	3.41	2.46	2.63	2.22	$2.88	1.89	2.45	1.68	2.25	$1.94
1964	2.36	2.92	3.55	2.53	2.71	2.29	3.03	1.96	2.52	1.75	2.30	2.05
1965	2.45	3.00	3.70	2.61	2.79	2.36	3.11	2.03	2.61	1.82	2.39	2.17
1966	2.56	3.19	3.89	2.72	2.90	2.45	3.24	2.13	2.73	1.91	2.47	2.29
1967	2.68	3.35	4.11	2.83	3.00	2.57	3.42	2.24	2.88	2.01	2.58	2.42
1968	2.85	3.61	4.41	3.01	3.19	2.74	3.64	2.40	3.05	2.16	2.75	2.61
1969	3.04	3.85	4.79	3.19	3.38	2.91	3.85	2.55	3.23	2.30	2.93	2.81
1970	3.22	4.06	5.24	3.36	3.55	3.08	4.21	2.71	3.44	2.44	3.08	3.02
1971	3.44	4.41	5.69	3.57	3.79	3.26	4.64	2.86	3.67	2.57	3.27	3.23
1972	3.67	4.72	6.03	3.81	4.06	3.47	5.03	3.01	3.88	2.70	3.42	3.46
1973	3.92	4.73	6.38	4.07	4.33	3.68	5.04	3.20	4.12	2.87	3.57	3.58
1974	3.92	5.21	6.37	4.08	4.34	3.68	5.43	3.20	4.12	2.87	3.58	3.76
1975 p	4.22	5.89	6.75	4.41	4.69	3.99	5.91	3.47	4.49	3.09	3.82	4.06

Average weekly earnings (dollars)

Year	Total private	Mining	Contract construction	Manufacturing			Transportation and public utilities	Wholesale and retail trade			Finance, insurance, real estate [2]	Services
				Total	Durable goods	Nondurable goods		Total	Wholesale	Retail		
1947	$45.58	$59.94	$58.87	$49.17	$51.76	$46.03	(3)	$38.07	$50.14	$33.77	$43.21	(3)
1948	49.00	65.56	65.27	53.12	57.25	49.50	(3)	40.80	53.63	36.22	45.48	(3)
1949	50.24	62.33	67.56	53.88	57.25	50.38	(3)	42.93	55.49	38.42	47.63	(3)
1950	53.13	67.16	69.68	58.32	62.43	53.48	(3)	44.55	58.08	39.71	50.52	(3)
1951	57.86	74.11	76.96	63.34	68.48	56.88	(3)	47.79	62.02	42.82	54.67	(3)
1952	60.65	77.59	82.86	67.16	72.63	59.95	(3)	49.20	65.53	43.38	57.08	(3)
1953	63.76	83.03	86.41	70.47	76.63	62.57	(3)	51.35	69.02	45.36	59.57	(3)
1954	64.52	82.60	88.91	70.49	76.19	63.18	(3)	53.33	71.28	47.04	62.04	(3)
1955	67.72	89.54	90.90	75.70	82.19	66.63	(3)	55.16	74.48	48.75	63.92	(3)
1956	70.74	95.06	96.38	78.78	85.28	70.09	(3)	57.48	78.57	50.18	65.68	(3)
1957	73.33	98.65	100.27	81.59	88.26	72.52	(3)	59.60	81.41	52.20	67.53	(3)
1958	75.08	96.08	103.78	82.71	89.27	74.11	(3)	61.76	84.02	54.10	70.12	(3)
1959	78.78	103.68	108.41	88.26	96.05	78.61	(3)	64.41	88.51	56.15	72.74	(3)
1960	80.67	105.44	113.04	89.72	97.44	80.36	(3)	66.01	90.72	57.76	75.14	(3)
1961	82.60	106.92	118.08	92.34	100.35	82.92	(3)	67.41	93.56	58.66	77.12	(3)
1962	85.91	110.43	122.47	96.56	104.70	85.93	(3)	69.91	96.22	60.96	80.94	(3)
1963	88.46	114.40	127.19	99.63	108.09	87.91	$118.37	72.01	99.47	62.66	84.38	$69.84
1964	91.33	117.74	132.06	102.97	112.19	90.91	125.14	74.28	102.31	64.75	85.79	73.60
1965	95.06	123.52	138.38	107.53	117.18	94.64	128.13	76.53	106.49	66.61	88.91	77.04
1966	98.82	130.24	146.26	112.34	122.09	98.49	131.22	79.02	111.11	68.57	92.13	80.38
1967	101.84	135.89	154.95	114.90	123.60	102.03	138.85	81.76	116.06	70.95	95.46	83.97
1968	107.73	142.71	164.49	122.51	132.07	109.05	148.15	86.40	122.31	74.95	101.75	90.57
1969	114.61	155.23	181.54	129.51	139.59	115.53	155.93	90.78	129.85	78.66	108.70	96.66
1970	119.46	164.40	195.45	133.73	143.07	120.43	155.66	95.66	137.60	82.47	113.34	102.28
1971	127.28	172.14	211.67	142.44	153.12	128.12	169.24	100.30	146.07	86.61	120.66	103.28
1972	136.16	187.43	222.51	154.69	167.68	137.76	187.92	105.65	154.81	90.99	126.88	110.14
1973	145.43	201.03	235.69	166.06	180.11	145.73	204.62	111.04	162.74	95.57	132.10	117.64
1974	154.45	220.90	249.08	176.40	190.88	156.01	218.29	118.33	174.66	101.04	140.19	127.46
1975 p	163.89	249.15	264.98	189.51	204.69	168.39	234.63	126.41	188.75	107.89	150.75	137.23

p Preliminary unweighted average.
[1] For mining and manufacturing, data refer to production and related workers; for contract construction, to construction workers; for all other divisions, to nonsupervisory workers.
[2] Excludes data for nonoffice salespersons.
[3] Separate data not available.

Source: U.S. Department of Labor, Employment and Training Administration, *Employment and Training Report of the President* (Washington: Government Printing Office, 1976), p. 296.

to incentive plans since they feel they pit worker against worker, are difficult to measure, and penalize employees who work in fixed pace positions. What the two parties do tend to agree upon is the fact that different jobs demand different pay levels given their relative contributions to production.

Differences between jobs can be negotiated into the contract, or the parties may agree on a system to determine relative worth across jobs. This system is called job evaluation and requires that jobs be analyzed

TABLE 9–5
Employee benefits as percent of payroll, by type of benefit and industry groups, 1975

Type of benefit	Total, all industries	Total, all manufacturing	Food, beverages and tobacco	Textile products and apparel	Pulp, paper, lumber and furniture	Printing and publishing
			Manufacturing			
Total employee benefits as percent of payroll	35.4	36.1	36.2	27.8	32.7	32.2
1. Legally required payments (employer's share only)	8.0	8.8	9.0	8.8	8.4	7.4
Old-age, survivors, disability and health insurance	5.7	5.8	5.8	5.8	5.8	5.5
Unemployment compensation	1.0	1.2	1.2	1.5	1.1	1.2
Workmen's compensation (including estimated cost of self-insured)	1.2	1.7	1.9	1.1	1.5	0.6
Railroad retirement tax, Railroad Unemployment and Cash Sickness Insurance, state sickness benefits insurance, etc.†	0.1	0.1	0.1	0.4	‡	0.1
2. Pension and other agreed upon payments (employer's share only)	11.6	11.6	11.7	7.3	9.7	9.4
Pension plan premiums and pension payments not covered by insurance type plan (net)	5.5	4.9	5.7	2.9	3.5	4.1
Life insurance premiums, death benefits, accident and medical insurance premiums, hospitalization insurance, etc. (net)	5.2	6.1	5.1	4.1	5.6	4.9
Salary continuation or long-term disability	0.2	0.2	0.2	0.1	0.2	0.1
Dental insurance premiums	0.1	0.1	0.2	0.1	0.1	0.1
Discounts on goods and services purchased from company by employees	0.2	‡	0.2	‡	‡	‡
Employee meals furnished by company	0.2	0.1	0.1	‡	0.1	0.1
Miscellaneous payments (compensation payments in excess of legal requirements, separation or termination pay allowances, moving expenses, etc.)	0.2	0.2	0.2	0.1	0.2	0.1
3. Paid rest periods, lunch periods, wash-up time, travel time, clothes-change time, get-ready time, etc.	3.6	3.7	4.2	4.0	3.1	3.0
4. Payments for time not worked	10.1	10.1	9.3	6.6	10.1	10.2
Paid vacations and payments in lieu of vacation	5.2	5.4	5.0	3.5	5.7	5.3
Payments for holidays not worked	3.3	3.5	3.0	2.6	3.5	3.6
Paid sick leave	1.2	0.8	1.0	0.4	0.7	1.1
Payments for State or National Guard duty, jury, witness and voting pay allowances, payments for time lost due to death in family or other personal reasons, etc.	0.4	0.4	0.3	0.1	0.2	0.2
5. Other items	2.1	1.9	2.0	1.1	1.4	2.2
Profit-sharing payments	1.1	1.1	0.4	0.6	0.7	1.6
Contributions to employee thrift plans	0.3	0.2	0.5	‡	0.1	0.1
Christmas or other special bonuses, service awards, suggestion awards, etc.	0.4	0.4	1.0	0.3	0.5	0.4
Employee education expenditures (tuition refunds, etc.)	0.1	0.1	‡	‡	‡	0.1
Special wage payments ordered by courts, payments to union stewards, etc.	0.2	0.1	0.1	0.2	0.1	‡

* Includes mining, transportation, research, hotels, and so on.
† Figure is considerably less than legal rate, as most reporting companies had only a small proportion of employees covered by tax.
‡ Less than 0.05 percent.
Source: U.S. Chamber of Commerce, *Employee Benefits*, 1975 (Washington, 1976).

industries										Nonmanufacturing industries							
Chemicals and allied products	*Petroleum industry*	*Rubber, leather and plastic products*	*Stone, clay and glass products*	*Primary metal industries*	*Fabricated metal products (excluding manufacturing and transportation equipment)*	*Machinery (excluding electrical)*	*Electrical machinery, equipment and supplies*	*Transportation equipment*	*Instruments and miscellaneous manufacturing industries*	*Total, all nonmanufacturing*	*Public utilities (electric, gas, water, telephone, etc.)*	*Department stores*	*Trade (wholesale and other retail)*	*Banks, finance and trust companies*	*Insurance companies*	*Hospitals*	*Miscellaneous nonmanufacturing industries**
42.2	39.2	40.4	35.1	40.6	35.1	36.1	35.0	39.9	34.8	34.4	37.5	28.4	28.2	37.3	35.2	24.0	32.2
7.9	6.4	9.3	9.4	9.5	9.3	8.3	8.1	10.3	8.1	6.9	6.4	7.9	8.0	6.9	6.3	7.0	7.7
5.8	5.2	5.8	5.8	5.8	5.8	5.8	5.6	5.8	5.8	5.4	5.3	5.5	5.6	5.6	5.3	5.6	4.9
0.8	0.6	1.2	1.4	1.0	1.2	1.1	1.5	1.3	1.0	0.8	0.5	1.5	1.0	1.0	0.8	0.5	0.9
1.2	0.5	2.2	2.1	2.7	2.2	1.4	0.9	3.2	1.0	0.6	0.6	0.6	1.4	0.2	0.2	0.9	1.1
0.1	0.1	0.1	0.1	‡	0.1	‡	0.1	‡	‡	0.1	‡	0.3	‡	0.1	‡	‡	0.8
13.3	13.5	15.6	11.4	15.8	11.1	12.2	9.9	14.1	10.3	11.4	14.1	9.4	6.6	11.0	11.8	6.6	9.6
6.5	9.3	6.7	4.7	7.2	4.4	4.7	3.8	5.3	4.4	6.9	8.7	2.7	2.6	6.4	7.0	2.5	4.2
5.8	3.7	8.0	6.3	8.1	6.2	6.9	5.5	7.8	5.4	3.8	4.5	2.5	3.3	3.7	3.3	2.9	3.8
0.2	0.1	0.4	0.1	‡	0.2	0.3	0.3	0.3	0.2	0.2	0.2	0.1	0.2	0.1	0.3	0.1	0.3
0.1	‡	0.1	0.1	0.1	0.1	‡	0.2	0.3	0.1	0.1	0.1	0.2	‡	‡	‡	‡	0.1
0.1	0.1	‡	‡	‡	‡	‡	‡	0.1	‡	0.3	0.2	3.9	0.2	0.1	0.1	0.3	‡
0.4	0.1	‡	‡	‡	‡	0.1	‡	‡	‡	0.3	0.2	‡	0.2	0.6	0.8	0.4	0.3
0.2	0.2	0.4	0.2	0.4	0.2	0.2	0.1	0.3	0.2	0.3	0.2	‡	0.1	0.1	0.3	0.4	0.9
5.2	5.0	4.0	4.5	3.2	3.4	3.4	3.8	3.4	4.0	3.5	3.5	3.6	4.1	4.2	3.8	2.0	2.9
12.3	12.2	10.7	9.4	9.6	9.7	10.0	10.6	10.5	9.7	10.3	12.1	6.8	7.3	9.8	10.5	8.0	9.9
6.2	6.5	5.8	5.5	5.6	5.5	5.5	5.4	5.4	5.2	4.8	5.7	4.1	3.8	4.4	4.8	3.3	4.6
3.8	3.4	3.5	3.2	3.0	3.6	3.6	3.8	4.0	3.4	3.2	3.4	2.0	2.3	3.4	3.6	2.4	3.1
1.9	1.9	0.6	0.5	0.4	0.4	0.5	1.1	0.8	0.7	1.8	2.2	0.5	1.1	1.7	1.7	2.1	1.8
0.4	0.4	0.8	0.2	0.6	0.2	0.4	0.3	0.3	0.4	0.5	0.8	0.2	0.1	0.3	0.4	0.2	0.4
3.5	2.1	0.8	0.4	2.5	1.6	2.2	2.6	1.6	2.7	2.3	1.4	0.7	2.2	5.4	2.8	0.4	2.1
1.6	0.8	0.1	0.2	1.8	1.0	1.3	1.7	0.8	2.0	1.1	0.1	0.7	1.7	3.2	1.5	‡	1.4
0.6	1.2	0.1	‡	‡	0.1	0.1	0.1	0.3	0.1	0.4	0.7	‡	0.1	0.5	0.3	‡	0.1
0.8	0.1	0.3	0.2	0.4	0.4	0.5	0.4	0.3	0.4	0.4	0.2	‡	0.2	1.2	0.4	0.2	0.4
0.1	‡	‡	‡	‡	‡	0.1	0.1	‡	0.1	0.2	0.1	‡	0.1	0.3	0.2	0.2	0.1
0.4	‡	0.3	‡	0.3	0.1	0.2	0.3	0.2	0.1	0.2	0.3	‡	0.1	0.2	0.4	‡	0.1

to identify underlying compensable factors. One general method called the factor comparison approach identifies five major components: skill, responsibility, mental effort, physical effort, and working conditions. Each of these, in turn, has a number of degrees attached, with equivalent points. Table 9–6 is an example of a scoring scheme

TABLE 9–6
Points assigned to factors and degrees

	Percent	1st degree	2d degree	3d degree	4th degree	5th degree	6th degree	Weight in percent
Skill	50							
1. Education and job knowledge		12	24	36	48	60	72	12
2. Experience and training		24	48	72	96	120	144	24
3. Initiative and ingenuity		14	28	42	56	70	84	14
Effort	15							
4. Physical demand		10	20	30	40	50	60	10
5. Mental and/or visual demand		5	10	15	20	25	30	5
Responsibility	20							
6. Equipment or tools		6	12	18	24	30	36	6
7. Material or product		7	14	21	28	35	42	7
8. Safety of others		3	6	9	12	15	18	3
9. Work of others		4	8	12	16	20	24	4
Job conditions	15							
10. Working conditions		10	20	30	40	50	60	10
11. Unavoidable hazards		5	10	15	20	25	30	5
Total	100%	100%	100%	100%	100%	100%	100%	100%

Source: Zollitsch and Langsner, *Wage and Salary Administration* 2d. ed. (Cincinnati: Southwestern, 1970), p. 186.

for a point method job evaluation study. Once jobs are identified and valued, grade levels are applied given the number of points each has associated with it and wages negotiated by grade. Table 9–7 shows point and grade levels.

TABLE 9–7
Grade structure

Grade	Points assigned
1	100–119
2	120–139
3	140–159
4	160–179
5	180–199
6	200–219
7	220–239
8	240–259

Pay may also depend on some other considerations. For example, a contract may specify a step increment based on seniority. Thus, two individuals performing within the same job may receive different pay levels based on differences in job tenure. Entitlement to vacations may be based on seniority, too. Sometimes pay for certain periods of time not worked requires earlier or later attendance. It may be common practice for a contract to require attendance the last working day preceding and the first working day following a holiday to receive pay for the day(s) off.

Some pay is determined by factors outside of the company's control or by custom and tradition. Some other types are determined by a company's profits or work unit's productivity. We will examine some of these next.

The first major subfactor is pay for time not worked. Holidays and vacations are broadly known examples. Other contracts may include sick leave. Probably the most important recent development here is to maintain incomes during temporary income downturns. This feature is supplementary unemployment benefits (SUB), a major part of past and present auto industry agreements. Figure 9–5 contains the current SUB provision for Ford Motor Company and the UAW. SUB provides income from a trust fund to add to required state unemployment insurance benefits. Typically the addition enables a worker to maintain income at levels between 90 percent and 95 percent of regular straight-time wages. Unfortunately, if layoffs are severe in magnitude and of long duration, benefits may exceed the funds available to pay them. This occurred during the 1975 cutbacks in the auto industry.

FIGURE 9–5
SUB section of UAW-Ford contract*

Part B
Supplemental unemployment benefit
plan
Article I
Eligibility for benefits

Section 1. Eligibility for a regular benefit

An employee shall be eligible for a regular benefit for any week beginning on or after **November 1, 1976,** if with respect to such week he:

a. Was on a qualifying layoff, as described in Section 3 of this article, for all or part of the week;

b. Received a state system benefit not currently under protest by the company or was ineligible for a state system benefit only for one or more of the following reasons:

1. He did not have prior to layoff a suffcient period of employment, or suffcient earnings, covered by the state system;

2. Exhaustion of his state system benefit rights;

3. The period he worked or because his pay (from the company and from any other employer(s)) for the week equaled or exceeded the amount which disqualifies him for a state system benefit or "waiting week" credit; or because he was employed full-time by an employer other than the company;

4. He was serving a "waiting week" of layoff under the state system during a period while he had sufficient seniority to work in the plant but was laid off out of line of seniority in accordance with the terms of the collective bargaining agreement; provided, that the provisions of this item (4) shall not be applicable to a layoff under the provisions of Section 16(d) or Section 21 of Article VIII of the collective bargaining agreement;

5. The week was a second "waiting week" within his benefit year under the state system, or was a state system "waiting week" immediately following a week for which he received a state system benefit or occurring within less than 52 weeks since his last state system "waiting week";

6. He refused an offer of work by the company which he had an option to refuse under an applicable collective bargaining agreement or which he could refuse without disqualification under Section 3(b)(3) of this article;

7. He was on layoff because he was unable to do work offered by the company while able to perform other work in the plant to which he would have been entitled if he had had sufficient seniority;

8. He failed to claim a state system benefit if by reason of his pay received or receivable from the company for the week such state system benefit would have amounted to less than $2;

9. He was receiving pay for military service with respect to a period following his release from active duty therein; or was on short-term active duty of 30 days or less, for required military training, in a National Guard, Reserve or similar unit, or was on short-term active duty of 30 days or less because he was called to active service in the National Guard, Reserve or similar unit by state or federal authorities in case of public emergency;

10. He was entitled to statutory benefits for retirement or disability which he received or could have received while working full-time;

11. Because of the circumstances set forth under Section 3(b) (4) of this article which existed during only part of a week of unemployment under the applicable state system; or

12. He was denied a state system benefit and it is determined that, under the circumstances, it would be contrary to the intent of the plan to deny him a benefit;

* SUB = **Supplementary unemployment benefits.**

FIGURE 9–5 (*continued*)

    c. Has met any registration and reporting requirements of an employment office of the applicable state system, except that this subparagraph shall not apply to an employee who was ineligible for a state system benefit or "waiting week" credit for the week only because of the reason specified in item (3) of Subsection (*b*) of this section (period of work, amount of pay or full-time employment by an employer other than the company) or the reason specified in item (8) of Subsection (*b*) of this section (failure to claim a state system benefit which would have amounted to less than $2) or the reason specified in the second clause of item (9) of Subsection (*b*) of this section (short-term active duty of 30 days or less, for required military training, in a National Guard, Reserve or similar unit, or was on short-term active duty of 30 days or less because he was called to active service in the National Guard, Reserve or similar unit by state or federal authorities in case of public emergency);

    d. Had to his credit a credit unit;

    e. Did not receive an unemployment benefit under any contract or program of another employer or under any other "SUB" plan of the company (and was not eligible for such a benefit under a contract or program of another employer with whom he had greater seniority than with the company or under any other "SUB" plan of the company in which he had credit units which were credited earlier than his oldest credit units under the plan);

    f. Was not eligible for an automatic short week benefit;

    g. Qualified for a benefit of at least $2; and

    h. Has made a benefit application in accordance with procedures established by the company hereunder and, if he was ineligible for a state system benefit only for the reason set forth in item (2) of Subsection 1(*b*) of this article, is able to work, is available for work, and has not failed (1) to maintain an active registration for work with the state employment service, (2) to do what a reasonable person would do to obtain work and (3) to apply for or to accept suitable work of which he has been notified by the employment service or by the company.

<h3 style="text-align:center">Article II
Amount of benefits</h3>

Section 1. Regular benefits

    a. The regular benefit payable to an eligible employee for any week shall be an amount which, when added to his state benefit and other compensation, will equal 95 percent of his weekly after-tax pay, minus $7.50 if the layoff began before January 1, 1977 and $12.50 if the layoff began thereafter, to take into account work-related expenses not incurred; provided, however, that such benefit shall not exceed $90 for any week with respect to which the employee is not receiving state system benefits because of a reason listed in item (2) or (6) of Section 1(*b*) of Article I and is laid off or continues on layoff by reason of having refused to accept work when recalled pursuant to the collective bargaining agreement or having refused an offer by the company of other available work at the same plant or at another plant in the same labor market area (as defined in Section 3(*b*)(3) of Article I); except that refusal by skilled tool and die, maintenance and construction or power house employees or apprentices of work other than work in tool room departments, maintenance departments and power house departments, respectively, shall not result in the application of the maximum provided for in this paragraph.

    b. An otherwise eligible employee entitled to a benefit reduced because of ineligibility (or eligibility for a leveling week benefit) with respect to part of the week, as provided in Section 3(*d*) of Article I (reason for layoff or eligibility for a disability, pension, or retirement benefit), will receive one fifth of a regular benefit computed under Subsection (*a*) of this section for each work day of the week in which he is otherwise eligible.

Source: *Benefit Plans and Agreements between Ford Motor Company and the UAW* (Dearborn, Mich.: Labor Relations Staff, Ford Motor Company, November 1976), pp. 148–51, 155–56.

Another subfactor in pay determination is profit or productivity gain sharing. Employers favor these types of plans because pay is related to their ability to pay and the fortunes of the company are of greater salience to the workers. Profit sharing has met with mixed success, largely because a large part of profitability is determined by factors external to the firm like raw material prices and finished product demand. Productivity gain sharing divides the benefits of the increased effectiveness of employees and introduction of new equipment between labor and management. Probably one of the better examples of this type is the 1959 USW-Kaiser Steel agreement which allowed the company to introduce new equipment in return for guaranteeing job security and sharing cost savings.

One type of plan which has been applied in a number of companies and has some track record of success is the Scanlon Plan. Under this arrangement labor cost reductions are specifically identified and divided between labor and management, usually in an 80/20 ratio. This establishes a high degree of contingency between labor efficiency and wages and reduces the likelihood of individual competition or recognition since the savings are generally shared plantwide. We will return to the Scanlon Plan in our discussion of bargaining strategies in Chapter 12.

Other considerations

As we mentioned previously, employers generally favor long-term contracts while unions generally oppose them because of the unpredictability of the economy. To obtain a long-term contract, a company may agree to a "wage reopener" clause enabling the union to enter a limited bargaining arrangement during specified subsequent periods to renegotiate wage levels only.

HOURS

Obviously, wage levels are tied in with hour issues to some extent, especially in relation to overtime. What we are primarily looking at here are restrictions, over and above those required by law, on the employer's scheduling of work and workers.

Overtime

Overtime is both a blessing and a curse. It is a blessing to persons desiring more income, but a curse to those desiring additional leisure. Generally, labor seeks to penalize management additionally for using overtime by attempting to raise the premium level from 50 percent to

100 percent or more, especially for weekends and holidays. While the federal wage and hour laws applicable to most employers require payment of an overtime premium after the first 40 hours in a given week, unions may seek to impose the premium after 8 hours in a given day. Contracts also specify rules for determining who is entitled to overtime when it is available. Recently, the UAW has negotiated the right of employees to refuse to work over 54 hours in a given week in the auto industry. Figure 9–6 portrays the overtime provisions of the current Ford-UAW contract.

Since the contract can specify the length of the working day before overtime is required, a union may negotiate for a less than eight-hour day. Little success has been achieved here, although Local 3 of the International Brotherhood of Electrical Workers in New York managed to set 25 hours as its work week during 1962 negotiations. Few workers actually worked as little as 25 hours, but overtime began at that point.

FIGURE 9–6
Ford-UAW overtime clauses

Appendix H
Memorandum of understanding
voluntary overtime

Introduction

The parties recognize that the operations of the company are highly integrated. An interruption at one stage of the production process, whether during the regular workday, workweek, or overtime or other premium hours, can cause costly interruptions of the process. Thus regular attendance not only on straight-time, but during overtime periods as well, is essential.

It is recognized that employes should be able to exercise discretion concerning the acceptance of certain overtime assignments consistent with the needs of the company. It is also recognized that management needs sufficient notice of employee availability to work in order to plan efficient operations.

The provisions of this memorandum of understanding represent an accommodation between the needs of the company and the desire of individual employees for an option to decline overtime work assignments.

Part A. Right to decline certain
overtime assignments

Except as otherwise provided in Part B hereof:

1. **Daily overtime**

    Hours in excess of nine (9) hours worked per shift shall be voluntary, except as otherwise provided in this memorandum of understanding, for an employee who shall have notified the company in accordance with Paragraph 16.

2. **Saturday Overtime**

    Employees may be required to work Saturdays; however, except as otherwise provided in this memorandum of understanding, an employee who has worked two or more consecutive Saturdays may decline to work the following (third) Saturday provided (a) he shall have notified the company in accordance with Paragraph 16, and (b) he has not been absent for any reason on any day during the week preceding the Saturday. For purposes of this paragraph, Saturday work shall not include hours worked on Saturday by employees regularly scheduled to work Saturday or any portion thereof as the normal fifth day worked

FIGURE 9–6 (*continued*)

such as (1) an employee whose shift starts Friday and continues into Saturday, or (2) an employee who is assigned to work on no. 1 shift (midnight) operations regularly schedule to start with the no. 1 shift (midnight) Tuesday.

3. **Sunday overtime**

Except as otherwise provided in this memorandum of understanding, overtime work on Sundays shall be voluntary; provided, however, that (a) the employee shall have notified the company in accordance with Paragraph 16, and (b) the employee has not been absent for any reason on any day during the week preceding such Sunday, except for a Saturday which he declined to work pursuant to Paragraph 2 above. For purposes of this paragraph, Sunday work shall not include those hours worked on Sunday which are part on an employee's normal five-day workweek (Sunday P.M. through Friday A.M.).

4. **Daily and Saturday overtime—Car and truck assembly**
   plants and tractor assembly operations
   Notwithstanding Paragraphs 1 and 2, above, the following procedure shall govern employees in the car and truck assembly plants and in the tractor assembly operations, except as otherwise provided in this memorandum of understanding.
   a. Management shall have the right to designate, during a model year period, beginning at the completion of the model launch exemption period stated in Paragraph 9, below, and ending two weeks preceding the announced model build-out date, six Saturdays as nonvoluntary overtime workdays. All other Saturdays are voluntary, except as otherwise provided in this memorandum of understanding, and employees may decline to work any other Saturday during such model year, provided (a) he shall have notified the company in accordance with paragraph 16 and (b) he has not been absent for any reason on any day during the week preceding any Saturday which he elects not to work.
   b. In such plants or operations, daily hours in excess of ten hours worked per shift and Saturday hours in excess of eight hours per shift shall be voluntary, except as otherwise provided in this memorandum of understanding.

5. **Employees working on necessary, continuous**
   seven-day operations
   Notwithstanding Paragraphs 1 through 3 inclusive employees on necessary, continuous seven-day operations shall be governed by the following:
   a. Daily overtime—Hours in excess of nine (9) hours worked per shift shall be voluntary except as otherwise provided in this memorandum of understanding for an employee who shall have notified the company in accordance with Paragraph 16.
   b. First regularly scheduled day off in the workweek—Employees may be required to work one of their regular days off in a workweek; however, except as otherwise provided in this memorandum of understanding, an employee who has worked one of his regular days off in two (2) or more consecutive weeks may decline to work one of his regular days off in the following (third) week provided (1) he shall have notified the company in accordance with Paragraph 16, and (2) he has not been absent for any reason on any of his five preceding regularly scheduled days of work.
   c. Second regularly scheduled day off in the workweek—Except as otherwise provided in this memorandum of understanding, an employee may not be required to work a second regularly scheduled day off in a workweek; provided, however, that (1) the employee shall have notified the company in accordance with Paragraph 16, and (2) the employee has not been absent for any reason on any of his five preceding regularly scheduled days of work.

6. **Exempt operations**

Employees on the following operations shall be exempt from the provisions of this memorandum of understanding: (a) those steel operations to which Article IX, Section 14 of the collective bargaining agreement applies, (b) railroad operations, and (c) over-the-road trucking operations.

7. **Emergencies**

The provisions of this memorandum of understanding that limit or restrict the right of the company to require employees to work daily overtime or Saturdays or Sundays shall be

FIGURE 9–6 (*continued*)

suspended in any plant whose operations are interrupted by emergency situations, such as single breakdowns of four hours or more,* government mandated work, power shortages, strike, fire, tornado, flood, or acts of God, for a period of time necessary to overcome such emergencies.

8. **Critical plants**

   a. Critical plants or parts of plants are those that are crucial to the integrated supply system of the company and whose output is essential to meeting the scheduled production of one or more other plants or of customers, and as a result, must operate, in whole or in part, seven (7) days a week.

   b. The company may, from time to time, designate plants or parts of plants as critical, provided, however, that fifteen (15) days prior to making such designations, it will inform the National Ford Department of the international union, which will indicate its objections, if any, to a plant or plants being so designated.

   c. Any plants or part thereof that the company designates as critical shall, for a period of ninety (90) days after it is so designated, be exempt from the provisions of this memorandum of understanding that limit or restrict the right of the company to require employees to work daily overtime or on Saturdays or Sundays or entitle employees to decline to work at such times.

9. **Changeover or model change**

   a. The provisions of this memorandum of understanding that limit or restrict the right of the company to require employees to work daily overtime or Saturdays or Sundays shall be ineffective in each of the car and truck assembly plants, and tractor assembly operations (a) beginning on a date two (2) weeks preceding the announced build-out date and ending on the build-out date, i.e., when the plant produces for sale the last unit of the model it has been producing; provided, however, the above mentioned provisions may be ineffective for up to two (2) additional weeks, provided the company gives advance notice of supply or other problems which would interfere with the build-out, and (b) for the week in which it launches, i.e., after the build-out, frames the first unit of a new model, and for three (3) weeks thereafter or until the line speed reaches scheduled production, whichever is later.

   b. Said provisions shall likewise be ineffective during model change time each year in plants other than car and truck assembly plants, or tractor assembly operations for periods to be designated by plant management that shall not exceed, in the aggregate, four (4) weeks. Local unions will be advised in advance of such designated periods.

10. **New plants, new car or truck line programs or new shifts**

   The provisions of this memorandum of understanding that limit or restrict the right of the company to require daily overtime work or work on Saturdays or Sundays shall be ineffective:

   a. At any plant the company builds or buys and remodels for a period of one year after regular production in such plant starts;

   b. At any car and truck assembly plant at which the company launches a new car line or new truck line or a car or truck line that is new to that plant for a period of one year after regular production starts in such plant and ending with that model year build-out, i.e., when the plant produces for sale the last unit of the model it has been producing, except an employee who has worked two or more consecutive Saturdays may decline to work the following (third) Saturday provided (1) he shall have notified the company in accordance with Paragraph 16; and (2) he has not been absent for any reason on any day during the week preceding the Saturday. For purposes of this paragraph, Saturday work shall not include hours worked on Saturday by employees regularly scheduled to work Saturday or any portion thereof

---

* Any breakdown is to be considered justification for suspending the limitations on the company's right to require overtime work for purposes of correcting the breakdown itself; the company's right to suspend such limitations for the purpose of making up lost production is, however, in the case of breakdowns, limited to production lost as the result of single breakdowns of four or more hours.

FIGURE 9–6 (*continued*)

as the normal fifth day worked such as (1) an employee whose shift starts Friday and continues into Saturday, or (2) an employee who is assigned to work on No. 1 Shift (Midnight) operations regularly scheduled to start with the no. 1 shift (midnight) Tuesday; provided, however, that in such a plant, a model change period specified in Paragraph 9(a) shall not be applicable at such plant at the beginning of the following model year.

 c. At any car and truck assembly plant for a period of six months from the time a production shift is added or restored at such plant.

11. Concerted activity

 a. Any right to decline daily overtime or Saturday or Sunday work that this memorandum of understanding confers on any employee may be exercised only by each employee acting separately and individually, without collusion, conspiracy, or agreement with, or the influence of, any other employee or employees or the union or pursuant to any other concerted action or decision. No employee shall seek by any means to cause or influence any other employee to decline to work overtime. Violation by any employee of the terms, purpose or intent of this paragraph shall, in addition to subjecting him to discipline, nullify for one month (not including the periods mentioned in Paragraph 9, above) his right to decline overtime.

 b. The company shall have the right to suspend for a period of two weeks (not including the periods mentioned in Paragraph 9, above) as to an affected plant the provisions of this memorandum of understanding that entitle employees to decline to work daily overtime or Saturdays or Sundays in each event employees collusively, concertedly, or in response to the influence of any employee, or group of employees, or the union (1) fail or refuse to report for daily overtime work or work on Saturdays or Sundays that they have not declined as herein provided or (2) decline, as so provided, daily overtime work or work on Saturday or Sunday. If employees who are scheduled to work daily overtime in a plant or department or on a Saturday or Sunday fail or refuse to work as scheduled in significantly greater numbers than the company's experience under this memorandum of understanding can reasonably lead it to expect, such evidence should be carefully considered by the impartial umpire in any decision involving the question of whether their failing or refusing to work the scheduled hours was collusive, concerted, or influenced by other persons. The union shall have the right specially to submit to the impartial umpire pursuant to Article VII, Section 9 any claim that the company has acted wrongly in suspending the provisions of this memorandum of understanding as to employees or a plant. If the umpire sustains the union's claim, the company shall, within 60 days of the date of the umpire's award, give each affected employee the right to decline overtime work on as many daily overtime days or Saturdays or Sundays as such right was suspended.

12. Local option

Nothing in this memorandum of understanding shall make ineffective any local past practice or agreement concerning voluntary overtime that is mutually satisfactory to the local union and the plant management. Local unions and plant managements may (1) continue in effect such practices or agreements as are now in effect, or (2) comply with the terms of this memorandum of understanding, or (3) agree from time to time to suspend the terms of this memorandum for a fixed period of time during which period production employees shall be governed solely by the provisions of Article IV, Section 6, excluding any reference therein to Appendix H, except for this subparagraph.

13. Work force supplementation

In order to implement this memorandum of understanding, the company may supplement the work force. The following are illustrative of actions which the company may take to do so:

 a. Temporary part-time employees may be hired in accordance with the terms of the memorandum of understanding—Temporary part-time employees, but shall not be entitled to Saturday or Sunday premium pay, except as required by law, until they are qualified to perform the work to which they are assigned, or for fifteen (15) working days, whichever is sooner.

FIGURE 9–6 (*concluded*)

    b. Nothing herein shall preclude a plant from expanding its work force beyond the normal requirements of its operations by hiring new employees and adopting a program pursuant to which employees of said plant may have one (1) or two (2) days off per week (which days need not be Saturdays or Sundays); provided, however, that work performed on Saturday or Sunday shall be at present premium rates. Plans for such a program shall be discussed in advance with the National Ford Department of the international union, and any system of rotating days off among some or all of the employees shall be by mutual agreement between the local union and the plant management.

14. Legal prohibitions

The optional overtime provisions in this memorandum of understanding shall not apply in any instance in which they would make it impossible to run an operation without violating a federal, state, or local law or ordinance.

15. SUB

Daily overtime hours or Saturday or Sunday work that an employee declines under the terms of this memorandum of understanding shall be deemed "compensated or available hours" within the meaning of the Supplemental Unemployment Benefit Plan.

16. Notice

With respect to all voluntary hours provided for in this memorandum of understanding in a given week, the employee may decline to work such hours if he notifies his supervisor on a form to be provided by the company before the end of the shift on the preceding Wednesday provided he has been notified of the overtime schedules for such week not later than the preceding day. If the employee is not so notified, he shall give such notice to his supervisor before the end of the shift following the day of such notice, provided that if he is not so notified until the week in which the overtime is scheduled, he shall give such notice by the end of the shift in which he receives such notice from the company.

    Source: *Agreements between Ford Motor Company and the UAW* (Dearborn, Mich.: Labor Relations Staff, Ford Motor Company, November 1976), pp. 148–57.

Shift differentials and preference

Normally, day shifts are preferred by workers. To compensate workers on other shifts, premiums over the normal rate are paid. Rules may also be devised to allocate people to shifts. Seniority may entitle one to a choice of shifts.

Other considerations

The contract may also call for a minimum pay period if workers appear for work and none is available. Rules may be devised to state where a shift will start and whether clean-up time is to be compensated. Rest and relief periods, as well as lunch breaks would be included in work schedule negotiations.

TERMS AND CONDITIONS OF EMPLOYMENT

Terms and conditions of employment are related to a variety of majority issues: job security, safety, work rules, union security, management rights, training, grievance procedures, and so on.

Job security

Job security issues are of critical importance to both employers and unions. Employers prefer flexibility in decision making. Generally, they would prefer to be free to hire or layoff employees as the work load requires. In the construction industry, this, in fact, is the norm. Employees work for a contractor as long as needed and then move on to projects undertaken by other contractors. In industrial employment the same norm generally holds, although there are usually some restrictions on how layoffs will be performed and what rights employees may have to transfer or bid on other jobs.

Because of many employees' long-term association with only one employer, workers perceive their position as holding future potential value, that they have, in fact, property rights. Thus, the greater one's investment of labor has been to an organization, the greater is its expected obligation to the employee. As a result, contract terms are negotiated to recognize property rights and to build in restrictions or rules constraining employer conduct in the use of labor.

Since job security may be either an individual or a collective issue, as in a layoff or a plant closing, we will arbitrarily divide them into those categories for our discussion.

Seniority systems. Seniority acts as an allocative mechanism for a variety of job protection and opportunity issues. In the opportunity area, unions may demand that employers post notices of vacant jobs and that persons eligible to fill that job and who volunteer be promoted on the basis of seniority, although employers may bargain for some showing of competence for promotion. Layoffs also usually take place in inverse order of seniority, thereby protecting the most senior worker for the longest period. Besides overall plant seniority, employees may have departmental seniority, although these may be suspect from a discrimination standpoint if minorities are underrepresented in certain departments.[6] Besides insulation from layoff, seniority may enable someone to "bump" a less senior employee in another department where the cutback impact is less. Figure 9–7 details the process in a typical layoff and bumping procedure.

Collective job rights. Any employer action which directly influences the job security of employees is a mandatory bargaining issue. This may involve issues such as labor-saving equipment, subcontracting, moving production facilities, plant closings, and so on. The NLRB and the courts generally take a very employee oriented view of what constitutes a job security issue. For example, the Supreme Court has held that unilateral subcontracting of bargaining unit work without

---

[6] *Franks v. Bowman Transportation*, 12 FEP Cases 549 (U.S. Supreme Court, 1976).

FIGURE 9–7
Seniority in layoff and bumping

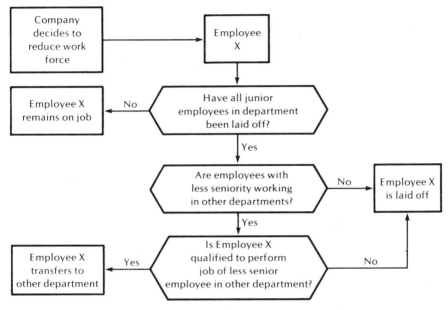

negotiating with the union is an unfair labor practice.[7] The Court further held that the closing of facilities (even if the closing is regulated by state agencies) must be bargained with the union, if it requests.[8] The union must be given the opportunity to propose alternatives and/or to bargain for severance benefits.

Safety and health

Safety clauses are of less importance recently since they have been largely superseded by the Occupational Safety and Health Act. Nevertheless, unions are free to demand standards higher than OSHA requirements. Typical issues related to safety might focus on periodic physical exams for persons in possibly toxic environments and the establishment of joint labor-management safety committees to identify and recommend action on potential hazards. Safety clauses may also allow employees to make individual decisions about whether to commence or continue a task where they believe unsafe conditions exist and proper protection against hazards has not been taken.

---

[7] *Fibreboard Paper Products Corp.* v. *NLRB*, 379 U.S. 203 (1964).

[8] *Order of Railroad Telegraphers* v. *Chicago and North Western Railroad Co.*, 362 U.S. 330 (1960).

Work rules

While management generally reserves the right to control production, the union may insist on retaining the opportunity to object to increased production rates, negotiate over production standards for new equipment, and bargain over the establishment or reduction of work groups and crews.

Work rules may also establish that certain job classifications are entitled to perform specific job tasks. These clauses will also restrict the use of supervisors in doing work of rank and file employees. The more different job classifications and the broader the set of tasks, the more likely these rules will be established. Another way of handling these problems is for the contract to specify that job descriptions will be jointly established by the union and management to define jobs within the bargaining unit.

Union security

The union usually desires some degree of security in its day-to-day operations to maintain its majority status. A number of different levels of union security may be negotiated. Except in states where right-to-work laws are in effect, a union can seek most of the following levels of security (ranging from most to least secure):

1. Closed shop—available only to the construction industry, this level requires the firm to hire only union members;
2. Union shop—requires that any bargaining unit employee who has been with the firm a specific length of time (but not less than 30 days) must become a union member as a condition of continued employment;
3. Agency shop—requires that any bargaining unit employee who is not a union member must pay a service fee to the union;
4. Maintenance of membership—any bargaining unit employee who becomes a union member must remain one as a condition of continued employment.

There are some variations on these, but the four listed above are the major levels of union security.

From a bookkeeping standpoint, the union's role is eased if it wins a checkoff. Here the company agrees to withhold union dues of consenting employees from their pay and forward the amount directly to the union.

Management rights

Management frequently insists on contract language which permits it to control the scheduling of work, hiring of employees, disciplining of employees for rule violations and so forth. These clauses preserve within management's discretion those decisions and actions which are not explicitly modified by the contract.

Grievance procedures

Since the management rights clause of most contracts retains for the employer the right to assign and to discipline employees, what happens if an employee believes that management has erred in its assignment or discipline? What recourse is available? As an individual, there may be none. As a union, some concerted action, like a strike, may gain redress. But the employer seeks to avoid unpredicted strikes. So there is motivation for both parties to devise a grievance procedure for settling differences.

Under the Taft-Hartley Act, employees may individually present grievances to representatives of management. As a practical matter, the grievance procedure specifies the steps available to the employee in getting a grievance heard and redressed. The positions of individuals involved and the number of steps vary. We will examine these variances in detail in Chapter 13, "Contract Administration." One procedure, however, is generally agreed upon by employers and unions, and that is to provide that a neutral third party resolve continuing disputes between the parties.

Allied with grievance procedures are provisions for union representation in the work place. We noted before in Chapter 5 that unions elected stewards to represent work group members. Contract terms may be devised to specify the rights of stewards to be away from their jobs to attend to union business, to be entitled to office space in the plant, and to have superseniority for job security reasons.

Strikes and lockouts

Labor and management may agree to avoid work stoppages during the contract by including no-strike no-lockout clauses. If a strike occurs, the union must take steps to convince its members to return to work.

Training and apprenticeships

These clauses specify the individual responsibilities of labor and management in the design and administration of programs for bargaining unit members. Methods used in hiring or promotion into these programs will also be included.

Duration of the agreement

The parties must also agree on the period of time the contract will be in effect and whether or not specific sections can be modified or renegotiated during the life of the agreement.

"Zipper" clauses

These are often inserted on the insistence of management. Essentially, a zipper clause states that the contract constitutes the entire agreement between labor and management and any issue not mentioned is solely within management's prerogative to change.

PREVALENCE OF CONTRACT PROVISIONS IN RECENT NEGOTIATIONS

Obviously, we have not dealt with every unique issue that might interest a given set of parties. Table 9–8 does, however. This table

TABLE 9–8
Basic clauses in union contracts (1976)

Clause	Percent containing
Contract term	
1 year	5
2 years	21
3 years	70
4 or more	4
Discharge and discipline	97
Insurance	
Life	97
Accidental death and dismemberment	65
Sickness and accident	82
Hospitalization	96
Surgical	93
Major medical	65
Doctors' visits	51
Miscellaneous medical expenses	62
Maternity benefits	69
Prescription drugs	16
Dental care	15
Optical care	3
Pensions (regulated by Pension Act of 1974)	99
Grievance and arbitration	99
Steps specified	96
Arbitration	96
Income maintenance	48
Severance pay	39
Supplemental unemployment benefits	17
Hours and overtime	99
Daily work schedules	82

TABLE 9–8 (*continued*)

Clause	Percent containing
Weekly work schedules	64
Overtime premiums	95
Sixth day premiums	17
Seventh day premiums	18
Pyramiding of overtime	64
Distribution of overtime work	58
Acceptance of overtime	33
Restrictions on overtime	35
Weekend premiums	69
Lunch, rest, and cleanup	42
Waiting time	16
Standby time	3
Travel time	14
Voting time	4
Holidays	
None specified	1
Less than 6	0
6, 6½	6
7, 7½	10
8, 8½	12
9, 9½	29
10, 10½	20
11, 11½	12
12 or more	10
Eligibility for holiday pay	85
Layoff, rehiring and work sharing	
Seniority	85
Sole factor	42
Notice to employees	
No minimum	9
1–2 days	36
3–4 days	22
5–6 days	8
7 or more	34
Bumping	
Manufacturing	63
Nonmanufacturing	30
Recall	75
Work sharing	20
Technical displacement	7
Leaves of absence	
Personal	73
Union	72
Maternity	38
Funeral	74
Civic	75
Paid sick	23
Unpaid sick	49
Military	66
Management and union rights	99
Management rights statements	69
Restrictions on management	81
Subcontracting	40

TABLE 9–8 *(concluded)*

Clause	Percent containing
Supervisory work	57
Technological changes	19
Plant shutdown or relocation	17
In-plant union representatives	45
Union access to plant	58
Union bulletin boards	68
Union right to information	58
Union activity on company time	39
Union-management cooperation	14
Seniority	92
Probationary periods at hire	71
Loss of seniority	77
Seniority lists	49
As factor in promotion	70
As factor in transfers	48
Status of supervisors	36
Strikes and lockouts	93
Unconditional pledges (strike)	57
Unconditional pledges (lockouts)	63
Limitation of union liability	43
Penalties for strikers	38
Picket line observance	20
Union security	97
Union shop	63
Modified union shop	11
Agency shop	4
Maintenance of membership	3
Hiring only	1
Checkoff only	15
Checkoff with other provisions	86
Vacations	96
Three weeks or more	85
Four weeks or more	76
Five weeks or more	42
Six weeks or more	10
Work requirement	55
Vacation scheduling	87
Wages	
Deferred increases	88
Cost-of-living adjustments	36
Wage reopeners	8
Shift differentials	82
Incentive plans	36
Hiring rates	27
Wage progression	43
Working conditions and safety	
Occupational safety and health	82
Hazardous work acceptance	15
Safety and health committees	39
Guarantees against discrimination	83

Source: Compiled from *Collective Bargaining: Negotiations and Contracts* (Washington: Bureau of National Affairs, updated as necessary).

contains basic contract provisions by type and frequency of appearance. In examining it, you may get a different perspective on the types of issues involved in bargaining and their likely appearance in a contract.

SUMMARY

Both labor and management have general goals they pursue in collective bargaining. Labor is concerned with economic gain and job security while management pursues greater predictability in relationships and freedom in decision making.

The law related to bargaining issues requires that labor and management be willing to bargain over wages, hours, and terms and conditions of employment. These relate to economics, scheduling, and job security.

Economic issues within these primarily relate to the magnitude, form, and determinants of pay. Scheduling relates to overtime, time not worked, and shift arrangements. Job security deals with a myriad of issues like promotions and layoffs, plant closings, seniority and the like.

Recent data show a broad spectrum of possible contract clauses. Most contracts contain procedures specifying the roles of each party in the agreement and procedures for peacefully resolving interpretive disagreements during the life of the contract.

SUGGESTED READINGS

Slichter, Sumner H., Healy, James J., and Livernash, E. Robert. *The Impact of Collective Bargaining on Management* (Washington: Brookings Institution, 1960).

Sloane, Arthur A., and Witney, Fred. *Labor Relations*, 2d ed. (Englewood Cliffs, N.J.: Prentice-Hall, 1977), chaps. 7–10.

DISCUSSION QUESTIONS

1. From either an employer or union standpoint, what do you see the advantages and disadvantages of longer contracts, say three years, as being?
2. How far should a union be able to go in negotiating job security for its members?
3. What are some long-run ramifications that have come to plague management as a result of their approach to or concession of certain bargaining issues?
4. How would you expect a craft union to differ from an industrial union in terms of the issues it emphasized?

5. From an employer's standpoint, point out the advantages and disadvantages associated with agreeing to a union shop clause.

6. Every likelihood exists that some significant national agreement will be renegotiated this year. Depending on which it is: United Mineworkers-Bituminous Coal Operators Association, United Auto Workers-A "Big 3" Auto Maker, Teamsters-National Freight Haulers, or Steelworkers and Basic Steel Industry; prepare a list of what you expect will be the major issues in this year's negotiations. Which will be the most difficult to resolve? Why?

10

CONTRACT NEGOTIATION

The negotiation of a labor agreement is of critical importance to both parties. Within its scope, the agreement will govern the relationship between the parties for a definite contractual period. For the organization, the agreement will have definite cost impacts and will specifically constrain management decision making. For the union, the contract will spell out the rights of its membership in their employment relationship.

Why does a contract emerge in the form that it does? What forces interact to lead to a certain specification in terms? What strategies are used by the parties to obtain features important to them? What is the usual sequence of activities that take place?

In this chapter, we want to step through the bargaining sequence first, so we can see the activities of both parties. Then we will look at the influence of bargaining power on the outcome. Finally, we will examine the tactics which may be used by the parties to support a position. All of these are inextricably intertwined, but we will separate them as much as possible in our explanation.

As you move through this chapter you should look for answers to some of the following questions:

1. How do both management and the union prepare for negotiations?
2. What are the methods both parties use to maintain control of a complex process like contract negotiation?
3. What are the consequences of using certain bargaining tactics on both the process and outcome of negotiations?
4. What are the differences between distributive and integrative bargaining, and what conditions appear necessary for integrative bargaining to take place?

BARGAINING ACTIVITIES

Except for initial contracts, the timing of bargaining activities is determined to a large extent by the expiration of a previous contract and the law. Under the law, if either party desires to modify the agreement at its expiration, it must give the other at least 60 days' notice. Thus, if the contract is not to be extended past its expiration date, the notice must come two months before the contract is due to run out. In all negotiations, initial or otherwise, the parties are required to meet at reasonable times to bargain.

Different strategies may be used across bargaining situations, but, in general, Figure 10–1 portrays the sequence of activities likely to be found in the bargaining process.

Prenegotiation activities

Both parties have some idea of how they would like a new contract to be shaped. They either have taken positions during an organizing campaign or have some experience with an existing agreement. Using Figure 10–1 as a general backdrop, let's examine the activities engaged in by the parties.

Union activities. During the term of the contract the union continually receives information about its effects on the membership. It also receives information about other agreements which may fairly be compared to its own.

Since the last contract was negotiated, local negotiating committee members have processed written grievances of the local's membership. The committee has probably reached some conclusions about portions of the contract (for example, allocation of overtime) which are susceptible to more than one interpretation or are viewed as inequitable by the membership.

Locals also are served by the international's field representatives. As a result, members learn about settlements reached by other locals in the same international. They also get more specific indications of the issues the international feels are critically important to include in all contracts.

Settlements by companies and unions in other areas or industries are also important. Certain agreements are seen as pattern setters. For example, the steel and auto agreements often serve as benchmarks against which other unions base their demands.

The relative performance of the employer, in terms of profitability, funding, and so on, is general public knowledge and may be used by the union to gauge the level of its economic demands. Trends in the introduction of new equipment or construction of plants in other geo-

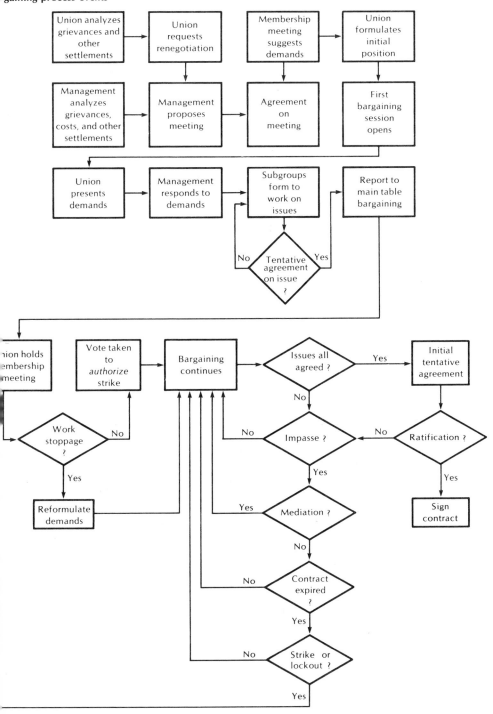

graphical areas may also signal to the local what the magnitude of its bargaining demand should be.

Management activities. Management information gathering parallels the union's. Information on grievances, areas where management is troubled by work rules, and difficulties in recruiting employees at negotiated wages, as well as other information, is gathered. From the pattern of grievances filed, management may be able to anticipate somewhat the thrust of union demands.

Since labor costs are an important aspect in an organization's ability to perform (for example, profitability, allocation of resources, and so forth), and since the employer accounts for these costs on a continuous basis, some estimate of the effects of different union positions should be assessed. These data may enable the company to help calculate how far it would be willing to go to meet economic demands of the union.

Management also assesses settlements in other organizations and industries to anticipate the pattern the union may desire to emulate in its initial set of demands. Besides this information, competitors' settlements provide information on how much of an increase an employer can give and still produce a marketable product while making a profit.

Negotiation requests

Section 8 (d) of the Taft Hartley Act requires the party desiring a renegotiation of the contract (usually the union) to notify the other of its intention and offer to meet to bargain a new agreement. This notice must come at least 60 days before the end of the contract if the requesting party intends to terminate the agreement at that point.

The usual management reply to the union's request is the proposal of a time and place for negotiations to begin. This is usually not immediate and may very often lead to the initial demands not being made until a month or less before the expiration date. After notice is served, both parties commence last minute preparations for bargaining.

Union activities. The activities which take place immediately before actually sitting down at the table begin to diverge between the parties. This divergence reflects the differing goals and organizational properties of the parties. The union is essentially an organization of relatively equal constituents, a political body, with some responsibility to an electorate included in the perceptions and duties of the leadership. The rank and file absolutely expect to improve their contract. They do not expect the negotiating committee to give away any benefits previously won. On the other hand, the company has more information about its own position in hand and can impose a more unitary purpose on its negotiators.

Immediately before going to the bargaining table, the union generally holds a membership meeting. Here the rank and file are told the major issues that the negotiating committee intends to pursue. Their views are solicited to gauge the strength of the rank and file's resolve to obtain these bargaining components. Individual members make suggestions about topics that are specific to their situations. The leadership notes these and may include them in the demands.

After the meeting, the negotiating committee puts together the information gathered from the membership along with its preliminary set of proposals and formulates the package of demands it will make of management at the first meeting.

Management activities.   Ryder, Rehmus, and Cohen suggest that four major areas concern management negotiators immediately prior to sitting down with their union counterparts:

1. Preparation of specific proposals for changes in contract language.
2. Determination of general size of the economic package that the company anticipates offering during the negotiations.
3. Preparation of statistical display and supportive data that the company will use during negotiations.
4. Preparation of a bargaining book for the use of company negotiators.[1]

The first three points are relatively straightforward, although the authors found some variance in their use depending on the company negotiator's assessment of their impact, usefulness, and commitment to a position. On the other hand, bargaining books are generally seen more positively by the bulk of negotiators.

What is a bargaining book? Simply put, it is a cross-referenced file that enables a negotiator to determine quickly what contract clauses would be affected by a proposed change in another area. It also contains the general history behind the development of these specific contract terms. The book may also contain a code alongside the proposals to indicate their relative importance to management. A fairly complex bargaining book might contain information on each of these classifications for a given clause:

1. The history and text of the particular clause as it was negotiated in successive agreements.
2. Comparisons of the company's clause with those of other companies in the industry, together with comments on similarities and differences.
3. The company's experience with the clause, both in operation and concerning the grievances arising thereunder.

---

[1] Meyer S. Ryder, Charles M. Rehmus, and Sanford Cohen, *Management Preparation for Collective Bargaining* (Homewood, Ill.: Dow Jones-Irwin, 1966), p. 53.

4. Legal issues pertaining to the clause, including both NLRB determinations and judicial decisions.

5. Points the company would like to have changed with regard to the clause, differentiated into minimum, maximum, and intermediate possibilities.

6. Points the union may have asked for in the past with regard to changes in the clause, the union's justification for the proposed change, and the arguments used by management to rebut the union's position.

7. Data and exhibits with regard to the clause, including cost, supporting analysis, and so on.

8. Progress with regard to the clause in the current negotiation, together with drafts of various company proposals.[2]

Management thus enters the negotiations with specific positions backed up by hard data. It also should have assessed settlements gained by others and formulated a final settlement it would be willing to live with. It should also have assessed the general tone of union activities. For its part, the union's position may not have coalesced as completely as management's due to the political nature of its demands and the lower degree of predictability of its constituency's response.

Costing contract terms. As noted in Chapter 9 when bargaining issues were discussed, the wage and fringe benefit demand and ultimate settlement will have a definite cost impact for the organization. To be able to make rational choices among possible demands and to counteroffer with an attractive package that will minimize its costs, management must accurately cost the contract.

There are a variety of methods that could be used, varying in their sophistication, but a good example of a mid-range approach is detailed by Richardson and portrayed in Figure 10–2.[3] As you examine the information there closely, you will realize that some of the dynamics in long-term contracts are important. For example, social security tax rates and taxable bases may change during the term of the contract. Unemployment insurance rates may rise or decline depending on the state of the economy and your firm's individual experiences in layoff rates.

Whatever system is used, its use should be systematically coordinated with the bargaining book in negotiations. The technique should allow management to calculate quickly the effects of various union

---

[2] Ibid., pp. 65–66.

[3] Reed C. Richardson, "Positive Collective Bargaining," in Dale Yoder and H. G. Heneman, Jr., eds., *Employee and Labor Relations*, vol. 3 of the *ASPA Handbook of Personnel and Industrial Relations* (Washington, Bureau of National Affairs, 1976), pp. 7–134 through 7–136.

FIGURE 10–2
Costing out changes in contract terms

Changes in costs	Increased cost
1. Direct payroll—annual	
Straight-time earnings—36¢ per hour general increase	
100 employees × 2,080 hours × 36¢	$74,800
Premium earnings—second shift established differential—10¢ per hour	
30 employees × 2,080 hours × 10¢	6,240
Overtime—overtime cost increased by increased straight-time rate—	
average straight-time rate increases 39¢	
39¢ × 12,000 overtime hours × .5 overtime rate	2,340
Bonus	None
Other direct payroll cost increases	None
Total increase in direct payroll costs	$83,460
2. Added costs directly resulting from higher payroll costs—annual	
F.I.C.A.—5.85 percent times increase in average straight-time	
earnings below $9,000 annual	
100 employees × 36¢ × 5.85% × 2,080 hours	$4,380.48
Federal and state unemployment insurance tax	
number of employees × 4,200 × 2.5% tax rate	No change
Workmen's compensation (total cost or estimate)	No change
Other	No change
Total additional direct payroll costs	$4,380.48
3. Nonpayroll costs—annual	
Insurance—company portion	
Health insurance	No change
Dental insurance	None
Eye care	None
Life insurance—added employer	
contribution $100 per year	
$100 × 100 employees	$10,000
Pension costs—fully vested pension reduced from 25 years and age	
65 to 20 years and age 62	
Estimated additional cost	52,000
Miscellaneous	
Tuition reimbursements (addition)	600
Service rewards	No change
Suggestion awards (addition)	350
Loss on employee cafeteria	No change
Overtime meals	No change
Cost of parking lots	No change
Company parties	No change
Personal tools	No change
Personal safety equipment (addition)	1,200
Personal wearing apparel	No change
Profit sharing	No change
Other	No change
Total additional nonpayroll costs—annual	$64,150
4a. Changes in nonwork paid time	
Holidays—2 new holidays added to 6 already in contract	
100 employees × 8 hours × 2 holidays × $3.96 average new wage	$6,336
Vacation—new category added—4 weeks	
(160 hours annual vacation) with 20 or more years service—former	
top was 3 weeks after 15 years	

Changes in costs	Increased cost
Average number of employees affected annually	
15 employees × 40 hours $3.96 average new wage	2,376
Paid lunch time—paid ½ lunch time added to contract	
100 employees × ½ hour × 236 days worked yearly × $3.96	
average new wage	46,728
Paid wash-up time	None
Coffee breaks	No change
Paid time off for union activity—new 1 hour per week per shop steward	
10 shop stewards × $4.20 shop steward average new wage	
× 1 hour × 52 weeks	2,184
Paid sick leave	None
Paid time off over and above workmen's compensation	
paid time	None
Jury service time off—no change	None
Funeral leave time off—no change	None
Paid time off for safety or training—no change	None
Other	None
Total change in hours paid for but not worked—annual	$57,624
4b. Financial data derived from costing out (Items 1–4, above)	
Total increase in contract costs	
Item 1 + item 2 + item 3	$151,990
Average total increase in contract costs per employee payroll hour	
Item 1 + item 2 + item 3 ÷ 2,080 hours	.73
Average total increase in direct payroll costs per man-hour	
Item 1 + item 2 ÷ 2,080 hours ÷ 100 employees	.422
Average total increase in nonpayroll costs per payroll hour per employee	
Item 3 ÷ 2,080 hours ÷ 100 employees	.308
Average total increase in nonwork paid time expense per payroll	
hour per employee	
Item 4 ÷ 100 employees	.277
Average total increase in direct payroll costs per productive (worked)	
hour per employee	
Item 1 + item 2 ÷ 1,888 hours ÷ 100 employees	.49
Average total increase in nonpayroll costs per productive (worked)	
hour per employee	
Item 3 ÷ 1,888 hours ÷ 100 employees	.34

Source: Reed C. Richardson, "Positive Collective Bargaining," in Dale Yoder and H. G. Heneman, Jr., eds., *Employee and Labor Relations*, vol. 3 in the *ASPA Handbook of Personnel and Industrial Relations* (Washington: Bureau of National Affairs, 1976), pp. 7–135 and 7–136.

proposals so that its hand won't be tipped in bargaining by dwelling on a certain proposal too long.

Bargaining meetings

As the parties meet at the table for the first time, the identity of the negotiators becomes known, the opening position of one of the parties (at least) is probably communicated, and a schedule for future meetings may be established.

The negotiators

The union negotiators include the members of the local's negotiating committee. Management is familiar with them since they have been responsible for processing grievances for the union under the old contract. Frequently, the local union's team is augmented by a field representative, regional director, or officer of the international union, depending on the importance of the negotiations.

The makeup of management's team is not as easy to predict. Typically, members will come from areas which have particular interests in the contract (production) or expertise in specific areas to be negotiated (employee benefits manager). The leader of management's team is frequently the top industrial relations executive in the organization, although the position may also be filled by the president of the organization or an outside consultant with experience in negotiations (often an attorney).

Union presentation

While it is not legally required, it is customary that the union presents its demands first. At this presentation, it is likely that it will specify all of the areas of the contract where change is desired. This initial session also allows the union to get all of the grievances or positions developed through the membership meetings onto the table. Obviously, the union does not expect to gain all of these, but as a political organization, it owes an obligation to state the positions of individual members.

Management response

Management may not reply to the union's demands at the initial session, but it does respond at an early session. Usually its response is substantially below what it would ultimately be willing to settle for. As management's position unfolds, if it adheres to its original positions or refuses to move past a particular position, it must provide information requested by the union which management claims would support its position where it is based on an inability to pay.[4]

Bargaining on specific issues

If the issues are complex or the company is large, the negotiating committee and company representatives will frequently divide themselves into subcommittees to negotiate specific issues. For example,

---

[4] *NLRB* v. *Truitt Mfg. Co.*, 351 U.S. 149 (U.S. Supreme Court, 1956).

the contract language on work standards may be handled by a subgroup.

Most of the time, the subgroups do not have the authority to sign off on the issues they discuss, since these issues may form part of a tradeoff package, but they may bring tentative agreements or positions back to the main table for their consideration.

At the main table, issues that will not form part of a combined package or not be used as tradeoffs may be initialed by the parties as finalized for the ultimate settlement. Thus, the final agreement is not necessarily related to a coalescing on all issues simultaneously, but a completion of negotiations on final areas where disagreement existed.

Strike authorization vote

After negotiations are underway, the union usually calls a membership meeting. The negotiating committee reports on the bargaining to the members and requests authorization to call a strike, if necessary. The membership traditionally gives overwhelming approval. This vote does not mean there *will* be a strike, only that the bargainers have the authority to call one after the contract expires.

Tentative settlement

When the negotiators have reached agreement on a new contract, the union team still has some responsibilities to fulfill before the final agreement is signed. In most unions, two hurdles remain to be cleared after the tentative agreement is reached. First, the international union must approve the agreement. This is to insure that a local will not negotiate an agreement substantially inferior to what comparable workers elsewhere or in other unions are receiving. Second, most unions require that a referendum be held among the local's membership to ratify the contract. To do this, the bargaining team conducts a membership meeting and explains the contract gains won in negotiations. The team then generally recommends settlement, and the members vote to accept or reject.

If the negotiating committee recommends acceptance, the membership nearly always votes to ratify. In a study by Burke and Rubin, only about 30 percent of contract rejections, in negotiations which had required a mediator, occurred after a unanimous recommendation by the bargaining committee.[5] Table 10–1 presents reasons for contract rejections as they found them. Figure 10–3 shows the mechanism they

---

[5] Donald R. Burke and Lester Rubin, "Is Contract Rejection a Major Collective Bargaining Problem?" *Industrial and Labor Relations Review*, vol. 26 (January 1973), pp. 820–33.

Table 10–1
Factors involved in 41 contract-rejection cases

Factor	Frequency of occurrence among cases*
Management rejection	1
Local-international conflict	5
Committee membership gap†	10
Lack of recommendation	28
Union elections	4
Other union(s) in plant	4
Other union(s) outside	13
Plant move impending	1
Youth versus age	6
Skilled versus unskilled	1
Poor labor-management relations	9
Company-employee gap‡	1
Misunderstanding of provisions	3
Rejection of unanimous recommendation§	12
Leadership imposed settlement	2
Racial factors	2
Uncoordinated committee	1
Refusal of anything	3
Engineered rejection	2
New leaders-no control	2
Weak union leadership	2

* In many cases, more than one factor was involved.
† No membership consensus was derived.
‡ Management was unaware of employee priorities.
§ In these cases, no discernible factor was present.
Source: Donald R. Burke and Lester Rubin, "Is Contract Rejection a Major Collective Bargaining Problem?" *Industrial and Labor Relations Review*, vol. 26 (January 1973), p. 827.

concluded as being related to contract rejection. These would include an inability to alter positions through bargaining, final positions outside the settlement range of the opponent, hostile relationships between the parties, poor coordination in bargaining, or a failure to estimate correctly the priorities of the membership.

When the negotiating committee unqualifiedly recommends ratification and the contract is rejected, union negotiators are placed in a precarious position. Management may rightfully question whether they actually speak for the union. During the negotiation process, management may have conceded on issues of seeming importance to the bargainers but of questionable relevance to the rank and file. The negotiating committee also may have difficulty selling a subsequent settlement to the membership since its credibility has been undermined by the earlier rejection.

210

Figure 10–3
Typology of variables in contract rejection

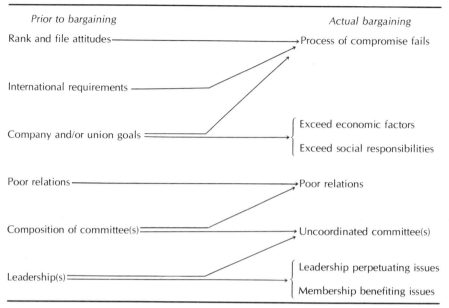

Source: Donald R. Burke and Lester Rubin, "Is Contract Rejection a Major Collective Bargaining Problem?" *Industrial and Labor Relations Review*, vol. 26 (January 1973), p. 831.

Occasionally, management will question whether the bargaining committee is representing the true wishes of the rank and file. Management bargainers may suggest that a package be submitted to the membership for ratification. The company may not insist on taking a proposal back, however, since this is not a mandatory bargaining issue.[6] If the negotiating committee is reasonably certain that a proposal will be rejected, they may take it back with a recommendation to reject. If this occurs, their bargaining position is substantially strengthened, since management is put on notice that its position is not acceptable.

Nonagreement

Occasionally, the parties may fail to reach a settlement, either before or after the expiration of the contract. A variety of activities may then occur, including mediation, strikes, lockouts, replacements, arbitration, and so forth. Impasses in negotiations lead to very complex issues which we will detail in the next chapter.

---

[6] *NLRB* v. *Wooster Division of Borg-Warner Corp.*, 356 U.S. 342 (1958).

We have now traced through the procedure of the negotiations. We now need to examine the power of the parties in the bargaining relationship.

BARGAINING POWER

Two separate aspects of bargaining power can be explored: (1) the power inherent in the economic positions of the parties, and (2) the skill of its negotiators. We could liken these aspects to those encountered in a poker game. If you were consistently dealt straights, flushes, and full houses, you should amass quite a pile of chips by the end of the evening. You also have probably known a card player who consistently wins even though the cards are shuffled thoroughly and no deck stacking is in evidence. This type of player has developed skills either to persuade others that his hand is more powerful than theirs or that his hand is weaker (when in fact it is a real crusher) to induce them to bet against him. In essence then, we could separate bargaining power into the relative capabilities for winning a position and bargaining behavior at the table. Our examination of bargaining power will concentrate on the former, while we will include the latter under the heading of bargaining tactics.

Economic aspects

In the last chapter we illustrated a situation where an employer would have greater bargaining power because of its capital intensive production process. We also noted that a union might propose certain issues or adhere to certain positions because of their effects on the wages of present members and the expansion of future membership. We will now introduce two key aspects related to bargaining power: (1) the elasticity of the demand for labor, and (2) the structure of the labor market from the standpoints of both purchaser and seller.

Elasticity of demand

When we ask questions about elasticity of demand for a good, we are asking: What will happen to the amount consumers will purchase if the price of that commodity increases (or decreases)? Demand is said to be inelastic if price changes (up or down) have relatively little effect on the amounts sold, while an elastic demand is highly sensitive to price changes. Figure 10–4 shows examples of relatively elastic (D_E) and inelastic (D_I) demand where Q is the quantity sold and P is the price.

212

FIGURE 10–4
Examples of elastic and inelastic demand

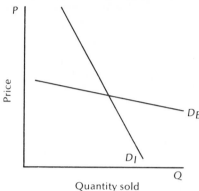

Quantity sold

Since employment of labor is necessary to produce most products and since the quantities of the product sold depend on an aggregation of individual purchases by the consumer, the utilization of labor is a derived demand influenced by the elasticity of demand for the employer's product.

There are a number of situations where derived demand for labor is inelastic, and the employer, therefore, would have little motivation to resist a wage increase. Alfred Marshall established four criteria under which the employer's demand for a service is likely to be inelastic: (1) the more essential the given item is in the production of the final product, (2) the more inelastic the demand for the final product, (3) the smaller the fraction of total cost accounted for by the item in question, and (4) the more inelastic the supply of competing factors.[7] These prescriptions would indicate that skilled trades in relatively small bargaining units where substitutes are not readily obtainable and where price has little influence over sales should have a high degree of economic bargaining power.

Within a given product market, demand may be inelastic or elastic depending upon the characteristics of the good. For example, we might expect the demand for salt to be rather inelastic since there are few acceptable substitutes, it is a small part of one's total budget, and it is a necessary ingredient in many recipes. On the other hand, the demand for stereo equipment could be expected to be elastic for just the opposite reasons.

Elasticity of demand is also of concern at the firm level. If there are many firms producing a given good, the market is said to be competi-

---

[7] Alfred Marshall, *Principles of Economics*, 8th ed. (New York: Macmillan, 1920), pp. 385–86.

tive, since an individual producer's output has little impact on the total amount of goods produced. But if its prices are above the market rate, it will sell nothing. Demand for goods of perfectly competitive firms would be characterized as elastic. Thus a competitive firm would find it difficult to pass the cost of a wage increase on to customers through higher prices.

We will also find that the character of the labor market will have an effect. If the supply of labor to the firm is not perfectly elastic, wage costs will increase as the work force's size increases. For example, if there are 10,000 workers of a particular skill level appropriate to your firm's needs who are willing to work at the wage rate being paid, and if you and your competitors are currently employing all 10,000, then a wage increase will be necessary to increase the supply. If yours is the only firm to increase, it may be able to hire away from competitors, but to increase the market supply quantity, all would have to raise wages.

When wage negotiations are taking place, employers may attempt to calculate the proportion of a wage increase that could be passed along to consumers as a product price increase. This amount and its effect depends on the elasticity of demand. Competitive firms with elastic product demand curves would be unable to pass on any cost increases while firms with inelastic demand could pass on the total cost. The following figures demonstrate the effects of a wage increase in a variety of situations.

Elastic demand.   A classic example of an organization facing an elastic demand curve would be a supermarket. Generally there are several in one city, and shoppers may determine patronage at least partially by price. All sell similar products of fairly equivalent quality. If one store raises its prices noticeably, customers would be expected to switch. On the other hand, if it took a strike to keep wages down, customers would also desert it as hunger ensued. Thus the power to adhere to its position for a firm facing an elastic demand curve is low.

Figure 10–5 shows the effect of a wage increase on employer behavior. The demand curve for the company's product(s) is D, and the supply (cost) curve for labor is S. Product prices and wage rates are on the P axis and quantities of goods sold and labor purchased are on the Q axis. A wage increase pushes the supply curve up to S', but the quantity of labor purchased simultaneously declines to Q_L' since the employer is powerless to increase the prices of its products without losing its market but will not pay wages higher than what can be recouped in the selling price of its output. Paradoxically, the situation where the employer has the least ability to bargain and pass along the effects of a wage increase also has a great likelihood of leading to deleterious effects for the union, since employment would be necessarily cut back.

FIGURE 10–5
Effects of a wage increase on labor demand for
the firm in a competitive market for its products

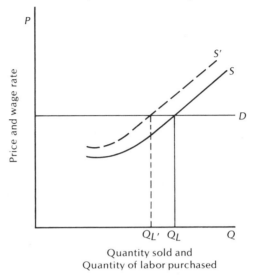

Quantity sold and
Quantity of labor purchased

Inelastic demand. An employer who has some monopoly power may be better able to pass on cost increases to consumers, particularly where no adequate substitutes exist and the good is essential. Now let's consider our supermarket from the elastic demand example again. Assume that it is the only supermarket within 50 miles. Let's also assume that customers cannot substitute lower priced goods since this store only stocks one item in each of the essential nutrition areas. Here, demand would become relatively inelastic, and the wage increase could be almost entirely passed on to consumers through higher prices. Figure 10–6 portrays the relationship. Prices would increase and employment would decline far less than for the elastic demand situations.

Thus, it is to the union's benefit, as well as the employer's, for the product market for the firm to be characterized by inelastic demand. Later we will see that this gives an underlying logic to unions' acquiescence to multiemployer bargaining units where the unit encompasses the product market (for example, a grocer's association).

A reconciliation of the economic theory paradoxes

Chamberlain and Cullen point out that bargaining power does not necessarily reside in the degree to which the employer controls the

FIGURE 10–6
Effects of a wage increase on demand for labor in a monopolistic situation where wages increase

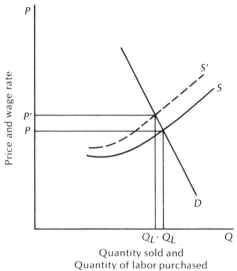

Quantity sold and
Quantity of labor purchased

market in which its goods or services are sold.[8] Instead they forcefully argue that bargaining power is "my cost of disagreeing on your terms relative to my cost of agreeing on your terms."[9] For example, a service station owner (in a highly competitive situation) may find that agreeing to a wage demand will push the cost of the gasoline sold over the receipts from its sale. Thus, the owner would object to agreeing with a union wage proposal in this area. The employees would be likely to pressure the union to lower its demands unless strike benefits were equivalent to present wages or unless alternative employment were available.

On the other hand, an employer who sells products in a less than competitive market may be motivated to accept a relatively large wage demand that could be resisted to forgo losing sales to competitors.

Ability to continue operations (or take a strike)

Besides the market conditions in which a firm operates, bargaining power is enhanced substantially by the ability to take a strike. A variety of conditions relate to this ability, including timing, technology,

---

[8] Neil W. Chamberlain and Donald E. Cullen, *The Labor Sector*, 2d ed. (New York: McGraw-Hill, 1971), pp. 225–36.

[9] Ibid., p. 227.

availability of replacements, and competition. We will examine each of these in turn.

Timing. An employer will be much more resistant to a strike if it comes during off-peak periods. Being facetious, a strike of Santa Clauses on December 26th would have little impact on an employer's stance. If timing cannot be controlled by the company, it can frequently be neutralized by anticipating a strike through stockpiling or accelerated deliveries. This has been the practice in the steel industry prior to entering into the Experimental Negotiating Agreement with the Steelworkers.

Technology. If the firm is highly capital intensive or automated, it frequently can continue to operate by using supervisors in production roles. For example, if there were a nationwide Bell Telephone strike tomorrow, a telephone user would likely not be aware of it in terms of telephone operations.

Availability of replacements. Strike replacements might come from either of two sources. First, supervisors may be able to perform enough of the duties of strikers to maintain concurrent operations. This would most likely be possible in capital intensive firms. Second, the looser the labor market (the more potential employees available to work) and the lower the skill level of the job, the easier it will be for an employer to hire and utilize replacements effectively.

Competition. Here we are not primarily concerned about the effects of competition or in the firm's ability to pass on a price increase. Instead, ability to take a strike increases if no adequate substitutes for the organization's goods or services are available. Revenues will then not be irrevocably lost, but only postponed to a later period when the firm will be back in operation.

Attributes of the parties.

While a great deal of speculation has been raised about the bargaining power properties related to the personalities of the parties involved, virtually no research on the effects of personal attributes on labor negotiations has been reported. However, some general conclusions have been reached on individual and contextual factors which are related to bargaining behavior in a variety of situations.

These conclusions are drawn by Rubin and Brown, as a result of their survey of the literature on bargaining and negotiation.[10] Here we would like to present some of their definitions and major conclusions. First, let us examine the social components of the bargaining struc-

---

[10] Jeffrey Z. Rubin and Bert R. Brown, *The Social Psychology of Bargaining and Negotiation* (New York: Academic Press, 1975).

ture. Labor negotiations are seldom conducted in complete privacy. While the general public and most union and management constituents are excluded, the negotiating teams witness the behavior of all the parties involved. This contextual aspect is important because the evidence suggests that audiences make it more difficult for bargainers to make concessions. This difficulty is increased if the bargainer has a high degree of loyalty to the group or there is a strong group commitment to the bargaining issue. If concessions are made and feedback to the conceder indicates that the other party views it as a weakness, retaliation is likely in subsequent negotiating.[11] Two tactical suggestions result from these findings. First, to promote a willingness to concede in an opponent, the bargainer's response to a concession should be one which increases the stature of the opponent in the eyes of his team members; perhaps a simultaneous concession on an area important to them, or an indication that what is a major concession is perceived by the negotiator to be hard bargaining. Second, the negotiator should be aware that public commitment to an issue will reduce the degree to which objective data may modify the position. The skilled negotiator must, however, be aware that public commitment may simply be a tactic used to justify support for an issue which is not really viewed as important.

A number of aspects related to the bargaining environment, the perceptions of the bargainers, and the complexity of the negotiations are important. Aspects of neutrality in the bargaining environment are important. There appears to be little willingness to make concessions if the negotiations are conducted on one's home ground. Unions would be advised to bargain away from the plant. Along with the setting, the perception one holds about the opposition's characteristics are important. If the opponent is perceived through status or other attributes as nondeferring, then gaining concessions will not be sought as vigorously. As more issues are injected into the bargaining, two processes are likely to occur. First, "logrolling" (trading off blocks of issues that appear to be of dissimilar nature, for example, union shop for wage increase) occurs frequently. Second, bargaining on issues assumes a more sequential character in terms of offers and counteroffers and issue settlement.[12]

Perhaps one of the most significant findings in their review relates to the interaction of personality and context variables and its effect on bargaining relationships. Three variables form this interaction: interpersonal orientation, motivational orientation, and power. Interpersonal orientation is seen as reflecting responsiveness to others, reacting

---

[11] Ibid., pp. 43–54.
[12] Ibid., pp. 130–56.

218

to, being interested in, and appreciating variations in another's behavior.[13] Motivational orientation refers to whether one's bargaining interests are individual (seeking only one's own interest), competitive (seeking to better an opponent), or cooperative (seeking positive outcomes in the interests of both).[14] Power refers to the range of bargaining outcomes that the other party may be moved through.[15]

Interpersonal orientation appears to be related to some extent to other individual differences. Table 10–2 summarizes Rubin and

TABLE 10–2
Summary of the individual differences in background and personality that appear to lie at opposite ends of the interpersonal orientation

High IOs	Low IOs
Older children and college students	Young children
Blacks	Whites
Females	Males
Low risk-takers	High risk-takers
Externals	Internals
Abstract thinkers	Concrete thinkers
Persons high in needs for affiliation and power	Persons high in need for achievement
Cooperators (premeasured)	Competitors (premeasured)
Persons low in authoritarianism	Persons high in authoritarianism
Persons high in internationalism	Persons low in internationalism
Persons high in machiavellianism	Person low in machiavellianism
"Normals" (remitted schizophrenics, nonparanoids, patients with good premorbid histories)	Abnormals (regressed schizophrenics, paranoids, patients with poor premorbid histories)

Source: Jeffrey Z. Rubin and Bert R. Brown, The Social Psychology of Bargaining and Negotiation (New York: Academic Press, 1975), p. 194.

Brown's conclusions on differences affecting interpersonal orientation. Motivational orientation may be affected by attitudes or predispositions to bargaining, the structuring of rewards and their attainability, and the roles that bargainers may be told to take by their constituents.[16] In terms of power, discrepancies between the parties in their amounts of power, and in the amount of abolute power (ability to inflict loss on the other) are also important parameters.[17]

Given these individual differences and contextual variables, Rubin and Brown suggest that bargaining effectiveness should be greatest where interpersonal orientation is high, motivational orientation is

[13] Ibid., p. 158.
[14] Ibid., p. 198.
[15] Ibid., p. 213.
[16] Ibid., pp. 201–13.
[17] Ibid., pp. 213–33.

cooperative, and power is equal and low.[18] The interaction of these variables may well have no effect on how the parties, independently, decide to structure their negotiating teams. Much of the structuring must depend on the goals of a party (for example, to break new ground on productivity issues which would require cooperation), and beliefs about the tactics an opponent may use (for example, assigning low interpersonal orientation bargainers).

One other aspect of bargaining considered by Rubin and Brown relates to the conduct of the concession process. They conclude that the type and level of concessions of a party convey important information about the party's true position. For example, a series of concessions on a given issue followed by no subsequent movement could signal that one's resistance point had been approached. Negative concessions or a retreat toward an original position may signal a toughening of a stand. Concessions which appear to reward the requester's behavior may well increase cooperation between the parties and appear to strengthen the role of an attractive counterpart to his constituency.[19]

Now that we have examined some of the psychological factors involving the bargainer, we need to look at the behavioral processes involved in complex negotiations. To do this, we will examine and summarize some of the work done by Stevens[20] and Walton and McKersie.[21]

BEHAVIOR IN COLLECTIVE BARGAINING

Obviously, the conduct of collective bargaining is a highly complex process. Each separate negotiation has some unique characteristics, but all fit an overall pattern to some extent. It is this overall pattern that we will use as a backdrop to examine the subtleties and nuances leading to the outcomes of the bargaining process.

Walton and McKersie suggest that there are four separable components within the bargaining process that may occur during any set of negotiations. The first is *distributive bargaining.*[22] Distributive bargaining takes place where the parties are in conflict on a particular issue and where the outcome will represent a loss for one party and a gain for the other. As an example, suppose the union wants a 60 cent

---

[18] Ibid., pp. 256–57.

[19] Ibid., pp. 276–78.

[20] Carl M. Stevens, *Strategy and Collective Bargaining Negotiation* (New York: McGraw-Hill, 1963).

[21] Richard E. Walton and Robert B. McKersie, *A Behavioral Theory of Labor Negotiations* (New York: McGraw-Hill, 1965).

[22] Ibid., p. 4.

hourly increase, and the parties ultimately settle for 30 cents. The 30 cent increase is a gain to the union and a loss to the company. This is not to say that the loss is greater than the company expected, however. The company may have felt that a settlement for anything less than 35 cents would be better than it expected to win. All that distributive bargaining means is that there is a fixed supply of some resource, and one's gain is the other's loss as to that resource.

The second is *integrative bargaining*. This type of bargaining takes place when the parties face a common problem.[23] For example, a company may be experiencing above average employee turnover. As a result, union membership may be eroded, and union officials have to spend an inordinate amount of time recruiting new members from the workers hired as replacements. Both parties may then seek a solution to their joint problem by attacking the causes of turnover that may exist in their present or previous agreement.

A third component is called *attitudinal structuring*.[24] This relates to the activities in a given negotiation that the parties engage in to create atmospheres such as cooperation, hostility, trust, respect, and so forth. The process is primarily related to changing attitudes of the parties in the expectation that changed attitudes will change predispositions to act. A number of the activities summarized in Rubin and Brown fall within this component.

The fourth component is *intraorganizational bargaining*.[25] This process is involved with achieving agreement within one of the bargaining groups. For example, it might relate to the efforts of a management bargainer to convince fellow management representatives that 40 cents per hour will be necessary to avoid a strike when management has determined previously that the union would likely settle for 35 cents. At the same time, intraorganizational bargaining may refer to the activities union negotiators may engage in to sell an agreement to the union's membership.

Distributive bargaining tactics

Obviously, bargaining takes place because either or both parties are not willing to accede to the demands of the other. In this regard, Stevens has suggested six rules which govern the conduct of bargaining.[26] In our examination of these rules, you will see that many overlap the conclusions of the studies relating to the psychology of bargaining summarized by Rubin and Brown.

---

[23] Ibid., p. 5.

[24] Ibid., p. 5.

[25] Ibid., p. 5.

[26] Stevens, *Strategy and Collective Bargaining Negotiation*, pp. 27–56.

Stevens's rules. *Rule 1* states that an impending contract expiration is necessary to the commencement of bargaining. During the course of the agreement, the parties have essentially agreed not to bargain, so the anticipated expiration serves as an enabling process for the renewal of bargaining.

Rule 2 states that the initial bargaining demand should be large. Even though both parties are fairly certain that the initial positions are at substantial variance from what each party would be willing to settle for, the large initial demand creates substantial room for bargaining and the making of what are relatively large concessions when the time is right.

Rule 3 explains that the negotiating agenda is set by the initial demands and counterproposals. In other words, the issues initially raised by the parties constitute the focus of the bargaining. There are seldom additions to the initial agenda, and offers made in regard to these items can seldom be effectively retracted.

Rule 4 is the strike or lockout deadline rule. Stevens notes that this rule precludes strikes before a certain fixed time and serves notice that a strike is likely after this point.

Rule 5 provides for a termination in negotiations as a result of an agreement. Within this rule may be a requirement that unresolved issues be arbitrated or operations continued to preclude an emergency while an agreement is reached.

Rule 6 requires that the parties negotiate in good faith. To do this the parties must respond to each other's demands and take no unilateral action to change the existing conditions prior to the end of negotiations.

Communicating intentions. Through the bargaining itself, both sides may pick up cues as to where the other is willing to settle. An important part of this process is identifying the finality of commitment a bargainer attaches to a bargaining position. Figure 10–7 portrays various management and union commitment statements and analyzes them as to their finality, specificity, and consequences for ignoring them. All of these help the parties to reach an agreement by providing cues as to the actual requirements of each party in the settlement.

Each side has to convince the other that the cost of disagreeing is greater than the gain or saving from continued adherence to a position if it is to get movement from the opposition. Next we will examine areas where integrative bargaining takes place.

Integrative bargaining

Integrative bargaining occurs in contexts where both management and union may accommodate the needs of the other without cost or

FIGURE 10–7
Interpretive comments about the degree of firmness in statements of commitments

Statement of commitment (1)	Degree of finality of commitment to a position (2)	Degree of specificity of that position (3)	The consequences or implications associated with a position (the threat) (4)
From a negotiation involving a middle-sized manufacturing plant in 1953: "We have looked very seriously and must present this (10-cent package) as our final offer."	The statement "must present this as our final offer" is not as strong as, for example, "this is our final offer." The strength of the word "final" is somewhat hedged by the more tentative phrase "must present this as."	The reference to the "10-cent package" was fairly specific.	No reference to the consequences. What the other party is expected to associate with the company's position would depend on the company's reputation or other confirming tactics. It would seem to imply that company is ready to take a strike.
A union replied later, "The membership disagreed" with the company's economic proposal. "The present contract will not extend beyond 12:00 tonight."	Significantly, the membership was reported as only having "disagreed"; it did not "reject."	Reference to "economic proposal" is not specific. Hence the degree of disagreement is unclear.	By stating "the present contract will not extend," they do not state that there would be a strike. And in the particular context it was not clear that they would strike.
From the public statements regarding the 1955 negotiations between the UAW and the Ford Motor Company: Henry Ford II suggested alternate ways of achieving security "without piecemeal experimenting with dangerous mechanisms or guinea pig industries. . . ." This was a statement of opposition to the union's GAW proposal.	The statement contained no hint about the finality of his commitment of opposition.	The phrase "piecemeal experimenting . . ." clearly avoided reference to just what was objected to.	There were no references to the consequences to be associated with ultimate failure to agree.

From the transcripts of a negotiation in the oil industry: Management stated, "If you say now or never or else (on a wage increase demanded by the union), I would say go ahead; we are prepared to take the consequences."	This was an explicit, binding commitment.	The company's position was also clear in this instance—it was not prepared to make any concession on the issue at hand.	Company was indicating its readiness for a work stoppage.
Later the union spokesman replied, "My advice to your employees will be not to become a party to any agreement which binds them to present wages."	Regarding what the union leader's advice will be, that is final. It says nothing about the finality of that position of the party, however.	The advice "not to become a party to any agreement which binds them to present wages" is hardly specific. Any increase would meet the test of this statement. In fact, even a reopening clause would avoid "binding the union to present wages."	Although at first glance this statement seems to commit the union to a wage increase "or else," it leaves them the option of continuing with no contract and with signing a contract which has a way of adjusting wages in the future. The context did nothing to clarify just what consequences were to be associated with the union's position.
"I don't believe that they (the rest of the union committee) can recommend acceptance" (of the company's offer).	"I don't believe" is more tentative than "I know they cannot."	"I don't believe that they can recommend acceptance" leaves unanswered whether the union committee would recommend that the membership not accept the offer or merely make no recommendation. Moreover, the reference is only to the company's *offer as it now stands.*	Not specified here, but the union had begun to refer to economic sanctions.

Source: B. M. Selekman, S. K. Selekman, and S. H. Fuller, *Problems in Labor Relations* (2d ed.) (New York: McGraw-Hill, 1958), 221, 226, 233: Material from these pages used in formulating table by Richard E. Walton and Robert B. McKersie in *A Behavioral Theory of Labor Negotiations* (New York: McGraw-Hill, 1965), 96–97.

through a simultaneous gain. Walton and McKersie suggest that these frequently involve desires to improve management flexibility while unions simultaneously desire increased job security.[27] Two noteworthy examples of integrative bargaining can be found in the International Longshoremen's and Warehousemen's Union (ILWU) contract with the west coast shippers and the Experimental Negotiating Agreement between the basic steel firms and used for the first time in the recent Steelworkers' negotiations.

The longshoremen and the maritime industry had faced what seemed to be an insurmountable problem before 1960. The Pacific Maritime Association (management) was concerned that restrictive work rules governing crew size would make the introduction of labor-saving equipment inefficient, since the rules would not allow crew sizes to be reduced. The union wanted to preserve jobs for its members and was reluctant to agree to a relaxation of the work rules. Over a series of contract negotiations, crew size requirements were reduced, wage guarantees for laid-off dockworkers were negotiated, and the ILWU even pressed for more mechanization to ease the physical loads on its members. In the 1966 negotiations, Kossoris summarized the outcomes as follows:

To the Union:

1. An immediate pay increase of 50 cents an hour, with an additional 20 cents in 1969 and again in 1970; basic pay will rise, as of July 1, 1966, from $3.38 an hour to $3.88, and to $5.82 per hour of overtime. Basic pay for an 8-hour day, with the last 2 hours paid at time and a half, amounts to $34.92. In the 5th year, basic hourly pay will rise to $4.28 and pay for an 8-hour day to $38.52.

2. Longshoremen may retire at 63 years of age for pension purposes instead of 65.

3. Upon retiring, with 25 years of service and age 63, a longshoreman will receive $13,000; if he drops out because of death or disability, the amount will be paid as prorated on years of service.

4. Pensions rise from $165 a month to $235 for the next 10 years, but only for men who retire after the new contract goes into effect. Men who retired before then remain at $165. But there is to be a general review of all pension amounts in 1971, with adjustments based on the BLS Consumer Price Index, local or national, or both.

   A widow will get half of the pension due if a longshoreman reaches age 60 with 25 years of service but has not retired before he dies. Previously, the widow received nothing if the longshoreman died before he retired.

5. All work on the docks belongs to longshoremen, including work now performed by other crafts. However, existing bona fide labor agreements will not be disturbed. Apparently they are not to be renewed.

---

[27] Walton and McKersie, *A Behavioral Theory of Labor Negotiations*, pp. 129 ff.

To Employers:

1. No work stoppages for 5 years.
2. Greater flexibility in the use of men, particularly skilled men. This, plus the right to move men around as needed under the 8-hour pay guaranty for every man dispatched on request, permits employers to shift men from dock to dock, ship to dock, and dock to ship, subject only to the restrictions of the preferential dock list. Furthermore, employers can now employ skilled men on a "steady basis" without their reporting back to the hiring hall after each job.
3. An actual reduction of gang sizes by the provision that two men out of every specified gang size be skilled men, which eliminates the need for one or more additional skilled men.
4. The possibility of reducing even the four-man basic gang in the hold to one by means of such devices as the robot. This puts teeth into the phrase "There shall be no unnecessary men."[28]

A more recent successful example of integrative bargaining resulted in the 1973 signing of the Experimental Negotiating Agreement (ENA). Because steel consumers had a strong belief that contract negotiations would be likely to lead to strikes, they normally stockpiled steel in advance of a contract expiration. The consequences of these activities were threefold. First, steel mills were utilized at very high rates prior to contract expiration but at inefficiently low rates immediately after, if no strike occurred. Second, steel workers were frequently laid off after a new contract was signed, leading to wage losses with or without a strike. And third, customers had money tied up in excess inventory they would not have needed. As a result, they frequently turned permanently to surer sources like foreign producers.

The ENA provides for the settlement of many unresolved issues by arbitration. To ensure that customers will not have to stockpile steel to meet anticipated strike shortages, the union has agreed not to strike but to have a panel of arbitrators determine terms for unresolved issues. Arbitration cannot determine local working conditions, checkoff of dues, cost of living clauses, union shop, or management rights clauses.[29]

Benefits accrue to steel companies in terms of cost savings from starting and shutdown avoidance. Officials estimate this saving at about $80 million per strike. Workers are assured that production will be more steady, hence chances of layoff are reduced, and the steel

---

[28] Max D. Kossoris, "1966 West Coast Longshore Negotiations," *Monthly Labor Review*, vol. 89 (October 1966), pp. 1073–74.

[29] William F. Maloney, "Experimental Negotiating Agreement: Development and Impact," unpublished paper, 1974.

companies are sharing some of the shutdown cost savings with workers.[30]

Attitudinal structuring

Walton and McKersie suggest that the relationship patterns occurring between labor and management will have an effect on or be a result of a party's action toward the other, beliefs about legitimacy, level of trust, and degree of friendliness.[31] As a result of these additional dimensions, they predict, as we show in Figure 10–8, that the predominant patterns would fall within the categories of conflict, containment-aggression, accommodation, cooperation, and collusion.

Conflict occurs where both parties seek to destroy the other's base. Neither acknowledges the legitimacy of the other, and activities are pursued to interfere with the other's existence. Containment-aggression occurs when either or both sides demonstrate a high degree of militancy while recognizing the other's right to exist. Accommodation takes place when each accords the other party a legitimate role and allows the other party to represent its position as a legitimate interest. Cooperation occurs when the other's position is seen as completely legitimate and where common issues are of simultaneous concern to both parties. Collusion takes place when either or both join together to subvert the goals of the parties they represent.[32] This occurs in situations where management may covertly assist a union in organizing in return for a nonmilitant stance on bargaining.

The way the parties relate to each other may frequently be expected to determine whether or not negotiations define an issue as distributive or integrative. The ENA, for example, took over six years to be adopted, partly because of the mutual suspicion of the contending parties.

Walton and McKersie suggest that a number of factors could affect the type of bargaining relationships likely to be found. A number of contextual aspects like the general state of business, whether the firm is a pattern setter or follower in bargaining, labor intensiveness, and so on, affect the degree to which the relationship is conflict or cooperation oriented. Personality factors related to the bargainers have an effect. Management personalities may have greater visibility since there is less apparent need for managers to represent a constituency directly. For the union's part, the leadership may reflect the type of personality the membership wants, but the type of image that, for example, I.W.

---

[30] Ibid., pp. 24–25.
[31] Walton and McKersie, *A Behavioral Theory of Labor Negotiations*, pp. 184–280.
[32] Ibid., pp. 186–88.

FIGURE 10-8
Attitudinal components of the relationship patterns

Attitudinal dimensions	Pattern of relationship				
	Conflict	Containment-aggression	Accommodation	Cooperation	Collusion
Motivational orientation and action tendencies toward other	Competitive tendencies to destroy or weaken		Individualistic policy of hands off	Cooperative tendencies to assist or preserve	
Beliefs about legitimacy of other	Denial of legitimacy	Grudging acknowledgment	Acceptance of status quo	Complete legitimacy	Not applicable
Level of trust in conducting affairs	Extreme distrust	Distrust	Limited trust	Extended trust	Trust based on mutual blackmail potential
Degree of friendliness	Hate	Antagonism	Neutralism-Courteousness	Friendliness	Intimacy—"Sweetheart relationship"

Source: Richard E. Walton and Robert B. McKersie, *A Behavioral Theory of Labor Negotiations* (New York: McGraw-Hill, 1965), p. 189.

Abel projected, definitely has had an effect on the type of bargaining that has taken place in basic steel.[33]

Intraorganizational bargaining

The negotiators for both sides frequently require that the initial positions be modified if a contract is to be reached. They also are going to be maintaining a continuing relationship. Both management and union negotiators must build up some sort of predictable relationship between themselves. To do this, convincing persons within their own organization to alter a position may be necessary.

On the union side, the union negotiating team must have the ability to sell an agreement to the rank and file once it's been reached. To do this, it has to be sensitive to the demands of the membership but be able to balance the competing needs of subgroups within the union. One tactic used by union negotiators is estimating to the membership some reasonable range of contract outcomes. Suggestions that excessive demands could damage the nature of the bargaining relationship (see attitudinal structuring) can have an effect on moderating opening demands.

Another tactic that may be used, particularly by management, is limiting participation. Persons who are likely to take militant stances, or be unwilling to modify positions as bargaining continues, may be excluded from the process. This way, the management negotiator is freer to respond during the bargaining process.[34]

A test of the model

Peterson and Tracy suggest that the four bargaining processes and their degree of use result from certain preexisting conditions and the behaviors of the negotiators.[35] Figure 10–9 shows the predictors of the processes. For example, conditions like bargaining power would be expected to be related to early commitment to a firm position. This, in turn, should lead toward the use of distributive bargaining.

To examine this model, Peterson and Tracy collected questionnaire information from union and management negotiators on their perceptions of the negotiations they were involved in. Their findings suggest that success in attaining one of the bargaining process goals did not depend on reaching another. The only exception was that negotiators

---

[33] Ibid., pp. 190–96.

[34] Ibid., pp. 281–340.

[35] Richard B. Peterson and Lane Tracy, "Testing a Behavioral Theory Model of Labor Negotiations," *Industrial Relations*, vol. 16 (February 1977), pp. 35–50.

FIGURE 10–9
Model of conditions and behaviors related to Walton and McKersie's four goals of bargaining

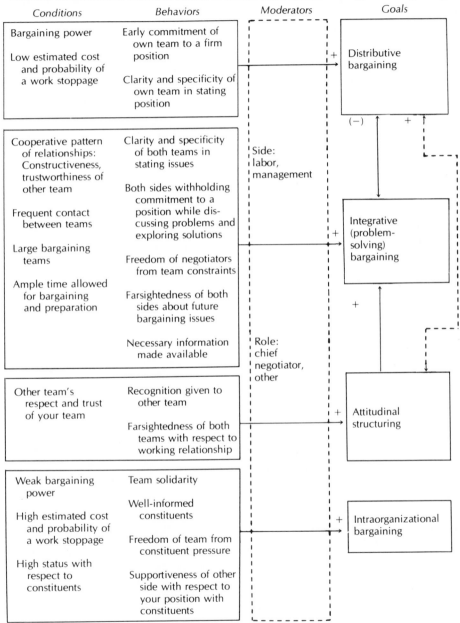

saw a relationship between integrative bargaining success and attitudinal structuring, which was reflected in improved working relationships. Distributive bargaining success was influenced by bargaining power and low probabilities of a work stoppage, and clarity in stating issues combined with the opponent's discussion of the basis for its position as behavior. Integrative bargaining success depended on conditions of trust, support, and friendliness by the opponent and a clear statement of issues with open discussion and plentiful information. Success in attitudinal structuring was related to management respect for the union, generally constructive relationships toward management, and a lack of criticism of the opponent. Intraorganizational bargaining success depended on the confidence bargainers had in their constituents' endorsement and high perceived costs of a stoppage. Behaviors relevant to success related to team solidarity and low outside pressures.

Peterson and Tracy conclude that the interpersonal processes in negotiations have an effect on bargaining outcomes as well as economic factors such as bargaining power. Tactics which lead to distributive bargaining success have some positive effects on integrative bargaining as well. Thus, we might conclude that experience and preparation have positive effects on negotiations. Finally, an important finding relates to the relatively significant relationship between attitudinal structuring success and integrative bargaining success. An aura of trust may well be necessary before problem solving can occur.

Thus, the economic, attitudinal, and experiential contexts in which negotiations are conducted have a major effect on their outcomes. The work of Walton and McKersie, the review by Rubin and Brown, and the test by Peterson and Tracy all help to explain why behavioral implications, the personalities of the negotiators, and their stream of experiences heavily influence the outcomes.

SUMMARY

Bargaining for a new contract begins as the parties express their initial positions. However, preparations by both parties precede the initial meeting. The union must assess the position its constituents want it to take, and management must anticipate union demands. At the table, the union usually proposes and management responds. The bargaining power and behavior of the parties influences the outcome of the process.

Bargaining power is defined by the degree to which the costs of agreeing for the employer or union on the other's terms relates to the cost to the opponent of agreeing on its terms. Bargaining power is influenced to some extent by the competitiveness of the market for the sale of the firm's products.

Four major behavioral components of bargaining have been suggested. The first is distributive bargaining in which one party's loss is the opponent's gain. Integrative bargaining occurs when both parties agree on a new position which simultaneously meets goals of each at lower costs to both. The third is attitudinal structuring. This process creates the climate among the parties for bargaining. The fourth is intraorganizational bargaining. Here negotiators work to convince members of their own organization to modify or accept a certain position.

OVERVIEW AND PREVIEW

In this chapter we have examined the general practice, background, and determinants of collective bargaining negotiations. To recap, both labor and management formulate their demands as a result of experience with the previous agreement and the desires of their constituents. Information on probable positions of both is kept and used for negotiating. Generally, contract negotiation results in an initial union demand and a management counteroffer follows. The parties then negotiate toward a solution. The final solution or contract is a joint product of each side's demands moderated by raw bargaining power, the talents and personalities of the bargainer, and the nature of the attitudes involved in the bargaining relationship.

Preview

Now that we have examined bargaining issues and negotiations in the last two chapters, we want to look at some bargaining and administrative topics. What happens if the two parties fail to agree? What is permissible conduct for each side in a potentially acrimonious atmosphere? To examine this, we will turn to impasse procedures in the next chapter.

We also are concerned with patterns of bargaining. Who sets trends in settlements? How do small employers bargain with big unions? How does an employer with many bargaining units cope? These will be covered in our chapter on special bargaining processes and topics.

Then we will move into the area of contract administration. What goes on between the parties after an agreement is reached? How are disputes during the course of the agreement resolved? What is the role of third parties in contract disputes?

These and other issues will face us as we move from the general to the specific in collective bargaining.

SUGGESTED READINGS

Chamberlain, Neil W., and Cullen, Donald E. *The Labor Sector*, 2d ed. (New York: McGraw-Hill, 1971), chap. 12.

Granof, Michael H. *How to Cost Your Labor Contract* (Washington: Bureau of National Affairs, 1973).

Richardson, Reed C. "Positive Collective Bargaining," in Dale Yoder and H. G. Heneman, Jr., eds., *Employee and Labor Relations*, vol. 3 in *ASPA Handbook of Personnel and Industrial Relations* (Bureau of National Affairs, 1976), pp. 7–111 through 7–143.

Rubin, Jeffrey Z., and Brown, Bert R. *The Social Psychology of Bargaining and Negotiation* (New York: Academic Press, 1975).

Ryder, Meyer S., Rehmus, Charles M., and Cohen, Sanford. *Management Preparation for Collective Bargaining* (Homewood, Ill.: Dow Jones-Irwin, 1966).

Somers, Gerald G. "Bargaining Power and Industrial Relations Theory," in Gerald G. Somers, ed., *Essays in Industrial Relations Theory* (Ames, Ia.: Iowa State University Press, 1969), pp. 39–53.

Stevens, Carl M. *Strategy and Collective Bargaining Negotiation* (New York: McGraw-Hill, 1963).

Walton, Richard E., and McKersie, Robert B. *A Behavioral Theory of Labor Negotiations* (New York: McGraw-Hill, 1965).

DISCUSSION QUESTIONS

1. To what extent should the union's leadership determine its demands? Should rank and file preferences have a major impact?

2. If an organization were ultimately willing to settle for a 50 cents per hour wage increase and the union was demanding 80 cents, what sequence of concessions would you suggest to the firm (assuming 50 cents was within the union's settlement range)?

3. Discuss the advantages and disadvantages of having a union or management negotiator who did not have the power to commit the party to a position.

4. What personality characteristics would you desire in your negotiator for distributive bargaining? For integrative bargaining?

Case

GMFC NEGOTIATING CASE

A. APPROACH

The mock bargaining case will be used to develop an appreciation of, and insight into, principles and problems of collective bargaining with special emphasis upon contract negotiation. The case aims to make the student aware of the nature and complexity of the issues, problems, and processes. In many respects these sessions will combine the advantages of the case method, incident process, and role playing.

The basic problem here relates to what collective bargaining on a contract means for an organization and a union. We will seek to develop such understanding through negotiation of a new contract between the General Manufacturing & Fabrication Company (GMFC) and Local 384. Your instructor will assign you to labor and management teams.

B. DEMANDS

1. The union's initial demands are as follows:
    a. A three-month sabbatical vacation with full pay every five years for those with ten years or more of seniority in addition to regular vacation.
    b. $1.50 an hour general wage increase; plus $0.30 an hour inequity increase for nonproduction employees (that is, maintenance and craft).
    c. A four-day week with time and one half for all hours worked over eight in any day.
    d. Double time for all other overtime and on all holidays worked.
    e. Two-week layoff notice.
    f. Vacations should be one week for 1 year service, two for 2, three for 5, four for 10 and five for 20.
    g. Paid lunch and relief periods should be increased to 40 minutes from 25 minutes.
    h. Increase in pension contributions from 5 percent to 7 percent; plus employer-paid dental insurance.
    i. Equal pay for equal work—move "B" job scale up to "A" job scale.
    j. One-year contract.
    k. Union shop with membership after 60 days.
    l. Friday after Thanksgiving added to holidays.
2. The company offers the following:
    a. Maintenance of membership—replacing union shop for new employees.
    b. Elimination of daily overtime pay except where required by law.
    c. Raise probationary period from 40 to 60 days.
    d. Seniority for layoff and recall—merit and ability only for promotion.
    e. No bumping across jobs.
    f. Supervisors will have right to do work of hourly employees.

g. Supervisors who are reduced to hourly ranks shall become members of union only if they so desire.

h. Steps one and two of grievance procedure shall be handled in five rather than two working days.

i. Expenses of arbitration shall be borne by the losing party.

j. $0.50 (first year), $0.20 (second year), and $0.15 (third year) an hour general wage increase plus profit-sharing plan in which 20 percent of profits over the average of past three years' profit be divided equally among all company employees.

k. A three-year contract.

l. Eliminate the SUB Plan.

C. ORGANIZATION OF NEGOTIATIONS

Each labor team will be headed by a chief steward and will have about eight members. Each management team will also have about eight members and will be headed by a labor relations director.

Prior to negotiations, each labor and management team will:

1. Determine relative priority of issues.
2. Select key issues (and identify "horse trading" issues).
3. Suggest compromise solutions for a "package" deal—for example, will company go to 38-hour week if union will accept $0.50 wage increase.
4. Devise strategies, develop reasons.
5. Keep bargaining book(s).
6. Cost the contract provisions.

D. MOCK NEGOTIATIONS

Negotiations will consist of:

1. Preparation of demands, counterarguments and proposals

Each labor and each management team will meet alone. For each issue they should lay out:

a. Present relevant contract provisions.
b. If the issue is a demand from their side (labor or management), they shall frame the demand giving reasons to support their position.
c. If the issue is a demand of the opposite party, they should anticipate the oppositions's arguments and prepare counterarguments.
d. Strategy for the bargaining sessions that will follow.
e. Assignment of individual team member responsibilities.

Emphasis throughout shall be upon policy, major objectives, and problems, rather than specific techniques and/or semantics per se.

2. First bargaining session

Labor and management teams will meet to negotiate. They shall first agree upon an agenda and order of presentation. If they cannot arrive at a mutually satisfactory agenda and order, the following should be used:

a. Agenda—the Demands assigned in Part "B" above in that order;
b. Order of presentation—each issue will be discussed separately—the party making the demand will first present its views and the other party will follow.
c. N.B. If stalled, see your instructor, but remember bargaining time may be lost in the process.

3. Intermediate sessions
   You may break into subgroups to bargain on separate issues, for example, benefits. Periodically you should convene the whole group to get an overall picture of negotiations to date and to reconcile and consolidate positions. This will serve to coordinate bargaining strategy. It should help define "horse-trading" items, demands they are willing to drop, to concede, "rock-bottom" positions, and so on. You may also develop new proposals to counteroffer. For example, you might introduce a wage reopener as a counter to a three-year contract demand. You may not exceed your initial position on an item, however.

4. Final bargaining session
   When agreement is reached, the labor and management teams will meet to initial the contract. Management should then determine the final impact of the contract, and labor should design a strategy for selling the agreement to its membership.

5. Report preparation and delivery
   Each team will meet separately (labor alone, management alone) to prepare its report for the "Reports on Bargaining" to be made to the entire class. Each team will be given 30 minutes to make its report. (There will be 15 minutes for labor and 15 minutes for management.) After both teams make their reports, there will be 20 minutes of general discussion.

6. Your instructor may impose costs for a failure to settle by a certain date.

GMFC seniority list

	Cumulative (number of employees)
20 years or more	42
15 or more	151
10 or more	218
9	329
8	486
7	601
6	732
5	835
4	954
3	1,068
2	1,179
1	1,208

**Consumer Price Index (BLS) Central City last contract
(1967 = 100)***

1977	
January	170.9
April	172.3
July	174.6
October	178.0
1978	
January	181.1
April	184.7
July	186.2
October	189.3
1979	
January	193.1

* Not actual CPI figures, constructed for this case only.

**BLS occupational wage survey (manufacturing) Central City,
January 1979**

	Average straight-time hourly wage
Maintenance carpenters (manufacturing)	$7.74
Truck drivers	7.19
Maintenance electricians	9.59
Forklift operators	6.51
Stationary engineers	8.43
Guards	6.30
Maintenance helpers	6.58
Oilers	4.86
Maintenance machinists	8.84
Machine tool operators	7.60
Millwrights	8.56
Painters, maintenance	8.29
Tool and die makers	8.63
Laborers, material handling	6.03
Packers, shipping	5.55
Shipping clerks	6.64

Average hourly pay GMFC production workers in 1978 was $6.85.

ADDITIONAL FACTS WHICH MAY BE RELEVANT FOR NEGOTIATIONS

1. While the contract covers only two plants, these are key contracts in that they set the pattern for following negotiations in others located elsewhere in GMFC.
2. Skilled employees constitute about 15 percent of the bargaining unit.
3. Currently health insurance premiums are $82.50 per employee per month.
4. Health insurance premiums have risen about 30 percent per year under the expiring contract.
5. Dental insurance has been quoted at $23 per month per employee for $100

deductible per year, $30 per month per employee for $10 deductible per visit, and $45 per month per employee for full coverage.

6. Overtime has averaged 212 hours per year for maintenance and craft employees and 293 per year for production.

GMFC—Selected financial information ($000 except amounts per share)

	1975	1976	1977	1978
Sales	700,039	754,899	881,072	979,375
Income before taxes	159,407	171,065	204,208	221,928
Provision for taxes	75,310	80,594	102,823	112,965
Net income	84,097	90,446	101,385	108,963
Earnings per share (common)	1.57	1.68	1.82	1.95
Common stock dividend	38,973	42,637	47,610	52,949
Dividend per share	0.72	0.80	0.88	1.00
Stockholders' investment	419,365	472,094	533,379	597,536
Market value per share				
(last stock split 1970)	47.38	57.25	43.75	41.50
Number of common stockholders	66,414	66,159	64,609	65,733
Number of employees	32,490	33,433	36,893	40,242
Salaries, wages and other compensation	196,662	213,988	248,120	275,225

AGREEMENT

between

GENERAL MANUFACTURING & FABRICATION COMPANY

CENTRAL CITY, INDIANA

and

LOCAL 384, UNITED STEELWORKERS OF AMERICA

AFL–CIO/CLC

Effective March 1, 1976

CONTENTS

Article 1. Purpose 240
Article 2. Recognition 240
Article 3. Checkoff of Union Dues 240
Article 4. Management 240
Article 5. Representation 241
Article 6. Hours 241
Article 7. Wages 242
Article 8. Seniority 245
Article 9. Grievance Procedure and No-Strike Agreement .. 249
Article 10. Vacations 251
Article 11. Sick Leave 252
Article 12. General 254
Article 13. Renewal 259
Appendix   Classified Base Rates 259

ARTICLE 1. PURPOSE

1.01 It is the intent and purpose of the parties hereto that this Agreement will promote and improve industrial and economic relations between the employees and the COMPANY, and to set forth herein a basic agreement covering rates of pay, hours of work, and other conditions of employment to be observed by the parties and to insure the peaceful settlement of disputes and to prevent stoppages of work.

ARTICLE 2. RECOGNITION

2.01 The COMPANY recognizes Local Union No. 384, United Steelworkers of America, AFL–CIO/CLC, as the exclusive bargaining agent for all hourly paid employees designated in the bargaining unit by the National Labor Relations Board for the Central City plant and warehouses, which includes all production and maintenance employees including machine shop employees and receiving department and warehouse employees, but excluding boiler room employees, clerical employees, watchmen, guards, assistant foremen, foremen and any other supervisory employees with authority to hire, promote, discharge, discipline, or otherwise effect changes in the status of employees, or effectively recommend such action.

2.02 Any employee who is a member of the UNION on the effective date of this Agreement shall, as a condition of employment, maintain his membership in the UNION to the extent of paying membership dues.

2.03 Any employee who on the effective date of this Agreement is not a member of the UNION shall not be required to become a member of the UNION as a condition of continued employment but shall be required to pay an amount equal to the UNION's regular monthly dues. Any such employee, however, who during the life of this Agreement joins the UNION must remain a member as provided in Section 2.02.

ARTICLE 3. CHECKOFF UNION DUES

3.01 Upon individual authorization from members, monthly UNION DUES in an amount to be determined by the UNION shall be deducted by the COMPANY from each member's first pay in each month. Such sums shall be forwarded by the COMPANY to the financial secretary of the UNION before the 15th day of the month.

ARTICLE 4. MANAGEMENT

4.01 The UNION and its members recognize that the successful and efficient operation of the business is the responsibility of management and that management of the plant and the direction of the working force is the responsibility of the COMPANY, provided, in carrying out these management functions, the COMPANY does not violate the terms of this Agreement.

4.02 The COMPANY retains the sole right to discipline and discharge employees for cause, provided that in the exercise of this right it will not act wrongfully or unjustly or in violation of the terms of this Agreement.

ARTICLE 5. REPRESENTATION

5.01 The UNION shall designate a UNION COMMITTEE of no more than ten members who shall represent the UNION in meetings with the COMPANY with no more than seven employees actively working in the plant as members of the committee.

5.02 The COMPANY agrees that during meetings held with management, members of the UNION required to attend shall be paid at their regular hourly base rate plus their departmental incentive for all time lost from their regularly assigned work schedule.

ARTICLE 6. HOURS

6.01 WORK DAY.   A day starts at the beginning of the first shift and ends at the close of the third shift. The first shift is any shift that starts after 12 o'clock in the evening. Normally the first shift starts at 7 A.M. or 8 A.M. Present shift schedules will continue unless mutually agreed to be changed by the COMPANY and the UNION.

6.02 PAYROLL WEEK.   The payroll week starts at the beginning of the first shift on Monday and ends at the end of the third shift on Sunday.

6.03 DAILY OVERTIME.   Time and one half shall be paid for all hours worked in excess of 8 in any one day. Time and one half shall be paid for all hours worked in excess of 8 in any 24 hour period whenever provisions of the Walsh Healy Act apply.

6.04 WEEKLY OVERTIME.   Time and one half shall be paid for all hours worked in excess of 40 in any one payroll week for which overtime has not been earned on any other basis.

6.05 SATURDAY WORK.   Time and one half shall be paid for work performed on Saturday between the hours of 7 A.M. or 8 A.M. Saturday to 7 A.M. or 8 A.M. Sunday.

6.06. SUNDAY WORK.   Double time shall be paid for work performed on Sunday between the hours of 7 A.M. or 8 A.M. Sunday to 7 A.M. or 8 A.M. Monday.

6.07 CONSECUTIVE HOURS OVER 8.   Time and one half shall be paid for all hours worked over 8 but less than 12.

6.08 CONSECUTIVE HOURS OVER 12.   Double time shall be paid for all consecutive hours worked over 12.

6.09 DISTRIBUTION OF OVERTIME.   Overtime shall be distributed on an equitable basis within the department in a manner to be decided by the supervision and the UNION representatives in that department, giving consideration to seniority and ability to perform the work. Refused overtime hours shall be credited as overtime hours worked for purposes of distributing overtime.

6.10 SHIFT PREMIUM.

    a. A shift premium of 30 cents per hour will be paid to all employees for all hours worked on a particular day if 50 percent or more of the hours worked on that day fall between the hours of 3 P.M. and 11 P.M.

    b. A shift premium of 40 cents per hour will be paid to all employees for all hours worked on a particular day if 50 percent or more of the hours worked on that day fall between the hours of 11 P.M. and 7 A.M.

    c. The incentive percent will not be applied to the shift premium.

6.11 HOLIDAYS.

    a. After completion of the probationary period an hourly employee not working on the holiday will be granted holiday benefit consisting of eight hours straight-time pay at his regular hourly base rate on the following holidays:

New Year's Day	Thanksgiving
Decoration Day	Christmas
Labor Day	December 24
Fourth of July	December 31
	Floating Holiday

    b. Double time in addition to the holiday pay, as stated in Section 6.11a, will be paid for all hours worked on the above holidays.

    c. The floating holiday will be designated by the COMPANY. The UNION will be notified at least 90 days prior to the day set by the COMPANY.

    d. A holiday starts at the beginning of the first shift and ends at the close of the third shift. When one of these holidays falls on Sunday, the holiday shall be observed on Monday.

    e. To be eligible the employee must be at work on the day for which he is scheduled prior to the holiday and following the holiday unless absence is established for any one of the following reasons:

        1. Unavoidable absence caused by sickness or injury.

        2. Emergencies in the immediate family.

        3. Any other justifiable absence previously approved by his foreman.

ARTICLE 7. WAGES

7.01 Effective March 1, 1976, all hourly rates will be contained in the Appendix.

7.02 Effective March 1, 1977, all hourly rates contained in the Appendix will be increased by 40 cents.

7.03 Effective March 1, 1978, all hourly rates contained in the Appendix as increased in 7.02 will be increased an additional 30 cents.

7.04 JOB CLASSIFICATION PLAN.   The principle of like pay for like work shall prevail. The rates for production jobs throughout the plant shall continue to be established or reviewed by the COMPANY and the UNION after careful rating under the job classification plan in proportion to all factors of skill, responsibilities, effort, and working conditions of each individual job. When a new job is established or the duties and responsibilities of any job have changed sufficiently to place that job in a different pay bracket, a special job rating to determine the proper rate will be made no later than 30 days from the rating request. A special form for this purpose will be supplied by the COMPANY.

7.05 RATES RETAINED ABOVE CLASSIFIED RATES.

    a. If, as a result of job classification, the classified rate for a job is lowered, the employee on the job will retain his current rate for that job. In the event of a wage increase, he will participate to the extent that it does not bring his rate above the proper classified rate. Future transfers, promotions, and demotions will conform to the new rate schedule established by job classification. If the higher rate is established as a result of job classification, the employee on that job will advance to the proper classified rate as provided in Section 7.07 unless the job increases two pay grades in which case it will be posted.

    b. An employee who retains a rate above the classified rate on a job that has been reclassified will be expected to accept promotion to a higher classified job within his department in accordance with his seniority when a vacancy occurs and he is considered qualified to handle the job. In the event the employee who is offered the promotion chooses to remain on his present job, he will receive the new rate for his job on the following Monday, except in cases where the promotion would result in changing from a fixed day shift to a shift operation.

7.06 NEW EMPLOYEES.   New employees shall advance from the starting rate for their job to the classified rate for their job on the Monday following completion of 40 days actually worked.

7.07 PROMOTIONAL INCREASES.   When an employee is promoted to a higher classified job, he will receive the classified rate for the job the first Monday on or after his promotion.

7.08 TEMPORARY SERVICE IN HIGHER JOBS.

    a. Temporary work or part-time service in a higher classified job for periods of less than one full payroll week will not be classified a promotion or a change of classification. Wherever possible departmental seniority will be given due consideration in assigning such temporary work.

b. When an employee has worked temporarily on a higher classified job for 50 percent or more of his scheduled hours in the week, he will receive the higher rate during that week. When an employee is assigned temporary work in a higher classification, he shall, whenever possible, be allowed to complete 50 percent or more of the week on the higher classified job.

7.09 TRANSFERS TO LOWER JOBS. When an employee is permanently transferred to a lower classified job, he will receive the rate for the lower classification the first Monday on or after transfer to the lower classified job.

7.10. TEMPORARY SERVICE IN LOWER JOBS. The COMPANY agrees that while an employee is assigned temporarily to a lower classified job, he shall receive his regular higher classified rate.

7.11 TEMPORARY TRANSFERS BETWEEN DEPARTMENTS. When in the interest of effective and economical operation or as a means of deferring layoffs, it is desirable to transfer employees temporarily from one department to another, such temporary transfers may be made for a maximum period of four weeks if mutually agreeable to both the COMPANY and the UNION. Wherever possible, departmental seniority will be given due consideration in determining employees to be transfered. The UNION agrees to cooperate with the COMPANY in arranging such temporary interdepartment transfers. The COMPANY agrees not to request temporary interdepartment transfers except in the interest of efficient and economical operation or as a means of deferring layoff.

7.12 EMPLOYEE REPORTING AND NO WORK AVAILABLE. Employees reporting for work according to their regularly assigned work schedules without being notified in advance not to report and work is not available shall be allowed a minimum of four hours' pay at the employees' regular straight-time hourly base rate except in cases beyond the control of the COMPANY.

7.13 CALL-IN PAY. Employees, who have been recalled to work after they have completed their regularly scheduled shift and have left the plant, shall be given a minimum of four hours' work if they so desire. If four hours' work is not available, the employee shall be paid for the hours worked according to the wage and premium pay policy, and the remainder of the four hours not worked shall be paid at the employee's regular straight-time hourly base rate.

7.14 JURY DUTY. The COMPANY agrees to pay the difference between jury duty pay and the employee's straight-time hourly base rate earnings when called for jury duty. When called, the employee will be scheduled to work on the first shift whenever possible. The employee shall be required to report for work whenever he is able to work four consecutive hours or more of the first shift.

ARTICLE 8. SENIORITY

8.01   PLANT SENIORITY.   Plant seniority shall be determined from the employee's earliest date of continuous employment with the COMPANY and shall apply to divisional and plant layoffs and plant recalls after layoffs.

8.02   DEPARTMENTAL SENIORITY.   Departmental seniority shall be determined from the employee's earliest date on continuous employment in the department and shall apply to promotions, demotions, reductions in force within the department.

8.03   TERMINATION OF SENIORITY.   Seniority shall terminate for the following reasons:

   a.   Voluntary resignation.
   b.   Discharge for proper cause.
   c.   Absence for three successive working days without notice, unless satisfactory reason is given.
   d.   Failure to report to work after layoff within five working days after being notified by registered letter (return receipt requested) at the employee's last available address, unless satisfactory reason is given. A copy of the written offer shall be sent to the UNION.

8.04   EMPLOYEES ON LAYOFF.
   a.   Employees who are or shall be laid off due to lack of work and later reemployed shall accumulate seniority rights except that, if an employee after the first six months of layoff declines to return to work when contacted by the production personnel office regarding an opening, his seniority rights shall be terminated.
   b.   Employees shall be given three working days' notice of impending layoff from the plant of three days' pay in lieu thereof.

8.05   PROBATIONARY EMPLOYEES.
   a.   A new employee shall be on probation without seniority for 40 days actually worked after date of employment by the COMPANY, during which period the COMPANY shall determine the employee's ability to perform satisfactorily the duties and requirements of the work. Layoff or discharge of an employee during such probationary period shall not be subject to the grievance procedure.
   b.   Upon satisfactorily completing the probationary period, the employee will be placed on the department's seniority list, and his departmental seniority shall date from the beginning of the probationary period. If an employee is transferred to another department during his probationary period, his departmental seniority shall date back to the date of transfer to the new department upon completion of the probationary period.

8.06   PROMOTIONS AND VACANCIES.   When vacancies are to be filled and increases are to be made in the work force, it shall be done on the following basis:

a. Departmental postings.
1. When vacancies occur in a department, notices shall be posted by the COMPANY for three working days in the department in which the vacancy occurs and a copy of the posting provided to the UNION representatives of the department. Any employee in the department wishing to fill the vacancy shall make written application on the form provided by the COMPANY and containing the following information: (a) department and location, (b) date and hour of posting, (c) serial number of notice, (d) job title and classified rate of vacant job, (e) date job becomes effective, and (f) date and hour of closing time for application.
2. The employee making application with the most departmental seniority shall be given the job provided he is qualified and has the experience to handle the job.
b. Plant postings. In the event the vacancy is not filled from the employees in the department as outlined above, the COMPANY agrees to post the vacancy in the plant entrances for three working days and employees will be selected in accordance with Section 8.06a–2. To expedite the processing time the opening adjudged to be the resulting vacancy may be posted concurrently with the departmental posting. To be eligible for consideration, an employee must make written application on the form provided for the purpose, a copy of which shall be retained by the production personnel office, and a copy to be given to the UNION. The rate of pay for the job and the date the employee's seniority shall commence in the new department will be included on the posting.
c. Transfers between "A" and "B" seniority groups will not be allowed.
d. A qualified applicant shall be given a chance to qualify on the job by a fair trial. Any employee who is disqualified for any reason may have his qualifications acted upon in accordance with the grievance procedure.
8.07 TRANSFERS.
a. When an employee leaves his department to accept a job in another department, his seniority rights in the department which he has left shall not be forfeited for a period of 90 days. If the employee chooses to return to his home department (home department is where he has recall and return rights) within 90 days from the date of such transfer, he shall be returned to his former job not later than the third Monday following his request, provided he has enough seniority, otherwise he will be placed in a classification to which his seniority entitles him, provided it is not higher than the job grade he left. If he requests transfer to another department within 12 months of his return to his home department, he shall, upon being transferred, forfeit all departmental seniority rights.

b. When an employee has been reduced from his home department and is working in another department, he may sign plant postings, but the above clause does not apply.

c. If an employee signs a plant posting, and during the 90-day period in that job signs another plant posting, he has the original 90 days to return to his home department but has no right of return to the second department he left.

8.08   LAYOFFS.

a. Departmental. When the number of employees in a department is reduced, reduction to lower jobs or layoffs shall be made on the basis of departmental seniority providing those remaining are qualified to perform the work.

b. Divisional. The employee ultimately laid off from a department shall be entitled to bump into the department of the least senior employee in the division on the basis of plant seniority, provided he has the necessary qualifications to perform the job to which he is assigned.

In multiple reductions involving the displacement of employees in the department in which reduction is taking place, the employees with the most departmental seniority of those on the original reduction schedule will be retained in the department providing employees in the reducing department do not have sufficient plant seniority to allow them to remain in the division.

Others reduced from the department will be assigned to one or two shifts according to plant seniority. Upon notification to the production personnel department special shift requests will be given consideration.

c. Plant. The employee laid off from his division shall be entitled to bump into the department of the least senior employee in the plant providing the claiming employee has the necessary qualifications to perform the job to which he is assigned and has more than six months of plant seniority to his credit. In case any of the jobs vacated by the least senior employees in the plant are on a one- or two-shift basis as opposed to the ordinary three-shift basis, the employees being laid off from a division who have the most plant seniority shall automatically be given these one- or two-shift jobs. Upon notification to the production personnel department special shift requests will be given consideration.

d. The employee so reduced or transferred shall accept, according to his seniority, the position vacated to make room for him. The foreman shall have the right to place the crew as he sees fit on jobs carrying the same classified rate in all cases of emergencies and vacancies, taking into account the most efficient utilization of his working force.

e. When a classification is eliminated, the employee(s) occupying that classification may exercise his seniority to claim any classification within the department to which his seniority entitles him. The employee(s) then affected will follow the normal layoff procedure.

    f. Bumping shall not be allowed between ''A'' and ''B'' seniority groups.

8.09 RECALL AFTER LAYOFF.

    a. When it is necessary to employ additional employees, employees laid off due to lack of work will be recalled in order of their plant seniority, providing they are qualified to handle the jobs, before new employees are employed.

    b. When an employee is recalled after layoff for a job in another department and accepts, he will retain his home departmental seniority until such time as he declines an opportunity to return to his home department, subject to Section 8.07. If a laid-off employee declines, he shall remain on recall to his home department for a period not to exceed six months after layoff date. If during the six months' period, the employee wishes to be considered for an opening in another department, he may do so by notifying the production personnel office. Thereafter, he must return to work when offered employment by the COMPANY or his seniority will be terminated.

8.10 LEAVES OF ABSENCE.

    a. Members of the UNION, not to exceed three in number at any one time shall be granted leaves of absence for the duration of this Agreement to work directly for the local UNION. It is further agreed that four additional leaves shall be granted to any employees of a COMPANY covered by this Agreement who have been or who may in the future be elected to or appointed to a full-time office in the international union or the state federation of labor, AFL–CIO, such leaves not to exceed the duration of this Agreement. Upon being relieved of their official positions, they will be entitled to full seniority rights as though they had been employed by a COMPANY continuously.

    b. Employees not to exceed 1 percent of the UNION's membership who are members of the UNION when delegated or elected to attend a UNION convention or conference shall be granted such leave of absence as may be necessary, providing reasonable notice is given the COMPANY.

    c. Any employee elected to or appointed to any federal, state, or city public office shall be granted a leave of absence during the period he is actively engaged in such service.

    d. Maternity leave.

        1. An employee who becomes pregnant will be granted a leave of absence upon request at any time during pregnancy and extended for three months after the birth of the child. Where leave of absence is taken, such employee shall not lose senior-

ity which was acquired before the beginning of such leave of absence.

2. All employees placed on maternity leave or absence shall have their seniority dates adjusted upon their return by an amount of time equal to the number of days absent prior to and after the birth of the child.

8.11 SUPERVISORY AND OTHER SALARIED POSITIONS.

a. It is recognized that all supervisory employees are representatives of management and the assignment of their duties, promotions, demotions, and transfers is the responsibility of the COMPANY and cannot be determined on the basis of seniority.

b. Any supervisory employees, including quality supervisors, promoted from any hourly job shall maintain seniority as follows:

1. Hourly employees promoted to supervisory positions prior to January 1, 1977, shall continue to accumulate seniority while holding a supervisory position.

2. Hourly employees promoted to a supervisory position after January 1, 1977, shall accumulate seniority until such a time that he holds a supervisory position continuously for six months. After six continuous months, his seniority in the bargaining unit shall be frozen as of the date of promotion.

If later reduced to an hourly job, he shall be assigned to the job to which his accumulated or frozen seniority entitles him in the department which he left to become a supervisor, providing he is qualified to perform the job and providing the job is not in a higher job grade than the job he left to become a supervisor. No supervisor as herein defined shall have posting privileges until 30 days following his reassignment to an hourly production job. In return for protecting an employee's seniority while he is in a supervisory position as well as allowing him the right to claim a job in the bargaining unit if reduced from his supervisory position, supervisors who are reduced to hourly jobs shall become members of the UNION within 30 days.

c. Supervisory and other salaried employees will not perform the work of hourly production employees except in cases of emergency.

ARTICLE 9. GRIEVANCE PROCEDURE AND NO-STRIKE AGREEMENT

9.01 DEPARTMENTAL REPRESENTATIVES. The UNION may designate representatives for each section on each shift and in each department for the purpose of handling grievances which may arise in that department. The UNION will inform the production personnel office in writing, as to the names of the authorized representatives. Should differences arise as to the intent and application of the provisions of this Agreement, there shall be no strike, lockout, slowdown, or work stoppage of any kind, and the controversy shall be settled in accordance with the following grievance procedures:

9.02 GRIEVANCES.

Step 1. The employee and the departmental steward, if the employee desires, shall take the matter up with his foreman. If no settlement is reached in Step 1 within two working days, the grievance shall be reduced to writing on the form provided for that purpose.

Step 2. The written grievance shall be presented to the foreman or the general foreman and a copy sent to the production personnel office. Within two working days after receipt of the grievance, the general foreman shall hold a meeting, unless mutually agreed otherwise, with the foreman, the employee, and the departmental steward and the chief steward.

Step 3. If no settlement is reached in Step 2, the written grievance shall be presented to the departmental superintendent, who shall hold a meeting within five working days of the original receipt of the grievance in Step 2 unless mutually agreed otherwise. Those in attendance shall normally be the departmental superintendent, the general foreman, the foreman, the employee, the chief steward, departmental steward, a member of the production personnel department, the president of the UNION or his representative and the divisional committeeman.

Step 4. If no settlement is reached in Step 3, the UNION COMMITTEE and an international representative of the UNION shall meet with the MANAGEMENT COMMITTEE for the purpose of settling the matter.

Step 5. If no settlement is reached in Step 4, the matter shall be referred to an arbitrator. A representative of the UNION shall meet within five working days with a representative of the COMPANY for the purpose of selecting an arbitrator. If an arbitrator cannot be agreed upon within five working days after Step 4, a request for a list of arbitrators shall be sent to the Federal Mediation & Conciliation Service. Upon obtaining the list, an arbitrator shall be selected within five working days. Prior to arbitration, a representative of the UNION shall meet with a representative of the COMPANY to reduce to writing wherever possible the actual issue to be arbitrated. The decision of the arbitrator shall be final and binding on all parties. The salary, if any, of the arbitrator and any necessary expense incident to the arbitration shall be paid jointly by the COMPANY and the UNION.

9.03   In order to assure the prompt settlement of grievances as close to their source as possible, it is mutually agreed that the above steps shall be followed strictly in the order listed and no step shall be used until all previous steps have been exhausted. A settlement reached between the COMPANY and the UNION in any step of this procedure shall terminate the grievance and shall be final and binding on both parties.

9.04   The arbitrator shall not have authority to modify, change, or amend any of the terms or provisions of this Agreement, or to add to or delete from this Agreement.

9.05   The UNION will not cause or permit its members to cause or take part in any sit-down, stay-in, or slowdown in any plant of the COMPANY or any curtailment of work or restriction of production or interference with the operations of the COMPANY.

9.06   The UNION will not cause or permit its members to cause or take part in any strike of any of the COMPANY's operations, except where the strike has been fully authorized as provided in the constitution of the international union.

ARTICLE 10. VACATIONS

10.01   The vacation year shall be from April 1 to and including March 31. Wherever possible, however, vacations should be taken before December 31 of any one year. Vacations for any two years shall not be taken consecutively.

10.02   ONE WEEK'S VACATION.   One week's vacation with pay (See Section 10.08) will be granted to an employee who has accumulated 12 months or more of service credit prior to September 30 of the vacation year, provided he has accumulated a minimum of 6 months' service credit during the 12-month period immediately preceding April 1 of the vacation year, and is actively working on or after April 1 of the vacation year.

10.03   TWO WEEKS' VACATION.   Two weeks' vacation with pay (See Section 10.08) will be granted to an employee who has accumulated 36 months or more of service prior to September 30 of the vacation year, provided he has accumulated a minimum of 6 months' service credit during the 12-month period immediately preceding April 1 of the vacation year, and is actively working on or after April 1 of the vacation year.

10.04   THREE WEEKS' VACATION.   Three weeks' vacation with pay (See Section 10.08) will be granted to an employee who will complete 120 months or more of service credit by December 31 of the vacation year, provided he has accumulated a minimum of 6 months' service credit during the 12-month period immediately preceding April 1 of the vacation year, and is actively working on or after April 1 of the vacation year.

10.05 FOUR WEEKS' VACATION. Four weeks' vacation with pay (See Section 10.08) will be granted to an employee who will complete 180 months or more of service credit by December 31 of the vacation year, provided he has accumulated a minimum of 6 months' service credit during the 12-month period immediately preceding April 1 of the vacation year, and is actively working on or after April 1 of the vacation year (effective 1977 vacation period).

10.06 FIVE WEEKS' VACATION. Five weeks' vacation with pay (see Section 10.08) will be granted to an employee who will complete 360 months or more of service credit by December 31 of the vacation year, provided he has accumulated a minimum of 6 months' service credit during the 12-month period immediately preceding April 1 of the vacation year, and is actively working on or after April 1 of the vacation year (effective 1977 vacation period).

10.07 FIVE WEEKS' VACATION. Five weeks' vacation with pay (see Section 10.08) will be granted to an employee who will complete 300 months or more of service credit by December 31 of the vacation year, provided he has accumulated a minimum of 6 months' service credit during the 12-month period immediately preceding April 1 of the vacation year, and is actively working on or after April 1 of the vacation year (effective 1978 vacation period).

10.08 One week of vacation pay shall consist of 40 hours' pay at the employee's regular straight-time hourly base rate plus the average incentive percentage of the eight weeks prior to April 1 of the department in which he is working at the time the vacation is taken.

10.09 If a holiday recognized within this Agreement falls within an employee's vacation period, he shall be granted an extra day of vacation, provided the employee is eligible for holiday pay on that holiday.

10.10 Any employee who is discharged for proper cause will not be eligible for a vacation.

10.11 Vacations will be granted at such times of the year as the COMPANY finds most suitable, considering both the wishes of the employee according to plant seniority and the requirements of plant operation.

10.12 Employees who are laid off will be granted the vacation to which they are otherwise eligible if they have worked a minimum of 1,600 straight-time hours since the previous April 1.

ARTICLE 11. SICK LEAVE

11.01 EMPLOYEES WITH ONE- TO FIVE-YEAR SERVICE CREDIT. Employees who have accumulated 12 months but less than 60 months of service credit shall be entitled to a maximum of four working days' sick leave (32 hours straight-time pay at the employee's regular hourly base rate) in any one year calculated from April 1 to March 1, inclusive. Such benefits, not to exceed eight hours in any day, will apply only to time lost from scheduled work for reasons of personal illness or injury except that no benefits will be paid for the first two scheduled working days of any period of such absence.

11.02 EMPLOYEES WITH FIVE OR MORE YEARS OF SERVICE CREDIT.

a. Eligibility. A five-year hourly employee who has accumulated 60 months of service credit will receive the difference between sickness and accident insurance or workmen's compensation benefits for which he is eligible and his regular hourly base rate for time lost due to unavoidable absence as defined in Section 11.02e, which occurs during the first 40 hours he is scheduled to work in any week, not to exceed 8 hours in any one day and subject to Section 11.02d.

b. Amount of benefits. The benefits made available each year shall be 80 hours. The year starts April 1. Combined benefits on any day of qualified absence shall total amount equal to the number of qualified hours multiplied by the employee's base rate. In no instance shall this payment total more than base rate earnings of 8 hours per scheduled work day, nor more than base rate earnings of 40 hours per scheduled work week. In other words, the COMPANY shall supplement with sick leave payments any compensation or insurance payments from a company-financed private or government plan with an amount of money sufficient to make the combined total payment equal to 8 hours of base rate pay per day of qualified absence or 40 hours per week of qualified absence.

1. If the employee qualifies for compensation from a company-financed private or governmental plan, his available sick leave benefits will be charged 19.9 hours per 40-hour week or 49.8 percent of the eligible working hours absent for part weeks. If the employee does not qualify for compensation from a company-financed private or governmental plan, his available sick leave benefits will be charged with 100 percent of the eligible working hours absent.

c. Accumulation.

1. Sick leave benefits unused in any year of the plan may be accumulated for possible use in the next two years. When fourth year benefits become available the unused benefits from the first year automatically cancel and so on for each succeeding year. Order of sick leave usage is—first—the current year's benefits, second—oldest year's benefits.

Employees out sick before April 1 whose absence due to that illness extends through April 1 will first use those benefits which were available at the commencement of the absence.

d. Waiting period. There shall be no waiting period for the first five days (40 hours) of sick leave usage in a benefit year. However, no ·benefits shall be payable for the first normally scheduled working day in any period of absence commencing thereafter.

e. Unavoidable absence is defined as follows:

1. Unavoidable absence caused by sickness or injury.
2. Emergencies in the immediate family.

f. Immediate family shall consist of the following with no exceptions:

Spouse	Son	Sister
Mother	Daughter	Mother-in-law
Father	Brother	Father-in-law

In addition, the death of the employee's grandfather or grandmother will be recognized as an emergency in the immediate family to the extent of allowing one day's benefit, provided it is necessary that he be absent.

11.03 a. A 15-year hourly employee will receive straight-time pay at his regular hourly base rate for time lost due to hospitalization in a recognized hospital or convalescence thereafter which occurs during the first 40 hours he is scheduled to work in any week, not to exceed 8 hours in any day. The total amount of such allowance will not exceed 80 hours in any one year, calculated from year to year. Benefits provided in this paragraph will not apply to days of unavoidable absence for which benefits are paid under the provisions of Section 11.02.

b. A 25-year hourly employee will receive straight-time pay at his regular hourly base rate for time lost due to hospitalization in a recognized hospital or convalescence thereafter which occurs during the first 40 hours he is scheduled to work in any week, not to exceed 8 hours in any day. The total amount of such allowance will not exceed 160 hours (an additional 80 hours to [a] above) in any one year, calculated from year to year. Benefits provided in this paragraph will not apply to days of unavoidable absence for which benefits are paid under the provisions of Section 2 above.

11.04 In order to obtain these benefits the employee shall, if required, furnish his supervisor satisfactory reason for absence.

11.05 The COMPANY and the UNION agree to cooperate in preventing and correcting abuses of these benefits.

ARTICLE 12. GENERAL

12.01 BULLETIN BOARDS. The COMPANY shall provide bulletin boards which may be used by the UNION for posting notices approved by the industrial relations manager or someone designated by him and restricted to:

a. Notices of UNION recreational and social affairs.
b. Notices of UNION elections.
c. Notices of UNION appointments and results of UNION elections.
d. Notices of UNION meetings.
e. And other notices mutually agreed to.

12.02 RELIEF PERIODS.
a. Relief periods of 25 minutes for every eight-hour work period will be on COMPANY time at such times in each department as will be most beneficial to the employees and the COMPANY. A lunch period on COMPANY time may be substituted for relief period, provided the total time allowed for lunch and relief period in an eight-hour work period does not exceed 25 minutes.
b. The relief and lunch periods in each department will be determined by the department supervisors and the UNION stewards considering both the wishes of the employees and the requirements of efficient departmental operation.

12.03 All benefits now in effect and not specifically mentioned in this Agreement affecting all hourly paid employees of the COMPANY shall not be terminated for the duration of this Agreement.

12.04 SICKNESS AND ACCIDENT.   The COMPANY agrees to maintain its current sickness and accident insurance plans, as amended, effective December 1, 1976. Benefits begin one month after the sickness and accident initially occurred and continue for six months. Benefits will be equal to 60 percent of the employee's straight-time wage at the time of the sickness or accident.

12.05 LONG-TERM DISABILITY PLAN.   Subject to the provisions and qualifications of the long-term disability plan, there will be available a monthly income benefit commencing after 26 weeks of continuous total disability and continuing until recovery or death, but not beyond the normal retirement date.
The monthly amount will be $25 per $1,000 on the first $10,000 of group life insurance.

12.06 GROUP LIFE INSURANCE.
a. The COMPANY will pay for the first $1,000 of group life insurance available to employees. Employees will have the option of purchasing an additional amount of insurance in accordance with their earnings class schedule.
b. The present permanent and total disability benefit is replaced by a disability waiver-of-premium provision under which coverage will be continued during periods of total disability, while long-term disability payments are being made, but reduced each month by the amount of the long-term disability benefit. Reductions will cease when the amount of insurance in force is equal to the greater of (a) 25 percent of the original amount or (b) the employee's post retirement life amount calculated as of the date of commencement

of LTD payments. Coverage will be reduced to the latter amount at the earlier of (a) normal retirement age or (b) commencement of any income under ERI.

12.07 RETIREMENT INCOME PLAN. Following is a brief description of the major changes to become effective January 1, 1977, in the employee retirement income plan as it applies to employees covered by this bargaining unit:

    a. The COMPANY will contribute an amount equal to 5 percent of each employee's straight-time earnings to the retirement trust fund administered by Commonwealth National Bank, Central City.

    b. Provide for 100 percent vesting in pension benefits after ten years service.

12.08 The COMPANY will contract with Indiana Blue Cross–Blue Shield to provide hospitalization and medical insurance for all employees and their family members residing at home (except children over age 21). The COMPANY will pay all premiums necessary to provide full coverage of necessary surgical, medical, and hospital care under Blue Cross–Blue Shield fee schedules when performed in a participating hospital.

12.09 Departmental agreements between COMPANY and UNION representatives shall not supersede provisions contained in this Agreement should controversies arise. In no case, however, shall any retroactive adjustment be made if and when such a departmental agreement is cancelled. Wherever possible, the UNION shall receive a copy of the agreement.

12.10 SAFETY.

    a. The COMPANY will make reasonable provisions for the safety and health of the employees of the plant during the hours of their employment. Such protective devices and other safety equipment as the COMPANY may deem necessary to protect employees from injury properly shall be provided by the COMPANY without cost to the employees. The foreman in each department will arrange for this equipment.

    b. Gloves and uniforms required on such jobs and in such departments as the COMPANY may deem necessary shall be furnished and maintained by the COMPANY.

    c. The UNION agrees in order to protect the employees from injury and to protect the facilities of the plant that it will cooperate to the fullest extent in seeing that the rules and regulations are followed and that it will lend its wholehearted support to the safety program of the COMPANY.

    d. Rotating UNION departmental representatives chosen by the UNION will participate in periodic safety inspections conducted by departmental supervision and safety staff.

    e. The COMPANY agrees that it will give full consideration to all suggestions from its employees or their representatives in matters pertaining to safety and health, including proper heating and ventilation, and if these suggestions are determined to be sound, steps will be taken to put them into effect.

f. It shall be considered a regular part of each employee's regular work to attend such safety meetings as may be scheduled by the COMPANY. Hours spent at safety meetings will be compensated for as hours worked.

g. It is understood that the COMPANY shall not be required to provide work for employees suffering from compensable or other injuries; the COMPANY, however, will offer regular work which may be available to such employees provided that they can perform all duties of the job.

12.11   Other than for the recall provisions of this Agreement and the privileges accorded an employee under the COMPANY group insurance plans, employees on layoff shall not be entitled to the benefits of this Agreement.

12.12   SUPPLEMENTARY UNEMPLOYMENT BENEFIT PLAN.

a. Objective. To provide a greater measure of income protection during periods of unemployment for all eligible employees by supplementing state unemployment benefit payments.

b. Principles.

1. To provide income protection for permanent full-time employees as mentioned (a) above.

2. Preserve necessary differential between amounts received while unemployed and straight-time weekly earnings while working so as to provide an incentive for the unemployed to become employed. (65 percent of straight-time weekly earning less any normal deductions that are not of the savings variety).

3. The COMPANY will pay the difference between 65 percent of straight-time weekly earnings less normal deductions and the state unemployment benefit for which the employee qualifies. In the event the state benefit check is reduced because of ineligibility, the SUB payment will be reduced in the same proportion. The straight-time weekly earnings will be based on the week of layoff. The number of weeks an employee qualifies for would depend on length of service.

c. Eligibility.

1. Permanent, full-time employees covered under this Agreement.

2. Five years or more of service.

3. On layoff from the COMPANY as per seniority provisions in the UNION-MANAGEMENT Agreement and with the following conditions present:

a. Be able and available for work.

b. Maintain an active and continuing search for work.

c. Register and maintain constant contact with the State Employment Office.

d. Accept referral by the COMPANY to other employers in the area and accept resulting employment offers if deemed suitable under terms of the existing state system.

e. Layoff not due to a strike, slowdown, work stoppage, or concerted action.

f. Layoff not due to a labor dispute within the COMPANY or labor picketing conducted on the COMPANY premises which interferes with the COMPANY's operations.

g. Layoff not due to voluntary quit.

h. Layoff not due to disciplinary suspensions or discharges.

i. Layoff not due to leaves of absence.

4. Weeks of eligibility.

0–5 years' service credit-0
    5 years' service credit—5 weeks of SUB.
    6 years' service credit—6 weeks of SUB.
    7 years' service credit—7 weeks of SUB.
    8 years' service credit—8 weeks of SUB.
    9 years' service credit—9 weeks of SUB.
    (1 week of SUB. per year of service credit up to a maximum of twenty-six (26) weeks of SUB.

d. Reinstatement. When an employee has received any benefits for which he is eligible under this plan as per the schedule, he will have his full benefits reinstated after 6 months of continuous active service.

e. To obtain benefits. To obtain benefits, the employee must initiate the claim by preparing the necessary forms and presenting his state unemployment compensation check weekly to the personnel office for verification and processing of claim.

12.13 In the event any section or article of this Agreement shall be found to be illegal or inoperable by any government authority of competent jurisdiction, the balance of this Agreement shall remain in full force and effect.

12.14 NONDISCRIMINATION AGREEMENT.

a. The COMPANY and the UNION agree that the provisions of this agreement shall apply to all employees covered by the Agreement without discrimination, and in carrying out their respective obligations neither will discriminate against any employee on account of race, color, national origin, age, sex, or religion.

b. In an effort to make the grievance procedure a more effective instrument for the handling of any claims of discrimination, special effort shall be made by the representatives of each party to raise such claims where they exist and at as early a stage in the grievance procedure as possible. If not earlier, a claim of discrimination shall be stated at least in the third stage proceedings. The grievance and arbitration procedure shall be the exclusive contractual procedure for remedying discrimination claims.

ARTICLE 13. RENEWAL

13.01   This Agreement shall become effective as of March 1, 1976, and shall continue in full force and effect until 12:01 A.M., February 28, 1979, and thereafter from year to year unless written notice to modify, amend, or terminate this Agreement is served by either party 60 days prior to the expiration of this Agreement, stating in full all changes desired.

13.02   After receipt of such notice by either party, both parties shall meet for the purpose of negotiating a new agreement within 30 days from the date of service of said notice, unless the time is extended by mutual agreement.

APPENDIX

A1.01   Classified base rates effective as of March 1, 1976
1.   "B jobs. Light assembly (production)

Job grade	Classified base rate
61	$4.40
62	4.465
63	4.53
64	4.595
65	4.66
66	4.715
67	4.78

2.   "A" jobs. Heavy fabrication (production)

Job grade	Classified base rate
7	4.905
8	5.00
9	5.095
10	5.19
11	5.285
12	5.38
13	5.475
14	5.57
15	5.665
16	5.76

3. Maintenance and machine shop rates will be as follows:

    Leadman .... Rate established at 18 cents above
    classification supervised

Tool and model maker	$7.74
Tool and die maker	7.53
Systems control technician	7.35
Jig grinder operator	7.26
Measurement and control technician	7.17
Instrument maintenance technician	7.17
Electrician	7.17
Machinist	7.08
Refrigeration and air conditioning mechanic	7.08
Steamfitter	7.08
Developmental electronics technician	7.08
Welder	6.99
Millwright mechanic	6.99
Maintenance mechanic	6.99
Millwright	6.99
Precision grinder	6.99
Layout and setup worker	6.90
Painter	6.90
Profile mill	6.57
Machinist trainee	6.57
Capital assembly worker	6.38
Weldment finisher	6.38
Metal fabricator	5.30
Grinder operator	5.30
Milling machine operator	5.30
Lathe operator	5.30
Cabinet maker	5.30
Head assembly worker	5.23
Locksmith	5.16
Specialist	5.07
Developmental assembler	4.93
Oiler	4.88
Steelroom handlers	4.855
Machine operator	4.855
Heat stockroom clerk	4.855
Yard worker	4.73
Stock service worker	4.73
Air conditioning cleaner	4.73
Truck driver	4.67
Experimental assembler	4.60
Tool crib attendant	4.60
Trades helper	4.60
Stockroom clerk	4.60
Assembler	4.385
Waste hauler	4.36
Yard laborer	4.36
Janitor	4.315

11

IMPASSES AND THEIR RESOLUTION

All negotiations do not result in an agreement. If you are looking for a car and the dealer is unwilling to sell at your highest offer, a sale is not made. The same thing happens in labor-management relations when the firm and the union cannot agree on the terms of a new contract. This inability to agree results in an impasse.

Most negotiations do not result in an impasse. The parties usually find a common ground for settlement, and strikes or interventions by third parties are not required. Recent data show that for the period from 1966 through 1975 about 41 million person-days per year were lost to strikes, only 0.23 percent of total time available.[1]

This chapter is directed toward situations where impasses are reached. We will examine the causes of impasses, the tactics available to either side after an impasse is reached, and the intervention of third parties. As a case study, we will focus on the rubber workers' strike of 1976 and examine the causes of the impasse, attempts to resolve the dispute, and the ultimate breaking of the impasse. Our focus here will be on the private sector. Public sector impasse resolution procedures are generally more complex and often only applicable to certain occupational classifications.

As you read this chapter, focus your attention on these issues:

1. To what extent is the federal government legally entitled to intervene in impasses? To what extent does it actually intervene?
2. What are the actions labor and management can legally take when impasse is reached?
3. What is involved in the mediation process?
4. What steps are taken by private enterprise and labor to reduce the incidence of impasses?

---

[1] U.S. Department of Labor, *Employment and Training Report of the President* (Washington: Government Printing Office, 1976), p. 363.

IMPASSE DEFINITION

A bargaining impasse occurs when the parties are unable to move further toward settlement. The impasse may result because the settlement ranges of both parties are nonoverlapping—the least the union is willing to take is more than the most the employer is willing to offer. It may also result because the parties have been unable or unwilling to communicate enough information about possible settlements for an agreement to be reached. The first type is relatively more difficult to overcome since it requires either or both parties to adjust their settlement ranges in order for a solution to be reached. The second type is more amenable to the injection of outside parties to facilitate communication and keep the parties working toward a settlement.

We will deal first with situations where impasses are resolved prior to strikes and examine the procedures used to open communications, allow reassessment and adjustment of bargaining stances, and lead toward settlement. Since employees in most public sector jobs are precluded from striking by law (although evidence is plentiful enough to demonstrate the law's general unenforceability), the use of third parties is more prevalent there. We will discuss the general types of third-party interventions used across both public and private sectors here and then explain in more detail their application in public jurisdictions in Chapter 15.

THIRD-PARTY INVOLVEMENT

There are three major types of third-party intervention: mediation, fact-finding, and arbitration. Each becomes progressively more constraining on the freedom of the parties, but in most private sector negotiations, the parties would have to agree voluntarily before any third-party involvement can be imposed on them (however, see Chapter 16, "Health Care Organizations"). The only major exception involves national emergency disputes under the Taft-Hartley Act where outside fact-finding is required.

Mediation

Mediation is a process in which a neutral third party attempts to assist the principals toward reaching agreement. The procedures used are tailored to the situation and are aimed at maintaining communications and pointing out settlement cues that the other party has missed. In our examination of mediation, we will learn the process and find out something about mediation, its successes and failures, and the situations mediators find themselves in.

Drawing on his experience as the director of the Federal Mediation and Conciliation Service (FMCS) during the Kennedy and Johnson administrations, William Simkin has discussed the functions of mediation.[2] The mediator is most often dealing with a difficult situation since his involvement would be unnecessary if the parties were able to agree on their own, although some parties use mediation as a matter of course. Frequently a mediator is brought in after an impasse has been reached and negotiations have been broken off. Not only does the mediator have trouble in getting a settlement but also in merely getting the sides back together. As a show of bargaining strength, both sides may refuse to propose a bargaining session; and as our earlier look at personality and behavior issues in bargaining showed us, if one takes a position that might be seen as demonstrating weakness, some form of retaliation could easily follow.

The mediator must ultimately get the parties together to reach a settlement, but often many sessions will be held between the mediator and a party to assess possibilities for movement. Changing the location of a meeting to the mediator's office may serve to increase his strength in the process. The basic requirements of mediation require that the parties continue to communicate and negotiate, but not at an intensity that will lead to a hardening of positions.

Since the parties have reached an impasse, the mediator not only has to keep communications open, but must also move the parties toward settlement, if possible. To get an assessment of settlement possibilities, the mediator may try out hypothetical settlements on the parties to see their reactions. The relative rigidity of a party's position must also be assessed so that the mediator knows whether or not there is a continued willingness to compromise on given issues.

As a strike deadine approaches, the mediator must communicate assessments of the likelihood of a strike, the possible settlement packages available, and the costs of striking versus nonstriking. In all of these the mediator must use great care not to commit the parties to positions since the mediator is a go-between, not someone with the authority to fix a position.

A few excerpts from Ann Douglas's classic book on mediation will help to show the role of the mediator in resolving disputes.[3] In the first excerpt, the mediator is giving the union caucus some background on negotiating in an attempt to make them see the processes that will be necessary to reach a settlement. (**M** stands for the mediator; **U1** is the

---

[2] William E. Simkin, *Mediation and the Dynamics of Collective Bargaining* (Washington: Bureau of National Affairs, 1971).

[3] Ann Douglas, *Industrial Peacemaking* (New York: Columbia University Press, 1962).

union's chief negotiator; **U2** is second in line; and so forth. **C1, C2**, and so on, are company negotiators.)

From the mediator's second caucus with the union:

> **M:** Well, look, fellows, to get this started, I don't know how much I rea— how much time I really need with you. I had a pretty good idea last time of just what you wanted, what were the basic demands, and, most prob'ly, I have more work to do with the company at this point than with you. However, I do want to do one thing tonight. I wanta go over with you what the company has responded with respect to each of the nine basic demands you substituted, plus get your thinking on each of the company's counterproposals. Now, before we get into that, I want to spend a minute or two with something else. I wanta remind you of something I used as a comparison of one of the early cases we had. You recall at that time I said that, in a sense, we all do bargaining in one form or another on many occasions, and I used the example of any one of you who might have an automobile that ya wanted to sell. What ya did was dress the thing up, make it look as attractive as possible, and put the highest price you felt you could reasonably ask on it. When a prospective purchase came around, you gave him the best sales talk you could give, but ordinarily you did not expect he was going to say "Yes." Ya expected he was going to haggle a little bit, and when he did, ya tried to think up some arguments to counter those that he advanced. Ya try to indicate to him that the lower price he was offering was not a proper price. Maybe you would even go back in the garage and dig up another spare tire or something else to make the car a little bit more attractive, and you would keep on haggling with him over price. And eventually he would offer something else to make the car a little bit more attractive, and you would keep on haggling with him over price. And eventually he would offer something that was worth- while to you, for which you would make the swap. Now, in that sort of thing, you didn't get overly mad. Ya took it as part of the game you were playing. I'm not saying, that in collective bargaining, where you're dealing with—with much more serious things, and things which are not quite within your control as is the sale of an automobile. You can either sell it or not sell it; you don't have to. With a contract, though, ya do have to conclude it, and ya have some compulsion here which was not present in any individual bargaining you might do over a personal effect. But there are a lot of elements of sameness; and just as you would do in a private transaction, so, in part, you must do here. When you make a proposal, until ya come right down to the end of the wire, where ya have most everything settled and it's a matter of saying "Yes" or "No" to a couple of final propositions, ya got to expect that what you're going to get is a tentative "Maybe," usually ah— to which is usually added a couple of other propositions, and it becomes a switch back and forth, a jockeying to try and get the most of what you want, knowing that the company is going to do the same thing. No, I mention these things because I want to remind you that last time I said that I did not think the company counterdemands, which you felt

pretty strongly about, were things to get too seriously concerned with, for, as far as I knew at that point—they may be, but as far as I know, they do not represent a final company position. If they did, then I think that you would be logically entitled to say—and holler every sort of implication you could think of. But I don't think that that's what they represent. I think what is called for after this is some further thinking, some further proposals on your part. What I want to do is to find out, how much that the company offered in connection with the counter-proposals they made to your nine proposals is acceptable to you, either as they have stated it or in some modified form. I want to find out, secondly, what there is in the company's additional nine proposals you think have any merit or that you're willing to go along with, either as they stated or in some modified form. This for my information. Tomorrow I have to do the same thing with management. How much of what the union—of what they said in their counterproposals did they say for bargaining purposes, how much closer to what they know the union wants are they willing to go?—that, again, is confidential with me. When I have those two things, then I can see how really far apart you are, and becomes a problem, then, of trying to get you to go a little bit this way on that business, gettin' the company to go a little bit your way on some other matter, until we reach the point where it looks like we have something that is an agreeable thing with you, something that's agreeable with them. And the only way we can do that is through this point-by-point discussion. I want to repeat that what you have to say concerning it is between you and I. Concessions that you tell me you are prepared to make are not told to the company. Concessions the company tell me they are prepared to make are not told to you at this point. For what you will be willing to do, what they will be willing to do will be perhaps to make concessions on one item, providing they get a counter-, or you get a counter-, concession on another item. So until the whole thing is squared up, I have to be the repository of your confidence and of theirs. So, to get to this, then (pause), let's start with their response in connection with no. I, two-year contract. And this is what I want to know. If you gave them a two-year contract, what would you want in return? Of what advantage is it to you to say, "We'll give you a two-year contract"? What can you get out of them in return?[4]

In an excerpt where the mediator meets with company negotiators he is asking them to examine positions, seeing where movement can be made, and stressing the difficulties that lie ahead. Notice also that he refuses to tip his hand about information he may have on the union's position.

From the second management caucus with the mediator:

M: Well, what I'd like to do today is go over the company's counter-proposals to the union's proposals and see how much it means, actu-

---

[4] Ibid., pp. 56–58.

ally, how much room there is to move around in connection with the various points you have made, and I want this for my own information. I've already discussed a good bit of this with the union, so I have some notions on what they will and will not do. I wanta get similar notions from you and see whether or not actually you're really closer together than you appear on the surface. I'll say this pretty frankly, that quite probably there's goin' ta have ta be a lot of shaking down before you get to an agreement. The union is undoubtedly holding out for more now than you're prepared to give, and they're going to have to come down (**C2**: Uh-huh) in a number of respects.

C2: Any particular areas?

M: U1—(slight pause) I won't say now. Just (**C2**: Uh-huh) as a general position, they would appear to be holding to some things which are unlikely to come their way. I mention this because I think in part they're holding to them out of a belief that you, in your counter-proposals, have advanced some rather unreasonable notion.

C1: You mean unreasonable to them.

M: Oh, of course (laughing). Not to me, never! (**C1, C2,** and **M** all laugh) Not for recording on tape.

M: No, but I expect to get at least part of it today.

C1: What you're tryin' to do is find out where the soft spots are.

M: Yeah, and without presenting as notions the union might have to you, I shall discuss these things from the point of view of softening your position. Again I say that this is between us and for my information to see where I can then approach the union to get them to do likewise, and if we can get enough of that done, why, the thing may not look quite as black as it appears to the union to be.[5]

Returning to the union caucus, the mediator is still not specific about the positions taken by management but does say that a gap exists in the settlement range. He also continues his lessons on bargaining. From the mediator's third caucus with the union:

U1: What's their attitudes on—their position as to our minimum demand? Are they altering those?

M: Well, you have their counterproposal which is very definitely not acceding to your minimum demand. See, I—I don't understand minimum demand (**U1**: Well, you gotta remember that—)—what you mean by minimum demands. If you have to have everything such as this, then there's no room for bargaining.

U1: No. But we'd like to know if their counterproposal to ours is their final position.

M: Well, I just explained it. I've just told you the answer to that.

U2: Which?

---

[5] Ibid., p. 91.

M: That I've found that there is things in their position (**U2:** That's what—) that are bargainable (**U2:** Well—), which merely means that they are not saying to you, or they're not saying to me that "What we have answered the union is as far as we'll go."

U2: See what's happened, U1? We—when we went through—pract'ly went through all of these here and gave 'em our minimum demands, now what they're doin' is just knockin' them down to where—

U1: Yeah!

U2: The way it is now, we want all of ours.

U3: That's where the stalemate is.

M: No! The stalemate is that after you gave the company this offer, the company made a counteroffer and then you quit bargaining.

U1: We didn't quit bargaining. They did.

U3: They did.

M: All right. There was no cause for further reaction on your part directly to what they had said and that's what I am trying to get. Ordinarily in these things, it's a series. You demand, they reply; you demand, they reply; you demand, they reply; you demand, they reply. Somewhere in there—and this is exactly the way it looks—you start here with your demand. They reply. Then on down, each counterdemand is met with a counterreply until you reduce the difference (**U2:** Well, the—) the point where you reach an agreement. Now—

U4: Fact, all the time we're in there, M, we're t— all the time we were talking about their proposals. We hardly, if ever, mentioned our own proposals, because we figured when they got through we'd have our chance, and we never got our chance to talk.

U5: (Over U4 above) U4, as far as language is—is concerned, the whole thing is in a package and what—C1 is sittin' back, little ah— oh, one of these here chess players with the idea he just—he can take and move us fellows like we's just pawns or somethin' there. He just tryin' to—

U4: We never ran into that before. I mean—

M: (Over U4 above) Well, look. How—how would you propose that you go about—about reaching an agreement? What's your idea of how you do these things?

U1: They never once discussed any of our demands, never (**M:** Well—), and that's what we were asking for. (**M:** And—) Uh—

M: If they didn't discuss them, it was because you didn't insist on it, because you certainly have a right to discuss your own demands. (**U1:** We insisted on those) If you start, then they got to respond. You'll haggle back and forth until you get what is reasonably satisfactory. Now, when you tell me that you'll take 4 cents plus—4-cent improvement factor each year plus the cost-of-living adjustment, I am not going to tell them that. If anything, I might tell 'em, well, you'll take 10 cent plus their—no, I won't tell them you'll take. I'll ask them, "Well, what do you say—give 'em 10 cent plus the cost-of-living, huh?" to give me some room to move around. I gotta bargain with them, so I can't—I'm not gonna give them minimums. (Laughs) I'll stretch the minimum so I can come back a little bit.[6]

The exchanges depicted above and the crisis atmosphere in which mediators operate appear to call for a special mix of experience, talents, and behavior. We will now explore the major sources of mediators, their backgrounds, personalities, and the prevalence of mediation.

Mediator backgrounds

There are no specific requirements for selection as a mediator or for appointment to the Federal Mediation and Conciliation Service. This is not to say that FMCS mediators are not carefully selected or are untrained. In his work on mediation, Simkin details the backgrounds of FMCS mediators. Of new hires, less than 40 percent had college degrees, but experience plays a big role. Of 295 mediators employed by FMCS in 1969, 203 had had significant union or management labor relations experience, and an additional 74 had been neutrals in labor relations disputes. Mediators in the FMCS are most often over 45, and many have long experience in the service. Turnover due to resignations from 1961 through 1969 averaged only 1.2 percent annually.[7]

Mediator attitudes and personalities

A study of mediator backgrounds and attitudes was completed in 1964 at Rutgers University.[8] Some of their significant findings related to attitudes toward the parties and processes in collective bargaining. Other areas of concern included an examination of the types of mediation strategies neutrals found most effective.

The mediators believed strongly that collective bargaining is an effective tool for settling differences and generally would not favor imposed settlements by third parties. They endorsed the need for unions to represent employees, but they also supported management's rights to introduce innovation and change.

Generally, mediators did not favor involvement in bargaining until an impasse is reached. The impasse cannot be complete, however, since mediators generally agreed that their appointment be mutually

[6] Ibid., pp. 59–60.

[7] Simkin, *Mediation and the Dynamics of Collective Bargaining*, pp. 57–69.

[8] Monroe Berkowitz, Bernard Goldstein, and Bernard P. Indik, "The State Mediator: Background, Self-Image, and Attitudes," *Industrial and Labor Relations Review*, vol. 17 (1964), pp. 257–75.

endorsed and requested by both parties. Mediators saw their role as attempting to bring the parties toward a settlement rather than injecting a public opinion or viewpoint into the proceedings.

Mediators generally favored an active rather than a passive role in negotiations. They saw themselves as often having to criticize an extreme position of one or both parties which was a major contribution to the impasse. When they were asked to rank coercion, expertise, reward, authority, and affect (creating an atmosphere of friendship and agreement) as strategies useful for successful negotiations, affect was ranked first by 75 percent, followed by reward (benefits of settlement), and expertise (mediator's ability).

How do the parties involved see the mediator's effectiveness? Landsberger asked union and management representatives' and mediators' collegues to rank the mediators they had worked with recently on the dimensions shown in Figure 11-1.[9] Interestingly, there was general agreement by both users (labor and management) and the colleagues of mediators regarding their effectiveness. Skills leading to success as a mediator appeared to be related to intellectual competence and an ability to structure the situation and keep the parties at work. Less emphasis was placed on human relations skills related to positive feelings about the mediator's personality. This finding does not square with the first strategy preference of the mediators responding to the Rutgers study. Perhaps the mediators themselves feel it is necessary to create a friendly atmosphere while the parties respond to perceived expertise and an ability to manage the situation.

In a more tongue-in-cheek vein, Simkin offers the following set of qualities necessary to be a successful mediator:[10]

1. The patience of Job.
2. The sincerity and bulldog characteristics of the English.
3. The wit of the Irish.
4. The physical endurance of the marathon runner.
5. The broken-field dodging abilities of a halfback.
6. The guile of Machiavelli.
7. The personality-probing skills of a good psychiatrist.
8. The confidence-retaining characteristic of a mute.
9. The hide of a rhinoceros.
10. The wisdom of Solomon.

Simkin's impressive list suggests that some training, in addition to careful selection, may be necessary to attain skills as a mediator.

---

[9] Henry A. Landsberger, "The Behavior and Personality of the Labor Mediator: The Parties' Perception of Mediator Behavior," *Personnel Psychology*, vol. 13 (Autumn 1960), pp. 329–47.

[10] Simkin, *Mediation and the Dynamics of Collective Bargaining*, p. 53.

FIGURE 11–1
Scales reflecting mediator behavior

1. *Originality of ideas*
   Rank according to the originality of the suggestions made by the mediator. Take into consideration: Did he come up with a new formula when the usual one for settling a point in dispute did not work? Did he give the parties good ideas on which they could build further to get a settlement? Was he able to alter and rearrange ideas already put forward by him or others to remove objectionable features and yet retain the acceptable parts? and so on.
2. *Sense of appropriate humor*
   Rate high the person whom you remember as the one with the most ability to introduce a light touch into a tense situation, and so on.
3. *The ability to act unobtrusively*
   Whom could you remember most as "letting the parties convince each other when they were making headway in doing so?"
4. *The mediator as "one of us"*
   Rate high the mediator about whom you would say, "He understood us," "He talked like one of us," "He was a good guy." (It was made clear that informality, not partiality, was implied.)
5. *The mediator as a respected authority*
   . . . [T]he person for whom you really felt some respect in the sense of looking up to him a little . . . deference . . .
6. *Willingness to be a vigorous salesman*
   . . . [D]id he tell you (or the other side) that it seemed to him that the other side was unlikely to make further concessions; did he press the two sides to tell him what it was they *really* wanted. . . .
7. *Control over feelings*
   Rank high the individual who rarely seems to feel, and even more rarely expresses, his irritation and annoyance with others . . . unless it served a good purpose. . . .
8. *Attitude toward, and persistent patient effort invested in, the work of mediation*
   . . . [S]tick with your case day after day and into the evening and night, as long as there was a chance that a settlement could be reached.
9. *Ability to understand quickly the complexities of a dispute*
   . . . [G]rasping both the *facts* which you put before him, and . . . grasping also the *issues, feelings, motives,* and complexities which often lie beneath the specific dispute.
10. *Accumulated knowledge of labor relations*
    . . . [T]he backlog of information which you feel the mediator had at his command before . . . he started out on a case with you.

Source: Adapted from Henry A. Landsberger, "The Behavior and Personality of the Labor Mediator: The Parties' Perception of Mediator Behavior," *Personnel Psychology,* vol. 13 (Autumn 1960), pp. 334–35.

Mediator training

Generally the FMCS mediator begins with a two-week training program in Washington and then is sent to a regional office to learn procedures and work with experienced mediators. By the end of the first year, a first case probably has been assigned. Summaries and specialized training supplement experience as the mediator is assigned to increasingly complex cases.

Mediator activity

Under the Taft-Hartley Act employers and unions are required to notify the FMCS 30 days before the expiration of a contract where renegotiation is underway and an agreement has not been reached. Table 11–1 shows the notification and case load for the FMCS during fiscal year 1975. The figures indicate that the FMCS is involved in just under 20 percent of cases in which 30-day notifications have been received. The proportion of cases requiring assistance and the caseload has remained about the same over several years as Table 11–2 indicates.

Thus, most cases are settled without the intervention of mediators. Data from the FMCS Annual Report Series show that mediation is needed more frequently where the parties are negotiating a first contract and when the term of the contract is for three years. Thus, the inexperience of the negotiators and/or the permanency of the terms of the agreement appear to detract from the ability of the parties to reach agreement without outside assistance.

Our look at mediation has explored one method of third-party intervention in labor disputes. We recognize the active nature of mediation in keeping the parties together and its neutral approach in not projecting mediator values into the terms of the settlement. Mediation is aimed strictly at enabling the parties to settle on their own terms when and where they have been unable to do so on their own.

Fact-finding

Fact-finding has a long history in U.S. labor relations. According to McDermott, fact-finding in the 19th century was used for fixing the blame on one party rather than finding the underlying causes of the dispute.[11] Rehmus defines present day fact-finding as a situation where a neutral party studies the issues in a dispute and makes a public recommendation of what a reasonable settlement ought to be.[12]

McKelvey stresses that fact-finding requires the use of neutrals without any connections with either side to act on behalf of the public.[13] In the private sector, if their published findings are not adopted in a settlement, the parties are free to return to bargaining as they see it.

According to Rehmus, fact-finding has been used in two major types of disputes in the United States. The first is within the Taft-Hartley emergency disputes requirements, which he characterizes as being relatively ineffectual, and the second are the presidential emergency

---

[11] Thomas J. McDermott, "Fact-Finding Boards in Labor Disputes, *Labor Law Journal*, vol. 11 (1960), pp. 285–304.

[12] Charles M. Rehmus, "The Fact Finder's Role," *The Proceedings of the Inaugural Convention of the Society of Professionals in Dispute Resolution* (October 1973), pp. 34–44.

[13] Jean T. McKelvey, "Fact-Finding in Public Employment Disputes: Promise or Illusion?" *Industrial and Labor Relations Review*, vol. 22 (July 1969), p. 529.

TABLE 11-1
Notifications processed by the service covering all types of mediation activity for fiscal year 1975

Receipt of notifications

Notifications received during the year		98,515
30-day notices required by LMRA	91,812	
Requests from union and/or company	2,609	
Certifications	4,086	
NLRB	3,907	
LMSA	179	
Intercessions by FMCS	8	
Cases pending at close of previous year		7,063
Total notifications		105,578

Disposition of notifications

Cases closed by mediators		21,385
Joint meeting cases*	8,795	
Nonjoint meeting cases†	10,976	
Technical assistance cases‡	935	
Information and education cases§	679	
Cases closed administratively after inquiry by mediators		5,219
Screened for lack of jurisdiction	645	
Settled prior to inquiry, erroneous notice, and so on	3,787	
Consolidated with other cases	787	
Screened for lack of jurisdiction		16,276
Consolidated with other notifications		56,151
Cases pending at end of year		6,547
Dispute cases, joint and nonjoint	6,403	
Technical assistance cases	126	
Information and education cases	18	
Total notifications		105,578

* Cases in which joint and separate mediation conferences were held.
† Cases followed closely by mediators from assignment until final closing, requiring only informal mediation with no joint conferences.
‡ Cases comprise training, education, consultation and problem-solving activities performed by mediators for representatives of labor and management, other neutrals in dispute resolution, professional associations, and academic institutions.
§ Cases include activities such as informational addresses to public and professional groups and associations; interviews with newspapers, magazines, radio and television media; film showings and appearance and participation in conventions, seminars, and similar occasions.
Source: Federal Mediation and Conciliation Service, *Twenty-Eighth Annual Report* (Washington: Government Printing Office, 1976), p. 41.

TABLE 11–2
Number and percent of closed dispute, technical assistance and information and education cases participated in by FMCS mediators for fiscal years 1971–1975

Type of case	All mediation activity									
	1975		1974		1973		1972		1971	
	Total number of cases	Percent of fiscal year total	Total number of cases	Percent of fiscal year total	Total number of cases	Percent of fiscal year total	Total number of cases	Percent of fiscal year total	Total number of cases	Percent of fiscal year total
Total	21,385	100.0	20,160	100.0	18,238	100.0	17,248	100.0	19,285	100.0
Dispute cases	19,771	92.4	18,809	93.3	16,930	92.8	15,994	92.7	17,608	91.3
Joint meeting*	8,795	41.1	8,479	42.1	7,238	39.7	7,215	41.8	7,991	41.4
Nonjoint meeting†	10,976	51.3	10,330	51.2	9,692	53.1	8,779	50.9	9,617	49.9
Technical assistance cases‡	935	4.4	642	3.2	515	2.8	523	3.0	851	4.4
Information and education cases§	679	3.2	709	3.5	793	4.4	731	4.2	826	4.3

* Cases in which joint and separate mediation conferences were held.
† Cases followed closely by mediators from assignment until final closing, requiring only informal mediation with no joint conferences.
‡ Cases comprise training, education, consultation and problem-solving activities performed by mediators for representatives of labor and management, other neutrals in dispute resolution, professional associations, and academic institutions.
§ Cases include activities such as informational addresses to public and professional groups and associations; interviews with newspapers, magazines, radio, and television media; film showings, and appearances and participation in conventions, seminars, and similar occasions.
Source: Federal Mediation and Conciliation Service, Twenty-Eighth Annual Report (Washington: Government Printing Office, 1976), p. 31.

boards created under the Railway Labor Act.[14] We will come back to say more about fact finding in the public sector in Chapter 15.

Taft-Hartley fact-finding

Section 206 of the Taft-Hartley Act specifies that in cases where a national emergency dispute exists, the president may name a fact-finding board to report to him. No recommendations are to be made in the report, but it is to be filed with the FMCS. Under Section 208, after the fact finders have made their report, the president can ask a federal district court to enjoin a strike or lockout if *it* finds the dispute falls within national emergency criteria. Thus, the use of the fact-finding board appears redundant, given the requirement of a court determination.

Rehmus notes that the use of Taft-Hartley fact finders has diminished over time.[15] Their determinations were generally reflected in the federal court's granting of injunctions, but neither the reports nor the injunctions appeared to be related to success in impasse resolution.

Railway labor boards

Rehmus argues that the presidential emergency boards have been successful in impasse resolution in critical transportation disputes. He cites as evidence the move toward settlement of nonoperating craft job security, the recommendations made on phasing out the fireman job in diesel engines, and the introduction of new equipment in the airline industry.[16]

On the other hand, Northrup and Bloom paint a gloomy picture of the effectiveness of emergency boards.[17] They feel that a historical analysis of the record would conclude that more and more railroad negotiations are designated "emergencies"; that the boards have not been very independent, but more likely politically expedient; and the existence and use of boards has reduced the parties' abilities to bargain.

Fact-finding and the issues

Private sector fact finders appear to be relatively unsuccessful on matters related to distributive bargaining. They have little authority to

---

[14] Rehmus, "The Fact Finder's Role," pp. 35–36.

[15] Charles M. Rehmus, "The Operation of the National Emergency Provisions, 1947–1954," in Irving Bernstein, Harold L. Enarson, and R. W. Fleming, eds., *Emergency Disputes and National Policy* (New York: Harper & Brothers, 1955), pp. 261–68.

[16] Rehmus, "The Fact Finder's Role," p. 36.

[17] Herbert R. Northrup and Gordon F. Bloom, *Government and Labor* (Homewood, Ill.: Richard D. Irwin Inc., 1963), pp. 327–30.

make more than recommendations and can do little to keep the parties together. Neither labor nor management may accord legitimacy to an outside group in determining or recommending what either is entitled to.

On the other hand, presidential emergency board fact finders appear to have had some success in integrative bargaining areas. Employers and unions in the rail industry, in particular, have been faced with many problems where innovations have raised job security issues for the union and survival issues for management, given competition, if they were not implemented. In general, it has been necessary to convene boards to propose solutions, and the proposal by a neutral group may legitimize possible avenues to resolution enough so that the parties may implement them without bearing as great an individual responsibility to their constituents. Thus, fact-finding boards allow integrative bargaining through the proposal of solutions and encourage intraorganizational bargaining by legitimizing positions the principal negotiators may be willing to raise but see as unacceptable to their memberships.

Interest arbitration

One method that has been proposed and that has seen considerable use in various forms in the public sector is interest arbitration. Arbitration differs from mediation and fact-finding. Where mediation seeks to get the parties to reach a settlement, the arbitrator determines the settlement terms. Where fact-finding recommends a settlement, arbitration dictates it.

Two major types of arbitration in terms of subjects are central to labor relations, "rights" and "interests." According to the Supreme Court, interest arbitration occurs where no agreement exists or a change is sought and where the parties have an interest in the outcome because the contract will specify future rights. Rights arbitration involves the interpretation of an existing agreement to determine which party is entitled to a certain outcome or to take a certain action.[18]

In the United States, interest arbitration was used by the National War Labor Board during World War II and has been imposed, essentially, on the railroad industry by Congress since the 1960s. Taylor and Witney argue that the imposition of interest arbitration eliminates the parties' needs to settle on their own because a settlement is certain through outsiders if an impasse is reached.[19] There are many more cases in the public than the private sector, and while there is some

---

[18] *Elgin, Joliet, & Eastern Railway Co.* v. *Burley,* 325 U.S. 71 (1945).

[19] Benjamin J. Taylor and Fred Witney, *Labor Relations Law,* 2d ed. (Englewood Cliffs, N.J.: Prentice-Hall, 1975), pp. 488–91.

evidence to support this view, it is not as clearcut as they maintain.[20] We will follow this controversy in some detail in Chapter 15.

The spectre of interest arbitration has recently been raised through the conclusion of the Experimental Negotiating Agreement (ENA) between the basic steel industry and the United Steelworkers. In the ENA, both parties agreed to submit certain types of issues unresolved by bargaining to an arbitration tribunal for settlement. Obviously, the parties had not had previous experience with interest arbitration, so the narcotic effect could not have been in effect, but the parties could have resorted to it in 1977. Instead, the USW accepted the final package proposed by the steel companies just prior to the deadline for arbitration submission. According to reports, the USW was more comfortable with its bargained position than what the arbitrators might have awarded.[21] In this instance, the threat of arbitration and its unknown consequences probably hastened, rather than retarded, agreement.

Review of "third-party" involvements

Of the three methods of third-party involvement, only one (arbitration) guarantees a solution to an impasse. But for various reasons, arbitration has not been embraced by the private sector to decide interest issues. Fact-finding also has a relatively checkered past. It has generally been imposed on the parties who are then free to ignore its recommendations. There are actually no "facts" in fact-finding, only values associated with the possible positions that could be taken on outcomes in the dispute. Mediation is neutral in the sense that it requires the parties to bargain their own terms. It has been relatively successful in keeping parties at the table, given the FMCS load and success rate reported earlier.

There is, however, a disturbing trend which involves the FMCS more and more in quasi–fact-finding or arbitration. When the parties appear to be headed toward an impasse, rather than letting bargaining power in major disputes determine the outcome, the parties are brought to Washington, and deadlines for settlement are strongly implied as government action is threatened. As more unions and industries experience this mandatory outside intervention, we may see greater initiatives taken toward ENA types of responses, with the parties increasing pressure on themselves to agree.

We should note, however, that strikes and lockouts account for relatively little lost time. Absences by employees are much more frequent.

---

[20] Hoyt N. Wheeler, "Compulsory Arbitration: A Narcotic Effect?" *Industrial Relations*, vol. 14 (February 1975), pp. 117–20.

[21] *John Herling's Labor Letter* (Washington, April 16, 1977).

This is a relatively small price to pay to preserve the right and obligation of the parties to settle their own differences. Ironically, advocates of free collective bargaining find themselves modifying well-thought-out positions when faced with the pressures of political offices. For example, Box 11–1A contains a 1963 quote from a paper by George Shultz, then professor of economics at the University of Chicago, to be compared with a later pronouncement in the 1970 rail negotiations when he was secretary of labor (Box 11–1B).

BOX 11–1A
Shultz's differing positions on national emergency strikes

"Now, perhaps you will say that the recent longshore strike, in which Taft-Hartley injunction was used, is a case against me. That may be, but I think it is worth noting that the president sought and got an injunction against such a strike on the grounds that, if the strike were permitted to occur, it would create a national emergency. But after the injunction expired, a strike did run for over one month and what did people talk about? All I read about in *The Wall Street Journal* was the bananas; you are not going to get bananas, they are doubling in price. My, oh my, should we throw away our freedoms for a handful of bananas? Just for fun, I ordered bananas with my shredded wheat to see if they would come. The waiter didn't even give me an argument; he brought the bananas. Or a banana, I should say. Maybe he only had one. This is not to deny the genuine economic hardship and public inconvenience that can be caused by a prolonged strike on the docks or in some other industries. But the allegations of hardship need the closest scrutiny, and the true costs must be balanced against the price of intervention."

Source: George P. Shultz, "Strikes: The Private Strike and Public Interest," selected paper no. 8, Graduate School of Business, University of Chicago, 1963.

Quite obviously there are instances where the parties do not use or have mediation, fact-finding, or arbitrations imposed. There are also instances where mediation or fact-finding fail to break impasses. Then, typically, a work stoppage occurs. If the stoppage is a withholding of services of labor, we have a strike. On the other hand, if an employer refuses to provide opportunities for work, we have a lockout. We will now examine each, in turn, as to when it is used, its effectiveness, and its legality.

STRIKES

There are a variety of different types of strikes, but all have one thing in common: a withholding of effort by the employees. In terms of

---

BOX 11–1B

Following is the text of the telegram to the presidents of the unions and the designated presidents of a smaller number of railroads that represent 76 rail carriers: (*official text*)

"It is apparent that the nation is threatened with an imminent railroad work stoppage because of a breakdown in labor contract negotiations between the industry and the shopcraft unions. The adverse effect on the nation coupled with the relatively narrow nature of the unresolved issue in dispute make it imperative that every reasonable step be taken to avoid such an occurrence. Accordingly, please advise me immediately of your agreement to proceed as follows:

1. The parties will not engage in any strike or lockout for the next seven days.

2. You and presidents of the other affected unions will meet with me and designated railroad company presidents on Monday, February 2, at 2 P.M. to explore further avenues of dispute settlement."

Source: Secretary of Labor Telegram reported in *Daily Labor Report* (Washington, D.C.: Bureau of National Affairs, January 30, 1970), p. A–9.

---

causes, we could probably identify four major types of strikes. First, the *economic strike* occurs as a result of a failure to agree on the terms of a contract. It is called to place pressure on the employer to settle on the union's terms. The union believes that the cost of the strike (both economic and political) is less to it than to the employer or the potential benefits of the expected solution are greater than the costs. Just because it is called an economic strike does not mean that the issues in dispute involve dollars and cents. An economic strike can occur over any of the mandatory bargaining issues mentioned in the labor acts. But, a union cannot insist to impasse on and strike on permissive issues, or it would commit an unfair labor practice.[22] It is the economic strike that results from a bargaining impasse, and as we will see, it involves unique rules.

Unfair labor practice strikes are undertaken to protest illegal conduct by the employer. If the employer has committed illegal acts, the employees' right to strike and be reinstated after its conclusion is absolutely protected by NLRB and court interpretation of the labor acts. A *wildcat strike* is an unauthorized strike occurring during the term of the contract. Strikers may face disciplinary action, and the union bears some responsibility in getting the strikers to return to their jobs. A *sympathy strike* occurs when one union strikes in support of the strike

---

[22] *Detroit Resilient Floor Decorators Union*, 136 NLRB 769 (1962).

of another union. This type of action normally takes place where more than one union represents employees in a single establishment. Although no dispute exists between the sympathetic union and the employer, the union's right to support another is guaranteed by the Norris-LaGuardia Act, *even* if its present contract contains a no-strike clause and arbitration of unresolved grievances.[23]

Economic strike activity

We will focus here on what takes place and what is normal and permissible conduct between the parties. A typical strike scenario would find the striking union establishing picket lines at the employer's facilities. These lines would discourage deliveries by organized transportation personnel. The processes in which the strikers would have been involved as employees are normally shut down.

Other nonunion employees continue to work and endure minor harassment. The parties resume negotiations, usually after some period and with some difficulty, because the strike is evidence of their inability to settle. Sooner or later an agreement is reached; the strikers ratify it and return to work.

There are obviously variants on this theme that are more exciting, and it is on these that we will focus. We will also look at the effects of strikes on settlements.

Strike votes and going out

As we noted in Chapter 10, the union generally takes a strike vote sometime during the negotiations to strengthen the union's bargaining position. This does not mean that a strike will be called. But if the contract expires, the union may go out. Usually a local union needs the approval of its parent international to strike. If it strikes without this approval, local officers may be disciplined, the local union may be disciplined, the international may place the local under trusteeship, or strike benefits may not be paid.

Unions generally require members to participate in strike activities, such as picketing, to receive strike benefits. The union also may discipline members who refuse to strike.

Picketing

One of the first and most pervasive activities occurring during a strike is picketing. In picketing, the union member is informing the

---

[23] *Buffalo Forge Co.* v. *United Steelworkers of America, AFL–CIO*, 92 LRRM 3032 (U.S. Supreme Court, 1976).

public about the existence of a labor dispute. The appeal may also ask that others refrain from business dealings with the struck employer during the dispute. In the past, before the passage of the Norris-LaGuardia Act, state laws and federal courts frequently enjoined picketing. After Norris-LaGuardia, federal courts could no longer enjoin these activities unless a clear and present danger to life or property through the actions of the strikers could be shown. A 1940 Supreme Court decision voided state picketing laws by holding that peaceful picketing was the equivalent of free speech.[24] Some restrictions on over various picketing procedures (such as recognitional picketing) have been imposed by amendments to the labor acts.

To be protected from employer reprisals, employees must publicize the fact that they are involved in a labor dispute when they picket or inform the public. For example, the Supreme Court decided that a group of TV technicians could be discharged for passing out handbills calling into question the quality of local TV coverage at the struck stations, where the handbills did not also state the employees were involved in a labor dispute.[25]

The site and manner of the picketing is also of concern since the union can be accused of illegal secondary activity in certain instances.

Situs picketing

The place at which picketing occurs may have an effect on secondary employers and on the expected benefits associated with picketing. This issue is of greatest importance in the construction industry where a prime and several subcontractors work simultaneously on a common site. Each utilizes different trades, may or may not be unionized, and may have different terms, wages, and expiration dates in contracts. If unions strike in sympathy with a primary dispute, then where a dispute exists with one contractor a whole site may be shut down.

Construction industry

The construction industry is most affected by common situs picketing since primary and neutral employers frequently work simultaneously on the same site. A primary employer is one involved in the dispute while a neutral is one affected by the picketing activity of the primary's employees. The rules governing common situs picketing in construction were laid down in 1951 by the Supreme Court in the *Denver Building Trades Council* cases.[26] Here, picketing was estab-

---

[24] *Thornhill* v. *Alabama*, 310 U.S. 88 (1940).

[25] *NLRB* v. *Local Union, 1229, International Brotherhood of Electrical Workers*, 346 U.S. 464 (1953).

[26] *NLRB* v. *Denver Building Trades Council*, 341 U.S. 675 (1951).

lished when it was learned that the prime contractor on the site had employed a nonunion subcontractor. One object of the picketing was to force the general contractor to drop the sub. When the picketing began, all other union workers refused to cross the picket line. The prime contractor maintained that the dispute was with the subcontractor and general picketing of the site was an illegal secondary boycott designed to force neutral parties to cease their dealings with the sub. The court agreed, and since that time construction unions have been forbidden to picket sites for the purpose of forcing a prime to cease doing business with a nonunion sub.

Ambulatory site

Sometimes the objects of a strike move from place to place. The precedent-setting case here is *Moore Dry Dock*.[27] In this case the union had a primary dispute with a shipowner. When the ship was moved to a dry dock for repairs, the union sought to picket by the ship. The dry dock management refused to allow this, and a picket line was set up at the company's entrance.

The NLRB ruled that such picketing would be legal if (1) the object is currently on the secondary employer's site, (2) the primary employer continues to be engaged in its normal business, (3) the picketing is reasonably close to the strike object, and (4) the picketing discloses the name of the struck employer and that this is whom the dispute is with.

Multiple-use sites

In the past an employer's site was usually easily identified. But recent changes in retailing, for example, have blurred this concept. The enclosed shopping center makes it difficult to picket a primary employer without disrupting secondary businesses. And the employer has usually leased the site from another company which owns the shopping mall.

A recent Supreme Court decision in this area severely restricts the ability of a union to notify the public of a labor dispute.[28] In this case store employees sought to picket their employer's shopping mall premises. The mall owner ordered them off, claiming that he could dictate what activities take place on his property. The union claimed that using the mall provided access to the source of the dispute and also fell within the area of freedom of speech. The court disagreed, accepting the owner's arguments.

---

[27] *Sailor's Union of the Pacific (Moore Dry Dock Co.)*, 92 NLRB 547 (1950).
[28] *Hudgens* v. *NLRB*, 91 LRRM 2489 (U.S. Supreme Court, 1976).

Off-site picketing

One other technique that has been used is to inform the general public of a labor dispute at a location where the struck business's products are sold. This type of activity borders on being a secondary boycott, however.

Consider the following. Suppose that one of the major TV and radio receiver manufacturers is struck by its production employees. In an attempt to pressure the employer to settle, the union picketed retail stores selling the TV sets. Their signs say: "Don't shop here. This store sells XYZ TV sets produced under unfair conditions. ABC union on strike for justice against XYZ." On the other hand, suppose that it uses a different message on its signs: "ABC on strike against XYZ Co. Don't buy an XYZ TV while shopping here today. ABC has no dispute with this store." Would either or both strategies be legal? The answer is that only the second is.

In the second instance the picket is calling attention to the labor dispute and the struck product, but not asking persons to boycott the neutral store. If the union follows the second strategy and does not impede customers or deliveries, the action is considered primary and legal.[29]

Employer responses

A variety of responses are available to the employer when struck. These generally fall into three categories: shut down the affected area, continue operating, or contract-out work during the duration. Each of these has its own consequences and can cause retaliatory action by the union.

Shut-downs

Shut-downs have the least consequences in terms of union activity since this was precisely what the strike was called to do. But a shut-down has consequences for the employer that it would like to avoid. First, revenues from production are lost during this period. Second, the employer may find that competitors gear up to take over the lost production, permanently reducing market shares. Third, if a firm is a sole supplier, the uses of its products may encourage others to enter the market to reduce the possibilities of temporary shortages since alternative sources would then be available. And fourth, during periods of scarcity, the firm may lose its suppliers as they fill more reliable orders.

---

[29] *NLRB* v. *Fruit & Vegetable Packers, Local 760*, 377 U.S. 58 (1964).

Continued operations

Continued operations may be accomplished by two strategies. Neither is relished by the union, but the second will amost certainly lead to some militant action. The first is to continue operating using supervisors and other nonproduction workers. This is feasible where the firm is not labor intensive and where maintenance demands are not high. Automated operations and continuous-flow industries such as the chemical industry fall into this category. One difficulty that will be encountered later if this strategy is used is that supervisor-employee relations may be strained following the strike because the supervisor's work may have enabled the company to prolong it.

The second strategy is to hire replacements for the strikers. Since this places the strikers' jobs in direct jeopardy, difficulties usually result. Strike replacements, themselves, face a possibly difficult position since they are reviled as "scabs" by the strikers (see Figure 11–2) and may find themselves vulnerable to layoff after a new contract is signed.

FIGURE 11–2
What is a scab?

After God had finished the rattlesnake, the toad, and the vampire, he had some awful substance left with which He made a *scab*. A *scab* is a two-legged animal with a corkscrew soul, a water-logged brain, and a combination backbone made of jelly and glue. Where others have hearts, he carries a tumor of rotten principles.

When a *scab* comes down the street, men turn their backs, and angels weep in heaven, and the devil shuts the gates of hell to keep him out. No man has a right to *scab* as long as there is a pool of water deep enough to drown his body in, or a rope long enough to hang his carcass with. Judas Iscariot was a gentleman compared with a *scab*. For betraying his Master, he had character enough to hang himself. A *scab hasn't!*

Esau sold his birthright for a mess of pottage. Judas Iscariot sold his Savior for thirty pieces of silver. Benedict Arnold sold his country for a promise of a commission in the British Army. The modern strikebreaker sells his birthright, his country, his wife, his children, and his fellowmen for an unfulfilled promise from his employer, trust, or corporation.

Esau was a traitor to himself, Judas Iscariot was a traitor to his God. Benedict Arnold was a traitor to his country.

A strikebreaker is a traitor to his God, his country, his family, and his class!

Source: Philip S. Foner, *Jack London, American Rebel* (New York: Citadel Press, 1947), pp. 57–58.

Rights of employers

Employers can legally replace striking employees if there is an economic strike in effect.[30] Operations may then resume. However, these new employees become members of the bargaining unit and are

---

[30] *NLRB* v. *MacKay Radio & Telegraph*, 304 U.S. 333 (1938).

represented by the striking union. Only a decertification removes this representation. As such, when a new contract is negotiated the new workers frequently lose their jobs if they are temporary replacements for striking employees.

Rights of strikers

If the strike involves an unfair labor practice, the striker retains his right to a job as long as the dispute is unsettled. Since employer misconduct led to the strike, the law does not allow the employer to subvert the union by hiring new employees on a permanent basis.

Economic strikers are in a different situation. Since the employer is free here to hire replacements, the jobs of strikers are in real jeopardy. A strike would be a true economic strike if the company bargained in good faith to an impasse. Then, if neither the company nor the union refused to move further, the gulf would remain permanently, and new employees would have to be sought to remain in business.

If replacements are being hired, the strikers may still get their jobs back. First, if they unilaterally offer to return to work before the strike is over and their jobs or others for which they are qualified are unfilled, it would be an unfair labor practice to refuse to rehire them since engaging in a strike is a protected Section 7 activity. Second, if they wait until the conclusion of the strike and ask for reinstatement, they are entitled to their jobs, if open, or to preference for rehiring when positions open up.[31]

This is not to say that employers are forced to take back employees guilty of offenses during the strike, such as sabotage and picket line violence, but these discharges would have to be for cause, and the grievance procedure would be open for hearing disputes over these discharges.

Contracting-out

For the employer who has several major customers who demand services or products at certain times, a strike can have serious consequences, particularly where competitive firms offer the same services. One strategy open to the struck employer is to arrange for a competing firm temporarily to handle the work.

On its face this would seem to be a foolproof strategy. No problems with strikebreakers and the union, and the customers get their work done on time by a subcontractor. It's not, however. If the subcontractor is unionized, its employees may legally refuse to perform the subcon-

---

[31] *NLRB* v. *Fleetwood Trailer Co., Inc.*, 389 U.S. 375 (1967).

tracted work where the struck employer has initiated the order. This is dealt with under the so-called ally doctrine.

In a recent case, a printing firm responsible for providing Sunday supplements to newspapers was struck by its employees. To maintain its ability to meet the weekly schedule, it subcontracted the work to another firm. When the second firm's employees learned why they were doing the work, they refused to perform it. The first employer charged that this was a secondary boycott, but the board reasoned that the dispute became primary through the handling of the struck work for the primary employer.[32]

Overview

Strikes can be powerful weapons where an employer has few options in terms of remaining open. They are not without their risks, however, since economic strikers may legally be replaced and some positive movement by the union may be necessary to get bargaining resumed.

There is one other weapon open to unions which is generally used only in extreme cases: the boycott. This is the area we briefly explore next.

BOYCOTTS

The boycott is a weapon that has been used seldom and with mixed results. As we noted in Chapter 2, the Danbury Hatters' and Buck's Stove boycotts were declared to be violations of the Sherman Act, leaving the unions responsible for treble damages. Later legislation has exempted unions from antitrust provisions, but the boycott strategy still remains infrequent in its use.

There are a number of reasons for this lack of use: (1) a boycott requires a great deal of organization and publicity to alert customers, (2) customers may not be sympathetic to union demands unless a clear-cut social issue is involved, (3) sometimes it is difficult to keep a legal primary boycott from having secondary boycott ramifications, and (4) it is not as easy to turn off the effects of a boycott as it is those of a strike since the public may continue to identify the producer with poor labor relations after a settlement.

Recently, boycotts have been used against Farah Manufacturing (to force recognition) and J. P. Stevens Co. (to force recognition and bargaining on initial contracts). The Farah boycott probably did have some effect on the ultimate willingness to recognize the union, but the

---

[32] *Blackhawk Engraving Co.*, 219 NLRB 169 (1975).

J. P. Stevens action will be much more difficult since many of its products are sold under labels that are difficult to identify with the employer.

An unanswered issue in boycotts is what responsibility unions have to the secondary employer who handles the goods. In a case involving J. P. Stevens products in a large department store, the impact may be minimal. But if the employer handled primarily J. P. Stevens products and the boycott was successful, the impact could be great.

The question of impact was dismissed in the *Tree Fruits* case mentioned earlier but has been raised again in a case where the impact of a successful boycott was much greater on the employer. The Steelworkers Local 14055 struck the Bay Refining division of Dow Chemical Company at Bay City, Michigan, in 1974. Among other products of the company was gasoline marketed through Bay gasoline stations in Michigan. To put pressure on Dow, pickets informed customers in heavily union areas that Dow (which was struck) supplied Bay Gasoline and asked consumers not to buy it when patronizing Bay stations. Over 80 percent of station revenues resulted from gasoline sales, so where the boycott was effective, the impact on the secondary employers was great. Since gasoline refining is only a small part of Dow's business, any sales loss would be minimal. Furthermore, the gasoline could easily be marketed through other firms. The appeals court dismissed unfair labor practice complaints against the Steelworkers since the *Tree Fruit* case said that impact was not a proper test. The Supreme Court, however, reopened the issue by overruling the appeals court and remanding the issue to the board. But the board did not reconsider its decision since by that time Local 14055 had been disestablished.[33] Thus, the impact test has not been decided.

So far we have talked primarily about union initiatives in impasses. One tactic has also been used by employers—the lockout. While the strike has been legal since Norris-LaGuardia, the lockout has a much murkier legal background. We will explore its uses and legitimacy next.

LOCKOUTS

Lockouts may be thought of as the flip side of the strike coin. Where a strike is a refusal of employees to provide labor, a lockout is a refusal by the employer to provide opportunities to work. While the right to strike without government intervention has been guaranteed since the passage of the Norris-LaGuardia Act in 1932, employers' rights to use lockouts have only been recently clarified.

---

[33] *Daily Labor Report* (Washington: Bureau of National Affairs, May 5, 1977), p. A–4.

After the passage of the Wagner Act, the NLRB declared lockouts to be unfair labor practices. The board felt the use of lockouts interfered with the employees' rights to engage in protected concerted activities. As such any refusal to provide work as the result of a labor dispute was presumed to relate to and interfere with workers' protected rights. Over time this board approach has been redefined by specific situational variables and court interpretations. Three distinct types of situations have been defined where lockouts may be legal if specific conditions are met: (1) perishable goods, (2) multiemployer bargaining units, and (3) single employer units.

Perishable goods

An employer dealing in perishable goods is frequently at the mercy of the union. For example, in 1976 the California vegetable canners were struck just before the harvest. Since their revenues depend on packing and selling the produce when it is available, a strike during the "pack" itself would cause the produce to rot. Thus, great pressure for a quick settlement on the employer's part exists.

Similar situations occur where the employer's goods and services are perishable, but the employer has more control over their perishability. For a packer, the timing of the crop's maturity is not within the firm's control. On the other hand, a brewer can decide when to start a new batch of beer, and a contractor can elect when a tract of houses is begun. In the brewer's case, if the beer is started, it must be bottled on a certain date or the batch will spoil, resulting in economic loss of an immediate nature. For the contractor, customers may become dissatisfied with the waiting period on an unfinished house and spread their displeasure by communicating with others. Thus, the long-term business interests of the contractor and the short-term economic losses suffered by the brewer can only be minimized by capitulating to the union on its terms. The lockout is a legitimate employer tactic to neutralize or decrease union power in situations involving perishable goods.

Duluth Bottling Association.[34]   The multiemployer Duluth Bottling Association bargained as a single unit with the Brewery Workers. All members agreed to lock out their employees if a strike was called. When negotiations failed, the union notified them of its intent to strike, whereupon the association locked out its employees. The employers argued that their actions were not designed to interfere with the rights of union members but to avoid economic loss since the production of soft drinks required the mixing of batches of syrup which would read-

---

[34] *Duluth Bottling Assn.*, 48 NLRB 1335 (1943).

ily spoil if unused. To avoid the loss, no syrup was mixed after the strike intentions became known and hence no work was required. The NLRB agreed that this was a legitimate business interest which only coincided with expected union activity.

Betts Cadillac-Olds.[35] In a situation where perishability was not an issue, but where customer goodwill was, the NLRB again decided in the employer's favor. This lockout involved a 21-member, multiemployer automobile dealers' association which bargained with a union representing its mechanics. In this case, they had bargained past the contract expiration date and had sought pledges from the union that it would not strike. The union, however, refused to give these assurances. As a result, when two of the dealers were struck, the remainder locked out their mechanics.

Before the NLRB, the association maintained that it would be disastrous economically to have customers' cars torn down and out of commission when and if a strike of uncertain duration occurred. Thus, when employees reported for work it was denied until a new contract was signed.

The board held that the lockout was legal since it protected the interests of the employers' customers. At no time had the mechanics indicated any specific length of time they would work after contract termination and, in fact, had struck two of the employers. The board also held that there was no evidence the employers were seeking to weaken the union since all mechanics were returned to work when a settlement was reached.

Multiemployer lockouts

As will be discussed in some detail in the next chapter, some employers bargain jointly. The most frequent situation occurs where several small employers engaged in the same business have employees represented by the same union. Here, the union has a high degree of bargaining power when dealing with a single employer, since a strike against one employer leaves its business vulnerable because the other unstruck companies remain open for customers. To get back into business, the employer may settle on terms very favorable to the union. After settlement the union selects its next victim and, in a whipsaw manner, increasingly favorable settlements are won. To counteract this, the employers band together and bargain as one. But what happens if the union only takes strike action against one or attempts to break the solidarity of the group through the use of a whipsaw strat-

---

[35] *Betts Cadillac-Olds, Inc.*, 96 NLRB 268, 1951.

egy? Is a lockout then an appropriate legal weapon for the multiemployer group? The Supreme Court's answer is yes. Two key cases will be examined in which this question was addressed.

Buffalo Linen[36]. The *Buffalo Linen* case was the first following the passage of the Taft-Hartley Act in which the Supreme Court rendered a decision on this issue. In this case a multiemployer linen supply group negotiated with a single union. When a new contract was not reached, the union struck one of the members. The remaining employers locked out their employees. The NLRB and the Court held that the lockout was defensive in nature and that without its use the continued integrity of the bargaining unit could not be assured.

Buffalo Linen explicitly recognizes the legality of the lockout in multiemployer units where an impasse in bargaining is reached and a strike follows against one of the members. As we learned earlier, employers involved in economic strikes are free to replace strikers. On the other hand, can an employer lock out its employees, then temporarily replace them for the duration of the lockout to continue operations? The court ruled that multiemployer groups could.

NLRB v. Brown[37]. In *NLRB v. Brown* a group of retail food stores bargained with their clerks. When an agreement could not be reached, the clerks struck one store, and the other employers responded by locking out their clerks. All stores continued operating using temporary replacements. When an agreement was reached, the replacements were discharged and the clerks were reinstated. The Supreme Court held that the action was legal and was simply one of a permissible group of economic weapons the parties might use in convincing the other to agree to its bargaining positions. The legitimate interest of the group in continuing multiemployer bargaining, given the tactics used here, outweighed any harm done to the employees through their loss of wages.

Single employer lockouts

Where a union negotiates with a single employer, a lockout can't be justified as a weapon to forestall whipsaw effects since a whipsaw requires a multiemployer group. Thus, the question of whether or not a lockout interferes with employee rights to engage in concerted activities must be much more closely scrutinized for single employers. There are fewer cases in this area, but the line is relatively clear and concludes with a Supreme Court decision.

---

[36] *NLRB* v. *Truck Drivers' Local 449*, 353 U.S. 87 (1957).

[37] *NLRB* v. *Brown*, 380 U.S. 278, U.S. Supreme Court, 1965.

Dalton Brick and Tile[38]. Dalton Brick and Tile had faced an increasingly competitive product market in its area and had incurred substantial recent losses. When contract negotiations opened, the company insisted that the old contract be renewed without wage increases or the firm would be forced permanently to close. The union did not agree, and the firm locked out the employees until the contract was signed on its own terms. The NLRB declared that the firm threatened the employees to compel them to accept the present contract, but the appeals court reversed. It held that the company had done nothing to interfere with rights to join or be represented by a labor organization, and that the company was only adhering to a bargaining position supportable by financial evidence.

Quaker State Oil[39]. This is a case where no impasse or imminent strike occurred. In an attempt to pressure the union to accept its conditions, Quaker State threatened to shut down and actually followed through even though the union had given assurances in writing that its members would continue to work while bargaining went forward. The NLRB held that the lockout by the company was coercive in nature since the union had always abided by its word in the past on continued work and the threat and action were taken before an impasse was reached.

American Ship Building[40]. The flagship decision in the single employer lockout area was handed down by the Supreme Court the same day it established the prevailing precedent in multiemployer lockouts (*NLRB* v. *Brown*). The company operated four shipyards on the Great Lakes. Most of the work done involved ship repair of a scheduled nature during the winter months and for emergency problems encountered during the heavy summer shipping season.

The company bargained with eight different unions and had experienced strikes during contract negotiations several times in the past. In 1961, it feared a repeat of this practice, especially when a ship had just entered its yards for emergency repairs or during the winter when workloads were heaviest. On August 11, after a bargaining impasse had been reached, and ten days after the expiration of the old contract, the Chicago yard was shut down, the Toledo work force reduced to two, and the Buffalo work force was gradually laid off as work was completed. The Lorain, Ohio, facility remained open to work on a major project.

The NLRB viewed this action as illegal since they felt it was only done to enhance a bargaining position. The Supreme Court overruled

---

[38] *NLRB* v. *Dalton Brick & Tile Corp.*, 49 LRRM 3099, 5th Circuit Court of Appeals, 1962.

[39] *Quaker State Oil Refining Corp.*, 121 NLRB 334 (1958).

[40] *American Ship Building Co.* v. *NLRB*, 380 U.S. 300, U.S. Supreme Court, 1965.

the board, holding that the employer does not necessarily discriminate against union membership or coerce workers in the exercise of their rights by the use of lockouts. The Court held that the lockout was the corollary of the strike and that unions had no legislated right to determine the starting date and duration of a work stoppage. It was suggested by Justice Goldberg in his concurring opinion that the legality of lockouts should be assessed in relation to the length, character, and prevailing relationships in the bargaining relationship. For instance, a refusal to bargain simply to gain an impasse which would allow the use of a lockout would be unlawful.

Requirements for the use of a lockout

The Court's decisions have substantially liberalized the conditions for the use of the lockout. As a weapon, it is not often used since an employer is normally reluctant to cease operations when employees proclaim their willingness to continue working. When it is used, what conditions appear necessary for it to be found legal?

The following criteria appear to be necessary conditions:

1. The contract must have expired,
2. A bargaining impasse must have been reached,
3. A legitimate economic or bargaining interest must be served,
4. Employees may not be permanently discharged or replaced (and replacement is apparently only permissible in multiemployer units), and
5. No subjective intent to discourage or interfere with union members' rights to engage in concerted activity may be undertaken.

THE 1976 RUBBER STRIKE

This strike is particularly interesting because it involves the following: (1) stockpiling by customers in anticipation of a strike, (2) operation of several smaller companies not subject to expiring contracts, (3) an internal political demand for craft severance by some union members, (4) a decline in the parity position of the union in relation to the auto workers, (5) a product boycott against Firestone, and (6) government intervention through mediation. Our purpose here is to give the background of the issues, the activities of the parties during the strike, and a comparison of the settlement with earlier settlements within the industry and across other major industries.[41]

---

[41] This background draws on the commentary included in the *Daily Labor Report* during 1976.

Toward the strike

Negotiations opened between the United Rubber Workers (URW) and the "Big Four" tire manufacturers (Firestone, Goodrich, Goodyear, and Uniroyal) on January 30, 1976. The existing contract was due to expire on April 20. Since the last contract was signed in 1973, the Rubber Workers had seen their traditional wage parity with the Auto Workers substantially eroded, since the Auto Workers had a cost-of-living allowance (COLA) in their contract while the URW did not. The union was demanding some hefty wage increases in an effort to catch up with autos and close the gap. From an economic package standpoint, the URW demanded immediate increases of $1.65 per hour for production employees and $2.00 per hour for skilled trades, other pay increases over the life of the contract, a cost-of-living allowance tied directly to the Consumer Price Index (CPI), additional contributions to the Supplemental Unemployment Benefit fund and other benefit improvements.

The negotiations were fraught with problems not usually found elsewhere and had significant national economic ramifications. From an internal problem standpoint, the union was facing an attempt by the International Society of Skilled Trades to sever craft employees. Already 30 percent of workers in skilled trades had signed cards for an NLRB election. Second, while the bargaining was to be done on a companywide basis, in the past locals had made some settlements on their own. The union's president, Peter Bommarito, was thus faced with difficult organization maintenance problems as the negotiations began.

From an economic standpoint, the Rubber Workers' negotiations were important on two counts. First, a large settlement could be a precursor for other major contracts due to be negotiated in autos and steel later in 1976 and 1977 (although the URW argued that any large increase would simply be a catchup). Second, since tires are essential to auto production, a strike of major length could disrupt production, cause layoffs, and reverse the recovery from depressed economic conditions.

As early discussions continued, one of URW President Bommarito's problems evaporated when the NLRB refused to consider the craft severance issue, saying there had been no previous bargaining history to support it.

As the contract expiration date neared, it became apparent that Bommarito did not have a great deal to say about the final terms of settlement since a 15-member advisory committee had been established to evaluate offers.

The approach of April 20

The advisory committee was to meet in Columbus, Ohio, on April 17 and 18 to consider management's offer and recommend action to the union. It was reported that thus far management had been offering wage increases over a three-year contract of 50 cents, 30 cents, and 25 cents with skill differentials of 15 cents and 10 cents in the first two years. No COLA was offered.

In their meeting a strike authorization was approved. Bommarito said that if a strike were to be called it would shut down all of the Big Four. The union would concentrate negotiating activities and other actions, including a consumer boycott, against Firestone. He emphasized that a strike would be long, lasting five to six weeks, but that the deadline could be extended if realistic proposals came forth. Mediators concentrated their activities at Firestone.

April 21–27—Week 1

The URW struck against all of the big four. The final prestrike proposal by Firestone was said to call for increases of 60 cents, 30 cents, and 25 cents during the three years of the contract with 15 cent and 10 cent skill differentials. COLA was offered at the rate of 1 cent for each 0.4 percent increase in the CPI. Pension increases of 50 cents for each year of service were offered, increasing pension credits from $10.00 to $10.50. Bargaining took place again on April 23, but talks at Firestone recessed until April 28.

Meanwhile the AFL–CIO endorsed the product boycott against Firestone and laid plans for its inauguration. On April 27, Bommarito flew to Geneva to urge the World Rubber Council to support the boycott. At the meeting officials of the International Federation of Chemical and General Workers' Union pledged that their members would work no overtime to make up U.S. production losses. Predictions were made by mediators that this would be a long strike. Some forecast that auto production would be affected in four weeks as tire supplies declined.

The URW publicly altered its demands to $1.65 immediately and "reasonable" second- and third-year increases. It also demanded wage equality for workers in both tire and nontire plants.

Week 2

The AFL–CIO boycott began with instruction packages being mailed to local union officials. The package is reproduced in Figure 11–3. Note the careful emphasis on primary rather than secondary impact.

FIGURE 11-3
Letter of AFL-CIO President Meany on Firestone boycott (text)

April 29, 1976

State and Local Central Bodies

Dear Sir and Brother:

On Saturday, May 8, 70,000 striking members of the United Rubber Workers will launch a nationwide boycott of all Firestone products unless a satisfactory settlement has been reached by that time.

They are on strike against all of the big four tire makers—Goodyear, Goodrich and Uniroyal, as well as Firestone—but they are concentrating their boycott effort against Firestone as the bellwether of the industry.

This action is completely justified and has the full support of the AFL-CIO. Its success depends on the wholehearted cooperation of every union member.

Therefore I call on you to rally your entire membership to mobilize their purchasing power behind the Firestone strikers and to join in bringing the boycott message home to the public at large.

Experience has proved that the best method for getting a boycott message across is by picketing and handbilling at retail stores.

The basic problem is organizational. A committee to direct the entire effort must be selected, pickets and handbillers must be secured, the materials they need must be prepared and primary targets—Firestone outlets and those independent retailers selling a large volume of Firestone products—must be identified. The task in each area will be somewhat different. In light of your experience, there is little point in reviewing what I am sure would be obvious steps. I know that whatever unforeseen problems arise, you will overcome them.

Here are some of the things that need to be done:

1. First, union members must be immediately informed about the boycott. The message —"Don't Buy Firestone"—should be spread by every possible means. Meetings, bulletin board notices in the union hall and in the plants, and flyers at plant gates should be utilized, and shop stewards should personally contact every member.

2. Handbills directed to consumers should be prepared and experienced picket captains should be given materials on the proper techniques for consumer picketing (samples are attached). These captains should see that the handbills are distributed at Firestone stores and independent retail outlets handling Firestone products. Informational picket lines should be established in front of all retail outlets featuring Firestone products.

3. Senior citizens and similar groups should be contacted to man these informational picket lines during peak shopping hours, especially during the day when members are working.

4. Retailers should be informed of the boycott, urged to stop selling Firestone products and allocate advertising and promotion to products of other manufacturers. We do not want to hurt retail sales. We want consumers to purchase what they need but not to purchase Firestone products.

5. Purchasing agents at every level of government should be urged to halt all buying of Firestone products.

6. Builders and contractors should be urged to halt all buying of Firestone products.

7. Local advertising—including newspapers, television, radio and billboards—should be used to every extent possible to spread the "Don't Buy Firestone" message.

8. Wherever possible, full-time union representatives should be detached from other duties to coordinate the "Don't Buy Firestone" campaign.

Firestone can still avert this boycott, if it chooses. All it has to do is engage in realistic collective bargaining and end the strike.

If the boycott takes place, it will be because Firestone forced it, just as it forced its workers to strike.

While the practical problems will vary, the basic legal problems will not. I, therefore, wish to note in summary form your basic rights in carrying out a consumer boycott and the legal restrictions that apply:

FIGURE 11-3 (continued)

You have a right to advise consumers by picketing and handbilling that there is a labor dispute with Firestone, that a retail store is selling Firestone products, and that you request the consumers not to purchase Firestone products.

You have a right to engage in such picketing and handbilling on the pedestrian walkways at the customer entrances of a retail store selling Firestone products during the hours that store is open for business.

You have the right to advise the manager of a retail store of your intention to engage in such picketing and handbilling.

You have the right to request the manager of a retail store to exercise his managerial discretion to make the business judgment to stop purchasing and selling Firestone products.

You are forbidden to address a retail store's employees and delivery men except to advise them that you are not requesting them to refrain from performing services.

You are forbidden to request a total boycott of a retail store selling Firestone products. The appeal must be limited to a boycott of Firestone products.

You are forbidden to use any form of physical interference with consumers, employees, or delivery men, or otherwise engage in any obstruction of disturbance.

You are forbidden to threaten a retail store manager with any form of economic reprisal for continuing to handle Firestone products.

Attached are five appendixes as follows:

Appendix 1—Brand names carried by Firestone products

Appendix 2—Suggested language for placards

Appendix 3—Suggested language for leaflets

Appendix 4—Suggested letter to store managers

Appendix 5—Instructions to pickets

You are advised to bring the boycott to a retail store's attention, before picketing or leafleting, at a meeting with the store manager and to hand him a copy of the attached letter (Appendix 4). During the meeting, the union spokesman should not make any statements other than those contained in the written letter. If the manager has any questions, you should refer him to a previously designated official at boycott headquarters.

You are advised to use the language of the attached picket sign (Appendix 2) and sample handbill (Appendix 3).

You are advised to supply every picket and handbiller with the instructions attached hereto (Appendix 5).

You are advised to retain, in advance, competent legal counsel to protect you against crippling restraining orders and potential damage suits. Counsel should be versed in local law and federal labor law and be thoroughly familiar with the *San Diego Building Trades* v. *Garmon*, 359 U.S. 236; *Local 438 Construction Union* v. *Curry*, 371 U.S. 542; *NLRB* v. *Fruit & Vegetable Packers*, 377 U.S. 58, and *NLRB* v. *Servette*, 377 U.S. 46.

A united labor campaign can bring the Firestone strikers the victory they deserve.

Sincerely and fraternally,

/s/ George Meany
President

Figure 1–3 (continued)

APPENDIX 1

Firestone tires are also marketed under Dayton and Seiberling labels and under at least 35 private-brand names. Where appropriate, as in the case of Montgomery Ward or J.C. Penney outlets, the brand name should be inserted in placards and leaflets publicizing the boycott. Following is a list of brand names included in the Firestone boycott:

Source: Who Makes It? And Where? Directory 1975 Tire Guide, Farmingdale, N.Y.

Firestone

Atlas	Falcon	O. K. Tires
Caravelle	Fruehauf	Shell
CBI	Getty	Triumph
Coast-to-Coast	Lancer	Union 76
Cordovan	Multi-Mile	Montgomery Ward

Firestone subsidiaries:

Dayton

Argyle	Dean	Schenuit
Carnegie	Duralon	Super Traction (truck only)
Co-op	J.C. Penney	Western Auto
Cornell	Road King	White

Seiberling

Award	Portage
Carvelle	Roger Ward
Holiday	Sterling
Buck Monroe	Zenith

APPENDIX 2—Suggested language for placards

DON'T BUY FIRESTONE (or brand name) TIRES

The United Rubber Workers of America, AFL–CIO, are on strike against the Firestone Tire and Rubber Co. Please do not buy Firestone or (brand name) tires made by Firestone. This is not a strike against this store.

APPENDIX 3

PLEASE DON'T BUY FIRESTONE TIRES

Members of the United Rubber Workers of America are on strike against the Firestone Tire and Rubber Co. for a new union contract governing their wages and working conditions.

They ask you to help them by refusing to buy Firestone tires or (brand name) tires made by Firestone until the company agrees to a just and fair settlement of the dispute.

The union contract that expired April 20 was negotiated in good faith in 1973 under President Nixon's so-called wage and price controls. Since those controls were rescinded, the company has raised its prices 35 percent—an increase that would have permitted wage increases of 114 percent. But no such wage increases were made.

Instead, because Firestone refused to make cost-of-living adjustments while prices went through the roof, Firestone workers have lost about $1.65 an hour in purchasing power. Firestone's "final" offer for three years was less than Firestone workers need to catch up to today's prices.

Obviously, Firestone workers badly need cost-of-living protection over the next three years. But the company's offer in this area would not begin to meet the projected increase in the

Figure 11–3 (*continued*)

consumer price index of 7 percent a year. At that rate, Firestone workers would be still further behind.

The company has also refused to improve pensions and health and safety programs.

Therefore we respectfully ask you not to buy Firestone products until Firestone agrees to treat its employees fairly.

Thank you for your support.

NOTE: When leafleting is conducted at Firestone's wholly owned outlets, no further language is necessary. Where independent stores selling Firestone products are involved, the leaflet should include the words: THIS IS NOT A STRIKE AGAINST THIS STORE.

APPENDIX 4

Dear Manager:

You are aware, of course, that there is currently in effect a strike against the Firestone Tire and Rubber Company by the United Rubber Workers Union and in order for us to win this strike we must ask the consuming public not to purchase Firestone tires.

Therefore, we are going to place peaceful pickets at the entrances to your store for the purpose of trying to persuade the public not to buy Firestone tires. These pickets are being instructed to patrol peacefully in front of the consumer entrance of the store; to stay away from the delivery entrance and not to interfere with the work of your employees or with deliveries to or pickups from your store. A copy of instructions which have been furnished to the pickets is attached hereto.

We do not intend that any of your employees cease work as a result of the picketing. We ask that you advise your employees of our intentions in this respect, perhaps by posting this notice on the store bulletin board. If any of your employees should stop work as a result of our program, or if you should have any difficulties as far as pickups and deliveries are concerned, or if you observe any of the pickets disobeying the instructions which they have been given, please notify the undersigned union representative at once, and we will take steps to see that the situation is promptly corrected.

Thank you for your cooperation.

(This should be signed by the member that will be in charge of this operation.)

APPENDIX 5

The instructions to the pickets should read as follows:

Dear Picket:

You are being asked to help publicize the consumer boycott against Firestone tires. To make this program a success, your cooperation is essential. Please read these instructions and follow them carefully:

1. At all times you are to engage in peaceful picketing. You are forbidden to engage in any altercation, argument, or misconduct of any kind.
2. You are to walk back and forth on the sidewalk in front of the consumer entrances to the stores. If a particular store is located toward the rear of a parking lot, you are to ask the store manager for permission to walk back and forth on the apron or sidewalk immediately in front of the store; but if he denies you this permission, you are to picket only on the public sidewalk at the entrances to the parking lot.
3. You are not to picket in front of or in the area of any entrance to the store which is apparently set aside for the use of store employees and delivery men. As noted above, you are to limit your picketing to the consumer entrances to the store.

Figure 11–3 (*concluded*)

---

4. We have no dispute with the store, and you are forbidden to make any statement to the effect that the store is unfair or on strike. You are also forbidden to request that the customers not patronize the store. We are only asking that the customers not buy Firestone tires when they are shopping at the store.
5. Similarly, you are not to interfere with the work of any employees in the store. If you are asked by these employees what the picketing is about, you are to tell them it is an advertising or consumer picket line and that they should keep working. Likewise if you are asked by any truck drivers who are making pickups or deliveries what the picketing is about, you are to advise that it is an advertising and/or consumer picketing and that it is not intended to interfere with pickups or deliveries (i.e. that they are free to go through).
6. If you are given handbills to distribute, please distribute these handbills in a courteous manner and if the customers throw them on the ground, please see that they are picked up at once and that the area is kept clean.
7. You are forbidden to use intoxicating beverages while on duty or to have such beverages on your person.
8. If a state official or any other private party should complain to you about the picketing, advise them you have your instructions and that their complaints should be registered with the undersigned union representative.
9. These instructions should answer most of your questions concerning this program. However, if you have any additional questions or if specific problems arise which require additional instructions, please call the undersigned.

It is imperative that the contents of this letter be read carefully and that the instructions to the pickets are followed explicitly for even with the cooperation on the part of the picket, if the employees refuse to work and if deliverymen refuse to make pickups and deliveries, we would then be engaging in a secondary boycott. Therefore, it is necessary that the pickets understand that the employees must continue working and that pickups and deliveries must continue. The only object of this publicity is to request the consuming public, through the placard and the leaflets, not to purchase Firestone tires.

(These instructions should be signed by the member who will be in charge of this operation.)

Source: Letter of AFL–CIO president on Firestone boycott, reprinted in *Daily Labor Report* (Washington: Bureau of National Affairs, April 30, 1976), pp. D–1 through D–3.

The URW called a special convention for May 27 in Chicago to consider a dues assessment to pay strike benefits. Benefits were to begin during week three at the rate of $35 per week.

Week 3

Strikers received their first $35 check. No news came from the negotiations. To moderate the effects of a long strike, auto makers began shipping cars without a spare tire.

Week 4

URW contracts with General Tire expired, but both agreed to continue negotiations subject to a five-day termination notice by either. Strikers got their second $35 check but were notified that the next check will be $25.

Weeks 5 and 6

Strikers got a $25 benefit. The special URW convention voted against a dues assessment for higher or longer benefits. No meaningful negotiations took place.

Week 7

The strike has now run longer than Bommarito predicted the duration of a "long strike" would be when negotiations began. FMCS Director James Scearce called the parties to Washington to negotiate. He cited local impacts and a possible dampening of the national recovery as reasons to settle. Little progress appeared to have been made. After the meetings, Bommarito reiterated the union demands for the catchup, COLA, improved pensions, and SUB improvements. Firestone's Vice President of Industrial Relations Cairns emphasized that the industry could withstand the strike pressures due to his estimates that auto industry tire supplies would last through July.

After the mediation efforts in Washington, negotiators returned to Cleveland to reopen negotiations as Week 8 began.

Weeks 8, 9, and 10

No news of progress came from Cleveland. On June 29, Secretary of Labor W. J. Usery, Jr., began his personal mediation attempts. Some concessions on COLA demands were reported to have been made by the URW.

Week 11

Management made its first major concession since the strike began offering increases of 75 cents, 30 cents and 25 cents over a three-year contract. COLA base periods were improved, and pension credits were raised from $10.50 to $10.75 for workers over age 45. Bommarito responded by calling the package inadequate.

Week 12

The twelfth week began with a rejection of management's proposal by the Firestone committee. By the end of the week Goodyear and Goodrich committees followed suit. The rubber companies viewed things grimly as a Goodyear spokesman said it was "the best possible offer that could be made." The companies also adopted a strategy to put pressure on the international union saying they would take subsequent proposals directly to the locals. Bommarito noted that locals aren't permitted to ratify, but rubber officials knew they had in the past.

Weeks 13, 14, and 15

The prospects for settlement continued to deteriorate. On July 19 company-paid health insurance ran out for strikers. Although the companies would continue to pay the premiums, the companies announced that premiums will be deducted from pay following the stoppage. The talks were moved back to Washington in an attempt to mediate the dispute. Secretary of Labor Usery met with each side separately on July 27, but the mediation failed.

As the strike moved past its 100th day, Goodyear announced plans to charge the URW with refusing the bargain by its insistence that the company could not bargain directly with the locals on economic issues. Bommarito responded by charging that the company was adopting a "divide and conquer" approach. The URW planned to sue the companies for accrued but unpaid vacation pay. The companies refused to pay it unless a worker had scheduled vacation during the strike. Firestone claimed that the union had still not spelled out its specific demands.

Meanwhile, auto production continued as tire shortages had not materialized.

Week 16

The week began with a strongly worded telegram from Usery practically ordering the parties back to Washington to negotiate and inferring that they would be closeted until an agreement was reached. A partial text of the telegram follows:

> Recognizing the union's legal right to demand, and management's legal right to resist, there comes a time when these rights must be tempered to reduce the harm being inflicted on employees and their families, the stockholders, the people in the communities involved, and the nation.
>
> Therefore, together with James Scearce, director of the Federal Mediation and Conciliation Services, I am calling for a resumption of negotiations in my offices at 10 A.M., Saturday, August 7, 1976. You are urged and expected to enter these negotiations with a determination to bring an end to this conflict.
>
> You are expected to come fully prepared to take the actions required to reach an agreement.
>
> You are expected to have with you all of those who are necessary to make pertinent decisions.
>
> Come prepared to remain in continuous bargaining.

Usery proposed a settlement to the parties on August 9, but neither side disclosed its contents or commented on progress.

Week 17

On August 12, the Firestone committee voted to accept the offer based on the Usery-Scearce recommendation. The catchup was not nearly achieved, but a large first-year wage increase was included. Economic terms provided for increases of 80 cents, 30 cents, and 25 cents; an uncapped COLA of 1 cent for each 0.4 percent increase in the CPI in the first two years, and 1 cent for 0.3 percent in the third; pension increases to $12.50 by the end of the contract, increased shift differentials for nonday shift employees of 3 cents, 2 cents, and 1 cent over the contract; 2 cents more for SUB contributions; 0.5 cents more for health and safety research; and full retirement benefits for 30-year employees displaced by plant shut-downs. Insurance was improved and health payments were made retroactive to July 19. The companies agreed to discuss discipline of strikers with the union and reserved the right to negotiate lower economic packages in nontire plants.

Aftermath

All companies had settled by the first week in September. Firestone reinstated all workers discharged for strike misconduct while Goodyear restored all but 20 who had earlier pleaded guilty to fire-bombing a guard shack.

ANALYSIS

The complexity of the strike defies total analysis, but we can examine some of the statements and behavior to see how they affected the outcome. We will divide these into three categories: union, company, and mediator behavior.

Initial positions and settlements

You will recall that the URW asked for $1.65 for production workers and $2.00 for skilled trades per hour at the beginning of negotiations as a catchup sum. They also demanded unspecified increases during the contract, an uncapped COLA clause, and benefits improvements. The final settlement had something to meet each demand except the catchup. The total hourly increase by the *end* of the three-year contract would be $1.35 per hour, 30 cents less than the catchup demand alone.

Union behavior. The union adopted a militant position, forecasting a strike. Emphasis on the international's influence in bargaining was emphasized. This probably occurred because the union was beset by both historical and current problems. First, the union typically encountered problems in solidarity in the past as locals circumvented the international in contract negotiations. The companies attempted to capitalize on this late in the strike. Second, at the beginning of the negotiations, the ISST was already into its craft severance campaign. Internal divisiveness was thus an overt issue.

The union estimated a long strike to be five to six weeks. By the time it reached that point, strike benefits had run out. The five- to six-week "long" estimate actually only turned out to be a third of the ultimate length.

The union's initial bargaining behavior, in terms of demand ambiguity and the close scheduling of the advisory committee report to the expiration deadline almost guaranteed a strike. What the union probably didn't reckon on was the company's preparedness.

The Big Four. Little came out of the early negotiations and pronouncements to let us assess the company's positions. But as time proceeded, it became continually more apparent that the rubber producers were extremely well prepared for a strike of major proportions.

In the past, the union had generally struck one target firm while the others continued to produce. If this was anticipated to be the strategy in 1976, no excess inventory or shipments would be necessary since the producing firms would take up much of the slack. It is apparent here, however, that the URW decision to strike all simultaneously did not catch the producers unaware.

No major movements in the negotiations came until close to the end. Automakers had stockpiled sufficient supplies to get them comfortably into the 1977 model run. As the end neared, the tire producers sought to break what was a more solid than usual front by filing the unfair labor practice charge. However, no major attempt was made to discredit Bommarito.

The mediators. Three times the mediators moved the negotiations onto their turf in Washington. The first two times they came up empty. The third time, Usery's telegram inferred that it was going to be harder to disagree than to settle. Undoubtedly Usery's strong point as secretary of labor was his ability as a mediator. His lack of success up to the August meeting compared with his other mediating successes may have redoubled his resolve to avoid the humiliation of being unable to orchestrate a settlement here.

Parallels to behavioral studies. Perhaps the most obvious parallel in these negotiations to the Rubin and Brown review relates to the publicity on the URW position and the mediators.[42] The URW had elected in 1973, as it had in the past, to forgo a COLA clause to get a large settlement. From 1973 to 1976, this proved to have been a bad strategy. Thus, URW officers were perceived to have been taken by the companies. Their intrasigence here can be partially explained by the public assessment of the relative positions of the rubber and auto workers. The same holds for the mediator. Obviously the intervention of high-level mediators is attended by publicity. When unable to deliver a settlement, the tactics got tougher than they perhaps would in a more normal or low-keyed situation.

REVIEW

The last three chapters have dealt with the issues and processes associated with contract negotiations. Here we have examined processes and behaviors where the parties have failed to agree. It is important to reemphasize the small number of situations in which strikes or lockouts do occur and the minute proportion of work days lost that can be laid to labor disputes.

Impasses do occur in negotiations. If they do, mediators are available and contribute to settlements. Strikes cannot occur until the contract expires and until 60 days after notification that renegotiation is requested. Lockouts cannot take place until contract expiration and unless an impasse has occurred.

Strikers run risks because they can be replaced in economic disputes, but the employer seldom does so because the union continues to represent bargaining unit members.

As labor relations between parties mature, the length and frequency of strikes decline. Both employers and union are interested in stable relationships in which both can reasonably predict their futures.

SUMMARY

As we noted in our introduction to this chapter, relatively few working days are lost to labor disputes in the United States. There are a variety of methods used to break impasses. First, the parties may be left to their own devices to solve the problem, possibly through bargaining power. Second, mediation may be used. Third, fact finders may highlight points of contention and propose solutions. Fourth, binding arbitration may be employed.

---

[42] Jeffrey Z. Rubin and Bert B. Brown, *The Social Psychology of Bargaining and Negotiation* (New York: Academic Press, 1975.)

Strikes may be divided into four major categories: economic, over conditions in the contract; unfair labor practices, in protest of a violation of the labor acts; wildcat, without authorization; and sympathy, in support of another union's demands.

Other tactics used in impasses include boycotts by the union and lockouts by management. Lockouts must be used judiciously and only after an impasse has been reached since retaliatory lockouts may arguably interfere with the employees' Section 7 rights.

SUGGESTED READINGS

Douglas, Ann. *Industrial Peacemaking* (New York: Columbia University Press, 1962).

Simkin, William E. *Mediation and the Dynamics of Collective Bargaining* (Washington: Bureau of National Affairs, 1971).

Walton, Richard E., and McKersie, Robert B. *A Behavioral Theory of Labor Negotiations* (New York: McGraw-Hill, 1965).

DISCUSSION QUESTIONS

1. In your estimation, why don't more firms use lockouts to break impasses?
2. To what extent should the federal government become involved in impasse resolution?
3. In the Rubber Workers' strike of 1976, why did the strike last as long as it did?
4. In what situations would the parties be most likely to benefit from mediation?

Incident

GMFC IMPASSE

Assume that you are director of industrial relations for GMFC. The company and the union have failed to agree on a new contract and the old contract expired last week. Two issues are unresolved and no movement has been made on these for over ten days. The union is demanding 10 cents an hour more than the company is willing to offer, and management will not accede to the dental care demand. This is the first negotiation in 15 years where a new contract has not been ratified prior to the expiration of the old one.

Local 384 voted a strike authorization about a month ago for its leadership, but they have not indicated at this point whether or not they intend to strike. In your own organization, production managers are lobbying for a lockout to avoid material losses if the heated steel treating process must be shut down rapidly. Marketing managers want production maintained to meet orders scheduled for shipment. They argue that the union doesn't intend to strike or they would have already.

In the executive council meeting this morning, financial officers briefed the top executives of GMFC and indicated that the company could accept a wage settlement of 5 cents an hour more, but only if this were a firm figure, not subject to increases over the term of the contract. Unfortunately, the union has appeared adamant on its dental care demand.

It is now your turn to recommend strategy to the company in this impasse. Considering the evidence, what course of action should the company take? Outline the action including processes used and timetables. Consider the possibility that some of your strategy may trigger a strike or other union activity.

12

SPECIAL BARGAINING PROCESSES AND TOPICS

In Chapters 9, 10, and 11 we examined many of the typical procedures and issues involved in bargaining and impasse resolution. This chapter is focused on some of the latest processes adapted to traditional bargaining and some of the major implementations of integrative bargaining. Many of these issues and procedures are primarily associated with large firms and industries but could be utilized wherever a mature bargaining relationship exists.

In a sense, we are going to reverse the approach we took in the last three chapters and move from processes to issues rather than the reverse in this one. The first subject we will deal with relates to alternative demand-offer sequences. The second will examine alternative bargaining structures such as coordinated bargaining, industrywide bargaining, and multiemployer bargaining. Finally, the third subject will relate to innovative and integrative issues such as productivity bargaining in construction, the Experimental Negotiating Agreement in the steel industry, quality of working life issues, and the Scanlon Plan.

As you read this chapter, ask yourself some of the following question:

1. What steps have or can a union take to deal with greater product or geographical dispersion within firms where it represents workers?
2. Which types of unions have been most willing to innovate in bargaining?
3. What are the conditions necessary for the products of integrative bargaining to be implemented?

ALTERNATIVE NEGOTIATING SEQUENCES

There are probably fewer variations or innovations in the sequences of offers or demands than in any area of the collective bargaining

306

relationship. Traditionally, the union communicates its demands first, and management responds with a counteroffer. This give-and-take iterative process continues until settlement.

There has been one important variation from this approach which was practiced from the late 1940s through the early 1960s. This variant, called "Boulwareism" and used by General Electric, was essentially a "last-offer-first" approach.

Boulwareism

This tactic got its name from Lemuel Boulware who held various high-level employee relations posts at General Electric starting in 1946. In his analysis of the GE bargaining approach, Northrup finds that Boulwareism had a number of key concepts.[1] First, GE felt that it was necessary to determine carefully what employees would prefer to have in a collective agreement. If GE felt it knew what employees needed in a contract, it did not want the union to specify the issues. Thus, the company embarked on a strategy in which it took the initiative in the process of bargaining. At the table, the company made but one offer, the package on which it was willing to settle and which it believed would meet the needs of bargaining unit members. It was open to a change in its position if management could be convinced by the union, on the basis of information the firm did not have when the offer was made, that the position was wrong. The company also increased its communication activity to the public and its employees to present its position and rationale.[2]

GE workers were primarily represented by the International Union of Electrical, Radio, and Machine Workers (IUE) but also had substantial numbers of its employees within the United Electrical, Radio, and Machine Workers (UE), the Machinists (IAM) and the Auto Workers (UAW). It also maintained open shops in its unionized plants and had several large operations which were not organized. Thus, the power of a given union may not have been as great as if it represented all production workers.

During the first decade of Boulwareism, the union was able to gain minor changes in the company offers, but generally the package was virtually intact when the contract was signed. IUE President James Carey complained that the company's general refusal to concede constituted bad faith bargaining.[3] On the other hand, Northrup argues that it was Carey rather than GE who was intransigent during the 1960

---

[1] Herbert R. Northrup, *Boulwarism* (Ann Arbor: Bureau of Industrial Relations, University of Michigan, 1964). Both spellings of the tactic are appropriate.

[2] Ibid., pp. 26–36.

[3] Ibid., pp. 51–60.

contract talks. He finds that several non-IUE unions agreed to GE's offer while the IUE went out and engaged in some strike violence.[4]

Boulwareism and the duty to bargain

As it had in the past, the IUE objected to GE's bargaining practices and filed an unfair labor practice charge with the NLRB. The board held that the totality of the conduct of GE's bargaining practices was such that it precluded true collective bargaining.[5]

The board found that GE's approach of offering the same settlement to all unions and insisting that certain parts of the package could not differ among agreements, coupled with its communication to the bargaining unit about negotiations and its avowed opposition to union representation in certification elections, amounted to an illegal pattern.

Even though GE made offers, participated in negotiations, and expressed a desire to reach a settlement, its conduct was unfair. The offer to change a position only on the basis of new information from some outside source was seen as placing the union in an advisory rather than a representative role. The board ordered the company to bargain in good faith.

The 2d Circuit Court of Appeals enforced the NLRB order and the Supreme Court refused to hear an appeal. In its decision, the appeals court further specified the board's order for subsequent bargainers: "In order to avoid any misunderstanding of our holding, some additional discussion is in order. We do not today hold that an employer may not communicate with his employees during negotiations. Nor are we deciding that the 'best offer first' bargaining technique is forbidden. Moreover, we do not require an employer to engage in 'auction bargaining,' or, as the dissent seems to suggest, compel him to make concessions, 'minor' or otherwise."[6]

The concerted campaign run by GE has not been practiced by a major U.S. employer since this decision. And as we'll see in the next section, GE encountered subsequent bargaining problems after the practice of Boulwareism was outlawed.

BARGAINING STRUCTURES

A variety of bargaining structures has been devised to overcome situational difficulties with the typical single employer-single union

---

[4] Ibid., pp. 81–90.

[5] *General Electric Co.*, 150 NLRB 192 (1964).

[6] *NLRB* v. *General Electric Co.*, 418 F.2d 766 (U.S. 2d Circuit Court of Appeals, 1969).

model. Recall that in the union organization chapter (Chapter 8), the bargaining unit specified for an election is not necessarily the unit for contract negotiations. Several other patterns can emerge. For example, several unions may bargain with a single employer (coalition or coordinated bargaining), several employers may bargain with a single union (multiemployer bargaining), and all employers in an industry bargain with a single union (industrywide bargaining). We will examine these structures in turn as we look at special processes.

Coalition bargaining

The GE case posed a substantial problem for the unions representing its employees since the settlement of one contract weakened the bargaining power of those still negotiating. If all unions bargained with GE together, this bargaining power in the employer could be reduced. To illustrate the differences between bargaining under Boulwareism where GE picked off the unions one by one and the results of the first coalition bargaining session, we will follow a case study reported by Schwarz.[7]

Seven unions affiliated with the AFL–CIO who bargained with GE formed the Committee on Collective Bargaining (CCB) in late 1965. The CCB was assisted in formulating demands by the industrial union department (IUD) of the AFL–CIO. Their initial contact with GE was rebuffed, but when GE and the IUE sat down for the first time to discuss prenegotiation matters, representatives of other CCB unions were there. GE refused to meet with the group.

Then a series of legal actions were begun by GE and the IUE, each accusing the other of refusing to bargain. The NLRB brought a complaint against the company which was never ultimately ruled upon since the completion of a new contract was seen by the Supreme Court as mooting the issue (having already provided any remedy the Court might award). As negotiations began and continued, the union initially gave an October 2 strike deadline but extended it to October 16 when it appeared that some IUE locals were lukewarm on the strike issue.

No general conclusion was reached as to whether or not the bargaining resulted in better outcomes for the union. In this and later negotiations, while GE permitted IUE negotiators to have observers and advisors from other CCB member unions, the demands made by and settlements with the IUE were seen by GE as applying only to the workers it represented.

To call what the unions put together at GE a coalition is to use the term loosely. From a strict standpoint, coalition bargaining is where

---

[7] Philip J. Schwarz, "Coalition Bargaining," *Key Issues Series*, no. 5 (January 1970), New York State School of Industrial and Labor Relations, Cornell University, pp. 13–16.

two or more unions negotiate a common master agreement with an employer or employees while coordinated bargaining takes place during joint negotiations involving two or more unions who wish to obtain common terms for some employees each represents.[8] Thus, GE's case is one of coordinated rather than coalition bargaining.

In an in-depth look at coalition and coordinated bargaining, Hildebrand discusses the impetus for bargaining, the types of situations in which it may become prevalent, and the tactics used by both labor and management.[9] He finds that the impetus for coalitions comes from a desire to reduce the power of the firm to whipsaw the unions where several of them represent employees in a variety of plants. Unless a coalition is formed, the organization with which it bargains would never be completely shut down. Hildebrand suggests that substitutability among plants leads to national level negotiations where a single union represents employees in a company. If a variety of unions represent workers in several plants, unions obtaining good settlements may be at a relative disadvantage as the firm shifts work to lower cost plants. Vertically integrated firms where the company handles most steps from the obtaining of the raw materials to marketing a finished product require coordination since nonstruck employers can make gains. Conglomerates also force a different type of strategy since choices may be made by the parent firm as to both plants and product lines it intends to emphasize.[10]

The tactics used by both parties have been the subject of a good deal of legal debate. Unions may use roving committees to keep track of separate negotiations, or they might simply bargain simultaneously with the company. For their part, the companies have generally tried to rebuff coalition but not necessarily coordinated bargaining. A variety of recent NLRB and court cases have dealt with the tactical issues and their congruence with the duty to bargain.

Decisions on coalition bargaining

Two major cases establish present permissible conduct in coalition or coordinated bargaining. The first is the *General Electric Company* case (partly in response to the dividing tactics of Boulwareism).[11] The NLRB required General Electric to bargain with a negotiating com-

---

[8] Lynn E. Wagner, "Multiunion Bargaining: A Legal Analysis," *Labor Law Journal*, vol. 19 (December 1968), p. 737.

[9] George H. Hildebrand, "Cloudy Future for Coalition Bargaining," *Harvard Business Review*, vol. 48 (November–December 1968), pp. 114–28.

[10] Ibid., pp. 114–17.

[11] *General Electric Co.*, 173 NLRB 46 (1968).

mittee made up of several representatives as long as each union represented GE employees. Outside representatives could not vote on any offers but could observe and comment.

The second case relates to the degree to which unions can commonly require an employer to agree to a standard agreement for all.[12] In the 1967–68 negotiations in the copper industry an interunion nonferrous industry conference was established to negotiate contracts with copper producers. One of the items it insisted on was a common contract expiration date for all unions. The unions did not demand changes in bargaining units other than their own, but each demanded the same termination date. The board ruled that this practice was illegal, but the appeals court refused to enforce the board's order and the Supreme Court declined its request to review.

Conglomerates and multinationals

A conglomerate is a business organization which has operations in a variety of distinct industries. For example, a firm may operate a chain of fast food franchises, market data processing time and services, manufacture and sell agricultural chemicals, and produce household appliances. This arrangement differs from a firm that specializes in a given product line such as autos, steel, and the like. By their nature, conglomerates are likely to deal with several distinct employee representatives since there would be distinct industrial jurisdictions within which unions would have organized. Because of its nature, a conglomerate may have a high degree of bargaining power since no single part of its business is very large relative to others, and it is unlikely that its distinct parts are dependent on each other for components or processes. Thus, the company could take a very long strike at almost any subsidiary.

Multinational organizations do not necessarily have the same characteristics as conglomerates in terms of product line diversity, but their bargaining power is also great because of the differing jurisdictions within which they have operations. Thus, UAW unions do not represent production employees of Ford Motor in Germany. To the extent that a firm's operations are spread across jurisdictions, it is able to withstand strikes through shifting production or simply foregoing small proportions of its revenues just as a conglomerate might.

In an analysis of bargaining involving plant shutdowns in Litton Industries, Craypo suggests that unions presently have little power in

---

[12] *AFL–CIO Joint Negotiating Committee for Phelps-Dodge* v. *NLRB* (3d Circuit Court of Appeals, no. 19199, 1972), p. 313.

bargaining but could profitably change some of their tactics.[13] He recommends that unions coordinate bargaining over contract terms and bargain with entire industry groups rather than single employers.

Multiemployer bargaining

In Chapter 11 we briefly discussed multiemployer bargaining from the standpoint of the use of lockouts as a tactic. Firms, especially small ones, may prefer to bargain as a group or employer association when they are dealing with a single union local. This preference is based in their motives to avoid whipsawing tactics by the union. If all firms bargain together, the costs of a strike to the union are much larger than if they bargain separately.

On the other hand, it would seem that there are few motives for the union to engage in multiemployer bargaining. If their costs go up and their bargaining power drops, it seems strange that it would consent to such a procedure. But unions may frequently want to avoid negotiated wage disparities between employers of the same types of employees it represents.[14] To do so, they must negotiate a similar agreement with all employers. To lessen the possibility of one group of employees prevailing where another does not, bargaining simultaneously in a multiemployer group is the answer.

Multiemployer bargaining takes place most often when there are several small employers bargaining with one large union. (Parenthetically, an employer association may bargain with several different unions representing different trades, but not simultaneously over the same terms.) Typical situations would include an association of retail food stores, a group of machine shops, or a number of construction contractors. Mills details the typical arrangements found in the construction industry.[15]

> Collective bargaining agreements in construction are normally negotiated between a local union in a single craft and an association of contractors who employ men of that craft. The agreement normally covers a geographic area (the geographic jurisdiction of the local) and specific types of work operations (the work jurisdiction of the craft). Wage scales, fringe benefits, and working conditions are established for the term of the agreement (generally two or three years), although wages

---

[13] Charles Craypo, "Collective Bargaining in the Conglomerate, Multinational Firm," *Industrial and Labor Relations Review*, vol. 29 (October 1975), pp. 3–25.

[14] Neil W. Chamberlain and Donald E. Cullen, *The Labor Sector*, 2d ed. (New York: McGraw-Hill, 1971), p. 205.

[15] Daniel Quinn Mills, *Industrial Relations and Manpower in Construction* (Cambridge, Mass.: MIT Press, 1972), p. 28.

may be increased in steps during this period. Because the agreement establishes uniform conditions that apply to all union contractors in the geographic area, it serves to regulate competition among firms with respect to wages and working conditions. Labor costs remain a major aspect of price competition among firms, but only in relation to the efficiency of the builder in his use of the labor force, not by virtue of differing wages and conditions of work.

Industrywide bargaining

Industrywide bargaining is a special case of multiemployer bargaining where several large employers constitute the entire industry and bargain as a group with a single union representing some or all of their unionized workers. Probably the best recent example of industrywide bargaining surrounds the practices of the basic steel producers and the United Steelworkers. The steel companies bargain together with the union on the economic package for the industry. This practice has been in effect since 1955 with some minor individual company breaks. Generally speaking, however, few industries bargain on a total basis with the union on any contract provisions.

Bargaining units: For representation and negotiation

By now you are probably fairly confused as to what a bargaining unit is. At its most elemental level, a bargaining unit is what labor and management say it is. This is a seeming tautology, but recall that in Chapter 8 we noted that NLRB consent elections were ordered where labor and management had no dispute over who would be included in a bargaining unit for representation purposes. But once we move past the representation stage, the parties are still free to make the bargaining unit more (but not less) inclusive in negotiations. Obviously, this may lead to novel bargaining structures which accommodate pecularities of the unions, firms, or industries involved. This is why we have industrywide and multiemployer bargaining and why coordinated or coalition bargaining only has advisory properties.

A recent decision involving Shell Oil Company and its benefits programs reiterated the voluntary nature of expanding bargaining unit size.[16] There the union asked the NLRB to force the company to bargain on a companywide basis over fringe benefits rather than locally as it had in the past. The board refused, holding that it had certified local units, and any expanded unit for bargaining purposes must be mutually agreed to. The 2d Circuit Court enforced the decision. Thus, the

---

[16] *Oil, Chemical, and Atomic Workers* v. *NLRB*, 84 LRRM 2581 (2d Circuit Court of Appeals, 1973).

scope of the bargaining unit for negotiating purposes is within the parties' control.

Figure 12–1 represents a flow chart which might predict the type of bargaining structures that could evolve in special situations.

FIGURE 12–1
Bargaining patterns

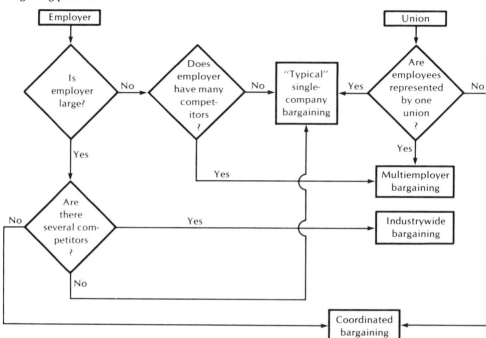

Now that we have looked at special bargaining structures, we need to examine some private sector bargaining topics that are important but not typically addressed in most contracts.

SPECIAL TOPICS AND METHODS

Two areas we will discuss here have been of continuing concern, especially to outsiders. These are innovations in dispute resolution and productivity. Another area which has become important in the last five years is the quality of working life.

Dispute resolution

There are two major types of labor disputes. One is disputes over contract terms during negotiations; the other is disputes over the interpretation of the contract during its effective period. When one examines labor history, the strike has been the weapon labor has used to try to get management to settle on its terms. For its part, management needs to continue operations to remain profitable so it is unlikely to shut down during a dispute unless leaving the timing of a closing to the union is economically more injurious than the shutdown itself.

Once the parties have reached an agreement, the company hopes that this will begin a period of predictable stable relations with the union. The union, for its part, wants to be able to have management live up to its agreement. If a dispute exists during the contract, procedures must be available for its resolution, short of a strike. Thus, the parties typically agree on a grievance procedure whose last step is binding arbitration. There have been some recent bargaining innovations here like expedited arbitration. We will examine the entire grievance and arbitration process in Chapters 13 and 14.

Experimental Negotiating Agreement

The Experimental Negotiating Agreement was included in the 1974 contract between the basic steel producers and the United Steelworkers. It is an excellent example of integrative bargaining on the part of the opponents and of intraorganizational bargaining in its later usage.

As background, the steel industry has seemed to engage in crisis bargaining ever since management and labor began their relationship. At each contract expiration, a long strike ensued or government intervention was necessary to gain a settlement. As Table 12–1 shows, from 1949 through 1971 for the eight negotiations, only two were settled without a strike or the threat of one. As a result, steel customers learned to stockpile steel prior to negotiations. This higher than normal demand caused steel mills to work at capacity and invited buyers to purchase foreign steel. If a strike ensued, even more pressure was placed on customers to make foreign orders. In cases where contract negotiations did not result in strikes, customer expectations that it would had led to so much stockpiling that mills frequently were forced to close and workers were laid off immediately after an agreement was reached. To prevent this "boom-or-bust" cycle which had negative effects on both labor and management, the ENA was negotiated in 1974. Just exactly what is provided for in ENA? And just exactly how did it come about?

The ENA didn't just drop out of the clouds as a gift from heaven. It was more like the gestation of an elephant, only more so. Maloney traced the history of the ENA back to union discussions following the 1965 contract.[17] The basic approach proposed was to arbitrate differ-

---

[17] William F. Maloney, "Experimental Negotiating Agreement: Development and Impact" (Unpublished Paper, Graduate School of Business Administration, University of Michigan, 1974), pp. 19–31.

TABLE 12–1
Steel industry negotiating history

Year	Result
1949	45-day strike—Pensions were established as a result of presidential board recommendations.
1952	59-day strike—Union shop provision emerged from government intervention settlement.
1956	36-day strike—Supplemental unemployment benefits and cost of living won by union in government-pressured pact.
1959	116-day strike—Management rights won by companies.
1962	No strike.
1965	No strike—Both sides invited to Washington for government dictated settlement. Union won early retirement provision.
1968	No strike.
1971	No strike—President Nixon threatened to remove import quota on foreign steel in attempt to leverage a settlement.

Source: Adapted from *Steel*, vol. 162, no. 8 (February 19, 1968), p. 40.

ences which were unresolved two months prior to the expiration of the present contract. The executive board of the USW refused to approve the proposal because the steel companies would not assure them that previously won contract features would not be subject to later renegotiation and that certain contract clauses would be immune to arbitration modification.

Interest in ENA was revived following the 1971 negotiations which were accompanied by one of the worst "boom-or-bust" buying cycles yet experienced. The continued layoffs and increased use of foreign steel served as motives for both parties to avoid their past bargaining conduct. The agreement on ENA was seen by the steel firms as contributing to cost reductions incurred as a result of shutdowns and reducing the reliance of domestic purchases on foreign steel. Union leaders saw the new approach as guaranteeing employment stability for the rank and file steelworkers.

The ENA was finally agreed to on March 29, 1973, and consisted of eight major sections. The first deals with strikes and lockouts and states that these will not be used on any national level bargaining issue. The second section agrees to provide basic wage increases over the life of the contract. Section three gives a lump sum payment to workers for reducing costs of shutdowns. Section four details proce-

TABLE 12–2
ENA national agreement bargaining sequence

February 1	Negotiations must begin by this date on the new contract.
April 15	By this date, the parties shall 1. Reach total agreement on all issues, or 2. Agree that certain specified issues are settled and certain other issues are to be submitted to the arbitration panel, or 3. Withdraw all offers and counteroffers and submit issues to the arbitration panel.
April 20	Submission of issues to the panel.
May 10	Submission of detailed position papers by both sides outlining their stands on the issues submitted to arbitration.
May 20	Submission of written replies to the other side's position paper.
July 10	Decision of the arbitration panel must be rendered not later than midnight.
July 20	Union and management sides must reach agreement on contract language and any other steps required for implementation of the arbitration panel's decision.
July 31	All unresolved issues must be resolved before midnight by the arbitration panel.
August 1	New three-year contract goes into effect.

dures for negotiation and arbitration if necessary at national and local levels. Table 12–2 covers the sequences and activities. Table 12–3 gives the subjects that were excluded from arbitration under the ENA. Section five specifies the makeup of and procedures to be used by the arbitration panel. Section six specifies the period within which the contract was to be effective. Section seven specifies that unchanged conditions would be carried over to a new contract. Finally, section eight specified that the ENA would expire on August 1, 1974, unless renewed by the parties.

The parties have continued to use the methods devised under ENA through their 1977 negotiations. Experience has shown that local lead-

TABLE 12–3
Items excluded from arbitration under ENA

a. Local working conditions provisions.
b. Union membership and checkoff provisions.
c. Cost-of-living adjustment provisions.
d. Wage parity and uniformity.
e. Wage increases and lump sum bonus granted under Sections B and C.
f. No-strike and no-lockout provisions.
g. Management rights provisions.

ers are less enthusiastic about it than national officers, but both the union and management appear to be more reluctant to go to arbitration than settle on their own. The boom-or-bust cycle has been reduced by this recent experience, and steel labor relations should be more predictable in the future. The ENA is still an extremely controversial issue within the union, however. During the last election for the union's executive officers, the Sadlowski faction made the ENA a campaign issue by arguing that it reduced Steelworker bargaining power through its deferral to arbitration.

Productivity bargaining

Another topic in bargaining that is of specific interest to both parties is productivity bargaining. In productivity bargaining, management is usually seeking a relaxation of some rules which will lead to an increase in output while the union is interested in maintaining job security for its members. The longshoring agreements we previously examined fall into this area. In this section we will discuss general issues in productivity bargaining and a specific system, the Scanlon plan, which has been used as a vehicle to implement increased productivity in both union and nonunion contexts.

What is productivity bargaining?

According to McKersie and Hunter, productivity bargaining is simply a system for allocating the rewards from increased productivity to the sources responsible for the gain. A formula is devised to state what proportion will go to labor, what proportion to capital, and so on. This system explicitly lays out steps that labor and management will be permitted to make to improve productivity.[18]

Within our study of productivity bargaining we will look at one example of steps taken in the contract construction industry and one example of an implementation system for allocation of savings from productivity gains, the Scanlon Plan.

The construction industry case is reported by Maloney and involves the Dallas–Fort Worth area.[19] Construction unions were concerned with productivity issues since wage costs were higher for unionized contractors than for open shop operations. As more and more nonresidential construction was being lost to these nonunion employers, increases in output would be necessary for high-wage firms to remain competitive. Management was concerned with remaining competitive, and also most did not want to go open shop since this would have

[18] Robert B. McKersie and Lawrence C. Hunter, *Pay Productivity and Collective Bargaining* (London: St. Martin's Press, 1973), pp. 4–5.

[19] William F. Maloney, *Productivity Bargaining: A Study in Contract Construction* (Unpublished doctoral dissertation, University of Michigan, 1976), pp. 262–85.

shifted the burden onto them in the employment and training area which the union had typically handled in the past.

Bargaining takes place at two levels in the multiemployer and multiemployer-coordinated bargaining format. The first involved members of one craft and the second included representatives of the area's building trades council. Various minor changes were negotiated such as a reduction in travel pay, elimination of age mix requirements, establishment of lower-paid helper classifications, and the reduction of double-time overtime. Starting times and holiday provisions were standardized. In addition, some of the masonry trades agreed to an additional contractual pay schedule calling for $2 less per hour on jobs that would have likely gone to open shop contractors.

Overall, however, the parties agreed that the changes had had little impact on productivity. Some costs had declined, but the rate of output and ability to compete had not changed. One possible reason for this is that the bargaining was not truly integrative in nature. Productivity bargaining here led to gains for management from what had been a very bad situation, but no gain for the union. Wages were cut in some instances, and no job protection was built in. One might say job security is an impossible demand in a fragmented industry like contract construction, but the also highly fragmented Pacific Maritime Association has made it work in the longshoring innovations. It appears that productivity bargaining does not work unless both parties can clearly see the benefits of a new approach and some system is established for sharing the benefits of increased productivity.

The Scanlon Plan

The genesis of the Scanlon Plan took place in the late 1930s in an obsolete steel mill. With profits close to zero and the employees demanding higher wages and better working conditions, their union leader, Joseph Scanlon, saw that gaining the demands would force the company out of business. To meet the profit goals of the company and the wage and working condition demands of the employees, he proposed that the parties work together to increase productivity while postponing a wage increase. But at a later date, if productivity were improved, the gains would be shared with the workers.

How does the Scanlon Plan work?

Frost and his co-workers detail the basics of a Scanlon Plan.[20] The two underlying foundations of the program are participation by all members of the organization and equity in reward distribution.

---

[20] Carl F. Frost, John H. Wakeley, and Robert A. Ruh, *The Scanlon Plan for Organization Development: Identity, Participation, and Equity* (East Lansing: Michigan State University Press, 1974), pp. 5–26.

FIGURE 12–2
Scanlon Plan production committee

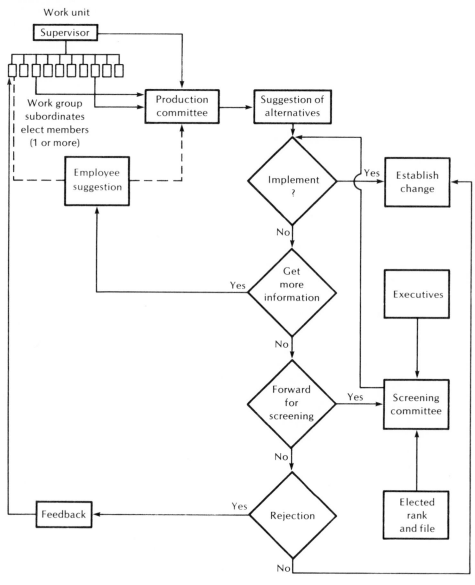

The participation system is based on a recognition that abilities are widely distributed in the organization and that change in the organization's environment is inevitable. Since change occurs and since persons at all levels may have possible solutions to change problems or suggested changes to improve productivity, the system includes an open suggestion procedure. These suggestions are evaluated and acted upon by joint labor-management committees who make recommendations up the line. Figure 12–2 details the typical composition of a committee and its actions.

When a suggestion is made, it is evaluated by the production committee of a given work unit. If it is implementable and has merit in that unit, the production committee can place it into effect. If the suggestion is questionable or has wide impact, it's forwarded to the screening committee (made up of executives and employee representatives) for evaluation and possible implementation.

The screening committee also has a very important additional function—determining the level of the bonus to be paid each month or quarter. Just exactly how is the bonus determined? A number of steps are involved, with a very simple approach examining labor costs in relation to production to establish the usual relative share of labor costs. For example, if, on the average, for each $1 of sales, it has traditionally required 30 cents in labor, then any improvement to, say, 29 cents or 25 cents, would represent a productivity improvement. Table 12–4 is a representation of a simple formula where labor costs are 30 percent of the total production value.

TABLE 12–4
Simple labor formula

Sales	$ 98,000
Returned goods	3,000
Net sales	$ 95,000
Inventory + ...	5,000
Production value	$100,000
Labor bill	
Wages	$ 16,000
Salaries	8,000
Vacations and holidays	1,800
Insurance	1,700
Pensions	500
Unemployment	500
F.I.C.A.	1,500
Total labor bill	$ 30,000
Ratio	

Source: Carl F. Frost, John H. Wakeley, and Robert A. Ruh, *The Scanlon Plan for Organization Development: Identity, Participation, and Equity* (East Lansing: Michigan State University Press, 1974), p. 103.

Companywide and individual bonuses can be calculated after the screening committee receives operating results for the previous period. Table 12–5 gives an example of a company and an employee report.

TABLE 12–5
Bonus report

a.	Scanlon ratio	0.40/1.00
b.	Value of production	$100,000
c.	Expected costs $(a \times b)$	40,000
d.	Actual costs	30,000
e.	Bonus pool $(c - d)$	10,000
f.	Share to company—20% $(e \times 0.20)$	2,000
g.	Share to employees—80% (adjusted pool) $(e \times 0.80)$	8,000
h.	Share for future deficits—25% of adjusted pool $(g \times 0.25)$	2,000
i.	Pool for immediate distribution $(g - h)$	6,000
j.	Bonus for each employee* as a percentage of his pay for the production period $(i \div d)$	20%

The June pay record might look like this for a typical employee.

Name	Monthly pay for June	Bonus percent	Bonus	Total pay
Mary Smith	$600	20%	$120	$720

* This example assumes that all employees are participating in the plan at the time this bonus is paid; for example there has been no turnover and no employees are in their initial 30-, 60-, or 90-day trial periods.

Source: Carl F. Frost, John H. Wakeley, and Robert A. Ruh, *The Scanlon Plan for Organization Development: Identity, Participation, and Equity* (East Lansing: Michigan State University Press, 1974), p. 15.

The major purposes of the plan are to increase the rewards to both parties for productivity gains, to encourage and reward participation, and to link rewards to employee performance. Notice that the system focuses on productivity improvements associated with lower *labor* costs—something more directly within the control of the workers. Thus, the behavior → outcome relationship is higher than profit sharing or other similar types of gain sharing systems. Notice also that productivity gains are shared across work groups, encouraging solutions which mutually benefit several departments.

Quality of working life

Quality of work is an issue that is receiving more and more publicity. The term has seldom been completely defined and its vagueness is wrapped in norms and values which may not be completely shared by everyone. On a general level, quality of working life has been described as more than present job satisfaction, including also opportunities for growth and self-development, freedom from tension and stress, and satisfaction of basic needs.[21] Aspects of work environments seen as contributing to increased quality include security, equity, individuation, and democracy.[22]

[21] Edward E. Lawler, "Measuring the Psychological Quality of Working Life: The Why and How of It," in Louis E. Davis and Albert B. Cherns, eds., *The Quality of Working Life*, vol. 1 (New York: Free Press, 1975), pp. 124–25.

[22] Neal Q. Herrick and Michael Maccoby, "Harmonizing Work: A Priority Goal of the 1970s," in *The Quality of Working Life*, pp. 64–66.

The enthusiasm of both academics and organized labor for quality of working life issues and interventions varies widely, with suggestions for and against legislation,[23] and for and against job enrichment as a specific course to follow.[24] And, to this point the evidence available to appraise quality of working life changes is sketchy and mostly anecdotal.

We do know, however that quality of working life changes fit basically into the integrative bargaining framework. Management's motive for changing working conditions toward the normative goals stated earlier would be related to cost and productivity measures. Macy and Mirvis suggest that employers are concerned with measures of absenteeism, tardiness, turnover, and strikes; productive volume, quality, grievances, accidents, downtime, and scrap variances.[25] The union should be motivated to change if it gains concessions on mandatory bargaining issues such as wages, hours, and terms and conditions of employment. Maccoby reports on a change site where piece-rate workers were given the option of leaving when they completed a certain output quota.[26] This would be an example of a change in a mandatory bargaining area.

Given that there is some controversy about the necessity for embarking on quality of working life (QWL) programs, if a company and union were interested, what would be the best vehicle for their inception? Using data gathered from union leaders in New York state, Dyer, Lipsky, and Kochan found that QWL programs were seen as best handled through joint programs with management outside of the collective bargaining agreement.[27] Of those responding, 63 percent favored a joint approach, 21 percent favored collective bargaining, and only 16 percent advocated a "hands-off" no-involvement approach. The preferred type of approach is similar to that advocated by the Scanlon Plan and may be preferred where the parties desire to innovate and not be locked in by a contract.

---

[23] Edward E. Lawler, "Should the Quality of Working Life Be Legislated?" *Personnel Administrator*, vol. no. 21 (January 1976), pp. 17–21; and Edwin A. Locke, "The Case against Legislating the Quality of Working Life," *Personnel Administrator*, vol. 21 (April 1976), pp. 19–21.

[24] Donald F. Ephlin, "The Union's Role in Job Enrichment Programs," *Proceedings of the Industrial Relations Research Association*, vol. 26 (Madison, Wis.: IRRA, 1974), pp. 219–23; and William Winpsinger, "Job Satisfaction: A Union Response," *The Federationist*, vol. 80 (February 1973), pp. 8–10.

[25] Barry A. Macy and Philip H. Mirvis, "A Methodology for Assessment of Quality of Work Life and Organizational Effectiveness in Behavioral-Economic Terms," *Administrative Science Quarterly*, vol. 21 (1976), p. 214.

[26] Michael Maccoby, "Changing Work," *Working Papers* (Summer 1975), pp. 43–55.

[27] Lee Dyer, David B. Lipsky, and Thomas A. Kochan, "Union Attitudes toward Management Cooperation," *Industrial Relations*, vol. 16 (May 1977), pp. 163–72.

A case study

As we have noted, QWL is an area which is presently long on theory, but due to its recency, relatively short on results. But a recent series of QWL experiments have begun which involve unionized firms, and some results are now being reported.

One of the first cases reported involved the United Mine Workers and the Rushton Coal Company.[28] Coal producing firms have faced declining productivity in underground mines for some time while the union has a continual concern for the safety of miners. Consistent with what Dyer, Lipsky, and Kochan found to be the preferred mode for QWL projects, the mine management and the UMW entered into a joint project which could be terminated unilaterally at any time by either party. An outside consultant, Dr. Eric Trist (with considerable mine work design experience) acted as the leader of a team to help the parties in the change.

In this and other studies two labor-management committees have been established. At the top level, high management and international union officials act as advisers and finalize site selection. At the level where a study is to take place, a joint management-union committee is also established. Further down the line, shop committees may also be established to actually implement the changes.

The Rushton study began slowly with management and the union having to overcome their traditional adversary roles and move toward a problem-solving approach. Their final agreement to proceed covered the following major points:

1. An experimental section would be established in the mine, comprising 27 volunteers, 9 to a shift.
2. Every worker in the experimental section would be on top pay. This meant the experimental section would cost at most $324 more each week than other sections, not a prohibitive cost factor to the mine's management.
3. All members of each crew would be, or would be trained by the company to be, capable of performing any job in the section, from continuous miner operation to roof bolting. The entire crew would also be given special training in state and federal mine safety laws, so each miner would know what constitutes a violation. Each crew of the experimental section, therefore, would be an autonomous work team.
4. Each of the three crew foremen in the section would henceforth have responsibility and authority primarily for the safety of the crew. The responsibility to management for the day-to-day production of coal by the crew was transferred to the entire work team of nine men now without a boss.

---

[28] Ted Mills, "Altering the Social Structure in Coal Mining: A Case Study," *Monthly Labor Review*, vol. 100 (October 1976), pp. 3–10.

5. Grievances by any member of the section would be dealt with primarily by the crew involved, in what is sometimes called "peer discipline." If the crew couldn't cope with a grievance itself, it would then be processed through the local union's formal grievance machinery.[29]

This document was then ratified by the union local, and a new experimental section was staffed with three all-volunteer crews.

Almost a year later, the restructured groups began to get feedback on their effectiveness. For January 1975, even though their mine face had been shut down almost 25 percent of the time due to a cave-in, they produced 25 percent more coal than the poorest section at a cost 40 percent less than that section. Their cost per ton of clean coal was 71 cents less than the mine average of $1.87. Results were even more striking for mine safety. Only 7 safety violations were accumulated in 1974 as against 37 and 17 in the other sections, and only 7 accidents against 25 in the other two.

A major difficulty began to emerge in late 1974, however. The mine management decided to expand and *unilaterally* chose the new work arrangement for a new mine face. Since few of the senior miners bid to switch, the new mine would be staffed primarily by apprentices making top wages under the agreement. Nonparticipating rank and file workers demanded that the local require top pay for all workers, not just the experiment's participants. A new agreement was drawn up offering top pay to all workers for a 90-day period while they received training in the autonomous work group arrangement. If they assimilated the training, they would be assigned to an autonomous group and continue at this high rate. But the rank and file rejected the agreement 79 to 75, and the UMW asked the company to take over the project in the autonomous work group sections.

The company announced that for one year all would receive the top rate (except apprentices) and then after that year nonautonomous groups would revert to the contract rate. The focus of change also expanded to management to introduce it to more participative systems. Expanded training to miners has been included, and dramatic safety improvements continue. Finally, a Scanlon-type gain sharing program has been proposed for later inclusion.

A number of issues are important to remember in this QWL study. First, the company was confronting a continued problem in declining productivity. Second, mine safety was an important union issue. Combining these, we have a basis for integrative bargaining—gains to both simultaneously realizable. Third, the union (in this case) faces a difficult political situation since two groups of employees (experimental

---

[29] Ibid., pp. 3–10.

and regular working method) groups are treated differently on a non-contractual and nontraditional basis (seniority). Fourth, when the project became successful, the Scanlon Plan negotiations indicate that workers expect to share in the gains they have helped to develop through a participative system. Unless these factors are recognized and acted upon, QWL or other nontraditional integrative bargaining areas are unlikely to be implemented successfully.

SUMMARY

In this chapter, we have examined nonroutine approaches to bargaining and special issues of an integrative nature which on occasion involve the parties. Large employers or collections of very small employers are more likely to be involved in special bargaining patterns. Remember that the parties can consent to bargaining arrangements that *expand* the original bargaining unit agreed to or determined by the NLRB. In cases where large employers do not wish to bargain with several unions, coordinated bargaining with other unions providing observers is still an available option. Both parties in multiemployer and industrywide bargaining have a stake in maintaining the relationship since this arrangement takes wages out of competition and reduces the possibility of whipsawing advantages.

Productivity bargaining involves primarily integrative processes to improve the positions of both parties, usually profitability for management and job security for the union. The industries using productivity bargaining most frequently have been contract construction and the maritime industry, both areas where the union has substantial involvement in providing workers to jobs. Major mechanisms for productivity agreement maintenance involve committees or work teams such as those found in the Scanlon Plan or QWL projects.

To an extent, the ability of the labor movement to adapt to changes in bargaining structures and issues will be a measure of its future vitality, free from government imposition of compulsory settlements. The ENA and other mechanisms auger well for the future.

SUGGESTED READINGS

Frost, Carl F, Wakeley, John H., and Ruh, Robert A. *The Scanlon Plan for Organizational Developmental: Identity, Participation, and Equity* (East Lansing: Michigan State University Press, 1974).

Hildebrand, George H. "Cloudy Future for Coalition Bargaining." *Harvard Business Review.* vol. 48 (November-December 1968), pp. 114–28.

McKersie, Robert B., and Hunter, Lawrence C. *Pay Productivity and Collective Bargaining* (London: St. Martin's Press, 1973).

Maloney, William F. *Productivity Bargaining: A Study in Contract Construction* (Ann Arbor: Industrial Development Division, Institute of Science and Technology, University of Michigan, 1977).

Mills, Daniel Quinn. *Industrial Relations and Manpower in Construction* (Cambridge, Mass.: MIT Press, 1972).

Mills, Ted. "Altering the Social Structure in Coal Mining: A Case Study." *Monthly Labor Review.* vol. 100 (October 1976), pp. 3–10.

Schwarz, Philip J. "Coalition Bargaining." *Key Issues Series.* no. 5 (January 1970), New York State School of Industrial and Labor Relations, Cornell University.

DISCUSSION QUESTIONS

1. What adaptations do you expect unions to make during the next decade to cope with the increasingly multinational character of many corporations?
2. Why don't more companies and unions practice some variant of productivity bargaining?
3. How does the ENA affect the bargaining power of the Steelworkers and the producers?
4. What are the advantages and disadvantages to the firm in engaging in industrywide or multiemployer bargaining?

Exercise

It is about three months since the effective date of the GMFC-Local 384 contract. In its executive council meeting this morning, financial officers made their report of an in-depth study on the profitability of the special order fabrication operations. Their recommendation was that GMFC take no more orders for this area and, when present commitments were shipped, close down the operation. Their data showed the operations losing money two out of the last three years, and they argued that the Speedy-Lift assembly lines could be expanded into that area for meeting the increasing demand for GMFC fork-lift trucks.

Top-level management in the special order fabrication operations conceded that profits were low, when earned, but pointed out that they had been among the best in the company, from a return on investment standpoint, during the 1968–1973 period. Besides, they argued that many of the special orders were from some of the largest customers in the standard product lines, and GMFC could ill afford to lose that business if it was dependent on occasional custom orders as well.

The finance people reiterated their recommendation to terminate the operation, pointing out that labor costs had risen over the last several contracts, and due to the custom nature of the work, productivity gains had been small since new technologies could not be introduced.

After both sides presented their final summations, the chief executive officer announced that the firm should make preparations necessary to terminate operations. After the announcement, the industrial relations director pointed out that GMFC would have to negotiate the termination with Local 384. The union may demand severance pay, job transfers, and so forth. The point was also raised that this decision offered the opportunity to the union and the company to devise a method for reducing and controlling labor costs.

The CEO designated the vice president of finance, the general manager of special order fabrications and the industrial relations director as the bargaining team to present the company's decision and bargain a resolution. The CEO also made it clear that the company intended to abandon these operations but could reverse its position with the right kind of labor cost reductions.

Although this meeting was not publicized, Local 384's leadership had been concerned about the special order fabrications area for some time. Management had frequently grumbled about low productivity, and stewards were frequently harassed about alleged slowdowns. The members in the shop grieved often about alleged work rule changes. The stack of grievances that had piled up coupled with management's inaction on them led the leadership to decide to request a meeting with the industrial relations director to solve them.

DIRECTIONS

1. Rejoin your original labor or management bargaining team.
2. Reach an agreement for the continuation or termination of the special order fabrication operations.
   a. Company negotiators must reduce labor costs by 10 percent and stabilize them for project bids if operations are to continue (labor costs are 30 percent of the total costs, and ROI would be 7 percent if costs were cut by 10 percent).
   b. Union members are unwilling to have their pay rates cut.
   c. All of the employees in this area are grade 15 or 16 production workers.
3. Use the agreement you previously reached or the contract listed in the book to specify current terms for these workers.

13

CONTRACT ADMINISTRATION

After the contract is negotiated and ratified, the parties are bound by its terms for the period of the contract. But the parties may interpret the contract clauses differently. Occasionally disputes occur and some mechanisms are needed to resolve them. This chapter is primarily aimed at identifying the causes of disputes and their resolution during the life of the contract. As you recall from Chapter 9, the parties usually negotiate a grievance procedure to handle these disputes. In this chapter we will see how the procedure works in practice.

We will examine some of the major issues in contract administration, the parties involved in disputes, and the processes followed. We will also introduce the procedures the parties include in the contract to resolve disputes as they surface.

As you read through this chapter, keep the following questions in mind:

1. What are the usual areas of disagreement that emerge during the course of the contract?
2. What actions by the parties are violations of the labor acts?
3. To what extent are disagreements solved by bargaining or by evaluating the "merits"?
4. What obligation does the union owe its individual members in grievance processing?

ISSUES IN ADMINISTRATION

You recall that the labor acts require the parties to bargain over wages, hours, and terms and conditions of employment. One might think that bargaining means arriving at a contract acceptable to both parties. But that would be a narrow definition. Bargaining, as the NLRB and courts interpret it, is the whole collective relationship from the time a union gains representation rights forward. Thus, a disagreement over what a term of the contract means cannot be dismissed by one side since this would ordinarily be considered an instance of refusing to bargain; in turn, an unfair labor practice. However, disagreeing on an interpretation is not, as long as the parties follow procedures they have devised to settle disagreements. In most cases contracts provide for handling of these disagreements, which normally arise in the form of employee grievances, so that interpretive disputes do not become disruptive. Later, we will examine situations where grievance procedures do not exist or where unions strike over grievances or unfair labor practices during the term of the contract.

A number of issues are encountered in contract administration. We will enumerate and explain these momentarily, but first, it should be recognized that the area of contract administration turns the tables on initiatives toward the company and away from the union. The reason for this is that the company generally does not file a grievance when the union or a worker allegedly violates the contract; it simply takes some action and waits for the union to respond. For example, if a worker swears at a supervisor, the company may suspend him for five days. If the union feels this is unjust, it protests the action through a grievance. The company does not contact the union and ask it to discipline its members. Now, we'll examine some aspects of contract administration that lead to grievances.

Discipline

One of the most frequently disputed issues relates to company disciplinary practices. Discipline can take the form of demotions, suspensions, and discharges. Frequently discipline is meted out for insubordination, dishonesty, or poor productivity. A discharge is the industrial equivalent of "capital punishment" and will very often be the focus of a grievance, regardless of its ultimate merit, since political solidarity often requires that the union extend itself to try to save a member's job.

Incentives

Occasionally a contract will have an incentive scheme where employees are paid by the piece or receive bonuses for production efficiency. Frequently these contracts will establish groups of jobs that work on incentive rates and identify others that don't. If an employee is moved from an incentive job to a nonincentive job, wages may very well decrease as a result. If the job seems to be highly similar to the incentive job, a grievance may result. A grievance might also result if the assignment is considered arbitrary or punitive.

Work assignments

Where a variety of job classifications exist, there may be disputes as to which job classification is entitled to perform certain work. For example, assume that we have an electrical generating plant powered by coal-fired boilers for steam generation. If a boiler is shut down for rebricking and a wall is to be knocked down with some care to avoid damaging other boiler parts, who should do the work? If we have a general helper category, they might do it with a supervisor's direction. On the other hand, since some care is required and the work is preparatory to rebricking, the job may rightfully be assigned to skilled masonry workers. The company may attempt to assign the job to the helpers because the cost is less and the skill requirements are believed to be low. But the masons may feel this is an integral part of their job and file a grievance. This is essentially a job security issue.

Individual personnel assignments

These grievances are most often related to promotions, layoffs, transfers, and shift assignments. Most contracts specify that seniority, seniority and merit, or experience on a particular job will be the governing factors in personnel assignments. The most frequent disputes relate to layoffs and shift preference. If a person is laid off, he may feel that he is entitled to the job of a more junior worker in another department who has been retained. While contracts normally specify that a person must be qualified for a job where he is "bumping" a junior employee, there may be a difference of opinion as to whether or not the claimed qualifications are actually possessed.

More grievances tend to be filed over promotions where the contract specifies some requirement in addition to seniority. For example, if seniority governs unless some junior employee is "head and shoulders" above the senior person, what exactly does the "head and shoulders" difference consist of? Is only a certain level of qualification, set against a standard, necessary; or are all persons, regardless of seniority, considered to arrive at the appropriate promotion? Thus, requirements over and above seniority invite grievances unless they are clearly spelled out.

Hours of work

Grievances in this area relate to overtime requirements and work schedules. For example, if the firm has maintained an 8 A.M. to 4 P.M. shift to mail customer orders and finds that its freight companies have moved their shipping schedule from 4 P.M. to 3 P.M., then a 7 A.M. to

3 P.M. shift would better meet its needs. The change can affect employees, however, and grievances may result.

Supervisor doing production work

Most contracts forbid supervisors from doing production work except where it is to demonstrate the job to a new employee or to handle an emergency. And an emergency is usually not considered to occur simply because an employee is absent. This is basically a job security issue, as is the work assignment area.

Production standards

Often management and the union will have agreed upon the rate of output in assembly line technologies or the underlying standard for an incentive system in piece-rate output. If management speeds up the line or reengineers the standards, then more effort is required for the same amount of pay, and grievances often result.

Working conditions

These issues often relate to health and safety questions. For example, if the workers believe that excessive amounts of fumes exist in their areas, grievances may be filed. If an existing convenience, like heating, fails, grievances often result.

Subcontracting

Unless the contract is specific in allowing the company complete discretion in subcontracting, any work that is done by bargaining unit members may not be subcontracted without bargaining if the union demands it.[1] The subcontracting can affect job security, and if a grievance results, management would be engaging in an unfair labor practice if it refused to discuss and bargain over the issue with the union.

Past practice

Often practices that involve labor and management are not written into a contract but are considered by the union to be obligations. For example, the company may operate a cafeteria where workers can obtain meals at costs below those at commercial operations. If the employer decides to close the cafeteria, the union may grieve even

---

[1] *Fibreboard Paper Products Corp.* v. *NLRB*, 379 U.S. 203 (1964).

though no contract language talks about the cafeteria. If it is common practice to stop work 15 minutes prior to the end of a shift to wash up, then extending working time to the shift's end is a change in past practice.

These types of grievances can be largely overcome if the contract contains a "zipper" clause (stating that anything not explicitly covered by the contract is within management's right ultimately to control).

GRIEVANCE PROCEDURES

Most contracts specify how interpretive disagreements will be resolved. These mechanisms are called grievance procedures. While there are variations among contracts, most procedures contain four or five steps. In the absence of a grievance procedure, the employee is still entitled to press grievances individually under guarantees contained in Section 9 of the Taft-Hartley Act. Employees may also do so if the contract has a procedure, but as a practical matter they generally do not.

Steps in the grievance procedure

The usual steps in the grievance procedure are as follows:

> *Step 1.* This step varies considerably across companies. In some an employee who believes the company has violated the contract (grievant) complains to his union steward who may accept or assist in the writing of a grievance. Then the steward will present the grievance to the grievant's supervisor who has the opportunity to answer or adjust it.

In some companies, few grievances are settled at Step 1, because the company will not delegate this power to supervisors since their decisions may be used later as precedents in similar grievances filed by the union. Thus, the supervisor simply "denies" the grievance and refuses the relief asked. In other companies, the grievant orally presents his complaint directly to his supervisor. (Figure 13–1 is an example of a complex grievance at its first step.)

> *Step 2.* After this step, most grievances have been settled. If the grievance is denied at Step 1, then the steward will pursue it to a plant industrial relations representative. Both are very familiar with the contract, and both are aware of how grievances have been settled in the past. The company is also willing, in most routine cases, to let the IR representative apply and create precedents.
>
> *Step 3.* If the grievance is likely to have major precedent-setting implications or involves possibilities of major costs, then the IR representative may deny it and send it to Step 3. The participants at Step 3 may

vary substantially depending on the contract. Typical arrangements would include the following parties. First, the grievance may be settled locally with the union being represented by its local negotiating committee and management by its top IR manager or plant manager. In more complex situations or in larger firms, the parties may be an international union representative with or without the local negotiating committee and a corporate level IR director. A fair share of unresolved grievances are settled at this level.

Step 4. When a grievance is unresolved at the third step, the parties submit the dispute to a neutral arbitrator who hears evidence from both sides and renders a decision in the favor of one side. A number of methods for choosing an arbitrator are available. First, the parties may designate a permanent arbitrator, by name, in their contract. Second, the parties may petition a private agency such as the American Arbitration Association for an arbitration panel. A panel consists of an odd number of names (usually five) from which each party rejects arbitrators in turn until one remains. He or she becomes the arbitrator unless one party objects, in which case a new panel is submitted. Third, the same process may be followed by petitioning the Federal Mediation and Conciliation Service (FMCS) which also supplies panels of arbitrators who are listed by this agency. A hearing date is then set, and the arbitrator renders a decision some time after the evidence is presented. We will examine arbitration as a separate area in the next chapter.

FIGURE 13–1

"I have just been given a job review, as a result of which I am now on the second highest eligibility list as against the top list. I now want clear and accurate answers with supporting information to the following questions:

"(1) Why was this job review given five months after its effective date and on the day before my vacation?

"(2) Why change my rating for 'manner and interest' from excellent to good? It was admitted that I am excellent in this category, but only to those whom I think will buy, and that the reviewer did not know of any mistakes in judgment I had made.

"(3) Why change 'alertness to service' from excellent to good? Since I was told by the reviewer that I was too 'selective' in both this and the previous category, I think that (a) one or the other should be eliminated, or (b) perhaps they should be combined, or (c) both reviewer and employees should be made aware of whatever difference there may be.

"(4) Why change 'cooperation' from excellent to good? Since I was told that my cooperation with the other eight people in the department was excellent, I should like to know exactly what incidents took place and who was involved, resulting in this change.

"It also seems that there is a clear, consistent pattern of downgrading everyone in the department from their previous ratings and that job reviews will be given just prior to going on vacation. It is my distinct impression that the present reviewers not only are ignorant of previous reviews but also feel that they do the job much better than the previous reviewers. If they can't come up with some better reasons for the changes than those I have heard, then I think they are doing a remarkably poor job."

Source: Maurice S. Trotta, *Handling Grievances: A Guide for Labor and Management* (Washington: Bureau of National Affairs, 1976), pp. 141–42.

Time involved

Generally the contract aims at a speedy resolution of grievances consistent with the amount of time that might be necessary to investigate the grievance. Typical contracts may allow 2 to 5 days for resolution at each of the first two steps and 3 to 10 days at Step 3. If management denies the grievance at this point, then the union has some time, 10 to 30 days, to demand arbitration. If it doesn't, the dispute may be nonarbitrable since it was not timely referred to arbitration. After arbitration is demanded, the time frame is less rigid since an arbitration panel must be requested and received, an arbitrator must be selected, hearing dates must be arranged, and the final award must be written and rendered. While it is conceivable that an arbitrated dispute could be resolved in two months or less, we will find in the next chapter that the time lapse is considerably longer in most cases. Figure 13–2 presents the flow of decisions in a typical grievance process.

Methods of dispute resolution

There are two major ways in which disputes during the life of the contract are resolved: arbitration and strikes. Arbitration is used far more often, but strikes are traditionally used by some unions or in some types of disputes.

Striking over grievances

Disputes which are not likely to be settled by arbitration are those that are not seen as affording the luxury of the time required for arbitration. Construction unions seldom use grievance procedures since their members frequently work short periods for a given employer. By the time a dispute would be settled if a grievance went to arbitration the job would be completed, with the employer dictating the working conditions.

The same frequently holds for grievances over safety and working conditions in industrial situations where employees enjoy a stable employment relationship. When these conditions occur, a strike may be used by the union to force the company to interpret the contract as it demands. With a contract in effect, these strikes may or may not be breaches of the agreement and may or may not be enjoinable by the courts.

Where the union and management have negotiated a no-strike clause, a strike during the period of the agreement is called a *wildcat strike*, since it is contrary to the contract and unauthorized by the parent international union. Wildcats are more prevalent in certain in-

336

FIGURE 13–2
Grievance procedure steps

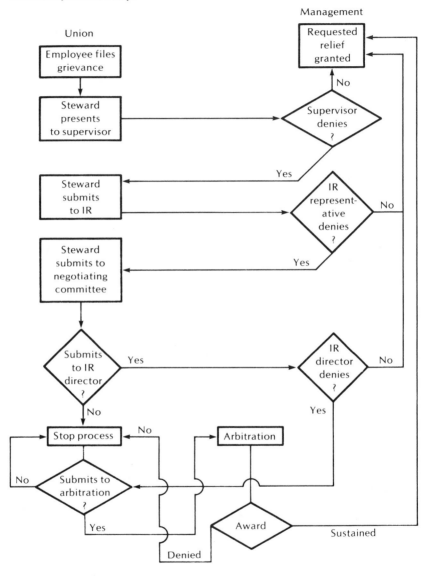

dustries, particularly the rubber[2] and wood by-products[3] areas. But in many instances a wildcat strike is not legally enjoinable since the

---

[2] James W. Kuhn, *Bargaining in Grievance Settlement* (New York: Columbia University Press, 1961).

[3] David R. Hampton, "Fractional Bargaining Patterns and Wildcat Strikes," *Human Organization*, vol. 26 (Fall 1967), pp. 100–109.

Norris-La Guardia Act essentially prohibits federal courts from enjoining most union activities, including strikes.

When companies agree to submit unresolved grievances to arbitration, they are giving up some of their initiative in changing conditions in their organizations. As a quid pro quo, they usually demand and win a "no-strike" clause. Under this provision the union agrees not to strike during the term of the contract since it has an arbitral forum available to it. But what if the union does strike? Does the company have a legal recourse? The answer was "no" for a number of years. The Supreme Court had interpreted the Norris-La Guardia Act in an absolute manner holding that unions could not negotiate away protections included in the legislation.[4] But this approach has recently been modified. In the Boys Markets case, the Supreme Court held that where a bona fide no-strike clause exists with a grievance procedure available and where the union has not sought to arbitrate its dispute federal courts could enjoin a wildcat strike in violation of the contract.[5] The Court explained that it would not apply this doctrine where the employer had been unwilling to include an arbitration agreement along with the no-strike clause.

Discipline for wildcat strikes

One question that one frequently encounters is what tool does management have to counteract a wildcat strike? First, if the strike is actually over an unfair labor practice and the union is correct in its judgment that the action was illegal, the strike is protected concerted activity under the labor acts, and the employer cannot legally retaliate. But if the strike is in violation of a no-strike clause, several factors come into play.

Recall that both the national and local unions participate in the ratification of the agreement. Both also share in the joint responsibility for enforcing it. If a wildcat ensues over a dispute and a no-strike clause exists and if after management requests it the union does nothing to get the workers to resume their job, it may be liable for monetary damages.[6] When the union demands that its members return, if they fail to obey they may be subject to union discipline as well as employer retaliation.

Due process in grievance initiation

One issue that is of increasing importance and has been largely resolved recently concerns an employee's right to union representa-

---

[4] *Sinclair Refining Co.* v. *Atkinson*, 370 U.S. 195 (1962).

[5] *Boys Markets, Inc.* v. *Retail Clerks Union, Local 770*, 398 U.S. 235 (1970).

[6] *Trap Rock Co.* v. *Teamsters, Local 470*, 91 LRRM 3022 (Federal District Court of Pennsylvania, 1976).

tion in disciplinary proceedings. Until recently, employees who were suspected of contract violations that could lead to discharge or other discipline had no inherent right to representation prior to filing a grievance. For example, if a supervisor suspected an employee of quitting early and this offense normally merited a suspension, the supervisor could confront and interrogate the employee with impunity. If the employee demanded union representation, the employer did not have to accede to this request until some action was taken against the employee. However, this type of employer conduct is no longer permissible since the Supreme Court ruling in the *Weingarten* case.[7] In that case the Court held that an employee who is suspected of an offense which could result in disciplinary action is entitled to union representation if he requests it. The employer cannot proceed with the interrogation unless a union steward is present to advise its member.

What is the employee entitled to?

Obviously not every grievance will be found to constitute a bona fide contract violation. And not every legitimate grievance may be worth pursuing to arbitration. For example, suppose a supervisor performed bargaining unit work during a rush, but not emergency, period. The union may have a legitimate grievance, and the workers might be entitled as a group to pay for the period the supervisor worked. But if it's an isolated incident, simply bringing the grievance to management's attention should reduce the likelihood of its recurrence even if management denies the requested relief.

Cases involving individuals will also vary in terms of the merits of particular fact situations. For example, a discharge case is more serious than one in which a grievant claims entitlement for two hours' pay for overtime given to another. How far is the individual union member able to go in the pursuit of a grievance or in an attempt to force the union to process it through arbitration, if necessary? This whole subject is not entirely resolved, but some direction is available through opinions of legal and labor experts and court discussions. The whole area tends to be referred to by terms like "individual rights" and "fair representation." We will use the latter and apply it at this point to the vigor of the union's advocacy, not necessarily its competence. This latter issue we will cover in the arbitration chapter since a vigorous approach in the face of management opposition will inevitably cause an unresolved grievance to arrive there.

---

[7] *NLRB* v. *J. Weingarten, Inc.*, 420 U.S. 251 (1975).

FAIR REPRESENTATION

The whole question of fair representation is a very complex issue and one in which the rights and duties of those involved are not completely spelled out. Legislation relating to grievance handling muddies the water as to the rights and obligations of the employee and the parties to collective bargaining. One thing we can say with certainty is that the unrepresented employee has no rights to process a grievance against an employer unless the employer grants that right by policy. That is not to say that employees are unable to seek redress for arbitrary employer decisions, but unless these decisions involve the use of criteria forbidden by the Civil Rights Acts (race, sex, age, and so on), wage and hour, or health and safety laws, the arbitrariness or merit of the decision is not reviewable.

As we noted before introducing the issue of fair representation, we are not talking here about the quality of the advocacy during arbitration, but in the process undertaken during the prearbitration grievance steps.

Individual rights under the contract[8]

The evaluation of precedents relating to individual rights under the contract consists of both judicial decisions and legislative modifications. Two major decisions prior to the passage of the Taft-Hartley modifications and additions to the labor acts helped to specify the rights of groups or minorities in grievance processing.

In *Elgin, Joliet and Eastern Railway* v. *Burley,* the Supreme Court held that an employer could not be immune from action by its employees simply because the employees' unions conceded a grievance.[9] The employees must have authorized the union to act for them, and some vigorous defense must be shown. Since the union is the exclusive bargaining agent for all employees, the courts will watch to ensure that all classes and subgroups are entitled to and receive equal protection and advocacy from their representatives.

The other case was decided by the NLRB.[10] In this case the board ordered a white union to process equally the grievance of a black employee within the bargaining unit.

Both of these decisions were rendered prior to the Taft-Hartley amendments. In that act, Congress enabled employees to file griev-

---

[8] For an excellent treatment of the legal issues involved, see Herbert L. Sherman Jr., *Labor Relations and Social Problems: Unionization and Collective Bargaining* (Washington: Bureau of National Affairs, 1972), pp. 184–97.

[9] 325 U.S. 711 (1945).

[10] *Hughes Tool Co.*, 566 NLRB 981 (1944).

ances directly to employers, even if represented. However, employers could not process their grievances in the absence of union observation, if demanded by the union, or adjust the grievance in a manner that is inconsistent with the contract. For example, if the contract entitles senior employees to promotions, a junior employee cannot personally insist on receiving a promotion a senior employee would be entitled to.

There is no widely established view of what an individual's rights are under the contract given the Taft-Hartley additions. Aaron suggests three possible positions: (1) Individuals have a vested right to use the grievance procedure through arbitration if they choose; (2) individuals should be entitled to grievance processing for discharge, seniority, and compensation cases; and (3) the union, as a collective body, should have freedom to decide what constitutes a meritorious grievance and how far a grievance should be pursued.[11]

A number of decisions by the NLRB and the Supreme Court since 1960 has helped to clarify somewhat the requirements for fair representation. Prior to these decisions there was a crazy quilt approach to the question of fair representation. In one decision, the courts refused to consider an unfair representation complaint of an employee where the union had bargained away her contractual rights.[12] Another state court decision held that an employee was entitled to demand arbitration.[13] If a court were to grant relief to an employee who had not gone through the contractual procedures, the employer could rightfully claim that the worker could shop for whatever forum was thought to offer the best chance for winning. As we will see later, the courts generally defer to a final arbitration award, so if every grievant were entitled to have a grievance formally settled, it would obviously be to the employer's advantage from a cost standpoint to go to arbitration on all grievances rather than have them taken to court.

However, there are some things that must be considered here to lessen the likelihood of wholesale court action. First, the company and the union would prefer to settle grievances early to gain certainty for their actions. Second, arbitration costs are jointly borne by the company and the unions, not the individual employee. Therefore, one who goes to court assumes greater risks of cost, even if the court agrees to entertain the action, than does one who uses the grievance procedure to arbitration.

There are, however, several precedents which reduce the likelihood of court involvement in grievance resolutions. The first is an

---

[11] Benjamin Aaron, "The Individual's Legal Rights as an Employee," *Monthly Labor Review*, vol. 86 (1963), pp. 671–72.

[12] *Union News Co.* v. *Hildreth*, 295 F.2d 658 (6th Circuit Court of Appeals, 1961).

[13] *Donnelly* v. *United Fruit Co.*, 40 N.J. 61 (1963).

NLRB case which was not enforced by the court of appeals while the last two are Supreme Court cases. The NLRB case was *Miranda Fuel Company,* decided in 1962.[14] In that case, an employee was given permission to start his vacation before the contractual date. Then when he returned late due to illness, the remaining bargaining unit members demanded that the union require that he be discharged. The NLRB ruled that this was an unfair labor practice since the union acquiesced to the majority demand even though the discharged employee was senior.

The second case involved the merger of two companies.[15] Here the same union represented employees of the acquired and surviving companies. After the merger, the union credited the seniority of the workers from the acquired company rather than beginning it at the date of acquisition. Several employees from the surviving company claimed they had been unfairly represented since their union had granted seniority to new employees for employment with the other firm. The Supreme Court held that the employees must use Taft-Hartley remedies for breach of contract rather than state court actions to gain redress for unfair representation.

The final case was *Vaca* v. *Sipes,* decided in 1967 by the Supreme Court.[16] Here, on returning from sick leave, an employee was discharged because the employer felt that he was no longer capable of holding a job. A grievance was filed and the union pressed his case, obtaining medical evidence and requesting that he be given a less physically demanding job. The doctors' reports conflicted on the question of whether the discharged employee could safely continue working. While the union vigorously pursued the grievance through the final prearbitration step, it did not demand arbitration when the company refused to reinstate the grievant.

The grievant sued his union for unfairly representing him and also sued his employer for breach of contract. The Court held that an employee may not go directly to court on a grievance unless the remedies provided by the contract have been exhausted; except that in cases where it is clear that the employer and/or the union has refused to allow these remedies to be used. If the grievant contends that the union has failed to represent him adequately, then he must prove this. The Court found that individual bargaining unit members have no inherent right to invoke the use of arbitration. As the representative of all bargaining unit members, the union is at once both an advocate and an agent that must decide whether certain claims are either frivolous

---

[14] 140 NLRB 181 (1962).

[15] *Humphrey* v. *Moore,* 375 U.S. 335 (1964).

[16] 386 U.S. 171 (1967).

or inconsistent with past practice or contract interpretation. If it weighs the merit of the grievance and treats the grievant similar to others in the same situation, it is not unfairly representing him.

Recently, the Supreme Court expanded the rights of grievants. In *Hines* v. *Anchor Motor Freight* the Court held that a group of discharged employees were entitled to court review of the grievance process where the union had not actively sought possible evidence which would clear them of wrongdoing.[17] Even though the contract established that an arbitral decision would finally dispose of a case, the courts may upset the finding.

While the unfair representation question has not been fully answered, we may draw the following conclusions. First, while the Taft-Hartley Act confers on individual bargaining unit members the right to present grievances, it does not impose any duty on the employer to respond to them. Second, if the employer does respond to an individual grievance, the bargaining agent is entitled to observe and participate in the process since the individual employee's settlement might be seen as involving a precedent for other members. Third, a union may not treat an employee or group of employees differently in grievance processing simply because of their group membership. Fourth, the union does not necessarily breach its duty of fair representation by settling a grievance on the company's terms prior to arbitration.

GRIEVANCES AND BARGAINING

Just as we have seen earlier in the chapters on union structure, organizing, and negotiation, while we can specify the processes involved, the actual behavior does not always exactly duplicate the description provided by the model. The grievance procedure, as we have described it, provides a method for resolving disputes over the meaning of the contract. We have examined it by tracing through the process for a single dispute. We also have consigned the union to the role of a respondent to management's actions and management as the initiator of some action which leads to the dispute. We have looked at grievance resolution as a serial process, both from the steps involved (which duplicates reality rather closely), and from the presentation order (first-in, first-out; which probably does not). In this section we will look at grievances from a political standpoint and as a bargaining tool. We will also examine some suggestions for assisting the process where it has become clogged.

---

[17] 424 U.S. 554 (1976).

Union responses to management action

In many cases, grievances have a number of ramifications for the union. A novel grievance may establish a precedent for or against the union if it is arbitrated. In the past the situation may have been informally handled on a case-by-case basis usually favorable to the union. The risks of losing here may be great. Other grievances may lead to internal disputes, such as entitlements to work or overtime. Politically powerful minorities within the union may also need accommodation. Smythe lists six considerations a union negotiating committee may examine in determining whether to process grievances or not and how far these should go.[18]

1. The immediate interests of the union as an organization in recognition and collective bargaining.
2. The immediate interests of the individual employee who will be directly affected by the grievance settlement.
3. The immediate interests of other employees as individuals or as a group who may be directly or indirectly affected by the grievance settlement.
4. The future interests of the union as an organization and of the employees as individuals or as a group, as affected by the law-making or precedent aspects of the grievance settlement.
5. The political interests of present union officers.
6. The political interests of aspiring union officers.

Besides the response of union officials to grievances, the rank and file members themselves may engage in tactics which affect the grievance process. As James Kuhn points out, if a large number of grievances build up, or if the settlement of grievances is slow (particularly those which allege a continuing violation), then pressure tactics like slowdowns, quickie strikes, and "working to rules," may be used to pressure management to settle or grant the grievances.[19] Thus, grievants may not passively wait for the ultimate response but use tactics to speed a favorable settlement.

"Fractional bargaining"

Since most grievances concern an individual employee, or a single work group, and relate to only one or a few contract terms, Kuhn calls

---

[18] Cyrus F. Smythe, "The Union as Arbitrator in Grievance Processing," *Personnel*, Vol. 40 (July–August 1963), p. 50, American Management Association.

[19] Kuhn, *Bargaining in Grievance Settlement.*

tactics aimed at modifying the practice of contract administration during its life "fractional bargaining."[20] Fractional bargaining exists for the work groups for the very same reasons that an employer with multiple bargaining units suffers a reduction in bargaining power. An organization consists of interdependent parts, and if one is embroiled in disputes which lessen its productivity, this will have an effect on the remainder.

Fractional bargaining raises problems for the union on occasion because one critical group may win grievances that others fail to achieve. If a union negotiating committee stops the grievances of a powerful small group, internal political pressures will increase. A steward of a powerful small group may successfully pressure for settlement at lower levels to avoid local officer involvement. The company may accede to this pressure to lessen chances of disruption in its production.

Management may also take the initiative by assigning work to political opponents of the existing union hierarchy, handling some disciplinary cases by the book and being lenient with others. These practices may increase the internal political pressures within the union and cause more of its energies to be devoted to healing these rifts rather than additional grievance activity. Thus, as in contract negotiations, each side pressures the other, but some mutual accommodation enabling survival of both is usually reached.

Union initiatives in grievances

There are a number of ways in which the union may take the initiative with grievances. Kuhn notes that the union steward may solicit grievances, looking for situations where the rank and file may see a contract violation.[21] A violation may not have actually occurred for a grievance to be filed, only the belief that one did and a linking of that belief to some contract clause. If the union believes that it is having problems with one area or supervisor, it may simply flood management with grievances. Grievances create work for management since they must be answered in a certain time under the contract. If higher management needs to spend more time on grievances, it may simply tell supervision to "clean up its act," resulting usually in a more lenient approach to demonstrate to management that supervision has "cured" the grievance problem.

Union stewards may also stockpile grievances to use as threats or tradeoffs for larger issues. If an important point comes up that the steward wants for that constituency, the foreman may simply be told

---

[20] Ibid., p. 79.
[21] Ibid., p. 14.

informally that unless a change is made grievances on a variety of matters will be filed with higher-ups later in the day.

In large plants, the union steward has a distinct advantage over the supervisor. Many contracts specify that the steward is a full-time union representative although paid by the company. As such, a steward's full-time work involves contract administration, while the supervisor is responsible for personnel, equipment, production, and other matters. The two are usually no match on interpreting the contract since the steward has studied it in far greater detail and finds it to be a much more integral part of the job.

Grievance types

From an overall standpoint, we can break grievances down into two major categories: (1) those influencing the job security of individual workers (discipline and discharge cases), and (2) those involving groups of workers in job assignments, work standards, or other precedent-setting issues. The first set tend to be handled in the straightforward manner we described earlier while the latter are much more subject to "fractional bargaining" tactics.

INNOVATIONS IN GRIEVANCE PROCESSING

As we will see in the next chapter, most of the recent innovations that have been reported relate to the final step, arbitration, rather than earlier points. One of the complaints made by union officials, and noted by Kuhn, is that grievances are seldom handled at lower levels but instead are bucked up the line for fear of a supervisor setting a precedent.[22] With this kind of problem or through poor relations between the company and the union, the grievance procedure can become clogged with unsettled grievances leading to disruptive tactics by the union and a lack of responsiveness by management.

In a study of congested grievance procedures, Arthur Ross concluded that most problems occur in large industrial organizations.[23] In one aircraft plant an arbitrator reported a backlog of 6,000 cases awaiting arbitration. Most of the arbitrators who saw this type of load mentioned faults within both management and the union but were more inclined to blame the union. Following is a list of the reasons they ascribed as union and management causes for clogging grievance procedures.[24]

---

[22] Ibid., p. 10.

[23] Arthur M. Ross, "Distressed Grievance Procedures and Their Rehabilitation," in Mark L. Kahn, ed., *Labor Arbitration and Industrial Change*, Proceedings of the 16th Annual Meeting of the National Academy of Arbitrators (Washington: Bureau of National Affairs, 1963), pp. 104–32.

[24] Ibid., pp. 107–8.

1. Refusal of international and local union officers to screen out the grievances; a feeling that most complaints should be taken to arbitration in order to satisfy the grievants.
2. A provision in the constitution under which the union cannot pass a resolution without unanimous approval of the numerous locals and therefore cannot pass the legislation required to control the affairs of these locals.
3. A shop committee, in order to perpetuate itself, first looks for trouble and files grievances at the drop of a hat.
4. A local union riddled with factional strife. "The local was large . . . and its treasury bountiful." The committee could not refuse to arbitrate weak grievances for fear that the opposition would make political capital.
5. Union investigation is initially poor and continues that way; poor steward training, newly changed officers, and so on.

A second set of causes lies within the management organization. For example:

6. Company hard line on practically all grievances; hard line called for by operating people; industrial relations people having weak status in corporate setup and not attempting to educate the operating people.
7. Top line management did not back up the industrial relations people. As a result, the IR men preferred to pass the buck to the umpire. . . .

Other causes of high unresolved grievance rates included rapidly changing jobs due to technological change, a bad bargaining relationship perpetuated from an acrimonious organizing campaign, and complicated contract language or job evaluation systems.[25]

When the load gets too high, grievances may not be decided for a year or more. Ross suggests that four types of solutions are most frequently used to deal with this type of situation.[26] First is the mass grievance settlement ("fire sale") where the union and management horsetrade grievances. This may lead to the setting of precedents both parties might prefer to avoid and might encourage the filing of non-meritorious grievances. Second, a screening procedure involving the company and union could concede or withdraw grievances that were likely to be nonwinnable at arbitration. Third, nonlocal, high-level company and union officials are involved in the screening process. Fourth, procedural changes like scheduling arbitration of grievances

---

[25] Ibid., pp. 108–9.
[26] Ibid., pp. 111–13.

on a "first-in, first-out" basis rather than the political explosiveness of an issue may reduce the stockpiling of cases awaiting arbitration.

One other approach that has been successful in reducing grievances is keeping them at the oral or informal stage long enough to settle them on the shop floor. McKersie and Shropshire report on the experience of International Harvester and the UAW in solving their huge grievance problem.[27] At one plant the grievance rate was so high that on the average each employee was submitting one written grievance per year. To alleviate the huge buildup, the company and the UAW agreed to keep grievances oral as long as possible, reducing their formality. If higher level management or union officials were necessary to help resolve a grievance, they were brought to the shop floor rather than having a written grievance brought to them. The backlog of grievances evaporated as the system became operational.

WHO FILES GRIEVANCES?

Our examination of the process thus far implies that some departments or individuals may be more heavily involved than others in grievance procedures. In the International Harvester case, for example, the forge department in one plant filed 22 percent of the grievances while comprising 6 percent of the population.[28] We should not draw a conclusion that grievances are filed frivolously by a group of malcontents, but there may be political differences among units which lead to differential use. What we are concerned with here is whether there are individual differences which distinguish grievants from nongrievants.

The first study we will examine reports the findings from a heavy machinery manufacturer located in Chicago.[29] The study found that grievants were more active union members, more often absent or tardy, earned less and had fewer pay increases, and were more highly educated.

The second study by Ash[30] found that grievances were filed more often by native white Americans than minorities or aliens, veterans than nonveterans, and younger employees. Ash also found (not unexpectedly) that supervisors with more grievances had longer processing

---

[27] Robert B. McKersie and William W. Shropshire, Jr., "Avoiding Written Grievances: A Successful Program," *Journal of Business*, vol. 35 (April 1962), pp. 135–52.

[28] Ibid., p. 138.

[29] Howard A. Sulkin and Robert W. Pranis, "Comparison of Grievants with Nongrievants in a Heavy Machinery Company," *Personnel Psychology*, vol. 20 (Summer 1967), pp. 111–19.

[30] Philip Ash, "The Parties to the Grievance," *Personnel Psychology*, vol. 23 (Spring 1970), pp. 13–38.

times. But he also found there were more group grievances for high frequency supervisors and fewer reversals by higher level management. Ash also found that the grievance rate for units with an experienced steward was less than for newly appointed representatives. He also found that an experienced steward had a higher favorable settlement rate. Maturity in office may mean that the steward does not solicit unmeritorious grievances and is more skillful in gaining favorable settlements.

The third study examined over 4,000 grievances to see whether or not there was a connection between filing a grievance and other characteristics.[31] The study found grievants had received more wage increases, were younger, better educated, with more derogatory personnel information in their files, fewer sick leaves, more likely handicapped, laid-off more, had more promotions and demotions, were more often absent and more likely to request leaves.

Those with multiple grievances were more likely only to have had more promotions than nongrievants. When disciplinary grievants were compared to nongrievants, they found that these grievants were younger, better educated, more likely to file grievances, more often terminated or suspended, more likely to have refused promotions, had fewer commendations, more derogatory personnel file material, and had more arrests, sick leaves, and absences.

These studies indicate that characteristics like youth and education which are normally considered desirable by employers also predict higher grievance rates. The Ash study also shows that mature leadership within the union at the steward level reduces grievances but increases the chances of winning those filed. The evidence points again to a mature relationship between the parties as contributing to success in collective bargaining.

SUMMARY

Contract administration is the joint activity with which labor and management are most involved in terms of time. Not only do the parties respond voluntarily to differences in contract interpretation, but they must, by law, bargain with each other on practices related to mandatory items over the life of the contract.

There are a variety of issues that both sides must deal with, job security issues, seniority, and discipline being among the most important. Methods for handling disputes involve the presentation and reso-

[31] John Price, James Dewire, John Nowack, Kenneth Schenkel, and William Ronan, "Three Studies of Grievances," *Personnel Journal*, vol. 55 (January 1976), pp. 32–37.

lution of grievances in a stepwise manner culminating in arbitration if necessary.

Unions must represent employees in a consistent manner in grievance proceedings, and employees who can show they were not accorded fair treatment may hold the union and the employer in breach of contract.

All grievances are not equally meritorious, and many are processed for political purposes. Some grievance processing arises at modifying contract applications within different work groups. Other times labor and management may "horsetrade" a backlog of grievances.

Grievants, as compared to nongrievants, are generally better educated and more highly paid but also are more likely to have had past disciplinary difficulties.

Our next chapter is on grievance arbitration and will examine the procedure and results of the final step of the grievance process when it is invoked.

SUGGESTED READINGS

Aaron, Benjamin. "The Individual's Legal Rights as an Employee," *Monthly Labor Review*, vol. 86 (1963), pp. 666–673.

Ash, Philip. "The Parties to the Grievance," *Personnel Psychology*, vol. 23 (Spring 1970), pp. 13–38.

Kuhn, James W. *Bargaining in Grievance Settlement* (New York: Columbia University Press, 1961).

McKersie, Robert B., and Shropshire, William W., Jr. "Avoiding Written Grievances: A Successful Program," *Journal of Business*, vol. 35 (April 1962), pp. 135–52.

Smythe, Cyrus F. "The Union as Arbitrator in Grievance Processing," *Personnel*, vol. 40 (July–August 1963), pp. 49–56.

DISCUSSION QUESTIONS

1. Should management be required to consult with the union about discipline before it is imposed rather than simply providing for grievance processing after imposition?

2. Should unions be allowed to agree with management about a particular disciplinary penalty for an employee at some point prior to arbitration?

3. How does the grievance procedure make possible subtle changes in the meaning of the contract over time?

4. What are the advantages and disadvantages of a program to reduce the number of written grievances?

Case _____

Carolyn Foster had just returned to her office from the weekly plant IR representative meeting. Her secretary had left a note to call George Lowrey, the superintendent of the fork-lift assembly operation. She called back right away and immediately recognized from the seriousness of George's tone that there must be a major problem brewing in his area. They both agreed that she would come right over.

After George had welcomed her into his office, he leaned forward and putting his chin in his hands, said, "Carolyn, I feel like I'm sitting on a powder keg here. Last year we put in the new Simplex Process assembly line for our fork lifts. It had a rated capacity of 35 units an hour. When we installed it, we started up at 28 units, the same as the old line, to shake it down and get the bugs out. The new line automates more of the assembly so each worker had less of a physical demand than before. Well, last week we figured we had everything ironed out on the bugs, so we raised the speed to 35. We figure that each worker has to put out about the same amount of effort as under the old system.

"This morning Ed Zeller, the shop steward, and three of my general supervisors came in, all arguing. Zeller had a fistful of grievances and was yelling about a 'speedup.' Anyway, the upshot is that he wants the job reclassified under 7.04 of the contract because he says effort and working conditions have changed.

"Carolyn, we can't give them a penny more and remain competitive. Besides that, if they get a raise the whole plant will paper us with classification grievances. Zeller is running for union president since the old one is retiring, and if he's successful with this grievance he's a shoo-in. All we need for a long strike over some penny-ante issue is a bunch of hotheads like him running the show. What can you do to help me?"

Carolyn had been busy taking notes about the problem. She asked, "Do you have the grievances?" George nodded and handed them to her. Then she said, "I'll study the grievances, the contract, and the union situation and get back to you in time for us to plan a Step 3 response. I'll be back to you tomorrow afternoon."

DIRECTIONS

1. Draft a strategy for the company to follow. Take into account the immediate problem and the possibilities of precedents being set by your actions. List the advantages and disadvantages of your chosen strategy.
2. Prepare a scenario in which your response is presented to Ed Zeller. How is he likely to react? What steps do you expect he will take as a result of your response?
3. What conditions do you feel are necessary for these grievances to be resolvable at Step 3?

14

GRIEVANCE ARBITRATION

This chapter is about the final step in most grievance procedures, arbitration. As we will see, arbitration is not solely a labor relations topic, and within labor relations it does not solely deal with grievances. Our organization of the chapter will deal, in turn, with the following topics: the definition of arbitration, its place in American labor relations, the process itself, difficulties associated with arbitration and its practice, and results associated with arbitration of employee discharge and discipline cases.

As you read this chapter, keep in mind the following questions:

1. What influence have the Supreme Court's decisions had on arbitration?
2. How is arbitration aided or interfered with by the NLRB?
3. What procedures occur during arbitration?
4. What problems do critics of arbitration point out?

WHAT IS ARBITRATION?

Arbitration is a quasi-judicial process in which the parties agree to submit an unresolvable dispute to a neutral third party for binding settlement. Both parties submit their positions, and the arbitrator decides which party is entitled to what types of relief. While we are only interested in labor arbitration, the method is also applied to disputes between buyers and sellers, contractors and real estate developers, doctors and patients.

Within labor arbitration, there are two major types: *interest* and *rights* arbitration. In this chapter we are primarily concerned with rights arbitration while we will explore interest arbitration in our next chapter on public sector labor relations. The Supreme Court distinguishes between rights and interest arbitration this way:

The first relates to disputes over the formation of collective agreements or efforts to secure them. They arise where there is no such agreement or where it is sought to change the terms of one, and therefore the issue is not whether an existing agreement controls the controversy. They look to the acquisition of rights for the future, not to assertion of rights claimed to have vested in the past.

The second class, however, contemplates the existence of a collective agreement already concluded or, at any rate, a situation in which no effort is made to bring about a formal change in terms or to create a new one. The dispute relates either to the meaning or proper application of a particular provision with reference to a specific situation or to an omitted case. In the latter event the claim is founded upon some incident of the employment relation, or asserted one, independent of those covered by the collective agreement. . . . In either case the claim is to rights accrued, not merely to have new ones created for the future.[1]

Thus, rights arbitration applies to interpreting and applying the terms of an existing contract, while interest arbitration decides future terms issues which are not resolved.

DEVELOPMENT OF ARBITRATION

As you recall, suggestions for the use of labor arbitration in the United States go back into the 19th century. We saw in Chapter 2 how the Knights of Labor advocated arbitration as a preferable method to strikes for the resolution of interest differences. No legislation mandates arbitration for any rights or interests in the private sector in the United States. The closest we come is the fact-finding requirements for national emergency disputes found in the Taft-Hartley amendments.

Arbitration in the United States got its biggest boost through the establishment and creation of the National War Labor Board during World War II. This board handled dispute cases during the war and required that the parties include clauses requiring arbitration for future disputes within the contract.[2]

The place of arbitration has been clearly established by the actions of the Supreme Court and the NLRB since the late 1950s. A string of cases decided by both have established the role of arbitration and its place in simultaneously deciding unfair labor practices.

---

[1] *Elgin, Joliet & Eastern Railway Co.* v. *Burley*, 325 U.S. 711 (1945).

[2] Frank Elkouri and Edna Asper Elkouri, *How Arbitration Works*, 3d ed. (Washington: Bureau of National Affairs, 1973), p. 15.

Lincoln Mills

The first case establishing the beginnings of arbitration as the final forum for contract disputes was the *Lincoln Mills* case.[3] In this case, the Supreme Court held that Section 301 of the Taft-Hartley Act meant that the federal court system could and should enforce agreements between labor and management, including those which provided for the arbitration of future grievances. The court held here that if the contract called for arbitration and if the court did not disagree with the arbitrator the award should be enforced if either party failed to comply with it.

Steelworkers' trilogy

The most important set of court cases involving the status and place of labor arbitration was decided by the Supreme Court in 1960.[4] The question facing the Court here was basically whether or not arbitrators' decisions are reviewable by the courts. The Supreme Court essentially said "no" in this set of decisions. The Court laid down three basic protections for arbitration. First, arbitration clauses in contracts require the parties to arbitrate unresolved grievances. Second, the substance of the grievance and its arbitrability is to be determined by the arbitrator, not the courts. And, third, if an arbitration clause exists, unless the dispute is clearly outside of the scope of the contract, the court will order arbitration. The decisions hold that the arbitrator is presumed to have special competence in labor relations and is thus better able to resolve labor disputes than courts.

In the *Warrior and Gulf* case the court held that where a broad arbitration clause was included in the contract, even if the dispute was not covered in other sections, it was still arbitrable. In this case the employer subcontracted work while the firm's employees were in a partial layoff status. While lower courts held subcontracting was a potential management right, the Court held that the broad arbitration agreement coupled with the no-strike provision brought the dispute within the arbitral arena.

The *American Manufacturing* case involved an employee who had been disabled and had accepted workmen's compensation. Later his doctor certified his ability to return to work. When the company refused to reinstate him, he grieved, and the company refused to process

---

[3] *Textile Workers Union* v. *Lincoln Mills*, 355 U.S. 448 (1957).

[4] *United Steelworkers of America* v. *Warrior & Gulf Navigation Co.*, 363 U.S. 574; *United Steelworkers of America* v. *Enterprise Wheel and Car Corp.* 363 U.S. 593; and *United Steelworkers of America* v. *American Manufacturing Co.*, 363 U.S. 564 (1960).

the grievance as frivolous. The Supreme Court, however, ordered arbitration.

The *Enterprise Wheel* case involved a situation where several employees had been discharged for walking out in protest of the firing of another employee. When the company refused to arbitrate the discharge grievances, the applicable federal district court ordered it, and the arbitrator subsequently ordered reinstatement and back pay for all but ten days' lost time. The award was rendered five days after the contract expiration date, but the Supreme Court ordered the company to comply with it.

Smith and Jones find four propositions laid down by the courts as a result of the Steelworkers' trilogy.[5]

1. The existence of a valid agreement to arbitrate and the arbitrability of a specific grievance sought to be arbitrated under such an agreement are questions for the courts ultimately to decide (if such an issue is presented for judicial determination) unless the parties have expressly given an arbitrator the authority to make a binding determination of such matters.

2. A court should hold a grievance nonarbitrable under a valid agreement to use arbitration as the terminal point in the grievance procedure only if the parties have clearly indicated their intention to exclude the subject matter of the grievance from the arbitration process, either by expressly so stating in the arbitration clause or by otherwise clearly and unambiguously indicating such intention.

3. Evidence of intention to exclude a claim from the arbitration process should not be found in a determination that the labor agreement could not properly be interpreted in such manner as to sustain the grievance on its merits, for this is a task assigned by the parties to the arbitrator, not the courts.

4. An award should not be set aside as beyond the authority conferred upon the arbitrator, either because of claimed error in interpretation of the agreement or because of alleged lack of authority to provide a particular remedy, where the arbitral decision was or, if silent, might have been the result of the arbitrator's interpretation of the agreement; if, however, it was based not on the contract but on an obligation found to have been imposed by law, the award should be set aside unless the parties expressly authorized the arbitrator to dispose of this as well as any contract issue.

Smith and Jones feel that these decisions enable arbitrators to determine first whether a dispute is arbitrable or not; and second, if arbitrable, what the award should be, free from federal court intervention.[6]

---

[5] Russell A. Smith and Dallas L. Jones, "The Supreme Court and Labor Dispute Arbitration: The Emerging Federal Law," *Michigan Law Review*, vol. 63 (March, 1965), pp. 759–60.

[6] Ibid., p. 761.

The Steelworkers' trilogy essentially protected a union's right to insist on arbitration and to have arbitral awards enforced without review by the courts. But could management also expect the same treatment, particularly where it agreed to arbitrate, received a favorable award, and the union struck to prevent enforcement? Remember that the Norris-LaGuardia Act broadly prevented federal courts from enjoining most labor organization activities, including strikes for any purpose as long as they did not threaten life or property.

The 1962 trilogy

The cases in the 1962 trilogy relate to the requirement for arbitration of damages for violation of a no-strike clause rather than taking them directly to the federal courts.[7] The *Drake* decision held that management should request arbitration where a no-strike clause existed to determine whether the contract had been violated. In the *Sinclair* cases, the Court first held that the federal court system could not enjoin a strike in violation of a no-strike clause since the Norris-LaGuardia Act prevented injunctions against labor union activities.

The decision in *Sinclair* v. *Atkinson* raises an important consideration for employees and the implementation of no-strike clauses. Without the opportunity for court enforcement, there is nothing that would penalize a union for striking over a grievance if an arbitrator ruled against it or for striking rather than using the agreed-upon grievance procedure. But, the Supreme Court has reversed itself on this issue. In the *Boys Markets* case, the Supreme Court held that a strike in violation of a no-strike clause prior to arbitration, where the company was willing to arbitrate the dispute, is enjoinable.[8]

NLRB deferral to arbitration

Occasionally, a grievance over a contract clause may simultaneously allege an unfair labor practice. For example, a work assignment may seem to the union to be covered by its contract, but the employer has given the work to nonunion employees outside the bargaining unit. The grievance may allege a violation of the contract on work assignments, and at the same time the union might accuse the employer of discrimination based on union membership before the NLRB. To prevent "forum shopping" and to reduce the number of cases it needs to hear, the board has adopted a systematic approach to

---

[7] *Sinclair Refining Co.* v. *Atkinson*, 370 U.S. 195 (1962); *Atkinson* v. *Sinclair Refining Co.*, 370 U.S. 238 (1962); and *Drake Bakeries* v. *Local 50*, 370 U.S. 254 (1962).

[8] *Boys Markets, Inc.* v. *Retail Clerks Union Local 770*, 398 U.S. 235 (1970).

cases where a simultaneous contract violation and unfair labor practice are alleged side by side.

In the first case, the NLRB held that where a grievance contained an unfair labor practice and the arbitration award had been adverse to, say the union, the union could not then pursue the same unfair labor practice before the board.[9] The board decreed that it would defer to arbitral awards as long as the parties had agreed in this contract to be bound by the decision, the proceedings were fair and regular, and the results were not inconsistent with the provisions of the labor acts.

In 1971, the board went a step further in its *Collyer* decision.[10] Here the board said that it would defer hearing an unfair labor practice charge until the arbitration had been completed as long as the process met the requirements it had spelled out in *Spielberg*.

In early 1977, the NLRB retreated somewhat from the *Collyer* doctrine. In two cases decided the same day, Chairman Murphy, essentially single-handedly established the present board policy on deferral since she concurred with the majority supporting a *Collyer*-type position on the first, then joined the dissenters to form a limited nondeferral approach on the second.[11] These two cases establish board policy to allow deferral only in cases where the alleged unfair labor practice is not a violation of an employee's Section 7 rights.

Arbitration and grievance settlement

The general direction of the federal courts and the NLRB is to give the arbitration process deference. What the parties have voluntarily included in their bargaining agreement as the means for resolving disputes will not be lightly overruled by the courts or board. As the Supreme Court stated in the Steelworkers' trilogy, the adjustment of grievances is best handled through the arbitration process because it is the system chosen by the parties and within the province and special expertise of the labor arbitrator who is schooled in the "law of the shop." The overall tenor of these decisions is to encourage the parties to devise and use processes to settle their disputes. Arbitration, as a means of settlement, will be considered to be binding on the parties and will be left undisturbed by the courts.

A judicial exception to deferral

Although the Supreme Court has led the way in the past in endorsing arbitration as the final step in contract disputes and the NLRB has

---

[9] *Spielberg Manufacturing Co.*, 112 NLRB 1080 (1955).

[10] *Collyer Insulated Wire Co.*, 192 NLRB 150 (1971).

[11] *Roy Robinson Chevrolet*, 228 NLRB 103 (1977); *General American Transportation Corporation*, 228 NLRB 102 (1977).

allowed arbitrators to decide cases which simultaneously alleged violations of federal law, one case has set limits on deferral.[12]

In this case Alexander was a black maintenance employee who bid on a skilled job. According to the seniority provisions of the contract, he was entitled to it and was promoted on a probationary basis like anyone else who moved into the job. After a period of time on the job, Alexander was warned that his performance was not up to standards and unless it improved he would be discharged. When his performance failed to improve, he was discharged.

The contract contained a clause whereby the company agreed to comply with equal employment opportunity laws and not discriminate on the basis of race, among other things. Alexander grieved his discharge and, citing this clause, said his superior discharged him because he was black. The case ultimately went to arbitration, and the arbitrator upheld the company's contention that the discharge was performance, not race-related.

Alexander then filed a charge with the Equal Employment Opportunity Commission (EEOC) claiming racial discrimination. The case was taken to court where it was dismissed because a final arbitration award had been rendered. On appeal, the Supreme Court ruled that the court system could not defer to an arbitral award where the grievance included a civil rights law issue. If an award was adverse to the grievant, he or she was still entitled to renew proceedings through the EEOC. If arbitration had taken place, the court could take the award into account in its decision but could not use the basis of an award as a final adjudication. The Supreme Court did not modify the NLRB's policy of deferral or its own findings that arbitral awards are final in strictly contract-related cases.

ARBITRATION PROCEDURES

In this section we will examine the processes that lead to arbitration, the selection of an arbitrator, the conduct of the arbitration hearing, the preparation and rendering of an award, and the magnitude of arbitration in the U.S.

Prearbitration matters

The parties have specified processes in their contract which govern how a dispute goes to arbitration. Normally, the case would have had to be handled through the preceding steps of the process. At the last step if management denies the grievance or fails to modify its position

---

[12] *Alexander* v. *Gardner-Denver Co.*, 415 U.S. 36 (1974).

sufficiently for the union to agree, the union can then demand arbitration.

If the parties have bargained some concessions prior to submission to arbitration these do not necessarily become the basis from which the arbitrator works. In most cases, the parties can retreat to their own initial positions without establishing precedents. Also, in cases which are settled prior to arbitration, the company may explicitly state in its settlement offer to the union that it will not consider the granting of that specific grievance as precedent setting.

The contract usually specifies time periods for each step. For example, a grievance must usually be filed within five days of its occurrence. A first line supervisor may have three days to answer it, and so it goes up the line. If management denies the grievance at the last prearbitration step, the union has a certain time period to demand arbitration. If it does not exercise its rights within this time period, management's decision becomes final.

Selection of an arbitrator

Procedures for the selection of an arbitrator are usually written into the contract. The most usual forms for arbitration hearings to take is to use either a single impartial arbitrator who hears the evidence and renders an award, or to have a tripartite board consisting of a company and a union representative and an impartial chairman.

How do the parties obtain an arbitrator or impartial chairman? These procedures are also specified by the contract. In large organizations or in some cases where a long-term bargaining relationship has existed, the contract may name a specific individual or group of persons from whom arbitrators are selected. When a specific individual is named, the position holder is called a "permanent umpire." Permanence, however, is a relative thing since the arbitrator continues to serve only so long as the parties rate performance to be satisfactory to both. Fleming notes that permanent umpires may be more vulnerable in situations where a militant union exists and where it brings a large number of cases to arbitration since there may be a greater likelihood that many cases are less meritorious than a union that saves arbitration for very important issues. The arbitrator would be likely, in that instance, to rule much more frequently for management; and, as a result, the union may rate performance unsatisfactory quite soon.[13]

A second, and more common, type of selection is called the "ad hoc arbitrator." The ad hoc arbitrator is appointed to hear only one particu-

---

[13] Robben W. Fleming, *The Labor Arbitration Process* (Urbana: University of Illinois Press, 1965), pp. 219–20.

lar case or set of cases. The appointment expires when the award is rendered. And the company and union may coincidentally appoint other ad hoc arbitrators to hear unrelated cases at or near the same time.

There are, obviously, advantages and disadvantages connected with either method of arbitrator selection. The ad hoc arbitrator is something of an unknown commodity although some information is usually available about potential arbitrators given resumes, previously published decisions, fields of expertise, and so on. But the appointment constitutes no continuing obligation by the parties. The permanent umpire has a better grasp of the problems the parties encounter because of continuing experience with both groups. But since the relationship is to be continuous, there may always be some question as to whether or not the umpire might engage in award splitting.

Sources and qualifications of arbitrators

Who can be an arbitrator, and how do the parties go about choosing one? There are no absolute qualifications to hold an appointment as an arbitrator. Any one of us could simply declare ourself to be an arbitrator and seek appointments. However, to be an arbitrator actually one must be selected by the parties to a grievance, and the parties might evaluate our qualifications differently than we do. Where, then, do arbitrators come from? Unfortunately, and somewhat tritely, arbitrators come from those who have arbitrated. Parties involved in ad hoc arbitration want someone with experience and expertise since some of the participants do little arbitrating of grievances and need an arbitrator who has experience to assist them in procedural matters. For firms having much experience with arbitration, a permanent umpire may be named, but this individual is likely to be someone with an outstanding reputation in arbitration.

Arbitrators generally come from three major sources, with the first two being used increasingly. The first group consists primarily of attorneys whose full-time occupation is labor arbitration. The second are academics who teach labor law, industrial relations, and economics. The third are respected impartial members of the community such as ministers, teachers, retired public officials, and so forth. This last group may be involved more often on tripartite panels where the labor and management members are highly experienced in arbitral matters.

Another source of arbitrators is new entrants. As we said before, we can simply declare ourselves to be arbitrators, but there are many who offer their services but are never chosen. One informal method for getting started is to serve an informal apprenticeship, gaining practice in writing decisions and learning hearing techniques, under an experienced arbitrator. This exposure with a highly regarded neutral may lead to later appointments. Another method is to attend training courses for arbitrators. But at the present, there are few of these available and most are still awaiting assessment as to their success in leading to later selection as an arbitrator.[14]

There are three major sources or bodies of arbitrators at the present time in the United States. Each serves a slightly different function, but all have interests in providing arbitration services in labor disputes.

National Academy of Arbitrators

This organization consists of the most highly regarded arbitrators in the country. Membership at present is around 400 and eligibility is limited to those invited by the current membership. The academy holds meetings and conventions and issues proceedings commenting on current difficult problems in arbitration and offering alternative solutions. For example, its membership has recently offered a variety of approaches to handling arbitration of matters having racial overtones given the *Alexander* v. *Gardner-Denver* decision.[15] The membership of the group is made up largely of full-time arbitrators, law school professors, and professors of industrial relations in major universities.

It does not offer arbitration panels to disputants, but its directory provides a source of recognized, highly qualified arbitrators the parties can contact directly.

American Arbitration Association

Many contracts specify that the parties will use the services of the American Arbitration Association for its unresolved grievances. The AAA does not employ arbitrators but acts more as a clearing house to administrate matters between the disputants and the arbitrators.

For example, if you were a party involved in a dispute, and your contract specified AAA as the organization to assist in the process, your activities (and those of your labor or management counterpart) would go something like this: First, you notify AAA that a contract dispute exists and request an arbitration panel. AAA responds with a list of arbitrators (usually five, and almost always an odd number). These arbitrators may have particular expertise in the disputed area, for example, job evaluation, or are likely to practice in your geographical area. Second, you and your counterpart reject names alternately until

---

[14] *Daily Labor Report*, no. 185, 1975, p. A–1.

[15] Harry T. Edwards, "Arbitration of Employment Discrimination Cases: A Proposal for Employer and Union Representatives," *Labor Law Journal*, vol. 27 (May 1976), pp. 265–77.

only one remains. This person will be the nominee unless one of you objects. In that case AAA will send out another panel. As a rule of thumb, referral agencies usually refuse to send more than three panels for any dispute. Third, after a name has been agreed upon, AAA will contact the appointee to offer the dispute. The appointee, in turn, accepts or declines. If accepted, arrangements are made directly with the parties for a hearing date. Fourth, if necessary, AAA will provide hearing facilities and court reporters if the parties request. Finally, the AAA follows up to see that decisions are rendered.

Federal Mediation and Conciliation Service

The FMCS maintains a roster of arbitrators from which it can select panels. The arbitrators are not FMCS employees but private practitioners. If our contract specified FMCS assistance, it would provide panels as AAA does but would not have available reporting or facilities assistance.

FMCS does some screening of persons seeking listing with it as arbitrators. People with obvious conflicts of interest (union organizers, employer labor consultants, and the like) are not included, and listees who fail to be selected over a period of time are purged from subsequent lists.[16]

FMCS also does some follow-up on referrals by requiring that appointed arbitrators render awards within 60 days of the close of the hearing and the receipt of posthearing briefs.

Once the arbitrator has been selected, processes related to the scheduled hearing itself begin. From a time standpoint we will break the procedure into three periods: prehearing, hearing, and posthearing processes.

Prehearing

Elkouri and Elkouri detail a number of steps both parties should go through prior to an arbitration hearing:[17]

> *a.* Review the history of the case as developed at the prearbitral steps of the grievance procedure.
> *b.* Study the entire collective agreement to ascertain all clauses bearing directly or indirectly on the dispute. Also, comparison of current provisions with those contained in prior agreements might reveal changes significant to the case.
> *c.* So as to determine the general authority of the arbitrator, and

---

[16] Title 29, chap. 12, part 1404, *Code of Federal Regulations.*

[17] Elkouri and Elkouri, *How Arbitration Works,* pp. 198–99.

accordingly the scope of the arbitration, examine the instruments used to initiate the arbitration.

d. Talk to all persons (even those the other party might use as witnesses) who might be able to aid development of a full picture of the case, including different viewpoints. You will thus better understand not only your own case but your opponent's as well; if you can anticipate your opponent's case, you can better prepare to rebut it.

e. Interview each of your own witnesses (1) to determine what they know about the case; (2) to make certain they understand the relation of your testimony to the whole case; and (3) to cross-examine them to check their testimony and to acquaint them with the process of cross-examination. Make a written summary of the expected testimony of each witness; this can be reviewed when the witness testifies to insure that no important points are overlooked. Some parties outline in advance the questions to be asked each witness.

f. Examine all records and documents that might be relevant to the case. Organize those you expect to use and make copies for use by the arbitrator and the other party at the hearing. If needed documents are in the exclusive possession of the other party, ask that they be made available before or at the hearing.

g. Visit the physical premises involved in dispute to visualize better what occurred and what the dispute is about. Also, consider the advisability of asking at the hearing that the arbitrator (accompanied by both parties) also visit the site of the dispute.

h. Consider the utility of pictorial or statistical exhibits. One exhibit can be more effective than many words, if the matter is suited to the exhibit form of portrayal. However, exhibits which did not "fit" the case and those which are inaccurate or misleading are almost certain to be ineffective or to be damaging to their proponent.

i. Consider what the parties' past practice has been in comparable situations.

j. Attempt to determine whether there is some "key" point upon which the case might turn. If so, it may be to your advantage to concentrate upon that point.

k. In "interpretation" cases, prepare a written argument to support your view as to the proper interpretation of the disputed language.

l. In "interests" or "contract writing" cases, collect and prepare economic and statistical data to aid evaluation of the dispute.

m. Research the parties' prior arbitration awards and the published awards of other parties on the subject of the dispute for an indication of how similar issues have been approached in other cases.

n. Prepare an outline of your case and discuss it with other persons in your group. This insures better understanding of the case and will strengthen it by uncovering matters that need further attention. Then too, it will tend to underscore policy and strategy considerations that may be very important in the ultimate handling of the case. Use of the outline at the hearing will facilitate an organized and systematic presentation of the case.

Besides these steps the parties may continue to meet to seek a settlement or to reduce the time necessary to settle a case. Just because a case has been submitted to arbitration does not mean an arbitrator will ultimately determine the outcome. Any time during the prehearing phase the party initiating the arbitration may withdraw it with the consent of the other party. Frequently the contract will specify how this is to be done, whether or not the withdrawal is "with prejudice" (nonresubmittable), and whether or not its withdrawal is precedent setting. The parties may also stipulate certain facts in the case, agree on what are applicable contract terms, and prepare joint exhibits.

Hearing processes

The actual hearing itself may take many forms. From the most simplified standpoint, a case may be completely stipulated with the arbitrator simply ruling on an interpretation of the written documents submitted. This option is not entirely up to the parties, however, since the arbitrator may insist on calling witnesses and examining evidence on site.

Representatives for the parties

The position of the parties may be advocated by anyone of their choosing. That means that the representatives may be attorneys, company or union officials, the grievant, and so on. In most cases involving smaller companies, we would expect to see an international union field representative or local union officer against an industrial relations director or personnel officer. There is no requirement for representation by attorney and no requirement for so-called equal qualifications across advocates.

Presentation of the case

Since the union has generally initiated the grievance, it has the responsibility to proceed with the case except in discipline and discharge cases. It presents joint exhibits relevant to its case, its own exhibits, and calls witnesses as necessary. During this period, management's representative may object to exhibits and cross-examine witnesses. When the union has completed its case, management offers its evidence in a similar manner.

The rules followed in arbitration cases for the presentation of evidence are more liberal than those in courts of law. We will examine these differences shortly.

At the end both sides may have an opportunity to present closing arguments. During the earlier presentation the arbitrator may question witnesses but is not required to do so.

Posthearing

Following the hearing the parties may submit additional material in the form of briefs to support their positions. When these are received, if anticipated, the arbitrator will study the evidence, take the briefs into account, and perhaps examine similar cases in which arbitrators were called upon for an award.

The arbitrator then prepares an award and forwards it to the parties for implementation. In some cases, the arbitrator maintains jurisdiction until the award has been completely implemented in case additional proceedings are necessary to iron out differences in its application.

Next we will examine aspects related to the receipt of evidence at the hearing and the form and preparation of the award.

Evidentiary rules

In courts of law, rules of evidence are rather strict. For example, hearsay evidence is not allowed. That is, one cannot testify as to what another told him, since this is not the best evidence. One instead must get the actual observer or witness to testify. One of the reasons for strict rules of evidence in criminal and civil proceedings is that a large number of them are heard by juries. Jury members may equally credit hearsay and direct evidence without realizing the distinction. In arbitral proceedings, however, it is presumed that the arbitrator can objectively give testimony the weight, or credit, that it is entitled to. Hence, the arbitrator may note a hearsay objection but allow the witness to continue.

In arbitration where AAA rules apply, Rule 28 states that: "The arbitrator shall be the judge of the relevancy and materiality of the evidence offered and conformity to legal rules of evidence shall not be necessary."[18] There are, however, several areas where arbitrators must consider the types of evidence they receive and their relevancy to the subsequent award.

Fleming has examined a number of problems arbitrators face when evidence is to be weighed.[19] First, companies often desire to introduce information about an employee's past misconduct to support their present actions. Fleming suggests that this evidence should be given

---

[18] 30 LA 1086, 1089.

[19] Fleming, *The Labor Arbitration Process*, pp. 165–98.

weight only in the following circumstances: (1) a basic case for the present offense has already been laid, (2) the offenses offered in evidence are substantially similar to those alleged in the present case (for example, past insubordination and present insubordination), (3) they are offered primarily to impeach the credibility of the grievant, (4) the offenses introduced are reasonably recent to the present one, and (5) the contract does not bar the introduction of such evidence.[20]

Occasionally one party will have information that would aid the other in the preparation of a case. Fleming offers four rules for the production of material held by one party: (1) if the arbitrator requests it, (2) if refused, the arbitrator may weigh the refusal as he sees fit in the award, (3) the document or information could be used to attack the credibility of a witness, and (4) the arbitrator may admit only parts relevant to the hearing.[21]

For cross-examination and confrontation, Fleming generally recommends that: (1) depositions and previous testimony be admitted where a witness is unavailable, (2) hearsay may be accepted when a direct witness declines to testify against a fellow employee, (3) investigation should generally not be attempted by the arbitrator, (4) where exposing the identity of a witness would damage legitimate interests of either party, the witness should be questioned by counsel in the sole presence of the arbitrator.[22]

Self-incrimination is prohibited in criminal trials and may also be an issue in arbitral proceedings. Fleming suggests that the arbitrator not grant an absolute immunity against self-incrimination, but weigh the refusal to testify as evidence would be. However, the arbitrator should not use a refusal to testify as sufficient to sustain a case by itself.[23]

Thus, the rules are relaxed somewhat, but the arbitrator's presumed competence in conducting the hearing and weighing the evidence should help protect the grievant's rights. It also should be remembered that while the grievant's employment is personally important, the same standard of proof necessary for conviction of an offense in a court of law is not necessary to sustain a charge in an arbitration proceeding. For example, in some instances where direct evidence may not be available to convict a grocery cashier of theft where there is a shortage, circumstantial evidence showing a strong likelihood that the grievant committed the offense may be sufficient to sustain a discharge.

---

[20] Ibid., p. 170.
[21] Ibid., p. 175.
[22] Ibid., p. 181.
[23] Ibid., p. 186.

Preparation of the award

The award basically conveys to the parties the arbitrator's decision in the case including (in most cases) a summary of the evidence presented, the reasoning behind a decision, and what action must be taken to satisfy the decision.

In preparing the award, the arbitrator must examine a number of issues. First, it must be determined whether or not the dispute was actually arbitrable. Did the grievance allege an actual violation of the contract? Were the grievance procedure steps followed in a regular and timely manner so the grievance was submitted soon enough and the union follow-up timely enough? If these arbitrability criteria are met, then the arbitrator may proceed with an examination of the merits.

While there is no statutory obligation on the arbitrator, it is important that the reason for a particular award be included for future guidance of the parties. Occasionally the grievance appears trivial on the surface, but the decision will govern employer and union conduct for some substantial future period. It is important then for them to know why the issue was decided as it was.

The arbitrator must also be careful to insure that an award draws from the essence of the contract since the arbitration itself is a creature of the agreement. Most contracts prohibit the arbitrator from adding to, subtracting from, or modifying the essence of the agreement. The arbitrator must show them how the interpretation made is within the four corners of the contract.

Occasionally an arbitrator will find a conflict between contract language and federal labor or civil rights laws or interpretations. There is no clearcut guidance for an arbitrator faced with this problem. Given a *Spielberg* approach, the arbitrator could expect a decision to be reversed for its repugnance to the labor acts, but then the Steelworkers Trilogy generally leaves the decision free from court intervention. Some suggest the arbitrator defer to the law, but that would alter the contract. Finally, an arbitrator may simply refuse to assert jurisdiction and find the manner nonarbitrable due to federal preemption of the issue.

PROCEDURAL DIFFICULTIES AND THEIR RESOLUTION

Probably the prime difficulty encountered in arbitration is the same problem found in our court system: time delays. A recent issue of the official AFL–CIO publication reported that the average time from the filing of a grievance through the submission of an arbitral award was

223 days.[24] While this is an average figure, it is not unusual to see some cases take up to two years for resolution. Table 14–1 provides the time data reported by the AFL–CIO.

While the arbitral process can take time, the data show an average of 104 days from appointment to award. The 43-day period from the

TABLE 14–1
Arbitration time delays

	Days
Grievance date to request for panel	68
Between request for panel and panel sent out	6
Panel sent out to appointment of arbitrator	45
Appointment of arbitrator to hearing date	61
Hearing date to arbitrator award	43
Total: Grievance date to award	223

Source: John Zalusky, "Arbitration: Updating a Vital Process," *American Federationist*, vol. 83 (November 1976), p. 6.

termination of the hearing to the award date is greater than the old 30-day limit previously established by the FMCS but may include time during which labor and management submit briefs. Thus, arbitrators may come fairly close to rendering decisions within 30 days of the receipt of all case material.

There are still problems with the length of time taken. The quote "justice delayed is justice denied" is not an empty platitude. For individuals who have been disciplined, it is important for them to have their cases finally disposed so they can make a new employment life or return to work made whole. For the firm, a grievance involving large numbers of persons could lead to substantial back pay liabilities if the findings are adverse after a long delay.

The costs of arbitration also cause problems, particularly for unions. Since management and unions usually share the cost of arbitration, a relatively poorly financed union may be reluctant to use arbitration as much as it would like. Figure 14–1 gives the costs for a union for a typical, relatively simple arbitration case. What can be done to reduce these time delays and high costs for arbitration?

Expedited arbitration

Since the early 1970s a fair number of larger companies and unions have moved toward a scheme called expedited arbitration. In expe-

---

[24] John Zalusky, "Arbitration: Updating a Vital Process," *American Federationist*, vol. 83 (November 1976), pp. 1–8.

FIGURE 14–1
The union's cost of traditional arbitration for a one-day hearing

Prehearing

Lost time: Grievant and witnesses @ $5/32 hours	$160
Lawyer:	
Library research @ $40/4 hours	160
Interviewing witnesses @ $55/4 hours	220
Filing fee: AAA (shared equally) $100	50
Total prehearing costs	$590

Hearing expense
Arbitrator:

Fee (shared equally) 1 hearing day	$100
Expenses for meals, transportation, and so on (shared equally)	50
Travel time one-half day (shared equally)	50
Total arbitrator	$200

Transcript: $2.75 per page with two copies and ten-day delivery of 200 pages (shared equally)	$325
Lawyer: Presentation of case @ $55/hour	330
Lost time: Grievant and witnesses @ $5/hour, 32 hrs.	160
Hearing room: Shared equally (Free under AAA)	25
Total hearing	$840

Posthearing Expense

Arbitrator: 1½ days study time (shared equally)	$150
Lawyer: Preparation of post-hearing @ $55/hour	440
Total cost to union	$2,220

Source: Averages estimated by AFL–CIO department of research.

dited arbitration time delays and costs are expected to be reduced. Very short written awards may be submitted. Rather than hearing only one case in a day, arbitrators might hear several. Most of the cases handled under expedited arbitration would be individual discipline and discharge cases or cases of an emergency nature.

One other expected advantage is that expedited arbitration may provide for the entry of new arbitrators since relatively simple and straightforward cases are generally handled by the expedited process. Figure 14–2 contains examples of expedited arbitration procedures presently in use.

Inadequate representation

In Chapter 13 we noted instances where employees successfully argued that they were not fairly represented by their unions in the grievance procedure. One other issue can arise in the arbitration

	Steelworkers—basic steel industry	American Arbitration Association Service	AIW Local 562 Rusco, Inc.	American postal workers—U.S. postal service	Miniarbitration Columbus, Ohio
Source of arbitrators	Recent law school graduates and other sources	Special panel from AAA roster	FMCS roster	AAA, FMCS rosters	Its own "Joint Selection and Orientation Committee" from FMCS roster
Method of selecting	Preselected regional panels. Administrator notifies in rotation	Appointed by AAA regional administrators	Preselected panel by rotating FMCS contacts	Appointed by AAA regional administrators	FMCS regional representative by rotation
Lawyers	No limitation, but understanding that lawyers will not be used	No limitation	No lawyers	No limitation but normally not used	No limitation
Transcript	No	No	No	No	May be used
Briefs	No	Permitted	No	No	May be used
Written description of issue	Last step grievance report	Joint submission permitted	No	Position paper	Grievance record expected
Time from request to hearing date	10 days	Approximately 3 days depending on arbitrator availability	10 days	Approximately 7 days depending on arbitrator availability	Not specified
Time of hearing to award	Bench decision or 48 hours	5 days	48 hours	Bench decision written award 48 hours	48 hours
Fees (plus expenses)	$100/½ day $150/day	$100 filing fee Arbitrator's normal fee	$100/½ day $150/day	$100 filing fee $100 per case	$100/½ day, 1 or 2 cases; $150/full day, 1 or 2 cases; $200/day, 3 or 4 cases

process—inadequate representation. Inadequate representation could be malicious in origin, or it could occur through ineptitude. Since arbitration proceedings are viewed as final determinations by the courts, the quality of the advocacy one receives is of substantial concern.

Recently the Supreme Court reversed an arbitration award upholding the discharge of an over-the-road trucker who was accused of padding expenses.[25] Adequate prehearing investigation would have disclosed that the seeming dishonesty was a result of a motel clerk's charging more than the generally published rate and pocketing the difference. The trucker was actually blameless.

Within the hearing itself, the arbitrator may become aware that there are differences in the quality of representation. While the arbitrator may question witnesses and probe into other matters, the umpire's impartiality in an essentially adversary hearing may be questioned as a result. One might ask whether it is ethical for an arbitrator to "make a case" for an advocate who has inadequately prepared a case. The issue is not settled.

ARBITRATION OF DISCIPLINE CASES

A large number of cases heard by arbitrators are appeals made by employees to reconsider the evidence related to employer discipline or to reassess the severity of the punishment. Any punishment which includes discharge is particularly likely to go to arbitration. We need to examine here the principles arbitrators apply to the evaluation of evidence and the establishment of fair punishment in industrial discipline cases.

Role of discipline

Under the contract, employees have certain rights and obligations as do employers. Employees have rights to their jobs as the contract reads, and employers are entitled to performance from their workers. Most contracts also include grievance procedures available to a union member.

Jones points out that an employer should be able to expect that employees will carry out orders, regardless of the employees' interpretation of the "rightness" of the orders, unless they would be unsafe, unhealthful, or illegal.[26] If the employees believe that the orders violate

---

[25] *Hines* v. *Anchor Motor Freight, Inc.*, U.S. Supreme Court, 74–1025, 1976.

[26] Dallas L. Jones, *Arbitration and Industrial Discipline* (Ann Arbor: Bureau of Industrial Relations, University of Michigan, 1961), pp. 17–18.

the contract, they are entitled to file grievances and gain relief. On the other hand, if the employees take matters into their own hands, they are guilty of insubordination and may be punished. The punishment may serve two basic purposes: (1) to motivate the individuals to avoid similar conduct in the future, and (2) by example, to deter others.

Evidence

Since discipline cases are extremely important to the grievant, arbitrators require that the company present evidence to show that the grievant actually committed the offense and that the punishment is consistent with the breach of the rules. The company must also show that it is not dealing with this employee in an arbitrary manner when compared to others involved in similar situations.

On the basis of this evidence, arbitrators may uphold or deny the punishment, or modify it downward (but not upward) to fit more closely the disciplinary breach. Arbitrators also require that the discipline be given for "just cause" and not on some capricious basis.

Uses of punishment

Jones suggests that punishment can be thought of in two contexts as it relates to discipline.[27] The first sees punishment as a legitimate exercise of authority as a consequence of a breach of rules. The second sees punishment as a corrective effort to direct the employees' attention to the consequences but also to change their attitudes toward the punished behavior. Arbitrators may be concerned with these approaches, but they are perhaps more concerned with the procedural regularity of the discipline in the case at hand, the evenness of application across persons in the same firm, and its fundamental fairness given societal norms.[28]

Wheeler examined recent arbitral decisions and, adding a category he defined as humanitarian (using rules only as guidance and taking into account individual intentions), he found that arbitration cases are split down the middle in applying authoritarian or corrective discipline. Table 14–2 gives his results. Corrective discipline appears to be used more often for absenteeism and incompetence while authoritarian approaches are used more often for dishonesty and illegal strike activity.[29]

---

[27] Ibid., pp. 2–4.

[28] Ibid., pp. 16–20.

[29] Hoyt N. Wheeler, "Punishment Theory and Industrial Discipline," *Industrial Relations*, vol. 15 (May 1976), pp. 235–43.

TABLE 14–2
Analysis of arbitration decisions relating to discharge and discipline reported in *Labor Arbitration Reports*, May 1970 through March 1974 by theory of discipline and type of offense

	Humanitarian	Corrective	Authoritarian	Total
Absenteeism, tardiness, leaving early	2	20	8	30
Dishonesty, theft, falsification of records	2	13	28	43
Incompetence, negligence, poor workmanship, violation of safety rules	1	27	9	37
Illegal strikes, strike violence, deliberate restriction of production	0	12	19	31
Intoxication, bringing intoxicants in plant	1	10	7	18
Fighting, assault, horseplay, troublemaking	3	16	15	34
Insubordination, refusal of job assignment, refusal to work overtime, also fight or altercation with supervisor	2	42	54	98
Miscellaneous rule violations	2	20	26	48
Totals	13	160	166	339
Percent	4%	47%	49%	

Source: Hoyt N. Wheeler, "Punishment Theory and Industrial Discipline," *Industrial Relations*, vol. 15 (May 1976), p. 239.

Given that corrective discipline appears to be used in about 50 percent of reported cases, is it effective? There are few data available to answer this question except for the small sample in Jones's comprehensive study. As a result of his analysis, he concludes that in no case did it turn an unsatisfactory employee into one whose performance was satisfactory. He suggests that there are a number of reasons for this finding. First, the individual is often restored to the original work group where behavior that resulted in the punishment is reinforced. Second, it may not have been closely pointed out to the grievant what behavior the punishment is related to. And, third, in some cases it may be reasonable to place an employee in a probationary status rather than punishing him so the contingency is on future rather than past behavior.[30]

ASSESSMENT OF ARBITRATION

We have included some assessments of arbitral processes as we have moved through this chapter. What we aim to do in this section is to get some idea of the relative occurrence of types of issues in arbitration and get some idea about how the parties perceive the process.

As one of the major suppliers of arbitration panels, the FMCS keeps statistics on the number of cases going to arbitration and the issues they involve. Table 14–3 shows the progression from 1973 through

---

[30] Jones, *Arbitration and Industrial Discipline*, pp. 71–74.

1975. There seem to be few trends in these data except that the number of awards has increased and issues related to arbitrability of grievances have expanded. The parties do not seem to be using arbitration less or to be more able to settle grievances without outside intervention.

But are the parties enthusiastic about the practices? We have seen complaints about cost and time delays in our look at the process. But how do labor and management feel about a process that has a third-party resolving their disputes?

An old joke holds that "Money doesn't buy happiness, but it's way

TABLE 14–3
Number and percent change in number of issues reported in applicable FMCS closed arbitration award cases for fiscal years 1973, 1974, and 1975.

Specific issues	1973 Total number of issues	1974 Total number of issues	1974 Percent change in number of issues from previous fiscal year	1975 Total number of issues	1975 Percent change in number of issues from previous fiscal year
Total	4,255	5,341	+ 25.5	5,243	− 1.8
General issues	1,130	1,255	+ 11.1	1,347	+ 7.3
Overtime other than pay*	204	237	+ 16.2	249	+ 5.1
Distribution of overtime	187	208	+ 11.2	198	− 4.8
Compulsory overtime	17	29	+ 70.6	25	− 13.8
Other	—	—	—	26	—
Seniority	653	708	+ 8.4	691	− 2.4
Promotion and upgrading	203	246	+ 21.2	260	+ 5.7
Layoff, bumping and recall	264	248	− 6.1	234	− 5.6
Transfer	96	104	+ 8.3	94	− 9.6
Other	90	110	+ 22.2	103	− 6.4
Union officers†	27	30	+ 11.1	20	− 33.3
Strike and lockout	19	18	− 5.3	18	no change
Working conditions‡	48	59	+ 22.9	45	− 23.7
Discrimination	—	—	—	48	—
Management rights	—	—	—	115	—
Scheduling of work	179	203	+ 13.4	161	− 20.7
Economic: Wage rates and pay issues	581	663	+ 14.1	729	+ 9.9
Wage issues	—	—	—	53	—
Rate of pay	—	—	—	107	—
Severance pay	—	—	—	11	—
Reporting, call-in and call-back pay	86	89	+ 3.5	92	+ 3.4
Holidays and holiday pay	119	117	− 1.7	101	− 13.7
Vacations and vacation pay	113	140	+ 23.9	108	− 22.9
Incentive rates or standards	82	96	+ 17.1	58	− 39.6
Overtime pay	181	221	+ 22.1	199	− 9.9

TABLE 14–3 (*continued*)

Fringe benefit issues	161	176	+ 9.3	164	− 6.8
Health and welfare	51	55	+ 7.8	66	+ 20.0
Pensions	24	23	− 4.2	21	− 8.7
Other	86	98	+ 13.9	77	− 21.4
Discharge and disciplinary issues	1,302	1,857	+ 42.6	1,812	− 2.4
Technical issues	400	499	+ 24.7	260	− 47.9
Job posting and bidding	—	—	—	56	—
Job evaluation	400	499	+ 24.7	204	− 59.1
Scope of agreement	186	211	+ 13.4	202	− 4.3
Subcontracting	95	93	− 2.1	104	+ 11.8
Jurisdictional disputes	40	45	+ 12.5	33	− 26.7
Foreman, supervision, and so on	42	63	+ 50.0	57	− 9.5
Mergers, consolidations, accretion other plants	9	8	− 11.1	8	no change
Arbitrability of grievances	252	397	+ 57.5	497	+ 25.2
Procedural	143	200	+ 39.9	235	+ 17.5
Substantive	70	121	+ 72.9	140	+ 15.7
Procedural and substantive	29	62	+113.8	90	+ 45.2
Other	10	14	+ 40.0	32	+128.6
Not elsewhere classified§	243	283	+ 16.5	232	− 18.0

* Overtime pay issues included under category Economic: wage rates and pay issues.
† Included in this classification are issues concerning superseniority and union business.
‡ This classification also includes concerning safety.
§ Issues classification as such nonexistent in this fiscal year.
Source: U.S. Federal Mediation and Conciliation Service, *Twenty-Eighth Annual Report* (Washington, Government Printing Office, 1976), pp. 52–53.

ahead of whatever's in second place." The same may be true for arbitration. It doesn't solve all of the problems of contract administration, but no one has devised a better substitute. In a study completed in the mid-1960s, Jones and Smith queried management and labor users on arbitration processes and came to a number of conclusions.[31]

They found that both parties prefer arbitration generally to bargaining over unresolved disputes. While most would leave the present process untouched, some prefer the possibility of a court review. A number were concerned with a lack of adherence to rules of evidence which make it more difficult to determine how testimony will be credited. In regard to procedural matters, Jones and Smith suggest that prehearing briefs could prove useful in focusing and shortening hearings. Finally, as to decision making, the parties want an arbitrator willing to act as a judge rather than a mediator and who is willing to stay within the contract in deciding a dispute. Given the court system's reluctance to review arbitral awards, the parties desire some

---

[31] Dallas L. Jones and Russell A. Smith, "Management and Labor Appraisals and Criticisms of the Arbitration Process: A Report with Comments," *Michigan Law Review*, vol. 62 (May 1964), pp. 1115–56.

certainty in how the proceedings will be conducted and what issues will be considered in rendering an award.

SUMMARY

Arbitration is a process for resolving disputes through the invitation of a neutral third party. The use of arbitration is encouraged by the courts and the outcome of arbitral awards is generally considered non-reviewable. Supreme Court decisions in the Steelworkers' trilogy laid the groundwork for the present status of arbitration.

Arbitral hearings are quasi-judicial in nature and relate to allegations that the contract has been violated. The arbitrator hears the evidence from both parties and rules on it.

A large number of arbitration proceedings are associated with individual discipline and discharge cases. Arbitration cases appear to split about evenly in applying authoritarian or corrective standards in the use of punishment.

Arbitration has been criticized for its time delays and costs and for the fact that some decisions go outside the scope of the contract or dispute. But opponents and proponents are relatively satisfied with the system.

SUGGESTED READINGS

Edwards, Harry T. "Labor Arbitration at the Crossroads: The 'Common Law of the Shop' versus External Law." *Arbitration Journal*, vol. 32 (June 1977), pp. 65–95.

Elkouri, Frank, and Elkouri, Edna Asper. *How Arbitration Works*, 3d ed. (Washington: Bureau of National Affairs, 1973).

Fleming, Robben W. *The Labor Arbitration Process* (Urbana: University of Illinois Press, 1965).

Jones, Dallas L. *Arbitration and Industrial Discipline* (Ann Arbor: Bureau of Industrial Relations, University of Michigan, 1961).

Landis, Brook I. *Value Judgments in Arbitration: A Case Study of Saul Wallen* (Ithaca, N.Y.: New York State School of Industrial and Labor Relations, Cornell University, 1977).

Prasow, Paul, and Peters, E. *Labor Arbitration and Collective Bargaining* (New York: McGraw-Hill, 1970).

DISCUSSION QUESTIONS

1. Given Supreme Court and NLRB rulings, what is the present scope and finality associated with rights arbitration in the private sector?
2. What possible drawbacks do you see associated with the expansion of expedited arbitration?

3. What duty, if any, does an arbitrator owe to the parties to see that both are competently represented?
4. Give arguments for and against the greater involvement of attorneys in arbitration both as advocates and umpires.
5. Forecast what you see to be the future of labor arbitration in terms of the expansion or contraction of issues within its jurisdiction and the finality of its decisions.

Cases

About six months after the new GMFC-Local 384 contract was ratified, three grievances were sent to arbitration by the union after a failure to resolve them. The company and the union agreed that all three grievances would be heard on separate dates by the same arbitrator. Your name was on the panel the FMCS sent to the parties, and they selected you to hear the grievances. You agreed and have just heard all three over the last three days. Now you have to prepare your awards.

Case 1

George Jones was a grade B production worker in the heavy components assembly department. He worked with six other assemblers of the same grade constructing cabs for power shovels. The supervisor, Ralph Barnes, was in charge of three of these heavy assembly crews. George Jones had been with the company for about a year, all of his time spent on this work crew. Up to this incident, his work record had been unremarkable. He had had two unexcused absences, but no problems with supervision.

On May 6, George had punched a co-worker, Elliot Johnson, and rendered him unconscious with one blow. As soon as Barnes arrived on the scene and after rendering first-aid, he asked the work crew what had happened. They had only seen Jones strike Johnson. After Johnson came around, Barnes asked him what happened. Johnson stated that he and Jones had been talking when Jones suddenly turned and swung at him. Barnes then asked Jones what had happened. Jones, who is the only black employee in his work group, said that Johnson had been making racial slurs toward him ever since he joined the crew, but this morning he had been pushed over the brink when Johnson had said, "Hey, black boy, you people have sure got the right rhythm for this pounding."

From his supervisor training course, Barnes knew it was company policy to discharge anyone who struck another employee or started a fight. Thus, he had sent Jones to the personnel department for termination. On the way, Jones filed a grievance with Ralph Murphy, the union steward in his area, alleging that the company had violated Section 4.02 of the contract by discharging him without cause. His grievance stated that the attack on Johnson was justified given his past harassment and that punching him seemed to be the "only way to get him off my back."

When Murphy gave the grievance to Barnes, it was immediately denied. Barnes said, "The rule is ironclad as far as I'm concerned. They said we supervisors didn't have any latitude on the issue."

Murphy then presented copies of the grievance to the shift IR representative, Carolyn Foster, and Neal Young, the general foreman. In her examination of the grievance, she called Johnson and Cronholm, Jensen, and Albers (three other employees in the work group) to her office separately. When questioned, Johnson repeated his allegation that Jones's attack was unprovoked. He adamantly denied ever making racial slurs toward him. Information from Jensen and Albers supported Johnson on his denial of racial slurs, but Cronholm said that he had repeatedly heard Johnson make disparaging remarks toward Jones. After weighing this information and considering company policy on discharges, she upheld Barnes's action.

The union continued to demand Jones's reinstatement with full back pay and management adamantly refused.

When the case was heard, the union's grievance alleged that not only had Jones been discharged without cause (Section 4.02), but that it had also been racially motivated, violating the EEO section (12.14a). In its opening argument, the company asked that you find the grievance to be nonarbitrable since Jones might file a charge with the EEOC under Title VII if your award upheld the discharge. They also said that the discrimination issue was not arbitrable because it had not been raised in Step 3 as provided by 12.14b. You noted their argument but reserved your ruling on arbitrability to the award you would prepare.

Both sides presented their evidence. All was in substantial agreement with what Barnes and Foster had found in their investigation. Jones and Johnson held to their stories as did Jensen, Albers, and Cronholm. The company introduced evidence to show that without exception employees had been terminated for fighting. It also provided statistics which showed that 12 percent of the 42 employees discharged for fighting over the past three years were black and that 14 percent of the production labor force was black.

In this case, your award should contain:

1. Your ruling on the arbitrability of the grievance.
2. Your rationale in finding on the merits of the case (if arbitrable).
3. If arbitrable, the degree to which you would grant the relief Jones is asking or uphold management.

Case 2

This case has the greatest ramifications for the firm from a cost standpoint. In the past, the company has always used its own janitors for cleaning and maintenance. Due to operational requirements, most of this work is performed on the third shift. About 50 janitors are required to maintain the Central City facilities. GMFC has always had problems with absences among its janitors, but since the last contract was signed, the rate increased from about 6 percent per day to 16 percent. Because of this increase, housekeeping was lagging, and GMFC officials were starting to worry about fire code violations resulting from the superficial cleaning. Management considered discharging those who were chronically absent but found on investigation that absences seemed to rotate systematically among members of the crew, as if they were planned.

As a result of its investigation, Carolyn Foster contacted Bud Allen, Local 384's president, and asked him to enforce the contract and get the janitors' absence rates down. She told Allen the company considered the action to be the equivalent of a wildcat strike and that strong action would be taken if absence rates weren't reduced. Allen protested, saying that there was no concerted activity behind the absences.

When the high rate and rotating pattern persisted, the company discharged the janitors and subcontracted their work to Dependa-Kleen, a full-time janitorial service. To the company's pleasure, Dependa-Kleen was able to take over the entire operation at a lower cost than their own in-house operation incurred prior to the absence problem.

On behalf of the janitors, Allen filed a grievance with the firm arguing that the discharges violated Section 4.02. He also filed an unfair labor practice charge with the NLRB claiming the company violated Section 8(a)(5) of the Taft-Hartley Act through its unilateral action in subcontracting the work without consulting or bargaining with the union.

The company argued that it was justified in replacing the janitors since their systematic absences were a violation of the contract's no-strike clause (Section 9.05). The company argued that it was entitled to replace the participants consistent with the management rights clause in the contract, Section 4.02.

Assume that the testimony at the hearing does not seriously challenge the evidence management has gathered on the increase in absences among the janitors. In this case, decide the following:

1. Would you find the grievance arbitrable given the unfair labor practice charge filed by the union?
2. Assume you find the grievance to be arbitrable, frame an award and justify it.

Case 3

The maintenance electricians in the unit are assigned to repair jobs around the Central City facilities shortly after they report to work at their central shop at the beginning of a shift. Up until the ratification of the most recent contract, it had been traditional for electricians to return to the shop for their afternoon coffee breaks. All of the electricians left their work so they would arrive at the shop to begin the break and leave at the end of the break to return.

The electrical shop supervisor, Ken Bates, issued a new policy after the new contract was approved stating that the break would commence once work stopped at the assigned location and end when it was restarted. This policy change meant some electricians would have insufficient time to return to the shop for their breaks.

The union filed a grievance alleging that the company had revoked a prevailing practice which had the effect of a contract term. It also argued that it had not been consulted as Article 12.03 requires. The company denied the grievance, citing the language in Section 12.02.

As the arbitrator, frame an award in this dispute.

15

PUBLIC SECTOR LABOR RELATIONS

To an extent public sector labor relations might be thought of as the set of exceptions to the general rules of collective bargaining or the "yes, but" situations to the person interested in details. As we will see in our exploration of public sector labor relations, there are more similarities than differences when we compare them with processes in the private sector. What we will find is that public sector labor relations is only in its adolescence when compared to the private sector and the rules surrounding its practice are much more complex.

The aim of this chapter is to provide you with information on the variety of settings within which collective bargaining is practiced in the public sector and to highlight the differences between public and private sector practices and within public sector levels. When we speak of the public sector, one may conjure up an image of a monolithic group of employees paid by government revenues and directly serving the general citizenry. However, we will soon see that there are a myriad of separate groups, by level and jurisdiction (federal, state, municipal, and so on) just as there are in the private sector. The one aspect that is much more pervasive for public sector labor relations is that the "customer" group affected by the outcomes is generally much larger (homeowners and apartment dwellers in a garbage collection strike), and the costs of settlement much more likely to be directly passed on to the customer in the short run.

While public employee unionization is not new in the United States, legislation enabling bargaining is. In general the collective relationship seldom dates back farther than the early 1960s as compared to the middle to late 1930s in the private sector. This means that most of the theory and research on public sector unionism is relatively recent. In fact, it would probably be fair to say that most of the research on unions in recent years has concentrated on the public, rather than the private, sector. This recency bias, coupled with the emphasis on this area should give us a good look at the public-private similarities and differences.

What do we intend to accomplish in this chapter? There are a variety of issues we will deal with, some parallel to earlier aspects we covered for the private sector. Enumerating them, we will cover: (1) the evolution of laws governing bargaining for public employees in the United States, (2) differences in coverage among jurisdictions, (3) differences in representation rights among employment levels, (4) differences in the application and comprehensiveness of laws relating to recognition, bargaining, and dispute settlement, (5) tripartite bargaining models and variables associated with bargaining outcomes, and (6) trends in public sector representation, bargaining and dispute settlement.

As you read this chapter, consider the following questions:

1. How do public and private sectors differ in their bargaining relationships, particularly for impasse procedures?
2. How do laws regulating labor relations in the public sector differ across both states and occupations?
3. How successful has the application of fact-finding been in the public sector?
4. What variables seem to have the greatest effect on bargaining outcomes?

JURISDICTIONS AND EMPLOYEES

While there are relatively few exceptions or exemptions from coverage for the private sector under federal labor law, this is not the case for the public sector. For example, in the private sector the law only identifies agricultural, domestic workers, and supervisors and managers as industrial and occupational classes exempt from coverage by the act. On the other hand, in the public sector we will see a variety of differences in coverage by types of employees, types of issues or strategies, and political jurisdiction.

Occupational groups

As you will notice shortly in Tables 15–1A, through 15–1E, the states very often distinguish between occupational groups in terms of the legislated rights to organize, bargain, and resolve disputes. Frequently firefighters, police, and teachers are specified as groups either entitled to certain rights or barred from using certain dispute resolution strategies.

Source of employment

Laws also may separate groups in terms of bargaining rights given other jurisdictional bodies and the manner in which jobs were obtained. Some states may distinguish between employees falling within a statutory civil service system and those who are outside its protection. Persons receiving jobs as the result of political appointments are usually unprotected although the Supreme Court has recently limited the ability of public officials to use political party membership as a criterion for maintaining a public employment position.[1]

Levels of government

There are also large differences in the jurisdictions or bargaining units involved. First, we have an obvious federal-state difference. Second, within states a variety of lesser jurisdictions and semiautonomous agencies exist. Frequently, for example, a statewide university system may be largely autonomous from a legislature in terms of its governance. Within states we find counties, cities, school boards, sewer districts, transportation authorities, and the like, all publicly governed, but each responsible to a different constituency and each perhaps dependent on a different source of funding.

While some public employee unions and associations, particularly the American Federation of State, County, and Municipal Employees (AFSCME) and the National Education Association (NEA), have lobbied hard for a federal public sector bargaining law, there is no great push in Congress at this point to standardize practice across the states and local jurisdictions.

For its part, the federal government has no legislated rules governing its labor relations. Here the requirements have been specified by a series of executive orders beginning with 10988 in 1962. We will examine this series shortly.

STATE LABOR LAWS

Just as the federal legislation in the private sector covers aspects such as union activities, representation, bargaining, dispute settlement, and administrative agencies, the same holds for state public sector laws. However, these are extremely varied across states and between employee groups within states. Tables 15–1A through 15–1E list public employee bargaining laws for teachers, police, firefighters, state, and municipal employees by state. Provisions related to recogni-

---

[1] *Elrod* v. *Burns*, U.S. Supreme Court, no. 74–1520 (1976).

tion, the duty to bargain, impasse procedures, and rights to strike are summarized. The table reflects statutory law, attorney general opinions and court rulings through the end of 1977. Thus, the provisions may now be different if the various legislatures, attorneys general, or courts modify them.

As you go through Tables 15–1A through 15–1E, you will notice that most states having provisions for recognition allow for exclusive representation. Only South Carolina, Texas, and Wyoming prohibited

TABLE 15–1A
Bargaining provisions for teachers (legislation, case laws, and attorney general opinions)

State	Recognition	Bargaining rights	Impasse procedures	Right-to-strike
Alabama	Exclusive	Consultation	N.P.	N.P.
Alaska	Exclusive	Mutual duty	M, FF	N.P.
Arizona	N.P.	Permitted	N.P.	N.P.
Arkansas	N.P.	Permitted	N.P.	Prohibited
California	Exclusive	Mutual duty	M, FF, A††	Prohibited
Colorado	N.P.	Meet and confer	N.P.	N.P.
Connecticut	Exclusive	Mutual duty	M, A	Prohibited
Delaware	Exclusive	Mutual duty	M, FF	Prohibited
Florida	Exclusive	Mutual duty	FF, M, Leg.	Prohibited
Georgia	N.P.	Permitted	N.P.	N.P.
Hawaii	Exclusive	Mutual duty	M, FF, A	Permitted
Idaho	Exclusive	Mutual duty	M, FF	N.P.
Illinois	N.P.	Permitted	N.P.	Prohibited
Indiana**	N.P.	N.P.	N.P.	Prohibited
Iowa	Exclusive	Mutual duty	M, FF, A	Prohibited
Kansas	Exclusive	Mutual duty	FF	Prohibited
Kentucky	N.P.	Permitted	N.P.	Prohibited
Louisiana	Permitted	Permitted	N.P.	N.P.
Maine	Exclusive	Mutual duty	M, FF, A	Prohibited
Maryland	Exclusive	Mutual duty	M, FF	Prohibited
Massachusetts	Exclusive	Mutual duty	M, FF	Prohibited
Michigan	Exclusive	Mutual duty	M, FF	Prohibited*
Minnesota	Exclusive	Mutual duty	M, A	Prohibited†
Mississippi	N.P.	N.P.	N.P.	N.P.
Missouri	N.P.	Consultation	N.P.	N.P.
Montana	Exclusive	Mutual duty	FF	Unfair practice
Nebraska	Permitted	Meet and confer	FF, CIR	Prohibited
Nevada	Exclusive	Mutual duty	M, FF, BFF	Prohibited
New Hampshire	Exclusive	Mutual duty	M, FF, Leg.	Prohibited
New Jersey	Exclusive	Mutual duty	M, FF, A#	Prohibited
New Mexico	N.P.	Permitted	N.P.	N.P.
New York	Exclusive	Mutual duty	M, FF, Leg.‡	Prohibited
North Carolina	N.P.	Prohibited	N.P.	N.P.
North Dakota	Exclusive	Mutual duty	FF	Prohibited
Ohio	N.P.	Permitted	N.P.	Prohibited
Oklahoma	Exclusive	Mutual duty	FF	Prohibited
Oregon	Exclusive	Mutual duty	M, FF	Limited§
Pennsylvania	Exclusive	Mutual duty	FF	Permitted
Rhode Island	Exclusive	Employer duty	M. A.‖	Prohibited*

TABLE 15-1A (continued)

State	Recognition	Bargaining rights	Impasse procedures	Right-to-strike
South Carolina	Prohibited	Prohibited	N.P.	Prohibited
South Dakota	Exclusive	Mutual duty	M, FF	Prohibited
Tennessee	N.P.	Prohibited	N.P. ·	Prohibited
Texas	Prohibited	Prohibited	N.P.	N.P.
Utah	N.P.	Permitted	N.P.	N.P.
Vermont	Exclusive	Mutual duty	M, FF, Leg.	Limited
Virginia	N.P.	Prohibited	N.P.	Prohibited
Washington	Exclusive	Mutual duty	FF	N.P.
West Virginia	Permitted	Permitted	M, FF#	Prohibited
Wisconsin	Exclusive	Mutual duty	M, FF	Prohibited†
Wyoming	Prohibited	Prohibited	N.P.	N.P.

Note: A = arbitration; BFF = binding fact-finding; CIR = court of industrial relations; FF = fact-finding; Leg. = legislative body action; M = mediation; and N.P. = no provision.
* But strikes will not be enjoined unless there is a danger to public safety or irreparable injury.
† Not prohibited if school board either refuses to arbitrate or implement an award.
‡ May agree to arbitration; some provisions do not apply to New York City employees.
§ Permitted where parties have not agreed to arbitrate.
‖ Arbitration binding on noneconomic issues.
Permitted.
** Law declared invalid by state supreme court
†† If agreed to by parties in previous contract or by parties at negotiation.
Source: U.S. Department of Labor, Labor Management Services Administration, division of Public Employee Labor Relations, *Summary of Regulations for Public Sector Labor Relations* (Washington: Government Printing Office, 1975); Deborah T. Bond, "State Labor Legislation Enacted in 1975," *Monthly Labor Review*, vol. 99 (January 1976), pp. 17–29; Deborah T. Bond, "State Labor Legislation Enacted in 1976," *Monthly Labor Review*, vol. 100 (February 1977), pp. 25–38; Richard R. Nelson and David A. Levy, "State Labor Legislation Enacted in 1977," *Monthly Labor Review*, vol. 100 (December 1977), pp. 3–24.

TABLE 15-1B
Bargaining provisions for police (legislation, case law, and attorney general opinions)

State	Recognition	Bargaining rights	Impasse procedures	Right-to-strike
Alabama	N.P.	Prohibited	N.P.	Prohibited
Alaska	Exclusive	Mutual duty	M, A	Prohibited*
Arizona	N.P.	Permitted	N.P.	N.P.
Arkansas	N.P.	Permitted	N.P.	Prohibited
California	Permitted	Meet and confer	M†	Prohibited
Colorado	N.P.	Meet and confer	N.P.	N.P.
Connecticut	Exclusive	Mutual duty	FF, M, A†	Prohibited
Delaware	Exclusive	Mutal duty	A†,§	Prohibited
Florida	Exclusive	Mutual duty	M, FF, Leg.	Prohibited
Georgia	N.P.	N.P.	N.P.	N.P.
Hawaii	Exclusive	Mutual duty	M, FF, A†	Permitted‡
Idaho	N.P.	Permitted	N.P.	N.P.
Illinois	N.P.	Permitted	N.P.	N.P.

TABLE 15–1B (*continued*)

State	Recognition	Bargaining rights	Impasse procedures	Right-to-strike
Indiana**	N.P.	N.P.	N.P.	N.P.
Iowa	Exclusive	Mutual duty	M, FF, A	Prohibited
Kansas	Exclusive	Meet and confer	M, FF, Leg.	Prohibited
Kentucky	Permitted	Permitted	N.P.	Prohibited
Louisiana	Permitted	Permitted	N.P.	N.P.
Maine	Exclusive	Mutual duty	M, FF, A§	Prohibited
Maryland	N.P.	N.P.	N.P.	N.P.
Massachusetts	Exclusive	Mutual duty	M, FF, A	Prohibited
Michigan	Exclusive	Mutual duty	M, A.	Prohibited‖
Minnesota	Exclusive	Mutual duty	M, A	Prohibited#
Mississippi	N.P.	N.P.	N.P.	N.P.
Missouri	N.P.	N.P.	N.P.	N.P.
Montana	Exclusive	Mutual duty	M, FF, A†	Permitted
Nebraska	Exclusive	Mutual duty	M, FF, CIR	Prohibited
Nevada	Exclusive	Mutual duty	M, FF, BFF	Prohibited
New Hampshire	Exclusive	Mutual duty	M, FF	Unfair practice
New Jersey	Exclusive	Mutual duty	M, FF, A	Prohibited
New Mexico	N.P.	Permitted	N.P.	N.P.
New York	Exclusive	Mutual duty	M, FF, A	Prohibited
North Carolina	N.P.	Prohibited	N.P.	N.P.
North Dakota	N.P.	Permitted	M, FF	Prohibited
Ohio	N.P.	Permitted	N.P.	Prohibited
Oklahoma	Exclusive	Mutual duty	FF	Prohibited
Oregon	Exclusive	Mutual duty	M, FF, A	Prohibited
Pennsylvania	Exclusive	Mutual duty	A	N.P.
Rhode Island	Exclusive	Employer duty	A	Prohibited
South Carolina	Prohibited	Prohibited	N.P.	Prohibited
South Dakota	Exclusive	Mutual duty	BFF	Prohibited
Tennessee	N.P.	Prohibited	N.P.	Prohibited
Texas	Exclusive††	Mutual duty	M, A	Prohibited
Utah	N.P.	Permitted	N.P.	N.P.
Vermont	Exclusive	Mutual duty	M, FF, Leg.	Limited‡
Virginia	N.P.	Permitted	N.P.	Probihited
Washington	Exclusive	Mutual duty	M, FF, A	Prohibited
West Virginia	Permitted	Permitted	M,† FF†	Prohibited
Wisconsin	Exclusive	Mutual duty	M, A	Prohibited
Wyoming	Prohibited	Prohibited	N.P.	N.P.

Note: A = arbitration; BFF = binding fact-finding; CIR = court of industrial relations; FF = fact-finding; Leg. = legislative body action; M = mediation; and N.P. = no provision.

* Except for nonessential employees.

† If agreed to by parties.

‡ Not permitted where public health or safety is endangered.

§ Not binding on economic issues.

‖ Not enjoinable unless public health or safety is endangered.

Except where employer refuses to arbitrate or comply with award.

** Law declared invalid by Indiana Supreme Court.

†† If allowed by local referendum.

Source: U.S. Department of Labor, Labor Management Services Administration, division of Public Employee Labor Relations, *Summary of Regulations for Public Sector Labor Relations* (Washington: Government Printing Office, 1975); Deborah T. Bond, "State Labor Legislation Enacted in 1975," *Monthly Labor Review*, vol. 99 (January 1976), pp. 17–29; Deborah T. Bond, "State Labor Legislation Enacted in 1976," *Monthly Labor Review*, vol. 100 (February 1977), pp. 25–38; Richard R. Nelson and David A. Levy, "State Labor Legislation Enacted in 1977." *Monthly Labor Review*, vol. 100 (December 1977), pp. 3–24.

recognition for at least some employee groups. Where exclusive representation exists, most states forbid the negotiation of union shops, but many allow agency shop clauses. A range of bargaining rights exist including the right to submit proposals, conferences with employers, and full bargaining rights. In Alabama, North Carolina, South Carolina, Tennessee, Texas, Virginia, and Wyoming, at least some employee groups are prohibited from bargaining. Impasse procedures

TABLE 15–1C
Bargaining provisions for fire fighters (legislation, case law, and attorney general opinions)

State	Recognition	Bargaining rights	Impasse procedures	Right-to-strike
Alabama	Exclusive	Proposals	N.P.	Prohibited
Alaska	Exclusive	Mutual duty	M, A	Prohibited
Arizona	N.P.	Permitted	N.P.	N.P.
Arkansas	N.P.	Permitted	N.P.	Prohibited
California	Permitted	Meet and confer	M*	Prohibited
Colorado	N.P.	Meet and confer	N.P.	N.P.
Connecticut	Exclusive	Mutual duty	M, FF, A*	Prohibited
Delaware	Exclusive	Mutual duty	A*†	Prohibited
Florida	Exclusive	Mutual duty	FF, M, Leg.	Prohibited
Georgia	N.P.	N.P.	N.P.	N.P.
Hawaii	Exclusive	Mutual duty	M, FF, A	Permitted‡
Idaho	N.P.	Permitted	N.P.	N.P.
Illinois	N.P.	Permitted	N.P.	Prohibited
Indiana**	N.P.	N.P.	N.P.	Prohibited
Iowa	Exclusive	Mutual duty	M, FF, A or A§	Prohibited
Kansas	Exclusive	Meet and confer	M, FF, Leg.	Prohibited
Kentucky	Exclusive	Mutual duty	FF	Prohibited
Louisiana	Permitted	Permitted	N.P.	N.P.
Maine	Exclusive	Mutual duty	M, FF, A†	Prohibited
Maryland	N.P.	N.P.	N.P.	N.P.
Massachusetts	Exclusive	Mutual duty	M, FF, A	Prohibited
Michigan	Exclusive	Mutual duty	M, A	Prohibited‖
Minnesota	Exclusive	Mutual duty	M, A·	Prohibited#
Mississippi	N.P.	N.P.	N.P.	N.P.
Missouri	Exclusive	Meet and confer	N.P.	Prohibited
Montana	Exclusive	Mutual duty	M, FF, A*	Permitted
Nebraska	Exclusive	Mutual duty	M, FF, CIR	Prohibited
Nevada	Exclusive	Mutual duty	M, FF, BFF	Prohibited
New Hampshire	Exclusive	Permitted	N.P.	Permitted‡
New Jersey	Exclusive	Mutual duty	M, FF, A	Prohibited
New Mexico	N.P.	Permitted	N.P.	N.P.
New York	Exclusive	Mutual duty	M, FF, A	Prohibited
North Carolina	N.P.	Prohibited	N.P.	N.P.
North Dakota	N.P.	Permitted	M, FF	N.P.
Ohio	N.P.	Permitted	N.P.	Prohibited
Oklahoma	Exclusive	Mutual duty	FF	Prohibited
Oregon	Exclusive	Mutual duty	M, FF, A	Prohibited
Pennsylvania	Exclusive	Mutual duty	A	N.P.

TABLE 15-1C (*continued*)

State	Recognition	Bargaining rights	Impasse procedures	Right-to-strike
Rhode Island	Exclusive	Employee duty	A	Prohibited
South Carolina	Prohibited	Prohibited	N.P.	Prohibited
South Dakota	Exclusive	Mutual duty	BFF	Prohibited
Tennessee	N.P.	Prohibited	N.P.	Prohibited
Texas	Exclusive††	Mutual duty	M, A	Prohibited
Utah**	N.P.	N.P.	N.P.	N.P.
Vermont	Exclusive	Mutual duty	M, FF, Leg.	Limited‡
Virginia	N.P.	Permitted	N.P.	Prohibited
Washington	Exclusive	Mutual duty	M, FF, A	Prohibited
West Virginia	Permitted	Permitted	M,* FF*	Prohibited
Wisconsin	Exclusive	Mutual duty	M, A	Prohibited
Wyoming	Exclusive	Mutual duty	A	N.P.

Note: A = arbitration; BFF = Binding fact-finding; CIR = court of industrial relations; FF = fact-finding; Leg. = legislative body action; M = mediation; and N.P. = no provision.
   * If agreed to by parties.
   † Not binding on economic issues.
   ‡ Except where public health or safety is endangered.
   § In civil service cities or in cities over 10,000 parties may go directly to arbitration.
   ‖ Not enjoinable unless public health and safety endangered.
   # Unless employer refuses to arbitrate or implement award.
   ** Law declared invalid.
   †† If allowed by local referendem.
   Source: U.S. Department of Labor, Labor Management Services Administration, division of Public Employee Labor Relations, *Summary of Regulations for Public Sector Labor Relations* (Washington: Government Printing Office, 1975); Deborah T. Bond, "State Labor Legislation Enacted in 1975," *Monthly Labor Review*, vol. 99 (January 1976), pp. 17–29; Deborah T. Bond, "State Labor Legislation Enacted in 1976," *Monthly Labor Review*, vol. 100 (February 1977), pp. 25–38; Richard R. Nelson and David A. Levy, "State Labor Legislation Enacted in 1977," *Monthly Labor Review*, vol. 100 (December 1977), pp. 3–24.

TABLE 15-1D
Bargaining provisions for state employees (legislation, case law, and attorney general opinions)

State	Recognition	Bargaining rights	Impasse procedures	Right-to-strike
Alabama	N.P.	Prohibited	N.P.	Prohibited
Alaska	Exclusive	Mutual duty	M	Permitted*
Arizona	N.P.	Permitted	N.P.	N.P.
Arkansas	N.P.	Permitted	N.P.	Prohibited
California	Exclusive	Meet and confer	M†	Prohibited
Colorado	N.P.	Meet and confer	N.P.	N.P.
Connecticut	Exclusive	Mutual duty	M, FF	Prohibited
Delaware	Exclusive	Mutual duty	A†	Prohibited
Florida	Exclusive	Mutual duty	M, FF, Leg.	Prohibited
Georgia	N.P.	N.P.	N.P.	Prohibited
Hawaii	Exclusive	Mutual duty	M, FF, A†	Permitted‡
Idaho	N.P.	N.P.	N.P.	N.P.
Illinois	Exclusive	Mutual duty	N.P.	Prohibited
Indiana‡‡	N.P.	N.P.	N.P.	Prohibited
Iowa	Exclusive	Mutual duty	M, FF, A	Prohibited

TABLE 15-1D *(continued)*

State	Recognition	Bargaining rights	Impasse procedures	Right-to-strike
Kansas	Exclusive	Mutual duty	M, FF	Prohibited
Kentucky	N.P.	Meet and confer	N.P.	Prohibited
Louisiana	Permitted	Permitted	N.P.	N.P.
Maine	Exclusive	Mutual duty	M, FF, A§	Prohibited
Maryland	N.P.	N.P.	N.P.	N.P.
Massachusetts	Exclusive	Mutual duty	M, FF	Prohibited
Michigan	Permitted	Permitted	M, FF	Prohibited
Minnesota	Exclusive	Mutual duty	M, A	Permitted‖
Mississippi	N.P.	N.P.	N.P.	N.P.
Missouri	Exclusive	Meet and confer	N.P.	Prohibited
Montana	Exclusive	Mutual duty	M, FF, A†	Permitted
Nebraska	Exclusive	Mutual duty	M, FF, CIR	Prohibited
Nevada	N.P.	N.P.	N.P.	N.P.
New Hampshire	Exclusive	Mutual duty	M,† FF†	Prohibited#
New Jersey	Exclusive	Mutual duty	M, FF, A†	Prohibited
New Mexico	Exclusive	Determined by employer	FF,** A**	Prohibited
New York	Exclusive	Mutual duty	M, FF, Leg.	Prohibited
North Carolina	N.P.	Prohibited	N.P.	N.P.
North Dakota	N.P.	Permitted	M, FF	Prohibited
Ohio	N.P.	Proposals	N.P.	Prohibited
Oklahoma	N.P.	N.P.	N.P.	Prohibited
Oregon	Exclusive	Mutual duty	M, FF, A	Permitted††
Pennsylvania	Exclusive	Mutual duty	FF, A†	Permitted‡
Rhode Island	Exclusive	Employer duty	M, FF, A§	Prohibited
South Carolina	Prohibited	Prohibited	N.P.	Prohibited
South Dakota	Exclusive	Mutual duty	BFF	Prohibited
Tennessee	N.P.	N.P.	N.P.	Prohibited
Texas	Prohibited	Prohibited	N.P.	Prohibited
Utah	N.P.	Proposals	N.P.	Prohibited
Vermont	Exclusive	Mutual duty	M, FF, Leg.	Prohibited
Virginia	N.P.	N.P.	N.P.	Prohibited
Washington	Exclusive	Mutual duty	M, A	Prohibited
West Virginia	Permitted	Permitted	M,† FF†	Prohibited
Wisconsin	Exclusive	Mutual duty	M, FF	Prohibited
Wyoming	Prohibited	Prohibited	N.P.	N.P.

Note: A = arbitration; BFF = binding fact-finding; CIR = court of industrial relations; FF = fact-finding; Leg. = legislative body action; M = mediation; and N.P. = no provision.

* For nonessential employees.
† By agreement of parties.
‡ Except if present danger to public health and safety.
§ Noneconomic issues.
‖ Where employer either refuses to arbitrate or to implement an award.
But not enjoinable unless danger to public health and safety.
** Only if approved by state personnel board.
†† Where arbitration is not provided.
‡‡ Law declared invalid by Indiana Supreme Court.

Source: U.S. Department of Labor, Labor Management Services Administration, division of Public Employee Labor Relations, *Summary of Regulations for Public Sector Labor Relations* (Washington: Government Printing Office, 1975); Deborah T. Bond, "State Labor Legislation Enacted in 1975," *Monthly Labor Review*, vol. 99 (January 1976), pp. 17–29; Deborah T. Bond, "State Labor Legislation Enacted in 1976," *Monthly Labor Review*, vol. 100 (February 1977), pp. 25–38; Richard R. Nelson and David A. Levy, "State Labor Legislation Enacted in 1977," *Monthly Labor Review*, vol. 100 (December 1977), pp. 3–24.

range from none to binding arbitration. Where arbitration is included, it is more often applied to police and firefighters than other occupations. Often arbitration can be invoked only through mutual agreement of the parties, and some laws limit arbitration to noneconomic issues, reserving pay questions to a legislative body. Finally, most states prohibit public employees from striking and have injunction or penalty provisions if they occur. However, some right to strike is granted certain public employees in Alaska, Hawaii, Minnesota, Montana, Oregon, Pennsylvania, and Vermont in certain situations.

Almost all states with public sector legislation grant exclusive recognition to a majority union, and most states prohibit strikes among public employees. Prohibiting strikes and enforcing the prohibition are two different things, however. There is a long enough history of

TABLE 15–1E

Bargaining provision for local employees (legislation, case law, and attorney general opinions)

State	Recognition	Bargaining rights	Impasse procedures	Right-to-strike
Alabama	N.P.	Prohibited	N.P.	Prohibited
Alaska	Exclusive	Mutual duty	M, A	Permitted†
Arizona	N.P.	Permitted	N.P.	N.P.
Arkansas	N.P.	Permitted	N.P.	Prohibited
California	Permitted	Meet and confer	M*	Prohibited
Colorado	N.P.	Meet and confer	N.P.	N.P.
Connecticut	Exclusive	Mutual duty	M, FF, A	Prohibited
Delaware	Exclusive	Mutual duty	A	Prohibited
Florida	Exclusive	Mutual duty	M, FF, Leg.	Prohibited
Georgia	N.P.	N.P.	N.P.	N.P.
Hawaii	Exclusive	Mutual duty	M, FF, A*	Permitted
Idaho	N.P.	Permitted	N.P.	N.P.
Illinois	N.P.	Permitted	N.P.	Prohibited
Indiana#	N.P.	N.P.	N.P.	Prohibited
Iowa	Exclusive	Mutual duty	M, FF, A	Prohibited
Kansas	Exclusive	Meet and confer	M, FF, Leg.	Prohibited
Kentucky	N.P.	Meet and confer	N.P.	Prohibited
Louisiana	Permitted	Permitted	N.P.	N.P.
Maine	Exclusive	Mutual duty	M, FF, A‡	Prohibited
Maryland	N.P.	N.P.**	N.P.	N.P.
Massachusetts	Exclusive	Mutual duty	M, FF	Prohibited
Michigan	Exclusive	Mutual duty	M, FF	Prohibited§
Minnesota	Exclusive	Mutual duty	M, A	Prohibited
Mississippi	N.P.	N.P.	N.P.	N.P.
Missouri	Exclusive	Meet and confer	N.P.	Prohibited
Montana	Exclusive	Mutual duty	M, FF, A*	Permitted
Nebraska	Exclusive	Mutual duty	M, FF, CIR	Prohibited
Nevada	Exclusive	Mutual duty	M, FF, BFF	Prohibited
New Hampshire	Permitted	Permitted	N.P.	N.P.§
New Jersey	Exclusive	Mutual duty	M, FF, A*	Prohibited
New Mexico	N.P.	Permitted	N.P.	N.P.
New York	Exclusive	Mutual duty	M, FF, Leg.	Prohibited

TABLE 15–1E *(continued)*

State	Recognition	Bargaining rights	Impasse procedures	Right-to-strike
North Carolina	N.P.	Prohibited	N.P.	N.P.
North Dakota	N.P.	Permitted	M, FF	Prohibited
Ohio	N.P.	Permitted	N.P.	Prohibited
Oklahoma	Exclusive	Mutual duty	FF	Prohibited
Oregon	Exclusive	Mutual duty	M, FF, A*	Permitted†
Pennsylvania	Exclusive	Mutual duty	FF, A*	Permitted†
Rhode Island	Exclusive	Mutual duty	M, A‡	Prohibited
South Carolina	Prohibited	Prohibited	N.P.	Prohibited
South Dakota	Exclusive	Mutual duty	M, FF	Prohibited
Tennessee	N.P.	Prohibited	N.P.	Prohibited
Texas	Prohibited	Prohibited	N.P.	Prohibited
Utah	N.P.	Permitted	N.P.	N.P.
Vermont	Exclusive	Mutual duty	M, FF, Leg.	Permitted†
Virginia	N.P.	Permitted	N.P.	Prohibited
Washington	Exclusive	Mutual duty	M, FF, A	Prohibited
West Virginia	Permitted	Permitted	M,* FF*	Prohibited
Wisconsin	Exclusive	Mutual duty	M, FF	Prohibited‖
Wyoming	Prohibited	Prohibited	N.P.	N.P.

Note: A = arbitration; BFF = binding fact-finding; CIR = court of industrial relations; FF = fact-finding; Leg. = legislative body action; M = mediation; and N.P. = no provision.
* If agreed to by parties.
† Unless danger to public health and safety exists.
‡ Noneconomic issues.
§ But not enjoinable unless danger to public health and safety exists.
‖ If employer refuses to arbitrate or implement an award.
Law declared invalid by Indiana Supreme Court.
** Except permitted to city of Baltimore.
Source: U.S. Department of Labor, Labor Management Services Administration, division of Public Employee Labor Relations, *Summary of Regulations for Public Sector Labor Relations* (Washington: Government Printing Office, 1975); Deborah T. Bond, "State Labor Legislation Enacted in 1975," *Monthly Labor Review*, vol. 99 (January 1976), pp. 17–29; Deborah T. Bond. "State Labor Legislation Enacted in 1976," *Monthly Labor Review*, vol. 100 (February 1977), pp. 25–38; Richard R. Nelson and David A. Levy, "State Labor Legislation Enacted in 1977," *Monthly Labor Review*, vol. 100 (December 1977), pp. 3–24.

public employee strikes to show that legally permissible steps to end strikes are not taken in most cases, and statutorily mandated reprisals, such as discharges, are almost never invoked. While the laws generally prohibit public employee strikes, they do occur. Table 15–2 gives you some idea of the incidence of recent strike activity in the public sector.

Table 15–2 shows that the largest number of strikes have occurred at the local level involving municipal or school district employees. With the exception of 1970 and 1975, more school employees were involved in strikes than any other jurisdictional level. With the exception of 1975, more days were lost by school employees to strikes. And, with the exception of 1973, the duration of strikes was longest for school disputes. One reason for the level and duration of school strikes is that they cost both employers and employees essentially nothing.

TABLE 15–2
Work stoppages in the public sector, 1970–1975

Employer and year	Number	Mean duration (days)	Employees involved (1,000)	Number of employee days lost (1,000)
Federal				
1970	3	NA	155.8	648.3
1971	2	6.3	1.0	8.1
1972	0	—	—	—
1973	1	12.0	0.5	4.6
1974	2	2.9	0.5	1.4
1975	0	—	—	—
State				
1970	23	NA	8.8	44.6
1971	23	7.6	14.5	81.8
1972	40	10.5	27.4	273.7
1973	29	22.4	12.3	133.0
1974	34	4.7	24.7	86.4
1975	32	5.4	66.6	300.5
County				
1970	45	NA	16.3	87.7
1971	29	7.0	6.7	30.1
1972	30	8.6	8.8	50.3
1973	40	9.3	13.4	89.2
1974	32	8.7	14.6	96.5
1975	44	7.5	15.0	78.8
City				
1970	166	NA	29.0	221.9
1971	115	5.9	47.4	205.0
1972	128	11.3	19.9	135.6
1973	95	8.6	17.2	102.8
1974	116	9.0	36.5	227.7
1975	252	9.9	192.3	1,419.4
School district*				
1970	174	NA	123.5	1,020.5
1971	159	10.3	82.9	576.4
1972	171	13.7	85.6	796.0
1973	210	19.1	149.2	1,920.4
1974	200	17.1	84.3	992.1
1975	150	12.9	44.7	405.7

Note: NA = not available.
* 1974–75 school district figures also include other special districts.
  Source: U.S. Bureau of Labor Statistics, *Analysis of Work Stoppages* (Washington: Government Printing Office, Annual).

Legislatures establish school years of certain lengths. If a strike disrupts the first three weeks of school, the year is simply extended three weeks. The only cost to the school or the teachers is the delay in school aid receipts and wages. Unless the strike lasts longer than the summer recess available to make up the lost days, there is little incentive to settle.

Impasse procedures

There are major differences among the states and across occupations when the question of impasse resolution is raised. Since public employees are not generally permitted to strike, some other mechanism must usually be created if bargaining power is to have some overall equivalency. When we look at impasse resolution in the public sector, we will see a greater use of fact-finding and interest arbitration (including some innovative methods applied particularly to public sector cases) than we find in the private sector. We will also see that where distinctions among occupations are made in state laws, the more stringent impasse procedures like arbitration are more often applied to public safety occupations such as police and fire.

This application is made not only to minimize the likelihood of public safety work stoppages, but is also a recognition of the relative political expertise and maturity of public safety unions, particularly those representing the firefighters. For example, in Wyoming public employees are denied representation rights, except for firefighters, since the state courts have interpreted legislation granting bargaining to firefighters as excluding others through its silence on their occupations. But, the firefighter law requires the mutual duty to bargain where recognition is gained through majority status and also mandates arbitration of unresolved contract issues. Thus, firefighter bargaining power is relatively high while other public employees are forbidden to bargain.

With this summary of state laws in the background, we turn to an examination of the evolution and present position of federal public employee labor policies.

FEDERAL POLICY

Federal policy applies to most of the employees in the executive branch of the federal government. To an extent, the employees are at the mercy of their employer from a "rules of the game" standpoint since the policies governing public sector labor relations have been promulgated through a series of executive orders rather than through legislation. The "at their mercy" term is probably too strong to use here though, since many of the provisions are close to other public sector policies and laws and are to be applied uniformly across agencies.

While federal labor policies date back to President Van Buren's administration, we will begin our look with the promulgation of Executive Order 10988 in 1962 by President Kennedy. While this order was the first set of regulations for federal employee labor relations, there had been attempts to pass legislation for several years. The order undercut and largely obviated the need for the legislation while simultaneously establishing ground rules for executive department labor relations by top management itself.

Executive Order 10988

The executive order established a variety of safeguards for labor organizations and specified negotiation rights. As in the private sector, federal employers were forbidden from restraining or interfering with organizing or other lawful union activity including testimony before Congress about employment matters. Employee organizations could be recognized if they were not discriminatory, did not advocate the overthrow of the government, and did not assert the right to strike.

Three levels of recognition were specified. First, an employee organization representing a majority of employees in a unit was entitled to exclusive representation and could negotiate written agreements with the agency, the contents of which were subject to approval by higher-level management. Since salaries are fixed through the civil service classification system, negotiations dealt with noneconomic matters. Second, groups representing 10 percent or more of the employees in units where no exclusive representative had been designated were entitled to formal recognition. Formal recognition entitled a labor organization to be consulted on personnel policies and to raise work-related issues. No power to negotiate agreements was conferred on groups holding formal recognition. Third, informal recognition was to be accorded to any group representing employees regardless of whether or not formal or exclusive recognition had been granted to another organization. These organizations were entitled to make their views on personnel matters known, but management was under no obligation to consult with them on proposed personnel changes.

The order also provided that contracts could contain grievance procedures terminating in arbitration. But the arbitral opinion was only to be advisory in nature, and the grievance would ultimately be decided by an agency head.

Unionization was allowed for most employees. Exceptions included managers and nonroutine personnel workers. Bargaining units could not include professionals and nonprofessionals without the consent of the former. Persons who formally evaluated another's work could not be included in the same unit with the evaluatee.

Over time several difficulties became apparent in the implementation of the executive order. First, the informal and formal recognition aspects contributed to fractionalizing bargaining units. Second, a great deal of discretion was still held by management as to how grievances would be resolved. And, third, economics were excluded from the bargaining process. Despite these drawbacks, the numbers of federal employees unionized grew from 897,000 in 1964 to 1,351,000 in 1968.[2]

As these difficulties became apparent, President Johnson appointed a review committee headed by Secretary of Labor Willard Wirtz to recommend changes in federal labor relations. Some of these recommendations were incorporated in Executive Order 11491 signed by President Nixon on October 29, 1969. This order was later amended by Executive Orders 11616 in 1971 and 11838 in 1975.[3]

Executive Order 11491 as amended

The major changes incorporated in these orders related to the creation of agencies and processes for administering the collective bargaining process and the modification of the 10988 recognition features.

Administration

A federal Labor Relations Council consisting of the chairman of the Civil Service Commission, the secretary of labor, the director of the Office of Management and Budget and other federal appointees was established to hear appeals from decisions and prescribe regulations and policies. A Federal Services Impasses Panel consisting of three appointees was established to act on negotiation impasses. An assistant secretary of labor for labor-management relations was designated. The responsibilities of the office include ruling on the appropriateness of bargaining units, supervising representation elections, deciding on the eligibility of labor organizations to represent federal employees, investigating and deciding unfair labor practice complaints, and deciding whether a grievance is arbitrable.

Recognition

The new executive order dispensed with formal and informal status and created machinery to determine majority status within a unit. Individual employees and interest groups such as veterans' organizations, professional, religious, fraternal, or other associations maintained their consultation rights, but nonmajority labor organizations lost them.

Labor organizations representing substantial numbers of employees nationally in an agency were entitled to national consultation where neither they nor another labor organization exclusively represented the agency's employees.

---

[2] U.S. Bureau of Labor Statistics, *Handbook of Labor Statistics* (Washington: Government Printing Office, 1975 and 1977).

[3] Murray B. Nesbitt, *Labor Relations in the Federal Government Service* (Washington: Bureau of National Affairs, 1976), pp. 130–33.

Agreements

The executive order provides that the parties may *meet and confer* about personnel practices and working conditions, and *may* conclude an agreement. This agreement cannot refer to staffing levels, pay, agency mission, budget, or a variety of other matters. If an agreement is concluded, it still must be approved by the head of the agency before becoming effective.

Other features of the order, as amended, provide for the inclusion of a grievance procedure in an agreement with arbitration as a last step and forbids the inclusion of union shop, agency shop, or maintenance of membership clauses.

Disputes and impasses

In case the parties cannot conclude an agreement, the FMCS can be asked to mediate. If mediation fails, the Federal Services Impasses Panel (FSIP) may recommend a settlement or approve the use of interest arbitration.

Unfair labor practices

The executive order forbids a number of unfair labor practices. These are shown in Figure 15–1.

U.S. Postal Service

As you studied Table 15–2, which reported public sector work stoppages, you probably noticed that strike activity in the federal sector has never come close to approaching the 1970 level. Postal workers walked off their jobs during the frenetic spring of 1970 just as students were closing down campuses over the invasion of Cambodia. While there has been no subsequent major postal disruption, postal workers are no longer covered by the executive orders since the postal service was established as a government corporation. Postal labor relations are now within NLRB jurisdiction. As federal employees they still are not permitted to strike, but they can collectively bargain on issues such as pay, staffing levels, and so on that are prohibited to civil service employees.

Overview

Federal sector employees do not generally have bargaining rights equal to those of other public sector employees. First, there is no provision for bargaining on economic matters. Their only recourse is

FIGURE 15–1
Unfair labor practices under Executive Order 11491

Sec. 19. *Unfair labor practices.*
a. Agency management shall not—
  1. Interfere with, restrain, or coerce an employee in the exercise of the rights assured by this order;
  2. Encourage or discourage membership in a labor organization by discrimination in regard to hiring, tenure, promotion, or other conditions of employment;
  3. Sponsor, control, or otherwise assist a labor organization, except that an agency may furnish customary and routine services and facilities under section 23 of this order when consistent with the best interests of the agency, its employees, and the organization, and when the services and facilities are furnished, if requested, on an impartial basis to organizations having equivalent status;
  4. Discipline or otherwise discriminate against an employee because he has filed a complaint or given testimony under this order;
  5. Refuse to accord appropriate recognition to a labor organization qualified for such recognition; or
  6. Refuse to consult, confer, or negotiate with a labor organization as required by this order.
b. A labor organization shall not—
  1. Interfere with, restrain, or coerce an employee in the exercise of his rights assured by this order;
  2. Attempt to induce agency management to coerce an employee in the exercise of his rights under this order;
  3. Coerce, attempt to coerce, or discipline, fine, or take other economic sanction against a member of the organization as punishment or reprisal for, or for the purpose of hindering or impeding his work performance, his productivity, or the discharge of his duties owed as an officer or employee of the United States;
  4. Call or engage in a strike, work stoppage, or slowdown; picket an agency in a labor-management dispute; or condone any such activity by failing to take affirmative action to prevent or stop it;
  5. Discriminate against an employee with regard to the terms or conditions of membership because of race, color, creed, sex, age, or national origin; or
  6. Refuse to consult, confer, or negotiate with an agency as required by this order.
c. A labor organization which is accorded exclusive recognition shall not deny membership to any employee in the appropriate unit except for failure to meet reasonable occupational standards uniformly required for admission, or for failure to tender initiation fees and dues uniformly required as a condition of acquiring and retaining membership. This paragraph does not preclude a labor organization from enforcing discipline in accordance with procedures under its constitution or by-laws which conform to the requirements of this order.
d. Issues which can properly be raised under an appeals procedure may not be raised under this section. Issues which can be raised under a grievance procedure may, in the discretion of the aggrieved party, be raised under that procedure or the complaint procedure under this section, but not under both procedures. Appeals or grievance decisions shall not be construed as unfair labor practice decisions under this order nor as precedent for such decisions. All complaints under this section that cannot be resolved by the parties shall be filed with the assistant secretary.

through the order's provision allowing representatives of employee organizations to testify and make proposals. Second, the meet and confer provisions which lead to a permissive bargaining relationship even where employees have an exclusive representative are less liberal than most states' mutual duty bargaining requirements. Third, the lack of a neutral dispute settlement procedure leaves the ultimate resolution of many issues to the decision of an agency chief. And, fourth, there is little available in terms of union security provisions given the proscription of agency and union shops even where exclusive representation exists.

When compared with the private sector, the federal regulations have moved toward allowing conduct which is close to bargaining. Impasse settlement still requires that the agency head agree with the conclusions. This substantially tips the scales toward management since an appointed executive branch government manager has to decide what rights management will relinquish.

PUBLIC EMPLOYEE UNIONS

Now that we have examined the laws and regulations that govern public sector labor relations, we need to look at the unions that represent government employees. Not surprisingly, public sector unions parallel those in the private sector in terms of their constituencies. And as you might suspect, several unions whose memberships are concentrated in the private sector also represent employees in the public sector.

In the public sector there are two major, exclusively public, industrial-type unions. One, the American Federation of State, County, and Municipal Employees, AFL–CIO (AFSCME) represents state and local unit employees across occupations. Another large industrial-type union, the American Federation of Government Employees, AFL–CIO (AFGE) represents federal employees.

Some public employees are represented by craft-type organizations, either exclusively for public sector employees such as the International Association of Fire Fighters (IAFF) or one of the AFL–CIO unions representing skilled tradespersons working for governmental agencies. The government oriented craft unions and associations are older but vary considerably in their original adoption of traditional trade union bargaining approaches. For example, some are called associations and did not originally engage in collective bargaining (for example, the National Education Association as compared to the American Federation of Teachers, AFL–CIO).

In his study on public employee unions, Stieber distinguishes between five classifications of nonfederal public sector organizations: all-public unions, mixed public and private sector unions, state and local employee associations, and unions and associations representing uniformed protective services.[4] The major mixed unions are the ser-

---

[4] Jack Stieber, *Public Employee Unionism* (Washington: Brookings Institution, 1973).

vice employees (SEIU, widely involved now in health care organizations which we explore in the next chapter), and the Teamsters. From the uniformed services, the IAFF and the Fraternal Order of Police (FOP) are both among the largest with the IAFF being more openly a labor organization. The largest of the associations is the California State Employees Association. Associations continue to be most prevalent where laws forbid bargaining but where legislative lobbying representing numerical strength is important. Professional associations are usually organized on an occupational basis and have only recently begun to bargain. At the time of his research, Stieber estimated that about 60 percent of all public employees in municipalities of over 10,000 population were organized with the figure approaching 100 percent for larger cities.[5] Among these cities, representation varies by occupation or function with firefighters having the greatest representation and public welfare workers the least. Table 15–3 shows representation as of 1968.

TABLE 15–3
Percent of municipal employees represented in various functions, by size of city, 1968

| | | City population, in thousands | | | | | |
| | | Over 500* | 250– 500 | 100– 250 | 50– 100 | 25– 50 | 10– 25 |
Function	All cities*						
Police protection	67(73)	79(87)	82	63	69	58	38
Fire protection	80(82)	95(97)	93	79	80	71	43
Public works	49(55)	66(77)	53	39	52	45	26
Public utilities	36(55)	39(70)	61	43	33	29	16
Public health and hospitals	38(57)	46(71)	38	48	23	23	12
Noninstructional education	40(61)	41(75)	72	36	60	29	28
Parks and recreation	38(46)	47(66)	57	33	38	28	14
Public welfare	31(69)	31(77)	50	25	38	26	4
All others	36(53)	47(73)	42	35	36	22	11
All functions . .	50(61)	59(77)	63	·47	53	42	25

* Percentages in parentheses include New York City; it is excluded from principal percentages because its size distorts averages.
Source: Jack Stieber, *Public Employee Unionism* (Washington: Brookings Institution, 1973), p. 228.

Because of the variety of unions and associations involved and the differences in dates when organization took place, we frequently find employers bargaining with several unions. Bargaining units are generally not as inclusive as we would find in industry, but more akin to the building trades in construction. In a given geographical area, pub-

---

[5] Ibid., p. 13.

lic employees also may bargain with a variety of statutory agencies. For example, a large city may have a local government, a school board, a transit authority, a sewer district, a public utility, and so forth; all with autonomous powers to bargain, levy taxes, and provide specific services. Within each of these, separate bargaining units may exist. For example, a school board may bargain with an AFT local representing teachers, a SEIU local representing custodians, an AFSCME local representing clericals, and a Teamsters local representing bus drivers. This situation creates the possibility for union whipsawing of an unsophisticated management, but ultimately the costs may result in requests for higher taxes bringing either legislative or taxpayer referendums or both into play. This fact identifies a critical difference between public and private sector bargaining, and that is that public sector bargaining is inherently a multilateral relationship.

PUBLIC SECTOR BARGAINING PROCESSES

Management in most public sector bargaining consists of two levels: appointed civil service officials such as city managers, school superintendents, and the like; and elected officials such as mayors, city councils, school boards, and so on. While appointed managers may have a direct responsibility for negotiations, pressure may be applied on them to modify positions toward the union by elected officials. (Obviously, these officials may also try to take a more intransigent position than appointed officials in other labor-management situations.) Recalling our earlier look at bargaining processes in Chapter 10, it might be reasonable to expect a necessity for more intraorganizational bargaining among management parties in public sector negotiations.

Kochan has proposed and tested a model of multilateral collective bargaining in the public sector.[6] Multilateral bargaining occurs where more than two groups with particular interests engage in the process simultaneously. In his model, he suggests that multilateral bargaining would be more likely to occur where there is internal conflict among management bargainers, where the union is politically active and involved, and where it attempts to use a variety of impasse procedures. His data, collected from 228 firefighter negotiations conducted in various cities across the nation, found four major aspects related to the incidence of multilateral bargaining (defined as the degree to which (1) city officials took actions outside the negotiations, (2) union representatives discussed contract terms with management members who were

[6] Thomas A. Kochan, "A Theory of Multilateral Collective Bargaining in City Governments," *Industrial and Labor Relations Review*, vol. 27 (July 1974), pp. 525–42.

not on the bargaining team, (3) community interest group involvement, (4) city officials did not implement the agreement, and (5) mediation attempts were made by elected officials). These were (in order of importance): (1) conflict among city officials in general, (2) union political pressure tactics, (3) union impasse pressure tactics, and (4) management commitment to collective bargaining.

Among environmental or situational variables, the age of the bargaining relationship was positively related to multilateral bargaining; but statutory differences in comprehensiveness, and the experience of management negotiators had virtually no effect.

Kochan concluded his study by suggesting that as public sector bargaining matures it will become less, rather than more, like private sector labor relations. The opportunities for a sophisticated union to use available tactics would move bargaining toward rather than away from a multilateral stance. Unions may exercise political power and be more able to bring community interest or public pressure to bear in public rather than private sector bargaining. Thus, he suggests we will see a divergence rather than a convergence between the two.

Since multilateral bargaining appears to be emerging rather than retreating and since it appears to result from conflict within management or purposeful union tactics, one might ask what its effectiveness is for positive bargaining outcomes for the union? Kochan and Wheeler followed this issue in a later study.[7] Using the degree to which a settlement duplicated the IAFF's national model contract as a measure of union bargaining outcomes, they examined environmental characteristics, union tactics away from the bargaining table, management characteristics, and degree of multilateral bargaining to see what their effects were on bargaining outcomes. Their results suggest that six variables are significantly related to positive union outcomes: (1) compulsory arbitration at impasse, (2) fact-finding at impasse, (3) comprehensiveness of the states' bargaining law, (4) the decision-making power of management's negotiator, (5) city council-negotiator goal incompatibility, and (6) elected official intervention at impasse. Thus, three of the variables (the most powerful) reflect the legal environment, two reflect management characteristics, and the last is a multilateral bargaining component. Interestingly, union pressure tactics were not significantly related to outcomes.

Since these legal environment characteristics appear to be so important in influencing public sector outcomes, we should explore what variables correlate with comprehensive legislation which includes impasse procedures. Using some of the same types of data included in

---

[7] Thomas A. Kochan and Hoyt N. Wheeler, "Municipal Collective Bargaining: A Model and Analysis of Bargaining Outcomes," *Industrial and Labor Relations Review*, vol. 29 (October 1975), pp. 46–66.

Tables 15–1A through 15–1E as a measure of comprehensiveness, Kochan identified several state environmental characteristics associated with the ultimate shape of the public sector law.[8] Generally speaking, he found more comprehensive legislation in states where per capita budget expenditures were higher, where incomes of its citizens were increasing more rapidly, and where legislation of an innovative nature is passed earlier than in other states. To a certain extent then, states with a greater ability to pay (higher expenditures, more rapidly growing income) are more likely to pass comprehensive bargaining laws. These laws and the ability to pay characteristics may go hand in hand in influencing bargaining outcomes.

Figure 15–2 represents the relationship between the environment, the bargainers, the process, and outcomes as Kochan and Wheeler conceive it. While their analysis examines the effects of laws on out-

FIGURE 15–2
The general conceptual framework

Source: Thomas A. Kochan and Hoyt N. Wheeler, "Municipal Collective Bargaining: A Model and Analysis of Bargaining Outcomes," *Industrial and Labor Relations Review*, vol. 29 (October 1975), p. 51.

comes, the outcomes may also be associated with legal aspects affecting the bargaining power of the parties. For example, Gerhart suggests that comprehensive state laws reduce the costs to management for recognizing a union and may legally decrease their ability to use tactics like refusing to bargain, rejecting a contract, and so forth.[9] Thus, the environmental characteristics affect not only the makeup of the bargaining teams and their interrelationships, but affect the bargaining power and tactics through enabling or prohibiting legislation.

Gerhart extended Kochan and Wheeler's analysis to point out that statutory law often lags public opinion. The presumption here is that voters elect legislators who reflect current public opinion and who will *subsequently* enact laws reflecting this opinion. Thus, statutes may follow changes in public sentiment by at least the period of time nec-

---

[8] Thomas A. Kochan, "Correlates of State Public Employee Bargaining Laws," *Industrial Relations*, vol. 12 (October 1973), pp. 322–37.

[9] Paul F. Gerhart, "Determinants of Bargaining in Local Government Labor Negotiations," *Industrial and Labor Relations Review*, vol. 29 (April 1976), pp. 331–32.

essary to change incumbents' minds or replace them with a more opinion-reflective group.[10]

Using legislation as a lagged variable, Gerhart analyzed a number of environmental and bargaining relationship variables and their effects on favorable bargaining outcomes to the union. On the basis of his results, he concluded that outcomes were more favorable where the bargaining took place in a moderate-size urban area (rather than large or rural), where only certain functions were involved (for example, sewer workers), where there was no statutory penalty for striking, where the union was affiliated with a public sector international, where strike activity in the state was above average, and where public opinion had led to or favored a bargaining law.[11] These results suggest that a favorable public opinion environment, coupled with a public employee oriented union, and lower management sophistication found in moderate-sized areas led to better union outcomes.

Unfortunately, we do not know the direct effect, at this point, of economic conditions and the state of the labor market on bargaining outcomes, but scattered evidence from beleaguered areas, such as New York City, suggests that contract favorability to the union is lessened by economic hardship.

Another area that is of vital importance to a study of bargaining outcomes is the question of impasse procedures. These are usually markedly different in the public sector, with most states and the federal government prohibiting strikes.

IMPASSE PROCEDURES

As was noted in our examination of state laws, there is a general prohibition on strikes for public sector employees among the states. Because of this general prohibition, there are several outcomes that can occur when an impasse is reached in the public sector. Among them are the following: Management may continue the past contract, mediation may occur, the employees may go out on an illegal strike or have a "sickout," fact-finding may take place, arbitration of differences remaining may take place, or a legislative body will mandate an agreement. We will focus primarily on fact-finding and arbitration of contract issues here since these are much more prevalent in the public than in the private sector. In the arbitration area, several variants have been developed for various reasons which we will discuss later. As you probably noted earlier, impasse procedures are more often legislatively prescribed for public safety employees and local unit em-

---

[10] Ibid., pp. 348–49.
[11] Ibid., p. 349.

ployees, with arbitration seldom being applied to other than the uniformed services (police and fire).

Fact-finding

In the United States, fact-finding has its roots in the private sector through the establishment of fact-finding boards in the Taft-Hartley Act and the emergency board procedures in the Railway Labor Act. However, its use is presently far more prevalent in the public rather than the private sector.

McKelvey distinguishes the role of the public sector fact finder from that of the private sector fact finder. Where an impasse exists, in the private sector, the fact finder's role is to establish a reasonable position for a settlement by objectively studying the context and issues and preparing a report of conclusions based on the setting. A primary end result sought by this process is the publication of the disputed issues and recommended settlements. In this way, public opinion may be galvanized to pressure a settlement on this "factual" conclusion. Fact-finding may also lead to economizing a legislature's time when it expects to impose a solution.[12]

The role of providing facts for the legislature is usually not appropriate in the public sector since the legislators are frequently a party to the dispute (school boards, city councils, and so on). Here, the role of the fact finder is frequently to educate the public as to what the costs of a reasonable settlement might be. McKelvey suggests that this and other roles are commonly adopted. For example, fact-finding may be sought where the union and management fear public opinion if they bargain a settlement when a fact finder would probably recommend a similar conclusion. The "facts" may seem reasonable coming from a neutral while a similar bargained settlement may seem collusive.[13]

Statutory role of the fact finder

Wisconsin was one of the first states to pass a comprehensive fact-finding statute. Stern has reported on aspects related to the application and success of this law. Under this law, fact-finding may be initiated by either party if an impasse exists or the other party refuses to bargain. The Wisconsin Employee Relations Board investigates the request and attempts to mediate. If the mediation fails, a neutral or neutral board is appointed to examine the evidence and make recommendations for a settlement. The recommendation is sent to the parties and

---

[12] Jean T. McKelvey, "Fact-Finding in Public Employment Disputes: Promise or Illusion," *Industrial and Labor Relations Review*, vol. 22 (July 1969), pp. 528–30.

[13] Ibid., pp. 530–31.

the WERB, which publicizes it. While the parties may have asked for fact-finding, they are under no obligation to accept the report's recommendation.[14]

In his study Stern found that fact-finding cases in Wisconsin took from between three months to two years from the initial request until a recommendation was issued. Fact finders usually had to fit cases into their schedules since they were usually university professors or attorneys appointed on an ad hoc basis rather than WERB examiners.[15] On the other hand, in Michigan where a strike situation led to a request for fact-finding, only about 26 days elapsed from a request to a fact finder's report.[16] However, as we will note later, the "success" of fact-finding, if dispute resolution is the criterion, is much lower in an emergency situation.

Fact-finding results

Does fact-finding accomplish what it is designed to do: lead to a settlement acceptable to both parties without a work stoppage? The answers are mixed depending on where the issue is examined.

Wisconsin. In his examination of the early Wisconsin experience, Stern concluded that the procedure was effective since only about 11 percent of the petitions for fact-finding were not resolved. But not all cases ultimately went to fact finders. Of those that did, about one quarter went unresolved after a report was issued by the fact finder. Both unions and managements were relatively positive about the procedure, but some managements complained that the fact finder was not sufficiently aware of local problems, while some union officials decried management's ability to disregard the award in areas where the union had little political power.[17] Since Stern's study, fact-finding has been replaced by arbitration in Wisconsin.

Michigan. In school fact-finding situations, fact-finding where strikes were underway resulted in negative perceptions of the process. Parties were not experienced enough with the procedure to present their cases adequately. Furthermore, the time pressures were great since strikes were usually already underway. Finally, unlike Wisconsin, the state paid for the process, reducing any cost-conscious reluctance for the parties.[18]

---

[14] James L. Stern, "The Wisconsin Public Employee Fact-Finding Procedure," *Industrial and Labor Relations Review*, vol. 20 (October 1966), pp. 4–5.

[15] Ibid., pp. 7–8.

[16] Russell Allen, "1967 School Disputes in Michigan," in *Public Employee Organization and Bargaining* (Washington: Bureau of National Affairs, 1968), chap. 9.

[17] Stern, "The Wisconsin Public Employee Fact-Finding Procedure."

[18] Allen, "1967 School Disputes in Michigan."

New York. McKelvey noted that about 50 percent of the early cases referred to the Public Employee Relations Board were settled by mediation before fact-finding was ordered. Of the other half, about 22 percent were mediated before a report was issued, 45 percent were settled by accepting the fact-finding report, and the other third required additional mediation or were unilaterally modified by the employer. Of a total of 316 impasses, 9 resulted in strikes. However, one should keep in mind that the statute defines an impasse as an inability to agree within 60 days of the required adoption of a budget, so the parties may still have been experiencing some movement in bargaining positions when an official impasse was declared.[19]

McKelvey concludes that fact-finding probably works better where the parties are unsophisticated in collective bargaining, since they may have difficulty defining a reasonable settlement. She also notes the complaints of some labor advocates that an employer may request the process and then reject the recommendations. Since the employer is often the legislative body that sets the rules, this may leave the union vulnerable if fact-finding is the only available impasse resolution procedure.

Criteria for recommendations

In early Wisconsin experiences with fact-finding, Stern suggests the fact finders have used wage comparisons as a most frequent criterion for their economic recommendations. Ability of the governmental unit to pay the increase sought is also frequently considered. Finally, some fact finders used their predictions of what the wage settlement would have been if the parties were bargaining in a situation where the union was permitted to strike as a criterion. Seldom mentioned were productivity and cost-of-living although management and labor raised these issues in their presentations.[20]

Fact-finding overview

Fact-finding is applied to several occupations on a mostly local level in several states. The process appears to resolve impasses where the bargaining relationship is relatively new or where the parties need external justification for making a particular settlement. On the other hand, either party is generally free to ignore the fact finder's recommendations. As such, a rejection will reduce fact-finding's effectiveness for future impasses.

---

[19] McKelvey, "Fact-Finding in Public Employment Disputes," pp. 536, 538.

[20] Stern, "The Wisconsin Public Employee Fact-Finding Procedure," pp. 15–17.

Arbitration

Some laws provide for mandatory arbitration of contract disputes. Where these exist, they generally apply only to public safety divisions, primarily for the uniformed services, and are considered as the equivalent to granting these areas the right to strike. With arbitration as an impasse procedure, the union is not faced with the prospect of management unilaterally continuing past terms without recourse to some other bargaining weapon. Some other laws allow unions and management voluntarily to agree to interest arbitration as a means for settling negotiation impasses. Another form of arbitration mentioned in the laws is advisory arbitration. This may be a misnomer, however, since the end result is similar to a fact finder's recommendations in that the award is not binding on the parties.

Arbitrators who handle public sector interest cases are normally selected in the same way as those in private sector *ad hoc* rights cases. The hearing procedure is also similar. Both sides present evidence supportive of their positions and the arbitrator determines the contract on the basis of the evidence and whatever criteria he uses for the award.

Interest arbitration variants

There are a number of different methods used in public sector interest arbitrations. The typical situation is as described above. The arbitrator hears the case and determines what an appropriate settlement should be. However, it has been argued that this approach has a chilling effect on bargaining since the parties believe an arbitrator will split differences between them. For example, if a union wants 50 cents an hour and management is willing to give 10 cents, an arbitrator may be believed to settle on 30 cents, half-way in-between. It is also argued that as the parties experience splitting, arbitration becomes habit-forming. The parties supposedly skip negotiations and go directly to impasse, thereby availing themselves of the more effortless remedy: arbitration. This is the so-called narcotic effect.

To what extent does the availability of mandatory arbitration chill the bargaining process? Wheeler provided an answer in a study of firefighter negotiations.[21] He found that negotiations make use of impasse procedures more frequently in states where arbitration is required.

Since arbitrators are believed to split the difference remaining between the parties at impasse and since collective bargainers that have

---

[21] Hoyt N. Wheeler, "Compulsory Arbitration: A 'Narcotic Effect'?" *Industrial Relations*, vol. 14 (February 1975), pp. 117–20.

used interest arbitration in the past may be more likely to use it in the future, some variants on the process have been contrived. Where the arbitrator is usually free to award any final package, there may be a tendency to split. To counter this tendency, final offer selection has been adopted in some jurisdictions as a remedy for the "narcotic" effect.

Final offer selection. Final offer selection differs from conventional interest arbitration in requiring that the arbitrator award the final offer of one of the parties. For example, if management offered a 20 cents hourly wage increase prior to impasse and the union was demanding 40 cents, the arbitrator would be bound to award either 20 cents or 40 cents, not any figure over, under, or in-between. Usually arbitrators independently decide each contract issue on which no agreement has been reached. Thus, the union may win an overtime clause while management's position prevails on a promotional issue. This system, however, is open to criticism of a between-issue-splitting rather than a within-issue-splitting nature.

A more extreme variant is one where the arbitrator is required to adopt one side's total final package. Thus, all issues would be decided in favor of labor or management. It is this last variant that is presumed to have the greatest effect on decreasing the reliance on arbitration for impasse resolution.

Feuille notes that some jurisdictions opt for the entire package approach (Massachusetts and Wisconsin) while others use an issue-by-issue approach (Michigan and Iowa).[22] He finds that package selection increases responsibility on a final offer submission since one unreasonable issue in an otherwise reasonable package may tip the scales toward the other party's offer in the mind of the arbitrator. He also finds that where final offer selection is available on an issue-by-issue basis more unresolved issues reach the arbitrator.

One area where interest arbitration may differ from rights arbitration is that many collective agreements and statutes permit the parties to settle after the arbitral process begins and to alter "final" offers. Since interest arbitration in the public sector is often conducted before a tripartite board (one labor, one management, and one neutral member), the partisans may sense which direction the neutral appears to be leaning and settle on a concession rather than lose the issue entirely.[23]

Feuille suggests that final offer procedures can be evaluated by examining whether the parties accept and comply with the awards and

[22] Peter Feuille, *Final Offer Arbitration* (Chicago: International Personnel Management Assn., 1975), pp. 35–48.

[23] Ibid.

by whether the process chills or encourages future bargaining.[24] A number of studies have been completed examining this issue. We will summarize them here.

Eugene, Oregon. Long and Feuille report that the "entire package final offer" procedure compares favorably with these evaluation criteria.[25] First, no rejections of the awards have occurred; and, second, fewer arbitrations have been invoked in succeeding years and the number of issues in the impasse package has decreased. Table 15–4 contains the details.

TABLE 15–4
Eugene negotiation–arbitration experience (1971–75)

Employee group	Arbitration invoked?	Items submitted to arbitrators	Outcome
1971–72 negotiations:			
Firefighters	Yes	Entire contractual package	City first offer selected
Police patrolmen	Yes	Entire contractual package	Agreement negotiated during arbitration proceedings
AFSCME	Yes (binding fact-finding)*	Union security; all other items agreed to in negotiations	Union position (agency shop) selected
1972–73 negotiations:			
Firefighters	Yes	Longevity pay dispute; all other items agreed to in negotiations	City alternate offer selected
Police patrolmen	No	—	Negotiated agreement
AFSCME	Yes	One-year economic package; non-economic issues agreed to in negotiations	City alternate offer selected but was moot because of three-year agreement negotiated during arbitration proceedings
1974–75 negotiations:			
Firefighters	No	—	Negotiated agreement
Police patrolmen	No	—	Negotiated agreement
AFSCME	No	—	Negotiated agreement

* The two sides agreed to use the fact-finding services provided free by the state and to be bound by the fact finder's decision. Since this arbitration did not take place under the city procedure, the final offer selection criteria did not apply in this case.
Source: Peter Feuille, *Final Offer Arbitration* (Chicago: International Personnel Management Assn., 1975), p. 17.

---

[24] Ibid., pp. 15–16.

[25] Gary Long and Peter Feuille, "Final Offer Arbitration: 'Sudden Death' in Eugene," *Industrial and Labor Relations Review*, vol. 27 (January 1974), pp. 186–203.

Michigan.[26] Michigan's form of arbitration is issue-by-issue final offer for economic aspects and conventional as to others. The study there concluded that the process has had no appreciable effect on the number of cases that went to arbitration over time or across functions in the uniformed services. There was a slight tendency for deputy sheriff negotiations to use the procedure more often than police or fire, but this was partially attributed to a relatively newer collective bargaining relationship.

Wisconsin.[27] Wisconsin uses a "package" type final offer procedure. While the earlier Eugene, Oregon, procedure seemed to decrease the usage of arbitration, the Wisconsin experience does not lend support to the idea that usage of arbitration declines in a "package" selection environment over time. However, the total extent of usage on a relative basis is less than in Michigan, an "issue-by-issue" state.

Evidence. While the Eugene, Oregon, experience suggests that final offer selection reduces the use of arbitration for impasse resolution over time, the larger share of the data are not that convincing. While the incidence declined in Eugene, the total number in Wisconsin was high enough to indicate that the message does not spread unless the results are personally experienced. Besides, the laws have been in effect for such a short period of time that it is impossible to conclude how long it takes the parties to forget an imposed settlement and use the process again.

The data are more clear-cut when the effects of "issue-by-issue" versus "package" selection procedures are legislated. States with issue approaches have more arbitrations and more issues going to impasse.

What is a final offer? Stern, and his colleagues note one problem that is encountered in final offer arbitration, and that is "What is a final offer?"[28] The Wisconsin law requires the parties to state their positions when an impasse is declared to the Wisconsin Employee Relations Board. But it has been the practice there, on occasion, and in Michigan (where mediation by the arbitrator appears to be encouraged) to allow negotiations to narrow the differences subsequent to the arbitration request. Some see this as an advantage since the parties settle the issues. But some disputants simply see it as a no-win situation because if they adhere to a well-thought-out final position and only the opposition expresses a willingness to move the arbitrator may award the point to the opponent because of apparent intransigence by the party. Thus, a party may provoke an impasse to achieve what it believed it could

---

[26] James L. Stern, Charles M. Rehmus, J. Joseph Lowenberg, Hirschel Kasper, and Barbara D. Dennis, *Final Offer Arbitration* (Lexington, Mass.: Lexington, 1975), pp. 37–75.

[27] Ibid., pp. 77–115.

[28] Ibid.

not get from true bargaining. As a result of their analysis, the researchers in the Stern et al. study concluded that unions gained 1 percent to 5 percent more in economic settlements as a result of arbitration than they would have from bargaining a settlement.[29]

Alternative to final offer selection. One argument that can be levied against final offer arbitration is that the arbitrator has knowledge of the parties' positions in bargaining through both public reports and their final offers. Wheeler argues that arbitrators should only be given information on the positions each party desires and not evidence on the previous negotiation.[30] Thus, either party might run the risk of getting less than it had already been offered in negotiations. As such, they may have a greater motive to settle on their own. No test has been made of this procedure in the United States, but some British experience appears to conclude that it reduces arbitration.

Arbitral criteria

Just as rights arbitrators apply criteria in deciding awards in grievance cases, so do arbitrators in interest arbitration. Some criteria are specified by law, while others are specified by the arbitrators. These criteria can cause problems for both arbitrators and the disputants.

One factor that is often considered is ability to pay. The state of Nevada statutorily requires its assessment in arriving at an award.[31] Recently an arbitrator in a New York City hospital award for voluntary hospitals (private, nonprofit) mentioned the same criteria for her low wage award during the city's acute financial crisis.[32] The ability to pay issue may retard wage gains where revenues would not support wage demands. However, there are suggestions that arbitrators are less concerned about the actual ability to pay than elected officials.[33] (This is hardly surprising since officials are generally closer to their management than to their rank and file who are coincidentally constituents).

TRENDS IN PUBLIC SECTOR BARGAINING

We have seen the growth of public sector representation explode over the last 20 years. Federal employees are now heavily unionized.

[29] Ibid.

[30] Hoyt N. Wheeler, "Closed Offer: Alternative to Final Offer Selection," *Industrial Relations*, vol. 16 (1977), pp. 298–305.

[31] Joseph R. Grodin, "Arbitration of Public Sector Labor Disputes," *Industrial and Labor Relations Review*, vol. 28 (October 1974), pp. 89–102.

[32] Margery Gootnick, Arbitrator, Award in League of Voluntary Hospitals and District 1199, Hospital and Health Care Employees, RWDSU, reprinted in *Daily Labor Report*, no. 181, (September 16, 1976) pp. D–1 through D–7.

[33] Raymond D. Horton, "Arbitration, Arbitrators, and the Public Interest," *Industrial and Labor Relations Review*, vol. 28 (July 1975), pp. 497–507.

State and municipal employees are close to 50 percent organized with an upward trend continuing. Bargaining and representation rights have not kept pace, however, with few jurisdictions allowing strikes and many offering no neutral impasse procedure.

What laws are being passed are more liberal rather than the reverse. Limited rights to strike are now granted in several states. A federal bargaining law regulating all public employee bargaining has been proposed, although its constitutionality is in doubt since the Supreme Court ruled that Congress could not extend overtime and minimum wage laws to the states.[34]

It is probably unrealistic to ban public sector strikes. The ban is essentially unenforceable. Employers can readily use other alternatives like replacing the strikers. The former has been proven often, and the latter has recently been successfully demonstrated with striking school teachers in Michigan.[35]

As bargaining experience and sophistication grow, strike incidence will probably decline. At the same time government employers will become more able to cope with strikes. Unions will attempt to exert more political pressure on elected officials as bargaining experience increases, but the success of multilateral bargaining will probably ultimately depend on the electorate's ability to pay.

SUMMARY

The legal environment is a critical factor in public employee unionization since management determines the scope of bargaining rights. The mood of the electorate predicts changes in these laws in some states, but generally rights are more restrictive than in the public sector. Legislation is most conducive to bargaining in the industrialized North and East and least in rural or southern areas. Right-to-work laws for the private sector predict statutes prohibiting union activity in the public sector.

Where bargaining is permitted, the issues are much the same as in the private sector. Unionization varies with AFSCME taking an industrial union approach and the uniformed services generally taking a craft union approach.

Impasse resolution varies widely by jurisdiction and occupation. In the federal government the Federal Services Impasses Panel resolves

---

[34] *National League of Cities et al.* v. *Usery*, U.S. Supreme Court, no. 74–878 and no. 74–879 (1976).

[35] *Crestwood Education Association* v. *Crestwood Board of Education*, Michigan Supreme Court, 89 LRRM 2017 (1975); certiorari denied by U.S. Supreme Court, 92 LRRM 2918 (1976).

disputes. In states providing for impasse resolution by statute, arbitrators usually handle uniformed services disputes. In other areas, fact-finding, mediation, and other methods are prescribed. Strikes are forbidden in most jurisdictions.

Because of our limited experience with interest arbitration, no real conclusions can be drawn at this point regarding the effectiveness of different arbitration processes. On a preliminary basis, if reducing a reliance on arbitration is important, final offer selection may be advantageous when compared to conventional methods.

SUGGESTED READINGS

Feuille, Peter. *Final Offer Arbitration* (Chicago: International Personnel Management Assn. 1975).

Lelchook, Jerry. *State Civil Service Employee Associations* (Washington: Government Printing Office, 1973).

Nesbitt, Murray B. *Labor Relations in the Federal Government Service* (Washington: Bureau of National Affairs, 1976).

Public Employee Relations Library (Chicago: International Personnel Management Assn., 1958–present).

Stern, James L., Rehmus, Charles M., Lowenberg, J. Joseph, Kasper, Hirschel, and Dennis, Barbara D. *Final Offer Arbitration* (Lexington, Mass.: Lexington, 1975).

Steiber, Jack. *Public Employee Unionism: Structure, Growth, Policy* (Washington: Brookings, 1973).

"Symposium: Public Sector Impasses." *Industrial Relations*, vol. 16 (October 1977), pp. 264–314.

DISCUSSION QUESTIONS

1. If government employees were to be given a limited right to strike, which occupations should be prohibited from striking, and under what conditions should the prohibition be enforced?
2. Since arbitrators are not responsible to the electorate, should they be allowed to make binding rulings on economic issues?
3. Civil service rules provide many public employees a large measure of protection from arbitrary action. Since this is the case, why should public employees be allowed to organize?
4. Since fact-finding publicizes the major areas in dispute and a proposed settlement, why has it not been more successful given the public's stake in the outcome?

Case _____

The annual contract negotiations between the Pleasant Ridge Board of Education and the Pleasant Ridge Classroom Teachers Association (PRCTA) were due to begin one week from now on July 1. Under state law, the new contract had to be signed by September 1 or an impasse would be declared. Following an impasse, state law provided for simultaneous mediation and fact-finding. The fact finder's report must be published no later than September 20. Under the law, the parties could arbitrate unresolved contract issues using a total package final offer selection approach if both agreed that arbitration would be binding. The state law prohibited teachers from striking, but about ten short strikes had occurred last year at the time school opened.

The contract at Pleasant Ridge was not signed until November 10 last year even though mediation and fact-finding had taken place. The PRCTA had repeatedly requested arbitration of the contract dispute, but the board refused. While there was no strike, there were two "sickouts" in October where teacher absence rates exceeded 90 percent. For the upcoming contract, there appears to be considerable sentiment for "hitting the bricks" if negotiations are unsatisfactory.

Presently there are about 5,000 students enrolled in the kindergarten through 12th grade program at Pleasant Ridge. There are 250 teachers of whom 240 are PRCTA members. Like many other established school systems, enrollment at Pleasant Ridge has been declining in recent years in response to lower birth rates. While the impact is greatest in the elementary grades with a recent drop of about 6 percent annually, the decline in the entire system is about 3 percent annually.

The school system's operating budget is funded from two sources: state school aid based on student enrollments and local property taxes. The state school aid was equal to 40 percent of the budget last year. The legislature has passed a 5 percent increase in per student funding for the upcoming school year. Local property taxes are presently providing the other 60 percent based on a 22-mill levy against assessed market value. Fifteen mills are permanent as required by state law. The other seven are supplemental and are periodically reconsidered by local voters. Five of the seven mills expire this November and will be subject for reapproval by the voters in the general election. Property values are presently appreciating by 8 percent annually.

School costs are approximately equally divided between salaries and plant, equipment and supplies. Of the 50 percent allocated to salaries, 80 percent is paid to the instructional staff represented by the PRCTA. Non wage costs are increasing at an annual rate of 6 percent.

The PRCTA bargaining committee has just completed its contract demands. Major areas in which they demand changes include: a 15-percent salary increase, a reduction in maximum class size from 30 to 25 in the elementary grades (K–6), and the granting of tenure after the second year of teaching instead of four. Since about 2,500 students are in the K–6 program, a reduction in class sizes would have a positive impact on teacher employment. The tenure change would affect 25 second and 25 third year teachers now uncovered. In case of a reduction in staff, tenured employees who are terminated are entitled to one year's pay under the contract. As part of their preparations for negotiations, the PRCTA has surveyed comparable schools and finds that its members' pay is about 5 percent below the market rate, that tenure is normally granted after three years, and that the median elementary class size (by contract) is 27.

The Pleasant Ridge Board of Education must ultimately approve the contract as the school's management if arbitration is not used, but the school system's superintendent, personnel director, high school principal, and two elementary principals form the management bargaining team. The school board is made up of five persons. Two of these are union members and three (including these two) were endorsed by the Pleasant Ridge Central Labor Union (PRCLU) at the last election. Two others endorsed by the PRCLU lost to the other present members. At that last election two mills of the supplementary property tax were reapproved, but the margin was only 500 out of 10,000 votes cast.

QUESTIONS

1. What should be the initial bargaining position of the school board? What data justify this position?
2. What should the PRCTA consider a reasonable settlement to be?
3. If fact-finding takes place, what should the fact finder use as criteria in recommending a settlement? What should the recommendation be?
4. Should the board go to arbitration if an agreement can't be negotiated?
5. What strategies should the management and union negotiators use to win their demands?
6. If the negotiations go to arbitration as a final offer package, what should each party's offer be for the arbitrator?

16

HEALTH CARE ORGANIZATIONS

The health care industry requires another special set of approaches in the field of labor relations. This specialization results from the variety of different corporate forms hospitals take, differences in jurisdiction over hospitals and health care, and the rather broad occupational mix of nonmanagerial employees.

Collective bargaining in hospitals is unique for a variety of reasons. First, the possibilities of disruptions in service have critical implications for the hospital's service: patient care. Partially completed automobiles may rest on the assembly lines for weeks with relatively little effect, but patients in intensive care can't suspend their state of health until a withholding of services is ended. Second, large distinguishable groups of professional employees are interested in organizing. And third, hospitals are frequently in the position where they face one large dominant purchaser of their services (insurance carriers) who may resist the pass through of bargained economic gains to the customer.

As you read this chapter consider the following questions:

1. Should hospital employees be allowed, by statute, to strike?
2. What safeguards has Congress introduced to reduce the possibilities of disruption while preserving traditional collective bargaining?
3. What patterns in the designation of appropriate bargaining units have emerged?
4. What are the emerging patterns of bargaining practices, particularly as they relate to multiemployer units?

JURISDICTIONS

National labor law initially placed most hospital employees outside of the jurisdiction of the NLRB. First, since the acts excluded public employees, all state and local hospitals operated by governmental

414

units were exempt from coverage. Second, throughout most of the history of the acts, nonprofit hospitals were specifically excluded. Thus, health care workers employed by charitable organizations, religious orders, and voluntary associations were exempted. Third, the NLRB declined to exert jurisdiction over proprietary (privately owned, for-profit) hospitals until 1967.[1] In 1974, however, the Taft-Hartley Act was amended to include health care workers employed by voluntary medical facilities within the jurisdiction of the NLRB.

In the public sector, labor relations in hospitals are governed by state statutes applicable to the facility. Thus, the same legislation that applies to other public employees applies to health care workers. Most states do not specifically mention publicly employed health care workers in their statutes, and as such they usually have organizing and bargaining rights equal to or slightly more restricted than other public employee classes.

What is a private nonprofit hospital?

This question was one of the first that had to be answered by the NLRB after the Taft-Hartley amendments. Obviously, any hospital owned and operated by a nongovernment agency was now subject to board jurisdiction regardless of the profit or nonprofit orientation of the facility.

But frequently hospitals are operated by private organizations where public agencies may own the assets. In the *Bishop Randall Hospital* case, although the physical assets of the hospital were owned by Fremont County, Wyoming, the facility was operated by the Lutheran Hospitals and Homes Society of America.[2] Since the Society's administration was responsible for day-to-day operations, was entirely responsible for personnel policies, and was largely independent of the hospital's public member board of trustees, the NLRB determined that it was, in fact, a private employer and subject to board jurisdiction. Thus, the body which employs and directs the management rather than the owner of the physical assets would seem to determine whether or not a health care facility is within the jurisdiction of the board.

What is an employee?

One problem that has plagued hospitals and employee groups is whether or not a member of the organization is a student or an em-

---

[1] *Butte Medical Properties*, 168 NLRB 52 (1967).

[2] 217 NLRB 185 (1975).

ployee. Hospital housestaffs are generally made up of interns and residents. While they perform significant medical duties, they are also simultaneously students carrying out these duties as part of their educational requirements. But while the duties have educational value, the hospitals compensate them for their work.

Recently the NLRB has held that hospital housestaffs are not employees within the meaning of the act.[3] In a split decision, the board reasoned that the members of the housestaff participated in hospital activities for primarily educational rather than employment reasons. The board held that the hospitals' programs were designed to meet the educational needs of the housestaff rather than the immediate needs of the hospital. Finally, housestaff members' tenure is related to the length of their curriculum rather than the employment needs of the hospital. In dissent, Member Fanning argued that the duties were often performed in the absence of the instructors, that their compensation was significant and taxable, that the act did not specifically exclude students as employees, and that the NLRB had previously certified all-student units in private industry.

While the NLRB decision is the governing precedent in the area, some sentiment exists in Congress specifically to include housestaffs as employees. There are also differences in how the states interpret their legislation. For example, housestaffs in public hospitals in Michigan are considered to be employees for bargaining purposes.[4]

BARGAINING UNIT DETERMINATION

The number and types of bargaining units in hospitals is a difficult issue for the NLRB. Congress wanted the board to avoid what it considered to be an unnecessary proliferation of units, but the act itself leads to the possibility of fragmentation.

One could easily agree that there are a variety of professions employed in health care facilities. Since the Taft-Hartley Act expressly forbids the inclusion of professionals in a larger unit without their majority consent, a number of units might be expected to result where organizing is active. Another issue relates to whether or not some designated supervisory personnel have jobs of a managerial nature. For example, is a head nurse a supervisor of personnel and resources or primarily responsible for judgments regarding patient care?

While the board has refused, on occasion, to certify separate units of engineering and maintenance personnel, it has generally severed or created separate professional units when requested. A general pattern

---

[3] *Cedars-Sinai Medical Center*, 223 NLRB 57 (1976).

[4] *Regents of the University of Michigan* v. *Michigan Employment Relations Commission*, 204 NW2d 875 (1973), 82 LRRM 2909.

would find four or five separate bargaining units in a fully unionized health care facility subject to NLRB jurisdiction.

First, a unit representing nurses, including head nurses, would be considered appropriate. As professionals, they are immediately entitled to separate representation. The board also includes head nurses within the unit since they generally direct patient care rather than hire, fire, or make other personnel decisions relating to the members of a nursing team.

Second, technicians and others with medical skills of a subprofessional nature might form a second unit. This unit is likely to include licensed practical nurses (LPN's) who are excluded from the professional registered nurse (RN) unit.

Third, service and maintenance employees involved predominantly in nonmedical duties are included in another unit. Most attempts to sever skilled trades from the service and maintenance units are disallowed by the board.

Fourth, the board generally finds clerical employees share a separate community of interests. In some instances, it also divides clericals into two units, one servicing medical records, the other office clericals dealing with billing and other administrative duties.

Although there are exceptions, the board generally does not require the merging of units having a separate bargaining history if communities of interest appear somewhat distinct.[5]

Bargaining structures

As in the nonhealth care private sector, health care bargaining may cover a broader spectrum of units than are designated in representation petitions. Abelow and Metzger note that in large cities, multiemployer bargaining across similar occupational groups is becoming more prevalent.[6] In New York multiemployer bargaining developed to cope with union whipsawing tactics and was encouraged by the union so that hospitals could present a united front when seeking payment increases from carriers like Blue Cross. On the other hand, the San Francisco multiemployer bargaining resulted from representation at the association rather than the establishment level. The Minneapolis–St. Paul situation is slightly different. In the past, hospitals belonged to an association which acted as a bargainer for each hospital. Thus, each hospital signed an individual, but nearly uniform, contract. Beginning in 1974, Health Manpower Management, Inc., a

---

[5] *St. Joseph Hospital and Medical Center*, 219 NLRB 161 (1975); but see also *North Memorial Medical Center*, 224 NLRB 28 (1976).

[6] William J. Abelow and Norman Metzger, "Multiemployer Bargaining for Health Care Institutions," *Employee Relations Law Journal*, vol. 1 (Winter 1976), pp. 390–409.

hospital bargaining firm, negotiated a single uniform contract. Thus, in cities where hospitals are heavily unionized and have been for some time, multiemployer bargaining seems to evolve as a relatively effective approach for both labor and management.

HEALTH CARE UNIONS

Because of the early organization patterns in health care, the mix of occupations, and the NLRB's policy on bargaining unit determination, the unions involved in health care do not strictly follow the patterns set elsewhere. From an overall standpoint, hospital union patterns fall midway between public and private sector approaches.

The one labor organization that comes closest to an industrial-type union in health care is District 1199 of the Retail, Wholesale, and Drug Store Workers Union, AFL–CIO. It gained its impetus in organizing through some very successful drives in New York City in the early 1960s. While it represents predominantly nonprofessionals, it also contains a nurse department.

Another union with some success in health care organizations is the Service Employees Internal Union, AFL–CIO (SEIU). Its organizing efforts have been concentrated primarily among maintenance personnel.

A third major group is one representing professional nurses—the American Nurses' Association. Throughout its history it has generally viewed itself as a professional association rather than as a bargaining agent. This orientation has changed recently, just as it has for the National Education Association and the American Association of University Professors.

SPECIAL BARGAINING RULES FOR HOSPITALS

In expanding bargaining rights to private sector nonproprietary hospitals, Congress recognized that the rights of employees to representation would have to be balanced against the special needs of patients to avoid a disruptive atmosphere which could accompany organizing and strike activities.

Organizing

Congress appeared to want to avoid disputes among unions in organizing through its wish that bargaining unit proliferation be avoided. To an extent, the NLRB has followed this so that it is fairly clear which separate groups could petition for elections.

You will recall from Chapter 8, the right of access to employees has been relatively easy for internal union organizers. However, hospital management (and patients) may feel that this degree of latitude is disruptive to the major mission of the hospital: providing an atmosphere conducive to the comfort and return to health of the patient. Contentious organizing campaigns could interfere with this mission.

Recently the NLRB held that a broad no-solicitation rule prohibiting union organizing from any area of the hospital where patient contact is possible is overly broad.[7] On an appeal for enforcement, the 10th Circuit reversed the board and held that the needs of patients outweighed the organizing rights of the employees.[8]

Passive activities may have more latitude, however. In a case where hospitals required nurses to refrain from wearing union membership pins on their caps as an alleged safety hazard, it was pointed out that the pins were not conspicuous compared to other approved jewelry items and that school pins of similar size and style could be worn with impunity.[9] In this case the pin only noted union membership or advocacy of representation and was not an active incident of solicitation.

Timing of bargaining activities

Because of its desire to avoid disruptions in health care, Congress provided for a more stringent notification procedure in its Taft-Hartley amendments. For example, whereas in other industries notification that a party desires to renegotiate must be given 60 days before expiration, a 90-day notice is required in health care. The FMCS must be notified 60 days prior to expiration if an agreement has not been reached.

If there is no settlement, the parties may be required to mediate their differences using FMCS representatives. In situations where a medical emergency might result, for example, a multiemployer unit or a single hospital area; an emergency dispute procedure is mandated when 30 days remain before expiration. A fact finder is appointed and a report is then due in 15 days. The parties then negotiate on the basis of this report. Little is available on the efficacy of hospital fact-finding, but we could expect its effectiveness to fall somewhere between the early Wisconsin public sector experience where one of the parties declared an impasse,[10] and the Michigan public schools' experience where fact-finding took place after a strike had already begun.[11]

---

[7] *St. John's Hospital and School of Nursing*, 222 NLRB 182 (1976).

[8] *NLRB v. St. John's Hospital and School of Nursing*, U.S. 10th Circuit Court of Appeals, 76–1130 (1977).

[9] *Baptist Memorial Hospital*, 225 NLRB 69 (1976).

[10] James L. Stern, "The Wisconsin Public Employee Fact-finding Procedure," *Industrial and Labor Relations Review*, vol. 20 (October 1966), pp. 1–17.

[11] Russell Allen, "1967 School Disputes in Michigan," in *Public Employee Organization and Bargaining* (Washington: Bureau of National Affairs, 1968), chap. 9.

One other important timing requirement aimed at reducing patient care disruptions is the rule that unions anticipating a strike or intending to picket must give the hospital a ten-day notice. This would allow for a cutoff in admissions and an orderly movement of long-term patients to other facilities. There is one exception to this requirement; unions are not required to give the notice where the walkout is over unfair labor practices. The NLRB has given a very broad interpretation to the congressional prohibition against strikes without notice. The clause requires a ten-day notice before "engaging in any strike, picketing, or other concerted refusal to work at any health care institution [8g]." If this clause is violated, the strikers are no longer legally protected in engaging in concerted activity, and employers may take reprisals against them.

What happens if the striking union does not bargain with the hospital? Frequently hospitals are involved in new construction. Labor disputes are not infrequent events in construction, and they usually involve strikes or picketing. Does a labor organization having a dispute with a nonhealth care employer on a hospital site have to provide notice? According to the NLRB's *Lein-Steinberg* decision, it does.[12] It views Congress's prohibition as absolute, even if the struck organization is a secondary employer. However the circuit courts have held that this cannot be applied to construction unions where no dispute exists with the hospital.[13]

Ally doctrine

Another major difference that exists in health care labor relations is the "ally doctrine." The ally doctrine basically holds that a previously neutral employer may become a primary employer for dispute purposes if struck work is accepted. If the ally doctrine did not exist, pressures on employers to settle would decrease, and job security might decline if the employer decided to continue by subcontracting. Also, a strike frequently does not result in any long-run loss of earnings where the work is not lost, but orders are simply made up on an overtime basis after settlement.

There are some real dangers in extending the ally doctrine to hospitals, however. Sick patients can't simply be made to wait for care until a strike is over. Hospitals accepting struck work (patient care) can't risk the extension of the strike to their facility. Congress recognized these problems in its modification of 8(b)(4) for health care facilities.

---

[12] 219 NLRB 837 (1975).

[13] *Laborers Local 1057 v. NLRB, 96 LRRM 3160; and IBEW, Local 388 v. NLRB, 94 LRRM 2536.*

If a hospital is struck and another health care facility supplies an occasional technician to assist the struck facility, an ally relationship is not established. On the other hand, if shifts of LPN's were provided by a group of hospitals, they would become allies. Thus, the magnitude of the assistance is the important factor.

HEALTH CARE BARGAINING ISSUES

A large share of the issues facing health care workers are similar to those in other industries. But one tack taken by professionals in health care has been seldom emulated except by unionized teachers. That relates to the standard and level of their services which the employer will be expected to provide.

While an R.N. or an M.D. is an employee of a hospital in some cases, he or she is also a member of a profession, personally and professionally committed to specific standards of health care. Hippocratic oaths and codes of practice may specify work rules which may be at variance with those preferred by administrators of the facility. Holloway notes that interns and residents have demanded a right to negotiate quality of training issues as well as working conditions.[14] Nurses in Ohio insisted that their nursing code of ethics be included, intact, in their collective bargaining agreement, recognizing professionally prescribed standards of care.[15] Thus, there is more input in negotiations as to how the standards of work performance will be set.

Physicians, in particular, also differ in negotiations by identifying third parties (insurance carriers) as a focus for their collective negotiations. Where results were not consistent with physician demands, it has been suggested that refusing to work for certain third parties, refusal to handle paperwork, or stopping treatment of marginally ill patients may be seen as a substitute for a strike.[16]

Professional health care workers have generally been reluctant to strike, although there are recent instances. Doctors in California withheld services in late 1975 to protest malpractice insurance increases. House officers in New York City struck Mt. Sinai Hospital recently after efforts to reach a new contract failed. There is, then, a reluctance on the part of labor and management to experience a work stoppage and considerable public interest in avoiding strikes. This leads to a greater use of formal impasse procedures in health care.

---

[14] Sally T. Holloway, "Health Professionals and Collective Action," *Employee Relations Law Journal*, vol. 1 (Winter 1976), p. 413.

[15] Ibid., p. 414.

[16] Mario F. Bognanno, James B. Dworkin, and Omotayo Fashoyin, "Physicians' and Dentists' Bargaining Organizations: A Preliminary Look," *Monthly Labor Review*, vol. 98 (June 1975), pp. 33–35.

IMPASSE SETTLEMENT

One of the major changes wrought by the Taft-Hartley health care amendments was the involvement of the FMCS in the contract negotiation process. The longer period for negotiations, the FMCS mediation involvement, the authority of the FMCS to establish boards of inquiry, and the ten-day strike notice requirement are all pieces of evidence indicating Congress's concern for health care impasse resolutions.

In its first year of experience under the changes, the FMCS handled 1,400 health care cases. Of these, boards of inquiry were established in 54 cases. A total of 37 cases of the 1,400 encountered strikes. Only four of these occurred where a board of inquiry was in operation.[17] Generally the evidence has been positive regarding the reduction of strikes as impasse strategies under the legislation. However, we must temper this conclusion with the observation that impasse procedures in the public sector have had an initial effect on reducing strikes but that over a longer run period this effectiveness has deteriorated.

PATTERNS AND EFFECTS OF UNIONS

In what types of hospitals and in what areas are unions most prevalent? Given that a hospital is unionized, what effect does this have on hospital administration? These and other questions are now beginning to be researched since jurisdiction over hospitals has expanded so greatly under the Taft-Hartley amendments.

In a survey conducted in late 1975 by the American Hospital Association, 6,199 hospitals responded to questions about their organizational characteristics. The results from the survey are summarized in Table 16–1. These indicate that about 23 percent of the hospitals had one or more organized employee groups. Given the NLRB's position on bargaining unit determination, it is unlikely that this means that 23 percent of the health care workers are unionized in a given sample of hospitals of the same size. It is likely, as the results show, that larger hospitals are more likely to have unions since almost half of the unionized facilities are in SMSA's (standard metropolitan statistical areas) of over 1 million population.

The results indicate that unionization is more prevalent in large cities, in larger hospitals, in federally controlled hospitals, and in hospitals located in the Northeast and West. Fewer church or proprietary hospitals are organized than one might expect.

In his study of these hospitals, Juris found that hospitals generally negotiated contracts of shorter duration with more wage reopeners and

---

[17] U.S. Federal Mediation and Conciliation Service, *Twenty-Eighth Annual Report* (Washington: Government Printing Office, 1976), p. 25.

TABLE 16–1
Extent and nature of unionization of U.S. hospitals, 1975 (percentage of hospitals reporting)

Hospital characteristic (SMSA size)	All U.S. hospitals (N = 7,165)	Responding hospitals (N = 6,199)	Unionized hospitals (N = 1,418)	Control sample (N = 576 hospitals)
Non-SMSA	46	46	26	27
Fewer than 250,000	9	9	10	8
250,000–1 million	17	18	18	14
More than 1 million	28	28	46	51
Bed-size category				
0–99	49	46	23	21
100–199	22	22	22	24
200–399	17	18	26	28
400+	13	14	29	28
Control				
Government, nonfederal	32	32	31	35
Government, federal	5	6	20	1
Church	11	12	7	11
Voluntary	39	39	36	49
Proprietary	13	11	6	4
Region				
West	13	12	22	18
Northeast	18	18	34	31
North central	28	30	28	31
Other	41	40	16	10

Source: American Hospital Association Survey reported in Hervey A. Juris "Labor Agreements in the Hospital Industry: A Study of Collective Bargaining Outputs," *Proceedings of the 1977 Annual Spring Meeting* (Madison, Wis.: Industrial Relations Research Assn., 1977), p. 505.

fewer deferred increases than private industry.[18] Union shops were negotiated in only about half as many situations as private industry (30 percent versus 63 percent). On the other hand, hospitals and industries are equally likely to use seniority as a criterion for personnel decision making, although health care occupations may also impose a state legal requirement for licensing. While shift differentials are paid less often, more paid time off is negotiated. A feature of health care contracts that seldom appears in private sector agreements is a provision for joint study committees consisting of health care professionals and hospital administrators to deal with allocation issues. About half of the contracts examined mentioned these committees. In a study of unionized hospitals in Illinois, Minnesota, and Wisconsin, Miller, Becker, and Krinsky found that hospital workers did not have typical

---

[18] Hervey A. Juris, "Labor Agreements in the Hospital Industry: A Study of Collective Bargaining Outputs," *Proceedings of the 1977 Annual Spring Meeting* (Madison, Wis.: Industrial Relations Research Ass., 1977), pp. 504–11.

TABLE 16-2

Manpower subjects covered by 126 hospital contracts in Illinois, Wisconsin and Minnesota

Issue	Percent of contracts mentioning
Subcontracting restriction	1
Crew-size control	7
Supervisor performing work in B.U.	0
Provisions for job-posting	45
Joint labor-management safety committee	9
Joint determination by job evaluation of wages	7
Joint determination by job evaluation of job content	4

Source: Richard U. Miller, Brian B. Becker, and Edward B. Krinsky, "Union Effects on Hospital Administration: Preliminary Results from a Three-State Study," *Proceedings of the 1977 Annual Spring Meeting* (Madison Wis.: Industrial Relations Research Assn., 1977), p. 518.

job security clauses included in their contracts.[19] Table 16-2 shows their findings on several typical private industry job security issues.

In terms of union penetration, it is too early to tell what proportion of hospitals will ultimately be organized. But the Miller study may provide some early answers. Both Minnesota and Wisconsin have had state laws asserting jurisdiction over charitable hospitals for several years longer than Taft-Hartley health care amendments have been in effect, and both states have unionization which has appeared to have stabilized at about 30 percent.[20]

SUMMARY

Health care organizations are of three major types: proprietary, voluntary or charitable, and public. Public hospitals are covered by state statutes while charitable and proprietary hospitals fall within Taft-Hartley provisions. Hospital employees form a number of distinct groups. Professionals include housestaffs and nurses. Nonprofessionals are clustered in technician, clerical, and maintenance groups. The NLRB has usually designated separate bargaining units for each. At the present time housestaff officers are considered students by the board and are not entitled to recognition in voluntary facilities.

Hospital unions are often organized along occupational lines. Pre-

---

[19] Richard U. Miller, Brian B. Becker, and Edward B. Krinsky, "Union Effects on Hospital Administration: Preliminary Results from a Three-state Study," *Proceedings of the 1977 Annual Spring Meeting*, Madison, Wis.: Industrial Relations Research Assn., 1977), pp. 512-19.

[20] Ibid.

dominant unions include District 1199, SEIU, and the American Nurses Association.

Bargaining is most often on a hospital-by-hospital basis, although mature bargaining situations tend toward multiemployer bargaining.

Hospital bargaining requires more stringent notice procedures with the FMCS which enables it to establish impasse panels where health care may be disrupted. Strike notices are required in health care ten days before picketing, and all organization and picketing activities are more circumscribed than in other private sector organizations.

SUGGESTED READINGS

Employee Relations Law Journal, vol. 1 (Winter 1976).

Metzger, Norman, and Pointer, Dennis D. *Labor-Management Relations in the Health Service Industry: Theory & Practice* (Washington: Science and Health Publications, 1972).

"Proceedings of the 1977 Annual Spring Meeting of the Industrial Relations Research Assn.", *Labor Law Journal*, vol. 28 (August 1977).

DISCUSSION QUESTIONS

1. What are the advantages and disadvantages to hospitals, unions, and patients in multiemployer bargaining?
2. Should professional groups be able to insist that codes of conduct or standards of practice authored by their professions be included in collective agreements?
3. Should Congress require an impasse procedure like arbitration for health care organizations rather than permitting strikes?
4. Since insurers may have a big stake in a settlement, should bargaining include representatives of health carriers?

Case

Mercy Hospital had recently opened negotiations for a new contract with the Professional Nurses Association, the registered nurses' (RN) bargaining agent. While the hospital anticipated the wage and hour demands of the PNA, it was surprised by the inclusion of a patient care issue.

The RN's demanded that Mercy equip each floor of the six-story hospital with cardio-pulmonary resuscitation (CPR) equipment. The hospital now has three units, one in intensive care, one in the operating room, and one portable unit for use as needed throughout the remainder of the hospital. The nurses accused the hospital administration of a callous disregard for patient care in its possession of only one portable unit. They pointed out that it could take up to eight minutes to get the unit from one end of the hospital to another, given elevator usage. With one on each floor, the maximum lag would be three minutes.

The hospital responded to the demand by asserting that it was responsible for patient care and decision making relative to necessary equipment provision. The nurses countered by arguing that their professional standards required that everything possible be done to provide patient care, and CPR units were *possible*.

DIRECTIONS

1. Take a management or union position on this issue, and justify your bargaining position.
2. Is this likely to be a mandatory or permissive issue? Can the nurses pursue this to impasse?

17

LABOR AND EQUAL EMPLOYMENT OPPORTUNITY

Since the passage of the 1964 Civil Rights Act, labor and management have become increasingly involved in equal employment opportunity issues. Management becomes immediately involved in hiring decisions while, except for the hiring hall unions, labor organizations become involved through the negotiation of seniority systems, job promotion and security provisions, and grievance processing.

In this chapter we will focus on a number of current equal employment opportunity issues. First, we will look at federal law and executive agency requirements as they relate to employer and union actions that may have a discriminatory impact on employment. Second, we will examine the remedies to discrimination that have been proposed, decreed, and implemented. Third, we want to examine differences between unions in the way in which they can and do react to discrimination. Fourth, and finally, we want to examine issues in fair representation of minorities and women by unions.

As you read this chapter, consider the following questions:

1. What has the effect of Title VII been on minority rights in unionized settings?
2. How has the application of Title VII modified the collective bargaining relationship?
3. How does the NLRB address discrimination claims?
4. What duties does a union have toward minority members in grievance procedures?

EQUAL EMPLOYMENT OPPORTUNITY

Title VII—1964 Civil Rights Act

Title VII forbids employers and unions from using race, sex, color, religion, or national origin as a basis for making employment decisions

427

except where possession of a particular characteristic is a bona fide occupational qualification. That is, an employer in the women's apparel industry could require that models be female, but a warehouse operator could not require that jobholders on the loading dock be male because of a *general* likelihood that males possess greater physical strength.

In most employment situations, unions do not have any say about who is hired and who is rejected. Union shop clauses cover workers after they complete a probationary period, not before or at hire. The only area where this is not the case is where unions refer individuals to jobs, as they do in the construction and maritime industries. There, the unions control entry into the hiring pool with employers being dependent on the unions' selection criteria.

After workers complete a probationary period, the union does become involved in promotion and transfer decisions through the application of the negotiated contract. This is true even where no agency or union shop exists since a majority union is the exclusive representative of all employees in the bargaining unit. As we will see, if a union and an employer negotiate a contract which is designed or intended to discriminate, then both may be required to remedy the effects of the discrimination.

The union generally bargains for seniority to be the prime criterion used in personnel decision making. Promotions, transfers, layoffs, and salary levels would all be influenced to a large extent by seniority if union preferences were incorporated into contracts. And they usually are. On their face, seniority requirements are certainly neutral in regard to race or sex. And Title VII explicitly permits personnel decisions to be made using a seniority criterion where the system is bona fide (see Section 703h which states: "Notwithstanding any other provision of this title, it shall not be an unlawful employment practice for an employer to apply different standards of compensation, or different terms, conditions, or privileges of employment pursuant to a bona fide seniority or merit system . . . provided that such differences are not the result of an intention to discriminate because of race, color, religion, sex, or national origin. . .").

Seniority issues

Seniority may be either a very simple or a complex issue. An example of a very simple seniority system is one in which an individual's rights are consistently related to the date of hire. Where seniority determines the outcome of a personnel decision among two or more employees, the first hired receives the most desirable or least undesirable outcome. Probably the most frequent example is one where the last hired is the first laid off during an employment cutback.

More complex systems often refer to departmental seniority. Various separate functions in a plant (within the same bargaining unit) may be designated as departments for seniority purposes. Generally, transfers between departments are not permitted except where they involve a promotion. Transfers between departments may also result in a loss of seniority since departmental seniority systems base employee rights not on the date of hire, but the date of assignment to that department. Thus, it becomes increasingly costly to the individual to move across departments as one accumulates seniority. Figure 17–1 gives examples of the two systems in operation.

Prior to the enactment of Title VII, many unionized firms had both

FIGURE 17–1
Departmental and plantwide seniority systems in use

*Assume: Hire dates of present employees**

Department A			Department B	
Employee	Hire date		Employee	Hire date
1	1/ 9/40		6	2/ 6/59
2	3/16/47		7	4/18/70
3	12/20/52		8	5/22/73
4	2/16/57		9	6/24/74
5	8/14/65		10	7/21/76

*Assume: Plantwide seniority with five layoffs
(remaining employees)*

Department A	Department B
1	6
2	
3	
4	

*Assume: Departmental seniority with 40 percent layoff
(remaining employees)*

Department A	Department B
1	6
2	7
3	8

* Entry to department is same as hire date.

black and white union locals or restricted black entrants to certain departments (usually those with few promotional opportunities and less desirable jobs). After the passage of the act, dual unions based on race became illegal. A difficult seniority question then required determination. As one union was merged into the other, how was seniority to be determined? Two approaches, merging and dove-tailing, were used, the latter with definite discriminatory impact. Figure 17–2 shows how the two approaches worked.

FIGURE 17–2
Merging and dovetailing

Pre–1964 Civil Rights Act			
Black local		White local	
Employee	Hire date	Employee	Hire date
A	1/6/37	F	2/7/39
B	2/7/43	G	4/2/42
C	6/18/51	H	7/21/49
D	12/10/55	I	10/12/62
E	4/6/62	J	4/16/63

Post–1964 Civil Rights Act			
Merged locals		Dovetailed locals	
Employee	Hire date	Employee	Hire date
A	1/6/37	F	2/7/39
F	2/7/39	G	4/2/42
G	4/2/42	H	7/21/49
B	2/7/43	I	10/12/62
H	7/21/49	J	4/16/63
C	6/18/51	A	1/6/37
D	12/10/55	B	2/7/43
E	4/6/62	C	6/18/51
I	10/12/62	D	12/10/55
J	4/16/63	E	4/6/62

Departmental versus plantwide seniority

Often an organization may believe departmental seniority will be to its advantage in retaining workers with particular skills in major functional departments during a cutback. Organizations may also find that departmental seniority exists because different bargaining agents represent different groups of employees. If an employee transfers from one bargaining unit to another, the representing union in the receiving unit is not likely to want to grant hire data seniority. Thus, employers and multiple bargaining agents may have some reason for preferring departmental seniority. Where departmental seniority is used, a worker runs a risk in transferring across departments in that one becomes more vulnerable to layoffs as a result of lost seniority.

Seniority systems and utilization

The Equal Employment Opportunity Commission (EEOC) has generally taken the position that if an employer either rejects for employment a larger proportion of a subgroup such as minorities than majorities, or that the rate of minority employment is less than in the relevant labor supply, it is presumed that the imbalances result from discriminatory practices unless the employer can show otherwise. In its 1978 Uniform Selection Guidelines the EEOC requires that the employer provide evidence that its techniques are non-discriminatory if its utilization of minorities is less than 80 percent of the proportion of minorities in its relevant labor supply. Table 17–1 is an example of the types of imbalances that are presumed to be discriminatory.

TABLE 17–1
Presumed discriminatory impact

	Applicants	Hires	Labor market	Firm
Hiring				
Blacks	100	20		
Whites	100	60		
Utilization				
Blacks			20%	5%
Whites			80%	95%

Given a nondiscriminatory hiring policy as it relates to post–1964 Civil Rights Act behavior, a seniority system used for apportioning layoffs may have a different impact across races. Figure 17–3 illustrates this possibility. Assume that a plant operates in an area which has a 25-percent minority representation in the population. In the past the company racially discriminated in hiring, but after Title VII became effective, these policies were dropped. The firm now faces a 50-percent cutback in personnel due to declining orders. Under the seniority provisions of the contract, people with hire dates after 1963 are furloughed. Thus, all minorities are laid off. Is this system racially discriminatory or bona fide under 703h in Title VII?

The Supreme Court and seniority

Recently, the Supreme Court has handed down a series of decisions which clarified what a bona fide seniority system requires and what

FIGURE 17–3
Layoff impact on minority utilization

Employee	Race	Hire date
A	W	1/9/40
B	W	12/26/41
C	W	9/2/42
D	W	6/26/49
E	W	8/30/51
F	W	4/13/56
G	W	6/14/59
H	W	12/2/61
I	W	11/15/62
J	W	2/7/63
		Layoffs
K	B	12/6/65
L	W	4/13/67
M	W	4/21/68
N	B	5/12/69
O	B	6/30/69
P	B	3/2/71
Q	W	4/8/71
R	B	7/10/72
S	W	10/10/72
T	W	8/16/73

the rights of unionized employees are under this type of system. While other aspects of employment, such as selection procedures, had been dealt with as early as 1971, the Court made no decisions regarding the status of seniority systems and their impact on equal employment opportunity until it handed down its decision in early 1976 in the *Franks* v. *Bowman Transportation* case.[1]

Franks v. Bowman Transportation

In the *Franks'* case, the Court found that a number of black applicants had been discriminatorily denied employment as over-the-road truck drivers by Bowman Transportation. In the appeals court's review action, it had been held that a grant of seniority retroactive to the date of discrimination was unnecessary to make the person discriminated against "whole." Back pay would be sufficient. But where most personnel decisions, for example, layoffs, promotions, and so on, are based on seniority, the Supreme Court held that back pay would be insufficient to constitute adequate relief since the effects of the discriminatory action would be manifest any time a decision was to be made on an individual with less seniority, due to earlier discrimination.

---

[1] *Franks* v. *Bowman Transportation Co.*, 424 U.S. 747 (1976).

Thus, victims of discrimination in selection decisions following the effective date of the 1964 Civil Rights Act were held to be entitled to seniority from the date of the discriminatory action because this grant was necessary to restore both competitive and benefit seniority status in relation to job and compensation rights, respectively. But what effect does this have on persons who had no part in the company's discriminatory decisions to hire, and who have acquired seniority as a result? Their competitive status is changed as a result of the Court's imposition of back seniority. Figure 17–4 diagrams this effect.

FIGURE 17–4
Seniority list effects of *Frank* v.
Bowman Transportation

Discriminatees and dates

6	1/21/72
7	2/23/72
8	3/24/73

Employees and hire dates

1	1/31/63
2	2/17/71
3	3/14/73
4	10/16/74
5	12/22/75

Employee and seniority date after decision

1	1/31/63
2	2/17/71
6	1/21/72
7	2/23/72
8	3/24/73
3	3/14/73
4	10/16/74
5	12/22/75

Ironically, with the exception of the fact that an employer would have to compensate actual damages in lost pay for the discriminatory action, the award of back seniority has no effect on the employer except that seniority lists must be reordered.[2] But it has a direct competitive effect on those with a seniority date after the discriminatory action took place since Figure 17–4 shows they are now more vulnerable to layoff and less likely to obtain promotions, preferred job assignments, and the like.

In a brief to the Supreme Court when it was considering the *Franks* case, the United Auto Workers (UAW) argued that only innocent bystanders were penalized by a retroactive seniority award.[3] The

---

[2] *Albermarle Paper Co.* v. *Moody*, 422 U.S. 405 (1975).

[3] *Local 862, UAW* v. *Ford Motor Co.*, No. 74–1349, discussed in *Daily Labor Report*, no. 112, June 10, 1975, pp. A–4 through A–7.

UAW took the position that earned seniority rights should be preserved and that instead of a grant of retroactive seniority, the employer should be required to provide "frontpay" for discrimination. This would work something like the following: Suppose A was denied the employment for which he was most qualified among 1973 applicants. A court requires that he be hired in 1979 due to discriminatory selection policies. At that point under *Franks* and *Albemarle* v. *Moody,* he would be entitled to seniority from 1973 and back pay since 1973 less the earnings he has received in other jobs. Under the UAW scheme, he would receive back pay but not back seniority. Instead, if A were in line for a seniority based promotion available to persons with a 1973 hire date, he would not get the promotion because his actual seniority would date from 1979, but he would get pay relief equal to the differential between his present pay and the pay for the advanced position. Thus, no worker's seniority status or economic benefits would be disturbed. The same would hold for layoffs. If all workers with seniority dates later than 1975 were furloughed, A would be entitled to full pay even though not working. He would lose his pay only when the layoffs involved people with hire dates earlier than the discriminatory action against him. But the Supreme Court did not adopt this argument.

In holding that seniority lists can be revised to accommodate victims of discrimination, the Court held that both public policy relating to accumulation of seniority while off-the-job on military duty and collective agreements going beyond these stands are legitimate and recognizable.[4] Thus, back seniority is appropriate as a remedy against discrimination.

Teamsters v. United States

As we noted before, one of the important considerations in the operation of seniority systems is the potential adverse effect that departmental seniority systems may have on minority persons, particularly where an individual must irrevocably surrender accumulated seniority when transferring to another department. A second important problem relates to the definition of a bona fide seniority system. Congress protected seniority systems in 703(h), but how far is this protection to extend? If the effects of decisions based on seniority have adverse effects on minorities, can the systems still be legal? These questions were answered by the Supreme Court in two decisions rendered on May 31, 1977.[5]

---

[4] *Ford Motor Co.* v. *Huffman,* 345 U.S. 330 (1953).

[5] *International Brotherhood of Teamsters* v. *U.S.* and *T.I.M.E.-D.C., Inc.* v. *U.S.* (75–636, 75–672); and *East Texas Motor Freight System, Inc.* v. *Rodriguez* (75–718), *Teamsters Local Union 659* v. *Rodriguez* (75–651), and *Southern Conference of Teamsters* v. *Rodriguez* (75–715).

In the *Teamsters* (*T.I.M.E.-D.C.*) case, the government charged that the union and company practiced discrimination against blacks and Spanish-surnamed applicants and employees. It was alleged that the company discriminated against minorities in hiring for line (over-the-road) driving positions and that the departmental seniority system included in the collective bargaining agreement with the Teamsters perpetuated this discriminatory impact. Under the contract, city terminal drivers and other employees lost accumulated seniority when promoted. Their promotional seniority was also subordinate to laid-off line drivers since they retained recall rights for three years after layoff under the contract.

First, the Court found that the company had violated Title VII by virtually refusing to hire minorities for line drivers' positions. Of the company's 6,472 employees in early 1971, 571 (9 percent) were minorities; but of the 1,828 line drivers, only 15 (.8 percent) were. The Court also noted that prior to 1969, only once had the company employed a minority line driver.

Second, the Court examined the effects of the seniority system and whether it met the bona fide requirement of 703(h). In this labor agreement seniority in terms of "benefit status" (entitlement to pay and benefits) runs from date of hire on a systemwide basis. But "competitive status" (entitlement to promotions, avoidance of layoffs, and so on) seniority dates from the beginning of one's tenure on a particular job at a particular terminal. Since competitive status seniority did not accrue across jobs, the system might be said to discourage city drivers from bidding for line driver jobs, particularly if job security were an issue for a city driver. For its part, the union argued that its seniority system was bona fide within Title VII since the act does not deal with preact, but postact discrimination and that the union is ready, willing, and able to press for back seniority for postact victims who avail themselves of the grievance procedures.

The Court held that persons discriminated against since the act were entitled to be made whole for discrimination by the company. In terms of preact behavior, however, the Court interprets the wording of 703(h) and the congressional debate behind it to insulate preact discrimination from relief. Thus, constructive (or back) seniority cannot be granted to a date prior to the effective date of Title VII. And persons who accumulated seniority prior to that date, even as a result of discrimination, could continue to use it for "competitive status" purposes.

The Court held that although the seniority system perpetuates preact discrimination, Congress intended that seniority rights accrued as of the effective date be undisturbed. Postact applications are bona fide as long as they do not treat different races (or other groups) unequally. The Court held that the departmental seniority system for jobs within terminals applied equally to majorities and minorities. The system was not negotiated to establish or maintain discrimination. Thus, persons suffering from the effects of preact discrimination are not entitled to relief even though the application of the seniority system, *at this time*, may reduce their opportunities or discourage their bidding for promotion.

The Court also extended its approach to discrimination remedies. Both *Albermarle* and *Franks* dealt with job holders or applicants, but what remedy (if any) should be made available to persons who don't apply out of futility because of the firm's reputation for bias? The Court held that if a nonapplicant could establish qualifications for a job and an interest in applying for a specific job vacancy at the time it was open, then that person may be entitled to back pay, a job when an opening occurs, and constructive seniority.

Summary

Thus, a seniority system is bona fide even if it serves to perpetuate preact discrimination if it is applied equally to all members of a department or plant, regardless of race, and the like, and is based only on length of service. Departmental seniority systems which may require accrual of "competitive status" seniority within the department (even in cases where "benefit status" seniority accrues from hire date) are also legal. Remedies which include constructive seniority for postact violations (up to, but not exceeding, the effective date of the act) are necessary and appropriate to make whole persons who have suffered from discrimination.

UNIONS AND DISCRIMINATION

Unions may be involved in discrimination at a number of points. One point we will not address in this section is the duty to represent equally employees in the exercise of their rights to redress grievances under the contract. That aspect will be examined under the heading of fair representation. Unions are able to discriminate in hiring only where they are an active part of the process, for example, as in the construction industry where labor is obtained by the employers directly from the union. After hiring, unions may collude with employers to reduce opportunities through departmental seniority systems which prevent bidding on jobs in other areas or through the establishment of separate bargaining units for "white" and "black" jobs. The last is seldom if every encountered since the vigorous enforcement of Title VII rights began.

Construction Industry

Mills finds that there is a relatively wide range of black employment across the building trades.[6] Table 17–2 shows high levels of black utilization in the trowel trades (bricklayers, cement finishers, and so on) and low levels in electrician and plumber trades.

TABLE 17–2
Proportion of minorities by trade (1890–1970)

	1970	1967	1950	1940	1930	1910	1890	Approximate percentage of total number in occupational category in employed construction	
								1966	1970
Bricklayers	15.5	13.5	10.9	6.0	6.9	7.5	6.1	74	93
Carpenters	6.6	6.1	3.9	3.9	3.5	4.3	3.6	77	84
Cement finishers ..	30.3	37.7	26.2	15.2	15.8	13.0	10.3	95	97
Electricians	3.4	3.6	1.0	0.7	0.7	0.6	n.a.	45	48
Painters	9.8	9.9	5.2	3.8	3.6	2.9	2.0	67	83
Plumbers and pipefitters	3.9	3.2	3.3	2.2	2.0	1.7	1.1	64	70
Excavating grading, and road machinery operators	5.0	6.9						78	81
Roofers	10.5	15.3						98	95
Structural metal workers	6.7	3.9						56	69
Tinsmiths, coppersmiths, and sheet metal workers		1.9						35	
Laborers in construction ...		26.9						100	100

Source: 1890–1950: F. Ray Marshall, *The Negro and Organized Labor* (New York: John Wiley & Sons, 1965), p. 157; 1967, 1970: Current Population Survey data; the last two columns contain estimates based on unpublished CPS data from Daniel Quinn Mills, *Industrial Relations and Manpower in Construction* (Cambridge, Mass.: MIT Press, 1972), p. 145.

Mills suggests that social imbalances in both occupational and geographical sectors of the construction industry occur as a result of several causes.[7] Smaller employers with a more stable work force may

---

[6] Daniel Quinn Mills, *Industrial Relations and Manpower in Construction* (Cambridge, Mass.: MIT Press, 1972), pp. 143–77.

[7] Ibid., pp. 153–63.

engage in discriminatory practices since they may have more control over retention of employed union members and a lower likelihood of involvement in government contracts which forbid discrimination. But unions appear to have a greater effect on racial discrimination. While some trade unions have a widespread past reputation for discrimination on a national basis, the major source of bias rests in the local unit rather than the international. Given that the local apportions employment opportunity among its membership, the moderate continuous threat of unemployment, coupled with the homogeneity of skills involved in the trade, probably serve to increase group cohesion to exclude dissimilar minority members.

Apprenticeship programs also serve as barriers. Candidates for these programs may be required to pass difficult entry examinations which frequently are not job-related. Deficits in schooling or cultural differences may impose hurdles in one's path to program entry. Backgrounds rooted in geographical areas where building trades are not prevalent, such as rural or nonindustrial areas, may reduce the information an individual might have about possible opportunities.

Efforts have been made by employers, internationals and some local unions, and the federal government to remove the barriers to minority entry to the building trades and to accelerate their inclusion through Affirmative Action programs.

Affirmative Action

Besides the nondiscrimination requirements that an employer must meet under Title VII of the 1964 Civil Rights Act, a firm seeking to do business with the U.S. government is required to have an agency approved Affirmative Action Plan which specifies the steps it intends to take to employ, train, retain, and promote underutilized groups such as minorities and women. This requirement is specified in Executive Order 11246 and expanded on in Revised Order No. 4 which details the form in which Affirmative Action Plans are to be submitted.

The plans must detail the voluntary efforts an employer will take to include underutilized groups at a rate closely equivalent to their proportion in the labor market for each major occupational category for which hiring is done. This means that an employer must be concerned with all jobs, not just an overall workforce. For example, the employer hiring 500 building trades workers cannot hire 50 minority laborers and be in compliance in an area which is 10 percent minority if only 100 of the jobs are assigned to laborers.

Where employers are underutilizing minorities, specific steps must be detailed to show how they will reduce underutilization, when they will do it, and by how much. This is the "goals and timetables" aspect of an Affirmative Action Plan. For example, if a labor market contains 10 percent minorities and a contractor now has only 2 percent minority carpenters, an Affirmative Action Plan may specify what activities will take place for affirmative recruitment of qualified minorities into the building trades, may provide for the expansion of apprenticeship programs, and specify when these will be accomplished and project a specific numerical impact.

Mandatory compliance

In 1969, the Office of Federal Contract Compliance (OFCC) promulgated a set of requirements for contract construction employers known as the Philadelphia Plan. In his examination of the program, Gould notes that bidders employing trades where underutilization was a problem were required to promise employment of minorities consistent with OFCC's guidelines for that area.[8] In their efforts to meet their promises, contractors were required to notify action agencies which would refer minorities, track minority applicants and note actions taken regarding them, inform the OFCC if a union interfered in minority employment, and participate in training programs.

A contractor who consistently fails to make progress in affirmative action may be debarred from federal contracting. This means that the employer becomes ineligible from bidding on or performing federal jobs.

Industrial unions

Under existing labor law industrial unions have no influence on discrimination in the hiring process since union membership cannot be a required condition for initial employment. However, they may be parties to later discriminatory actions through the negotiation of contract terms which serve to "lock-in" minorities in jobs where they are overutilized because of departmental seniority clauses.

While the building trades control entry to contract construction occupations and the industrial unions do not control or influence initial employment, they often represent workers who learn skills within an industry. For example, the United Auto Workers (UAW) does not represent only unskilled assemblers, but also skilled plant maintenance workers such as electricians, millwrights, and model makers. Entry to these jobs occurs through initial hiring, and a bidding and testing procedure in which unskilled employees may apply for apprenticeship programs. Preference is given to present employees where a sufficient number have bid to fill the open positions.

---

[8] William B. Gould, *Black Workers in White Unions* (Ithaca, N.Y.: Cornell University Press, 1977), pp. 299–303.

440

There are a number of situations in which contractual agreements may lead to an adverse impact on minority attainment of skilled jobs. First, entry requirements on tests may be higher than necessary or nonjob-related, both having a disproportionate impact on minorities. Second, many contract clauses require the forfeiture of "competitive" seniority when one elects a transfer to another job classification. In cyclical industries, this imposes a greater penalty on unskilled workers bidding for an apprenticeship program than it does on "off-the-street" applicants. And third, where jobs are allocated first to internal bidders, an employer's past exclusionary policy at entry level is perpetuated into higher level jobs.

Remedies for discrimination

Besides the constructive seniority awards which have been granted by the Supreme Court, a number of other "make-whole" remedies for discrimination have been used by employers, unions, and the courts. We will see that some of the remedies used have resulted in conflicts between the union contract and requirements of regulatory agencies which employers have acceded to. The priorities of the conflicting claims and redress of discrimination and seniority entitlements have not been entirely resolved by the courts.

Consent decrees and judicial determinations

There are two major ways in which remedies for discrimination are imposed on employers and/or unions. The first is through a determination by a federal court that discrimination prohibited by Title VII has occurred. The second is through an agreement between the EEOC and an employer or union alleged to have discriminated. This latter type, a consent decree, specifies what an employer will do to remedy the alleged discrimination and is a negotiated settlement which has a federal court overseeing its implementation.

Major remedies have usually been fashioned in class action cases where the alleged discrimination has involved many members of a definable group such as blacks, women, persons over 40, and so on. These usually include monetary awards for class members, priority in hiring and promotion for affected classes, and the active removal of employment barriers. Where the remedies are prescribed by the courts, the monetary awards are equal (as closely as possible) to actual damages for persons who can show they were victims of discrimination. Under consent decrees, class members receive lump sum settlements without a requirement that they show actual discrimination against them. For the firm, the amount is usually less than the actual costs, and the class member is precluded from suing the firm for the actual amount as part of the settlement.

As examples of what occurs in discrimination cases where remedies are ordered, we will examine two court orders and two consent decrees: *Albemarle* v. *Moody;* and *EEOC et al.* v. *Detroit Edison, American Telephone and Telegraph, and Bethelehem Steel.* Although none of the four mention a union in its title, the last three involve unions as co-defendants or affect its members in the implementation of the order or decree.

Albemarle Paper Co. v. Moody[9]

Prior to this decision in 1975, it was unclear what the federal courts would require an employer to do to remedy past discrimination. In this case, a variety of problems including segregated departments, the employer's testing system for selection, and possible supervisory rating bias against minorities all served to reduce opportunities for black workers. The company argued that its practices were not intentionally discriminatory or designed to circumvent the act. The argument suggests that a proper remedy would be for the Court merely to enjoin further conduct which is discriminatory. However, the Supreme Court held that Title VII does not direct itself primarily at determining whether or not to punish an employer's discriminatory action but rather to make whole the victim of the action, whether intended or not. Thus, an employer may well be liable for the *actual* amount of the damages related to a discriminatory action.

EEOC et al. v. Detroit Edison Co. et al.[10]

This action alleged that Detroit Edison and unions representing its employees, particularly Local 233 of the Utility Workers Union of America (AFL–CIO), and Local 17 of the International Brotherhood of Electrical Workers (AFL–CIO), had systematically discriminated against blacks in hiring (company) and negotiated promotion policies.

A number of important principles emerged from this case (which was recently remanded to the 6th Circuit Court of Appeals for additional hearings). First, an individual or an organization named as a plaintiff in a Title VII suit must actually have suffered an injury to have standing to sue. Second, unions can be found guilty of violating Title VII if they have promoted or acquiesced in allowing contract terms like departmental seniority which serve to lock minorities out of

---

[9] 10 FEP Cases 181 (1975).

[10] 10 FEP Cases 239 (1975).

more desirable jobs. Third, companies found to be discriminating against minorities can legally be required to hire on a quota basis until the effects of past discrimination are remedied.

The quota requirement was a remedy instituted by the district court[11] and upheld by the 6th Circuit Court. The remedy required that for many jobs in the company hiring and promotions must be made on a 3/2 black/white ratio until 25 percent of the employees in these classifications were black (close to the proportion of blacks in Edison's labor market). For promotions to supervisory positions, the ratio was to be 1/1.

While the district court ordered punitive damages against the Utility Workers, the appeals court refused to enforce this provision since granting of punitive damages requires a jury trial which the defendants had requested but did not receive.

American Telephone and Telegraph[12]

This is an example of a consent decree rather than a court judgment. As a result of conciliation procedures between the EEOC, the OFCCP (Office of Federal Contract Compliance Programs) and AT&T, a consent decree was written which contained a series of actions AT&T would take to remedy race and sex discrimination. While this was not a court order, compliance with the decree is monitored by a federal district court.

Among the elements of the decree were the following: First, AT&T would pay about $15 million to approximately 13,000 women and 2,000 minority males who were denied pay and promotions. Pay increases of about $23 million were also to be given to women and minorities. Second, goals for the increased utilization of women and minorities in previously male jobs and males in previously female jobs were established. Third, the qualification and seniority requirements contained in the collective bargaining agreement could be subordinated to promotion goals if sufficient numbers of minorities and women were not available using contract procedures.[13] Thus, negotiated collective bargaining agreements appear to be subordinate to negotiated consent decrees. However, an employer cannot, in the absence of a consent decree, impose a quota on hiring and/or promotions to maintain or restore racial balance, regardless of whether it is unilaterally instituted or negotiated.[14]

---

[11] 6 FEP Cases 612 (1973).

[12] See FEP 431: 71–72a and 73–124k (Washington: Bureau of National Affairs).

[13] Upheld in *EEOC* v. *AT&T*, U.S. Court of Appeals (3d Circuit), certiorari denied by U.S. Supreme Court.

[14] *Weber* v. *Kaiser Aluminum & Chemical Corp.* U.S. District Court, Eastern District of Louisiana, 12 FEP Cases 1615 (1976).

Steel industry consent decree[15]

This decree involved nine major steel producers and the United Steelworkers (USW). Among other things, the decree requires that almost $31 million be apportioned among 34,000 minority employees and 6,000 women. Goals were established for craft job hires to be 50 percent women and minorities. Promotions to supervision were to be 25 percent minority or female. Where seniority was to be used as a basis for promotion, it was to be on a plantwide rather than a departmental basis.

Summary

The court decisions and consent decrees are clear on two major issues which are important to employers and have implications for collective bargaining. First, employers may be motivated to seek settlements with the EEOC through conciliation rather than risking a court judgment awarding actual damages. Second, remedial action required of an employer may legally override some aspects of a collective bargaining agreement.

Two final areas will now be examined. Both of these have greater impacts on unions and their members than on employers. These areas relate to certification of a union alleged to discriminate and the duty to represent bargaining unit members fairly under a grievance procedure.

CERTIFICATION AND DISCRIMINATION

There are three major cases in the certification area which determined the NLRB's present position on alleged racial discrimination of unions and the duty of employers to recognize and bargain with these unions.

Mansion House[16]

In this case a building management firm refused to recognize a painters' union which it charged with discriminating against racial minorities. The NLRB ordered Mansion House to bargain, but when Mansion House refused to comply, the circuit court declined to enforce the board's ruling.

The court held that the labor acts could not be used to force recognition of a union which is apparently discriminating against an identifi-

---

[15] FEP 431: 72a–b and 125–152.

[16] *NLRB* v. *Mansion House Corp.*, 82 LRRM 2608 (1973).

able protected subgroup. It also held that when a company raises the issue of discrimination and produces statistical evidence indicative of bias the union is obligated to rebut this evidence if certification is to be granted and bargaining ordered.

Bekins Moving and Storage Co. of Florida[17]

In this case Bekins argued that the Teamsters local which was seeking to represent its employees discriminated against women and Spanish-speaking minorities. Certification of a discriminating union by the NLRB would then place the weight of the federal government behind this organization and diminish a represented employee's right to fair treatment by a bargaining agent.

The board held that an employer could raise a postelection claim that a union would be likely to discriminate or unfairly represent. If the NLRB found evidence of discrimination, it could refuse to certify the results.

Handy-Andy, Inc.[18]

This decision has seemingly brought the board back full circle to its position prior to *Mansion House* (before enforcement was denied by the appeals court). The change in position can be explained to some extent by the changed composition of the board since *Bekins* and its generally greater willingness to allow the parties to settle things without outside interference, just as we saw in the *Shopping Kart* decision.[19]

In the *Handy-Andy* case, a Teamsters local was seeking representation rights for a group of grocery warehouse employees. When the election was held, the vote was 108 for representation and 66 against, from a total of 198 eligible employees. After the election, Handy-Andy filed an objection to certification alleging that the local either practiced discrimination in membership or would not fairly represent employees.

The board held here that it was not obligated to determine whether or not a union was likely to discriminate, but rather whether the actions it took *after* certification were discriminatory. In its decision the board recognized a recent Supreme Court ruling in which the Court held that a regulating body is to police the activities within its purview (in that case, rate setting for utilities; in this, certification of bargaining agents).[20]

---

[17] 211 NLRB 138 (1974).

[18] 228 NLRB 59 (1977).

[19] 228 NLRB 190 (1977).

[20] *NAACP* v. *Federal Power Commission*, 425 U.S. 662 (1976).

Further, denial of certification to a union elected by a majority of persons in an appropriate unit may actually subvert the wishes of minority members who voted in a secret ballot election. In the Handy-Andy election unit there were 211 employees. Almost 82 percent (172) were minorities. The union won the election by 108 to 66 carrying 62 percent of the votes. If all 39 majorities had voted for the union, it would still mean that in the most extreme case possible, minorities had endorsed the union by a 69 to 66 margin. The NLRB majority argued that the electorate should be free to determine whether or not a union will represent its best interests and whether a "discriminatory" bargaining agent is a better alternative than a "punitive" employer.

Thus, the focus on minority representation is again essentially aimed at the issue of fair representation of individual rights or group rights under a contract and away from the reputation or pattern of past conduct of a bargaining agent.

FAIR REPRESENTATION

We have already discussed the area of fair representation from a general standpoint in Chapter 13, but we want to focus here on specifics related to race, sex, and representation. The focus we will take looks at group representation, individual representation, and finally self-help by represented groups in dealing with employers without using the designated bargaining agent. While the principles adduced here can be applied to any individual or subgroup within the union, the development has been substantially related to the securing of minority group rights (race).

While the NLRB did not directly deal with the general subject of fair representation until the *Miranda Fuel* decision in 1962, the Supreme Court decided its first case relating race to fair representation in 1944.

Steele v. Louisville & Nashville Railroad[21]

This case held that an exclusive bargaining agent responsible for a mixed group of black and white employees, who denied membership to blacks, must equally represent both groups. The responsibility devolved upon the union because of its majority status and the statutory inability of the minority group to obtain its own representative. The decision did not, however, prohibit unions from forbidding membership of minorities.

---

[21] *Steele* v. *Louisville & Nashville Railroad*, 323 U.S. 192 (1944).

Two important points to remember about *Steele* are: first, the case is a Railway Labor Act case, not a Wagner Act case; and, second, in 1944 (before the passage of the Taft-Hartley amendments) the statutes did not recognize union unfair labor practices. Therefore, there was no relief grantable by the NLRB until 1947 to one who alleged unfair representation.[22]

Hughes Tool Company[23]

This 1964 case was the first which required unions under Taft-Hartley jurisdiction to represent blacks and whites equally in a bargaining unit. The union's failure to process grievances of blacks was found here by the NLRB to be an unfair labor practice.

Local 12, United Rubber Workers v. NLRB[24]

The *Rubber Workers* case involved the layoff of more senior black employees while junior whites remained on the job. When the blacks filed grievances, Local 12's grievance committee refused to process them. The appeals court, in its ruling on the *Rubber Workers'* case, held that the refusal to process the grievances restrained the black members Section 7 rights to bargain collectively using a representative of their own choosing, the majority choice for that unit.

A question remains as to how far a union must go in advocating the grievances of individual members and whether the rights of individuals or groups must necessarily be represented by the union in some situations where the individual may feel this is inappropriate. We will discuss the leading case in this area next.

Emporium-Capwell v. Western Addition Community Organization[25]

The Emporium is a department store located in San Francisco. Employees there were represented by the department store union. In the collective bargaining contract there were clauses which related to no-strike no-lockout agreements, nondiscrimination and grievance processing, including arbitration.

In 1968 a group of employees presented a grievance alleging discrimination against blacks. The union leaders agreed to take the grievance to arbitration, if necessary to redress the discrimination. When the

---

[22] Gould, *Black Workers in White Unions*, p. 36.

[23] *Hughes Tool Co.*, 147 NLRB 1573 (1964).

[24] *Local 12, United Rubber Workers v. NLRB*, 368 F.2d 12 (5th Circuit, 1966).

[25] See Gould's discussion of this case and related issues in *Black Workers in White Unions*, pp. 246–67.

grievance was being heard by an adjustment board (step immediately prior to arbitration), one black read a statement asking that the grievance be handled directly between the individuals involved and the president of the firm. Minority group members of the union attended no further hearings and did, in fact, go to the president who referred them to the personnel director. Since they had already seen the personnel director and no action had been taken, no further attempt was made there.

The following weekend, on their own time, two black employees picketed the store carrying banners alleging racial discrimination by the store and urging a consumer boycott of the store. When they reported for work at the beginning of the next week, they were warned that repeated conduct of that nature would result in their discharge. When they persisted, they were fired.

The NLRB was asked to rule on whether or not the individual picketing was protected concerted activity under Section 7. The board held that it was not. The union was taking affirmative steps to adjust the grievance and the actions of the picketers were not taken at the union's behest. Since the contracted grievance procedure which would address the negotiated nondiscrimination clause was not used by this group, the conduct was unprotected.

The court of appeals for the District of Columbia refused to enforce the NLRB ruling. They held that the action taken to picket the store was Civil Rights activity, not concerted activity within Taft-Hartley provisions. The fired employees' peaceful protest would be protected under Section 704(a) of Title VII of the 1964 Civil Rights Act. In its decision the court held that a specific minority group should have the opportunity to engage in activities it may feel will be more successful than the union's in obtaining its goal.

The Supreme Court reversed, endorsing the NLRB position.[26] Given the Court's earlier strong endorsement of the grievance procedure culminating in arbitration as the appropriate forum for the settlement of industrial disputes (compare, the Steelworkers trilogy), the Court held that the minorities' picketing activity was unprotected. Since the contract provided for arbitration of discrimination claims, it was premature for the fired employees to use other avenues for redress. The Court was also concerned over the possibility that a union might not internally be capable of resolving differences among competing employee subgroups if other prearbitration self-help procedures were available.

It is interesting to note that under the 1974 *Alexander* v. *Gardner-Denver* decision on arbitration awards as not precluding later Title VII

---

[26] *Emporium-Capwell* v. *Western Addition Community Organization*, 420 U.S. 50 (1975).

action, the picketing employees might have avoided discharge and later won the discrimination claim if they had allowed the charge to proceed to arbitration.[27] If unsuccessful there, they could have charged the store with discrimination under Title VII. While Gould might conclude self-help for particular subgroups is reduced by the *Emporium* decision, the avenues still remain relatively uncluttered as long as the subgroup observes due process and the issue is one which is related to Title VII rights.

SUMMARY

In this chapter we have observed the rapid and pervasive increase in activity by governments and unions to enhance equal employment opportunity. The most important federal requirements are contained in Title VII of the 1974 Civil Rights Act and Executive Order 11246 (1965) which specifies employment requirements for federal contractors. Evidence exists that both employers and unions have contributed to historical patterns of discrimination; employers primarily through initial hiring or assignment, unions through the negotiation of departmental seniority clauses or restrictive apprenticeship programs.

Recent court remedies for discrimination include back pay, constructive seniority, and quota hiring. However, seniority accrued during a period of discriminatory hiring prior to the effective data of Title VII cannot be disturbed in the awarding of constructive seniority. Only postact discrimination is redressable. Where patterns of discrimination have existed, both employers and unions may be responsible to take action to eliminate it.

Under present NLRB and court decisions, unions cannot discriminate among individuals in representing their contractual rights, members or not, minorities or majorities. The NLRB does not now, however, refuse to certify unions as bargaining agents because of a likelihood of discrimination. Rather it will review actual behavior on a case-by-case basis where unions are charged with unfair labor practices related to representation.

In general, international unions have advocated nondiscrimination for some time. Locals, however, have not been ardent, in some cases, in protecting individual rights due to the makeup of the union and prejudices of local members.

SUGGESTED READINGS

Hill, Herbert. *Black Labor and the American Legal System: Vol. I, Race, Work, and the Law* (Washington: Bureau of National Affairs, 1977).

---

[27] *Alexander v. Gardner-Denver*, 415 U.S. 36 (1974).

McKelvey, Jean T., ed. *The Duty of Fair Representation* (Ithaca, N.Y.: New York State School of Industrial and Labor Relations, Cornell University, 1977).

DISCUSSION QUESTIONS

1. Since the labor acts confer exclusive representation rights on a majority union for a given bargaining unit, how carefully can minority members expect the union to represent their interests?
2. Should minority employees be entitled to their own representation rather than relying on the majority union?
3. What are the ramifications of the Supreme Court's seniority decisions for minority inclusion in more skilled jobs? Was the decision equitable?
4. Should "forum shopping" for discrimination grievances granted in *Alexander* v. *Gardner-Denver* have been awarded?

Case

In 1975 GMFC was awarded a large defense department subcontract to fabricate turrets for the new X–84 tank. One of the requirements made of the prime contractor, United Motors Company, was that it prepare an acceptable Affirmative Action Plan (AAP) detailing its specific plans, goals, and timetables for the utilization of women and minorities in jobs where they were underrepresented. The contract also required subcontractors to prepare AAP's, too. One part of the AAP portrays the firm's utilization of women and minorities and compares this to their prevalence in the labor force.

The data for GMFC's 1975 employment clearly showed underutilization of both women and minorities in skilled positions. These data are contained in Exhibit 1. As part of their AAP, GMFC established a goal to double utilization of females and minorities by 1980.

EXHIBIT 1
Utilization and availabilities of women and minorities for skilled jobs

| | Present (1975) | | | Goal (1980), GMFC | |
| | GMFC | | Labor force | | |
	Number	Percent	Percent	Number	Percent
Skilled labor	1,375	100%	100%	1,450	100%
Male	1,350	98	88	1,395	96
Majority	1,305	95	72	1,305	90
Minority	45	3	16	90	6
Female	25	2	12	55	4
Majority	22	1.8	9	44	3.2
Minority	3	0.2	3	11	0.8

One of the first procedures GMFC undertook was an attempt to convince senior minorities and women in unskilled jobs to bid on skilled openings. This produced only two people willing to be upgraded. Others were deterred by the departmental seniority system which would deprive them of competitive status seniority upon promotion.

GMFC industrial relations staff members participated in a Central City Personnel Association conference on AAP problems late in 1975. The conference revealed that an unwillingness to accept promotions was pervasive across employers where departmental seniority existed. The GMFC participants recalled that the union had been unwilling to change the departmental seniority system since its members counted on the permanency of the process to maintain job security rights. To the union, job security was a more important issue than promotions.

As a result of the conference, representatives of GMFC and three other heavy industries in Central City agreed to meet again to try to find an innovative, workable solution to their problem. The first prong of their solution was to establish a four-firm consortium to fund and operate a skills training center in an area of Central City suffering from severe unemployment. Places in the training program were allotted on the basis of application date and need. Of the enrolled students, 80 percent were racial minorities and 30 percent were women.

The program consisted of two phases: a remedial course to bring verbal and math skills up to a level necessary to complete the craft part of the course, and a craft training program which offered opportunities to gain skill at welding, metal forming, and other fabrication work. The whole program required about two years, and students were subsidized by federal grants.

In early 1978, the first ten students were graduated. GMFC and the other three employers offered jobs to all ten (eight minorities, six males and two females; and three women, two minority, one majority). Of the ten, GMFC was able to hire three. These three were placed directly into skilled jobs with the firm.

When news of this action became known to Local 384's negotiating committee, it asked for a meeting with John Colestock, the IR vice president. At the meeting George Curtis, the leader of the negotiating committee, demanded an explanation for how the company had decided to place these employees directly. Colestock said that it was an attempt by the company to meet its AAP goals which were necessary to retain government business and guarantee continued high levels of employment.

Curtis did not seem impressed. Stabbing the air with his finger, he said, "Listen, Colestock, we owe our senior employees who were by-passed our representation. I don't care how little seniority anyone working here has, but it's a hell of a lot more than any of these skills training center people have. Our members are entitled to those jobs. If I don't get a satisfactory explanation from you and a plan of action to keep you management people from violating our contract, I'll take this thing clear to arbitration, understand?"

DIRECTIONS

1. Prepare a strategy that you expect will meet Curtis's objections and save the AAP.
2. If you had it to do over again, what strategy would you design?
3. Assume Curtis takes the case to arbitration; how would you defend the company's actions?

18

COLLECTIVE BARGAINING
IN THE FUTURE

It's customary to speculate about what the future holds for any area where we have acquired information about its past history and its present practices. Labor relations and the practice of collective bargaining are no exceptions. We have examined some major evolutionary changes and how both labor and management have adapted to them. We can expect many major changes to take place in the relatively near future. In this chapter, we will point out some new directions that we should expect collective bargaining to take. These new directions will be influenced by a number of factors. Among the most important are (1) the long-run secular change in the distribution of workers across the various industrial sectors of the economy, (2) the increasingly white-collar nature of employment, (3) demographic changes in the makeup of the labor force, (4) the migration of individuals and industries from the traditionally industrialized states to the South and West, (5) significant legislative initiatives on the federal and state levels, (6) the impact of high levels of inflation on wage demands and income maintenance programs, and (7) the makeup of the unions' hierarchies and the evolution of the overall philosophy of the labor movement.

As you read through this chapter, try to connect present day practices and their deficiencies to adaptations that you expect in the future. Try also to apply the past history of the labor movement to predicting where future changes will take place. While we are living in the present, we are part of a continuous flow of time and the practices that are occurring in the present will be seen in the future as simply a segment on the trend line of progress in union-management relations.

INDUSTRIAL CHANGE

As you examine the distribution of workers by industry in the economy since the beginning of this century, you can see some dramatic changes which influence the patterns of union organization. Table 18–1 shows the total numbers of employees and their distribution by major nonagricultural industry classification from 1947 to 1975. Table 18–2 shows the breakdown between production and nonproduction workers within these industries over the same period of time. Table

TABLE 18–1
Total employment on payrolls of nonagricultural establishments, by industry division: Annual averages, 1947–1975.

| Year | Total | Private | | | Manufacturing | | | Transportation and public utilities | Wholesale and retail trade | | | Finance, insurance, real estate | Services | Government | | |
		Total private	Mining	Contract construction	Total	Durable goods	Non-durable goods		Total	Wholesale	Retail			Total government	Federal[1]	State and local
								Number (thousands)								
1947	43,881	38,407	955	1,982	15,545	8,385	7,159	4,166	8,955	2,361	6,595	1,754	5,050	5,474	1,892	3,582
1948	44,891	39,241	994	2,169	15,582	8,326	7,256	4,189	9,272	2,489	6,783	1,829	5,206	5,650	1,863	3,787
1949	43,778	37,922	930	2,165	14,441	7,489	6,953	4,001	9,264	2,487	6,778	1,857	5,264	5,856	1,908	3,948
1950	45,222	39,196	901	2,333	15,241	8,094	7,147	4,034	9,386	2,518	6,868	1,919	5,382	6,026	1,928	4,098
1951	47,849	41,460	929	2,603	16,393	9,089	7,304	4,226	9,742	2,606	7,136	1,991	5,576	6,389	2,302	4,087
1952	48,825	42,216	898	2,634	16,632	9,349	7,284	4,248	10,004	2,687	7,317	2,069	5,730	6,609	2,420	4,188
1953	50,232	43,587	866	2,623	17,549	10,110	7,438	4,290	10,247	2,727	7,520	2,146	5,867	6,645	2,305	4,340
1954	49,022	42,271	791	2,612	16,314	9,129	7,185	4,084	10,235	2,739	7,496	2,234	6,002	6,751	2,188	4,563
1955	50,675	43,761	792	2,802	16,882	9,541	7,340	4,141	10,535	2,796	7,740	2,335	6,274	6,914	2,187	4,727
1956	52,408	45,131	822	2,999	17,243	9,834	7,409	4,244	10,858	2,884	7,974	2,429	6,536	7,277	2,209	5,069
1957	52,894	45,278	828	2,923	17,174	9,856	7,319	4,241	10,886	2,893	7,992	2,477	6,749	7,616	2,217	5,399
1958	51,363	43,524	751	2,778	15,945	8,830	7,116	3,976	10,750	2,848	7,902	2,519	6,806	7,839	2,191	5,648
1959	53,313	45,230	732	2,960	16,675	9,373	7,303	4,011	11,127	2,946	8,182	2,594	7,130	8,083	2,233	5,850
1960	54,234	45,881	712	2,885	16,796	9,459	7,336	4,004	11,391	3,004	8,388	2,669	7,423	8,353	2,270	6,083
1961	54,042	45,448	672	2,816	16,326	9,070	7,256	3,903	11,337	2,993	8,344	2,731	7,664	8,594	2,279	6,315
1962	55,596	46,706	650	2,902	16,853	9,480	7,373	3,906	11,566	3,056	8,511	2,800	8,028	8,890	2,340	6,550
1963	56,702	47,477	635	2,963	16,995	9,616	7,380	3,903	11,778	3,104	8,675	2,877	8,325	9,225	2,358	6,868
1964	58,331	48,735	634	3,050	17,274	9,816	7,458	3,951	12,160	3,189	8,971	2,957	8,709	9,596	2,348	7,248
1965	60,815	50,744	632	3,186	18,062	10,406	7,656	4,036	12,716	3,312	9,404	3,023	9,087	10,074	2,378	7,696
1966	63,955	53,163	627	3,275	19,214	11,284	7,930	4,151	13,245	3,437	9,808	3,100	9,551	10,792	2,564	8,227
1967	65,857	54,459	613	3,208	19,447	11,439	8,008	4,261	13,606	3,525	10,081	3,225	10,099	11,398	2,719	8,679
1968	67,951	56,106	606	3,306	19,781	11,626	8,155	4,311	14,099	3,611	10,488	3,381	10,622	11,845	2,737	9,109
1969	70,442	58,240	619	3,525	20,167	11,895	8,272	4,435	14,704	3,733	10,971	3,562	11,228	12,202	2,758	9,444
1970	70,920	58,359	623	3,536	19,349	11,195	8,154	4,504	15,040	3,816	11,225	3,687	11,621	12,561	2,731	9,830
1971	71,222	58,334	609	3,639	18,572	10,597	7,975	4,457	15,352	3,823	11,523	3,802	11,903	12,887	2,696	10,192
1972	73,714	60,373	625	3,831	19,090	11,006	8,084	4,517	15,975	3,943	12,032	3,943	12,392	13,340	2,684	10,656
1973	76,896	63,157	644	4,015	20,068	11,839	8,229	4,614	16,674	4,107	12,568	4,041	13,021	13,739	2,663	11,075
1974	78,413	64,235	694	3,957	20,046	11,895	8,151	4,646	17,017	4,223	12,794	4,208	13,617	14,177	2,724	11,453
1975 p	76,984	62,213	745	3,455	18,344	10,676	7,668	4,499	16,950	4,177	12,773	4,222	13,997	14,771	2,748	12,023
								Percent distribution								
1947	100.0	87.5	2.2	4.5	35.4	19.1	16.3	9.5	20.4	5.4	15.0	4.0	11.5	12.5	4.3	8.2
1948	100.0	87.4	2.2	4.8	34.7	18.5	16.2	9.3	20.7	5.5	15.1	4.1	11.6	12.6	4.2	8.4
1949	100.0	86.6	2.1	4.9	33.0	17.1	15.9	9.1	21.2	5.7	15.5	4.2	12.0	13.4	4.4	9.0
1950	100.0	86.7	2.0	5.2	33.7	17.9	15.8	8.9	20.8	5.6	15.2	4.2	11.9	13.3	4.3	9.1
1951	100.0	86.6	1.9	5.4	34.3	19.0	15.3	8.8	20.4	5.4	14.9	4.2	11.7	13.4	4.8	8.5
1952	100.0	86.5	1.8	5.4	34.1	19.1	14.9	8.7	20.5	5.5	15.0	4.2	11.7	13.5	5.0	8.6
1953	100.0	86.8	1.7	5.2	34.9	20.1	14.8	8.5	20.4	5.4	15.0	4.3	11.7	13.2	4.6	8.6
1954	100.0	86.2	1.6	5.3	33.3	18.6	14.7	8.3	20.9	5.6	15.3	4.6	12.2	13.8	4.5	9.3
1955	100.0	86.4	1.6	5.5	33.3	18.8	14.5	8.2	20.8	5.5	15.3	4.6	12.4	13.6	4.3	9.3
1956	100.0	86.1	1.6	5.7	32.9	18.8	14.1	8.1	20.7	5.5	15.2	4.6	12.5	13.9	4.2	9.7
1957	100.0	85.6	1.6	5.5	32.5	18.6	13.8	8.0	20.6	5.5	15.1	4.7	12.8	14.4	4.2	10.2
1958	100.0	84.7	1.5	5.4	31.0	17.2	13.9	7.7	20.9	5.5	15.4	4.9	13.3	15.3	4.3	11.0
1959	100.0	84.8	1.4	6.6	31.3	17.6	13.7	7.5	20.9	5.5	15.3	4.9	13.4	15.2	4.2	11.0
1960	100.0	84.6	1.3	5.3	31.0	17.4	13.5	7.4	21.0	5.5	15.5	4.9	13.7	15.4	4.2	11.2
1961	100.0	84.1	1.2	5.2	30.2	16.8	13.4	7.2	21.0	5.5	15.4	5.1	14.2	15.9	4.2	11.7
1962	100.0	84.0	1.2	5.2	30.3	17.1	13.3	7.0	20.8	5.5	15.3	5.0	14.4	16.0	4.2	11.8
1963	100.0	83.7	1.1	5.2	30.0	17.0	13.0	6.9	20.8	5.5	15.3	5.1	14.7	16.3	4.2	12.1
1964	100.0	83.5	1.1	5.2	29.6	16.8	12.8	6.8	20.8	5.5	15.4	5.1	14.9	16.5	4.0	12.4
1965	100.0	83.4	1.0	5.2	29.7	17.1	12.6	6.6	20.9	5.4	15.5	5.0	14.9	16.6	3.9	12.7
1966	100.0	83.1	1.0	5.1	30.0	17.6	12.4	6.5	20.7	5.4	15.3	4.8	14.9	16.9	4.0	12.9
1967	100.0	82.7	.9	4.9	29.5	17.4	12.2	6.5	20.7	5.4	15.3	4.9	15.3	17.3	4.1	13.2
1968	100.0	82.6	.9	4.9	29.1	17.1	12.0	6.3	20.7	5.3	15.4	5.0	15.6	17.4	4.0	13.4
1969	100.0	82.7	.9	5.0	28.6	16.9	11.7	6.3	20.9	5.3	15.6	5.1	15.9	17.3	3.9	13.4
1970	100.0	82.3	.9	5.0	27.3	15.8	11.5	6.4	21.2	5.4	15.8	5.2	16.4	17.7	3.8	13.9
1971	100.0	81.9	.9	5.1	26.1	14.9	11.2	6.3	21.6	5.4	16.2	5.3	16.7	18.1	3.8	14.3
1972	100.0	81.9	.8	5.2	25.9	14.9	11.0	6.1	21.6	5.3	16.3	5.3	16.8	18.1	3.6	14.5
1973	100.0	82.1	.8	5.2	26.1	15.4	10.7	6.0	21.7	5.4	16.3	5.3	16.9	17.9	3.5	14.4
1974	100.0	81.9	.9	5.0	25.6	15.2	10.4	6.0	21.7	5.4	16.3	5.4	17.4	18.1	3.5	14.6
1975 p	100.0	80.8	1.0	4.5	23.8	13.9	10.0	5.8	22.0	5.4	16.6	5.5	18.2	19.2	3.6	15.6

p Preliminary.
[1] Data are prepared by the U.S. Civil Service Commission and relate to civilian employment only, excluding the Central Intelligence and National Security Agencies.

Source: U.S. Department of Labor *Employment and Training Report of the President* (Washington: Government Printing Office, 1976), p. 293.

18–3 shows the degree to which major industrial sectors are organized. When taken together, we can extrapolate some trends which might be likely to occur in union organizing abilities and levels in the future.

Employment distribution by industry

In terms of raw numbers, Table 18–1 shows that total payrolls grew by about 75 percent between 1947 and 1975. However, many industries did not grow at a rate anywhere near that level. Over the period, employment in mining fell by 22 percent, while small increases were registered for nondurable goods manufacturers (7 percent), transportation and public utilities (8 percent), durable goods manufacturers (27 percent), and the federal government (46 percent). Industrial growth patterns for contract construction (75 percent), wholesale trade (77 percent), and retail trade (95 percent) were close to the overall growth rate of 75 percent. Areas where growth was much more rapid than that of total employment were: finance, insurance, and real estate, 141 percent; services, 177 percent; and state and local government, 236 percent.

Production and nonproduction workers

We can also see that there were some marked changes over time in the internal makeup of the industrial work force. There has been a relative change toward the use of nonproduction workers over time. Table 18–2 shows these changes quite clearly.

In no industry for which data were reported, was there a lower ratio of nonproduction to production employees in 1975 than there was in 1947. Industries where the relative proportion of nonproduction workers increased the most rapidly were mining, contract construction, durable goods manufacturing, and wholesale trades. Increases were slowest for transportation and public utilities, retail trade, and service sectors.

Union penetration

Table 18–3 shows the level of union penetration in several major industrial areas. Here we note that the greatest degree of penetration is generally in areas where growth has been slower than the national average. High levels of organization are found in mining, contract construction, and transportation. Lower levels are found for services, finance, insurance, and real estate, and retail trades.

TABLE 18-2

Production or nonsupervisory workers and nonproduction workers on private payrolls, and nonproduction workers as percent of total employment, by industry division: annual averages, 1947-1975

Year	Total private	Mining	Contract construction	Manufacturing			Transportation and public utilities	Wholesale and retail trade			Finance, insurance, real estate	Services
				Total	Durable goods	Nondurable goods		Total	Wholesale	Retail		
Production or nonsupervisory workers (thousands)												
1947	33,747	871	1,759	12,990	7,028	5,962	(3)	8,241	2,165	6,076	1,460	(3)
1948	34,489	906	1,924	12,910	6,925	5,986	(3)	8,629	2,274	6,355	1,521	(3)
1949	33,159	839	1,919	11,790	6,122	5,669	(3)	8,595	2,267	6,328	1,542	(3)
1950	34,349	816	2,069	12,523	6,705	5,817	(3)	8,742	2,294	6,448	1,591	(3)
1951	36,225	840	2,308	13,368	7,480	5,888	(3)	9,091	2,365	6,726	1,649	(3)
1952	36,643	801	2,324	13,359	7,550	5,810	(3)	9,333	2,439	6,894	1,711	(3)
1953	37,694	765	2,305	14,055	8,154	5,901	(3)	9,510	2,459	7,051	1,771	(3)
1954	36,276	686	2,281	12,817	7,194	5,623	(3)	9,456	2,442	7,014	1,837	(3)
1955	37,500	680	2,440	13,288	7,548	5,740	(3)	9,675	2,479	7,196	1,920	(3)
1956	38,495	701	2,613	13,436	7,669	5,767	(3)	9,933	2,547	7,386	1,994	(3)
1957	38,384	695	2,537	13,189	7,553	5,638	(3)	9,923	2,541	7,382	2,031	(3)
1958	36,608	611	2,384	11,997	6,579	5,419	(3)	9,736	2,477	7,259	2,063	(3)
1959	38,080	590	2,538	12,603	7,033	5,570	(3)	10,087	2,562	7,525	2,121	(3)
1960	38,516	570	2,459	12,586	7,028	5,559	(3)	10,315	2,605	7,710	2,181	(3)
1961	37,989	532	2,390	12,083	6,618	5,465	(3)	10,234	2,584	7,650	2,225	(3)
1962	38,979	512	2,462	12,488	6,935	5,553	(3)	10,400	2,625	7,775	2,274	(3)
1963	39,553	498	2,523	12,555	7,027	5,527	(3)	10,560	2,656	7,904	2,329	(3)
1964	40,589	497	2,597	12,781	7,213	5,569	3,484	10,869	2,719	8,151	2,386	7,974
1965	42,309	494	2,710	13,434	7,715	5,719	3,555	11,358	2,814	8,544	2,426	8,331
1966	44,281	487	2,784	14,297	8,370	5,926	3,632	11,820	2,911	8,909	2,476	8,786
1967	45,169	469	2,708	14,308	8,364	5,944	3,712	12,121	2,971	9,151	2,566	9,287
1968	46,506	461	2,786	14,514	8,457	6,056	3,751	12,542	3,036	9,506	2,687	9,764
1969	48,243	472	2,973	14,767	8,651	6,116	3,857	13,094	3,139	9,954	2,836	10,246
1970	48,197	473	2,951	14,020	8,042	5,978	3,907	13,379	3,206	10,174	2,921	10,546
1971	48,202	455	3,023	13,467	7,622	5,845	3,861	13,630	3,192	10,438	2,995	10,772
1972	49,992	472	3,166	13,957	8,005	5,952	3,916	14,188	3,299	10,889	3,092	11,201
1973	52,334	488	3,315	14,760	8,691	6,069	4,019	14,709	3,433	11,266	3,184	11,769
1974	53,029	527	3,234	14,613	8,641	5,972	4,058	15,065	3,526	11,540	3,240	12,293
1975 P	51,087	566	2,761	13,068	7,541	5,528	3,858	15,005	3,462	11,542	3,221	12,608
Nonproduction workers (thousands)												
1947	4,660	84	223	2,555	1,357	1,197	(3)	714	196	519	264	(3)
1948	4,751	88	245	2,672	1,401	1,270	(3)	643	215	428	308	(3)
1949	4,763	91	246	2,651	1,367	1,284	(3)	669	220	450	315	(3)
1950	4,847	85	264	2,718	1,389	1,330	(3)	644	224	420	328	(3)
1951	5,234	89	295	3,025	1,609	1,416	(3)	651	241	410	342	(3)
1952	5,574	97	310	3,273	1,799	1,474	(3)	671	248	423	358	(3)
1953	5,893	101	318	3,494	1,956	1,537	(3)	737	268	469	375	(3)
1954	5,995	105	331	3,497	1,935	1,562	(3)	779	297	482	397	(3)
1955	6,261	112	362	3,594	1,993	1,600	(3)	860	317	544	415	(3)
1956	6,635	121	386	3,807	2,165	1,642	(3)	925	337	588	435	(3)
1957	6,895	133	386	3,985	2,306	1,681	(3)	963	352	610	446	(3)
1958	6,917	140	394	3,948	2,251	1,697	(3)	1,014	371	643	456	(3)
1959	7,149	142	422	4,072	2,340	1,733	(3)	1,040	384	657	473	(3)
1960	7,365	142	426	4,210	2,431	1,777	(3)	1,076	399	678	488	(3)
1961	7,459	140	426	4,243	2,452	1,791	(3)	1,103	409	694	506	(3)
1962	7,727	138	440	4,365	2,545	1,820	(3)	1,166	431	736	526	(3)
1963	7,924	137	440	4,440	2,589	1,853	467	1,218	448	771	548	(3)
1964	8,146	137	453	4,493	2,603	1,889	481	1,291	470	820	571	735
1965	8,432	138	476	4,628	2,691	1,937	481	1,359	498	860	597	756
1966	8,882	140	491	4,917	2,914	2,004	519	1,425	526	899	624	765
1967	9,290	144	500	5,139	3,075	2,064	549	1,485	554	930	659	815
1968	9,600	145	520	5,267	3,169	2,099	560	1,557	575	982	694	855
1969	9,997	147	552	5,400	3,244	2,156	578	1,610	594	1,017	726	982
1970	10,162	150	585	5,329	3,153	2,176	597	1,661	610	1,051	766	1,075
1971	10,128	151	616	5,105	2,975	2,130	596	1,722	631	1,091	807	1,131
1972	10,381	152	665	5,133	3,001	2,132	601	1,787	644	1,143	851	1,191
1973	10,823	156	700	5,308	3,148	2,160	625	1,875	674	1,202	907	1,252
1974	11,306	167	723	5,433	3,254	2,179	638	1,952	697	1,254	968	1,324
1975 P	11,126	179	694	5,276	3,135	2,140	641	1,945	715	1,231	1,001	1,389

(3) = Data not collected.

p = Preliminary.

Source: U.S. Department of Labor, *Employment and Training Report of The President* (Washington: Government Printing Office, 1976), p. 294.

What could we conclude from the combination of these three tables? First, it is relatively clear that employment in the most heavily unionized industries is not increasing as rapidly as elsewhere. Thus, other things being equal, the percentage of workers who are unionized would be expected to decrease over time. But on the other hand, those areas which have the fewest union members at the present are also

TABLE 18–3
Union membership proportions by industry

75 percent or more	25 to 50 percent
Transportation	Printing, publishing
Contract construction	Leather
Ordinance	Furniture
Paper	Electric, gas utilities
Electrical machinery	Machinery
Transportation equipment	Chemicals
50 to 75 percent	Lumber
Primary metals	Less than 25 percent
Food and kindred products	Nonmanufacturing
Mining	Textile mill products
Apparel	Government
Tobacco manufacturers	Instruments
Petroleum	Service
Manufacturing	Local government
Fabricated metals	State government
Telephone and telegraph	Trade
Stone, clay, and glass products	Agriculture and fishing
Federal government	Finance
Rubber	

Source: Adapted from U.S. Department of Labor, Bureau of Labor Statistics, *Directory of National Unions and Employee Associations, 1973* (Washington: Government Printing Office, 1974), p. 81.

those that are growing most rapidly. Successful organizing campaigns in these industries could increase the relative share of workers who are unionized. Success in organization may not come easily, however, since workers in some industries (finance, insurance, and real estate) may resist unionization given their attitudes toward labor; and other industries (services) have employment patterns which will make organization expensive where employers are relatively small.

We might tentatively conclude at this point that the proportion of workers who will be unionized will decline slightly in the future as the more heavily unionized industries lose both their relative share of employment and as the ratio of production to nonproduction employees declines.

OCCUPATIONAL DISTRIBUTION

The pattern of employment by occupation in the United States has also changed markedly over time. Table 18–4 details some of the major shifts in the proportion of people in major occupational categories over the first seven decades of the 20th century. Major changes reveal the decline of agricultural employment and the redistribution of jobs between the blue- and white-collar occupations.

TABLE 18-4

Occupational distribution of the economically active population, by sex, selected years, 1900–1974

Major occupation group and sex	1900	1910	1920	1930	1940	1950	1974 (April)
BOTH SEXES							
Total: Number (thousands)	29,030	37,291	42,206	48,686	51,742	58,999	85,192
Percent	100.0	100.0	100.0	100.0	100.0	100.0	100.0
White-collar workers	17.6	21.4	24.9	29.4	31.1	36.6	48.8
Professional, technical and kindred	4.3	4.7	5.4	6.8	7.5	8.6	14.6
Managers, officials, and proprietors, except farm	5.8	6.6	6.6	7.4	7.3	8.7	10.4
Sales workers	4.5	4.7	4.9	6.3	6.7	7.0	6.4
Clerical and kindred	3.0	5.3	8.0	8.9	9.6	12.3	17.4
Blue-collar and service workers	44.9	47.7	48.1	49.4	51.5	51.6	47.6
Blue-collar workers	35.8	38.2	40.2	39.6	39.8	41.1	34.3
Crafts, supervisors, and kindred workers	10.5	11.6	13.0	12.8	12.0	14.2	13.3
Operative and kindred workers	12.8	14.6	15.6	15.8	18.4	20.4	16.1
Laborers, except farm and mine	12.5	12.0	11.6	11.0	9.4	6.6	4.8
Service workers	9.0	9.6	7.8	9.8	11.7	10.5	13.3
Private household	5.4	5.0	3.3	4.1	4.7	2.6	---
Service workers, except private household	3.6	4.6	4.5	5.7	7.1	7.9	---
Farmworkers	37.5	30.9	27.0	21.2	17.4	11.8	3.6
Farmers and farm managers	19.9	16.5	15.3	12.4	10.4	7.4	---
Farm laborers and supervisors	17.7	14.4	11.7	8.8	7.0	4.4	---
MALE							
Total: Number (thousands)	23.711	29,847	33,569	37,933	39,168	42,554	51,927
Percent of total	81.7	80.0	79.5	77.9	75.7	72.1	61.0
White-collar workers	14.4	16.1	17.0	19.6	20.2	22.0	24.7
Professional, technical, and kindred	2.8	2.8	3.0	3.6	4.4	5.2	8.5
Managers, officials, and proprietors, except farm	5.8	6.2	6.2	6.8	6.5	7.6	8.5
Sales workers	3.7	3.7	3.6	4.8	4.9	4.6	3.7
Clerical and kindred	2.3	3.5	4.2	4.3	4.4	4.6	4.0
Blue-collar and service workers	33.3	36.1	38.3	38.9	39.1	39.4	33.2
Blue-collar workers	30.7	33.0	35.4	35.2	34.6	34.9	28.2
Crafts, supervisors, and kindred workers	10.3	11.3	12.7	12.6	11.7	13.7	12.8
Operative and kindred workers	8.5	10.0	11.5	12.0	13.7	14.8	11.0
Laborers, except farm and mine	12.0	11.7	11.2	10.6	9.2	6.3	4.4
Service workers	2.5	3.1	2.9	3.8	4.6	4.5	5.0
Private household	.2	.2	.1	.2	.3	.1	---
Service workers, except private household	2.4	2.9	2.8	3.6	4.3	4.4	---
Farmworkers	34.0	27.8	24.2	19.3	16.4	10.8	3.1
Farmers and farm managers	18.8	15.8	14.6	11.8	10.1	7.2	---
Farm laborers and supervisors	15.3	12.0	9.6	7.5	6.3	3.6	---
FEMALE							
Total: Number (thousands)	5,319	7,445	8,637	10,752	12,574	16,445	33,265
Percent of total	18.3	20.0	20.5	22.1	24.3	27.9	39.0
White-collar workers	3.7	5.2	7.9	9.8	10.9	14.6	24.1
Professional, technical and kindred workers	1.5	1.9	2.4	3.0	3.1	3.4	6.1
Managers, officials, and proprietors, except farm	.3	.4	.5	.6	.8	1.2	1.9
Sales workers	.8	1.0	1.3	1.5	1.8	2.4	2.7
Clerical and kindred	.7	1.8	3.8	4.6	5.2	7.6	13.5
Blue collar and service workers	11.6	11.6	9.7	10.5	12.4	12.2	14.4
Blue-collar workers	5.1	5.1	4.9	4.4	5.3	6.2	6.0
Craft, supervisors, and kindred workers	.3	.3	.2	.2	.3	.4	.6
Operatives and kindred workers	4.4	4.6	4.1	3.8	4.7	5.6	5.1
Laborers, except farm and mine	.6	.3	.5	.3	.3	.2	.4
Service workers	6.5	6.5	4.9	6.1	7.1	6.0	8.3
Private household	5.3	4.8	3.2	3.9	4.4	2.5	---
Service workers, except private household	1.2	1.7	1.7	2.1	2.7	3.5	---
Farmworkers	3.5	3.2	2.8	1.9	1.0	1.0	.5
Farmers and farm managers	1.1	.7	.7	.5	.3	.2	---
Farm laborers and supervisors	2.4	2.4	2.1	1.3	.7	.8	---

NOTE: Prior to 1940, the term "the economically active population" refers to civilian gainful workers, 10 years old and over; for 1940 and 1950, it refers to persons 14 years old and over in the civilian labor force and thereafter to persons 16 years old and over.

Source: U.S. Department of Labor, *Employment and Training Report of the President* (Washington: Government Printing Office, 1976), p. 387.

Major changes in the white-collar area have included increases in professional employees and clericals. The proportion of people working in blue-collar occupations, in the aggregate, has not changed markedly over the course of the century, with most of the loss from agriculture being redistributed in the blue- and white-collar areas.

TABLE 18–5A

Employment by occupation group, 1974 and projected 1985 requirements (numbers in thousands)

Occupation group	Actual 1974		Projected 1985 [1]		Change 1974–85		Average annual rate of change, [2] 1974–85
	Number	Percent distribution	Number	Percent distribution	Number	Percent [3]	
Total employment [4]	85,936	100.0	103,400	100.0	17,464	20.3	1.7
Professional and technical workers	12,338	14.4	16,000	15.5	3,662	29.4	2.4
Managers and administrators, except farm	8,941	10.4	10,900	10.5	1,959	21.6	1.8
Sales workers	5,417	6.3	6,300	6.1	883	15.7	1.4
Clerical workers	15,043	17.5	20,100	19.4	5,057	33.8	2.7
Craft and kindred workers	11,477	13.4	13,800	13.3	2,323	19.9	1.7
Operatives	13,919	16.2	15,200	14.7	1,281	9.0	.8
Nonfarm laborers	4,380	5.1	4,800	4.6	420	8.8	.8
Service workers	11,373	13.2	14,600	14.1	3,227	28.0	2.3
Farmers and farm laborers	3,048	3.5	1,900	1.8	−1,148	−39.0	−3.0

[1] Among the assumptions underlying these projections is a 4-percent unemployment rate. More detailed assumptions will be described in an article scheduled to be published in the *Monthly Labor Review* in mid-1976.
[2] Compound interest rate between terminal years.
[3] Percentages were calculated using unrounded numbers.
[4] Represents total employment as covered by the Current Population Survey.

Within the blue-collar occupations, there has been an increase in the proportion of operatives through 1950, then a decline; a long-term decline in the use of laborers and an increase in the proportion in service occupations. These trends for the blue-collar labor force are consistent with the peaking of labor union penetration in the early 1950s. The fall-off in the proportion of workers in lower skilled blue-collar occupations is consistent with the decline in union proportions in the population.

TABLE 18–5B

Total employment[1] by major industry sector, 1960, 1974, and projected 1980 and 1985 (numbers in thousands)

Industry sector	Actual		Projected [2]		Percent distribution				Number change			Average annual rate of change [3]		
	1960	1974	1980	1985	1960	1974	1980	1985	1960–74	1974–80	1980–85	1960–74	1974–80	1980–85
Total	68,869	90,958	101,866	109,565	100.0	100.0	100.0	100.0	22,089	10,908	7,699	2.0	1.9	1.5
Government [4]	8,353	14,177	16,800	19,350	12.1	15.6	16.5	17.7	5,824	2,623	2,550	3.9	2.9	2.9
Total private	60,516	76,781	85,066	90,215	87.9	84.4	83.5	82.3	16,265	8,285	5,149	1.7	1.7	1.2
Agriculture	5,389	3,466	2,750	2,300	7.8	3.8	2.7	2.1	−1,923	−716	−450	−3.1	−3.8	−3.5
Nonagriculture	55,124	73,315	82,316	87,915	80.0	80.6	80.8	80.2	18,191	9,001	5,599	2.1	1.9	1.3
Mining	748	710	788	823	1.1	.8	.8	.8	−38	78	35	−.4	1.8	.9
Contract construction	3,654	4,783	5,178	5,798	5.3	5.3	5.1	5.3	1,129	395	620	1.9	1.3	2.3
Manufacturing	17,197	20,434	21,937	22,597	25.0	22.5	21.5	20.6	3,237	1,503	660	1.2	1.2	.6
Durable goods	9,681	12,093	13,148	13,661	14.1	13.3	12.9	12.5	2,412	1,055	513	1.6	1.4	.8
Nondurable goods	7,516	8,341	8,789	8,936	10.9	9.2	8.6	8.2	825	448	147	.7	.9	.3
Transportation and public utilities	4,214	4,926	5,186	5,381	6.1	5.4	5.1	4.9	712	260	195	1.1	.9	.7
Transportation	2,743	2,973	3,049	3,081	4.0	3.3	3.0	2.8	230	76	32	.6	.4	.2
Communication	844	1,193	1,308	1,423	1.2	1.3	1.3	1.3	349	115	115	2.5	1.5	1.7
Public utilities	624	760	829	877	.9	.8	.8	.8	136	69	48	1.4	1.5	1.1
Wholesale and retail trade	14,177	19,797	22,457	23,187	20.6	21.8	22.0	21.2	5,620	2,660	730	2.4	2.1	.6
Wholesale	3,295	4,568	5,029	5,109	4.8	5.0	4.9	4.7	1,273	461	80	2.4	1.6	.3
Retail	10,882	15,229	17,428	18,078	15.8	16.7	17.1	16.5	4,347	2,199	650	2.4	2.3	.7
Finance, insurance, and real estate	2,985	4,531	5,392	5,964	4.3	5.0	5.3	5.4	1,546	861	572	3.0	2.9	2.0
Other services [5]	12,152	18,134	21,378	24,165	17.6	19.9	21.0	22.1	5,982	3,244	2,787	2.9	2.8	2.5

[1] Employment in this table is on a "jobs" rather than a "persons" concept and includes, in addition to wage and salary workers, self-employed and unpaid family workers. Employment on a job concept differs from employment on a person concept by separately counting each job held by a multiple jobholder.
[2] See footnote 1, table E–9.
[3] Compound interest rate between terminal years.
[4] Includes domestic wage and salary workers and government enterprise employees; does not include employees paid from nonappropriated funds.
[5] Includes paid household employment.

Source: U.S. Department of Labor, *Employment and Training Report of the President* (Washington: Government Printing Office, 1976), p. 336.

Where the proportions in occupations with relatively moderate skill requirements have increased, such as service workers or clericals, either difficulties in organizing large numbers of small employers or in overcoming negative attitudes toward unions has probably contributed to the declining labor share.

Department of Labor projections continue to forecast larger than average growth rates for occupational areas where unions have not been particularly successful or active in the past, such as professional and technical workers, clericals, and service workers. Slower than average growth rates are found for areas in which they have done well such as operatives and nonfarm laborers. Table 18–5 contains these employment projections by occupational group.

DEMOGRAPHIC CHANGES

The changing composition of the labor force in terms of population characteristics may also affect the degree to which employees become or remain organized in the future. We have recently witnessed a paradoxical period in American employment history. Beginning in 1976 we have experienced employment at record levels while unemployment rates remain at or above the 6 percent figure. The reason for the paradox is the influx of large numbers of new jobseekers which resulted from two major factors. First, birth rates during the period beginning in 1946 through the middle 1960s were at higher levels than earlier periods. As these individuals reached their late teens and early twenties, they created a bulge of jobseekers. Second, increasingly large proportions of women are either remaining in or reentering the labor force. Participation rates among women have steadily increased over the last several years without a corresponding decline for male participation. Between 1947 and 1975, participation rates for women jumped from about 32 percent to over 46 percent while male participation declined from 87 percent to 79 percent. Overall, these changes were reflected in a 3-percent increase in the total participation rate from 59 percent to 62 percent.

As the birth rate declined in the late 1960s and the 1970s, this will mean that workers entering the labor force in the middle 1980s through at least the middle 1990s will be in relatively short supply in comparison to the past. Changes which could reduce the short supply problems would be a continuing increase in participation rates among women and a willingness of older workers to take advantage of legislation prohibiting forced retirements before age 70.

What might these demographic changes mean for the labor movement? We can only speculate, but issues related to rewards and job security would be expected to have a major effect. For example, as there are increasing numbers of individuals at any given job level, the competition for promotions becomes more intense. If the criteria used by the organization for making employment decisions for promotions, layoffs, and so forth are either not consistently applied or are not consistent with the belief systems of the involved employees, we might expect some push for organization. This could have a major impact in professional areas if opportunities for promotion into management positions decline. For example, if large numbers of engineers find themselves blocked from exits from their occupations at traditional career change points, and management makes moves to replace them with more recently trained people, then a likely reaction will be organization. Career planning systems and careful attention to promotional criteria will be necessary in the near future to reduce the necessity for employees to organize if firms desire to remain nonunion.

GEOGRAPHICAL SHIFTS

We recognize that there are large differences among states in terms of public reactions to and legislation regulating labor organizations. Most of the differences in legislation relates to the public sector since federal law preempts the states in most private sector areas. But you should recall that the Taft-Hartley amendments allow the states the option of prohibiting union and agency shops through the passage of "right-to-work" laws. Up to this point, most of these laws are in states that have not been heavily industrialized, that have strong ties to agriculture, and are in the South or West. With the exception of Texas, no state with a major industrial base has a right-to-work law.

We have recently seen an upsurge in the movement of industrial facilities from the North and East to the South and West. Some of these moves have been to capitalize on the lower wage costs associated with these areas, others to take advantage of more favorable tax situations, and still others in reaction to the increased interest of the American population in living in "sunbelt" areas. One reason that is also mentioned is that the attitude of the general populace toward unions is not favorable. Companies may believe that they have a lower risk in being organized in the sunbelt than they do in their present locations. Evidence at this point seems to bear them out, but it will be hard to predict whether sunbelt workers will be satisfied making lower wages for doing the same work as workers in heavily industrialized areas. At the present time, we would have to forecast that geographical move-ment to sunbelt areas would reduce the proportion of people unionized. First, the attitudes in the area to which the moves are being made are less positive toward unions. And, second, if a move is made from a unionized plant to a new facility, there normally has to be a new organizing campaign, with concommitant risk of loss by the union in the new facility. So any move is likely to reduce a union base, but a move to the sunbelt would be likely to have greater effect.

LEGISLATION

As you have obviously noted, legislation has had a major effect on the conduct of labor relations in the United States. Thus, major changes in labor statutes could influence both the ability to organize the bargaining power. By the time you read this text, the first piece of proposed legislation we will examine may have been enacted. It may not be in the same form as we discuss here, as it may be amended during congressional debate or in conference committee proceedings after passage by both houses.

Labor Reform Act of 1977

In October 1977, the U.S. House of Representatives passed a bill to amend the Labor Management Relations Act. During the 1978 session of Congress, the U.S. Senate was to debate its version of the bill and act upon it. Prior to this debate and coincidental to the house passage, many individuals and groups testified for or against it. Most business groups denounced it as a bill which would make union organizing activities so easy that the proportion of employees who would be unionized would rapidly increase to the 50 percent level. On the other side, organized labor cited a need for legislation to stop delaying tac-tics it alleged that management used when faced with organizing ac-tivity. They also argued that the NLRB's "make whole" remedies for persons who were illegally discharged by employers were not sufficient to deter illegal conduct. They asked for greater penalties to be levied against employers for violations of individual rights under Section 7 of the LMRA.

Following are some of the major provisions of the Labor Reform Act:

1. The NLRB would be expanded from five to seven members. As in the past, three members would be sufficient to render a decision of a given case, but all members of the board would have to be willing to clear the decision (as in the past).

2. The legislation would enable a prevailing party to ask the NLRB for summary affirmance of an administrative law judge's decision within ten days after the decision is rendered. The losing party would have up to 20 days to file exceptions.

3. A major provision of the bill would give employee union organizers equal access to other employees for campaigning at any point where an employer addressed its employees about union representation. There is no change in the act which appears to alter the judiciary's stance according nonemployee organizers a lesser degree of access to employees by enabling employers to forbid their access to company facilities.

4. The bill directs the NLRB to hold representation elections within 25 days of the receipt of a petition where evidence shows that a majority of the employees support the petition, within 50 days where there is not a majority but sufficient interest, and 75 days as an absolute maximum where the situation is extremely novel or complex. The Senate version of the bill also forbids the setting aside of elections solely because one or both of the parties made noncoercive statements which were not factual during any period of the campaign except the 48-hour period immediately preceding the election.

5. Where an employer was determined to have violated the act willfully and committed an unfair labor practice, that employer could be debarred from federal contract work for a period of up to three years.

6. Where employers have committed unfair labor practices against individuals, back pay awards could be doubled rather than using a simple "make whole" procedure. Where an entire bargaining unit is to be made whole because of an employer's refusal to bargain, they are to be made whole for the difference between the pay they were receiving before the refusal to bargain and that they received after, multiplied by a factor equivalent to the increase in prevailing settlements near the time of the violation.

7. Under this act, board orders would be self-enforcing instead of requiring the board to seek an enforcing petition with an appeals court.

8. The act would require that injunctions against employee discharges be rendered by the federal courts where there is reasonable cause to conclude that the discharge was motivated to blunt an organizing campaign. The discharge would be voided by the injunction, and the worker would be reinstated.

9. Injunctions could also be granted to employers against unauthorized wildcat strikes and sympathy strikes where the picketing is not related to a labor dispute. However, employers could not

seek injunctions against strikes authorized by the union but which are in violation of a nonstrike clause in a labor contract.

The future of the act is in limbo as of the end of 1978. A Senate filibuster during the summer led to the bill being referred back to committee for additional work.

Public employee bargaining laws

In 1975 there appeared to be some sentiment for a national public employee bargaining law. This law would have established statutes governing the conduct of labor relations for federal employees and state and local employees as well. But public opinion shifted toward opposition to the proposed legislation as public employees become more successful in gaining wage increases on a state and local level. It is also probable that such a law may be unconstitutional since the Supreme Court overturned legislation extending overtime and minimum wage provisions to state and local employees.

However, there has been activity on a state-by-state basis as we noted in Chapter 15. There does appear to be a recognition that public employee strikes are not the major catastrophes most people have projected in the past. States are more willing now to grant limited rights to strike to public employees and to offer some type of arbitration procedures to resolve impasses for public safety employees. We would expect that unionization among public employees will continue to increase, but we also will probably note that multilateral bargaining procedures will be less successful over time as settlements favorable to unions lead to tax increases.

INFLATION

Except for the period immediately after World War II, management and labor have never experienced inflation at the rate we have seen during the 1970s. Inflation causes difficulties for both. Management encounters problems in accurately forecasting what its cost will be at some future point because wages are often tied to the rate of inflation as well as to some negotiated flat figure. Labor also encounters difficulties. These occur most frequently among retirees. Retirement benefits are seldom indexed but figured as some rate against earnings made during the last few years of employment and multiplied by the number of years of service a given employee had provided. Thus, if an employer paid $2 in benefits for every $100 in earnings an employee averaged over the last five years and multiplied that by years of service, we could find that someone who averaged $15,000 per year would receive a $9,000 yearly pension ($2 × 150 × 30). If the cost-of-living were to rise at a rate of 8 percent annually, the real value of the $9,000 pension would be less than $4,000 by the end of ten years.

To preserve the real purchasing power of pension benefits, the union may attempt to bargain up the rate of employer benefits—say from $2.00 to $2.16 to offset the 8 percent inflation. But the employer encounters difficulties with this even if it were to agree to the demand, because the Employee Retirement Income Security Act requires that all pension plans be funded on an actuarially sound basis. The employer would probably have to come up with a lump sum immediately to restore the fund's deficiency given the benefit increase. Problems also occur for the union since the present membership may find the amount of money available for an increase in pay, if pension benefits increase, will be substantially less than they expected.

THE LABOR MOVEMENT

In the 1980s, the American Federation of Labor will celebrate its 100th anniversary. That same decade the Congress of Industrial Organizations will note its 50th. How much has the underlying philosophy of the labor movement changed in the interim? Conclusions on the degree of change may vary broadly across observers, but the underlying philosophy and approach of organized labor probably has not. We noted in Chapter 3, at the merger of the AFL and CIO, that George Meany kept the faith by his statement of a set of goals for organized labor that was entirely consistent with anything Samuel Gompers would have said. The American labor movement has survived because it has listened to the workers it represents rather than the general public. It has not always been as successful when it was devising tactics to secure these goals since some depend on the reactions of the public. Is the approach that Meany restated in 1955 still labor's approach? The answer is probably "yes." Box 18–1 contains an excerpt from a speech delivered by Thomas Donahue, executive assistant to the president of the AFL–CIO at the International Conference on Trends in Industrial and Labour Relations in Montreal on May 26, 1976. This excerpt again endorses the long-run approach taken by the American labor movement.

The leadership

Many of the leaders of the labor movement are old. George Meany is in his 80s. Others are approaching mandatory retirement as established by their union constitutions. This means that new leadership is inevitable in many unions. Many observers of the union scene predict

BOX 18-1

"There are those who view collective bargaining as a narrowing of workers' interests. It is, after all, a self-interest mechanism. So they call for collective bargaining to tackle a broader range of social concerns, as if the contracts between individual employers and unions can resolve what are truly national issues—discrimination, poverty, inflation, recession, safety, health care, and on and on.

They look for some sort of revolutionary unionism, welfare unionism or uplift unionism—none of which has ever been acceptable to the majority of U.S. workers—which is why our unions are an unusual mixture of job unionism and social unionism.

Our structures focus first and foremost on the representation of workers in their dealings with employers. Unions are, of course, special interest organizations whose first and principal function is to organize workers and represent those workers in an effort to improve their job conditions—in other words, to bargain collectively.

Only when this function is successful can our unions pursue their secondary function—the expression of social unionism. That is, the effort to improve the general condition of their members by improving the general condition of everyone in the community, be it local, state, national or international.

It is in the pursuit of those larger goals, and in the unification of the more than 45,000 local labor organizations in that pursuit, that American labor can be seen as a movement with a social philosophy. . . .

That equality is established through the collective bargaining process, a conflict relationship, where equals talk with equals. And because American unions have won equality at the bargaining table, we have not sought it in corporate board rooms.

We do not seek to be a partner in management—to be, most likely, the junior partner in success and the senior partner in failure.

We do not want to blur in any way the distinctions between the respective roles of management and labor in the plant.

We guard our independence fiercely—independent of government, independent of any political party, and independent of management.

Similarly, we guard our strength and our militance, and when we bargain, we bargain on all issues—whether they are mandatory subjects for bargaining under our laws or not—because realistically, they are all on the table.

And we probably bargain on as many, if not more, issues than the number we might have any impact on as members of a board of directors.

We've watched co-determination and its offshoot experiments with interest, and will continue to do so, but it is our judgment that it offers little to American unions in the performance of their job unionism role (given our exclusive representative status and our wide-open conflict bargaining) and it could only hurt U.S. unions as they pursue their social unionism functions—seeking through legislation, political action, community involvement, and a host of other approaches, to improve our members' lot by improving society generally."

Source: Thomas R. Donahue, "Remarks," International Conference on Trends in Industrial and Labour Relations, Montreal, Canada, May 26, 1976.

that these leadership changes will cause some major redirections in the thrust of the labor movement. I think they are wrong.

In the past we have seen individual union leaders who have had great impact on the course and outcomes of collective bargaining. Some whose names immediately come forward are people like Walter Reuther, John L. Lewis, Jimmy Hoffa, and Philip Murray. These people all had major impacts on their organizations. But none of them could singlehandedly have a major impact on the ultimate success or failure of his organization. Regardless of the charismatic aura that John L. Lewis carried, the United Mine Workers were in a continually declining position throughout most of his presidency. And none of their unions were radically changed when they passed from leadership roles. Granted, the stewardship of Lewis's successors was poor, but for the others, the underlying trends present in their organizations were not greatly altered by their replacements.

American labor may in many ways be similar to American management. If we looked at General Motors' past history, we would have seen periods during which one person held the role of chief executive officer for extended periods, for example, Alfred P. Sloan. Recently, however, top management at General Motors has been turning over every three years or so, because of the corporation's mandatory retirement age. Chief executives do not reach that position until their sixties, so their tenure is short. The same holds true to some extent in many of the more mature unions. Stability in philosophies and interests is insured by the relatively short tenure of those on top.

CONCLUSION

There are many factors which will influence the future of collective bargaining and the shape of the labor movement. Demographics, economics, and legislation are three major factors. At the present time, none of these seems to support rapid union growth. In fact, we might predict a moderate decline in the relative proportion of persons who will belong to unions in the future. Some legislative initiatives like the Labor Reform Act could make organizing easier and reduce the ability of firms to use delaying tactics which might inhibit a majority's choice for organizing, but the underlying factors which contribute to organization like large numbers of unorganized workers performing the same types of duties in single facilities do not often exist in the present day situation. The last major outpost for organization, the state and local public sector, has already received a good deal of emphasis and activity. From here on, labor will have to penetrate professional and clerical employment in large private sector firms. To do this, it will require a situation where either fewer opportunities exist than in the past for professional workers, or stability in employment increases for clericals. The latter is more likely than the former.

The underlying philosophy of the labor movement will probably not change. Some issues may become increasingly important to its members. Most of these won't relate to more interesting work, but more freedom in using one's waking hours. It is unlikely that we would come back to look at labor in 50 years and not still see its direction as being, "More, more now."

SUGGESTED READING

Somers, Gerald G., ed. *The Next 25 Years of Industrial Relations* (Madison, Wis.: Industrial Relations Research Assn., 1973).

AUTHOR INDEX

A

Aaron, Benjamin, 340, 349
Abelow, William J., 417
Abodeely, John E., 143–44, 146, 160
Allen, Russell, 403, 419
Applebaum, Leon, 102
Ash, Philip, 347–49

B

Barbash, Jack, 78, 107
Becker, Brian B., 423–24
Berkowitz, Monroe, 268
Bernstein, Irving, 59
Blaine, Harry R., 102
Blood, Milton R., 124
Bloom, Gordon F., 274
Bognanno, Mario F., 421
Bok, Derek C., 107
Bond, Deborah T., 383–84, 386–87, 389
Brecher, Jeremy, 27
Brown, Bert R., 216–19, 232, 303
Burke, Donald R., 208–10

C

Campbell, John P., 118
Cartter, Allen M., 165–66
Cartwright, Dorwin, 102, 126
Chamberlain, Neil W., 15, 25, 103, 107, 215, 232, 312
Cherns, Albert B., 322
Cohen, Sanford, 203–4, 232
Coleman, James S., 102
Commons, John R., 11
Cook, Alice H., 103, 107
Craypo, Charles, 311–12
Cullen, Donald E., 15, 25, 103, 107, 215, 232, 312
Curtin, Edward, 105

D

Davis, Louis E., 322
Dennis, Barbara D., 408, 411
Dewire, James, 348
Donahue, Thomas R., 464
Douglas, Ann, 263–68, 304
Dulles, Foster Rhea, 13–16, 18–20, 22, 24, 28, 31, 34–36, 44–46
Dunlop, John T., 107
Dunnette, Marvin D., 118
Dworkin, James B., 421
Dyer, Lee, 323

E

Edwards, Harry T., 360, 375
Elkouri, Edna Asper, 352, 361–62, 375
Elkouri, Frank, 352, 361–62, 375
Ephlin, Donald F., 323
Estey, Martin, 108

F

Fashoyin, Omotayo, 421
Feuille, Peter, 406–7, 411
Fine, Sidney, 32, 59
Fleming, Robben W., 358, 364–65, 375
Foner, Phillip S., 283
Fossum, John A., 176
Fox, Arthur L., II, 94, 101
Frost, Carl F., 319, 321–22, 326
Fuller, S. H., 223

G

Gannon, Martin J., 32
Gerhart, Paul F., 400–01
Getman, Julius, 129, 147, 149, 155–57, 160
Goldberg, Stephen, 129, 147, 149, 155–57, 160

Goldstein, B., 268
Gompers, Samuel, 23
Gootnick, Margery, 409
Gould, William B., 439, 446
Granof, Michael H., 232
Grodin, Joseph R., 409

H

Hackman, J. Richard, 124
Hampton, David R., 336
Healy, James J., 197
Heneman, Herbert G., Jr., 172, 204, 206, 232
Herman, Jeanne B., 129, 147, 149, 155–57, 160
Herrick, Neal Q., 322
Hildebrand, George H., 310, 326
Hill, Herbert, 448
Holloway, Sally T., 421
Horowitz, Morris A., 85
Horton, Raymond D., 409
House, Robert J., 118
Howe, Irving, 59
Hoxie, Robert F., 26
Hulin, Charles L., 124
Hunter, Lawrence C., 318, 326

I–J

Indik, Bernard P., 268
Jackson, Louis, 150–51, 160
Jones, Dallas L., 24, 354, 370–72, 374–75
Jones, Mary, 28
Juris, Hervey A., 422–33

K

Kahn, Mark L., 345
Kasper, Hirschel, 408, 411
Kilpatrick, Joan G., 99
Kochan, Thomas A., 323, 398–400
Kossoris, Max D., 225
Krinsky, Edward B., 423–4
Kuhn, James W., 336, 343–45, 349
Kutler, S. I., 23

L

Landsberger, Henry A., 269–70
Langsner, Adolph, 180
Lawler, Edward E., III, 118, 126, 322–3
Lawrence, Paul R., 124
Lelchook, Jerry, 411
Lens, Sidney, 28
Levy, David A., 383–84, 386–87, 389
Lewis, Robert, 150–51, 160
Lipset, Seymour M., 102

Lipsky, David B., 323
Livernash, E. Robert, 197
Locke, Edwin A., 323
Long, Gary, 407
Lowenberg, J. Joseph, 408, 411

M

Maccoby, Michael, 322–23
McDermott, Thomas J., 271
McKelvey, Jean T., 271, 449
McKersie, Robert B., 219–20, 223–24, 226–27, 232, 304, 318, 326, 347, 349
Macy, Barry A., 323
Maloney, William F., 225–26, 315, 318, 327
March, James G., 108
Marshall, Alfred, 212
Marshall, E. Ray, 28, 437
Meany, George, 45
Metzger, Norman, 417, 425
Miller, Richard U., 423–24
Mills, D. Quinn, 312–13, 327, 437
Mills, Ted, 324–27
Mirvis, Philip H., 323
Morris, Richard B., 28

N

Nelson, Richard R., 383–84, 386–87, 389
Nesbitt, Murray A., 58, 393, 411
Northrup, Herbert A., 274, 307–8
Nowack, John, 348

P

Peters, E., 375
Peterson, Richard B., 228–29
Pointer, Dennis D., 425
Porter, Lyman W., 118
Pranis, Robert W., 347
Prasow, Paul, 375
Price, John, 348

R

Rayback, Joseph G., 21, 23, 31–33, 37–38
Rehmus, Charles M., 203–4, 232, 271, 274, 408, 411
Reuther, Victor G., 59
Richardson, Reed C., 108, 172, 204, 206, 232
Romer, Sam, 94
Ronan William, 348
Rosen, Hjalmer, 124, 126
Ross, Arthur M., 345–46
Roth, Herrick, 108
Rothman, Stuart, 76

Rubin, Jeffrey Z., 216–19, 232, 303
Rubin, Lester, 208–10
Ruh, Robert A., 319, 321–22, 326
Ryder, Meyer S., 203–4, 232

S

Sayles, Leonard R., 78–81, 103, 108
Schachter, Stanley F., 121
Schenkel, Kenneth, 348
Schlossberg, Stephen I., 133, 135, 160
Schwab, Charles M., 25
Schwarz, Philip J., 309, 327
Seidman, Joel, 108
Selekman, B. M., 223
Selekman, S. K., 223
Selvin, David F., 31
Sherman, Fredrick E., 133, 135, 160
Sherman, Herbert L., Jr., 76, 339
Shropshire, William W., Jr., 347, 349
Shultz, George P., 277
Sikorski, John C., 94, 101
Silverberg, Louis G., 160
Simkin, William E., 263, 268–69, 304
Slichter, Sumner H., 197
Sloane, Arthur A., 23, 197
Smith, Russell A., 354, 374
Smythe, Cyrus F., 343, 349
Soltow, Martha Jane, 28
Somers, Gerald G., 232, 466
Stagner, Ross, 124, 126
Stanley, Miles C., 99
Stern, James L., 403–4, 408, 411, 419
Stevens, Carl M., 219–20, 232
Stieber, Jack, 84, 396–97
Strauss, George, 78–81, 103, 108
Suffern, Arthur, 39
Sulkin, Howard A., 347
Suttle, J. Lloyd, 124

T

Taft, Philip, 25, 28, 38–40, 46, 51
Tannenbaum, Arnold S., 108
Taylor, Benjamin J., 33–34, 36, 57, 76, 275
Tosi, Henry L., 118
Tracy, Lane, 228–29
Treckel, Karl F., 98
Trotta, Maurice S., 334
Trow, Martin A., 102
Turner, Arthur N., 124

U–W

Ulman, Lloyd, 88
Vroom, Victor H., 118, 127
Wagner, Lynn E., 310
Wahba, Mahmoud A., 118
Wakeley, John H., 319–321–22, 326
Walton, Richard E., 219–20, 223–24,
    226–27, 232, 304
Wanous, John P., 124
Weick, Karl E., 118, 127
Wery, Mary K., 28
Wheeler, Hoyt N., 276, 371–72, 399, 405.
    409
Widick, B. J., 59
Williams, Jerre S., 12–3
Witney, Fred, 23, 33–34, 36, 57, 76, 197,
    275
Winpisinger, William, 323

Y–Z

Yoder, Dale, 172, 204, 206, 232
Zalusky, John, 367–69
Zander, Alvin, 102, 126
Zollitsch, Herbert, 180

SUBJECT INDEX

A

Abel, I. W., 88–90, 226, 228
Affirmative Action programs, 438–39
AFL–CIO
  convention, 95
  creation, 44–45
  internationals affiliated with, 81–83, 95, 99
  leadership, 463–65
  merger of AFL and CIO, 44–45
  officers, 95–96
  per capita tax, 105
  philosophy, 44–45
  rubber boycott, 293–98
  staff departments, 96–97
  state and local central bodies, 98–99
  structure, 95–99
  trusteeship, 98
AFL–CIO Joint Negotiating Committee for Phelps-Dodge v. *NLRB*, 311
Agency relationship, 81, 123–25
Albemarle Paper Co. v. *Moody*, 433, 441
Alexander v. *Cardner-Denver Co.*, 356–57, 448
Alliance for Labor Action, 84, 98
Ally doctrine, 284–85
  in health care facilities, 420–21
American Arbitration Association, 360–61
American Federation of Government Employees (AFGE), 396
American Federation of Labor; *see also* AFL–CIO
  founding, 16
  merger with CIO, 44–45
  philosophy, 17–18, 30
American Federation of State, County, and Municipal Employees (AFSCME), 381, 396
American Federation of Teachers, 396

American Plan, 24–25
American Railway Union, 20
American Ship Building Co. v. *NLRB*, 290
American Telephone & Telegraph, 442
Anheuser-Busch, Inc., 145
Appropriate bargaining units, 140–46
  bargaining history, 144
  community of interests, 143
  employee desires, 144
  extent of organization, 144
  functional integration, 143–44
  geographic proximity, 143
  health care facilities, 416–17
  interchange of employees, 144
  jurisdiction of organizing union, 141
  legal constraints on NLRB, 140–41
  NLRB policy, 143–46
  territorial or administrative divisions, 143
Arbitrability, 353
Arbitration, expedited, 367–69
Arbitration, final offer selection, 406–9
  closed-offer, 409
  criteria for final offers, 408
Arbitration, interest
  criteria for award, 409
  defined, 351–52
  under Experimental Negotiating Agreement, 225, 276
  narcotic effect, 405–6
  under National War Labor Board, 275
  in public sector, 405–9
  variants in practice, 405–9
Arbitration, procedures, 357–72
  awards, 366
  evidentiary rules, 364–65
  hearing process, 363
  post hearing briefs, 364
  prearbitration matters, 357–58
  preparation for hearing, 361–63

Arbitration, procedures—*Cont.*
  presentation of case, 363–64
  representatives of parties, 363
  selection of arbitrator, 358–61
  time delays, 366–67
Arbitration, rights, 351–75
  costs apportioned, 340, 368
  defined, 351–52
  discipline cases, 370–72
  of discrimination cases, 356–57, 447–48
  exception to deferral to, 356–57
  legal status of, 353–55, 356–57
  level of use, 373–74
  NLRB deferral to, 355–56
  procedures, 357–72
  of unfair labor practices, 355–56
Arbitrators
  "ad hoc," 358–59
  permanent umpires, 358
  qualifications, 359–61
  sources of, 359–61
Atkinson v. *Sinclair Refining Co.*, 355
Attitudinal structuring, 220, 226–30
Authorization cards, 129–36
  agency relationship created, 129,
    135–36
  distribution, 132–36
  example, 131

B

Baptist Memorial Hospital, 419
Bargaining, coalition, 309–11
  decisions involving, 310–11
Bargaining, coordinated, 309–10
  defined, 309–10
Bargaining, good-faith, 207
  information required, 207
Bargaining, industry-wide, 313
Bargaining, multiemployer, 312–13
  bargaining power, 312
  contract construction, 312–13
  health care facilities, 417–18
  lockouts, 287–89
Bargaining, multilateral, 398–401
  comprehensiveness of state laws, 399–
    400
  environmental characteristics, 399–400
  health care insurers, 417–18, 421
Bargaining, public sector, 380–411
  levels of government, 381
  trends, 409–10
Bargaining activities, 200–210
  attitudinal structuring, 220
  contract rejections, 208–10
  intraorganizational bargaining, 228
  management activities, 203–6
  meetings for negotiations, 206–8

Bargaining activities—*Cont.*
  negotiation requests, 202–6
  prenegotiation, 200–202
  ratifications, 208
  strike authorization votes, 208
  tentative settlements, 208–10
  union activities, 202–3
Bargaining books, 203–4
Bargaining issues
  distributive issues, 219–20
  economic issues, 173–84
  in health care facilities, 421
  hours of work, 184–89
  job security, 88, 168–69, 190
  mandatory issues, 68, 171–73
  and negotiations, 207–8
  permissive issues, 171
  productivity, 88, 176, 184, 318–19
  prohibited issues, 171–72
  seniority, 190
  superseniority, 79
  terms and conditions of employment,
    189–94
  union security, 168, 192
Bargaining power, 211–19
  ability to take a strike, 215–16
  and bargaining unit, 142
  behavioral aspects of, 216–19
  economic aspects of, 211–14
  and interpersonal processes, 228–30
  as related to cost of disagreement,
    214–15
Bargaining tactics, 219–28
  Boulwareism, 307–8
  communicating intentions, 221
Bargaining units
  accretion, 146
  appropriateness, 143–44
  and bargaining power, 142, 212, 215
  craft severance, 144–45
  definitions, 70, 78
  and democracy, 102–4
  determination, 140–46
  elections, 137–38
  health care facilities, 416–17
  reorganization and reclassification, 146
  representation and negotiation, 313–14
  successor organizations, 146
Beck, Dave, 47–50
*Bekins Moving and Storage Co. of
  Florida,* 444
Betts Cadillac-Olds, Inc., 288
Bishop Randall Hospital, 415
Blackhawk Engraving Co., 285
Blue Flash Express Co., 151
Bommarito, Peter, 292–303
*Borden Co., Hutchinson Ice Cream Divi-
  sion,* 144

Bourne v. *NLRB,* 152
Boycotts, 23, 285–86
  Bucks Stove, 23
  Danbury Hatters, 23
  rubber strike of 1976, 293–98
  secondary, 51, 282, 286
Boys Markets, Inc. v. *Retail Clerks Union, Local 770,* 337, 355
Brooks v. *NLRB,* 154
Brown, Thomas, 31
Buffalo Forge Co. v. *United Steelworkers of America,* 279
"Bumping," 331
Bureau of Labor Statistics, 113
  Consumer Price Index, 113, 176
Business agent, 78–79
Butte Medical Properties, 415

C

Canadian Labor Congress, 88
Carey, James, 307
Carpenters' Union, 85–87
  executive branch, 87
  jurisdiction, 85
  staff departments, 87
Carter, Jimmy, 52
Cedars-Sinai Medical Center, 416
Central Hardware Co. v. *NLRB,* 133
Certifications, 130, 153–54
  and discrimination by race, 443–45
  election bar, 153–54
Civil Rights Act of 1964, Title VII, 113
  and representation, 443–45
  and rights arbitration, 356–57
Coalition bargaining, 309–11
Collective bargaining; *see also headings beginning* Bargaining defined, 329–30
Collyer Insulated Wire Co., 356
Committee on Political Education, 106
Commonwealth v. *Hunt,* 12–13
Conglomerates, 311–12
  and bargaining power, 311
  bargaining tactics, 311–2
Congress of Industrial Organizations, 3, 30–33; *see also* AFL–CIO
  membership, 33
  merger with AFL, 44–45
  UAW affiliation, 84
  USW affiliation, 88
Consent decrees, 440–43
Conspiracy doctrine, 11
  legislatively outlawed, 64–65
Consumer Price Index, 113
Continental Baking Co., 143
Contract negotiations, 164–65, 199–231
  bargaining meetings, 206
  federal service, 394

Contracts
  enforceability, 353–55
  federal agreements under Executive Orders, 394
Coordinated bargaining, 309–10
Corruption in unions, 46–51
Cost-of-living allowances (COLA), 176
  historical, 38
Costing contract terms, 204–6
Craft severance, 144–45
  rubber industry, 292
Craft unions defined, 16
Crestwood Education Association v. *Crestwood Board of Education,* 410

D

Debs, Eugene, 20, 30
Demand for labor, 211–14
  derived demand, 212
  elastic demand, 213
  elasticity of, 211–14
  inelastic demand, 214
Demographic characteristics of labor force, 458–59
Discipline, 330
  arbitration awards, 370–72
  wildcat strikes, 337
Discrimination
  backpay, 432–34
  contract construction, 437–38
  front pay, 433–34
  in grievance processing, 339, 445–46
  quotas, 441–42
  remedies, 440–43
  representation, 443–45
  seniority, 428–36
  for union activities, 68
Distributive bargaining, 219–22, 230
District 1199, Retail, Wholesale, and Department Store Workers Union, 418
Donnelly v. *United Fruit Co.,* 340
Drake Bakeries v. *Local 50,* 355
Dual allegiance, 123–25
Dubinsky, David, 30
Dues, fees, and assessments, 79, 105
  United Steelworkers, 93
"Dues Protest," 88
Duluth Bottling Association, 287
Dunlop, John, 52
Duplex Printing v. *Deering,* 23
du Pont de Nemours & Co., 145

E

East Texas Motor Freight System, Inc. v. *Rodriguez,* 434–36
Economic issues, 173–84
  determinants of pay, 177–84

Economic issues—*Cont.*
  form of pay, 173–76
  fringe benefits, 174–76, 178–79
  job evaluation, 177, 179–81
  magnitude of pay, 176–77
  overtime, 175–76
  Supplementary Unemployment Benefits (SUB), 181–84
  wage reopeners, 184
Economic theory
  and bargaining issues, 165–66
  and bargaining power, 211–14
EEOC v. *American Telephone & Telegraph*, 442
EEOC et al. v. *Detroit Edison Co., et al.*, 441–42
Elgin, Joliet & Eastern Railway v. *Burley*, 275, 339, 352
Elrod v. *Burns*, 381
Employee responses to election campaigns, 155–57
  characteristics of prounion voters, 155
  threats, 156–57
Employee Retirement Income Security Act of 1974 (ERISA), 106
  Labor Management Services Administration involvement, 111
  Pension Benefit Guarantee Corporation, 116
  pension negotiations, 175
Employment by industry, 451–53
Employment by occupation, 455–58
Employment Standards Administration, 113
  Office of Federal Contract Compliance Programs, 113
  Wage and Hour Division, 113
Employment and Training Administration, 111
  Bureau of Apprenticeship and Training, 111
Emporium-Capwell v. *Western Addition Community Organization*, 446–48
Equal Employment Opportunity Commission (EEOC), 431, 441–43
  creation, 113
  functions, 113
Excelsior Underwear, Inc., 137
Exclusive representation, 34
  and racial discrimination, 443–45
  and union democracy, 103–4
Executive Order 10988, 57, 392–93
Executive Order 11236, 438
Executive Order 11491, 57, 393–95
Executive Order 11616, 57
Executive Order 11838, 57–58
Expectancy theory, 118–21

Experimental Negotiating Agreement, 225–26
  described, 315–18
  interest arbitration provisions, 276
  issues excluded from arbitration, 317

F

Fact-finding, 271, 274–75, 402–4
  criteria for recommendations, 404
  effectiveness, 403–4
  issues and success, 274–75
  Presidential Emergency Boards, 275
  public sector, 402–4
  statutory role, 402–3
  Taft-Hartley emergencies, 271, 274
Fair representation, 339–42
  adequacy of representation, 368, 370, 341–42
  group rights, 339
  individual rights, 339
  racial discrimination, 445–48
  redress for unfair representation, 340–41
Federal Labor Relations Council, 57–58
  duties, 393
Federal Mediation and Conciliation Service (FMCS)
  arbitration roster, 361
  creation, 41, 71, 113–14
  duties, 71, 113–14
  health care disputes, 419
  involvement in national disputes, 276–77
  involvement in negotiations, 272–73
  involvement in 1976 rubber strike, 299–301
  notification requirements, 270–71
  Taft-Hartley emergencies, 274
Federal Services Impasse Panel, 57, 393–94
Fibreboard Paper Products Corp. v. *NLRB*, 191, 332
Firestone Tire and Rubber Co., 291–303
Flemming, Harvey, 31
Ford, Gerald R., 52–54, 59
Ford Motor Company
  limitation on overtime, 185–89
  private police, 32
  Supplementary Unemployment Benefits, 182–83
Ford Motor Co. v. *Huffman*, 434
Fractional bargaining, 343–44
Franks v. *Bowman Transportation*, 190, 432–34
Fraternal Order of Police, 397
Frick, Henry, 19

Fringe benefits, 174–75, 178–79, 181–84
  historical development, 38
Front pay, 433–34

G

General American Transportation Corp.,
  356
General Electric Co., 307–10
  Boulwareism, 307–8
  coalition bargaining, 309–10
General Electric Co. (1964), 308
General Electric Co. (1968), 310
General Motors Corporation, 32, 37, 465
General Shoe Corporation, 151
Geographical shifts in employment,
  459–60
Goals in bargaining, joint, 170–71
  grievance procedures, 170–71
Goals in bargaining, management, 169–70
  certainty, 170
  competition effects, 170
  fringe benefits, 174–75
  management rights, 170
Goals in bargaining, union, 165–69
  ability-to-pay, 167–68
  economic theories, 165–66
  equity, 167
  job security, 168
  standard of living, 168
  union security, 168
Gompers, Samuel, 17–18
Good-faith bargaining, 207
Gould, Jay, 15
Green, William, 44
Grievance administration
  union democracy, 81
Grievance procedures, 333–48
  as bargaining issue, 193
  employee rights of access to, 337–40
  explained, 333–34
  in federal service, 392–93
  individual characteristics of users,
    347–48
  innovations in use of, 345–47
  problems with, 345–47
  public employer response to, 409–10
  racial discrimination, 445–48
  steps within, 333–34
  time involved, 335
  union decisions within, 343
  union initiatives within, 344–45
  use as a bargaining tool, 343–44
Group behavior, 121–23
  cohesiveness, 121–23
Group cohesiveness, 102, 121–23
  external threats, 122–23
  productivity, 122

H

Handy-Andy, Inc., 444
Haywood, "Big Bill," 20–22, 30
Health-care facilities, 414–25
  defined, 414–15
Hillman, Sidney, 30
Hines v. *Anchor Motor Freight*, 342, 370
Hitchman Coal & Coke v. *Mitchell*, 33, 64
Hoffa, James R., 46, 465
Hollywood Ceramics Co., 157
"Hot cargo" clauses, 51
Hours of work, 184–89
  clean-up time, 189
  in contract administration, 331–32
  overtime, 184–89
  shift differentials, 189
Housestaffs, 416
Howard, Charles, 30
Howard Johnson Co., Inc. v. *Detroit Local
  Joint Executive Board*, 146
Hudgens v. *NLRB*, 133, 281
Hughes Tool Co. (1944), 339
Hughes Tool Co. (1964), 446
Humphrey v. *Moore*, 341
Hutcheson, "Big Bill," 30–31

I

IBEW, Local 388 v. *NLRB*, 420
Ickes, Harold, 38
Immigrants, 11
Impasse resolution, 261–304
  definition, 262
  procedures in health care facilities, 422
  procedures in public sector, 391, 401–9
Incentives, 330
Industrial composition of the work force,
  453
Industrial unions, defined, 30
Industrial Workers of the World, 20–22
Industry-wide bargaining, 313
Inflation, 462–63
Injunctions, 23–4
  prohibited, 33, 64–65
Inland Steel Co. v. *NLRB*, 173
Integrative bargaining, 220–21, 224–26,
  230
  and quality of working life, 323
International Association of Fire Fighters
  (IAFF), 397
  multilateral bargaining, 398–400
International Association of Machinists,
  307
International Brotherhood of Electrical
  Workers (IBEW) Local 3, limitation
  on overtime, 185

International Longshoremen &
 Warehousemen Union, 224–25
International representatives, 85, 92
International Union of Electrical, Radio,
 and Machine Workers, 307–9
International unions, 81–95
 conventions, 82
 officers, 82
 size, 81–83
 structure, 83–95
Interpersonal orientation, 217–19
Interrogation
 in discipline cases, 338
 in election campaigns, 151–52
Intraorganizational bargaining, 220, 228,
 230

J

Job design, and individual characteristics,
 124–25
Job satisfaction
 and organizing success, 129, 155–56
 and quality of working life, 322
Joint goals in bargaining, 170–71
Jurisdictional disputes
 defined, 37, 87
 outlawed, 68
 representation elections, 141

K–L

Kaiser Steel, productivity bargaining, 88,
 184
Knights of Labor, 14–16
Labor law, federal
 Clayton Act, 23–24
 Erdman Act, 23
 health-care amendments, 52, 415–16
 Labor Reform Act of 1977, 460–62
 Landrum-Griffin Act, 51, 72–75
 National Industrial Recovery Act, 34
 Norris-LaGuardia Act, 33–34, 63–65
 permissible conduct, 2
 Railway Labor Act, 61–63
 Taft-Hartley Act, 40–44, 65–72
 Wagner Act, 34–35, 65–72
Labor laws, state, 381–89
 health care facilities, 415
Labor Management Relations Act (Taft-
 Hartley), 65–72
 breach of contract, 337, 341
 definition of employee, 66–67
 definition of employer, 67
 employee rights defined, 67
 FMCS created, 71
 Landrum-Griffin amendments, 51
 mandatory bargaining issues, 69

Labor Management Relations Act (Taft-
 Hartley)—*Cont.*
 national emergency disputes, 71–72
 NLRB established, 67
 NLRB orders, 70
 negotiation requests, 202, 270–71
 professional employee defined, 67
 purpose, 66
 refusal to bargain, 69
 representation, 69–70
 right-to-work, 41, 70
 suits by and against labor organizations,
 72
 supervisor defined, 67
 Taft-Hartley Act, 40–44
 unfair labor practices, 67–69
 Wagner Act, 34–35
Labor-Management Services Administration, 111
 Landrum-Griffin Act responsibilities,
 111
 Executive Order implementation, 111
Landrum-Griffin Act, 51, 72–75
 disclosure requirements, 73–74
 election requirements, 74
 fiduciary responsibilities, 74–75
 Labor-Management Services Administration, 111
 trusteeships, 74
 union members' Bill of Rights, 73
Lein-Steinberg, 420
Lewis, John L., 30–31, 37–38, 44, 84, 465
Livingston Shirt Corp., 152
Local unions, 78–81
 business agent, 78–79
 Carpenters' union, 87
 committees, 78–79
 convention delegates, 82
 dues, 79, 93, 105
 elections, 101–2
 government, 79–81
 jurisdictions, 78
 meetings, 79–81
 officers, 78–79
 stewards, 79
Lockouts
 multiemployer, 288–89
 no-strike, no-lockout clause, 193
 perishable goods, 287–88
 requirements to legally use, 291
 single employer, 289–91
Loewe v. Lawlor, 64

M

McBride, Lloyd, 89–92
McClellan, John L., 46
McDonald, David, 88

McGovern, George, 97, 106
McMahon, Thomas, 30
McParlan, James, 18
Mallinckrodt Chemical Works, 144–45
Management goals in bargaining, 169–70
Mandatory bargaining issues, 69, 171–73
Marsh v. *Alabama*, 132
Martin, Homer, 32
May Department Stores, 152
Meany, George, 44–45
Mediation, 262–73
Mediators, 268–74
  activity, 271–74
  attitudes and personalities, 268–70
  backgrounds, 268
  effectiveness, 269
  training, 270
Miranda Fuel Co., 341, 445
"Mohawk Valley" formula, 36
Molly Maguires, 18
Moore Dry Dock Co., 281
Motivation, 117–21
  expectancy theory, 118
  to organize, 119–21
  Scanlon Plan, 322
Motivational orientation, 217–19
Multiemployer bargaining, 312–13
Multinational corporations, 311–12
Murphy, Frank, 32
Murray, Philip, 31, 44

N

NAACP v. *Federal Power Commission*, 444
National Academy of Arbitrators, 360
National Education Association, 396
National emergency disputes, 71–72
National Labor Relations Board (NLRB)
  bargaining orders, 154
  coalition bargaining, 309–11
  constitutional basis, 36
  duties, 35, 114
  election certifications, 153–54
  establishment, 35, 114
  health care facilities, 414–15
  jurisdiction, 129–32, 414–15
  organization structure, 115
  powers, 69–70
  rules for representation elections, 129–32, 135–39, 151–53
  totality of conduct, 153
  unit determinations, 140, 143–46
National Labor Union, 14
National League of Cities v. *Usery*, 410
National Mediation Board (NMB)
  emergency boards, 63
  establishment, 61, 63, 114–15

National Mediation Board (NMB)—*Cont.*
  interest arbitration, 63
  mediation function, 63
National Railroad Board of Adjustment (NRBA)
  establishment, 63
  grievance settlements, 63–64
  relation to NMB, 114–15
National Typographical Union, 13–14
  union democracy, 102
National War Labor Board
  interest arbitration, 275
  required arbitration clauses, 352
  World War I, 24
  World War II, 36–37
Negotiating committee, 79, 200–203
Negotiations, 200–211
  bargaining meetings, 206–8
  Boulwareism, 307–8
  management response, 207
  preparation, 200–202
  requests for negotiation, 202–206
  specific issues, 207–8
  settlements, 208–11
  union presentation, 207
Negotiators, 207
Nixon, Richard M., 57, 106
NLRB v. *Jones & Laughlin Steel Corp.*, 36
NLRB v. *LeTourneau Co.*, 132
NLRB v. *McKay Radio & Telegraph*, 283
NLRB v. *Mansion House Corp.*, 443–44
NLRB v. *Metropolitan Life Insurance Co.*, 144
NLRB v. *Seamprufe, Inc.*, 132
NLRB v. *St. John's Hospital and School of Nursing*, 419
NLRB v. *Truck Drivers, Local 449*, 289
NLRB v. *Truitt Mfg. Co.*, 207
NLRB v. *Virginia Electric & Power Co.*, 153
NLRB v. *J. Weingarten, Inc.*, 338
NLRB v. *Wooster Division of Borg-Warner Co.*, 210
NLRB v. *Babcock & Wilcox Co.*, 132
NLRB v. *Brown*, 289
NLRB v. *Burns International Security Services*, 146
NLRB v. *Dalton Brick & Tile Corp.*, 290
NLRB v. *Denver Building Trades Council*, 280
NLRB v. *Exchange Parts Co.*, 152
NLRB v. *Fleetwood Trailer Co., Inc.*, 284
NLRB v. *Fruit & Vegetable Packers, Local 760*, 282
NLRB v. *General Electric Co.*, 308
NLRB v. *Gissel Packing Co.*, 154
NLRB v. *IBEW, Local 1229*, 280
No-strike clause

No-Strike clause—*Cont.*
  Boy's Markets, 337
  strikes, 279
  wildcat strikes, 335–37
Norris-LaGuardia Act, 33–34, 63–65
  injunctions permitted for violence, 65
  prohibitions, 64–65
    application of conspiracy doctrine, 64
    injunctions, 64–65
    yellow-dog contracts, 64
    wildcat strikes, 337
North Memorial Medical Center, 417

O

Occupational Safety and Health Act, 111
  in bargaining, 191
  Occupational Safety and Health Admin-
    istration, 111
  Occupational Safety and Health Review
    Commission, 116
Occupational Safety and Health Review
  Commission, 116
  establishment, 116
  duties, 116
Office of Federal Contract Compliance
  Programs (OFCCP), 113, 439, 442
Oil, Chemical, & Atomic Workers v.
  NLRB, 313
Order of Railroad Telegraphers v.
  Chicago and Northwestern Railroad,
  191
Organizing
  authorization cards, 129–33
  campaigns, 129–39, 146–53, 155–57
  dissatisfied employees, 129
  employer and union conduct, 133–35,
    146–51
  employer's desired bargaining unit, 142
  in health care facilities, 418–19
  by international union, 128–29
  motivation, 119–21
  and the NLRB, 129–39, 155–57
  union's desired bargaining unit, 141
Organizing campaigns, 129–57
  communications in general, 153
  employee response, 153, 155–57
  employer communications, 152
  interrogation, 151
  management strategy, 149
  management tactics, 149–50
  24-hour rule, 153
  union communications, 153
  union strategy, 147–48
  union tactics, 149–50
Organizing issues, 128–29
  management issues, 149
  union issues, 147

P

P. Q. Beef Processors, Inc., 66
Pacific Maritime Association, 224–25
Past practice, 332–33
Peerless Plywood, 153
Pension Benefit Guarantee Corporation,
  116
  establishment, 116
  functions, 116
Personnel assignments, 331
Philadelphia cordwainers, 11–12
Philadelphia Plan, 439
Picketing
  ambulatory site, 281
  common situs, 52–54, 280–81
  in economic strikes, 279–82
  extortionate, 75
  health care industry, 69
  multiple-use sites, 281
  off-site, 282
  recognitional, 68–69
Powderly, Terence, 15–16
Preparations for negotiations, 200–206
  bargaining books, 203–4
  costing contract terms, 204–6
  management activities, 202–6
  membership meetings, 203
  union activities, 200–203
Production standards, 332
Productivity bargaining
  in construction industry, 318–19
  defined, 318–19
  Scanlon Plan, 184, 319–22
Protestant work ethic, 124
Public employees
  political appointees, 381
  federal, 391–92
Public opinion, labor organizations, 2
Public sector bargaining, 380–411
  levels of government, 381
  trends, 409–10
Public sector unions, growth, 56–58,
  392–93, 409–10, 462

Q

Quaker State Oil Refining Corp., 290
Quality of working life, 322–26
  defined, 322
  handled through joint programs, 323
  opposing positions, 322
  results in coal mining, 324–26
Quotas, race, 441–42

R

Race quotas, 441–42
Railway Labor Act, 61–63

Railway Labor Act—*Cont.*
  bargaining, 61–63
  jurisdiction over air carriers, 63
  National Mediation Board, 61–63
  National Railroad Board of Adjustment,
    61–63
  representation, 61
Ranco, Inc. v. *NLRB*, 132
Recognition requests, 130, 135–36
  in federal service, 393–94
  federal service types under 10988,
    392–93
Regents of the University of Michigan v.
  *Michigan Employment Relations
  Commission*, 416
Representation elections
  balloting, 138–39
  bargaining orders, 154
  certifications, 131, 139, 153–54
  federal government, 392–94
  legislation, 61, 69–70
  outcomes, 157–59
  petitions, 137
  procedures, 135–39
  setting aside, 154
Republic Aviation Corp. v. *NLRB*, 132
Reuther, Walter, 44
  Alliance for Labor Action, 98
  political action by, 106, 465
  presidency of UAW, 84
  vice-president of AFL-CIO, 84
Right-to-work, 41, 70
Roosevelt, Franklin D., 34, 37–39
Roth, Herrick, 97–98
Roy Robinson Chevrolet, 356
Rubber industry
  craft severance, 292
  strike of 1976, 291–303
Rushton Coal Co., 324–26
  quality of working life, 324–26

S

Sadlowski, Ed, 89–92
  and Experimental Negotiating Agree-
    ment, 318
St. John's Hospital and School of Nursing,
  410
St. Joseph Hospital and Medical Center,
  417
Scanlon Plan, 184, 319–22
  defined, 319–22
  motivation to produce, 322
  quality of working life, 325–26
Scearce, James, 299–301
Schechter Poultry Corp. v. *U.S.*, 34
Shopping Kart Food Markets, Inc., 152,
  157

Seniority
  bargaining issue, 190
  benefit status, 435
  bona-fide systems, 434–36
  competitive status, 435
  departmental, 429–31
  discrimination cases, 428–36
  utilization of minorities, 431
Service Employees International Union
  (SEIU), 397, 418
Sinclair Refining Co. v. *Atkinson*, 337, 355
Sloan, Alfred, P., 465
Solicitation rules, 132–3
  broad no-solicitation rules, 152
  health care facilities, 419
Southern Conference of Teamsters v. *Rodriguez*, 434–36
Spielberg Mfg. Co., 356
State and local central bodies, 96–99
  affiliation with AFL-CIO, 96–99
Steel industry consent decrees, 443
Steel industry seizure, 44
Steel Workers Organizing Committee, 31,
  88
Steele v. *Louisville & Nashville Railroad*,
  445–46
Steelworkers trilogy, 353–54
Stephens, Uriah, 15
Stewards, 79
  involvement in fractional bargaining,
    343–45
  role in grievance processing, 333–34
Strasser, Adolph, 17
Strikes
  ability to take, 215–16
  ally doctrine, 284–85
  over arbitration awards, 355
  bargaining issue, 193
  benefits to strikers, 298–99
  contracting-out, 284–85
  Cripple Creek, Colorado miners, 20
  economic strike, 278–79
  employer responses to, 282–85
  frequency, 261
  government intervention, 18–20
  over grievances, 335–37
  health care facilities, 420
  historical usage, 12, 15
    incidence in 1941, 38
    incidence in 1945, 38
  Homestead Steel of 1892, 19
  incidence in public sector, 390
  Lawrence, Massachusetts textile work-
    ers, 1912, 22
  no-strike clause, 193
  Paterson, New Jersey, 1913, 22
  process, 279
  Pullman of 1894, 19–20

Strikes—*Cont.*
  railroad of 1877, 19
  reconversion after World War II, 39–40
  rights of employers, 283–84
  rights of strikers, 284
  rubber industry in 1976, 291–303
  sit-down, 32
  under state laws in public sector,
    382–91
  steel industry, 316
  strike votes, 279
  sympathy strikes, 278–79
  unfair labor practice strike, 278
  Wabash Railroad of 1885, 15
  wildcat strike, 278
Subcontracting, 332
Supervisors
  in contract administration, 333–34,
    344–45, 347
  doing bargaining unit work, 332
Supplementary Unemployment Benefits
  (SUB), 181–83
"Sweetheart" contracts, 46
Sylvis, William, 14

T

Taylor, Myron, 31
Teamsters, International Brotherhood of,
  94–95
  affiliation with Alliance for Labor Ac-
    tion, 98
  conferences, 94
  corruption, 46–50
  democracy, 94–95
  international convention, 94
  Joint Councils, 94
  jurisdiction, 94
  officers, 94
Teamsters v. *U.S.*, 434–36
Teamsters Local Union 659 v. *Rodriguez*,
  434–36
Terms and conditions of employment,
  189–94
  collective job rights, 190–91
  duration of agreement, 194
  grievance procedures, 193
  job security, 190–91
  management rights, 192–93
  plant closings, 190–91
  safety and health, 191
  seniority, 190
  subcontracting, 190–91
  training and apprenticeships, 193
  union security, 192
  work rules, 192
  "zipper" clauses, 194

Textile Workers Union v. *Lincoln Mills*,
  353
Thornhill v. *Alabama*, 280
T.I.M.E.-D.C., Inc. v. *U.S.*, 434–36
Title VII, Civil Rights Act of 1964, 113
Totality of conduct
  bargaining under Boulwareism, 308
  organizing campaigns, 153
Trap Rock Co. v. *Teamsters, Local 470*,
  337
Truax v. *Corrigan*, 33
Trusteeship
  by AFL-CIO, 97–98
  Landrum-Griffin requirements, 74

U

UAW Local 862 v. *Ford Motor Co.*, 433
Unfair labor practices
  employer, 68
  under contract administration, 329–30
  federal government, 395
  in organizing campaigns, 154, 156–57
  union, 68–69
Union
  conventions, 82
    Carpenters, 86–87
    USW, 88–90
  democracy
    dual governance, 103
    functional democracy, 102–3
    grievances, 78–9
    local level, 80–81
    Teamsters, 94
  discipline, and wildcat strikes, 337
  finances, 104–6
    ERISA, 106
    pension administration, 106
    receipts and disbursements,
      105
  government, local, 79–81
  meetings
    attendance, 79–80
    content, 79–80
    during negotiations, 203
    during organizing, 153, 156
    ratification, 208–10
    strike authorizations, 208
  officers
  law on elections, 74
    pay, 101–2
  penetration, 3
    federal service, 56, 393, 409
    health care facilities, 422–23
    by industry, 453–5
  political action, 106
    Committee on Political Action, 106

Union—*Cont.*
  security
    agency shop, 192
    bargaining issue, 168, 192
    checkoff, 192
    closed shop, 51
    democracy, 103–4
    maintenance of membership, 192
    union shop, 192
  structure, 4
    federations, 16–17, 95–100
    international, 83–95
    local, 78–79
Union News Co. v. *Hildreth*, 340
Unionism
  business, 16–18, 26
  predatory, 26
  revolutionary, 20–22, 26
  uplift, 14–16, 26
Unions, international, 81–95
Unions, local, 78–81
Unions, public sector, 56–58, 393–93,
    409–10, 462
United Auto Wrokers (UAW)
  affiliation with CIO, 84
  alliance with ALA, 98
  Boulwareism, 307
  departments, 84, 86
  disaffiliation with AFL-CIO, 84
  formation, 32
  international representatives, 85
  jurisdiction, 84
  limitation on overtime, 185–89
  National Councils, 85
  regional staffs, 85
  structure, 84–86
  Supplementary Unemployment Ben-
    efits, 181–83
United Electrical, Radio, and Machine
    Workers (UE), 307
United Mine Workers (UMW), 30
  pensions, 175
  quality of working life project, 324–26
United Rubber Workers (URW), 291–303
United Rubber Workers, Local 12 v.
    NLRB, 446
United Steelworkers of America (USW)
  convention, 88–90
  departments, 90, 93
  election of president, 88, 93
  Experimental Negotiating Agreement,
    315–18

United Steelworkers of America
    (USW)—*Cont.*
  finances, 93
  industry conferences, 88–89, 93
  jurisdiction, 88
  politics, 88–92
  productivity bargaining, 184
  structure, 89–90, 92–93
U.S. Department of Labor, 109–13
  bureaus, 111–13, 176
  purpose, 109–10
U.S. Postal Service, 394
Usery, W. J., Jr., 299–301
USW v. *American Mfg. Co.*, 353–54
USW v. *Enterprise Wheel & Car Corp.*,
    353–54
USW v. *Warrior & Gulf Navigation Co.*,
    353
Utility Workers Union, Local 233, 441–42

V

Vaca v. *Sipes*, 341–42
Viele & Sons, Inc., 66
Violence, 18–20
  enjoinable, 65
  Haymarket Square, 19
  Little Steel, 31, 35
Wage and hour laws, 175
Wage re-openers, 184
War Labor Disputes Act, 38
Weber v. *Kaiser Aluminum & Chemical
    Corp.*, 442
Western Federation of Miners, 20–21
Wiley, John & Sons, Inc. v. *Livingston*,
    146
Wilkie, Wendell, 37
Wilson, Woodrow, 24
Work assignments, 331
Working conditions, 332
Workingmen's parties, 13
World War I, 24 .
World War II, 38–39

W–Z

Yellow-dog contract, 24–25
  prohibited, 33, 64
Zaritsky, Max, 30
"Zipper" clauses, 194
  past practice, 333